THE FEMINIST
PROMISE

Praise for *The Feminist Promise*

"Christine Stansell's *The Feminist Promise* is a unique, elegant, learned sweep through more than two centuries of women's efforts to overcome the most fundamental way that human beings have been wrongly divided into the leaders and the led. It's full of surprises from the past and guiding lights for the future."
　　　　　　　　　　　　　　　　　　　　　　　　　—Gloria Steinem

"Christine Stansell's *The Feminist Promise* is a landmark in women's history—a remarkable and thoughtful narrative of the many movements and struggles that have shaped the lives of American women (and men) over two centuries and into our own time."
　　　　　　　　　　　　　　　—Alan Brinkley, Allan Nevins Professor
　　　　　　　　　　　　　　　　of American History, Columbia University

"It is with an evocative, even poetic, sense of saga that Christine Stansell infuses this epic work, a heart-moving journey over the last three centuries. Drawing distinctions between the 'mothers' and the 'daughters' of the feminist movement, Stansell gives fresh clarity and nostalgic immediacy to the breakneck pace with which women have changed their lives. This is to feminism the definitive account—the motherlode."
　　　　　　　　　—Sheila Weller, author of the *New York Times* bestseller *Girls Like Us:*
　　　　　　Carole King, Joni Mitchell, Carly Simon—and the Journey of a Generation

"It's all here—over two hundred years of history, down to the perplexities of the present day, in which a feminist might be an Afghan teenager fighting for an education or an American lawyer wondering how she ended up as a stay-home mother. *The Feminist Promise* is women's history for the twenty-first century—a magnificent and compelling work."
　　　　　　　　　　　　　　—Katha Pollitt, author of *The Mind-Body Problem*

"Never before has the whole scope and breadth of feminism's democratic promise been so arrestingly and memorably surveyed. Stansell unifies the long history of fractious and unruly generations of feminist endeavor with precise arrows of insight and luminous reflections. Her book is a must for anyone who wants to understand the situation of women in the world today."
　　　　　　　　　—Nancy F. Cott, Jonathan Trumbull Professor of American History,
　　　　　　　　　　Harvard University, and author of *The Grounding of Modern Feminism*

"A landmark book from a brilliant and insightful historian. Stansell brings pioneering feminist thinkers like Mary Wollstonecraft thrillingly alive and places contemporary American women activists in the contexts of two centuries of feminist argument. Assured, ambitious, and stirring, *The Feminist Promise* delivers the authoritative intellectual history needed to ground and launch a new era of global women's emancipation."
　　　　　　　　　—Elaine Showalter, Professor Emeritus of English, Princeton
　　　　　　　　　University, and author of *A Jury of Her Peers: Celebrating*
　　　　　　　　　American Women Writers from Anne Bradstreet to Annie Proulx

ALSO BY CHRISTINE STANSELL

American Moderns

City of Women

CHRISTINE STANSELL

THE FEMINIST PROMISE

1792 TO THE PRESENT

THE MODERN LIBRARY

NEW YORK

2011 Modern Library Paperback Edition

Copyright © 2010 by Christine Stansell

Published in the United States by Modern Library, an imprint of The Random House
Publishing Group, a division of Random House, Inc., New York.

MODERN LIBRARY and the TORCHBEARER Design are registered
trademarks of Random House, Inc.

Originally published in hardcover in the United States by Modern Library, an imprint of
The Random House Publishing Group, a division of Random House, Inc., in 2010.

Grateful acknowledgment is made to W. W. Norton & Company, Inc., and
Adrienne Rich for permission to reprint four lines from "Natural Resources" from
The Fact of a Doorframe: Selected Poems 1950–2001 by Adrienne Rich, copyright © 2002
by Adrienne Rich. Copyright © 1978 by W. W. Norton & Company, Inc.
Reprinted by permission of the author and W. W. Norton & Company, Inc.

Library of Congress Cataloging-in-Publication Data
Stansell, Christine.
The feminist promise: 1792 to the present / Christine Stansell.
p. cm.
Includes bibliographical references and index.
ISBN 978-0-8129-7202-3
eBook ISBN 978-1-58836-916-1
1. Feminism—History.   2. Women's rights—History.
3. Women—Social conditions—History.   I. Title.
HQ1150.S723 2010
305.4209—dc22   2009026662

Printed in the United States of America

www.modernlibrary.com

2 4 6 8 9 7 5 3 1

To

Deborah Epstein Nord
Stephanie McCurry

Crystal Feimster
Eileen Kane

Hannah Wilentz

There is no mark on the wall to measure the precise height of women.

—Virginia Woolf

Contents

INTRODUCTION

FEMINISM IS ONE OF THE great and substantial democratic movements, a tradition of thought and action spanning more than two hundred years. Its reach is huge, because it addresses the claims and needs of half the population. At its best, feminism incorporates men as well, to make it a politics of universal aspiration. The fact that feminism's hard-won achievements—the vote, women's education, legal contraception—now seem prosaic and humdrum speaks to its phenomenal success in many parts of the world, certainly in the United States. Yet here and abroad, the rights of women are targets of denunciation and violence, testimony to feminism's continuing urgency and the fundamental, dismaying fact that the battles are far from over.

While "democracy" is ingrained in our sense of prerogatives and rights, democracy has long been an honored ideal—much discussed, worth fighting for, with a history worth reading about. But feminism, democracy's younger sister, is easily shoved aside, dismissed as a chronicle of complaints that progress long ago made irrelevant. This is too bad, because feminism's successes, along with its chronic shortfalls, illuminate so much about both democracy's possibilities and its chronic limitations. There is little we can understand about the character of modern life, modern nations, or modern aspirations—from patterns of global migration to the war in Afghanistan to the latest round of the perennial American debate over work and the family—without taking into account the effects of feminist hopes and conundrums.

What is the feminist promise? At different times, feminism has promised to bring about world peace, end prostitution, and abolish pornography, the sexual double standard, and the nuclear family. Feminists have promised to make women more like men and to teach men to be more like women; and to make sexual difference irrelevant altogether. They have sought a world where there was less sex, more sex, better sex, and better marriages, no marriage, gay marriages. In other words, feminism has encompassed a wide variety of social views and positions, sometimes antagonistic to one another. A Protestant tradition for a good part of its history, feminism promised in the nineteenth century to spread the Christian message by using the world's women as evangelists; in the twentieth century, it swore to emancipate women from the patriarchal yoke of religion, be it Christian, Jewish, or Muslim. Feminists have embraced women's traditional loyalties to children and kin as a fundamental value, and they have also heralded individualism as the one basis for true freedom. Like any long-lived and durable political tradition, feminism has always promised more than it could deliver. But it has also produced stunning successes, challenging institutions and presumptions that have been in place for centuries.

Modern feminism dates from 1792, the year the young English writer Mary Wollstonecraft, enthusiastically following the French Revolution from London, took the rights of man into new territory in *A Vindication of the Rights of Woman*. At the time, women's rights was a preoccupation of ultra-radicals on the margins of politics.* More than two hundred years later, feminism is a staple of public debate and an element of geopolitics, as human rights groups as well as the occasional diplomat fasten on the abrogations of women's rights as matters of international concern. *The Feminist Promise* traces this arc from the margins to the center and asks a simple question: How did it happen?

The answers are various and complicated, but one place to begin is with the fundamental contradiction in the natural rights revolutions that Wollstonecraft and her peers lived through in the late eighteenth century. Revolutions in France and North America overturned the centuries-old belief that some were born to rule, others to submit: They toppled the reign of kings and replaced it with an order based on the

---

* In the book, I adhere loosely to the different terms in use over time: "women's rights" before 1900, "feminism" thereafter.

natural rights of man and government by consent. Thenceforth, and around the world, men who saw themselves as a brotherhood of equals would seize those principles of liberty and representative government to supplant the rule of the father—as embodied in king, emperor, overlord, or dictator. Republican ideology, however, harbored great exceptions: in the United States, chattel slavery, and everywhere the subordination of women to male authority. Women's exclusion from the political community of deliberating, consenting, liberty-loving men was an unspoken or barely spoken part of the political compact. The tremendous importance given to those male citizens, whose fraternal bonds knit together the revolutionary nation, bequeathed a huge problem to modern democracy—although at the time, it went mostly unnoticed. What about the women, the would-be political sisters? Could they join the fraternity of citizens? Surely they, being human, also had a natural right to liberty and equality?

The feminist tradition has been a long attempt to address these questions. From the beginning, feminists have had to expose injustices and inequalities considered to be perfectly natural. Women's lack of political and civil rights, particularly in marriage, led the list, followed by the indignities they suffered in sexual relations (including unwanted pregnancy), the psychology of deference ingrained in the task of pleasing men (what we would now call low self-esteem), and labor discrimination. All these perceptions can be found in Wollstonecraft, far less worked out than they would be in Simone de Beauvoir's *The Second Sex* (1949), but present nonetheless. The combinations have changed, and the stress has shifted: In the nineteenth century, the absence of political rights and the critique of marriage dominated the women's movement; in the late twentieth and early twenty-first centuries, it has been injuries of labor (housework and paid work), sexuality, and the psychology of gender relations. But there has also been a remarkable continuity, as if certain problems of gender are lodged in the very foundations of liberal democratic politics.

This is a long and large story, but not a chaotic one: Several themes connect developments widely separated in time. First, I trace the tensions between what one might call the politics of the mothers and the politics of the daughters, orientations of the feminist imagination that have been a perennial feature—from Wollstonecraft, a daughter and mother-hater of the first order, up through today's postfeminists, uneasy daughters trying to reinvent the maternalist stance. The politics of the mothers, the book argues, lean toward responsibility, propriety, and pragmatic expectations of what can be done; look to increase the admiration and power that accrue to women in their family roles; accept customary limitations on women's freedom to act like men; acknowledge the comforts and compensations of domestic life; and take patriarchal privileges for granted but work to make men more accountable to wives and children. The politics of the mothers, in short, have sought to enhance women's power without radically challenging the way things are.

The feminism of the daughters has contempt for the status quo. The approach is utopian, flamboyant, defiant, insisting on claiming men's prerogatives. It batters on the doors to power and demands dramatic rearrangements in marriage, motherhood, sex, and male psychology. It is animated by imagining a kind of equality that would free women to act in the world exactly as men do.

The categories are more descriptive than analytic, and they are never hard-and-fast. But the divide does help elucidate trends over time and explain conflicts between feminists that have been described as generational but in fact go beyond age demographics to deeper political philosophies: The mothers often achieved tangible results and greater acceptance for feminism, although to the impatient young they seemed pathetically grateful for a few scraps. In volatile moments, when deep-going transformation was possible, it was typically the daughters who stepped to the forefront, endowed with a will to change that outstripped the prescience of mothers who had more to lose. But the book also shows that feminism's biggest victories have come about when the efforts of mothers and daughters have converged: in the coalition, for example, that finally won the vote in 1920, and in the campaign to legalize abortion that culminated in the Supreme Court's decision in *Roe v. Wade* in 1973. Conversely, when one element or the other monopolizes the field, the result is usually stalemate and quietude.

Second, the book investigates structures of male government in the family as they changed over time. Grounded in British common law, which held that wives were "covered" by their husbands, family government was a relic of the social hierarchy of the ancien régime that passed unnoticed into the legal and political culture of the American republic. Over time, feminists were the main force that brought to light the autocratic arrangements that constrained women from acting as sovereign individuals. Some provisions of family government fell in the nineteenth and early twentieth centuries—most auspiciously, the winning of suffrage overturned the principle of virtual representation, by which men voted in place of their dependent wives. Still others remained, however, translated into modern idioms and upheld by newly minted rationales. The effects of family government tie together nineteenth-century disabilities, such as married women's inability to buy and sell property, to twentieth-century problems, such as the notorious difficulties women encounter in prosecuting domestic abuse and marital rape. Across the world, struggles over family government continue, ferocious and increasingly bloody. Writ large in global politics, attempts to impose despotic, atavistic forms of male governance in the name of tradition lie at the center of conflicts that pit feminists and liberal democrats against religious extremists in South Asia, the Middle East, and parts of Africa.

Third, the book follows the uses of universal Woman, the symbol that stands at the very center of feminist bids for power. "She, who is so different from myself, is really like me in fundamental ways, because we are both women": This is the feminist habit of universalizing extravagantly—making wild, improbable leaps across chasms of class and race, poverty and affluence, leisured lives and lives of toil to draw basic similarities that stem from the shared condition of sex. The penchant for comparisons far afield goes back to the nineteenth century, when feminists filled in the outlines of universal Woman with images of female slaves, prostitutes, and impoverished seamstresses. In the twenty-first century, extravagant universals reach around the world, plucking out Third World sex workers, Cambodian entrepreneurs, and African female farmers, among others, to add to the imagined figure of Woman.

Inevitably, the imagined Woman fell short of the actualities of the actual woman it was supposed to describe, and inevitably, the identification between the feminist who spoke and the woman she spoke for turned out to be wishful, once those other women spoke up. Even as feminism consolidated a following, it was always headed for a breakup into component parts, with new groups of women entering the political scene to challenge presumptions of unity. But although the Woman at the heart of feminism has been a fiction like any political fiction ("workers of the world," "we the people"), it has been a useful fiction, and sometimes a splendid one. Extravagant universalizing created an imaginative space into which otherwise powerless women could project themselves onto an unresponsive political culture. Representatives of a voiceless constituency, they could search out new audiences, recruit female speakers, and assemble evidence for their case (the book stresses that one of the great achievements of feminism has been simply to compile a substantial body of truth about women's lives).

Fourth, I am interested in the play of the feminist tradition across the political spectrum. Women's rights originated on the democratic left and feminism's natural home has always been there, but conservatism has had its own feminist impulses. The defense of women has come from the right as well as from radicals and liberals, and has involved moralistic, repressive, antidemocratic mobilizations against both sexes when they have failed to fit the bill of virtue that feminists issued. In the name of rescuing, protecting, and championing women, feminists have sometimes done their part for racist, colonialist, and nativist politics, as well as for the emancipatory struggles that are their more usual province. At times these different trajectories have converged.

The Feminist Promise begins with the American and French revolutions and ends with the war in Afghanistan. I have worked to integrate my account with other events, developments, and watersheds in national and world affairs. In this the book differs from many others on the subject, which focus exclusively on the internal development of the women's movement. There is no feminism that does not derive from and play into men's politics and institutions and does not involve male protagonists, whether we are considering the schisms in antislavery ranks before the Civil War or Richard Nixon's veto of the Child Development Act in 1971.

The Feminist Promise primarily concerns the United States, although the scope expands at particular times. I have tried to pay ample attention to the international context whenever precision demands it and space allows; inevitably, this is much easier to do in the early period, when women's rights movements were primarily British and American, than after 1870, when the ideas and goals became international currency. The popularity of global feminism after 1980 as a singular (although not exclusive) American export offers one opportunity to investigate the international scene at length, and I have devoted a chapter at the end to the subject. This means, though, that domestic developments after 1980 receive short shrift—one of several unavoidable omissions. I proceed mostly chronologically, but I jump over some periods and drastically compress others. The turning point of 1919–20 receives close attention, for example, but I skate over the next quarter century to arrive at 1945. And as I wrap up the book, the increasingly long present after September 11, 2001, shows me every day that another book could be written, and then another. I hope mine will encourage more to come.

To show feminism's reach and traction, I have broadened the cast of characters beyond the usual heroines. While Elizabeth Cady Stanton and Betty Friedan are here, I also cast my net wide to capture a polyglot and often contentious crowd: African-Americans as well as whites, men as well as women, trade union leaders and middle-class moralists, antipornography crusaders and sex radicals, urban sophisticates and rural teetotalers, lesbian and gay radicals, and World Bank economists. Not all these figures and constituencies made the women's movement their one great cause: Most had other loyalties and affiliations. But it is the "lesser" feminists, I have found, those for whom the cause of Woman was not the only cause, who sometimes discovered another road to the future or pointed to roads not taken.

Feminism is an argument, not received truth; it is an entrée into a fuller engagement with America and the world, not an exit visa out of a male-dominated society into utopia. It cannot end all the afflictions that women suffer, nor find a remedy for all the problems that arise between women and men. But since its inception, feminism has contributed more to the world's store of human happiness than it has taken away, and has undone some of its most banal and many of its insufferable oppressions without significantly increasing others. It is an extraordinary, productive, and moving past, and understanding it is part of democracy's patient work.

CHAPTER ONE

WILD WISHES

THERE IS NOTHING NEW about men's power, or women's recognition of it. Men have dominated, ruled, lorded over, and subjugated women as long as there has been recorded history. But the ways people have understood the preeminence of one sex over the other have changed through time. Western beliefs are rooted in a Christian schema that divided human beings into ranks according to a divine plan. As God ruled the world and man ruled beasts, so monarchs (usually kings) ruled subjects, fathers ruled children, masters ruled apprentices and servants, and men governed women. Rebelling against one's place in this order amounted to defying the will of God.

In the late eighteenth century, the great world-transforming revolutions in America and France overturned these assumptions, overthrowing monarchical rule first in the American colonies and then in France and installing governments based on the consent of the governed and the rights of man. The subordination of women survived the American and French revolutions, as did slavery, whose colossal expansion in the seventeenth and eighteenth centuries introduced another stark relationship of domination. In the American Revolution, patriots barely considered the question of women, nor did they debate the emancipation of the slaves (although the British offered emancipation as an enticement to join their side). Women joined the revolution in full force, but they never pressed for clarity about their own relation to the rights the patriots claimed, and soon most of those rights were out of bounds. In the French

Revolution, women were present in all phases. Some pursued rights for their sex, and in the early days they were partially successful, but in the end, they made no headway.

The outcomes were different: a stable republic in the United States, based on the political rights of white male property holders and a compromise that resulted in the Constitution's tacit protection of slavery; in France, bloodshed and repression followed by Napoleon's dictatorship. As to the universal application of the rights of man, however, the answers were the same: Women would be acknowledged as mothers, not sisters, present at the edges of the political community in their families and safely under the governance of men.

For centuries in Europe, women spoke of the indignities of being subject to men. Their laments were a kind of underground tradition in women's culture, winding through songs, proverbs, and tales. "Hard luck is the fortune of all womankind," mourns the singer in an old Anglo-American ballad. "She's always controlled, she's always confined / controlled by her father until she's a wife / then a slave to her husband the rest of her life." A sixteenth-century female poet gave a sharp, pragmatic piece of advice in "Unyoked Is Best! Happy the Woman Without a Man." "Don't hurtle yourself into marriage too soon," she urged:

> *Wedlock's burden is far too heavy.*
> *They know best whom it harnessed.*
> *So often is a wife distressed, afraid. . . .*
>
> *A man oft comes home all drunk and pissed*
> *Just when his wife had worked her fingers to the bone*
> *(So many chores to keep a decent house!),*
> *But if she wants to get in a word or two,*
> *She gets to taste his fist—no more.*[1]

Women had their place in the great chain of submission and authority like everyone else. Many ideas specified how men's and women's natures differed and why these differences placed men over women. But the determining premises came from the story of the Garden of Eden in the third chapter of Genesis, the Bible's second account of Creation, when God makes Woman from one of Adam's ribs. Disobeying God, she succumbs to the serpent's enticements and eats the fruit of the Tree of

Knowledge, bringing catastrophe on humankind. Eve's weak-mindedness set the pattern: Women were judged to be by nature unruly and prone to wreck the divine order with their lust, their fickle characters, their susceptibility to Satan's wiles. Women, too, understood things this way. "Girls were brought up to believe that they ought to obey their husbands," stresses Natalie Zemon Davis, "and boys were brought up to believe that they had the power of correction over their wives."[2]

It was only possible to imagine otherwise by conjuring up a fantastic scenario when the normal order of things was turned upside down—on festival days and in communal rituals, when life went topsy-turvy and women acted like men and sometimes vice versa.[3] But except for those extraordinary moments, men's power over women was a fact of life. Status was complicated and power was never divvied up tidily, with all men holding power over all women: The lady of the manor lorded it over male commoners. But no matter how highborn the woman, she was first and foremost subject to her husband. And because it was impossible to live outside family networks, virtually all adult women were destined for marriage.

Political authority was explicitly modeled on male authority in the family. British common law—which was, of course, the law of the North American colonies—designated the family a realm of government in itself, a kind of gendered jurisdiction where fathers and husbands ruled and (theoretically) protected women, children, laborers, and servants. In a satisfying marriage, a woman saw herself as a man's helpmate, his support and complement, her talents and labor put to the uses of their joint household. Nonetheless, she had no legal standing: Husband and wife were one, with the husband being the "one" before the law. "The very being or legal existence of the woman is suspended during the marriage, or at least is incorporated and consolidated into that of the husband," explained Sir William Blackstone, whose section on marriage in his 1765 *Commentaries* codified English common law.[4] Blackstone gave common law pride of place over other jurisdictions in England—church law and courts of equity—that at times did recognize women's separate legal identity. He thus authorized a body of law especially hostile to women. A husband had rights to any property his wife brought to the marriage, the fruits of her labor, the property they accumulated together, and custody of their children. The principle of coverture pertained: A man "covered," or stood in place of, his dependents before the outside world, including the law and the church (a reminder of coverture today is the custom of a woman taking her husband's name). A wife owed her husband compliance and labor; in return, husbands owed wives economic support and protection. Each owed the other sexual fidelity: Legal monogamy seamlessly bound the couple to Christian doctrine.

But in any social order there are cracks that thoughtful people notice and probe, widening the distance between what is supposed to be and what is. Isolated and unaware of each other, investigators and skeptics over the centuries wondered about women's place. Challenges to prevailing notions of female incapacities began to appear with some regularity in seventeenth-century France and England, from learned ladies who were well connected—Marie le Jars de Gournay, Mary Astell—but also from open-minded men: François Poullain de la Barre, influenced by the principles of Descartes, proposed in the 1670s that the mind had no sex. Although isolated from one another by time and geography, these writers made similar defenses of women's education and criticisms of their position in marriage. Mary Astell, writing in an era when the transatlantic trade in human beings boomed, compared marriage to slavery. "If all Men are born free, how is it that all Women are born slaves?" she inquired.[5]

Beginning with the North American colonies in 1776 and culminating in the Latin American wars of independence in the 1820s, revolution reshaped the Atlantic world. The intellectual origins lay with political philosophers of the British and French Enlightenments who, harking back to the idealized republics of Greece and Rome, proposed that reason and not obedience to God was the basis for proper human relations; that the origins of just government lay in the consent of the governed; and that people possessed certain immutable rights by virtue of being human.

Through the eighteenth century, republican ideas moved growing numbers of critics of monarchy in France, Britain, and British North America, firing their indignity at the way things were and setting in motion plans for what might yet be. The abstract ideas of treatises took on heat as they passed through arguments and conversations in coffeehouses and taverns, newspapers and pamphlets, drawing rooms and kitchens. Revolution fed on revolution. The establishment of the United States of America in 1789 emboldened the French, and the outbreak of the French Revolution inspired the uprising in the West Indian French sugar colony of Saint-Domingue in 1791, which resulted in the world's first republic of emancipated slaves.

These were revolutions made by men who saw themselves as brothers overthrowing tyrannical fathers—as the Americans and later the French labeled their kings.[6] In the crisis that led up to the American Revolution, hot-blooded patriots lambasted George III's abnegation of the role of just patriarch; Tom Paine's sensational *Common Sense* of January 1776 railed against the king as the "wretch . . . with the pretended title of FATHER OF HIS PEOPLE." The colonists in rebellion came to believe that the overthrow of the unnatural father and the triumph of a virtuous people would effect a great change in hearts and minds, "a renovation of the natural order of things." In France, the king's bond with a much maligned queen intensified the sense of ill usage by bad parents. As Lynn Hunt writes, the French "imagined replacing them—the king and the queen—with a different kind of family, one in which the parents were effaced and the children, especially the brothers, acted autonomously."[7]

No one mentioned the analogue, sorority, because sorority was the void at the other end of the ubiquitous idea of fraternity. To be sure, women were not the only people whom the revolutions left in a liminal position. Only in Saint-Domingue did constitution makers recognize the total denial of natural rights that chattel slavery represented. But free women's exclusion is a bit more difficult to grasp because they were not seen as so far outside the polity that they lacked rights altogether, as were slaves, but neither were they seen as full members of the political community.[8]

In the American Revolution, women's subordination was so deeply ingrained that questions about their place in the postrevolutionary order were barely raised. Writers of the British Enlightenment had little to say about women's relationship to liberty and equality, and what they did say tended toward the negative: Women were the agents of foolishness and social retrogression.[9] Their absence in the political theory that legitimated the revolution does not mean, however, that they were marginal to the actual war. Their contributions were crucial: They worked as nurses, spies, couriers, and prison wardens, housed troops, and ran farms, shops, and businesses. A few disguised themselves as men and fought in the army.[10] Here and there one catches a fleeting sense of entitlement, without the words to articulate protest: "I have Don as much to Carrey on the Warr as maney that Sett now at ye healm of government," objected the widow Rachel Wells, a patriot supporter, in 1786 (she had purchased New Jersey war bonds that the state subsequently refused to honor). She called herself a "Sitisen."[11] But in the colonies there was no flood of pamphlets and petitions from women as there would be in France, no learned ladies demanding to be included in political discussions, no intense debates about women's place.[12]

Insofar as patriot leaders thought about women, which was seldom, they thought about their weak characters and the need to keep them in line for everyone's good. "Are not women born as free as men? Would it not be infamous to assert that the ladies are all slaves by nature?" demanded James Otis of Massachusetts in 1764; he was virtually the only patriot to ask the question.[13] No, ladies were not slaves. They were citizens; so were freeborn children. But they were certainly not slated for the generous, activist conception of citizenship the patriots embraced. Tom Paine, whose *Common Sense* was the match to tinder, scoffed at any hereditary basis for rank and distinction but, in a commonsensical spirit, noted that the one basis in nature for social differences was sex. Unlike king and commoner, or the aristocracy and the people, "male and female are the distinctions of nature."[14]

Women were minimal citizens, not energetic participants. Citizenship was so thin for them because wifeliness was so thick. Marriage mediated their relationship to the self-governing nation. Marriage was deemed their normative state, and marriage made them dependents of husbands, putting them in the same category as children. In the republican vocabulary, dependence and its shining opposite, independence, were as much moral states as they were economic categories. To be independent, a person must own property and head a household; propertyless men could not vote, either. Thus single, property-owning women had some rights in the early years of the republic. But wives, like propertyless men and children, were too little acquainted with public affairs to form a right judgment and too dependent on men to have a will of their own. So maintained John Adams, who, we will see, spent some time working out the logic of women's exclusion.[15] Sons grew to adulthood, however, and apprentices, servants, and poor men could in theory acquire the property that conferred independence. Women were dependents for life.

Independent men represented their dependents in public affairs. This was the principle of "virtual representation" that passed intact from the British political system into the new republic. Women had no direct relationship to those who legislated for them, just as the colonies did not elect representatives to Parliament. While Americans repudiated the principle of virtual representation on which British rule was predicated, they retained virtual representation in regard to women. Virtual representation would have a long and hardy life in democratic-republican thought, lingering in various guises around the world well into the twentieth century as the chief argument against women's political rights.

One exception to the silence about women is the famous "remember the ladies" argument that occurred at the very beginning of the American Revolution, in the spring of 1776, between John and Abigail Adams, the future president and his wife. Abigail Adams was at home in Massachusetts, running the family farm as she would for a good decade while her husband served the new government. John Adams was in Philadelphia as a delegate to the Second Continental Congress, which would soon issue the Declaration of Independence. They wrote each other constantly, on matters large and small. The exchange on women is remarkable because the spouses confronted directly a question that everyone else ignored. Their writing has the bite of intimacy: In a sense, it was an argument between a brother and sister—in the ways that long-time spouses can turn into siblings—about the future of the republic.

Abigail Adams was not a learned lady. She was, however, a woman of great intelligence. Born in Massachusetts in 1744 to a prosperous country family, she educated herself in her father's library. When she married the rising lawyer and politician John Adams in 1764, the year before the Stamp Act crisis, she joined a circle of Boston lawyers and merchants who operated at the center of protest. As a woman, she did not strategize and debate with the men, but she shared their republican ardor and their disgust with the English crown. In all this, she was a goodwife, a helpmate to her husband, devoted to domestic affairs and bearing and raising five children. Being a well-behaved woman, however, did not preclude imagining another life, or noticing the limits hers imposed: "Had nature formed me of the other Sex, I should certainly have been a rover," she mused to a family friend in 1771.[16]

In the turbulent months leading up to the Declaration of Independence, that roving habit took her down an intellectual path John Adams considered off limits. In March 1776 she wrote him of her desire to hear that Congress had declared independence. Anticipating the new government, she suggested—she took a helpful tone—that the delegates "remember the ladies, and be more generous and favourable to them than your ancestors." On the subject of tyranny—much on the minds of George III's unhappy North American subjects—she reminded him that everyone knew that ordinary men, too, had a disposition to be tyrants when it came to their wives: "a Truth so thoroughly established as to admit of no dispute." The new laws should restrain such power by preventing "the vicious and the Lawless to use us with cruelty and indignity with impunity."[17]

Abigail probably had in mind the beatings, or "chastisement," that husbands, as masters of their household, could legally inflict on wives, so long as they did not injure them.[18] She did not challenge this system: She opposed men's abuse of their power, not the power itself. Such objections were not out of line for a well-behaved woman, since neighbors and female kin did their best to manage the social order of their communities by bringing the force of disapproval to bear on cruel husbands and intervening when they could. Goodwives, too, had a stake in well-administered family government.

It would not have been the description of men's behavior, then, but rather the suggestion that the Congress take action that riled the delegate from Massachusetts. It was a preposterous thought, and in such testy times it could not be entertained. In asking that the new government protect women by restraining men, Abigail Adams raised disturbing possibilities. In this light, the whole edifice of male governance in the family might be considered an anomaly in a republic. If it was not right to leave women subject to husbands' whims, then should they not exist in a more direct relation to the body politic?[19]

Those mental openings are what John Adams spotted, and why he hauled out the heavy artillery. He blustered, feigning disdain even as his intensity showed how seriously he judged the threat. The tone is heavy-handed mockery, a tactic used against smart argumentative women long before and ever since. "As to your extraordinary Code of Laws, I cannot but laugh." Really, he bantered, it was men who were in the power of women, although it might look the other way around, men who were subject to "the Despotism of the Peticoat." He mused with a patronizing rhetorical chuckle that her proposal seemed to prove their enemies were right when they predicted that the rebellion would create chaos, stirring up children and apprentices, Negroes and Indians. But no one in his wildest dreams thought that women would get riled up, too. "Your Letter was the first Intimation that another Tribe more numerous and powerfull than all the rest were grown discontented."[20]

Insofar as his wife was concerned, he seems to have considered the subject closed. But to fellow Bostonian James Sullivan, Adams confided his worries. The only proper foundation of government was consent. But then, who had to consent? "Shall we say that every individual of the community, old and young, male and female, as well as rich and poor, must consent, expressly, to every act of legislation? No, you will say, this is impossible." But here was the sticking point: "How, then, does the right arise in the majority to govern the minority, against their will? Whence arises the right of the men to govern the women?" Finally, he asked the real question: "Why exclude women?"[21]

Why, indeed? The sparks struck between husband and wife momentarily illuminated a vexing problem. Adams understood that women's uneasy place signified a greater irresolution; it was the contradiction that led to all other contradictions. Natural rights, taken this far, would destroy all distinctions and ranks. "It is dangerous to open so fruitful a source of controversy," he fretted. "There will be no end of it." "New claims will arise." Women would demand the vote; so would young boys, and "every man who has not a farthing, will demand an equal voice with any other." The question opened the door to democracy, at the time associated with the rule of the rabble—a possibility no one at the Continental Congress would entertain.[22]

As for Abigail, she backed down, writing back with a coy couplet about women charming and submitting. She took a different tone, though, when she wrote her friend Mercy Otis Warren. "He is very sausy to me," she complained irritably. Warren was the closest the colonies had to a woman of letters, a counterpart to the literary ladies of Paris and London. The daughter of one prominent patriot and the wife of another, Mercy Otis Warren was at the time publishing (under a pseudonym) anti-British satirical plays, and she would go on to write a major history of the American Revolution. "So I have help'd the Sex abundantly," Abigail concluded, as if knowledge of "the Sex" and its need for help was something she and Warren talked about often. She toyed with the possibility that the two of them might pursue the matter. "I think I will get you to join me in a petition to Congress"—petitions being the one political right women had.[23] But they never did.

Thirteen years later, the first words of the United States Constitution majestically invoked the voice of an entire people agreeing to form a government. The document begins, "We the People of the United States." It did not say "We the Founding Fathers" or "We the politically active minority of white men who have been sent to Philadelphia by our colleagues in the states," historian Linda Kerber wryly observes. In other words, "We the People" was a fiction, an imaginative projection, not a sociological reality.[24] Yet despite their contributions to the revolution, patriot women lacked the means to enter that fiction and reap its benefits.

The revolutionary settlement left the British law of domestic relations untouched. Coverture was retained; if anything, some features actually worsened, although judicial and legislative applications varied by state, in part because the publication of Blackstone's *Commentaries* in the 1760s codified what had been informal legal precedents and the system tightened up. The one exception was divorce. Here the states broke with the harsh British law, which required an act of Parliament to dissolve a marriage (and granted only 325 complete divorces between 1670 and 1857). Laws and courts varied state by state, but overall, looser divorces emerged by 1799, with women as well as men taking full advantage. Still, no one could enter and exit marriage at will. States retained control and a marriage could only end because a judge found that one person had failed to fulfill his or her duties. Typically, only the "wronged" spouse could remarry. The basics remained in place until after 1965, when laws for no-fault divorce began to appear.[25]

The relative liberality of divorce reflected the value Americans placed on marriage as a freely chosen state. Marriages in the New World, after all, were not arranged or coerced. As a model of consenting relations whereby individuals joined together out of love and common interest, marriage took on added ideological freight as a metaphor for the nation. The conjugal ideal recast female subordination as a chosen state, softening the hierarchical connotations of family government, although it did little to change the reality.[26]

The Constitution was mute on the subject of sex: There was nothing in it that spelled out the masculine basis of the political community. Indeed the word "male" was not mentioned until the Fourteenth Amendment in 1868. Yet except for the customary right to petition, women had no political rights, and their civil rights were also constrained. With a few exceptions they couldn't vote, make contracts or recover debts owed them, or buy, own, or sell property.[27] They also lacked the obligations to government that were the corollary of rights and defined the citizen: paying taxes (since they were not householders), working on the public roads, and serving on juries and in the militia. The last was more important than it seems: The exemption from the duty to bear arms in defense of the republic devolved from the facts of female irresolution, fickleness, and weakness. Thus John Adams thought the most obvious answer to Abigail's challenge was that women's delicacy made them unfit for "the hardy enterprises of war, as well as the arduous cares of state."[28]

In sum, the nation as yet had no use for women. The enfranchised citizenry was a minority legislating for a majority, an archipelago of white male property holders surrounded by a sea of the voteless.

Later in the 1790s, a cultural reevaluation came into play, a way to confer on women an ideological part to play, as mothers. Ideas about republican motherhood assured Americans that women too could add to the sum of citizenly virtue. As mothers and helpmates exercising reason, they could pass on the capacities for civic engagement to their sons. Thus the mother could be a silent partner to the active male citizen. Republican motherhood was a small gain that did not address women's enforced absence from the affairs of the nation, but it did have important consequences. In the short run, the enthusiasm of prominent gentlemen and a few ladies for enhancing female reason through education—the Philadelphia physician Benjamin Rush, signer of the Declaration of Independence; Judith Sargent Murray, a Massachusetts patriot and essayist; the popular novelist Susanna Rowson—promoted the establishment of girls' schools. And in the long run, the image of the virtuous mother implanting civic benevolence in her sons (only secondarily her daughters) undercut the older misogynistic disdain for the sex who bore the guilt of Eve. In the emerging middle class, women began to radiate natural virtue, a cultural acquisition that would over the next century work to enhance their access to broader participation in public affairs. Stereotypes of lustful, depraved, unruly women began to gravitate toward poor laboring women and slaves.[29]

In contrast to American women's acquiescence to their marginal place, women in the French Revolution forcefully engaged in the Revolution's tumult, surprising and shocking onlookers with their patriotic fervor and militant demands. Not all, but some called for rights for women, and their claims played an important role in both the brightest hopes of the Revolution and its dark outcome. To the political right, they were harpies, and in time republican men also drew from the old playbook of misogyny to condemn them as dangerous and out of control. Countering the animosity, revolutionary women trumpeted their patriotism; they were *les citoyennes*, conscientious members of the new order.

French women in 1789 entered the revolutionary crisis with a store of ideas and traditions to draw upon in presenting themselves as political actors. Women of all classes were accustomed to political roles, from aristocratic ladies engaged in machinations at court to street sellers who rioted for bread when prices soared. Intellectual and literary women reigned over semi-public, semi-private salons where conversation set the terms for political debate at large. A few worked as journalists in the crackling scene of Paris newspapers. Finally, the French Enlightenment theorists—*les philosophes*—whose ideas inspired and fed popular agitation, had long considered the place of women in a just society. This literature was hardly a brief for women's rights. Quite the opposite. Eighteenth-century writers made women's deference to men a keystone of good government, most famously Jean-Jacques Rousseau, whose philosophical novels linked female submission and domestic duty to the state of nature that underlay the common good.[30] But the work nonetheless brought issues of women's place in the polity to the surface of discussion.[31]

This meant that women entered the revolutionary crisis primed by questions that had already been asked, even though the answer was always the same: They belonged at home. From the first outbreak of agitation, bands of women sought to join the revolutionary fraternity. The 1789 women's march on the court at Versailles launched the revolt against the monarchy: Clamoring for lower food prices, the crowd looked both backward to the ancient tradition of the food riot and forward to the demands of empowered citizens, by actually moving the seat of government when they brought the king and queen back to Paris. Women's activity swelled thereafter—unrestrained, seemingly impetuous, but in actuality organized and purposeful. For years afterward on two continents, images of French viragoes would be used to smear women who went too far.

In 1791, women poured into the National Assembly, the representative body of the constitutional monarchy, and from the galleries joined in debates and votes. They joined a number of the revolutionary clubs and formed a few of their own. Women in the clubs watched closely the National Assembly's deliberations and worked to endow *la citoyenne* with virtue, reason, and responsibility. Well-to-do *bourgeoises* called them to serve the republic by supervising state-run facilities for poor women, beefing up traditional feminine charity work as a kind of republican social service administration. But others lobbied for political equality and civil reforms: an equitable divorce bill, equalization of inheritance, and (here it is again, Abigail Adams's hope) protection from wife beating. The French joined the United States in liberalizing divorce, but with a more radical twist. A couple could be divorced by common consent rather than because one spouse charged the other with malfeasance, a provision that carried with it the shocking implication that marriages could be dissolved at will. The next year, two and a half times as many women as men took advantage of the new law, most frequently because of a husband's abuse.[32]

The high-water mark came in the months before and after the constitution of 1791. Arguments about female equality surged back and forth. The Marquis de Condorcet, a leading *philosophe*, published *A Plea for the Citizenship of Women*, which made the case for full political rights on the basis of universal reason: "Now the rights of men result only from this, that men are beings with sensibility, capable of acquiring moral ideas, and of reasoning on those ideas. So women, having these same qualities, have necessarily equal rights." He concluded sharply that "either no individual of the human race has genuine rights, or else all have the same."[33]

The next year, Olympe de Gouges published her remarkable "Declaration of the Rights of Woman." Gouges was a Paris playwright of common birth, and royalist in allegiance. Her relationship to democratic aspirations was uneasy—she addressed her "Rights of Woman" to the queen. Yet she reached further than any contemporary, to expose the hypocrisy of radical rationales for masculine sovereignty. Gouges sardonically questioned the very basis of male authority—"Tell me, what gives you sovereign empire to oppress my sex?" she demanded of male readers. "Man" was for her no abstraction but rather the literal man of the revolutionary clubs who "pretends to enjoy the Revolution and to claim his rights to equality" but dodged his responsibility for women's situation, preferring "to command as a despot." She called for a national assembly of women to draw up their own declaration of rights.[34]

In 1793, Gouges was imprisoned for circulating tracts critical of the Terror and executed as an enemy of the republic. Her death and the ultimate crushing of women's demands condemned her "Declaration" to obscurity. But the fact that her ideas had no immediate consequences should not obscure what they show about the revolutionary process. For a moment, the republican brotherhood seemed contingent and assailable. The Declaration was "both compensatory—adding women where they have been left out," observes Joan Wallach Scott, "and a critical challenge to the universality of the term 'Man.'"[35]

From the beginning, opposition came from both the political right and the left. Women's historic power in the French court left a toxic association in the popular mind between female political involvement and aristocratic decadence and guile; this cluster of images joined perennial anxieties about unruly women to stir up antipathy, even in the earliest heady days. Even Condorcet thought women should refrain from undue political activity lest they neglect their domestic duties. "You take care of your household government," the editor of a widely read radical newspaper lashed out against the women's clubs, "and let us take care of the republic; let men make the revolution."[36]

In the end the National Assembly did not consider women's suffrage, and the 1791 constitution divided the republic into active and passive citizens. Active citizens were male and could vote and hold office. Passive citizens could not. The category included all women along with men of the lower ranks of property, age, occupation, status, and color. French women gained more civil rights than did their American peers. Along with divorce, the constitution made marriage a civil contract and remedied discrepancies in inheritance and property rights that had debilitated widows and daughters.[37]

As other European powers united against the Revolution and the republic called its men to arms, the requirements for total citizenly dedication intensified; and the standards for sacrifice, virtue, and purity in defense of the nation became weapons of political reprisal. When the Terror began with its executions and imprisonments, female political activity became a lightning rod for accusations. The Jacobins had long distrusted the more moderate and bourgeois Girondins for their tolerance for women. Now their opposition hardened into enmity and with it, charges of being counterrevolutionary: The Girondin women were labeled sirens and harpies whose monstrous lust for power endangered the republic. In 1793, the Committee of Public Safety shut down the women's clubs. In 1795, when the Committee was overthrown and the Revolution entered its next phase, the Directory prohibited women from joining any public gathering at all. A version of republican motherhood emerged. What was a conservative response in the United States to tensions about woman's place thus came from darker origins in

France. There, Bonnie Smith concludes, "a combination of bloodshed and legislation helped usher in domesticity."[38]

At the end of this first phase of the natural rights revolution, a kind of national motherhood was the ideological resolution to the problem of woman's place. In years to come, too, wherever other revolutions triumphed, ideas about enhanced roles for mothers in the nation's service helped to rein in the female participants whose assent—if not formal consent—to the political compact was still required.

From the first convulsions in Paris in 1789, the attention of a young writer in London, Mary Wollstonecraft, was fixed on the French Revolution and all it augured. Wollstonecraft was part of a group of English and American writers and artists, ultra-democrats and fervent supporters of the French. She was the only woman writer among them and in fact one of a handful of women in Britain earning a living with her pen. She had been churning out book reviews, essays, and political commentary since she arrived in London in 1787. In 1790 she rose to the challenge of Edmund Burke's attack on the Revolution with *A Vindication of the Rights of Men,* preceding Tom Paine's far more famous *Rights of Man* by a month.

In 1792 she followed with *A Vindication of the Rights of Woman.* There had really never been anything like it in length or ambition, although it was published a year after Olympe de Gouges' pamphlet and two years after Condorcet's defense of women's citizenship. It appears that Wollstonecraft had read neither, but a similar sense of urgency pervades her text: Like them, she knew she was living through a sea change in history. She did not venture as far as the French did into the subject of political rights; indeed she did not mention political rights at all. But being in London, not Paris, and having more mental space and time, she went deeper, to excavate and catalog the material of women's subjection.

At once magnificent, impetuous, repetitive, and tedious, the book was one of many radical proposals that appeared in the early 1790s, but it was the only one that spoke to the problem of women. There was a serious male as well as female readership, radicals and enlightened Anglo-Americans who believed that the hopes of the era lay not only in perfecting government but in bringing harmony and virtue to the relations of the sexes.[39] Over the next fifty years, the *Vindication* would acquire a reputation in Europe and America as the book of all books for those considering the plight of women. As it turned out, it laid out the themes and approaches that would structure half a century of feminist thought and more.

It is a long book, circular and rambling, written at a time when reading was a chief form of popular entertainment and readers could follow lengthy clause-laden disquisitions as easily as they could listen to two-hour Sunday sermons. Some of Wollstonecraft's dense paragraphs consist of one sentence that unwinds for a full page. But the text retains the excitement of ideas being worked through for the first time, showstopping declarations put forth and fiercely argued. There's a headlong rush to the prose, ideas tumbling over one another to stand up and be heard. Wollstonecraft rambles, takes up a subject, drops it, and then recurs to it four, six, eight times; she denounces, accuses, laments, complains, and blames. In a way, taking so long on the topic was in itself a form of vindication.

Wollstonecraft was little more than thirty years old when she wrote the *Vindication*. Born in 1759, she was slated for a life very different from the one she ended up with. Her father, a gentleman farmer, was an alcoholic who wasted his patrimony and dragged the family into poverty. She learned young about unfettered male power; an early memory was of lying outside her parents' bedroom door pleading with her father to stop beating her mother. At nineteen, she left home to earn her own living. Had she kept to that track, the best that could have happened would have been a marriage to a kindly gentleman of modest means. More likely, she would have continued to cycle through the weary round of underpaid employments available to genteel impoverished women. Teacher, governess, ladies' companion, seamstress: She worked in all those capacities, fearing she was becoming a "very poor creature" as she trudged through the vast, sad netherworld of nervous, obsequious gentlewomen of reduced means.

In her Pilgrim's Progress through the trials of women, though, she veered off the track when at the age of twenty-eight and slipping past marriageability, she went to London to try her luck as a writer. She was already writing short essays on education and morals; now she intended to make a living from them. "I am then going to be the first of a new genus," she bragged to her sister in 1787. "You know I am not born to tread in the beaten track—the peculiar bent of my nature pushes me on."[40] In London, her kindly editor and publisher Joseph Johnson took her under his wing and served as her protector in a city where a single woman, alone and unchaperoned, was sure to be thought a prostitute. She was energetic and argumentative enough to succeed in a world where speed, prolixity, and a polemical style brought literary assignments and reputation, and she was confident enough to function on her own. Wollstonecraft became a regular at Johnson's dinners for his shabby, brilliant friends, a circle of radicals and rationalists that included Paine, the naturalist Erasmus Darwin (grandfather of Charles), and the philosophical anarchist William Godwin.[41]

They were keyed to a pitch for news from across the channel. It was the high tide of hope: The Americans had just established a constitutional republic, the first in history; the Bastille had fallen, the French had drawn up a liberal constitution; revolution in Britain seemed close; and perhaps an end to despotism in human history was imminent. The Terror was not yet in sight. Having written her *Rights of Men* in the vein of the men around her, Wollstonecraft seems to have been freed up to bring the spirit of the day to a preoccupation that was hers alone. She dashed off *A Vindication of the Rights of Woman* in six weeks.

The focus of her ire was Talleyrand's proposal to the French for a system of public education that expelled girls from school at the age of eight, to return home to apprentice in the domestic arts until they married. Her real polemical enemy, however, was Rousseau, whose views on women's nature underlay Talleyrand's scheme. Rousseau's description of sexual difference was so extreme that it was as if men and women were fashioned out of different stuff altogether, with man as humanity's standard issue and woman a grace note to complement and please him. Rousseau's work cast doubt on whether natural rights and liberty even pertained to such docile, childish people. But though he was Wollstonecraft's chief antagonist, Rousseau was also her inspiration. For all his certainty, his fanciful concoctions of the ideal female gave Wollstonecraft the means to show that conventional femininity was a product of male fantasy. Much of the *Vindication* is taken up with a point-by-point rebuttal of Rousseau's views—difficult for us to read now, but interesting for eighteenth-century readers who could watch a female David take on the Gallic Goliath.[42]

The *Vindication* strenuously argued for education for girls in order to cultivate their reason, and thus their moral strength and virtue. Wollstonecraft decried the assumption that there was nothing wrong with leaving girls in ignorance. She picked apart the premises of a system that made women so psychologically and materially dependent on male approval that they turned into housebound ninnies. This was the point at which she took on Rousseau's premise that female dependency was a felicitous state. "Women are told from their infancy, and taught by the example of their mothers, that a little knowledge of human weakness, justly termed cunning, softness of temper, outward obedience, and a scrupulous attention to a puerile kind of propriety, will obtain for them the protection of man; and should they be beautiful, every thing else is needless." Woman "was created to be the toy of man, his rattle, and it must jingle in his ears whenever, dismissing reason, he chooses to be amused."[43] It was Wollstonecraft's brilliance both to acknowledge that there was truth in these descriptions of women's limitations and to show that the truths were arbitrary, enforced by social arrangements and male power.

Women learned to be women, she insisted, in order to survive in a society that made marriage their sole destiny. There was nothing natural about female character; it developed out of fear of being left alone, shunned and penniless—a reject of the marriage market. Wollstonecraft dissected the grim psychology of seduction that Rousseau celebrated. "Gentleness, docility, and a spaniel-like affection," she sarcastically observed, "are, on this ground, consistently recommended as the cardinal virtues of the sex."[44] The coy, yielding character that Rousseau praised was, in actuality, pounded into women and turned rancid as girls matured: Coquetry became manipulation, innocence went flaccid and became stupidity, and the obsession with pleasing men flowed into a narcissistic preoccupation with fashion and beauty fatal to a well-conducted home life and virtuous motherhood. Lassitude and vanity rendered women incapable of taking part in humanity's great aims. The solution? Relieve women of the crippling task of being feminine. "The only method of leading women to fulfill their peculiar duties, is to free them from all restraint by allowing them to participate in the inherent rights of mankind." Educate them, cultivate their reason, and there would be a huge payoff for humanity: "Make them free, and they will quickly become wise and virtuous, as men become more so; for the improvement must be mutual."[45]

One of her most prescient and touching proposals was for bodily freedom for girls. Wollstonecraft thought girls should play with boys and run wild, not be kept indoors to play with dolls and fidget with picky needlework. When female frailty was seen to be beautiful, it followed that girls would be trussed up and tamped down: "The limbs and faculties are cramped with worse than Chinese bands, and the sedentary life which they are condemned to live, whilst boys frolic in the open air, weakens the muscles and relaxes the nerves."[46] She wanted girls to use their bodies and minds instead to develop active, vigorous reason, so that women too could take part in the world, discharging "the higher duties" to the public good.

Although she wrote in defense of her sex, Wollstonecraft accepted the more hateful images of women that the eighteenth century offered. For all its hopes for a better future in store, the *Vindication* is a highly unsympathetic portrait of actual women. The book is peopled with schemers, sluts, man chasers, sloppy housekeepers, unfeeling mothers, and faithless wives. She understood why men disparaged women, and she usually agreed with them. "Men complain, and with reason, of the follies and caprices of our sex." "That women at present are by ignorance rendered foolish or vicious is, I think, not to be disputed."[47] Men's absolute power over women made them tyrants, she explained, echoing the antislavery argument being broached at the time that masters' power over slaves turned them into despots. Nevertheless, it was women who were the culprits. A reader can be forgiven if she comes away thinking that women are the crux of the problem and that the model to emulate is male.

Wollstonecraft's own life gives depth and poignancy to these images. She knew conventional femininity and its perils intimately in the persons of her battered, humiliated mother and the forlorn sisters she left behind—usually needling and always needy. In her years eking out a living at the edges of society, she saw how low women could sink even when they had money and position. In 1786–87, before she took off for London, she worked as a governess in a family where the mother, a horsey Anglo-Irish aristocrat, cared little for her children and everything for her dogs. There's a great deal of Lady Kingsborough in Wollstonecraft's portraits of bad mothers (and something of the memory of the dogs in the recurrent phrase "spaniel-like affection"). As a lady's companion at the edges of English ballrooms in high season, a spectator at the marriage mart, she watched women angle and maneuver to catch husbands. She was smart and pretty, and she would turn out to have a loving, sexual nature; yet she had to hold those qualities in check while she bided her time watching far less appealing women get on in life. It is no surprise that she harbored a sense of injured superiority. Her letters show that she felt those infirmities within herself even as she projected them onto other women; bitter self-denigration alternated with high-flying self-importance.

The problem that snagged Wollstonecraft was not solely biographical, however, but intellectual. It remains embedded in the feminist tradition. How much can the feminist identify herself with her sex when she sees women swamped by infirmity? The desire to escape womanhood waxes and wanes, but it is acute in the thinker who confronts the damage. What does she lose by siding with women and acknowledging that she shares their lot?

Over two hundred years, feminists have found different solutions to the dilemma of how to write powerfully about the powerless. To simplify, one can divide them into two camps: those who liked other women and those who didn't. Betty Friedan never much liked other women; Virginia Woolf did. Elizabeth Cady Stanton, for all her towering brilliance, always wrote *with* women as well as *to* them. Simone de Beauvoir wrote majestically about the wrongs done to women, but like Wollstonecraft she held herself apart, the special one who rose above the common issue of womankind to rival men. As for Wollstonecraft, dislike of womanhood shoots through her book, and it is difficult to see, given her scheme, how such limited creatures can really change. Writing about women and for women, and seeking earnestly to improve their standing, she simultaneously distanced herself from the common lot.

Intellectually and emotionally, she identified reason and virtue as male. In her personal life, it was to men, not women, she appealed as "fellow creatures," the makers of freedom. "I entreat them to assist to emancipate their companion." She lived in a world that was so bifurcated by sex that it was hard to imagine ambition, drive, and a thirst for liberty as anything but theirs. Musing on the problem, she wondered if "the few extraordinary women who have rushed in eccentrical directions out of the orbit prescribed to their sex, were *male* spirits, confined by mistake in female frames." But the idea of repudiating her sex altogether was not appealing either. Barbara Taylor, Wollstonecraft's most tender and insightful modern critic, has this to say about her dilemma: "Attacking the 'factitious' femininity foisted on women, she tried to see herself as a woman sans Woman, a self undivided by sexual distinctions, a genderless soul forged in God's image."[48] Her sense of superiority allowed her to draw closer to the radical brothers as a peer, assimilable to their mental world and conversations. She could foresee being a mother, and her plans for womankind depended on elaborating that role in a republican framework. But for the moment, in writing the *Vindication,* it was from the vantage point of the sister that she could most easily glimpse more equitable relations and a common project with men.

Occasionally, though, she did consolidate a sense of women as fully developed beings worthy in themselves, not creatures in need of an overhaul. Education would be the means. "I wish to see women neither heroines nor brutes, but reasonable creatures," she averred. The simple, monumental hope is tucked away in a footnote.[49] Her recurrence to the Aristotelian distinction between humans and animals—"brutes"— shows just how dismal was the prevailing opinion of women. Were their minds and capacities really equal to the fullest measure of humanity's— that is, men's? Those mental capacities remained, we will see, an item of contention not for decades but for centuries.

"A wild wish has just flown from my heart to my head," she wrote at one juncture: She vowed she would not hold back, even if she were ridiculed.[50] Her sense of a guffawing presence—it seems to be just behind her, looking down censoriously at what she's writing — anticipates by 140 years Virginia Woolf's image in *A Room of One's Own* of an invisible committee of critical gentlemen hovering over every female writer's shoulder.[51] "I do earnestly wish to see the distinction of sex confounded in society," Wollstonecraft went on to state. The formu- lation is plain, but it is daring. Wollstonecraft ventured right up to the thought that the differences between men and women should not count at all. And then (depending on how one sees it) she pulled back, or saw the complications, or came to her senses. She backtracked and qualified: "Unless where love animates the behavior." Sexual desire itself, the ani- mation of love, comprised the irreducible difference.

The passage about wild wishes offers a glimpse into a less visible strain of Wollstonecraft's thought, her attempt to understand the force of sexual desire between men and women. Wollstonecraft grappled as hard with the grip of passion and sexual love as any woman of her time (or ours). As much as ambition, her need for sexual happiness and men's love pushed her on. "On examining my heart," she once confessed, "I find that it is so constituted, I cannot live without some particular affection—I am afraid not without a passion."[52] Traveling to Paris in 1793, she fell in love with an American adventurer, Gilbert Imlay, a charming ne'er-do-well and womanizer. As danger mounted in the cap- ital, the two retreated to the countryside. There she had a child with him out of wedlock, suffered through his lengthening absences and growing coldness, tried to win him back by sailing the miserable stormy north- ern seas to Denmark to help his business affairs, her toddler in tow, and deluded herself for months about his devotion. In the agonizing last act of the affair, she twice tried to kill herself.

Yet something more was in store for her, a relationship that was at once a love affair and writers' partnership. Recovering from her last suicide attempt in London, Wollstonecraft fell in love with and married the con- firmed bachelor William Godwin, the ascetic middle-aged philosopher who frequented Joseph Johnson's evenings. "Friendship melting into love" was how Godwin memorably described the affair. The union was happy, productive, and erotic, and it produced some of the most enchanting love letters a great feminist ever wrote and received. Him: "And now, my dear love, what do you think of me?" Her: "Men are spoilt by frankness, I believe, yet I must tell you that I love you better than I supposed I did, when I promised to love you forever."[53] With Wollstonecraft's daughter, they made a family, living side by side in two little houses in London, meeting for meals, spending the nights together. In 1797, she died giving birth to their child.

The anguished Godwin paid tribute to her memory by publishing the next year a memorial biography. Blinded by grief, oblivious to convention, he thereby revealed to an appalled Anglo-American readership the scandalous facts: her passion for another man, the child born out of wedlock, the suicide attempts. Appearing as conservative reaction against the French Revolution gathered force, the book had the effect of turning Wollstonecraft into an exemplar of the low morals and dangerous excesses of the revolutionary years, an English stand-in for "the revolutionary harpies of France, sprung from night and hell"—Edmund Burke's fevered image. Abhorrence for all things revolutionary linked ideas of sexual equality to the dreadful time when blood ran in the streets of Paris. Wollstonecraft's life, intimately associated with that period of "wild wishes," was treated as an instance of female passion run amuck, the author a "hyena in petticoats," Horace Walpole charged.[54]

Between 1798 and 1820, the ideas dropped out of public discussion. The *Vindication* was a fugitive text, circling in eddies of radical dissent and private grievances, artifact of an abandoned project. Sometime in the early 1800s, for instance, Anna Wheeler, a young wife trapped on her alcoholic husband's estate in Ireland, read the book and thereby started to assemble the mental resources that eventually helped her escape.[55] In America, copies were scarcer but the old editions had long lives, passed around and pondered over. From Maine in 1801, Eliza Southgate, an astute teenage reader, fired off mettlesome letters to a supercilious male cousin about women's proper role. Anticipating mockery when she mentioned Wollstonecraft, she was careful not to associate herself too closely. Yet even as she wobbled back and forth in her allegiances, she insisted there was more to Wollstonecraft than people granted. "Though I allow her to have said many things which I cannot but approve, yet the very foundation on which she builds her work will be apt to prejudice us so against her that we will not allow her the merit she really deserves."[56]

Democratic-radical workingmen, eager young women such as Southgate, and enlightened gentlemen in Britain and the United States fastened onto the ideas of the *Vindication*.[57] Over several generations, the life and the book, the love affairs and the ideas would inspire gratitude and fellow feeling.

Margaret Fuller, the New England Transcendentalist who herself knew what it was to work and love on terms far in advance of her times, was the first to rise to the defense. In 1845, Fuller used a Romantic vocabulary of the inner life to cast Wollstonecraft as a gifted being "rich in genius, of most tender sympathies, capable of high virtue and a chastened harmony." Such women should be allowed space, Fuller insisted, "room in the world," "light and air." They "ought not to find themselves, by birth, in a place so narrow, that, in breaking bonds, they become outlaws." Much later, Virginia Woolf, reflecting on Wollstonecraft from the vantage point of the 1920s and her own literary marriage, found her still a living presence, wonderfully "high-handed and hot-blooded," above all in the marriage to Godwin: "She is alive and active, she argues and experiments, we hear her voice and trace her influence even now among the living."[58]

Today, Wollstonecraft's life and work still bear scrutiny and admiration. She lived and wrote at the far edge of what was possible and tangled with all the confusions which that position confers upon the brave and foolhardy. Yet while she has been held up as First Feminist for some two centuries, Wollstonecraft has always been an unsuitable founding mother. Her untidy life, her naked need for love, her failures and vagaries, militated against her reliability as symbol of rectitude and fidelity to her sex. "Nervous and commanding" was how Eliza Southgate described her: Nervous and commanding she still stands.[59] Wollstonecraft never did bear idealization, nor did she seek it out. Barbara Taylor points out that while she held herself above other women, she was also leery of heroines. Regardless of boasting about being special, she drew back from romanticizing the singular woman, because she believed the great majority of women were so oppressed that simple right-minded behavior was beyond them: the ability to act as "reasonable creatures."[60]

A Vindication of the Rights of Woman laid the intellectual basis for modern feminism. For all the hostilities to actual women embedded in its pages, the achievement was to announce, in a hundred different ways and from many different angles, that power, not nature, determined the relations of women and men. Expectations about how women should think and act were in truth born of a system of male privilege and tyranny as corrupt as any monarchy.

A pattern emerged that held for the next century, at the least. Women's rights could be sidelined and rebuked by the very democratic forces that gave rise to the ideas. The fact was that those democratic forces were in the hands of men, who continued to have difficulty remembering the ladies. Liberal democracy as it emerged was fragile, incomplete, and halting; feminism was all the more fractured. The tradition that Wollstonecraft announced would drop out of sight, reappear, branch, divide, and recombine many times over. The understanding of the Woman to be vindicated and her "rights" was never straightforward. The relationship to liberal and radical politics was always tense and often hostile.

Feminist theorists, looking back on this opening chapter of democracy, have stressed that liberalism was always premised on women's subjection; that the female sex was the exception to equality that made equality imaginable. Liberal democracy's abstract promises were—and remain—resistant to extending their benefits across the sex line. Whether this limitation is inherent in liberalism, as they maintain, the liberal rights-bearing citizen remained paradigmatically male for more than a century.

At the same time, it was only democratic movements that offered sanctuary to the aspirations of women. Far into the future, the converse would also be true: Feminism would harbor battered democratic hopes. Democracy and feminism: It was an asymmetrical relationship, with the brothers always claiming the ground of genderless humanity, the sisters forever asserting their importance yet finding themselves pushed into the corner where exceptions to the universal belonged. But in fact, we will see that one did not proceed long without the other.

CHAPTER TWO

BROTHERS AND SISTERS

*Women's Rights
and the Abolition of Slavery*

In 1840, British and American leaders of the movement to abolish slavery met together for the first time at the World Anti-Slavery Convention in London. The occasion called for unity, but a conflict broke out before the meeting even began when the British hosts refused to seat eight American female delegates. Worse, they put all the women bystanders plus rejected delegates—in a section behind a curtain in order to avoid exposing them to a public that included strange men. The episode was the culmination of ten years of women's participation and conflict in the American branch of abolitionism. "Am I not a man and a brother?" the kneeling slave on the abolitionist emblem hauntingly cried. The question buried in the fraternal ideal rose to the surface: What about the sisters?

The movement to abolish slavery originated with Quakers in the late eighteenth century. It gained the devotion of free American blacks after the American Revolution, and emerged as a force in the United States in the 1830s. In Britain and the United States, women were drawn to abolition; and in America the logic of natural rights and abolition's abhorrence of human subjugation led them to see their own situation as akin to the slaves'. "Since I engaged in the investigation of the rights of the slave, I have necessarily been led to a better understanding of my own," avowed Angelina Grimké, whose public speaking on the subject in 1837 would set off a crisis.[1] With their fervor and iconoclasm, female abolitionists emblazoned the claims of Woman with the brilliant radicalism of the era.

Despite their identical goals and their many ties, the British and American movements were very different. In Britain, abolition was a broad-based movement aligned with moderate public opinion. British abolitionists succeeded in ending slavery in the British West Indies in 1833. In the United States, it was a radical cause carried on by an unpopular minority, representing what many saw as an intolerable affront to political culture. Slavery in the United States was not a remote fact of faraway colonies, as it was in Britain, nor were people of African descent a neglible presence as they were there. Slavery and racial prejudice were ingrained in the country's economy, society, politics, and Constitution. In 1830, there were more than two million enslaved people in the United States, some three hundred thousand free blacks, and a booming internal slave trade between the upper and lower South. The stakes were much higher than in England, and the questions of citizenship and rights for free blacks unavoidable. American abolition, with its mix of black and white advocates, was besieged by virulent hostility.

Antislavery activity among whites in the earlier nineteenth century took the form of the influential American Colonization Society, founded in 1816, which advocated manumitting (partially freeing) slaves and sending them to Liberia in West Africa. In the early 1830s, a handful of white reformers repudiated colonization and embraced the black demand for immediate abolition and civil rights. Led by William Lloyd Garrison, a Boston printer and reformer of unflagging zeal, a cadre of antislavery Quakers, Unitarians, and evangelicals joined with free African-Americans in Boston to form the group that became the nucleus of the American Anti-Slavery Society (AASS). British West Indian emancipation in 1833 gave inspiration and hope. By 1837, the high point of the AASS, there were tens of thousands of supporters in New England, the Middle Atlantic, Pennsylvania, and Ohio and some two thousand chapters. The organization flooded Congress with petitions calling for measures such as the abolition of slavery in the District of Columbia and the abolition of the Constitution's three-fifths clause, which gave extra representation to the South in the House of Representatives and the Electoral College.[2]

On both continents, women formed their own abolitionist societies. But in the United States, female participation was much more daring. Black women founded the first all-female society in Salem, Massachusetts, in 1833. The associations were concentrated in Massachusetts, New York state, and the Philadelphia area, and stretched out through northern Ohio and Indiana. While white middle-class women dominated the membership, with a sprinkling of the wealthy, the societies also included women of modest means, white and black. Female abolition was strong in the Massachusetts industrial towns, for instance: Lynn, Lowell, and Fall River. Women from the tiny black urban middle class were present throughout, comprising about 10 percent of the membership in the Philadelphia Female Anti-Slavery Society (PFASS), one of the strongest chapters.[3]

Abolitionist women believed that salvation, their own and the nation's, required that they no less than men answer God's call. Many had been born again in God's grace in the Second Great Awakening, the Protestant revivals that swept through America in the 1820s and '30s. In emphasizing the believer's unmediated relationship to God and the urgency of carrying the message of salvation to others, the revivals authorized new forms of female action and speech in, for example, crusades to ban alcohol, observe the Sabbath more strictly, and organize Sunday schools. Evangelicalism enhanced their ability to speak and act with authority in the churches, testifying to their experiences of grace, in Christian associations, and in their families, leading prayers and struggling with the souls of loved ones. Ministers tried to contain them, devoting sermons and making rules to delineate their proper role. But their zeal forced church authorities to be flexible in interpreting the passages of scripture used for centuries to sideline them—above all Paul's injunction to the Corinthians, echoed in the epistle to Timothy: "Let your women keep silence in the churches."

Women's enhanced role in the revivals spurred energetic discussion. From the pulpits and press in the 1820s and 1830s, ideas about Christian domesticity refashioned republican motherhood into an explicitly Protestant and implicitly middle-class understanding. The home was no longer an adjunct to public life where women reared educated sons; it was a sphere of its own, a separate source of national values and morality, flourishing under the authority of women and, by its very distance from worldly matters, close to God.

Female abolitionists worked the tenets of domesticity into a justification of unconventional outspokenness and unpopular views. Theirs was a defense that combined the older view of the genderless soul—in Christ there is no male or female—with new assertions about the distinct moral understanding conferred on their sex. They believed they brought an intensified understanding to the cause by virtue of their piety and identification with female slaves, as they reached out in their imaginations—some spoke of the transmigration of souls—to women who were in chains. They spoke elliptically of masters' sexual degrada- tion of slave women and bluntly described the desecration of mothers' souls when owners tore them from their children. "By day and by night, their woes and wrongs rise up before us, throwing shades of mournful contrast over the joys of domestic life."[4]

Domestic ideology could thus serve antithetical ends. It was a conser- vative understanding compatible with longstanding patriarchal beliefs and an ideology of extreme sexual difference, but it also undercut some of the most toxic eighteenth-century assumptions about women's weak characters and dignified their advance into quasi-political space. Rather than slated simply to be mothers of future citizens, they became paramount moral actors with some limited authority beyond the home.

But how limited? British abolitionist women did not press the matter but hewed to a conception of their work as charity, much like minister- ing to distressed sailors or poor widows. They deferred to male author- ity and did not angle for a role in the men's organization (which was really the main organization).[5] American abolitionist women found them irritatingly timid and conventional when they met one another in London: "They had little to tell us," complained the Philadelphian Sarah Pugh, "and had but little desire to hear anything we had to say . . . fearing they might get 'out of their sphere' should they speak aloud even in a social circle."[6] But in the more democratic political culture of the United States, abolitionism opened up the contradiction between women's influence and the power of men and the churches to limit their compass. Was it enough for female societies to exist as an outgrowth of the domestic sphere, or did God ask them to do more?

The AASS struggled with these questions, seeking to calibrate social convention with God's will. At first, men in the organization did not admit women as full members; then women could be members but could not speak. Later, they could speak but not in mixed meetings; then they could speak in the meetings but not serve on committees. Then they could serve on some committees but not on others. And so it went through the 1830s.

In each controversy, women and their male supporters pressed to make room for the sexes to work together. Christianity provided the lan- guage for a coequal relationship: "Your brother in Christ." "Your sister in Christ." So they signed their constant letters to each other. The sibling metaphor sanctioned relationships between the sexes outside marriage and family ties. It made possible working partnerships between the sexes and put friendship between a man and a woman, that most anomalous of relationships, onto an elevated basis.

The achievement may seem modest. A small group of high-minded people infused a scriptural phrase with new meaning. Yet the idea that people could hold loyalties that transcended kin and country had appalled conservatives since Wollstonecraft's day, when detractors accused her of urging women to desert their children to pledge their energies to their sex instead.[7] Now it seems counterintuitive, but feminism in its first American phase came out of a sensibility that bestowed meaning and purpose on ties between the sexes. Sisterhood was indeed powerful for early feminism, but sisters had brothers as well.

One of the first women to profit from the sibling relations of abolitionism was Maria Stewart, a young African American living in Boston who briefly came to prominence in the early 1830s with the help of William Lloyd Garrison. Stewart was the first American woman to speak out publicly on the woman question (although the fact is little known). She began her brief but astounding public career as an exhorter and a prophet, and her protests on women's behalf always returned to abolitionist and racial themes: the wrongs of prejudice and slavery, and the moral lapses of the free black community. But her attention to the plight of the race did not subsume her care for women.

Born in Connecticut in 1803, possibly to free parents, Stewart was orphaned as a small child and grew up in the most miserable of circumstances, an indentured servant—which is really to say a drudge—from the age of five. She only had six weeks of formal schooling; like many poor children, she learned the rudiments of reading in Sunday school but apparently little of writing, for when she wrote her first essay she dictated it to an amanuensis, a ten-year-old girl. In 1826, she married a ship's chandler in Boston who was a navy veteran of the war of 1812 and a man of property. Stewart thereby lucked momentarily into fortune, joining the city's minuscule black middle class. She almost certainly would have known David Walker, another shopkeeper on the wharves, whose 1829 *Appeal . . . to the Coloured Citizens of the World* stirred African-Americans in the North and horrified whites with a militant call for black insurrection, if necessary, to end slavery. But prosperity, even solvency, eluded her: Her husband died and white executors defrauded her of the estate. In 1831, when she approached Garrison, she was impoverished and despondent.[8]

Regardless of her troubles, some confluence of events—a conversion experience, the tumult around David Walker's pamphlet and then, the next year, his mysterious death (many blacks believed he was poisoned), and Nat Turner's 1831 slave rebellion in Virginia—inspired her to write. With a manuscript in hand on religion, morality, and black freedom, she sought out Garrison at the cluttered offices of his print shop and antislavery newspaper *The Liberator*. Garrison and Stewart were almost the same age, in their late twenties, both deeply religious, and both "all on fire," as Garrison once described himself, with the urgency of ending the sin of slavery. Although they lived on opposite sides of the color line, she must have found something congenial in his hardscrabble Baptist background and the egalitarian spirit he brought to all his dealings, a trait that earned him respect and trust from Boston's black people. He in turn would have recognized a promising writer and a Christian sister. She was lovely, he recalled in paying tribute to her decades later: flush in "a ripening womanhood, with a graceful form and a pleasing countenance." Others too remembered "one of the most beautiful and loveliest of women." Having just arrived in Boston himself, Garrison extended fellowship to an impoverished, bereft woman by publishing her essay.[9]

The pamphlet made her a public figure. She gave public lectures at important places: the First African Baptist Church and the African Meeting House, where the New England Anti-Slavery Society met. These were important venues, evidence that for a brief moment she commanded an audience. She mostly held forth on religious and moral questions, taking care, though, to address the "daughters of Africa," thus expanding her community of listeners beyond men. She touted mothers' influence on the little souls in their care—a staple of domestic ideology, which black women were turning to their own uses. But she also departed from the standard line about female moral influence to toss in grievances about black women's destiny scrubbing pots and pans in the kitchens of haughty white women. "How long shall the fair daughters of Africa be compelled to bury their minds and talents beneath a load of iron pots and kettles?"[10]

Stewart seems to have walked trustingly into a position that was inevitably embattled. At first, Garrison's backing seems to have protected her from criticism: In 1831, God and Garrison were already a formidable pair. And the contemporaneous examples of a few itinerant black women preachers, respected and honored by Northern blacks, would have softened the audacity of putting herself before the public.[11] But Stewart appears to have pushed beyond the role of preacher, to presume to speak to the community about worldly matters as well. Her status as a widow would have given her some protection from social ostracism for stepping out of place, but as she proceeded, her disinterest in the meek quietude of grief would have been obvious. From the defensiveness that flares up in her writing, we can infer that audiences grew hostile. She was in tune with advanced opinion about race and slavery, but she was far out in front of even the most advanced opinions about women.

Although there is no record of what her critics said, Stewart may have suffered from the bugaboo of Frances Wright, a radical British advocate of workingmen's causes who had two years earlier scandalized America by defying the cultural prohibition against speaking before "promiscuous" audiences—that is, audiences that included men. Public space was male, and the only women who "exposed" themselves there were "public women" who were "on the town," that is, prostitutes. On an 1829 lecture tour, the unabashedly showy Fanny Wright drew accusations of being a prostitute for her audacity; pornographic fantasies swirled around her presence at the podium, as if she were literally exposing her body to strange men. As for Stewart, a bitter sense of ill usage drove her to leave Boston in 1833. The object of her rage is unclear, but the tone is unmistakably aggrieved. "Thus far has my life been almost a life of complete disappointment," she announced to her audience, blame suffusing the plaint.[12]

Over the course of her brief time in the limelight, her declamations on behalf of her sex moved front and center. In this she foreshadowed a line of black women to come who did not separate their commitments to the race from their grievances on their own behalf and whose experiences of black men's indifference strengthened their defense of women. In Stewart's last speech, she gave the topic undivided attention. "What if I am a woman?" she defiantly inquired. It was a resonant turn of phrase. Over the next three decades, abolitionist women would habitually use the inverted phrasing—not "I am a woman" but "what if I am?"—to defend themselves against charges that they had stepped out of their place. The language originated with the beautiful British female antislavery motto "Am I not a woman and a sister?" (analogue to the men's "Am I not a man and a brother?") and Stewart would have been echoing that query, already in the air. Over time, American women adapted, twisted, and rearranged the words, most famously when Sojourner Truth was said to have demanded at an 1850 women's rights convention, "Arn't I a woman?"[13]

Questioning Paul's injunction—let the women keep silent in churches—Stewart insisted, "Did but St. Paul but know of our wrongs and deprivations, I presume he would make no objection to our pleading in public for our rights."[14] She threw at listeners her righteous biblical predecessors: Deborah the judge, Esther the savior of her people, and Mary Magdalene, who announced Christ's resurrection to his disciples. The list, with a few additions, would reappear over the years in other briefs for the defense, a women's rights roll of honor compiled as a record of divine sanction for women who stepped out of line. Yet there was a more surprising list of names in Stewart's "Farewell": great women of the Middle Ages and Renaissance who were notable not so much for their Christian virtue as for their wordly achievements.

Stewart found them in a history of women through the ages published in London in 1790, the marvelously titled *Woman, Sketches of the History, Genius, Disposition, Accomplishments, Employments, Customs and Importance of the Fair Sex In All Parts Of The World Interspersed With Many Singular And Entertaining Anecdotes By A Friend Of The Sex*. Wherever she unearthed the old book, which was written in the palmy days of the French Revolution, she thought the information about women's upward course was important enough to copy straight into her own text. Through the lens of this book, optimism about the future banished her own afflictions in the present. An epoch of distinction for women was in the works, she predicted, and African-American women would be included. The past, after all, provided examples of magnificent figures of learning and independence who were honored in their own times: Anglo-Saxon seers, Greek oracles, Jewish prophetesses, and daredevils of Renaissance erudition who occupied university chairs of philosophy and advised popes. "Nuns were poetesses, and women of quality Divines," she marveled, and demanded, "What if such women as are here described should rise among our sable race?" "It is not impossible," she concluded.[15] Caution tinted the hypothetical question—after all, her own experience as a "Divine" in the "sable race" did not bode well—but the conjecture still glimmered with hope in an otherwise gloomy assessment of the present.

Stewart was fundamentally a Christian thinker. Except for the tome on women's history, the only book she used in her writing was the Bible. In all likelihood, she knew nothing about Mary Wollstonecraft or the demands women made in the French Revolution. Yet she benefited from the Age of Revolution's massive authorization of new historical subjects such as "Woman." She delighted in chronicling creatures of such importance that they could vie with kings and popes. An epic composed in 1790 could be adjusted to transform an impoverished black woman into a protagonist just arriving on the stage of history.

Across the Charles River in Cambridge, another young woman in quite different circumstances also contemplated the demands of the age. Margaret Fuller, ten years younger, lived in the same city yet worlds apart and no doubt knew nothing about Maria Stewart, so separate was black Boston from intellectual (white) Cambridge. Fuller was another reader but one blessed with the privileges of a strenuous education, loving parents, a white skin, and all the books her heart desired. Though they were unknown to each other, Fuller shared Maria Stewart's sense that the times issued a special invitation; she thought about "such a person of Genius as the nineteenth century can afford." Fuller imagined a genderless genius; Stewart, a female *savante*. Fuller depended on an untrammeled Soul; Stewart, on God. Fuller went on to become a brilliant transatlantic intellectual and revolutionary; Stewart dropped into obscurity.[16] But at the time, both drew mental fortitude from imaginative possibilities generated by American reform movements. In these years when feminism was quiescent, Woman in the Nineteenth Century—as Fuller would later title a book—was already bent on what her celebrants believed to be a world-changing mission.

Maria Stewart and Margaret Fuller were creatures of a new era for female readers and writers. In the Northern states, rising rates of literacy had created a substantial female literary public (although few Southern white women and virtually no enslaved women were literate). Women readers and writers favored religious literature, fiction, and poetry, especially the sentimental effusions of women's sphere. But they also read nonfiction, and the more forthright took up the great political subjects of the day—slavery, political representation, class inequality, and Woman.

Print culture was an entrée into the brothers' deliberative affairs. Women made themselves active citizens of the republic of letters long before they were full citizens of the nation. Linked revolutions in transportation and printing technology vastly increased the number of books, newspapers, journals, pamphlets, and tracts available to ordinary people.

The change rippled around the Atlantic but it was most marked in the United States, where neither the old guild organizations (as in Britain and on the Continent) nor censorship constrained the print media.[17]

Rising literacy was tied to a growing acceptance of women's education. This change was the one solid institutional gain for women since the American Revolution, and still it was very limited. Between 1800 and 1820, ideas about republican motherhood strengthened the regimen in girls' academies beyond the standard curriculum of a little French, a little music, and a little geography. Fuller, for example, was tutored by her father, Timothy, a believer in Wollstonecraft's views on education. In the 1830s, basic education for both sexes spread with the establishment of common schools. Reformers also created a few secondary schools intent on offering girls an education equivalent to the best boys' schools: Elizabeth Cady attended one, Emma Willard's seminary in Troy, New York, where she graduated in 1832. Indeed, in the far future and around the globe, improved education for girls was often the first change that nascent women's movements achieved, since reformers could pitch girls' education as training future mothers for the nation's service. In Iran in the 1910s, for instance, reformers established the first girls' schools in the wake of the Constitutional Revolution, and in China the number of girls in school nearly tripled after the 1911 revolution.[18]

This is not to suggest there was steady progress in education in the United States or anywhere else. In 1840, Fuller, by then the preeminent female intellectual in the country, surveyed the American field and found it badly wanting. Girls' schools had no interest in intellect or critical reasoning, she charged. There were two obstacles, she believed: men's fear that education would strip women of their femininity and women's own dislike of the life of the mind.[19] Subsequent developments bore out the first, but not the second, since contrary to Fuller's pessimism, girls and women consistently pressed for more rigorous, broad educations. But Fuller's basic criticism held: Nowhere did education adhere to the principle that the mind had no sex. Once girls surmounted one barrier, skeptics threw up another.

In Fuller and Stewart's time, they were thought to be incapable of learning Greek or Latin. Later, they could study Greek and Latin, but mathematics and science were deemed too taxing. In the twentieth century, biology was acceptable, but physics and engineering were far afield. And so on. Ohio's Oberlin College, a hotbed of evangelical religion and abolitionism, was the first coeducational institution of higher learning anywhere in the world when it opened in 1833. Land-grant colleges, the bases for state universities, opened to women after the Civil War, and philanthropists established women's colleges beginning with Mount Holyoke in 1837. Still, as late as 1900, many American universities slotted women into home economics courses (dressed up with the pseudo-scientific label "euthenics"). And on both sides of the Atlantic, the great universities remained closed. In Britain, benefactors established women's colleges at the universities of Oxford and Cambridge—against pitched resistance from the men—in the 1880s. After contentious discussions the students were allowed to sit for examinations, but they were not allowed to take degrees until 1920 and 1947, respectively.[20] Yale and Princeton did not admit women until 1969.

Even so, versions of republican motherhood sifted down through the years, adulterating the belief that women deserved an education for their own sakes. When I went to Princeton in 1969 in the first class of women, a fellow "coed" explained to me that she was not there to advance herself but to educate herself to be a good wife and mother. And in 2005 the president of Harvard University, Larry Summers, set off a furor when, in an unguarded moment, he offered his opinion that women's brains might be less capable of scientific research than men's.[21]

On balance, though, gains in literacy and schooling strengthened women's engagement in public issues. A constituency absorbed and pondered ideas with increased confidence in their own judgment: We see one expression in tens of thousands of women's signatures on antislavery petitions to Congress.[22]

In the AASS, reading and writing brought women into dialogue and fellowship with men. Relationships on paper were less cumbersome and fraught with fear of exposure than actual encounters. Angelina Grimké came to public attention this way in *The Liberator*. Print launched her into a public career as an abolitionist orator, a move that touched off a storm of controversy and precipitated the first full-fledged discussion in the United States about the rights of women.

Angelina and her older sister Sarah were renegade daughters of a great South Carolina slaveholding family. Sarah was born in 1792; Angelina, the youngest girl of the family, in 1805. By the early 1830s, both were self-exiled from the South, living as antislavery Quakers in Philadelphia. They were old enough to be anomalous single women: In the calculus of their times, Angelina was approaching middle age and Sarah was already there, a certified spinster. The deeply religious sisters came to oppose slavery through a long, tortuous series of events, leaving behind their middle-of-the-road colonization sentiments when they joined the PFASS. In 1835, in response to a spate of mob attacks against abolitionists, Angelina sent Garrison a letter avowing her solidarity with the male victims and pledging her dedication to the cause—a cause worth dying for, she wrote. Such was the sensation of a planter's daughter from a great Southern family allying herself with the radical wing of antislavery that other abolitionist papers reprinted the *Liberator* letter and the AASS published it as a pamphlet.[23]

Although the Quakers had led the antislavery fight in the United States since the eighteenth century, most Friends at the time, frightened by Nat Turner's 1831 rebellion, were backpedaling from the call for immediate emancipation.[24] The Philadelphia Quakers, leery of Garrison's red-hot views, pressed Angelina to repudiate the whole affair. Even her sister Sarah judged her badly for the unseemly attention she drew. Fortifying herself with prayer, Angelina stood firm even as she struggled against an undertow of terrible shame. The worst accusation, she felt, was that she brought disgrace on her family.

It was a pass at which other radical women would arrive, a turn in the road with bleakness and isolation up ahead and a dismayed gaggle of friends and family calling her to turn back. The psychology of a moment of radical choice affected every person who broke with the Northern consensus that slavery was an ineradicable institution. But for women, whose identities were so entangled with ensuring others' well-being, the choice between the demands of conscience and the wishes of loved ones could be overwhelming. Female moral influence could only take one so far before it collapsed as a justification, with the transgressor stranded in the wilderness outside respectability. Usually, a steely faith was necessary to armor oneself against others' disapproval and one's own shame at having brought on so much trouble. For abolitionist women, that structure was Christianity. For rebels in the future, it would be socialism, or anarchism, or art, or feminism itself. As for Angelina, a pained letter to Sarah conveys the resolution she struggled for and found: "Tho' condemnd by human judges, I was acquitted by him whom I believ qualified me to write it, & I feel willing to bear all, if it was only made instrumental of good. I felt my great unworthiness of being used in such a work but remembered that 'God hath chosen the weak things of this world to confound the wise.'" Prayer shored up a female self that felt inadequate—literally too small—for the burden. She took confidence from God's directions to her, a mere woman, to enter the battle whatever the costs.[25]

In the months after the scandal broke, invitations to speak to women's groups proliferated. Angelina learned she was a strong and persuasive speaker. Sarah too became convinced that the call to greater action came from God. In 1836, the sisters went to New York City to join the Seventy, an elite cadre of men the society had chosen to prepare for a blitz of agitation on the road for unconditional abolition. In New York, the Grimkés helped organize the first national convention of the female societies.

It was a valiant but dangerous idea. New York was a "withering atmosphere" for abolitionists, Sarah thought, its economy and tourist trade heavily dependent on the slaveholders who visited there to broker their cotton shipments. The Grimkés were appalled at the racism of the New York Female Antislavery Society, white women who treated their African-American co-workers like servants. At the convention, tensions pushed the subject of color prejudice into the proceedings. The meeting's leaders—the Grimkés were prominent—insisted that the rights and duties of women included white women's obligation to divest themselves of prejudice and treat black women as equals. Still, no black woman was asked to speak.[26]

In New York, the Grimkés moved to a larger stage. At first they spoke in parlors to women, white and black; when the audience grew too large, they moved to churches. While African-American listeners would have heard itinerant women preach before, most white people had literally never heard a woman stand up and talk in public except for testifying in revival meetings. Audiences were amazed at reasoned speeches coming from a woman. "My auditors literally sit some times with 'mouths agape and eyes astare,'" Angelina reported, "so that I cannot help smiling in the midst of 'rhetorical flourishes' to witness their perfect amazement at hearing a woman speak in the churches."[27] Here and there, men slipped in to listen, turning the meetings into "promiscuous assemblies." While the sisters anguished over their steps into prominence, they steadily proceeded. In New England in 1837, the sensation of turncoat Southern women lecturing on the evils of slavery drew hundreds— 1,500 in Lowell, Massachusetts, where factory girls came in force. A sharp question took shape and pushed its way through the decorum of domesticity—really, why shouldn't Christian women speak out publicly about the great evil of slavery? It edged into a corollary: Why shouldn't they join men in deliberating about the affairs of the world when worldly power impinged on what was right? The point of departure was the absolute moral equality of all human beings, the fundamental principle abolitionists used to call for an end to slavery. The Grimkés and other women, following the logic, ran up against a stark contradiction. Was not sex, like skin color, a mere circumstance that had nothing to do with the moral equality of a person?

This was American abolition's distinct contribution to women's rights. Mary Wollstonecraft, working within the terms of republican thought, was too encumbered by a negative imagery of womankind to come close to the idea that the essence of woman—as she existed in the present, not in some better future—was identical to the essence of man. The problem with making reason the founding principle of equality was that women were always found to be so deficient in it. But moral equality existed here and now. Every person was a moral being: slaves, yes, and women, too. It was only power, pure and simple, that prevented them from exercising their full humanity. It was a religious argument, although it had clear ramifications in a democratic society with a highly developed political culture. "This regulation of duty by the mere circumstance of sex, rather than by the fundamental principle of moral being, has led to all that multifarious train of evils flowing out of the anti-Christian doctrine of masculine and feminine virtues," Angelina avowed in her riposte to Catharine Beecher's attack on the behavior of FASS women in general and the Grimkés in particular. Female abolitionists were guilty of deserting their duties, Beecher maintained, and of abnegating the domestic virtues that gave women true power. "Woman is to win everything by peace and love; by making herself respected, esteemed, and loved. . . . But this is all to be accomplished in the domestic and social circle," she scolded.[28]

Her platitudes give a sense of what abolitionist women were up against: smug insinuation and pious condemnation, as if the lifelong church members, revered matrons, and Quaker ladies who constituted the FASS were not respected, esteemed, and loved. But against such adversaries, Angelina's recourse to God's call to moral action irrespective of sex was a stalwart defense. The sisters' challenge to the unwritten rule barring women from public speaking galvanized antislavery troops, especially women.

In New England, "the whole land seem[ed] roused to discussion on the province of woman, & I am glad of it," Angelina rejoiced to a woman friend. "Sister Sarah does preach up woman's rights most nobly & fearlessly, & we find that many of our New England sisters are ready to receive these strange doctrines, feeling as they do, that our whole sex needs an emancipation from the thraldom of public opinion." The "strange doctrines" were their reflections on the moral equality of the sexes, braided through disquisitions on the sin of enslaving other human beings.[29]

The association of women's rights with the preeminent issue of the day pushed it into proslavery discourse as well. Women's rights reformers would turn into Exhibit A for the slaveholders' case: that abolition was an insult to the God-given order of master governing slave, husband governing wife. Up to the Civil War, the South held on to the link between abolition and women's rights; politically, it was a peerless device to advertise abolitionism's intent to destroy everyone's family along with the slave owner's brood: the white women and children and the black people under his benevolent care and protection. "Ideas about the natural inequality of women contributed not a little to the ideological and political cohesion of the proslavery cause," points out Stephanie McCurry.[30]

In the North, the radical opposition to slavery, coupled with the challenge to gender rules, provoked the most powerful clerical body in New England to issue a condemnation of the Grimkés that ministers were to read at Sunday services. The "Pastoral Letter" was so assured and clear in its point-by-point prescriptions for correct womanhood that it amounts to an antifeminist manifesto, the nation's first. The ministers reminded congregants that women were by nature weak and dependent on men, like vines winding their tendrils around trees. "The power of woman is her dependence, flowing from her consciousness of that weakness which God has given her for her protection." When a woman presumed to speak about matters outside the domestic sphere (the Grimkés' identities were thinly veiled), she usurped the place of man and "her character becomes unnatural": withered, sterile, falling "in shame and dishonor into the dust."[31] Such was the punitive portrayal with which the devout Grimkés contended.

In the crunch, abolitionist brothers proved to be disappointing allies. Holding much in common, they still worked with a different calculus of the importance of women's demands. We can see the fault lines developing in letters between the Grimkés, who were on the road speaking, and Theodore Dwight Weld, a leader in the Seventy. Weld was quietly in love with Angelina. Two years older than her, he was a veteran organizer and a superb orator, one of the rebels dismissed from Lane Seminary in Cincinnati in 1834 because they refused to temper their abolitionist activity. Months on the road agitating for the AASS, facing down violent crowds in the process, had steeled his commitment. A man among men, he had little experience—perhaps none—of heterosexual love; and like any of his generation, he had no experience until then working with women as collaborators in public affairs.[32] There was a considerable emotional and intellectual leap from his all-male world to the association he developed with the Grimkés, and Angelina in particular.

Weld agreed with them in principle but thought the sisters head-strong and overly preoccupied with an issue that was extraneous to the cause. Women had every right to speak, yes, but there were ways to make their actions more palatable. Positioning himself as a kindly older brother who knew best—"my dear sisters," he called them—Weld struggled to contain his disapproval as the Grimkés shocked New England. In thick letters, pages and pages penned in furious disputation, he urged them to stick to their appointed topic—slavery—and stay away from the rights of women. At first he was courteous and jocular, but as the opposition mounted, he scolded, lectured, and harangued, some-times firing off two long letters a day. Their strategy should be tactful, change-by-example, he told them. Let intelligent women act with dig-nity and modesty, and "men begin to be converted." In response, Angelina, usually lachrymose and conflicted, for once turned tart. "What is the matter with thee," she fired back. The problem was unavoidable, she flatly stated. "How can we expect to be able to hold meetings much longer when people are so diligently taught to despise us for thus step-ping out of the sphere of woman?"[33]

In a conflict that called not for men's abstract principles but their forthright solidarity, the sisters' disappointment with the comrades crept in. Weld at least tried to work out some basis for agreement, but other men jumped ship. The sisters came to believe that their interest in women cut too close to the private interests of colleagues: "It will touch every man's interests at home," reflected Angelina, "in the tenderest relation of life." Then "WHO will stand by woman in the great struggle?" she wondered.[34]

They turned to other women. Shifting coteries backed them, protect-ing them from social ostracism. Boston abolitionist women stepped in: Anne Weston came out to Groton to fortify them, and the president of the Boston FASS, Mary Parker, wrote to assure them that they would stand by them, even "if every body else forsook us," Angelina informed

Weld with a hint of reproach.[35] The crusade to free the slaves intensified the meaning of the bonds of womanhood: They spoke of feeling different when women met together, of something new happening. Of the convention of the ladies' societies in New York, Angelina rejoiced that the gathering "very soon broke down all stiffness & reserve, threw open our hearts to each other's view, and produced a degree of confidence in ourselves & each other which was very essential & delightful." The resolutions they passed would "frighten the weak and startle the slumbering," she crowed to a friend.[36] It was not the sentimental ties of domesticity and benevolent work she celebrated, but their involvement in a great cause. That women alone could work together to vindicate the sex was something that Mary Wollstonecraft had not imagined.

The clash with New England ministers, coupled with male co-workers' disapproval, provoked Sarah Grimké to work out an impassioned rebuttal. Her *Letters on the Equality of the Sexes,* published first in *The Liberator* and then as a pamphlet in 1838, was an unapologetically defiant book. Had she read Mary Wollstonecraft? Perhaps not: The *Vindication*'s association with the godless French Revolution might well have repelled her. On the other hand, it would have been available. Grimké's fellow Quaker Lucretia Mott, also a member of the PFASS, kept it on her parlor table, a token of sympathy for an unfashionable topic. The book bobbed around working-class democratic-radical circles, too, in the 1830s: We have a sighting of a striking worker in a New England mill town who climbed on top of a pump to give "a flaming Mary Wollstonecroft speech" (so the local paper reported).[37] But regardless of whether Sarah Grimké had read it or not, the book's very existence may have encouraged her. Perhaps it seemed, like other important feminist books since (Simone de Beauvoir's *The Second Sex,* for instance), more hospitable with its cover closed, evoking some undefined mental place where the keywords of the title—*Woman—Rights—Vindication*—signaled the need for change without having to get there by trudging through the text.

The *Letters* make no reference to Wollstonecraft, though. They plunge off in a different direction, to elaborate on women's absolute moral equality. The prose leaps with the excitement of novelty and invention. "Men and women were CREATED EQUAL," Sarah proclaimed, the capital letters announcing unassailable truth. "They are both moral and accountable beings, and whatever is right for a man to do, is right for a woman." And again, lest readers missed the point: "WHATSOEVER IT IS MORALLY RIGHT FOR A MAN TO DO, IT IS MORALLY RIGHT FOR A WOMAN TO DO."[38]

The contention threw her up against not only the Massachusetts clergy, formidable enough, but also more fearsome antagonists: Saint Paul, centuries of scriptural interpretation, domestic ideology, and the institution of marriage. She faced them all squarely. No woman ever wrote like this; certainly not Wollstonecraft, whose ever-present sense of objections glowering at her from the edges of the page kept her proclaiming from the high ground of dispassionate reason. Grimké wrote aggressively, momentarily blessed by that obliviousness to danger on which startling courage depends. The *Letters* glow.

The light comes from several sources. First, Grimké lined herself up squarely with her subject as "we"—"we" women—as Mary Wollstonecraft would not. In the shift, the significance of the empathetic female voice in feminism becomes evident: Grimké liked women and wrote *with* them as well as to them and about them. It took time; in the first letters she pronounced from on high. But soon the sentences enveloped the writer in a "we" at once injured and noble: "the majesty of our immortal nature," "the wrong we suffer." And, on the other side of the equation, she identified the problem as "them," that is, men: Even among the abolitionist brethren she discerned a collective gender disposition. "Whether our brothers have defrauded us intentionally, or unintentionally the wrong we suffer is equally the same."[39]

Second, she located the damage not in women's failures, but in men's power. She believed that women had all the internal resources to obey God's will. But men impeded them; they "usurped"—the word is singular to her—a power that was rightfully God's to try to make themselves masters of women's consciences. In the abolitionist manner, she described that power as physical coercion of another, just as the master physically overpowered the slave. Her most powerful metaphors were of sexual inequality as bodily submission. Climactically, she declared, "I ask no favors for my sex," and she insisted, "All I ask of our brethren is, that they will take their feet from off our necks and permit us to stand upright on that ground which God designed us to occupy."[40]

Third, abolition taught her how to unpeel the accretions of the status quo so that what people considered natural in human relations could be held up to scrutiny. "Mastery" linked slavery to women's subjection. Here, Grimké drew on the idea of the "slave power," gaining credence in the 1830s, which pictured slave owners as conscious practitioners and defenders of a system that benefited them rather than, in the older manner, as reluctant heirs to a difficult situation.

At the time, though, Grimké's Bible readings were probably more influential than those political ideas for which we value her today. This was an age when the Bible, not anatomy, biochemistry, or genetics, was the final word on why women were different from men and why that difference made them subordinate. Her wit and fluency are striking, especially because she had the haphazard education of a Southern lady, consisting of a short spell at a Charleston female academy and second-hand lessons she culled from her brother's tutor. Yet she shows a mind playful and learned as she sidles around pitfalls, clambers over walls, and strikes out on obscure byways, working her way through exacting readings of the Bible to reach ingenious conclusions. There was, for instance, the old problem of the Fall. Was not Eve, after all, the instrument of mankind's fall from grace, a willful creature who needed Adam to keep her in check? Yes, but Adam was every bit as much a weak character, maybe more so, since Eve was tricked by Satan, while Adam went along of his own free will. How to get around Paul, who ordered women to keep silent in churches? It was only a tip to leaders of the early churches, she suggested, because they contended with women who were so excited to be liberated from strict Jewish ritual that they interrupted services too often with questions.[41]

The Grimké controversy and the spread of women's rights thought fueled anti-abolitionist fires. Sexual imagery conflated the two causes: It was "old maids" and "nigger-lovers" who made up the female societies. Rhetorical violence in newspapers and pamphlets fed mob violence—indeed, a mob murdered the abolitionist editor Elijah Lovejoy in Alton, Illinois, in 1837. Women were not exempt. In 1835 in Boston, a crowd of several thousand threatened members of the BFASS who were thought to be hiding a visiting British abolitionist in their meeting rooms. The mayor had to intervene and escort the women out of the building past enraged onlookers roaring threats and insults. Afterward, Maria Weston Chapman, a leading member and daughter of the prominent and wealthy Weston family, could not walk in the streets of her own city without passersby and shop clerks hurling abuse at her. The Boston women noted acidly the double standard that divided acceptable female behavior from activity that was reviled. They were all involved in several reform causes, they observed, and when they staged a benefit for the blind at Faneuil Hall, "we basked in the sunshine of popular favor." Female altruism on behalf of the blind was one thing: "No one said then, 'women had better stay home.'" Doing the same thing on behalf of the slaves, though, was another matter, bringing threats bordering on lethal.[42]

In Philadelphia in 1838, violence again broke out. There, in a private ceremony, Angelina Grimké married Theodore Weld before a racially mixed group of guests. Newspapers denounced the gathering and drummed up popular rage, abetted by city authorities and gentlemen of standing. Three days later, the second national convention of the female societies met in downtown Philadelphia. A mob went after them, smashing windows at Pennsylvania Hall, where they were meeting, and screaming threats. Finally, the women retreated, linking arms—white and black women paired, it was said, the better to protect the latter— before a drunken, enraged crowd that then proceeded to burn down the building.[43]

Violence is not usually seen as a factor in American feminist politics but at this early moment it had a chilling effect. The Philadelphia riot marked a rupture, driving a generation back into private life and political semi-retirement. African-American women almost disappeared from the female societies. The *Colored American,* the country's one black newspaper, sided with critics of the Grimkés and cautioned black women not to stray from their sphere, criticizing Sarah Grimké's *Letters* and calling up the bugaboo of Fanny Wright. The editor Samuel Cornish took the occasion to accuse women of letting down the race: "Colored females, from education, are more especially deficient in fulfilling their appropriate duties, and in redeeming the character and carrying forward the interests of their oppressed and injured people. As wives, as mothers and as daughters, they are too inert, and not sufficiently self-sacrificing." Conscientious black mothers were meant to exert their influence at home, building up their families and salving the wounds that prejudice inflicted on their men.[44]

The convergence of the Grimké controversy, the Pastoral Letter, and violence in Philadelphia proved an unsupportable burden for the female societies. Garrison defended the sisters—and women's participation— adamantly. But Garrison was an uncompromising leader who admitted no half measures, and his "come-outer" defiance of the established churches put off AASS members not inclined to "ultraist" views. Some resisted the Garrisonian defense because they themselves believed that women's place was in the home. Others had sympathy but thought that women's rights discredited the cause with moderates who needed to be won over if abolitionism was to make political headway.

The conflict erupted in 1838–40, with members splitting over the issue of whether women could participate in AASS conventions and whether or not to seat Abby Kelley on the society's business committee. Kelley was a young Quaker of incorruptible conscience who, in the wake of the violence in Philadelphia, continued to lecture by herself in New England and New York state, enduring accusations of being a prostitute and a Jezebel. When the Garrisonians prevailed in the Kelley matter, the other faction walked out to form a rival organization, the American and Foreign Anti-Slavery Society, the nucleus of what became the Liberty Party.[45] Theodore Weld sided with the dissenters. He, Angelina, and Sarah retreated to Red Bank, New Jersey; Weld and Angelina began a family, and they all worked together on Weld's compendious exposé *Slavery as It Is*. All three lived until after the Civil War; Weld, until 1895. But neither sister ever revived her public career.

In 1840, the Garrisonians included eight women in their delegation to the World Antislavery Convention in London. They had no reason to expect the British would seat the women, but the female delegates were seasoned veterans, and they considered the contacts they would make abroad and the debate they would provoke as worth the journey. The newlywed Elizabeth Cady Stanton, a novice to antislavery work, accompanied them to London; she was not a delegate but her husband, Henry Stanton, was. On the voyage over, Elizabeth Stanton, always drawn to intelligence and power, took especially to the much older Lucretia Mott, who was as close to powerful as a woman could get in 1840. At the convention from behind a curtain, the women followed the debate about seating them; and to the end of her very long life, Stanton remembered who of the American men sided with them and who lined up with the British position.

Stanton's retrospective account of what happened next has her and Lucretia Mott thick as thieves, fuming and fulminating and making plans. Mott's diary from the trip, however, sketches a different picture of passing contact with Stanton, who was an outsider to a tightly knit political clan. Mott was preoccupied with consultations with longtime colleagues and behind-the-scenes machinations. But however self-dramatizing Stanton's story was, one thing is likely: In London, someone—and maybe it was Stanton—had the idea to hold a convention about women's rights, and women's rights alone, when they returned to America.[46]

Thus abolitionism opened a line of development for women's rights, even as it also hindered. Events of the 1830s provided the basis for an understanding of Woman as morally sovereign person whose highest duties lay outside the family jurisdiction. Originating in domestic ideology, these ideas went beyond domesticity's acceptance of the male citizen as the gold standard of civic virtue. Tyranny could lodge in men, too, the Grimkés argued—and fascinated hundreds with the proposition. Women-as-they-were, not women-as-they-might-be, were judged quite able to take up rights and duties in a Christian republic.

CHAPTER THREE

NEW MORAL WORLDS

"OH NO DON'T let us get married," Antoinette Brown, a twenty-two-year-old abolitionist, urged her best friend, Lucy Stone, in 1847. The pair were about to graduate from Oberlin College in one of the early classes of women. They were preparing to go out into the world as teachers, advancing the cause of the slaves, of course, but also the cause of women. Reviewing their guiding precepts, Brown thought their single state would serve notice of great things to unnamed doubters. "Let them see that woman can take care of herself & act independently without the encouragement & sympathy of her 'lord & master,'" she boasted. Women were taking the stage of world history, the two agreed: crusaders in particular reforms but also leaders in a quest for the general good, the "great reform which is about to revolutionize society."[1] And indeed, the next year, participants at a meeting on women's rights at Seneca Falls, New York, did rally to a great reform, a new Declaration of Independence for the sex.

The principle of the moral equality of the sexes inscribed a clear line of development from the Grimké sisters, through antislavery women such as these two, to the 1848 Seneca Falls convention on women's rights and the movement that came after it. But in Europe, where, after all, women's rights began, the situation was very different because there were so few channels for popular politics of any sort. There, feminist thinking also stirred with life in the 1830s and 1840s, but several degrees off the main lines of political development. Where the subject flared up in political discourse, it was stoked by radical republicans, utopians, and socialists, especially in France and Britain: working-class people and middle-class dissenters. Heirs to the aspirations of the French Revolution, they struggled to resurrect dreams of equality and the rights of man in the face of political repression and the brutal exploitation of early industrial capitalism.

A continuing fascination with utopias was part of this European generation's quest to change the world through peaceful means outside traditional politics, to chart a course that repudiated blood in the streets and also circumvented intransigent regimes. Nourished by literary Romanticism and the rudiments of early socialist economic thought, reformers of many tints discovered the inner life—subjectivity, imagination, and emotion—as one resource for birthing a new, moral world. As repression eased after 1820 in France and Britain, the democratic-radical project of vindicating women revived, with the aim of changing marriage and family structure and thereby transforming mass psychology. Women's equality emerged as a precondition of, not an option for, social improvement, thereby turning women into leaders, not followers, in the coming revolution. At least in theory.

On the face of it, European utopian socialism was an ocean and a world away from little Oberlin College out in the Ohio fields. But echoes of treatises emanating from London and Paris can be heard in the convictions of the two students. Unconventional, independent, and committed to the greater good, their kind of women, they thought, were inaugurating a new era in history.

The major utopian prophets of the early nineteenth century were the French writer Charles Fourier and the British thinker Robert Owen. The two were very different in their personalities and preoccupations. Fourier was a solitary adept of strange and far-fetched schemes, including plans for "phalansteries," cooperative communities that abolished private property and marriage and raised children communally. Fourier's writings traveled around Europe from 1808, when he published his first work, until his death in 1837, inspiring in the course of these decades—and even more after his death—a farflung assortment of followers.

Owen was a moral and economic thinker, well connected to the liberal British elite and, in the 1830s, the leader of a populous movement of working people. A Welsh-born factory owner turned socialist, he came to believe in the early days of his intellectual and political journey that human happiness necessitated not only the end of private property and the death of capitalism, but also a profound alteration in family arrangements and the relations of men and women. Owen's utopia would reorganize society into networks of cooperative communities, run by working people for working people, where members shared labor and reinvested profits for the common good. At the heart of the twisted impulses that drove the capitalist system of greed and acquisitiveness, Owen believed, was the tyranny of marriage and the subjugation of women within it.

Both Fourier and Owen drew on an Enlightenment faith that reasoning human beings could infinitely improve, even perfect themselves. Both spun their plans from a hatred of industrial capitalism and a belief in people's ability to live in harmony, not competition; in abundance, not want; and for the social good, not selfish acquisition. Both saw private property, marriage, and the church as pillars of despotism. Both sought to organize people in ways that would swiftly transform a poverty-ridden, corrupt, violent society, where a few prospered and many suffered, into one of peace, productivity, and equality. Finally, both believed that humankind could attain perfect well-being and enduring happiness. It now seems a faith of dizzy naïveté, but in the early nineteenth century others, too, held to it. Felicity on such a scale required deep changes in the psyche, which meant re-creating the families in which the human psyche is formed. Changes could only come from altering the ways children were raised and sex and marriage were organized. To women's rights, then, Fourierism and Owenism proved obliquely hospitable.

Fourier predicated his plan on synchronizing social relations with what he posited as the laws of the universe. He proposed that "passionate attraction"—by which he meant sexual attraction, but also friendship and family feeling—was the true basis for human affinities, the glue of all relationships. Yet society repressed the passionate attractions. Marriage stamped out sexual feeling for others and, in an age before the advent of contraception, inflicted continual pregnancies on women. Both sexes suffered, but women bore the brunt of the burdens of loneliness, monotony, and the injuries of men's sexual infidelity.

Fourier devised a plan to utilize and sustain passionate attractions, entwining a theory of labor with a theory of sexual love. A network of cooperative communities of work and love—"phalanxes"—would replace all forms of government. Phalanxes abolished private property and profit along with nuclear families and marriage: In order to put labor and wealth on a cooperative basis, intimate relations had to be communal. Residents were to share domestic labor and child rearing along with productive work, with everyone pitching in: men, women, and children. Couplings would be transitory and end voluntarily—a kind of serial monogamy. Women, set free from economic dependency on men, would pursue their own passionate attractions. And it was on women's freedom that the fortunes not only of the phalanxes but of humanity rose or fell: "Social progress and change," wrote Fourier, "are brought about by virtue of the progress of women towards liberty, and social retrogression occurs as a result of a diminution in the liberty of women."[2]

The critique of marriage dated back to Wollstonecraft and, before her, to Mary Astell in the 1600s. But Fourier went those writers one better by inventing a form of heterosexual attachment beyond marriage. Unlike his feminist predecessors, he gave these concerns a basis in an entire science of society, an all-encompassing plan to put society on a rational basis, in part by enshrining men's customary sexual wandering as a rule of community service. In the 1830s, disciples (mostly male) preached Fourierism in France, Britain, Germany, Italy, and Spain. Not all emphasized sexual reorganization, but in France, followers of the liberal aristocrat Claude Saint-Simon replicated elements of Fourier's system in their scandalous practices. The Saint-Simonians lived in communes and encouraged women to break loose from abusive marriages and sleep with men in the group.[3]

Owen embarked on his road to socialist thought through attempts to remedy the poverty of the workers in a textile factory he managed and partly owned in the Scottish industrial center of New Lanark. There he experimented with humane labor practices, with the aim of creating a model other industrialists could follow. In an 1816 speech in New Lanark, he mentioned the "Millenium," indicating that his thinking had already shifted from a model factory town to something much larger: "What ideas individuals may attach to the term 'Millenium' I know not; but I know that society may be formed so as to exist without crime, without poverty, with health greatly improved, with little, if any misery, and with intelligence and happiness increased a hundredfold; and no obstacle whatsoever intervenes at this moment except ignorance to prevent such a state of society from becoming universal." In the 1820s, having left New Lanark to move to London (where he moved in the circle of liberal thinkers around Jeremy Bentham), he worked out specifications for what he termed a New Moral World, where laborers took production away from capitalists to manage it themselves on a cooperative basis, sharing profits equitably.

The New Moral World would require profound changes in private life, although Owen only briefly advocated abolishing marriage (he later backpedaled). Like Fourier, he believed that marriage was analogous to private property, an institution that implanted selfishness in everyone and practically guaranteed male selfishness. "It is my house, my wife, my children, or my husband, our estate, and our children.... No arrangement could be better calculated to produce division and disunion in society," he asserted.[4] Love, whether platonic or erotic, was a natural impulse, but it could not flourish when relations were based on ownership and women were subject to men's arbitrary will. The end of Mammon and materialism could only come when love ran freely through human connections.

Until 1829, small groups of disciples sustained Owenism, but as militant labor sentiment spread, the British working-class movement became its home. Enthusiasm for cooperative stores and labor exchanges tied to trade unions spread in Britain, especially in London and the industrial north, growing into a mass movement in the 1830s that overlapped with Chartism. Owenism appealed to active and thoughtful people of the middling sort, artisans and shopkeepers who were the shock troops of dissent everywhere in Europe, their ranks augmented by middle-class sympathizers and a few renegades from the gentry.[5]

In the Owenite movement itself, women were numerous and vocal, attracted by these perceptions of injustice in the family. They were tailoresses, seamstresses, bonnet makers, weavers, domestic servants, shopkeepers, ladies of small means, and runaways from the upper classes. In London, for example, Anna Wheeler, that Irish reader of Wollstonecraft, had by this time fled her husband, children in tow, and ended up in London, a devotee of Owen's, after passing through a Saint-Simonian community in Normandy (in France she met Fourier and tried to arrange a meeting between the two great men). Frances Wright was another Owenite; her theatrical deportment spoke to her self-presentation as a heroine of a new epoch.[6]

In the 1830s, Owenite women interjected their own voices into the movement, lecturing and writing about the desolation of unwanted pregnancies and the perennial issue of domestic abuse. They tackled economic problems, trying to make men care about women workers' particular debilities. Owenite women were the first wage earners to write about the ruthless underpayment of women, when even skilled seamstresses might earn half of unskilled men's pay. Applying the principle of cooperation to domestic work, they chided workingmen for exempting themselves from housework. Remarkable extrapolations from Owen's theories about marriage sailed forth. In 1831, Robert Dale Owen, his son, advocated contraception on the grounds that women's happiness, which was necessary to everyone's well-being, could only be ensured when they could choose when to have children and how many to have.[7] Owenites discussed making marriage a civil contract, dissoluble like any other, thus making divorce a civil matter (rather than ecclesiastical, as it was in Britain, which effectively made marriage a life sentence).

Men were the public face of this early European feminism, the prominent speakers, writers, journalists, and (eventually) legislators and members of Parliament. Their relationship to those women who were also thinking about these matters was asymmetrical, but it was fruitful. We can see the gravity and force of these half-hidden collaborations in the first written defense of women's rights since the *Vindication,* authored by William Thompson in partnership with Anna Wheeler. An eccentric and genial Irish landholder, William Thompson was another wealthy gentleman who had come to be tormented by the miseries of the people—his tenant farmers—whose labors enriched him. He too went to London to sit at Bentham's feet, but he ended up an Owenite champion instead. In 1825, Thompson published his grandly titled *Appeal of One Half the Human Race, Women, Against the Pretensions of the Other Half, Men, to Retain Them in Political, and Thence in Civil and Domestic, Slavery.* The co-author whom Thompson acknowledged in his preface was his friend and fellow reformer Anna Wheeler.[8]

The book was primarily an attack on the preeminent philosopher James Mill, Bentham's heir, who in a famous 1819 treatise on government denied that women had any claim to political rights. Mill's essay was a locus classicus of liberal British reform, which sought to fight a corrupt oligarchy by extending the franchise to responsible men of property and denying it to everyone else. Mill dismissed female suffrage with hauteur: Like children and workingmen, women could be "struck off from political rights without inconvenience," he professed with cold candor. This was virtual representation updated for an age of the widened franchise.

Thompson's *Appeal* is a closely deduced, flat-footed treatise swept along by fiery indignation. He pulled together Fourierist and Owenite ideas about women into an argument that was by no means easy or obvious to make at the time. He was much harder on men than Wollstonecraft had been. Male power, far from being the benevolent force that James Mill supposed, was really despotic; it was a "monstrous fiction" that men could legislate for wives and daughters when in fact they could easily abuse and exploit them. Like Wollstonecraft, he believed that women were victimized by bad education and narrow lives, but he saw the problem really coming back to men, who appeared to him not as avatars of republican virtue but as tyrants, their power girded by the law of marriage, which put women in a state worse than West Indian slaves. Woman's destiny was determined by "the never-closing eye of a domestic tyrant, jealous and brutal, because having power with impunity to be so, hemming round not only her actions but her words and thoughts at his pleasure, and invested by law with all the uncontrolled power requisite to keep life in such a constant state of torment, that the morning sun that calls her to a renewal of existence may be cursed for its summons to a renewal of misery." The clauses and metaphors tumble over each other, a grammatical hodgepodge that testifies to the white-hot outrage that drove the prose.[9]

Thompson's name was on the cover but he copiously acknowledged his debt to Anna Wheeler. It was Wheeler, he wrote, who fired his thoughts about women into something bold and big. It was impossible for him, as a man, to *feel*—Thompson italicized the verb—Wheeler's "lofty indignation." He knew that his sex limited him; he could write for women and to them, but not with them. So he presented the book's ideas as if they were "joint property." It was as if the two of them had managed to create an equitable marriage in which they held ideas in common when, in literal fact, coverture made a marriage of joint property impossible.

Thompson would have heard Anna Wheeler's story of her miserable marriage in Ireland—the beatings she endured from the drunken husband, the constant pregnancies, how the man wasted the dowry she'd brought to the marriage. Her firsthand understanding gave an intensity to the *Appeal* that abstractions about marriage and the family could never confer on their own. Thompson the bachelor stormed with anger at the coercion of marriage, to which women must submit or starve and which threw them legally into a class with children and idiots. What was the way to happiness, given this dire state of things? He hoped for male generosity and sympathy and offered his own. It was—and remains—a vision of what fellow creatures could do for one another, a fraternal renunciation of sexual privilege. If men voluntarily relinquished their power, they could overcome the only two natural obstacles he saw—women's inferior strength and their destiny as child bearers—and bring about a reign of perfect equality. Then enlightened women could breathe free.

After 1838, Chartism subsumed the energies of Owenism. The critique of marriage and the family petered out, receding to circles of sexual adventurers and middle-class bohemians. We can see the lingering effects in the South Place circle, a group of radical Unitarians in a breakaway congregation in London, where conjugal arrangements were so unusual they would have meant social death in respectable circles. The flamboyant minister left his wife to live with his onetime foster child; another household consisted of an ex-clergyman, his mistress, her sister, and the sister's male partner. Harriet Taylor lived with her husband but formed an intimate, apparently nonsexual partnership with John Stuart Mill, whom she would eventually marry when John Taylor died. "Most of these people are very indignant at marriage," huffed Thomas Carlyle about the men, "and frequently indeed are obliged to divorce their wives, or be divorced."[10]

In part because the radical Unitarians were connected to influential men, elements of their ideas passed into powerful circles. Reforming lawyers and members of Parliament pared down the Owenite attack on conjugal tyranny into the more modest cause of ameliorating the draconian provisions of British marriage law. Exposés of the horrors of coverture appeared routinely in the popular press in the 1840s, and the legal disabilities of married women entered English public awareness more or less permanently: Dickens's chilling portrait in *Dombey and Son*, for example, of the beautiful, tormented Edith Granger, imprisoned in a bleak marriage to a wealthy, heartless older man, is an artifact of this discussion.[11]

Utopian socialism dissipated and then disappeared, banished by the violent conflict of the revolutions of 1848 and thereafter, by a socialist movement that turned on economic theory. Early socialism's reputation for connecting disparate things and making odd pairs—love and labor, housework and the overthrow of capitalism, sex and the social good—was nothing but a burden to Karl Marx and Friedrich Engels, who as young radicals in exile on the eve of 1848 struggled to divest their hard-edged, scientific socialism and vision of violent class struggle from the soft pacific models of Saint-Simon, Fourier, and Owen. "Castles in the air," they called their predecessors' doctrines.[12] Their *Communist Manifesto* had its own messianic message of a world to win, but it disabused followers of any lingering notion that a new world would come about peacefully and include all classes. No, they preached, real revolution had nothing to do with "harmony" or "small experiments": It was an earthquake, a cataclysm that should instill fear in those it would dispossess. It was clearly going to be led by men. Feminism's close association with those utopian hawkers of flimflam dreams and sexual liberation would forever remain a reason that the Marxist left was leery of the woman question, unless it was treated strictly as a problem of the oppressed female proletariat.[13]

In America, too, utopian ideas found followers. Owenite cooperative communities came and went; disciples transported to the United States a Fourierist doctrine heavy on economic cooperation, inspiring phalanxes peopled by middle-class idealists and labor radicals from Massachusetts to Iowa. Margaret Fuller visited one outside Boston, Brook Farm, where Bronson Alcott and other Transcendentalists tried to run a farm together. American devotees toned down the theory of passionate attraction, although suspicions always dogged communitarian experiments, their assortment of residents serving as grist for neighbors' gossip. No matter how straightforwardly economic, they drew sexual rebels, malcontents, and outcasts, including women shunned by polite society because they had left husbands or taken lovers. Nathaniel Hawthorne, for one, picked up the erotic associations of the phalanxes in his portrait of the wayward Zenobia in *The Blithedale Romance*, his fictional depiction of Brook Farm. At the extreme were John Humphrey Noyes and his followers in the Oneida, New York, phalanx, who did take Fourier's sexual theories seriously and set up a commune that dictated a strict regimen called "complex marriage." Everyone shifted heterosexual pairings regularly and practiced rudimentary birth control, their couplings and uncouplings monitored by Noyes himself.[14]

The utopian socialist critique of marriage also led to bills for married women's property rights. Ernestine Rose, a Polish Jewish emigré, absorbed Owenism when she lived in London; when she moved to the United States she helped publicize a bill first introduced in the New York legislature in 1836. Finally passed in 1848, it represented a historic break with coverture, although, given the fact that women actually owned so little property, its main effect was to create an instrument whereby men threatened by creditors could protect their holdings by transferring them to wives.[15] Elizabeth Cady Stanton, who lived in Seneca Falls, New York, after 1843, spent her first political efforts after she returned from the World Anti-Slavery Convention in pressing acquaintances in the legislature to pass the bill. Stanton's father was an eminent jurist, and she remembered sitting in his law office listening to the teary stories of women who came to see him about reclaiming property lost when husbands absconded or died. Her father could offer them no recourse, she recalled with indignation. Stanton and Rose became friends and co-workers in the women's rights movement that burgeoned after 1850; Stanton would try for the next fifty years to bring about divorce and marriage reform in the United States.[16]

Stanton's turn to themes of marriage and sexuality, however, came later. In the 1840s, the most influential translator of European avant-garde thought and literature, including utopian socialism, was Margaret Fuller, whose book on the situation of the sex, *Woman in the Nineteenth Century*, was an unexpected popular success in 1844. Fuller, the leading female intellectual in America—really, the only female intellectual—gleaned her material from far and wide: from abolitionist debates about the women question, to be sure, but also from European Owenites and Fourierists.

Fuller had thought about women's position for some time. A luminous writer and beloved teacher of adult classes for Boston's female elite, she was editor of the Transcendentalist journal *The Dial* from 1840 to 1844, a labor taken on in collaboration with, among others, her friend and interlocutor Ralph Waldo Emerson. *Woman in the Nineteenth Century* was a work of transition, written after *The Dial* folded but before Fuller moved to New York City, where she began a different life as a journalist for Horace Greeley's *New York Tribune*—again she was practically the only woman in the field. In 1846, she sailed to Europe as the *Tribune*'s foreign correspondent.

But in 1844, when *Woman in the Nineteenth Century* appeared, Europe and the revolution were ahead of her. She was adrift, having come to a dead end in Boston, emotionally and professionally, but as yet having found no home elsewhere. Her relationships with family and friends in Boston, especially male friends and even more especially Emerson, were tangled and unsatisfactory. In this time of uncertainty, she turned to a matter that was central to her life as the sole woman of stature in a culture in which women were said to wither outside the home. The book was an expansion of an essay she had written for *The Dial*. Putting it into book form, tripling the length, and giving it the gravitas of a magnificent title made it an intellectual event. It was as if she were saying that the whole century belonged to women. *Woman in the Nineteenth Century* invited American women to take up a role in a magnificent historical narrative, to rise to the most daunting challenges of the age: "Let them be sea captains," she urged magnanimously.

Although Fuller detested slavery, she had not written about or taken part in antislavery politics. At heart, she disliked the Garrisonians' self-righteous temper and she believed they were wrong in assuming that recognizing women's moral equality would inevitably lead to sexual equality. In the book she took up questions she thought were more important and revealing. What was the nature of women's psychology, apart from their moral character? How best to educate them? How could the trait of female benevolence be reconciled with social ethics that were free of gender? As for rights, how could women acquire enough power to claim them? The writer of a retrospective sketch of Fuller around this time—possibly Elizabeth Cady Stanton, who may have heard her speak in Boston—recalled that she put two profound and simple questions to her female listeners: " 'What were we born to do?' " and " 'How shall we do it?' "[17] The book was a sustained reflection on these matters.

Woman in the Nineteenth Century appealed to the inner faculties of imagination and intellect: to the sense of self, not to moral duty. Into a Protestant discourse that turned on moral sovereignty and accountability to God, Fuller injected a language of imaginative exploration inflected with European Romanticism. She praised Fourier's sexual egalitarianism and applauded his belief that "harmony in action" between people was the corollary of individual freedom. The ideal of Owenite marriage intrigued her for the "aspiration of soul, of energy of mind, seeking clearness and freedom" that it brought into men's and women's relations. She cited a prominent Owenite couple, Catharine and Goodwyn Barmby, as partners in a marriage devoted to the common good. Equality in marriage emancipated repressed energies so that a woman "might dignify and unfold her life for her own happiness, and that of society."[18]

The quest for self-realization was a staple of Transcendentalism, but Fuller directed readers down a path that was gender-specific. Women must cease deferring to men, and rather "retire within themselves and explore the groundwork of life til they find their peculiar secret. Then, when they come forth again, renovated and baptized, they will know how to turn all dross to gold, and will be rich and free though they live in a hut, tranquil, if in a crowd." Garrisonian abolitionists insisted that the soul had no sex; Fuller instructed readers about the marvelous things the sexless soul could do: "Sweet singing shall not be from a passionate impulse, but the lyrical over-flow of a divine rapture."[19]

More than any other writer of her time and, for that matter, more than most since, Fuller stressed that sexual equality would benefit men, too; here again she followed the Owenites and Fourierists. The sexes were interdependent and gender roles were malleable. "I believe that the development of one cannot be effected without that of the other." Masculinity and femininity were unstable, complementary, and commingling. "Male and female represent the two sides of the great radical dualism.... [T]hey are perpetually passing into one another. Fluid hardens to solid, solid rushes to fluid."[20] Her father's treasured daughter and a token woman in a man's world, she could not imagine women's freedom without men's. The rushing, overflowing currents of her Romantic faith, despite painful disappointments in her friendships with Emerson and other male intellectuals, buoyed a democratic romance of sisters and brothers: "Improvement in the daughters will best aid in the reformation of the sons of this age," she believed. Living as she had with the New England eminences of the day, men who in their genteel way preened and pontificated and ordered women around, she was not naïve about their investment in the way things were.[21] But if men could tolerate the change, then divine energy would radiate outward: "The sexes should not only correspond to and appreciate, but prophesy to one another." Men should think of themselves as kindly brothers, encouraging women and recognizing their particular gifts. Like a good brother, they were to call out "'you can do it, if you only think so.'"[22]

Today *Woman in the Nineteenth Century* is difficult to read, with its New England mysticism, its scrim of inscrutable references to classical literature, and its preoccupation with an ideal brother figure. Fuller was one of the few nineteenth-century feminists to imagine women in a vibrant relationship with men and to plan for a good time coming that the sexes would spend together. In the next decades, the book did not fit easily into a tradition that marched along the lines of female separatism, with women anointed as the makers of change and men imagined as a surly crowd, trailing behind. Moreover, Fuller's interest in psychology, love, and pleasurable heterosexual exchanges and her insistence that women go out into the world to find their "gold" rather than burrow into the home was at odds with an American movement whose default mode would be improving women's sphere rather than leaving domesticity behind.

Fuller introduced into women's rights a preoccupation with introspection and imagination that would go into abeyance as an active principle, to surface only much later, when twentieth-century feminists again turned to the psyche as a critical ground of change. Her Romantic celebration of the female self broke open the citizen/individual of liberal democratic discourse to reflections about what the sovereignty of self actually required when women were involved. How to discover that self was—and remains—a problem, given how ideals of selflessness were—and are—instilled in the female sex from a very early age. Fuller understood the need to change laws, education, and marriage, but she was also one of the first feminists to grasp the importance of expressiveness, reflection, and subjective exploration to women's emancipation. This Romantic current would, in future years, nourish American feminism's ventures into personal transformation that outstripped the liberal paradigm of women's rights.

Given what happened with feminism in the United States, it is interesting to ponder what Fuller might have done had she remained in the country. Instead she sailed for Europe, embarking on an extraordinary journey of cosmopolitan awareness, political consolidation, and sexual awakening that took her to the barricades of the revolutions of 1848. Arriving in London in 1846, she stayed with radical Unitarians, whose unusual ideas were that much more striking because her hosts were not oddballs holding forth in the phalanx parlor but eminent writers, lawyers, and journalists. The women she met—including Harriet Martineau and George Eliot—made bracing company after her years as the standout female among Boston's brilliant young men. Moving on to Paris, she met George Sand, the female literary celebrity whose openly acknowledged love affairs shocked but also fascinated the public.[23]

There too she met the exiled Polish poet Adam Mickiewicz, who believed he spotted in her the incarnation of the Saint-Simonian female messiah. He urged her to take up her eschatological role. Mickiewicz was tender and praiseful, skirting the line between friendship and eros. But unlike Emerson, whose attention to her was also mixed, the poet was capacious in his encouragement and never undercutting. She had written about the rights and freedoms of women, he reminded her, and now she must live out those freedoms: to love and realize her potential in service to the world.[24] In short, the stodgy Old World embraced the American woman and offered her sumptuous materials to reinvent herself as the genius she had long thought about. What she saw of women taking cultural leadership and what she took from the admiration of leading men like Mickiewicz transformed what remained of her life.

The revolutions of 1848 tore across the Continent from France to Hungary and through every major city, with coalitions of middle-class republicans and radical workers fighting to overturn monarchies and feudal regimes and establish republics. Women joined the forces on the barricades, and here and there, they rose to prominence. In Germany, for instance, Mathilde Anneke was at the forefront of the revolt in Baden. The daughter of a wealthy bourgeois family, she was married off to a nobleman sometime in the early 1840s when she was still a teenager. Shortly thereafter, she so appalled her family by divorcing him that they cast her out. On the eve of 1848, she was a working writer; her "Woman in Conflict with Social Conditions" was an early German tract on the subject. In 1848 she rode into battle beside her second husband, Fritz Anneke, to defend the republican uprising in Baden.

The most concerted activity was in Paris. Led by Pauline Roland and Jeanne Deroin, both former Saint-Simonians, feminists produced in the headiest days of the revolution a newspaper, *La Voix des Femmes*, which became the center of women's independent organizing. The journal published news about the women's clubs and made the case for political rights, equal education, and women's inclusion in the republic's labor cooperatives. A self-proclaimed group of Vésuviennes—a name proclaiming their volcanic energy—published a manifesto calling for the reorganizaiton of family and home life in line with republican principles. Fourier's and Saint-Simon's legacy is evident in their belief that the key to the future lay in private life; but they reversed the older association of revolution with free love by calling for mandatory marriage and the equal division of domestic responsibilities. Most likely speaking as disenchanted veterans of liaisons with working-class men, they called others to join them: "Let us force men to share the duties of the hearth and they will no longer be able to arm themselves with ridicule and use it against us."[25]

But they did not strike a sympathetic chord among the men. Vitriol and misogyny congealed in newspaper cartoons by the city's best-known illustrators—the most famous was Honoré Daumier—who turned revolutionary women into old maids, viragoes, man haters, delinquent mothers, unfaithful wives, and armed maniacs. Lampooning feminists' ideas, the cartoons were the talk of the town and acted as a "brake on the revolutionary imagination," an art historian observes. The message was that revolution was a man's business, and women who dared participate were only evading their duties. "It makes no sense to leave me here with three kids to watch," protests a henpecked husband, loaded down with infants, to his termagant wife in one Daumier cartoon. "Oh! So you're my husband!... Well! It's my right to throw you out the door of your own house.... Jeanne Deroin proved it to me last night!" an enraged woman informs her man as she shoves him out the door.[26] Socialist Pierre-Joseph Proudhon voiced a common sentiment when he sneered at Deroin's campaign for a legislative seat: Women could no more govern than men could be wet nurses. Margaret Fuller, who followed events in Paris from her new home in Rome, resigned herself to the plain fact that "woman's day has not come yet."[27]

Leaving Paris, Fuller traveled on to Rome to take in the sights, like any American on the Grand Tour. But she also acted surreptitiously as an emissary for Guiseppe Mazzini, whom she had met in London. Mazzini was the leader of Young Italy, preparing to return to lead the revolution in Rome. In winter 1849, with the revolutionary tide elsewhere receding, Mazzini made his triumphal return to establish the short-lived republic. Fuller plunged in to help. In a city electric with expectation, she stepped out of Mickiewicz's utopian mythology and her own airy-mystical prose into living history, the "springtime of the peoples." Seized by the justice of the Roman cause, Fuller fired off a volley of passionate reports to the *Tribune* that tried to counter antirevolutionary sentiment in the States and fire up Americans' sympathies for a struggle that paralleled their own. Indeed, she believed that at the moment, Europe was leading the battle for democracy, since Europe was free from slavery. She fell in love with Giovanni Ossoli, a minor noble and dedicated republican, an officer in the Civic Guard defending the city. With Ossoli, she conceived a child almost certainly out of wedlock, a daring affirmation of free love. She gave birth to a son, whom they took to the countryside for safety. Fuller and Ossoli, now secretly married, returned to a city under siege by the French army, dispatched by Louis-Napoleon—the counterrevolutionary victor in France—in response to the pope's call to Catholic Europe to crush the republic.

Ossoli was no intellectual, but the two forged a marriage based on shared devotion to a noble cause, a partnership of the kind that Fuller had extolled in *Woman in the Nineteenth Century*. He fought courageously on the barricades and Fuller ran a hospital for the wounded, risking her life under constant bombardment: "May God help us," the letter giving her the commission is signed. But regardless of the danger the nurses faced, the very existence of the corps of female volunteers irritated some officials, who grumbled and carped about the women's authority. Mazzini upheld their standing, and the nurses retained their positions, officially honored as women of "high democratic ideals."

Musing on the spirit of 1848, Fuller imagined an even greater role for herself—"I might ask to be made an Ambassador"—though she knew that such a possibility would have to wait "another century." She had remade her life as a sexually emancipated woman; and now she took a place in the revolution as a woman and citizen. The only American to remain in the city during the siege, she and Ossoli stayed until the end, when the French marched through the city gates on one side and the revolutionaries poured out the other. If we look back to the symbolic sibling relationship she sketched in her book, it's as if Mazzini and the other republican brothers had assured her, " 'you can do it, if you only think so.' "[28]

In the ten months of revolution and counterrevolution between spring 1848 and the fall of the Roman republic, American reactions ran from excitement to condemnation. Antislavery supporters took the revolutions as a spur to their own labors to rid their country of the ultimate form of tyranny. In New York state, antislavery men precipitated their own rebellion within the Democratic Party, the Barnburners insurgency that led to the formation of the Free Soil Party, which ran former president Martin Van Buren for president on a third-party ticket that fall.

In the thick of the antislavery turmoil, Lucretia Mott paid a visit to her sister Martha Coffin Wright in Auburn, New York, and took the occasion to renew her friendship with Elizabeth Cady Stanton, who had moved from Boston to nearby Seneca Falls. Based in Seneca Falls, Henry Stanton was close to the antislavery uprising and deeply involved.[29] But while the Barnburners occupied Henry, Elizabeth chafed under the constraints of small-town life and three small children. Sitting around a table drinking tea with Lucretia Mott, Martha Wright, and two other women, Stanton jumped at the chance to call a women's rights meeting.

Stanton was convinced that there, in the middle of rural New York in 1848, they were on the edge of another revolt of historic significance. She knew exactly the place in history she wanted to stake out: "The first women's rights convention that has ever assembled," she stressed to a neighbor.[30] It was easy enough to put something together. Many years later, wanting to stress their heroism, Stanton told the story as if the idea were a bolt from the blue and the organizers scarcely knew how to proceed, so naïve and untutored were they in public life. The fact was that they were all reformers involved in organizing temperance, antislavery, and church meetings, renting halls, composing resolutions, and putting out notices for years.[31] They worried that attendance would be small: It was high summer, busy on the farms, hot and slow in town. Yet throngs of people gathered on the first day, about three hundred, mostly women but with a large contingent of men.[32]

From the European news, many in attendance would have had manifesto making on their minds. The organizers issued their own, a "Declaration of Sentiments," which inserted women into the formulations of the Declaration of Independence. "We hold these truths to be self-evident: that all men and women are created equal; that they are endowed by their Creator with certain inalienable rights."[33] Compared to Sarah Grimké's account of women's wrongs ten years earlier, the Declaration's tally of grievances was much more extensive and systematic: taxation without representation, the civil death women suffered under common law, the lack of maternal custody rights in cases of separation or divorce, and their exclusion from the ministry, law, and medicine. The document pointed out that freeborn American women were still the subjects of husbands and fathers; that divorce was a social and economic disaster for them; that a "double standard of morals" banished women from respectable society for actions that were deemed unimportant in men; and that no decently paid work was open to them. The culprit was man: "He has usurped the prerogative of Jehovah himself, claiming it as his right to assign for [woman] a sphere of action, when that belongs to her conscience and her God."

By using the language of 1776, the authors of the Seneca Falls resolutions drew authority from natural rights theory rather than Christian doctrine. The proposed remedies cohered as specific demands: to attend university, hold political office, have access to male employments, and end the worst features of coverture. All were premised on the proposition "that woman is man's equal—was intended to be so by the Creator, and the highest good of the race demands that she should be recognized as such." The most concrete resolution was for women's suffrage, a proposal Elizabeth Stanton put forward. It was the only one that was controversial.

It was not that the issue was unknown. The Owenites had raised it sporadically and to no avail in Britain. In Paris a few months earlier, a Committee for the Rights of Women petitioned the provisional government for the franchise (voted down 899–1).[34] In the United States, women's suffrage was far-fetched but still a logical extension of a system that had already undone the tight fit of virtual representation for men. With universal white manhood suffrage in place, it was not the lack of property but sex and race that stripped adults of political rights. And even race was debatable. Although effectively disenfranchised in most of the country, free black men voted in some states in the North. During the conventions in the 1840s held by most states to revise their constitutions, measures for black disenfranchisement occasioned lengthy debate. In New York state, the constitutional convention of 1846–47 received several groups of petitions for women's suffrage, although it ignored them. Commenting on the response, Unitarian minister Samuel May, a Garrisonian and a Liberty Party man, preached from his pulpit in Syracuse that one would never know that "there were any women in the body politic."[35]

Elizabeth Cady Stanton, well connected to leading men and well-versed in the day's political developments, had just seen the Married Women's Property Act pass the New York legislature. Now she seized the chance to introduce the subject of suffrage into debate. She encountered resistance on strategic grounds: "Those who took part in the debate feared a demand for the right to vote would defeat others they deemed more rational, and make the whole movement ridiculous." Lori Ginzberg suggests that the other organizers knew that the preponderance of Quakers and Garrisonians who were bound to be at the meeting saw voting as participation in a corrupt political system and would reject the resolution out of hand. But Stanton prevailed, probably with the help of the Free Soilers at the meeting, who would have been alert to the importance of voting. The balance tipped when Frederick Douglass threw his weight behind the resolution. Douglass, who was editing his *North Star* in nearby Rochester, was "a disfanchised man," as he wrote six months earlier when the state convention took away the vote from black men. Now he kindled to the principle of universal suffrage articulated from another direction.[36] Forty years later, at an anniversary celebration of Seneca Falls, he spoke with unmistakable pride of his action that day. "When I ran away from slavery, it was for myself; when I advocated emancipation, it was for my people; but when I stood up for the rights of woman, self was out of the question, and I found a little nobility in the act."[37]

Seneca Falls launched a fleet of women into public life. The impulse toward organization led to continuous activity, and the republican language provided the ideological basis to sustain an ongoing enterprise. Through the 1850s, women in the Northeast and Midwest held women's rights conventions with regularity. All told there were more than thirty held up to the outbreak of the Civil War, with interest running along channels of abolitionist sympathy.[38]

Like abolitionism, women's rights was a Northern phenomenon. The ideas were anathema in the South, where the power that upheld human bondage pervaded all human relations—slaves, slaveholders, and nonslaveholders alike. Men's customary power over women's labor, persons, and bodies derived from the same ancient sources as did slavery, a fact that did not escape feminists, beginning with Mary Astell, and that was of course a central insight of abolitionist-feminists.

But the analogy dwindled in power the closer one got to the slave system, because slave-owning women were nothing like slaves. Mastery was a status that also incorporated mistresses, who could dispose of the persons and labor of the women and children under their control as they would, especially in their own domain of the household. There they held the power of life and death and they did not shirk from using violence to enforce it. Regardless of their own subordination to men, Southern planter women were loyal to a ruthless social order antithetical to the principles of universal rights and moral equality on which feminism depended.[39]

Women's rights featured in Southern thought as a demonstration of all that was wrong with Northern society. Famously, George Fitzhugh maintained in *Cannibals All!* (1857) his defense of slavery as a positive good, that the kindly paternal care that enveloped childlike Africans also enfolded women, who were similarly weak and vulnerable. Planter women were aware of Northern arguments; the terms of women's rights thought flicker in Mary Boykin Chesnut's caustic observations in her diary of the 1850s about Southern men: their sexual liaisons with slave women, their bullying ways about money. But such private allusions to their sufferings functioned as tokens of planter women's stoic allegiance to the system.

Nowhere in the South did women's complaints about men amount to more than the carping of a loyal opposition: loyal, that is, to the class of which they were paid-up members. No Southern women except for the Grimkés spoke out against slavery. As a result, affiliations with women's rights were missing in the South until well after the Civil War.

In the North, though, the fight against slavery gave cover to feminist organizing, giving women space to gather in the interstices of antislavery clamor, away from withering scrutiny. The call for suffrage, a daring departure at Seneca Falls, became a standard demand. In Salem, Ohio, an abolitionist hotbed near Youngstown, participants in an 1851 convention were unequivocal about the universal right to vote, which they merged with black enfranchisement, concurrently being debated in the state constitutional convention: "'White male' must be stricken out of our State Constitution ... and person substituted in its place."[40] Legal reform of married women's position was a leading concern, routed through the call for married women's property acts.

Discussions ranged over the general debilities of wives, although they stopped short of contemplating the Owenite idea of marriage as a civil contract. Rather, the plight of the "drunkard's wife," a figure lifted from the temperance movement, was a more palatable way to talk about the gross inequities of marriage without coming uncomfortably close to the institution itself or the taboo subject of divorce. In passing, and in stately Victorian language that floated high above the gritty realities of workingwomen's lives, participants also considered paid labor: pervasive discrimination and women's drastically limited opportunities. "The number of her industrial avocations is unnecessarily restricted ... and, when she is engaged in the same occupations with men, her remuneration is greatly below what is awarded to her stronger associates."[41]

This flourishing field in America stands in sharp contrast to the situation in Europe. After the defeats of 1848, feminism there persisted as threads of thought and aspiration rather than streams of energy; strands woven through cultural elites and working-class movements as they regrouped. Radicals scattered. Only the Germans immigrated to the United States in significant numbers. Mathilde Anneke fled Bavaria with her husband and started a German-language newspaper in Newark, New Jersey. Anneke was one of the few '48ers who became prominent in the American suffrage movement; a colleague of Stanton and Anthony, she proselytized after the war to German immigrants.

In Paris in the aftermath, Jeanne Deroin and Pauline Roland spent six months in prison. From their cells, they comforted themselves by thinking about events abroad. How they got the news is not clear, but they somehow knew about the 1850 women's rights convention in Worcester, Massachusetts, and a Chartist women's petition for suffrage to the House of Lords.[42] The two prisoners believed something of great historic import was abroad in the world. In a long letter dispatched to each group of "sisters," they rehearsed the whole sad tale in Paris, including the rebuffs of the brothers, but ended on the upswing with a salute to those elsewhere who were taking up the great endeavor. Calling· up Wollstonecraft's language, they promised that "your socialist sisters of France are united with you in the vindication of the right of Woman to civil and political equality." Carry on! they entreated. "Faith, Love, Hope" and "Sisterly salutations."[43]

Colloquies across borders were evanescent but important, because they gave the conversants a sense that women together were operating in world politics, making the cause of liberal democracy their own. The transatlantic connections, however, remained thin. This was in part because of the death of Margaret Fuller Ossoli, who, returning to America in 1850, drowned with her husband and son off Fire Island, New York, on the last leg of their journey.

Unquestionably, Fuller's death was a loss to the nascent American movement. Only Elizabeth Cady Stanton would come close to Fuller's intellectual stature, her ability to hold her own with male luminaries, and her vision of a greater scope for women—and it would take Stanton years to get her footing. But even Stanton, brilliant as she was, lacked Fuller's intellectual breadth and cosmopolitan politics. We can only speculate about what might have happened had Fuller returned and taken her place again at the center of her culture. With her grasp of international politics, her fluency in French, German, and Italian, and her experience in combining the most advanced female liberties with the cause of democracy, she might have served as an intermediary between the American women and Europe. She might have opened the American movement to labor causes; or she could have returned to her writing on women's subjectivity. She might have revived the democratic themes of sibling relationships that, in Rome, she had lived out.

In 1850, America was at once the only functioning democracy left standing in the North Atlantic world and the one nation to harbor slavery. In the space that the contradiction wrenched open, American women mounted a small but energetic political initiative. These were the singularities of the American situation. Europe, the defeated hopes of 1848, and socialist castles in the air were very far away.

While there were men at the edges—friends, fathers, brothers, and sons—the American movement increasingly defined itself as a female affair. We are now in a time of women friends. The relative ease of travel in the North meant that women formed political friendships across distances. Letters spun homely intimacies across miles and between women's rights conventions: worries about children, stories of sickness and aging parents, preoccupations with servants and anxieties about money, along with tales of meetings organized and speeches given, fulminations on the Fugitive Slave Act, and plans for temperance campaigns.

It was a solidly middle-class group, with virtually no working-class women and few rich women, either, although middle-class was a fragile status. Lucy Stone, for example, the Oberlin graduate and in the 1850s an abolitionist lecturer, would land solidly in the middle class when she married Henry Blackwell, from a well-to-do Anglo-American reform family. But Stone, like many of these middle-class women, came from a modest farm family, and had she not married, she would have been a hard-pressed teacher scrabbling out a living.[44] Regardless of the liminal class identities, though, the milieu was overwhelmingly white. By 1840, black and white women had separated, a fact that should surprise no one; what is remarkable is the extent to which they had once overlapped.

This is not to say African-Americans were closed to women's rights, and any full account of feminist history must include the rising generation of black women abolitionists who operated from independent positions outside marriage, supporting themselves by lecturing and writing: the indomitable Sojourner Truth (once a slave); Frances Ellen Watkins (an Oberlin graduate); Sarah Parker Remond (daughter of a leading abolitionist family); and Mary Ann Shadd Cary (also a child of abolition). All these women brushed against women's rights ideas and organizations. While their public presence was tenuous, they established a foothold for feminist principles in African-American life to which Northern black women after the Civil War returned.[45]

At the center of the women's rights movement were Susan B. Anthony and Elizabeth Cady Stanton. The Anthony/Stanton partnership inaugurated a female political collaboration previously unimaginable. A demon organizer, Anthony, from a farm family in upstate New York, had not been at Seneca Falls, but she met Stanton shortly after, in 1850. They became political partners and friends, although the abiding desire they shared was not for intimacy but for women's power. Stanton's mobility and time were constrained by a growing family: She had three more children in the 1850s, bringing the total to six. If it had not been for their partnership, Stanton might well have fallen into the role of brilliant, bitter small-town housewife, firing off idiosyncratic letters to the editor; and Anthony could have slipped into the position of peripatetic spinster, a figure like Miss Birdseye, the aging reformer in Henry James's novel *The Bostonians,* immensely admirable and vaguely pitiable. The work of Anthony, who did not marry, often consisted of helping with Stanton's children so that their mother could write a speech. But between them they gave unfailing, steady, strong direction to what might otherwise have been a momentary upswelling of sentiment. As it was, their busy, productive fifty-year partnership was packed with events, travel, ideas, high aims, and political wrangling.

British feminists also came together as a distinct circle in the 1850s, but theirs was an elite, metropolitan affair, coalescing around Barbara Leigh Smith and Bessie Rayner Parkes, both from radical Unitarian families. The loosely knit group of fellow spirits met at a house in London that provided space for a newspaper office, meeting rooms, a library, and classrooms, "everything that could be desired by a new reform or lobby group." While the principals were genteel, the group continued the Owenite stress on women's labor, transposing it into a middle-class register in calling for professions for women. Barbara Leigh Smith's lengthy "Women and Work" decried the equation of feminine propriety with idleness and put the need for decent, fairly paid labor at the center of women's equality; the group held classes to train young women as accountants, bookkeepers, and printers. Smith and Parkes were prescient in their goals and ideas. But theirs was a select circle, with few connections to the wider world of women and no means to attract a mass constituency.[46]

Gone were the male/female partnerships so important to earlier feminism. Except for John Stuart Mill, whose *The Subjection of Women* (1869) was heavily indebted to Harriet Taylor (now his wife), the germinative relationships would be between women. Although the democratic brothers remained important presences in all feminists' lives and provided critical aid, they were not known as writing partners, collaborators, co-conspirators, or enthusiasts. The compelling problem of sisters and brothers receded, to be replaced for long stretches of time by a different aspect of feminism's family romance, negotiations between generations and factions imagined as mothers and daughters.

In Europe, feminist assertions were attached to popular insurgency. After 1848, the lifeline was gone. Women's rights retreated to small enclaves, such as the Langham Place circle, or lodged in literary sensibility, as in the work of Charlotte Brontë, Elizabeth Barrett Browning, and (more ambiguously) George Eliot. When women's rights movements emerged in the 1860s and 1870s in Britain, the Netherlands, and France, it was among middle-class women, connected to republican ideas that were purged of socialism and any hints of sexual impropriety.

In the United States, in contrast, antislavery politics gave women's rights a line of support and a raison d'être. For a time the fact that the women's cause was subsidiary did not raise troubling contradictions. The American feminist movement was small but pragmatic, with ideas about how to respond to pressing needs, hold men accountable, and seize a measure of self-representation in politics. The connection to antislavery propelled the subject into national conversation. Going down the Mississippi River on her wedding trip in 1857, Barbara Leigh Smith (now Bodichon) found that Southerners were ready to denounce women's rights at the drop of a hat.[47]

At the same time, however, the more public, Protestant, middle-class character of the American movement meant that avant-garde thinking about sexuality, marriage, and labor was more truncated than in Europe. Aside from Stanton and a few of her intimates, the movement absorbed only mild elements of the European marriage critique and spurned the rest as licentious free love.

The American women had no ties to Congress and few hopes of immediate changes they might effect. They were not adjuncts to a political elite. Yet neither were they on the fringe. They made themselves political actors, even though they were only playing bit roles. The diffuseness of their activity and aims generated the dynamics of future expansion. A freewheeling conversation began about the causes of women's difficulties. Amelia Bloomer, for instance, a supporter in Ohio, developed a theory about the role that clothes played in women's oppression. The long skirts and multiple petticoats of Victorian fashion literally dragged women down. Hems collected dust and mud, and the dirt made travel difficult. Workingwomen were turned away from skilled mechanized trades because their skirts might catch in the machinery. The most serious feminists flirted with wearing blousy pants underneath their dresses, "bloomers," named after their inventor. Bloomers never gained many converts; the mockery that greeted them was too harsh. But the thinking was typical of the American movement: an attempt to redress very large injustices with small measures.

The emphasis on the emancipation of the body, running alongside the call to the vote, owed something to European dreams, now subsided. With some ability to withstand the periods of lassitude and indifference that were (and remain) feminism's worst enemy, the American movement entered the second half of the nineteenth century able to articulate intense aspirations and imagine how they might come to pass.

CHAPTER FOUR

LOYALTY'S LIMITS

The Civil War, Emancipation,
and Women's Bids for Power

THE ASSOCIATION OF women's rights with antislavery was keenly felt. No antislavery activist could help but think that one good cause fed another. When war came, veterans of the women's conventions threw themselves into the battle for a republic whose preservation, they believed, depended on the efforts of all: mothers and sisters no less than the fathers and brothers who enlisted. And when the war ended, the emancipation of the slaves augured to them a huge expansion of democracy. The hopeful believed that loyal women would enter the Union as enfranchised citizens right alongside the freedpeople, recognized for the part they had played for thirty years in the battle that determined the republic's fate. They met with bitter disappointment.

"Such was the war. It was not a quadrille in a ball-room," Walt Whitman observed with dry understatement about his months nursing wounded and dying men.[1] Like most who wrote about the war, Whitman construed the experience as male. But the Civil War was no quadrille for women, either. Northern women did all in their power to join their efforts to the troops'. Since the battleground was almost entirely in the South, they were far from the fighting, and since it was a modern war, with the government supplying the wants and needs of the Union Army, they were distant from the actual operations (as women were not during the American Revolution). But the massive mobilization and soaring casualties meant that no one was untouched.

When Lincoln was elected, leaders agreed to put aside women's rights for the duration to attend to the crisis at hand. "I have felt that it would be very unwise, at this time," reasoned a sensible Martha Wright about not holding a convention in 1861, "when the nation's whole heart & soul are engrossed with this momentous crisis." She described what must have been the daily life of most households: "Every body now is absorbed in watching the course of our politicians, calculating the effect of every action on the future of the nation, reading with anxiety the account of battles, in which so many of us have a personal interest— How then is it possible to think of a Convention."[2]

Once the war began, the women who had thrown themselves into anti-slavery agitation were assigned to the sidelines along with the rest of their sex, knitting and rolling bandages. They found their political feet in the difficult spring of 1863, when the prospects for Union victory were dim. After a string of defeats and two months before the New York City draft riots and Gettysburg, Anthony and Stanton found a way to take action by issuing a call to the "Loyal Women of the Nation" in the *New York Tribune*. The call urged women to insert themselves as partisans into the issues of the war:

> Thus far there has been no united public expression from the women of the North as to the policy of the war. Here and there one has spoken and written nobly. Many have vied with each other in acts of generosity and self-sacrifice for the sick and wounded in camp and hospital. But we have, as yet, no means of judging how and where the majority of Northern women stand.

The organization they formed, the Women's National Loyal League, was their bid to join the Republican effort to shore up flagging Northern support and stave off the growing power of the Peace Democrats. Five months after the partial freedom of the Emancipation Proclamation, the Loyal League was a parallel to the influential Union Leagues for men, formed a year earlier to rally support for the government and amplify the demand for emancipation.[3]

The Loyal League did not tell anyone to stop making bandages and knitting. But its point was to encourage women to address the politics of the war directly. The message went against the grain: By this time, antislavery was a moral position tolerable for women to adopt, but party politics was thought to be men's business. The whole idea of women *as women* advocating war and defending the Republican Party flew in the face of assumptions about their peace-loving nature: They were supposed to be too busy with household concerns and too frail to take part in the rough-and-tumble affray of party debate. The premise reworked the principle of virtual representation for a more democratic age: Women should leave these fractious matters to husbands or their congressmen. Caroline Dall, an opinionated, high-handed women's rights leader in Boston, expressed the views of even open-minded people when she chided Stanton about the Loyal League. Women should confine themselves to moral influence and stay away from the down-and-dirty business of base partisanship, she scolded.[4]

Partisanship was exactly what the Loyal League called for. Speaking passionately at the first meeting, Stanton denounced the call for peace with slaveholders and vehemently affirmed the war aim of immediate and unconditional abolition. "For if there is a God in heaven, if there is a law of justice in the earth, if there is a law of cause and effect in the universe, this war can never be suppressed, this nation can never know peace, until slavery—the cause of the war—is wholly and for ever removed." Stanton spoke as a citizen, not a moral subject, and she sought to rally women on that basis. She declared the League to be "the first and only organization of women for the declared purpose of influencing politics," thus differentiating it from the aspirational, resolution-passing women's conventions of the 1850s.

Carried along by the momentum of crisis, Stanton and Anthony seem to have thought they could vault over obstacles by dint of sheer determination, willing themselves into political equality. In a war fought very far away, they meant to extend the home front by making women into influential citizens at the leading edge of public opinion, using what was still the only political right available to them after all these years, the right of petition. In the summer following Gettsyburg, the League set itself the task of getting a million signatures on a petition to Congress for immediate emancipation.[5]

It sounds simple, but it required complicated, hectic organization—important people contacted and urged into action, envelopes and paper purchased, free mailing privileges obtained from Massachusetts abolitionist senator Charles Sumner. The goal of a million signatures was unrealizable (it would have represented more than 10 percent of the adult population of the North). But they were phenomenally successful, collecting 100,000 names: Sumner brought the first group to the Senate floor in February 1864, laying the groundwork for the Thirteenth

Amendment, which passed the Senate two months later. More rolled in: Sumner introduced them in lots to keep up pressure on the House, which passed the amendment in December. The final tally is an impressive 400,000 signatures, one for every twenty-four adults in the Northern states.[6]

The Thirteenth Amendment petition drive inspired among women leaders conviction about their own efficacy. It seemed that they could take on political weight by virtue of hard work and determination. Looking back, we could call the approach willed equality: a faith that has often come to activist women working in the throes of a political crisis and convinced that their efforts cannot help but win recognition. Women had petitioned before, in the abolitionist campaigns of the 1830s. This time, however, they were working with the party in power. They helped shore up the Union at a dire moment and contributed to the passage of a constitutional amendment. "Women will undoubtedly be a power in the coming presidential campaign," Stanton happily predicted in 1864. They were "already speaking on all phases of the question, hence the importance that we know whereof we speak."[7]

In sum, "loyalist" was a position they imagined as inside, not outside formal politics, and bound to bring them political rewards.[8] For Stanton, the war was a hinge between a before of women's political quiescence and an after of robust engagement. Northern women had shown a "want of vigilance," but now, called to duty, they proved they were capable of taking up the obligations of citizens—the corollary of holding political rights. Stanton and Anthony's correspondence from 1864 shows them scheming avidly with friends male and female about the Republican presidential nomination, for all the world as if they were backroom wheeler-dealers.

It is impossible to overstate the immensity of the task the country faced at the war's end, or the severity of divisions about how to proceed. Six hundred thousand dead, four million slaves freed, the president murdered, and the rebellious states to be reintegrated into the Union. What was to be done with Confederate officeholders, leaders of a treasonous government? What was the civil and political status of the freedpeople? An armed South raised the stakes as white vigilantes went on the offensive against the former slaves, using terror to reimpose white rule. Skirmishes boiled over into full-scale attacks on freedpeople in New Orleans and Memphis in 1866. With the border state president Andrew

Johnson, who favored leniency so extreme it would mean readmission of the former Confederate states with the same senators and congressmen who seceded in 1861, consternation in the North spread. The vote for blacks was an absolute necessity to change the structure of power in the Southern states, but black suffrage on what terms?

Once a Republican Congress took control of Reconstruction in 1866, women's rights proponents were among those calling for black manhood suffrage. Only biracial democracy, shored up by the freedpeople's votes, could fend off the nightmare scenario of the former potentates of the slave power reinstalled in statehouses and Congress. In May, women's rights leaders combined with the Garrisonians to form the American Equal Rights Association (AERA), dedicated to universal suffrage. "As women we can no longer *seem* to claim for ourselves what we do not for others—nor can we work in two separate movements to get the ballot for the two disfranchised classes—the negro and woman—since to do so must be at double cost of time, energy and money." It was a clarion call for "the true basis of the reconstruction of our government, not the rights of woman, or the negro, but the rights of all men and women." The "citizen" whose outlines had appeared during the war seemed to them big enough to encompass both the freedman and the white woman, with the freedwoman presumably trailing along. Specifically, they saw Northern women loyalists as counterparts to the black soldiers, the humbled and excluded who had done their part, and whom a grateful nation would now welcome to full citizenship.[9]

Political exigency pulled the issue away from them. For Republicans, Congressional Reconstruction hinged on whether the political rights of the republic would be extended to black men, not whether those rights could be reinterpreted to belong to women. Assumptions that the new black citizens were male had already entered debate over the Thirteenth Amendment. So deeply inscribed in antislavery politics was the notion that freedom would redeem black manhood—a manhood crushed by slavery—that congressmen praised emancipation in just those terms: The former slaves could govern their women and children as white men did in their family jurisdictions.[10]

With each alarming report from the South, the importance of black suffrage rose, while women's claims languished. The Fourteenth Amendment, passed in 1866 and ratified in 1868, was a compromise between moderates and radicals: Federal power would defend the freedpeople's civil rights but stopped short of guaranteeing the vote. But there was no mistaking the direction: Section Two instituted penalties designed to punish states that abrogated the voting rights of any adult *male* inhabitant.

It was the first time the word "male" appeared in the Constitution. In a nation where now neither lack of property nor race disqualified one from voting, womanhood stood as a primary marker of disenfranchisement. The Loyal League women were firm supporters of black manhood suffrage, but this they had not expected. "If that word 'male' be inserted [into the Constitution], it will take us at least a century to get it out," Stanton balefully predicted. She supported the amendment but wanted the language changed to "persons." Although she would have mentioned the one-hundred-year time line for dramatic effect, she turned out to be on the mark. Women got the vote in 1920, but not until the 1970s did the Supreme Court apply the Fourteenth Amendment's equal protection guarantee to women.[11]

As participants in the AERA, women's rights leaders worked on the assumption that a grateful nation would abolish the markers of prejudice and "bury the woman & the negro in the citizen," as Stanton predicted to Sojourner Truth. Aiming for the lofty heights of gender-neutral citizens, they shucked the "woman" in women's rights, not because it was "odious," Martha Wright stressed, countering a charge that was sometimes made: No, every good cause was odious at one time, she observed wisely. It was because the war had transformed them, put flesh on their gender-neutral citizenly personae. "We take the new name for the broader work, because we see it is no longer woman's province to be merely a humble petitioner for redress of grievances, but that she must now enter into the fullness of her mission, that of helping to make the laws, and administer justice."[12]

The political situation was supercharged, but at first old alliances held firm. Frederick Douglass once again lent his moral authority to the women's cause. At one tense meeting, he and Stanton stood together as they had twenty years before at Seneca Falls—this time to oppose Henry Blackwell, Lucy Stone's husband and a man no one much liked or trusted. Blackwell proposed that equal rights forces endorse an educational qualification for voters, a provision that, Stanton pointed out, would disenfranchise the former slaves. Douglass followed up on her sharp rebuttal, arguing that voting required "no qualification beyond that of common humanity, manhood and womanhood," and pointedly contrasting the loyalty of uneducated freedpeople with the treason of Confederate officers educated at West Point.[13]

The problem was that only a few Republicans in Congress showed any interest in universal suffrage. When Sumner dutifully introduced a petition for women's suffrage to the Senate in 1866, he nullified his own gesture by instructing his colleagues to pay it no mind: "I do not think this a proper time for the consideration of that question."[14] The women picked up a few Democrats, but the support was cynical. Democrats seized on votes for women as a ploy to undercut black suffrage by holding up the demonstrably most ridiculous element of universal suffrage to public view: If you give the vote to black men, well then (ha ha) why not give it to women?[15]

Pushed aside by black manhood suffrage, the women turned more oppositional and partial. Ignored despite their best efforts, they drew for the first time a distinction between the freedmen, whom they defined as privileged males, and themselves, victims of male despotism. The freedwomen were eerily absent in their counterarguments, as they were in most deliberations. Northern champions of emancipation were fixated on the stature of black soldiers, and in the South, evolving discussions within the freedpeople's communities also made the ex-soldiers paramount representatives of their communities. There was no group of prominently placed black women in the AERA to press home the capabilities and needs of the freedwomen. Sojourner Truth, one exception, pointed to the road not taken: "There is a great stir about colored men getting their rights, but not a word about the colored women." Truth minced no words to the men in the audience, black and white: "You have been having our rights so long that you think, like a slaveholder, that you own us."[16]

This was all in the background of the infamous Kansas campaign of summer and fall 1867, when Stanton and Anthony turned against the Republican Party and took up with the flamboyant Democratic businessman and political hopeful George Francis Train. The rupture in Kansas caused a schism in the ranks that lasted for twenty years. In Kansas, a new state constitution was up for a vote, with separate amendments to be approved for black male suffrage and women's suffrage. The vote had national importance: Republicans feared that the Democrats would make a strong comeback in the 1868 presidential election, and were counting on free states to ensure black manhood suffrage. Looking to make black suffrage palatable, Kansas Republicans distanced themselves from women's suffrage. Lucy Stone and Henry Blackwell traveled to the state first for the AERA to stump for women's suffrage and found a mixed situation: enthusiasm among white voters in strongholds of antislavery sentiment, but opposition from free blacks and white Republicans elsewhere.[17]

When Stanton and Anthony went to Kansas to help, no one had any reason to expect anything except a common effort with the other two AERA representatives. Stone and Blackwell had also broken ranks with Republicans by wooing Democrats, and Stanton and Anthony joined in, looking for support wherever it cropped up. But they went very far indeed, stunning friends and colleagues when they fell in with George Train, a rich, publicity-hungry entrepreneur from the political demi-monde. In an era that abounded in loose fish and fast fish, Train was at the head of the school. A character out of a rags-to-riches tale, he started out as a shipping clerk in Boston and rose to make a fortune in Anglo-American-Australian commerce. That summer, he was operating as advance man for the Credit Mobilier venture to extend the Union Pacific railroad westward—an investment scheme that would end up as one of the great scams of a scandal-ridden era. But to Boston abolitionists, Train was already known as the despicable heckler carted off to jail in 1862 after he tried to incite a racist mob to attack Charles Sumner at a speech celebrating President Lincoln's preliminary Emancipation Proclamation. During the war, Train moved in the shady region between Peace Democrats and Copperheads; in Kansas he pitched himself as a Unionist who opposed emancipation. This was not the company Stanton and Anthony usually kept.[18]

Train was an outsize borderline personality and over-the-top self-promoter. Mark Twain, who made the man the subject of one of his send-ups of the era's bombast and opportunism, quipped that "the same God that made George Francis Train made also the mosquitoes and the rats" and inquired if there was "ever such a world of egotism stuffed into one carcass before?"[19] Train wanted a stage respectable enough that he could attract serious attention but loose enough that the venue would not cramp his style. In Stanton and Anthony's errand he spied opportunity. Charged with egomaniacal energy, he mysteriously and incredibly entranced two middle-aged women who were not given to naïveté, especially about the male sex.[20] The trio made up a women's suffrage entourage, with Train tossing the issue into his fantasies of running for president as third-party champion of the ten-hour day, Irish freedom from British rule, greenbacks, and free land. Rambling on cheerfully and disjointedly, Train seems to have transfixed audiences with the sheer fascination of watching a man hold a conversation solely with himself as he ricocheted from one topic to another, interrupting the boat ride of consciousness downstream when he hauled up every now and then to deliver his slogan "Woman first and negro last" or a little ditty mocking the "nig."[21]

Neither measure on the Kansas ballot passed, and neither attracted much support. The loss confirmed Republican fears that women's suffrage would doom black men's enfranchisement.[22] But the defeat hardly bothered Stanton and Anthony. On the contrary, their spirits lifted. Freedom to make their own choices and mistakes redoubled their energy. They thrived in the Western setting, surrounded by new companions, including Train, "the most wonderful man of the century," Stanton effused; she felt as if she were "fastened to the tail of a comet."[23]

They were far away from the confounding and burdensome debates of the past two years, the conflicted choices, the rock-ribbed, stiff-necked, high-minded colleagues, the necessity of compromising and giving ground, the chronic irritation that came from working with the same people for years—in sum, the burdens of political negotiations when you have a weak hand. In defeat they were happy and excited. "I feel as if I had just begun to live," marveled Stanton, who toyed with moving her family to Kansas and getting away from it all. Anthony bubbled with plans: "I want to get canvassers for our paper—women who can lecture for woman—go into the manufacturing villages—hold free meetings—show the factory girls their need of the ballot & then at the close of meeting solicit subscriptions," and so on.[24]

Friends back home were horrified. Garrison shot off a letter blasting their association with a "ranting egotist and low blackguard . . . fast gravitating toward a lunatic asylum"—a charge that hovered around Train until his death. Frederick Douglass could not stomach their tolerance for Train's racial slurs on the platform. Others questioned their use of AERA money—insulting, since Susan B. Anthony held the purse strings and her thrift and honesty were well-known, but more understandable given that they traveled with a dubious character who made a point of throwing money around.[25]

Bonds this old were not easily broken, and the AERA stayed together for more than a year. Tensions worsened as the opposition between universal manhood suffrage and universal suffrage hardened. Douglass tried to sustain his commitment to women's suffrage but the danger of the freedpeople's situation consumed him. In 1869, with the Fifteenth Amendment before the states for ratification, anger exploded. Douglass charged at the AERA convention that opponents of the amendment— with Stanton and Anthony the most prominent—were indifferent to the emergency in the South. "With us, the matter is a question of life and death, at least, in fifteen States of the Union," he perorated in trademark august style.

> When women, because they are women, are hunted down through the cities of New York and New Orleans; when they are dragged from their houses and hung upon lampposts; when their children are torn from their arms, and their brains dashed out upon the pavement; when they are objects of insult and outrage at every turn; when they are in danger of having their homes burned down over their heads; when their children are not allowed to enter schools, then they will have an urgency to obtain the ballot equal to our own.[26]

Yet the matter was not as simple as Douglass would have it, not at the time nor in retrospect. Even Douglass, so eloquent, could not bring the room around to his position that day, so difficult was the choice of supporting an amendment that was plainly insufficient as the only measure that could be won. Someone from the crowd brought the discussion back down from the oratorical heights with the question "Is that not true about black women?" "Yes, yes, yes," Douglass countered—with, we might guess, the impatience of knocking away a nagging contradiction. "It is true of the black woman, but not because she is a woman, but because she is black."[27]

Douglass was the one speaker to address the menace at hand, the epidemic of violence in the South, most visibly in the Memphis and New Orleans riots. In this he was at odds with his women's rights colleagues, who seem to have seen the freedpeople as rhetorical ciphers, not living Americans. They were not without contacts with the emancipated slaves—Northern women reformers white and black did relief work in the freedpeople's camps. But the freedwomen's fierce battles to reassemble their families and negotiate fair wage contracts with former masters who owned the land; to keep children out of semi-peonage indenture arrangements with those same men; to defend themselves against white violence, which came in many forms; to establish schools and literacy classes and churches—these did not draw the attention of Northern reform women.[28]

The reformer mind was accustomed to dealing in abstractions, not specifics. Even Frances Ellen Watkins Harper, herself African-American and a champion of black women, rose at the moment of the face-off over the Fourteenth Amendment to move the chess pieces of race and sex around the board: "The white women all go for sex," she charged, "letting race occupy a minor position."[29] The political distance conferred by linguistic generalities handicapped Northern reformers in general and white women in particular. Stanton, who often sailed aloft in abstractions, once criticized an adversary's mind as being limited to "the region of facts" and incapable of making generalizations. But in 1868–69, Stanton, along with the others, would have done well to spend more time in the region of facts.[30]

Facts or no facts, for those who believed women's suffrage could not be set aside, the way forward was the way out. In 1869, Stanton and Anthony formed a new organization, the National Woman Suffrage Association (NWSA), based in New York City, and severed their ties to the antislavery leadership. Supporters introduced a Sixteenth Amendment to Congress to enfranchise women. The AERA dissolved. Those loyal to the Republican Party formed the American Woman Suffrage Association (AWSA), led by Lucy Stone and Henry Blackwell and based in Boston. More accommodating to women's suffrage as a second priority and favoring a states' rights approach to winning the vote, the AWSA drew women from the ranks of former New England abolitionists. The NWSA depended on a more geographically dispersed membership and younger women and men, many of them in the West and Midwest, who had reform proclivities but little direct experience of antislavery politics.[31]

The break has long been described as between a group committed to the freedpeople's cause and a racist, all-white Stanton-Anthony faction, but the judgment is facile and ignores the facts.[32] Neither Stanton, Anthony, nor the NWSA opposed black manhood suffrage. Nor were the lines so neatly drawn. Prominent African-American supporters and advocates of women's rights—Harriet and Robert Purvis, Mary Ann Shadd Cary, Charles Lenox Remond, and Sojourner Truth—tended to refrain from taking sides, some showing up in NWSA actions after the fracas subsided.[33] Nor were the Bostonians such principled defenders of the freedmen. Henry Blackwell, a moving force in the AWSA, had already in 1867 come up with his "statistical argument" to attract white Southern support, which promised to restore "the political supremacy of your white race." Shot down by Stanton and Douglass when he floated it in the AERA, he pursued it in the AWSA for years to come. It was Blackwell's idea, not Stanton and Anthony's, that became the basis for the "Southern strategy" in the 1890s, when suffragists tried unsuccessfully to woo Jim Crow support by showing that women's votes would double the white vote in the South.[34]

For Stanton and Anthony, it was the caste system of sexual privilege that was appalling, not black manhood suffrage per se: the replacement of the white man's democracy with "an aristocracy of sex," Anthony explained in an 1869 letter to *The New York Times*. They denounced the antidemocratic rationales that underlay this great democratic triumph, the reasoning that held that the exclusion of one half of the adult population was unimportant, simply because of their sex. Yet despite their principled allegiance to popular democracy, it is also true that this was the moment when Elizabeth Cady Stanton exploded with racist and nativist gibes, inveighing in public and private against ignorant degraded Negro and foreign men who got to vote instead of noble "Anglo-Saxon" educated women (as one critic objected at a meeting, you would think there were no ignorant American-born men). For a time, she tossed around a standard quartet of caricatures—Patrick (Irish), Sambo (black), Hans (German), and Yung Tung (Chinese)—to demonstrate how outrageous it was that men such as these were voting rather than distinguished women.[35] But in time, the epithets dropped away. Over the next two decades, Stanton was more likely to resort to generalized denunciations of the lower orders and immigrants than she was to deride black men. She never again understood women's cause to be merged with that of African-Americans. But she maintained that the fundamental problem was that democracy was so limited, not that black men voted.[36]

In the aftermath of the split, Stanton's anger was at once political and personal, poured into scornful cynicism about close male colleagues. She had discovered how little loyal women's efforts really mattered to them. The abolitionists' towering sense of superiority enraged her as only intimates can enrage. Of Edward Davis (Lucretia Mott's son-in-law) and Wendell Phillips, a longtime friend, she dissected the combination of condescension and moralism: "To have E.M.D. [Davis] pounce on one like a shark, with sarcasm & logic & ridicule all mixed up & simmered down to gall and bitterness, to have W.P. [Phillips] withdraw his velvet paw as if you were unworthy to touch the hem of his garment, it is enough to raise one's blood to the white heat of rebellion against any 'white male' on the continent." It is one of the few times that Stanton, who had always lambasted man in the abstract, blamed men she knew (and loved) personally for the wrongs of women. "When I think of all the wrongs that have been heaped upon womankind," she concluded, "I am ashamed that I am not forever in a condition of chronic wrath."[37]

As for Frederick Douglass, after that dramatic 1869 public rebuke to Stanton and Anthony, he returned to unequivocal support for women's suffrage. He remained their colleague for the rest of his long life. Even in 1870, amid the joyous celebrations among blacks North and South that greeted the ratification of the Fifteenth Amendment, Douglass advised African-American women to prepare themselves to be ready to vote when the hoped-for Sixteenth Amendment became law, the very amendment that Stanton and Anthony had introduced.[38]

Why did the suffragists lose women's suffrage? The question has dominated the scholarship about the postwar years. But one can also ask, really, why did they ever think they could win? From any angle, the prospects were faint. True, a dozen Radical Republicans introduced amendments to state constitutions for universal suffrage, but on the other hand, there was no widespread discussion of the issue. A few congressmen supported suffrage, and there was no hard-core opposition—but this was because it was never likely to pass. Even if the word "male" had been omitted from the Fourteenth Amendment, the implications of a gender-neutral language would never have slipped past the public and the amendment would surely have faced an uphill ratification battle in the states. The principle of virtual representation was too entrenched in the nation's political culture to be abandoned without anyone noticing.[39]

The suffrage leadership's confidence came from a giant miscalculation of the political salience of the loyalist to the Republican Party, when the loyalist was female. The problem they were left with was almost insoluble. The principle of universal suffrage alone was not going to be enough to float women into the harbor of full citizenship, but without the franchise, how could they ever get there?

Despite the losses of longtime co-workers and fellow spirits, there were gains for Stanton and Anthony in the rift. Setting off on their own hook allowed them much more autonomy and creativity. In the NWSA, they elaborated on women's grievances and put forth remedies without the constraints that the exigencies of Reconstruction imposed on the AERA. There would be no more talk of the Fifteenth Amendment, for or against, Anthony declared at a Chicago meeting: They were done with it. The question now was "Woman suffrage, and Woman suffrage alone."[40]

The concentration of effort bore fruit in *The Revolution,* the newspaper they published from New York City between 1868 and 1870 (backed by

George Train's money). The Stantons were living in the city, and locating the paper there shifted the locus of energy from New England and upstate New York, seedbeds of antislavery and moral reform, to the country's hustling commercial capital. The brazen title, followed by the motto "Men Their Rights and Nothing More—Women Their Rights and Nothing Less," declared that this paper was not business as usual. Even the advertising campaign spurned feminine decorum: Mark Twain (who spotted the invisible hand of George Train) was appalled at the sight of girl newspaper sellers on the streets of New York decked out in flashy uniforms of red, white, and blue, their belts emblazoned with "Revolution."[41]

The Revolution claimed any number of issues as the province of women's rights. It discussed discrimination against female workers and celebrated female vocational accomplishments (a new postmistress where there had never been one!). Most sensationally, the paper broached the subjects of sex and marriage. One inspiration was John Stuart Mill's *The Subjection of Women,* published in 1869. Mill's writing on marriage as an institution of despotism followed several decades of critiques from British reformers and brought the discussion into the mainstream of liberal thought. Stanton revered Mill and used his ideas to hone her own.

Stanton had briefly tangled with criticisms of marriage in 1860, at the last women's rights convention before the war, when she provoked consternation among listeners by floating the idea that marriage was a contract that could be made and broken like any other. Antoinette Brown Blackwell had once been a severe critic of marriage herself, but by 1860 she was married and an ordained minister to boot. She rose to defend the institution on Protestant grounds, as a fusion of two souls ordained by God, to approbation from the crowd. Afterward, Stanton had to beat back the bogeyman of free love, and the newspapers accused her of trying to turn respectable women into prostitutes.[42]

In 1869, though, Stanton was left to herself in the pages of *The Revolution.* With the challenge of locating a new constituency, she returned with gusto to themes of marriage and sexuality. The same zestful spirit that sent newsgirls into the streets to drum up business led her to seize on a local New York scandal as a polemical platform: the trial of Daniel McFarland for the murder of his ex-wife Abigail's fiancé, Albert Richardson, a popular writer for Greeley's *Tribune.* The story served Stanton's determination to break through the hypocrisy that prevented frank discussion of marriage by bringing the steamy facts of desire, jealousy, and extramarital sex uncomfortably close in a way that oblique discussions about coverture could not.

Stanton served up to readers a dementedly jealous, abusive husband, a virtuous wife who did everything in her legal power to throw off the chains of her marriage, and a charming, sympathetic lover. McFarland, who was an abusive alcoholic (if we believe Abby—Stanton certainly did), shot Richardson on two occasions. The first time, he wounded him only slightly; he followed up on his attack with two lawsuits, one against Abby for custody of their children and the second against Richardson, the man he nearly killed, for alienation of affections. Meanwhile, Abby went to Indiana to secure a divorce under the state's relatively liberal law and returned to New York to marry Richardson. On hearing that the lovers were about to marry, the enraged ex-husband went to the *Tribune* offices and shot Richardson, this time mortally wounding him. At the trial, McFarland's attorney described him as a responsible, loving man tormented by loss of hearth and home. Abby was a willful, careless woman led astray by a free-love cabal around the newspaper, and Richardson was her wily seducer. The judge refused to recognize Abby's divorce, and thus prevented her from testifying against her former husband. The jury acquitted McFarland on grounds of insanity, despite the obvious fact that he presented a clear danger to his ex-wife. A divorced man could literally get away with murder.[43]

Stanton used the verdict as an opportunity to call for changing an institution that could still be a life sentence. Practically, she called for divorce laws to be revamped along the lines of contract, citing luminaries in the British debate as her authorities—Bentham, Dickens, and Mill. She also used the occasion to sketch her thoughts on what relations between the sexes could be at their best, picking up on the older utopian idea that love flourishes free of coercion. Citing the Mills as models, she celebrated a "true union of the soul and intellect, which leads, exalts, and sanctifies the physical consummation." Regardless of the falling-out with her political brothers, Stanton came back to her faith that men, whatever their present failings, were always to be considered companions in making a better future.[44]

The core of her developing vision in the 1870s was individualist and egalitarian, applying the precepts and guarantees of liberal rights and possessive individualism—the ownership of the self—further into the domain of the household than Mill ventured, calling into question the entire edifice of male governance as Mill did not. She spoke for the sovereignty of the individual, the right of women to realize their potential away from the interposition of husbands' directives. On this her favorite subject, marriage, she worked in black and white, not grays: Legal scholar

Hendrik Hartog has shown that in fact the application of coverture was, in rulings of American judges, incomplete, highly varied, and contested, not monolithic as women's rights polemicists made it out to be. Stanton, however, was never one to be troubled by inconvenient social facts. She hypostatized marriage as if only Blackstone determined social reality, to represent it in schematic form as her best target.[45] For her, coverture was the grossest manifestation of the power that shrouded women's personhood, even to themselves. Indissoluble marriage was a remnant of feudal, hierarchical society that had no place in a democracy.

Emancipated women, she believed, would create a new form of marriage, freely chosen and companionate. "I think divorce at the will of the parties is not only right, but that it is a sin against nature, the family, the State, for a man or woman to live together in the marriage relation in continual antagonism, indifference, disgust. A physical union should in all cases be the outgrowth of a spiritual and intellectual sympathy; and anything short of this is lust not love," she told an audience at a meeting protesting the McFarland verdict, sounding very much like Margaret Fuller thirty years earlier. On the road, she met listeners eager for these views. "I am speaking every night to fine audiences," she wrote a friend in 1870 from Michigan. "Sometimes on suffrage, sometimes on marriage, sometimes on marriage & divorce. I shall be a reservoir of sorrows! O! the experiences women pour into my ears!" Plantation slavery was nothing next to these "unclean" marriages, she averred—she meant marriages where husbands used their wives sexually—so "let the press howl,"[46] she would persevere in speaking.

NWSA recruits tended to be too young or distant from political hot spots in the 1850s to have been in the thick of antislavery battles, but the Civil War prepared them for bold action. A younger generation came to the fore: Membership extended beyond the middle-class wives and mothers who made up the antebellum movement to a new demographic, workingwomen. They had slipped through small openings in the paid labor force, including the professions, to establish themselves as hotel and boardinghouse keepers, ranchers, schoolteachers, journalists, professional lecturers, homeopathic physicians, newspaper editors, and attorneys. Their interest in national and state politics was keen, since both the Republican and Democratic parties supported female auxiliaries, and the third parties all welcomed female supporters.[47]

Many of the most engaged NWSA members were representatives of an evolving social type: vocationally oriented, tied to political parties through husbands or kin and poised to take up a part in a man's world. The comparatively unknown Belva Lockwood, an NWSA member in Washington, D.C., is a good example. Lockwood is remembered for being the first serious female contender for the presidency; she staged a third-party campaign on the ticket of the minuscule National Equal Rights Party in 1884 and 1888. The candidacy was no novelty act but rather the culmination of years of involvement in Washington politics. Lockwood's plainness, audacity, and tireless pragmatism maneuvering in an all-male political world, along with her hard-won achievements, exemplify the possibilities of the 1870s and '80s as much as the Grimké sisters' moral passion sums up the 1830s.

Lockwood's rise was not unusual in the years after the war, when economic expansion, migration, and the deaths of so many men pushed and pulled women out of the places they were born into situations where enough was yet to be settled that unusual initiatives could yield startling results. A woman from the far reaches of the country, by dint of a little education, hard work, connections to a sympathetic man, and engagement in women's organizations managed to scramble to local repute: The story can be told about newspaper editors, homeopathic physicians, educators, writers, and actresses. In Lockwood's case, the arc was from a farm in a remote county in upstate New York to the nation's capital, running for president and being the first woman to win entry to the bar of the U.S. Supreme Court.

Forced by a hard-pressed father to leave school when she was fifteen and work as a teacher to bring in money, Belva Bennett married young and was left a widow in 1853 at the age of twenty-three, with a small child to support. Now Belva McNall, she resumed teaching and went to school, earning a college degree in 1857 from the institution that became Syracuse University. In 1866, by then the head of her own school, she made the bold choice to move with her daughter to Washington, D.C. The city was a muddy, shambling town, flooded with demobilized soldiers and freedpeople and electrified by the impeachment of President Andrew Johnson and debates over Reconstruction. Avid for political intelligence, she watched from the "Ladies Gallery" in the new Senate chamber. There were few ways for a woman of modest resources without connections to make a living, but she found enough to establish herself. She acquired a boardinghouse and married an older man, becoming Mrs. Lockwood. It was an economic partnership, not a love match, but the marriage was sturdy and supported her through many difficulties and battles. By 1871, she was president of the local NWSA branch.[48]

Lockwood brought to suffrage work an interest in workingwomen that was notably lacking in a movement that historically had been composed of women economically dependent on their husbands. Before the war, women's rights conventions gave only cursory attention to the difficulties of earning a living: the issues of stark discrimination in wages and the segregation of the labor market that forced women into a few low-paid, overcrowded fields. These subjects were braided through European discussions, with different solutions. Socialists sought to remove women altogether from the labor force, to be supported at home by a man making a decent family wage; a few feminists followed Barbara Smith Bodichon in calling for the skilled trades to admit women; and in a few places, among more highly skilled workers, women organized into unions, although this was rare. But in the United States, Susan B. Anthony, the self-supporting woman who was the exception to the rule, was the one leader to address questions of labor. Anthony had little success, however, in broadening the movement's sense of "Woman" to the laboring classes or even to middle-class women who worked.[49]

In the United States and Europe, the problems were similar: a labor market strictly segmented by sex, with most jobs deemed men's and a few seen as properly women's. This meant that women were crowded into a few sectors of the industrial labor force, most prominently the sewing trades and textile manufacturing; barred from higher-paid skilled trades or segregated to subsidiary tasks within them; and paid about half the wages of the lowliest male workers. Everywhere, domestic service remained the largest female employment, with its grinding physical labor (in an age that lacked labor-saving domestic technologies that came with gas stoves, running water, and electric appliances). For women outside the cities, domestic service and farm labor were the only paid work. Except for teaching, available to women since the late eighteenth century, white-collar jobs deemed female only appeared in the United States after the Civil War when retail stores and businesses expanded to require an army of clerks and salespeople. But white-collar work, while deemed men's preserve before the war and ostensibly more skilled and higher-status than manual labor, nevertheless presented women with the same problems: no trade unions, long hours and low wages, and jobs seen as less valuable once they moved in.[50]

Lockwood, who supported herself in Washington as a boardinghouse keeper, had before her in the city a living demonstration of working-women's wrongs in the white-collar sector. During the war, when male labor was scarce, the federal government hired female clerks to carry on the work of a vastly expanded bureaucracy, but paid them a fraction of men's wages. In the Treasury Department, women, previously barred from jobs there, earned half of the men's salary for doing exactly the same work. Lockwood decided to try to outlaw sex discrimination in federal employment. With the NWSA's backing, she worked her congressional connections to put forth legislation that would outlaw pay discrimination on the basis of sex in federal jobs. She had enough sympathizers to make passage of the bill a real possibility. The strong words of Samuel Arnell, a Tennessee congressman who was its sponsor, show how far women's rights thought pervaded some corners of the Republican Party. "Man has been unjust to women," Arnell stated starkly in the House debate. Echoing NWSA language, he lectured his colleagues on man's subjugation of woman as an atavistic remnant of barbarism, abhorrent to republican government: "The poor pay of woman is an undervaluation of her as a human being." The bill passed in 1870, although conservatives watered it down. Nonetheless, the diluted provisions helped female clerks, who were able in a short time to quadruple their numbers in the top pay grade.[51]

As for Lockwood, she went to law school. One of a handful of women pressing in the 1870s to be credentialed, she fought for and won admission to the Washington, D.C., bar in 1873, the second woman to be admitted after Charlotte Ray, an African-American graduate of Howard University. It took six years of wrangling and another act of Congress to win her next battle, admission to the bar of the Supreme Court; but in 1879, after years of pushing recalcitrant authorities and pestering reluctant supporters in Congress, she succeeded and was sworn in, the first woman to be admitted to argue before the Court.

Finally, Lockwood ran for president in 1884 on the ticket of the National Equal Rights Party, a third party founded by women on the West Coast who were tired of being knocked around by the Republicans. Lockwood took her candidacy seriously and meant others to do the same. Her experience in Washington taught her that there was no getting power unless women grabbed it, and the time was ripe. "The country is prepared to-day for a boldly aggressive movement on the part of the women of the country," she judged.[52] She did not know how dead wrong she was. Others would follow on the third-party track, but no woman would make a serious bid for the presidency for 120 years, until Hillary Rodham Clinton ran in the 2008 Democratic primaries.

While the movement was proudly separatist—that is, composed of women and led by women—the "woman's rights man" took shape as a distinct identity. Supporters like Samuel Arnell were important to the NWSA as strategists, co-conspirators, and sympathizers who provided emotional and material aid. These "new men" took the place of the male abolitionists the NWSA jettisoned in 1869. Isabella Beecher Hooker's husband, John, for instance, submitted to the Connecticut legislature a married women's property bill that he co-authored with his wife. Henry Olney and Eugenia Wilde Olney, publishers of *The Silver World* in the Colorado Rockies, hosted Susan B. Anthony when she came to the state to lecture: "both in full sympathy with our movement," she found.[53] These people were no longer brothers and sisters in Christ; no, these new partnerships were of this world, vocational and practical. And the aid of woman's rights men made the prospects for change in this world that much more plausible.

The NWSA's most important activity in the 1870s was to push a militant strategy of constitutional change called the New Departure. Legal scholars Reva Siegel and Robert Post, surveying the long history of constitutional battles, argue that in volatile periods in American history, new interpretations of the Constitution move up from the bottom, from citizens to the Court, as well as in the usual way, from the Court down to the people. Americans revere the Court, Post and Siegel observe, but "they also expect their own constitutional beliefs to matter, and will, in extraordinary circumstances, mobilize to secure recognition of their views."[54] The early 1870s were such extraordinary circumstances, and the NWSA women were such citizens. Their sense they could change something as remote from them and abstruse as constitutional interpretation came from witnessing the war's enormous augmentation of federal power and the transformations wrought by the Reconstruction amendments: "For if amending the Constitution could abolish slavery, what could it not do?" as Ellen Carol DuBois describes the mindset. Those years were an education in the Constitution. "Such a schooling in the principles of government, in the fundamental law of the land, in the broad principles of human freedom, had never perhaps come to any people," Belle Squire, a feminist who lived through the period, declared in 1911. "No longer were such questions academic, or mere idle problems to be used for idle discussion, for they were found to be vital issues for which men were willing to give up their lives."[55] Suffragists became experts in constitutional theory.

In St. Louis in 1869, Francis and Virginia Minor—Francis was a Princeton-educated attorney, Virginia the local NWSA president—devised a strategy for winning the vote called the New Departure. The startling idea was that women already had the right to vote. The Minors argued on Fourteenth Amendment grounds; despite the use of "male," they were drawn to the first section's generous language of citizenship, equal protection, and due process. The Constitution made all people born or naturalized in the United States citizens; women were people and therefore citizens; the Fourteenth and Fifteenth amendments protected the rights of all citizens, including the right to vote; ergo, women had the right to vote. Women were to go to the polls and exercise their right, defying voter registrars, courting arrest, and throwing the matter into the courts.[56]

The vote was women's; they had only to take it. The contest was already in motion. Since 1868, groups of women had been trying to vote, in pairs, clumps, and crowds. They showed up at the polls in Passaic, New Jersey; Lewiston, Maine; White River, Washington; South Newbury, Ohio; Hyde Park, Illinois; and Detroit. African-American women participated in South Carolina; Washington, D.C.; Portland, Oregon; and Vineland, New Jersey. In 1868 in Vineland, 172 women, white and black, tried to vote, bringing their own ballot boxes with them. Two elderly sisters in Connecticut, a hotbed of protests, refused to pay local taxes, on the grounds of "no taxation without representation." Their milk cows were pointedly named "Taxey" and "Votey." In Johnson County, North Carolina, in 1871, two hundred black women dressed in men's clothing registered and voted. Sojourner Truth went to the polls alone in Battle Creek, Michigan, in 1872; Angelina Grimké Weld and Sarah Grimké tried to vote with fifty others outside Boston.[57]

The New Departure offered a way to seize the attention of Congress. Independently of the suffragists, Victoria Woodhull testified before the House Judiciary Committee, presenting the Fourteenth Amendment argument at the behest of committee chair Benjamin Butler, a Republican supporter of women's suffrage. Woodhull was a mysterious, magnetic outsider from the Midwest. Trailing rumors of blackmail, fraud, and prostitution, and gifted with a genius for attracting powerful men, Woodhull and her sister Tennessee Claflin had appeared out of nowhere in New York City, an entourage of dodgy relatives in tow. The two wended their way into the good graces of Commodore Vanderbilt, the richest man in the city, and set up shop on Wall Street in 1870 with his backing, becoming the first women stockbrokers. With Woodhull's suspicious liaisons and shady background (her parents operated a traveling medicine show in the Midwest, selling the Elixir of Life), she scandalized the suffrage movement. But Stanton was charmed and saw the opportunity that Woodhull's notoriety and testimony presented.

Woodhull's appearance was the opening act for the appearance before the committee of Stanton, Anthony, and Isabella Beecher Hooker a few months later. They gave a sensational performance, offering "a dazzling fusion of constitutional theory and political oratory" to a packed room.[58] There was reason to believe the New Departure could work. Eighteen seventy-two was an election year, and the Republican Party was actively courting suffragists. Henry Wilson, the Massachusetts senator who was the vice presidential candidate, advocated women's suffrage, and the platform included a plank nodding to women without actually committing to the vote. If either a federal court could be convinced and its decision implemented nationwide or Congress passed a declaratory bill, the New Departure would lead to a quick victory without the bother of another constitutional amendment.[59]

New Departure tactics were not for the fainthearted. Going to vote required a steely will: Polling places were notoriously masculine, brimming with rowdiness and liquor. Generally women went in groups; Sojourner Truth was the exception when she went alone in Michigan. The largest urban demonstration was in Washington, D.C., where Belva Lockwood and Frederick Douglass went with seventy white and black women to the polls. In Missouri, the Minors brought suit after the registrar turned Virginia away. Francis pushed the case up through the appeals process and in 1873 the Supreme Court agreed to hear it.[60]

Excitement rippled through the ranks. In 1872, Chicago NWSA member Myra Bradwell sued Illinois when it rejected her application for admission to the bar because she was a woman. Bradwell's battle was an offshoot of the New Departure and her appeal led to *Bradwell v. Illinois* (1873), which, along with *Minor v. Happersett* (1875), was the Court's first consideration of women's constitutional rights.

Married to a prominent Chicago attorney who taught her the law, Myra Bradwell was a successful professional, already a force in the Midwestern legal community as the founder, chief analyst, and editor of the *Chicago Legal News,* the most important legal publication west of the

Alleghenies. Her husband, James, was a member of the state legislature and a woman's rights man, the moving force behind several bills that secured legal remedies for Illinois women. Politically adept and well connected, Myra Bradwell nonetheless failed to gain entrance to the bar—despite the Iowa bar's first-ever admission of a woman, Arabella Mansfield, earlier that year.[61]

The *Bradwell* decision is famous, or infamous, as a textbook case of the Court's beliefs about the special nature of women. When the case reached the Supreme Court, the justices were already considering Fourteenth Amendment arguments in the Slaughterhouse Cases and they knew that a women's suffrage case was in the making. The justices were undoubtedly thinking ahead when, in 1873, they upheld the lower court's decision, declaring the question of Bradwell's qualifications for the bar to be under state jurisdiction. In his concurrence, Justice Joseph P. Bradley proceeded to a more sweeping judgment, denying that the Constitution guaranteed a married woman the right to pursue lawful employment of any sort. Justice Bradley summoned up the Founding Fathers to affirm coverture and women's subordination to male governance: The common law established that "a woman had no legal existence separate from her husband, who was regarded as her head and representative in the social state."

> The civil law, as well as nature herself, has always recognized a wide difference in the respective spheres and destinies of man and woman. Man is, or should be, woman's protector and defender. The natural and proper timidity and delicacy which belongs to the female sex evidently unfits it for many of the occupations of civil life. . . . The paramount destiny and mission of woman are to fulfill the noble and benign offices of wife and mother. This is the law of the Creator.[62]

Ruth Bader Ginsburg, arguing before the Court a hundred years later, cited *Bradwell* as an example of the faulty reasoning that justified sex discrimination, wryly observing that the 1873 Court did not explain how God communicated His views to the justices: "Laws delineating 'a sharp line between the sexes,' were sanctioned on the basis of assumptions unnecessary to prove, and impossible to disprove, for their lofty inspiration was an article of faith."[63]

Bradwell set the stage for *Minor* two years later. In that decision, the justices rejected Virginia Minor's claim that voting was one of the rights of national citizenship. The states conferred suffrage and the states alone could determine if sex disqualified a citizen from voting. The decision crushed the New Departure strategy. Moreover, it lent the Court's authority to the increasingly popular view that the federal government bore no responsibility for enforcing voting rights. *Minor*'s understanding of the Fifteenth Amendment was so narrow it did not even protect the freedmen. All this was a prelude to the end of Reconstruction and the collapse of biracial democracy in the South.[64]

In 1877, the federal government withdrew U.S. troops from the South, opening the door for the unrestrained reimposition of white rule. Retrenchment in the South galvanized disenfranchisement politics nationwide, fueling hostility to blacks', immigrants', and workers' rights and as a result throwing up nearly insurmountable obstacles to women's suffrage. At the cutting edge of disenfranchisement campaigns were Southern Democrats, who organized across the former Confederacy to "redeem" their states from biracial democracy. But in the North and West, too, grave doubts about popular democracy joined with Social Darwinist rationales to legitimate suffrage restrictions on workingmen and immigrants. "Universal suffrage can only mean in plain English the government of ignorance and vice," wrote the Bostonian Charles Francis Adams, grandson of one president, great-grandson of another. "It means a European, and especially Celtic, proletariat on the Atlantic coast; an African proletariat on the shores of the Gulf, and a Chinese proletariat on the Pacific."[65] The numbers of the voteless everywhere increased in the 1880s, not just in the South. Despite nominal enfranchisement, voting men were still in the minority in the United States. Well over half the country's adults could not vote, including all women, large sections of the male immigrant population, and most Southern black men.

It was a changed climate, an almost impossible environment in which to hold firm to the call for universal democracy that distinguished the NWSA in 1869, even though that call was compromised by the belief in white women's superiority. Stanton often veered off course, yet she did not reverse herself. She stuck to calling for universal suffrage and a stringent insistence on the obligation of the federal government to uphold the Fourteenth and Fifteenth amendments. The United States must protect the humblest citizen, she insisted—although in her rage at women's exclusion, her description of that humble citizen often fell into the class-driven language of the times.[66] She did not call for any group of men to be disenfranchised, but she did insist that women were more than worthy, compared to the less than worthy men who could already vote.

In crowning all men with this dignity, denying it to all women, we have established here the most odious form of aristocracy the world has ever seen—an aristocracy of sex, that exalts vice and ignorance, above virtue and intelligence, the unwashed, unlettered foreigner, who knows nothing of the grandeur of our free institutions, just landed on our shores, above the thousands of educated women in our public schools, who have taught American history and the United States constitution for near a century, an aristocracy that exalts brute force above moral power, the son above the mother who bore him.[67]

Such polemics—and none were better than Stanton's—attacked the use of sex to naturalize a profoundly antidemocratic theory that legitimated the exclusion of one class of citizens from political rights. Yet it was the anger of both sex and class—and thus implicitly race—that delivered the emotional punch: outrage that middle-class women like herself should be excluded. The politics of outrage could build on its own logic, ignoring inconvenient facts. Who, exactly, were those women schoolteachers who supposedly taught the Constitution for a hundred years? Were all immigrant men unwashed and unlettered? And for those who were, did that mean prima facie that better-bathed and -educated women should be before them in line? In an age when the call for educated suffrage was so widespread that even middle-class black reformers adopted it as a way to hold on to some sliver of enfranchisement, there was no one to argue with Stanton about the political costs or alternatives. Were there alternatives?

Meanwhile in the South, the vote was the linchpin of the freedpeople's struggles. There black women participated directly and indirectly in the battle for the franchise. At least three times, in an unspecified place in South Carolina in 1870, in Charleston in 1871, and later that year in Johnson County, North Carolina, freedwomen mounted their own direct actions at the polls, a little-noticed initiative that overlapped with the New Departure. More often, they acted in consort with men. In Richmond, Virginia, they attended the state constitutional convention in the fall of 1867, chiming in from the gallery. In Mississippi, they flaunted Republican campaign buttons during the 1868 election, incurring employers' anger and risking vigilante attacks when they walked to meetings. In South Carolina, where black voters took their lives in their hands, they accompanied men to the polls, both sexes armed for self-defense. But men did not always welcome them. In some places, Republicans white and black wanted to ban them from meetings. They should stay home and hoe cotton, one hostile man maintained.[68]

Some women may have seen the vote as their possession as much as men's, although men were the ones to do the voting: "It was that sense of suffrage as a collective, not an individual, possession that was the foundation of much of women's political activities," suggests historian Elsa Barkley Brown. "These women were speaking, however, not of whether they each individually had voice and representation but of whether their community had a voice."[69] Their support for manhood suffrage was an affirmation of the community's political rights, not a compromise driven by necessity.

If Brown is right, then freedwomen did not see virtual representation as exclusionary. Certainly all evidence from the immediate postwar years shows that the sense of self for both men and women was inseparable from the black political community; women saw membership in the polity as continuous with membership in families and households. Families were the ground of race solidarity and integrity, sanctuaries of desire and possibility, living repudiation of the slaveowners' haughty pretensions to being parents and protectors of a childlike race. The overwhelming desire was to be bound to and with others in freedom, with kin and also lovers, orphans, friends, and old people. "They began by attempting to assemble their immediate families and close kin, to lend those relations civil legitimacy, and to find circumstances in which those relations could establish meaningful and useful foundations," writes Steven Hahn about the aftermath of the war.[70]

An ethos of common concern drawn from enmeshment in the lives of others suffused the freedwomen's lives as it did all women's, but the extraordinary circumstances gave the family a democratic charge it did not carry for Northern suffragists. The communal associations complicated the meanings of women's rights in the Southern context, distancing black women from the possessive individualism of the Northern movement. Northern suffragists tried to untangle women's civic identity from their families, because it was their family position that disabled them from voting. The freedwomen viewed themselves as political actors by virtue of their family positions: Wives and mothers were leaders in race work.

It was a very different account of marriage and family from suffragists' emphasis on men's privileges and women's disadvantages. Yet it was undeniable that the sexes were in different positions in the South, too, and the extent and degree of men's authority and women's submission was by no means decided. Everything was in flux after the war, including the terms of marriage. What did freedom mean for women? To the freedmen, it was authority over the labor and persons of household members that signified their recovery of a manhood crushed in slavery. But when family conflicts came before Southern courts and Freedmen's Bureau agents, a woman might call that very understanding into question. Did the precious "marriage right" really mean submitting to a husband's authority? Sometimes a woman said no. Could a husband assign the labor of his wife without her consent and take her wages as his own? Black women might object, but Freedmen's Bureau authorities, all men, tended to think so.[71]

The powerful disposition to honor family solidarities and emphasize manhood as the centerpiece of race pride meant that freedwomen's difficulties were submerged in public discussions. As hedged-in as freedom was for a man, it was still polyvalent: It meant self-ownership, the ability to work for wages and make contracts and to do the same for his family, and the right to vote and run for office. Freedom for a woman was stingier. Bodily integrity was the bedrock for her, too—freedom from physical coercion, corporal punishment, and rape—yet the law was averse to confirming the principle. Even in terms of family violence, freedwomen—like white women—had no legal recourse against marital abuse, a grievance that cropped up when women asked bureau agents to stop husbands from whipping them.

Black men filtered women's problems through a discourse of moral and sexual honor. Given the long history of masters' abuse of enslaved women, it was paramount that they ensure women's safety. Sexual violence was exploding, with white vigilantes everywhere in the South using rape as a weapon of terror. Honorable black men, then, had a pressing duty to protect women from degradation and humiliation. In this way, an assertion of racial integrity also involved an assertion of women's dependency. The mission of protecting women, defined ideologically, suppressed other gender tensions and rifts.[72]

No Northern women's rights leader grasped the embattled and precarious situation of black citizens in the South, the political assertiveness of women, or the ferocity of the violence. The same indifference afflicted much of the Northern Republican Party, but in the case of suffragists, the abstract opposition they made between men and women exacerbated the inattention: By inserting the generalities of patriarchy into a context driven above all by white revanche, the suffragists plastered over their ignorance with faux knowledge. The logic of the NWSA idea of the aristocracy of sex, if extended, lumped all men together, black and white, freedmen along with, say, members of the Ku Klux Klan. The category was thus inadequate to describe, let alone illuminate, the situation. The indifference to facts on the ground lent a touch of demagoguery to suffragists' pronouncements whenever they touched on the topic of black men. The chasm between reality and ideology is evident in an 1874 NWSA written protest to the Senate asking for federal laws protecting women's freedom of movement, free from intimidation, in public space. The operative stereotype was the man plump with liberty, with black men folded into the cartoonish depiction. The memorial harped on black men's merry, easeful lives as compared to the restricted, fearful lives of women: Oh that women could walk the streets, go to the theater alone, or "ramble in the forests, or beside the lakes and rivers, *as do colored men,* without fear of molestation or insult from any white man whatsoever" (emphasis added).[73] The caricature was grotesquely out of touch: In the North black men risked beatings if they ventured into white theaters and hotels, and in the South those out alone at night courted lethal attacks. For these reasons and more, the dichotomy of powerful man/powerless woman did not resonate with Southern black women. It was not that they were immune to men's power or their own powerlessness; it was that they knew how variable it was, and how powerless black men themselves were in the face of white supremacy.

While the suffrage cause made no headway in Congress or the states, the women's rights movement could still claim solid achievements in the forty years since Seneca Falls. Most important, higher education opened up. Wealthy men and women endowed the first women's colleges: Mount Holyoke, established by Mary Lyon in western Massachusetts in 1837 as a higher order girls' school, paved the way (although it was not a real college until 1893). Matthew Vassar, a brewer in Poughkeepsie, New York, founded Vassar College in 1861; Sophia Smith endowed Smith College in 1871 near Mount Holyoke; and the Durants, Henry Fowle and his wife, Paulina, gave the money for Wellesley College in 1875. More modest institutions with religious affiliations dotted the Midwest: Jane Addams, a yearning, idealistic girl in Cedarville, Illinois, went to one nearby in 1877, high-minded Rockford Female Seminary. Federally funded land-grant colleges in the Midwest and West were coeducational from the start, opening prospects for girls of lesser means.

In the South, the freedpeople's hunger for education led to the establishment of schools at all levels, including colleges and seminaries funded by denominations: for instance, Spelman Seminary (eventually Spelman College), founded in 1881 as the Atlanta Baptist Female Seminary; the Methodist school in Greensboro, North Carolina, founded in 1873 by Albion Tourgee, which became Bennett College. Serious higher education for Southern white women was scarce, but among blacks, determination to give girls an education equipped a generation of African-American girls to take up service to the race. The trajectory of Mary McLeod (later Bethune) illustrates the dramatic consequences for the lucky. Fifteenth of seventeen children from a family of former slaves in South Carolina, McLeod would have ended up a tenant farmer were it not for her iron-willed Christian mother and her education, first at a local mission school and then at a Presbyterian female seminary. She became a leading educator, college president, and, in 1924, president of the National Association of Colored Women.[74]

Most white college graduates married and took up the life of middle-class matrons. But the skills learned in college and the momentary independence gained living away from home led them to look at public life as rightfully theirs. In the next two decades, these were the women whose efforts helped carry forward the Progressive movement, as well as innumerable literary and music clubs, self-improvement societies, art museums, symphony halls, parks, and public health campaigns. Cracks in the professions slightly widened. Increasing numbers of women graduated from law schools: Belva Lockwood was one and Phoebe Couzins another. Couzins, the first woman to be admitted to law school at Washington University, was a co-strategizer with the Minors on the New Departure. For black women, race prejudice narrowed the openings into the professions even more than the straitened access Northern white women had, but nonetheless a tiny cohort of African-American lawyers and doctors won professional accreditation. Charlotte Ray, for instance, was admitted to the Washington, D.C., bar a year before Lockwood; the former abolitionist Mary Ann Shadd Cary was at Howard University Law School along with Ray; Rebecca Lee graduated from a women's medical college in Boston in 1864 and practiced in the city; Rebecca Cole was a doctor who worked in Elizabeth Blackwell's infirmary in New York.

By 1887, there were enough female attorneys nationwide—about 250 in the 1890 census—to form a correspondence club for mutual support. In letters, members debated issues such as whether a woman should wear a hat in court. It was a problem, since propriety required it (only prostitutes left their heads uncovered in public), but on the other hand, attorneys had to remove their hats before judges. So seldom did women attorneys appear in court, though, that the point was still unresolved in 1961, when Raya Dreben worried about whether to wear a hat when she argued before the Supreme Court in *Hoyt v. Florida*. More to the point, there was disagreement about whether women should go into court at all, but instead limit themselves to working in law offices (courtrooms being another rough-and-tumble masculine venue that women entered at their peril). Charlotte Ray, for example, practiced real estate law, a common tack for those unwilling to face the open derision and prejudice they would assuredly encounter in courtrooms.[75]

The faith in willed equality that wells up in volatile periods also comes to women who gather at a threshold, waiting and waiting for a door that has cracked open to swing all the way. In the correspondence club, the attorneys' tone was jolly and strenuously confident that hard work and merit would banish the intransigent opposition that was every-where evident. "My experience thus far is but limited," conceded a new member recently admitted to the D.C. bar. But things were going well. "One, by one, the doors are thrown open, very wide to woman; and, I am fully convinced, that the time is at hand, when woman's ability to fill the chair, of professor of Law, in our colleges, sit beside her brother . . . and even grace the 'White House' in our city, as the nation's choice and its Chief Executive," she wrote with determined optimism in 1887, three years after Belva Lockwood ran for president.[76]

Women entered medical school in better circumstances than had Elizabeth Blackwell, the first to try in 1847, who could not study anatomy at Geneva College in upstate New York because it was thought immoral for her to look at a cadaver. Interest in women's health spread through the women's movement, leading several wealthy women to endow a half-dozen women's medical colleges, which in turn made med-ical education that much more plausible. When Jane Addams graduated from college in 1882, trying a career in medicine was respectable enough that even her highly conventional stepmother tolerated her enrolling in the Women's Medical College in Philadelphia. In 1881, 115 women were members of state medical societies; the number climbed over the next twenty years to more than 7,000 in 1900, 5.6 percent of the total.[77]

Educated women—purposeful, hardworking, and ethically committed—could begin to conceive of themselves as inhabiting a story their sex was only beginning to write, in which the female protagonist made a life of meaning and purpose that did not depend on having a husband and children.

These were accomplishments in which feminists could take pleasure, solid gains from forty years of activity. Yet at the same time, the deepening conservatism of the times shot through the women's movement. For Stanton and Anthony, the work could be drab. They both lectured and traveled incessantly: thousands of miles of train trips around the Midwest and far West, out to the Pacific coast, hundreds of miles in wagons and carriages over (as they described their journeys) awful roads, dreadful roads, long, terrifying, and horrible roads. Separately and together, they worked the circuit, sometimes speaking to crowds, more often to knots of the faithful, and sleeping in supporters' houses, fleabag hotels, and on trains. In the 1880s, they pulled back from lecturing and embarked on more gratifying trips: Stanton on jaunts to visit the two children who had settled in Europe, Anthony following her, to converse with reformers and women's rights leaders in Britain and France.

But while they traveled to new places and attracted converts, the work was tiresomely similar from year to year: lectures, more lectures, meetings and conferences, more meetings, pointless machinations to move the women's suffrage amendment along in Congress. Stanton, who saw herself as a reader and writer, not an organizer, complained about boredom as early as 1873. She was so weary of conventions, she wrote Martha Wright, the old friend who had been with her since Seneca Falls, that "I feel as if I would rather go to Heaven this spring than attend another. . . . Two days full of speaking & resolving & dreading lest some one should make a fool of us all, rehearsing the same old arguments in the same old way, must this be endured to the end of our slavery?" That was 1873; by 1889, writing to another friend, she really meant it. She was "sick of all organizations. . . . Once out of my present post in the suffrage movement I am a free lance to do and say what I choose and shock people as much as I please."[78]

One wonders if this woman, who spent heady years in the middle of the movement that both invented women's rights in America and ended slavery, was fretting at the limits of not only the issue but the co-workers. Although her long friendship with Susan B. Anthony, a restrained woman who put a premium on the steady virtues, was essential to her life's work, she had always thrived on rubbing up against other powerful political personalities: her husband, Henry, Lucretia Mott, Frederick Douglass, George Train, Wendell Phillips, Victoria Woodhull. These were high-stakes schemers, bold strategists, and fascinating outsiders. The suffrage movement lacked such people, precisely because it was so far from the institutions where powerful people—men—operated.

The Northern movement's estrangement from Reconstruction politics, coupled with the collapse of the New Departure and the rise of disenfranchisement measures, rendered militant suffragism politically insignificant by 1880. Although the two postwar suffrage organizations continued, they were eclipsed by the women's temperance movement, the most important sponsor of votes for women in the Gilded Age. The political landscape was so barren that in large parts of the country, temperance was the main vehicle for women's rights; in some places it was the only one. Promoting an ideology of maternalism and female moral superiority, temperance won great numbers to the cause even as it laid down a conservative basis for the vote.

The Woman's Christian Temperance Union (WCTU), formed in 1874, quickly became the premier women's organization in the United States, assuming a place at the center of unenfranchised women's civil society that it did not lose until after World War I. In league with its sister organization, the British Women's Temperance Association, the WCTU had an international impact as well. It spread its message of abstinence from alcohol and "social purity"—reformed sexual behavior—through Protestant missions and British colonists. By 1891, when a World's Woman's Christian Temperance Union formed, Americans were in touch with reformers in Canada, Australia, South Africa, Japan, and India.[79]

The WCTU usually drops out of histories of feminism, since few writers like to remember feminism as a movement of teetotalers and prudes. Temperance as ideology, however, was more than a passing chapter in feminism, and it's impossible to understand subsequent developments in feminist history without it. In the United States, the temperance crusade dominated the suffrage movement for a good twenty years, driving it into a period of political paralysis. More important, temperance injected a strain of conservatism into the tradition that, while latent for most of the twentieth century, episodically resurfaced, sometimes in the most unlikely radical settings. When we come upon images of lustful male predators, hapless women who are unable to escape their clutches, and wise, powerful women who by dint of their superior understanding can rescue them, there is the historic legacy of temperance.

The temperance movement dates back to the 1820s. It always had an affinity for women's rights, since the campaign against alcohol addressed by its very nature a prevalent form of male irresponsibility and violence. Susan B. Anthony started out her career in the 1850s in the New York state temperance association, and Elizabeth Cady Stanton pulled off some of her earliest maneuvers there. After the Civil War, temperance gained ground with white and black women in the South; and in the West, it followed Anglo settlers to sparsely settled states where male drinking was endemic. Frances Willard took over the WCTU presidency in 1879 and transformed what had been a federation of shrill bands, breaking into saloons and smashing bars, into a well-behaved, streamlined mass organization.

Willard was an organizational genius with a catholic view of women's politics. A happily unmarried woman herself (she lived most of her adult life with first one woman friend in a "Boston marriage" and then another), she developed a strategy for power that depended on marriage and motherhood. For her, the crusade against alcohol was an instrument to protect women and children from unrestrained male power. The WCTU tapped an evangelical faith in women's moral suasion and amplified it into a brief for their superiority. The emotional lure was the hope of converting unregenerate men, and the instrument of salvation was Christian marriage. Ushered in by a helpful woman, Jesus would enter the heart of the drinking man and take the family into "the next wider circle" of grace.[80]

At its height, the WCTU put forth an ambitious agenda, striving for a Christian feminism that was socially efficacious. A "Do Everything" policy stretched female benevolent ambitions as far as they could go. The WCTU woman was a doer as well as a gentle exemplar. The program of reform incorporated several score "departments." In 1889 in Chicago, the national headquarters, the WCTU sponsored two day nurseries, two Sunday schools, a vocational training school, a shelter for homeless women, a free medical clinic, a cheap lodging house for men, and a low-cost restaurant. Membership increased fivefold under Willard; in 1890 there were 150,000 dues-paying members, with an additional 28,000 young women signed on to a youth auxiliary and 135,000 children in the children's club. In 1886, six full-time, paid WCTU organizers traveled the country and there were chapters in more than half the nation's counties.[81] Neither the NWSA or the AWSA came close to these numbers.

The WCTU was the first—and for many years, the only—organization outside the two suffrage associations to endorse votes for women. Willard pushed through the first resolution in 1880, against great opposition, and over the years brought her membership along with sweet reasonableness and her message that the ballot would ensure "home protection." With a dense network that incorporated small Midwestern towns, the Western backcountry, and the rural South, the WCTU in the 1880s and '90s provided troops on the ground for state suffrage campaigns (although on the downside, it also linked votes for women to the prospect of prohibition, so that every year the brewers and saloon owners came out in force to defeat them). In the South, temperance was one of the few public forums open to black women as white supremacy strengthened its grip. Long popular among Northern blacks, temperance work was a means for community uplift, a showcase for middle-class black womanhood, and the sole model of biracial Christian cooperation, albeit cooperation as determined by white women's racism. As for Southern white women, temperance was the one entrée into a political culture that held that female political involvement was a Yankee monstrosity.[82]

In a conservative era, temperance softened and domesticated women's suffrage by ladening the issue with religiosity and maternal moralism. It was not because of women's natural rights but because of their motherly virtues that they *deserved* political rights. The pitch was in the short run persuasive. Temperance platforms in third-party campaigns and state referenda on prohibition drew home-abiding women into activity they would otherwise have shrunk from as a masculine domain, and made voting seem like it could be a Christian duty. The WCTU made suffrage safe. Vivian Gornick captures the change: "An intelligent, good-looking woman of the middle classes who worked for the vote no longer had to fear the stigma of caricature. She could now be experienced as lovely even if strong-minded, her work in the movement posing no real threat to her primary duties in society."[83]

To improve women's situation, the WCTU turned away from goals like coeducation, integrating the professions, and undoing coverture. Instead it concentrated on changing men, the source of women's problems, by bringing them to Christ—which meant bringing them around to respect and honor women. As things stood, men were free to wreak havoc on family finances and female bodies, and a licentious culture grotesquely enhanced their ability to damage women and children. Shutting down the liquor trade was the first step, but the vision of a world purified of male vice was more comprehensive. The WCTU aimed to end prostitution, which went hand in glove with saloons; to rescue and reform the degraded women who were its victims; to abolish the "white slave trade"—later generations would call it trafficking in women—which ensnared innocent girls; to eradicate venereal disease by inspiring men to pledge themselves to "social purity," that is, celibacy before marriage and sexual fidelity in marriage; and to abolish the male vices of tobacco and gambling.[84]

Yet despite all this, the WCTU refrained from directly challenging male authority, in the family or anywhere else. "Willard did not condemn the sexual contract; she aimed to salvage it," writes Suzanne Marilley, the WCTU's most astute historian. Temperance was "not an organized protest against the married relation," Clara Parrish, a WCTU organizer in Japan in 1896–98, assured her home audience "Instead of being organized to make women dissatisfied with the home, it is calculated to make them far better mothers." Wives would improve men by virtue of their shining example and the gospel truth, thereby leading them to a more equitable partnership. On family finances, for instance, the WCTU preached that a woman was due a fair share of the male wage: "It is her income as well as yours," the organization instructed husbands straight-out. "To dole out money grudgingly to your wife is more than ungenerous, it is unjust." But the leadership did not address the question of women's miserable wages, or what happened in cases of divorce or separation.[85]

The contradiction lay in the simultaneous commitment to conventional marriage and scorn for male depravity. The WCTU managed to reconcile the incompatible views by projecting the loathsome qualities it attributed to the male sex onto working-class, black, and immigrant men, as well as men of the dark-skinned races of Asia and Africa. Middle-class men were more likely to be seen as "brother-hearted" allies, partners in a middle-class Christian elite that would rescue vulnerable women from the depraved tyrants who held them in thrall. In other words, mothers and fathers were to collaborate in a Christian enterprise that was also a class and imperial mission.[86]

Frances Willard understood how potent were women's fears of men's power. She calculated correctly that political mobilization could flip that fear into anger, self-righteousness, and Christian bellicosity, a conviction of moral superiority that would shore up an otherwise timid public persona. Despite their own powerlessness, women could imagine themselves through temperance ideology as powerful mothers saving working-class daughters and younger sisters—ignorant, gullible, and frightened—from drunken, dangerous, dirty, diseased men: brutes in lumber camps, Negro pimps, Chinese procurers in red-light districts.

The problem with this politics of redeemed women and unredeemed men was that it could be adapted so easily to antidemocratic uses. In the American South, the contradictions of temperance were extreme. Even as black women gravitated to the WCTU, white temperance workers were among those who whipped up fears of a supposed legion of black rapists roaming the countryside threatening to rape and murder (white) women on the farms. The temperance watchword of "home protection" thus helped to legitimate a reign of terror against African-Americans in the 1890s, when lynchings reached an all-time high. Mob violence, too, could be an instrument of home protection.[87]

The politics of female protection and rescue proved to be hardy and adaptable. Surveying the globe, temperance activists depicted girls and women as victims of male despotism and savage custom. WCTU chapters cropped up among British women in outposts of the empire (especially India and South Africa) and American women in the Pacific islands and (after the Spanish-American War) the Philippines. Temperance women stressed the power and respect that Christian nations supposedly gave them, contrasting it to the oppressions of their sisters in foreign lands, itemizing atrocities that colonized men inflicted on hapless women: the harem, daughter selling, female infanticide, and bound feet. Women thus conceived of themselves as soldiers in the battle for civilization, especially trained to spot the female victims of barbarism.

By 1890, Gilded Age conservatism saturated women's politics. Christian redemption replaced the Constitution as the centerpiece of the suffrage campaign.[88] The suffrage movement did, unquestionably, incorporate a broader spectrum of opinion than it did before the Civil War. Such is the definition of coalition, but such is also the stuff of frustration for intellectuals. Elizabeth Cady Stanton never tangled with Frances Willard, but she was allergic to the sentimentality and idealizations of femininity that emanated from the WCTU.

The adoption of motherhood as the central value of the women's movement also precluded the discussion of marriage and divorce Stanton had carried on in *The Revolution*. Temperance ideology promised women power through shaming men, disciplining them within marriage rather than changing marriage itself. The difference in emphasis marks the distance between, on the one hand, a conservative stance that quietly maligned men even as it preserved the legal and economic bases of their privilege, and, on the other, a viewpoint that retained the hope for a better future that the sexes could share. No one was more aggressive than Stanton in attacking men for the injuries they inflicted, but her hatred was of male domination as it congealed in institutions, not of male character. Women were no better than men, she insisted at her most forthright and honest: "The talk about women being so much above men, celestial, ethereal, and all that, is sentimental nonsense." While she fulminated against "white males" and men in general, her touchstone remained faith in a common life. Men and women enriched one another, she believed. "The real woman is not up in the clouds nor among the stars, but down here upon earth by the side of man. She is on the same material plane with man, striving and working to support herself." One feels in these passages the presence of Stanton the mother of sons as well as daughters, Stanton the friend of men as well as women—and even, perhaps, Stanton the disaffected, distant but still-affectionate spouse, after thirty-five years of marriage.[89]

Stymied on the political front, Stanton turned to the deeper sources of resistance to women's freedom, engaging criticisms of organized religion that had compelled her decades earlier when the Garrisonians had attacked the churches for their equivocation on slavery. The free thought movement, a loose intellectual network of agnostics and atheists, intensified her interest in organized religion as a font of tyranny. At NWSA conventions, she ruffled feathers by introducing resolutions condemning the church as an institution that taught that woman was an afterthought in creation, marriage was a condition of subordination, maternity was a curse, and that to be Christians, women must remain silent before male ecclesiastical authority.[90] The movement she had helped to found, however, had little use for her probing thoughts.

The politics of the mothers tapped middle-class desires for more egalitarian families and drew middle-of-the-road women into the once-fearsome issue of suffrage. Political motherliness promised an accommodation with marriage and the prospect that still-covered but enfranchised citizens could nonetheless improve their marriages, thereby protecting their social interests. The problem was that the approach shunted women back into a structure of male governance that remained intact. An awareness of women's real vulnerabilities and the importance of exposing men's power in its most dangerous and secretive manifestations were legacies of this strain. But so was a sensibility of women's power that was soaked in self-righteousness, race and class superiority, and fantasies of rescuing other women.

CHAPTER FIVE

THE POLITICS OF THE MOTHERS

CRISES RACKED America in the 1890s: labor battles, the Panic of 1893, massive unemployment, racial violence in the South, the Spanish-American War. Yet to read through reports from women's organizations is to paddle in the mental backwaters. The America that was represented in their pages was a fundamentally calm place, steadily advancing into a better future by virtue of the wives and mothers who were busily improving their communities and gently prodding the recalcitrant toward the path of right living, even as they pressed politely for the vote. The approach to power is cautious and accommodating, advertising an acceptance of women's dependent position in the family.[1]

The ideology of separate spheres and female virtue allowed suffragism to survive in a conservative time. But it was also a liability. By 1900, opponents were turning it against them, charging that their ladylike incursions into the public sphere were in truth unwomanly. If suffragists took stock, they saw a political impasse. But few took stock.[2]

In 1890, the two rival American suffrage organizations (Stanton and Anthony's NWSA and the Boston-based AWSA) merged into the National American Woman Suffrage Association (NAWSA). Unification augured well for the combined forces, but it turned out instead to mean a softened tone and diminished goals. Elizabeth Stanton was elected president—although she was titular head, put forward because of

Susan B. Anthony's insistence, having already alienated conservative women with her combative ideas. Two years later Anthony, much more popular and assimilable, took over; she headed the association until 1900. Meanwhile, the democratic meanings of the vote steadily contracted.

NAWSA did profit sporadically from the old sterling currency of genderless natural rights. That view was identified with Stanton, who articulated the principles with lofty certainty in a magnificent final speech when she left the presidency in 1892. "The Solitude of Self" distilled Stanton's lifetime of work trying to pry women loose from family encumbrances so they could stand as liberal individuals. The intimate relations of the family, avowed Stanton (who was now seventy-seven), were precious but nonetheless incidental to the real business of life. Women's purpose was, like men's, to do the largest work of which they were capable.

The speech is both a majestic summation of nineteenth-century liberal feminism and a charter that heralds the modern era. Beginning with a classic liberal trope of autonomy, Stanton posed her exemplary woman as Robinson Crusoe, responsible for her own fate. The stoic tone evoked the lonely soul, not the social contract. Stanton contended that individual integrity of purpose was the most important requisite to give meaning to any individual's life, since God, if present at all, was distant from the turmoil of any one human being.

> The strongest reason for giving woman all the opportunities for higher education, for the full development of her faculties, her forces of mind and body; for giving her the most enlarged freedom of thought and action; a complete emancipation from all forms of bondage, of custom, dependence, superstition; from all the crippling influences of fear—is the solitude and personal responsibility of her own individual life.

Women no less than men endured tragic losses; the solitude of old age; the terrors of mortality. They must be equipped with sources of enduring meaning in order to bear these vicissitudes.[3]

The speech is all the more moving if we think of Stanton as a person who became an adult in a culture that pictured her sex as tendrils twining around the sturdy oak of male authority. Now, at the end of the century, she depicted them as erect and commanding. "No matter how much women prefer to lean, to be protected and supported, nor how much men desire to have them do so," avowed Stanton, "they must make the voyage of life alone, and for safety in an emergency they must know something of the laws of navigation." With metaphors of masculine hardihood and action—captain, pilot, engineer, soldier—she recurred to the need to chart one's course. "It matters not whether the solitary voyager is man or woman." Both must be equipped for the journey. And that equipment *must* include citizenship, for in the endeavor of self-realization humans, however lonely, require one another and can work together for the common good. It is the fullest statement of American feminism in the nineteenth century as well as a profound description of the psychological responsibility that democracy entails. With Stanton making women the captains of their ships, it is good to remember that long before, Margaret Fuller had urged, "let them be sea-captains." Perhaps Stanton remembered, too.

Stanton was not alone; like-minded suffragists clustered around her: NWSA co-worker Matilda Joslyn Gage, newspaper editor Clara Bewick Colby, novelist Helen Gardener, and others. But they fought a losing battle in NAWSA. Stanton's 1895 publication of *The Woman's Bible*, an astringent critique that came out of her freethinking investigations, appalled members with its castigation of Christianity for its mistreatment of women. They rose en masse at the 1896 convention to pass a resolution tantamount to censure over Anthony's pained objections.

Living in conservative times for which she was ill-fitted, Stanton "swung like a pendulum through the decade," historian Ann Gordon concludes, "hopeful and infuriated, expansive about rights and narrowly class centered." The road ahead was not to open in her lifetime, yet melancholy was not a state she entertained. She was doing the planting, she reasoned; others would bring in the harvest. Of that she was sure. After 1895, she returned to her family and writing, publishing in national magazines and producing her memoir *Eighty Years and More* (1898) and the second installment of *The Woman's Bible* (1898), just as much a "hornet's nest" as the first. She died in her sleep in 1902, having just written President Theodore Roosevelt urging him to support suffrage.[4] Susan Anthony died four years later.

By 1900, suffragists trucked almost exclusively in women's special traits as the basis for the claim to voting. Women were so different from men—superior, really—that they had a special role to play in politics. "It is because a woman loves her home that she wants her country to be pure and holy, so that she may not lose her children when they go out from her protection. We want to be women, womanly women, stamping the womanliness of our nature upon the country," declared Reverend Ida C. Hultin at the 1897 convention. Disenfranchisement was thus not a denial of rights but rather an insult to maternal authority.[5]

Ideas of mothers' preeminence gained strength from the pseudoscientific theories of human evolution developed in tandem with Darwin's science by Herbert Spencer and his American followers. Suffragists turned Spencer's thought to their purposes, giving the virtues of Protestant domesticity a pseudoscientific gloss. Social Darwinism adapted domestic womanhood to an aggressive racial ideology, a cluster of ideas and assumptions that purported to explain away human conflict and inequality as inevitable results of the triumph of the fittest. Humans were first and foremost members of separate races—Africans, Slavs, Orientals, Celts, Caucasians, and so on—each with distinct moral, intellectual, and physical traits. These differences placed groups on respective rungs of an evolutionary ladder: lower, higher, more primitive, or more civilized, with Anglo-Saxons at the top.[6]

There were different schools of thought about where women stood on the evolutionary scale. Hard-line Spencerians assumed that men's dominance in education, politics, war, and intellectual life showed their superiority, and that women's childbearing was an animal function that mired them in the primitive depths of humanity. But women's advocates squeezed out an optimistic reading that put women at the top of their respective races. Traits were mutable. Highly evolved Christian women transmitting their desirable traits to their offspring hauled everyone a rung or two up the ladder. Women from all the races—the lowly Africans, the weird Chinese, the vulgar Italians, the suspicious Jews—thus helped the civilizing mission.

In the 1890s, a generation of black suffragists came to national prominence, ushered in by uplift ideology and a pragmatic attitude toward white women reformers. They saw themselves as race women but at the same time they posited black women's separate position in African-American life, at a distance from men. With very sparse resources to work with, they found political traction in the maternal enterprise of uplift, refitted from evolutionist premises.

Although the voting rights of African-American men had been under attack since Reconstruction, black men voted and exercised limited political power in many Southern locales through the 1880s. In 1890, Mississippi set out to rectify the situation with a sweeping program to push blacks out of politics altogether, using poll taxes and residency and literacy requirements. The other states of the former Confederacy followed. There was initial anxiety among Southern elites about whether Jim Crow laws would stand up in federal courts, but the Supreme Court's decision in *Plessy v. Ferguson* (1896) gave constitutional legitimacy to segregation. The 1890s came to be known as the "nadir" of African American history.

At that moment, a book heralded the women's advent in national affairs. In 1892, Anna Julia Cooper, a Washington, D.C., educator and classics scholar educated at Oberlin, published *A Voice from the South, By a Black Woman of the South,* a searching meditation on race relations, women's power, and black America. In a period when hard-pressed African-Americans put a high premium on race solidarity and male leadership, Cooper's suggestion that women bore a double burden of race and sex broke new ground. Cooper was the first to sound the theme of black women's unique position in America. "To be a woman of the Negro race in America, and to be able to grasp the deep significance of the possibilities of the crisis, is to have a heritage, it seems to me, unique in the ages." Written at a bleak time for blacks and composed in a segregated city, Cooper's book is suffused with a striking sense of promise. "The race is young and full of the elasticity and hopefulness of youth. All its achievements are before it."[7]

Pitched as prophecy and program, *A Voice from the South* revived the antebellum idea of women's epochal importance. "We are living in what may be called, a woman's age," declared Fannie Barrier Williams, a Chicago leader who echoed Cooper in a landmark speech on black women at the 1893 World's Columbian Exposition. "The old notion that woman was intended by the Almighty to do only those things that men thought they ought to do, is fast passing away." Williams's words had a lyrical turn, picking up on Cooper's view that the very neglect of black women, their exclusion from sentimental idealizations and codes of chivalry, made them the newest of New Women. "The Negro woman is really the new woman of the times, and in possibilities the most interesting woman in America," Williams maintained with élan. "She is the only woman whose career lies wholly in front of her." The affirmation at once looked back to Maria Stewart and forward, to Toni Morrison's reflections many years later about the existential solitude that was the ordinary black woman's lot: "And she had nothing to fall back on; not maleness, not whiteness, not ladyhood, not anything. And out of the profound desolation of her reality she may very well have invented herself," Morrison wrote in 1971. The black woman would be the new century's heroine, making herself up as she went along.[8]

Cooper's emphasis on the singular character of a rising generation of women was related to a fascination with modern life and the changes it wrought in human character—an interest that rose among Americans in the 1890s, with the year 1900 anticipated as a historical caesura. Cooper's "new woman of the times" played off of the iconic "New Woman" who cropped up in Anglo-American popular culture in the decade. Ubiquitous in journalism, theater, novels, and magazine illustrations, New Woman imagery both absorbed changes in female education, work, and consciousness and heightened their meaning to individuals who embraced them. The New Woman type was single and uninterested in marrying; she was civically engaged, college educated, idealistic, and often professionally trained. Female physicians and lawyers were deemed New, as were artists, actresses, journalists, and settlement house workers—or any woman, for that matter, trying to make a go of it in service to the higher truths of Art, or Revolution, or Service to the Poor. The New Woman gestured toward a different life course—detractors said she was foolish, enthusiasts thought her marvelous. She saw herself as the heroine of a story (the details were vague) that would break with the paradigmatic marriage plot—inscribed in culture and art in a million ways—in which the woman's destiny unfolded through the twists and turns of courtship and romance and ended either happily-ever-after in marriage or tragically in death, despair, or shame.

The same year *A Voice from the South* was published, a thirty-year-old journalist from Memphis, Ida B. Wells, catapulted to international attention with a riveting exposé of mob violence in the South. Wells was a New Woman who could have stepped off the pages of Cooper's book. Born into slavery in Mississippi—she was three when the war ended—she had worked since she was orphaned at fifteen, first as a teacher and then, in the 1880s, as a journalist in the flourishing black press. In 1889 she became editor and part owner of a newspaper in Memphis. Three years later, three successful black men in the city who had angered white business competitors were arrested on trumped-up charges and lynched. Faced with certain death for a scathing editorial calling for a mass exodus of blacks from the city, Wells fled to New York, where she joined the staff of *The New York Age* and researched, wrote, and published "Southern Horrors: Lynch Law in All Its Phases." Followed several months later by news of a horrible torture-lynching of a black man in Paris, Texas, Wells's piece grabbed the attention of Northern whites who either knew little about lynching or accepted the Southern explanation that black men's lust provoked these regrettable but understandable reprisals.[9]

Wells was not an explicitly feminist writer, but in speaking of unspeakable things, she breached the protocols that made the subject of sex off-limits to respectable black women. Since the end of the Civil War, sexual violence had pervaded Southern politics, although open discussion was impossible, so omnipresent was the threat. Wells connected lynching to sexual violence, showing how the myth of the black man's lust for white women worked to legitimate torture and murder. "Southern Horrors" attacked head-on the premises of the politics of protection, including those held by white women. Not only had Rebecca Latimer Felton and her temperance troops contributed to the lynching rationale with tales of how alcohol fueled black men's lusts (although by this time Felton was recoiling from the violence she helped incite), but in an 1890 interview that shocked black temperance women, Frances Willard described the victims of lynching as rapists and murderers "whose rallying cry is better whiskey, and more of it." White women's safety was so precarious, Willard remarked, that white men "dare not go beyond the sight of their own roof-tree" lest drunken black marauders set upon their wives and daughters.[10]

Wells broke into this self-ratifying white conversation by daring to state openly what African-Americans already knew: The defense of white women's honor and sexual virtue was a mythology that went to the emotional core of white supremacy, a self-aggrandizing fiction that allowed Southern white men to get away with murder by projecting their own dark history of sexual violence onto black men. But white Americans, including Northern reformers, were resistant, and Wells had to take her crusade to Britain to find a receptive white audience. The clout she gained in a lecture tour in 1893–94 allowed her to take on the formidable Frances Willard when she returned. She forced Willard to retract her earlier statements. The explosion Wells touched off cleared a small political space for black women. When a Southern editor charged her with being a lying "Negro adventuress," Josephine St.

Pierre Ruffin, a well-to-do Boston journalist, issued a call to upstanding black women to unify in self-defense. It was their duty, she wrote, "to teach an ignorant and suspicious world that our aims and interests are identical with those of all good aspiring women."[11]

There was an organizational network to call into play. Clubs had spread among black women as well as white women since the 1880s. Some were literary and cultural, others altruistic and religious, and still others worked in a progressive spirit, campaigning for public health, education, and poverty relief. African-American women established church circles and raised funds for schools and parks; they ran kindergartens and housekeeping classes; in the South, they purchased screen doors for poor people's houses in order to keep out disease-bearing flies, and established vocational schools to train country girls in nursing and secretarial work.[12] Ruffin's call not only rallied support around Ida B. Wells, it led to the formation in 1896 of the National Association of Colored Women (NACW), a federation that gave clubwomen a national platform. The NACW motto, "lifting as we climb," evoked evolutionist precepts—highly developed women could improve themselves and thereby elevate the race. Influential women stepped into the limelight: Mary Church Terrell, the first president, a classmate of Anna Julia Cooper's at Oberlin; Margaret Murray Washington, a veteran teacher and administrator of the famous Tuskegee Institute in Alabama; Lugenia Burns Hope, founder of the dynamic Neighborhood Union in Atlanta, a city-wide organization that served in a Jim Crow city as an alternative municipal structure and funding agency.

The leaders, described by Paula Giddings as radical interracialists in the temperance tradition, worked to forge useful ties with white women even as they endured their racism and condescension. Adella Hunt Logan, another Tuskegee educator, used her light skin to pass as white in NAWSA to operate as a kind of race spy—she was the only black member from Alabama—in order to bring back information from segregated meetings to her colleagues. Fannie Barrier Williams suffered through an uproar in Chicago when she applied for admission to the Chicago Woman's Club. They took humiliation in stride, Giddings maintains, as the price of integration. Fannie Barrier Williams described an approach that was both shrewd and long-suffering: "The colored women have kept themselves serene while this color-line controversy has been raging around them. They have taken a keen and intelligent interest in all that has been said for and against them, but through it all they have lost neither their patience nor their hope in the ultimate triumph of right principles." The calculation was that the benefits to be derived outweighed the insults.[13]

This commitment to collaboration even when racism determined the context underlay black women's dedication to suffrage, including their efforts to be included in NAWSA. Support for women's suffrage was firm among African-Americans of both sexes. The NACW endorsed votes for women and worked to promote the issue, joining the WCTU and NAWSA in the cause well before the white General Federation of Women's Clubs signed on in 1913. African-American women did not need much persuasion to see the need for the vote in this age of black disenfranchisement.[14]

The image of the moral mother anchored the sense of political usefulness, but there were important differences between white and black understandings. Among African-American women, motherhood was not freestanding, as it was for white women; rather, it was crosscut with positive meanings adhering to marriage. What white temperance women viewed as a marital ideal to be reached through male conversion, black women understood as a living relationship: Marriage was a fellowship of Christian laborers, with husbands as collaborators in race work. Surrounded by contemptuous and pathological images of black men, middle-class women formed a protective cordon around their husbands and brothers as virtuous partners in uplift.

There was a social dimension. Marital partnerships were salient in black political culture to an extent inconceivable in white society: Margaret Murray Washington and Booker T. Washington, for example; Lugenia Burns Hope and John Hope; Mary Church Terrell and Robert Terrell, a leading attorney and the first black judge in Washington, D.C.; Fannie Barrier Williams and S. Laing Williams, Chicago assistant district attorney; Ida B. Wells and Ferdinand Barnett, whom she married in 1895, owner of a Chicago newspaper. To be sure, the actualities of these marriages were complex. No less than white people, couples harbored conflict, unhappiness, and asymmetries of power that belied assertions of marital harmony. But—and here is the point—a romance of political mothers and fathers held firm, and African-American women leveraged the ideal to establish independent standing.

Loyalty to men was not without complications. When Josephine St. Pierre Ruffin called black clubwomen to defend their honor in the Wells affair, she was asking them to take over a job that had been men's since Reconstruction. It was an article of faith that strong race men would protect women from sexual slurs and assaults. Yet in the 1890s it seemed to black women that men were not always up to the task. Nannie Helen Burroughs, leader of the national auxiliary of black Baptist women, was blunt: "White men offer more protection to their prostitutes than Black men offer to their best women." Women leaders always acknowledged the racist menace that rendered men impotent, but at times they came close to accusing them of dereliction of duty. "For the most part the chivalry of colored men for colored women has in it but little heart and no strength of protection," lamented Fannie Barrier Williams. Hints of a quarrel between the sexes, always kept away from white eyes, surfaced in clubwomen's reflections on the need to defend themselves.[15]

Thus the NACW's declaration of a woman's era had two faces: a public one, looking toward a fuller partnership with men; and a veiled one, glancing toward a rueful autonomy, confronting responsibilities that men were unable or unwilling to fulfill. The official language was familial, not individualist, stressing the roles of wives and mothers, husbands and fathers as co-guardians of African-American pride. Respectability required cordiality and harmony between the sexes. Discord, sexual anger, and resentment: Respectable African-American women kept such expressions of unhappiness in check, projecting them onto the unruly poor, those rough-talking, hard-living black women who needed to be instructed in gender courtesy along with thrift, housekeeping, hygiene, and temperance. But there was an undertone of unease.

On the main point of women's suffrage, however, the issue did not meet opposition from men. The franchise was still understood as community property. Thus black women's rights remained embedded in heterosexual alliances in the years when the white movement was wilting in a hothouse atmosphere of female separatism and self-congratulation.

In the postbellum decades, women's suffrage did have isolated successes. In Wyoming, Colorado, Idaho, and Utah, women could vote in all elections by 1896. Those places were among the few in the world where women had full voting rights. The others were also settler societies: New Zealand was the one nation that granted women the vote (in 1893) before 1900, and the Australian states soon followed.[16]

Nowhere was women's suffrage achieved because pure principle triumphed. In the Western breakthroughs, women succeeded because men latched onto suffrage to further particular interests. In Wyoming territory in 1869, boosters gave women the vote to lure them to join an overwhelmingly male Anglo population. Like New Zealanders and Australians, Wyoming men wanted to increase a small white population and were willing to be politically generous to attract female emigrants. In Colorado, victory came because the Denver workingwomen and rural temperance workers who led the suffrage push were Populists and insisted that the state victory in 1892 confer the vote on women. Idaho followed suit in 1896, when the Populists won power there.[17]

The Utah case is more complicated. Utah women won and then lost and then won the vote. In 1870, Mormon officials enfranchised women in order to ensure Mormon control of the territory (there were enough polygamous wives to triple the Mormon vote). National outrage was so intense that Congress revoked Utah women's suffrage in 1887. When the Mormons officially renounced polygamy, Congress reenfranchised them in 1896.

Outside the West, though, the situation did not improve. There were female auxiliaries to both the Republican and Democratic parties, but they had no effect on the parties' opposition to suffrage. Politicians, alert to the WCTU and third-party prohibition initiatives, paid lip service to home influence, but neither party formally endorsed suffrage.[18] With the collapse of the Populists after 1896, NAWSA lost its only significant third-party ally. They paid for the vanished association, though Antisuffragists capitalized on the defunct link by conflating votes for women with Populist anarchy. Suffragists reacted by redoubling their efforts to appear conventional and unthreatening.[19]

Facing the impasse, a cabal of dedicated white women from the South moved to the front ranks of NAWSA with a strategy that took the search for allies as far as it could go to the political right. An outspoken, confident band from the planter class, members of the ruling elite who were barred by their sex from wielding power, argued that they could convince Southern men that women's votes would ensure the stability of white supremacy—even though the hatred of women's rights had, if anything, intensified in the region since the Civil War. To NAWSA, they promised a huge dividend, the eleven states of the former Confederacy delivered to the suffrage cause.

In the period before *Plessy v. Ferguson,* when it was not yet clear that the federal courts would let legal segregation stand, the Southern suffrage strategy proposed a way to shore up white rule without the bother of unwieldy laws that risked being struck down. The idea was essentially the "statistical argument" Henry Blackwell had been making since 1867, now revved up for the Jim Crow South. "The South, true to its traditions, will trust its women," predicted the regal, rabidly racist Kate Gordon from New Orleans. "Thus placing in their hands the balance of power, the negro as a disturbing element in politics will disappear." In 1892, Laura Clay from Kentucky, daughter of the state's reigning planter clan, persuaded NAWSA leaders to establish a Southern Committee composed of women from leading families of South Carolina, Arkanas, Louisiana, and Georgia.[20]

In the South, the very idea of votes for women was a Yankee insult to a noble way of life: that is, the South's supposed chivalric respect and protection for its women (meaning white women). Virtual representation took on added meaning in the region as a means by which white men could restore the honor tragically besmirched by the war, in taking up the task of governing their women and their Negroes. So no matter how draped Southern suffragists were in Confederate laurels, they met vilification as traitors to the Lost Cause, trampling the way of life for which their fathers and brothers had fought and died. "Woman's suffrage comes from the North and West. . . . I do not believe the state of Georgia has sunk so low that her good men can not legislate for the women," huffed the head of the United Daughters of the Confederacy. "If they succeed then indeed was the blood of their fathers shed in vain," an Alabama state senator intoned.[21]

Regardless of the animus, Southern suffragists pushed on. In their case, racism and women's rights were entwined: To be a public-spirited white woman in the New South—like Rebecca Latimer Felton, Kate Gordon, or Belle Kearney of Mississippi—was to ally oneself with a civilizing enterprise identified with white supremacy. Middle-aged, savvy, and civic-minded, they wanted to take up a part in white supremacist rule alongside their fathers, brothers, cousins, and husbands. Kearney, Mississippi WCTU president, hated the constraints that the Southern elite put on women; Felton was a planter's wife, freed by the collapse of their plantation after the war to take up her true calling in politics, serving informally as her politician husband's campaign manager; Kate Gordon's crusade to modernize New Orleans's water supply freed the city from perennial yellow fever epidemics; Nellie Nugent Somerville was a Methodist leader from Greenville, Mississippi, with an anti-tuberculosis campaign (which included an anti-tobacco-spitting rider) and public library to her credit.[22]

All were political dynamos (Nellie Somerville and Belle Kearney went on to serve in the Mississippi legislature; Rebecca Felton was the first woman to be seated in the Senate—for one day, on a technicality, to serve out the term of Georgia's senator Tom Watson, who had died). Like women in the North, they wanted to angle in on men's politics via partnerships in public health schemes, social services for the poor, and prison reform. Theirs was the combination of feminism, racism, and modernization that characterized Southern Progressives. The bad old days of lynching and mob violence must be abandoned for a supposedly peaceful white supremacy backed by the law. Courts would regulate and restrain both races, by keeping black brutes in check and protecting their properly behaved fellows from the mayhem that rabble of both races stirred up when segregation was precarious.

Signaling cooperation with the Southern strategy, NAWSA held its national convention in Atlanta in 1895 and New Orleans in 1903, the meetings packed with former Confederate officers giving honorific speeches. In New Orleans, delegates sang a rousing chorus of "Dixie" and listened politely to Belle Kearney's denunciations of semi-barbaric blacks. It had to be the nadir of the American women's movement. I can only speculate that those older women with abolitionist pasts would have felt uneasy. Ten years earlier, even as the Southern strategy was gaining favor, Susan Anthony solicited the good offices of Frederick Douglass to give a speech to NAWSA on the virtues of popular democracy.[23] What was she thinking in New Orleans? The only evidence comes from one outward act of polite resistance to Jim Crow etiquette. Anthony reached out to old allies, old principles, and her own conscience when she took time out from the convention to pay a visit to an African-American women's club.

It was a modest act of collegiality across the color line—you could even call it pathetic. Regardless of Anthony's timidity in our eyes, though, the gesture would have sat badly with her New Orleans host-esses, because it violated the unwritten Southern prohibition of interra-cial contact outside the mistress-servant relationship. The significance of Anthony's visit wasn't lost on the black women, who responded with requisite phrases of deference. "When women like you, Miss Anthony, come to see us and speak to us it helps us believe in the Fatherhood of God and the brotherhood of Man, and at least for the time being in the sympathy of women." *At least for the time being:* The African-American suffragists allowed themselves that one dig. And Sylvanie Williams, club president, did not leave matters at that. She wrote to NAWSA's *Woman's*

Journal afterward, protesting the injustice the Jim Crow convention had done to "10,000 intelligent colored women."[24]

The question of how a once-proud democratic movement ended up warbling "Dixie" in New Orleans has to be understood in the broader context of disenfranchisement campaigns. NAWSA was latching on to a trend across a wide swath of American opinion, from Northern conservatives to liberal reformers. The tragedy was not that suffrage was uniquely racist, as Ellen Carol DuBois has put it, but that "the women's suffrage movement, which had begun in the visionary, perfectionist years of the mid-nineteenth century, dragged on into the early twentieth, into the very nadir of American race relations."[25]

Disenfranchisement reasoning pushed middle-class black women into a corner, which they tried to escape by using the legitimacy conferred by educated suffrage, fashioning themselves as redeemers of ignorant men's misused votes. By the 1890s, Southern reactionaries had succeeded in so maligning and distorting the history of Reconstruction that champions of the race had difficulty breaking through reigning depictions of tragic Negro domination, rife with vice and corruption, that supposedly followed the war. Black men were said to have sold their votes to the highest bidder—so went the story of the postwar South, as whites told it. White men redeemed state governments sodden with black iniquity.

Seeking a foothold in suffrage discussions, African-American women adapted condemnations of "vote-selling" for their own purposes—departing from the narrative promoted by male leaders, who depicted black men as loyal citizens thwarted and vilified by racist whites. Women declared that they, unlike men, would use the vote for noble purposes. "You do not find the colored woman selling her birthright for a mess of pottage," scoffed Anna Julia Cooper. "The Negro woman needs to get back by the wise use of it, what the Negro man has lost by the *misuse* of it," maintained Nannie Burroughs, a Baptist leader. However equivocal the approach now seems, educated suffrage held out the hope that middle-class blacks could hold on to some vestige of power by allying themselves with whites against the ignorant masses. Women made the case that they deserved their fair share of it. "Seeking no favors because of our color, nor patronage because of our needs, we knock at the bar of justice, asking an equal chance," professed Mary Church Terrell in this vein in an 1898 speech before NAWSA.[26]

Mostly, however, disenfranchisement energies in the early twentieth century encouraged white women to see themselves as presiding from their Anglo-Saxon pinnacle over social and racial inferiors. Xenophobic, racist language that shocked reformers when Stanton and Anthony used it after the war turned into standard NAWSA rhetoric. Suffragists routinely deprecated the ignorant foreign vote and bewailed the humiliation of being ruled by degraded men. In Germany, German men governed German women; in France, French men did the same, "but in this country, American women are governed by every kind of man under the light of the sun," complained Anna Howard Shaw, successor to Anthony as NAWSA president, at the 1914 convention—praise that was weirdly blind to the fact that Germany and France were about to descend into the maelstrom of World War I. "There is no race, there is no color, there is no nationality of men who are not the sovereign rulers of American women," she added. Carrie Chapman Catt, the no-nonsense leader who took over in 1915, used language indistinguishable from that of Southern whites, lamenting Reconstruction's government by "illiterate men, fresh from slavery." Black women were NAWSA's absolutely dependable supporters, but for their own reasons, and no thanks to white women.[27]

Conservative domination of the movement did not, however, serve it well. While the imagined face-off between high-minded women and coarse, debauched immigrants and blacks catered to the prejudices of the day, there were no victories and over time the ranks dwindled. The Southern strategy fizzled: Southern Democrats were quite able to shore up white supremacy without any help from women.[28] In 1903, the year of the New Orleans meeting, NAWSA had nine thousand members and a strapped treasury. In contrast, the main British suffrage organization, the National Union of Women's Suffrage Societies (NUWSS), established in 1897, had about the same number of members in a much smaller population. American women's suffrage lacked the animated debates, tactical flexibility, and alliances to push, prod, or pull itself out of the doldrums, as the period came to be called. The politics of the mothers, permeated with disdain for the foreign lesser stock and crude "Africans," was supposed to be a big tent, but the crowd inside was sparse.

Suffrage restrictions on men only made women's disenfranchisement look more, not less, logical and sensible. Antisuffragists drew strength politically and ideologically from other disenfranchisers. Members of the leading Northern "anti" group, for example, came from the same social set and in some cases the same families as the statesmen, blue-bloods, businessmen, and Harvard professors of the influential Boston-based Immigration Restriction League. This meant that in the first decade of the century, the antisuffragists held their ground and then some. Their platform was virtual representation: Antis repeated what defenders of the male franchise had been saying for more than a hundred years. "Faithful to the doctrine of the old Bible and true to the teachings of the new, our fathers founded this Government upon the family as the unit of political power," declared an Alabama congressman in 1915, "with the husband as the recognized and responsible head." (Actually, about the Founding Fathers he was correct.)[29]

While few in number, antis' wealth and connections gave them access to the press and local elites. Men dominated the movement, but eminent women also spoke out. Antis shifted ground, depending on the audience, with appeals that exploited several kinds of conservative beliefs about women's proper relationship to men and the body politic. They correctly saw the democratizing tendency that votes for women represented, and warned businessmen that suffrage would strengthen the labor and reform vote. But they also tailored their message to nonelite audiences when the occasion warranted. With saloonkeepers, brewers, and workingmen who liked their liquor, they warned that suffrage would bring prohibition. Where there were Catholic immigrants, they allied with the Church hierarchy; where there were nativists, they inveighed against foreign influence.

Sometimes the antis depicted women as upright moral arbiters, to be protected from the hurly-burly of electioneering, sometimes as dupes of their husbands, incapable of making their own decisions about candidates: Disenfranchisement was a protection for the country, as it was with ignorant blacks and immigrants, since it prevented demagogues from gaining control of foolish females who acted as shills for Democratic machine pols or Mormon polygamists.[30] Sometimes they posed disenfranchisement as an elixir of femininity that made women deferential and desirable. Virtual representation heightened sexual chemistry, and, conversely, eros would fizzle if women got the vote. The suffrage question "was making women less attractive to men," warned an Ohio representative in a 1915 congressional debate about the suffrage amendment.[31]

Mostly, however, the antis managed to avoid any disparaging suggestions that women's deficits were the reason they should not vote. In this respect they adjusted to feminist gains over the preceding fifty years. Antifeminism proved tenacious, as it often has, because proponents were shrewd enough to cede ground and reorganize their assault. The spread of women's higher education and their array of civic roles weakened the older anti position that women lacked the capacities to reason. So in the new century, the antis regrouped: "No question of superiority or equality is involved in the opposition to votes for women," Annie Nathan Meyer, a wealthy philanthropist and vocal anti, assured followers.[32] Instead, women's exclusion was a privilege. Electoral politics were dirty, distasteful work that men shouldered because they wanted to protect pure women. Women could do good, but party politics, with its corrupt deals and pandering to squalid self-interest, weakened the virtues of equanimity and moral understanding that made them valuable to their country. Men must protect women's freedom to stay clear.

The antis had considerable success. After the last state victory, in Idaho in 1896, the suffrage movement ground to a halt. There was little to show for the years of unified efforts and kowtowing to the Southerners. The federal amendment languished in congressional committee. Presidents McKinley and Roosevelt froze out NAWSA. As for the states, measure after measure went down in defeat. The numbers were depressing: 480 campaigns over fifty years to get legislatures to submit amendments to voters, forty-seven to get state constitutional conventions to include suffrage, and so forth. Although the numbers inflated the actual efforts invested—many campaigns involved only two or three women working the state—they were still dispiriting.[33]

Harriot Stanton Blatch, younger daughter of Elizabeth Cady Stanton, returned to the United States in 1900 after twenty years in England working in the flourishing suffrage movement there. The inertia dismayed her. "Friends, drummed up and harried by the ardent, listlessly heard the same old arguments. Unswerving adherence to the cause was held in high esteem, but alas, it was loyalty to a rut worn deep and ever deeper." Aging suffragists admitted in private that they had no purchase on a wider public: It was not the antisuffragists who were their greatest obstacle, but American women's apathy. "They have thought very little about it," Anna Howard Shaw confided to a European compatriot.[34]

Suffragism nestled in a corner of political culture where idealism presented itself as disenfranchisement. It harbored women whose political abilities were calcified and whose understanding of democracy was crippled by an overweening sense of their own superiority. Like many good ideas that had been around too long, women's suffrage was irritating to everyone but the faithful, boring yet elusive.

Internationally, asking for the vote was common by 1900, a marker of modern women's aspirations. Steamships and railroads hauled women's rights ideas and enthusiasts around the world; newspapers and books trekked across borders. In the British Empire, continental Europe, China and Japan, and parts of the Middle East, the ideas touched the middle classes and modernizing elites. Europeans and Americans, invested in the prospects of a global movement with themselves at its head, believed that women, in all their national variations, were a constituency recognizable to one another, a political bloc that might play a part in international diplomacy: a collective Woman of the Twentieth Century to follow the Woman of the Nineteenth.[35]

By 1900, women in Scandinavia, Iceland, and virtually all the countries of northern and central Europe and several outposts of the British Empire had called for the vote. The International Woman Suffrage Alliance (IWSA), formed in 1904, brought together suffragists from some two dozen North Atlantic countries.[36] Over time, Europeans and Americans became friends, mulling over tactics in letters, visiting, traveling together, and attending international conferences. Mutually congratulatory leaders praised their transnational sisterhood, which on paper seemed close to the international proletariat socialists claimed as their world-transforming force. The imagined affiliations across national borders sparked a sense of extravagant likeness across divides of country, language, and even faith.

Yet the reality belied these paeans to progress. Across Europe (with the exception of Scandinavia), suffrage movements were blocked, weak, or politically impotent—not unlike in the United States. Each country had its own reasons, story, and cast of characters, but some patterns are clear.

First, the issue could not make headway where the male franchise was sharply delimited. It is difficult now to appreciate how unusual it was before World War I for European men to vote or, alternatively, have their votes count. In the United States, universal male suffrage was at least nominal, guaranteed by the Constitution, although in practice disenfranchisement campaigns drastically eroded voting rights. But in Europe, the very idea had yet to succeed. Universal male suffrage only existed in France. Enfranchised populations were small, in some countries minuscule. In Belgium, until a general strike in 1893 forced reform, less than a tenth of adult men could vote. In England, the second most democratic nation in Europe, only 60 percent of adult men voted, and this was after two reform bills had extended the franchise.[37]

Second, the left/liberal formations in which women's suffrage movements originated were in retreat. Everywhere in Europe in the late nineteenth century, liberals lost support and momentum to workers', peasants', and right-wing nationalist parties. As for the left, the socialist parties had an on-again, off-again relationship to feminist organizing, their sympathy for women's rights undercut by a left-wing version of patriarchy (honest workingmen supporting virtuous wives at home) and fear that suffrage would take proletarian women away from the class struggle. Socialist women in Germany, Austria, and France had to grope their way through comrades' condemnation of the bourgeois women's movement, finding a way between class solidarity and their own sense that all classes of women shared certain problems.[38]

Third, in the autocratic regimes of Russia and the Austro-Hungarian Empire, women's rights ran up against insuperable obstacles. Civil rights, including a free press and free assembly, were weak or nonexistent. Austria banned women from joining political organizations in 1867, so no female suffrage society existed. Suffragists linked up with nationalist forces in Bohemia and Hungary but gained nothing from the partnership. In Russia, the intelligentsia had ruminated on the woman question since the 1860s. But in the absence of representative government there was no ground for a movement to develop. At first separately and then in unison, female factory workers and women of the liberal and left parties broached female enfranchisement during the Revolution of 1905, but the ascendant liberals shunted women aside, and the electorate that resulted from the czar's concessions was male. Infuriated, women organized, but as the czar undermined liberal gains, those organizations collapsed. In 1908, the main feminist organization counted only 1,000 members, down from 12,000 the year before.[39]

Finally, in countries dominated by Catholics, suffragists ran up against opposition from both left and right. Republican France was fiercely anticlerical, and liberals and socialists alike believed that women were ineluctably entangled with the superstitions and antidemocratic traditions of the Church: dupes of the priests and the pope. Conservatives, braced by Catholic tradition, thought women had no place in the polity.

In Belgium and Italy, the same convergence proved lethal; in Spain, women's rights had no purchase whatsoever.[40]

It was in Scandinavia that women's suffrage had the greatest success. Although these countries were small and marginal to Euro-American affairs, their women's movements came to serve as advertisements for dreams come true. A combination of Protestant sensibility, middle-class political vigor, and successful independence struggles carried on by liberals and radicals resulted in wide tolerance for women's rights. In Finland, the 1906 breakthrough came because suffragists were part of a left-liberal coalition that brought about independence from Russian rule. In Norway the same pattern held: Independence from Sweden brought votes for women in 1913. Tiny Iceland in the early 1900s provides the touching example of a population of 50,000 people producing 12,000 signatures on a petition for women suffrage. In Sweden and Denmark, both sovereign states, prolonged struggles against intransigent aristocracies strengthened the liberal politics that gave women's suffrage sway. Old regime forces kept suffrage blocked in both countries until after World War I, but women's rights ideas resonated in the populations.

Typically, suffragists were either affiliated with political parties or members of small, free-floating circles of advanced women. The large single-issue mass movements of Britain and the United States were the exception, not the rule. At the turn of the century, British suffragists commanded a robust movement, situated at the center of a far-flung empire with influence over feminist thinking worldwide. Their problem was that at home, a long dependence on the Liberal Party had come to nothing. In 1886, Liberals followed the general European trend of decline and lost their parliamentary majority, to remain out of power for twenty years except for a brief interregnum. In 1900, the NUWSS counted some ten thousand members and a hundred active local societies, which more than quadrupled in the next decade. But, as a veteran campaigner complained, the petitions, meetings, and demonstrations were to no avail: "All melt off Parliament like snow-flakes."[41]

Unlike the Americans, the British movement, while predominantly middle-class, also included workingwomen. An energetic labor contingent centered in the factory districts of the north carried on an association between women's rights and labor that went back to the Owenites.[42] The issue facing the British was whether to go for the final goal or a way station: a bill that enfranchised women property owners (meaning widows and single women)—the moderate measure—or one that called for full enfranchisement, which would mean challenging coverture. The latter tack, because it inevitably involved universal suffrage, was a proposition that in Britain—with its long attachment to the propertied franchise—smacked of dangerous radicalism. Moreover, coverture in Britain was much stronger than in the United States, where state statutes had whittled away the family jurisdiction over the years.[43]

Beginning in 1903, the Pankhursts—mother Emmeline and daughters Christabel and Sylvia—shook up the British movement. The Pankhursts were a middle-class family of reformers from the north, loosely tied to labor and workingwomen's suffragism. Their organization, the Women's Social and Political Union (WSPU), burst onto the scene when Christabel and another member heckled the Liberal home secretary at a 1905 election meeting. For well-bred ladies to stand up and scream in public, let alone at a high official, was riveting news. Over the next few years, the unrepentant WSPU whipped up a media frenzy with demonstrations of outrageous defiance, braving vitriol, derision, manhandling, and police brutality. Their tactics of enraged confrontation and wild civil disobedience pushed suffrage to the fore, provoked a series of showdowns with parliamentary Liberals, and revolutionized strategy throughout the world, including in the United States.[44]

The WSPU was brilliant at channeling middle- and upper-class women's convictions of superiority and selflessness into rebellion. Using a language of ladyhood, the Pankhursts transformed ideas about Christian women's purity and nobility into justifications for daring and violent acts. Members could be womanly in their righteousness and at the same time wreak havoc—all for the greater good. At first there were degrees of commitment. For the nonlawbreaking, the WSPU staged colorful marches, playing to media spectacle—exposing oneself to the public eye, in itself a transgression. Members harangued crowds from soapboxes in the streets and parks and decked themselves in enchanting regalia designed by feminist artists (the multicolored sash the comically earnest suffragette Mrs. Banks sports in *Mary Poppins* is one artifact).

The true militants, generally young and single, took on extreme challenges. In the 1906 election, the WSPU disrupted meetings around the country; after 1908, militants diversified to breaking windows of government offices, throwing acid at polling booths, chaining themselves to the Ladies' Gallery in Parliament, hurling stones at the prime minister, tossing bombs, and setting fires at official residences. The point was to disrupt business as usual—to stage a guerrilla war—until women were no longer second-class citizens. Militants were arrested and convicted, went to jail, went on hunger strikes, and suffered force feeding. It was a spectacle of martyrdom at the hands of cruel men, amply covered by a press feeding on the melodrama.

As the organization took on an increasingly authoritarian character, controlled by Christabel and Emmeline, it tightened into a cadre of zealots. In 1913, WSPU member Emily Wilding Davison committed suicide for the cause, hurling herself in front of the king's racehorse at the 1913 derby crying "Votes for women!" In 1914, Mary Richardson slashed an Old Masters treasure in the National Gallery, Velázquez's *Rokeby Venus*.[45]

Most British suffragists deplored WSPU tactics, but the crusade nonetheless inspired activity across the board. New organizations formed, and the moderate, constitutionalist NUWSS benefited from WSPU defections. Working-class women in particular were appalled by the Pankhursts' lawbreaking and what they saw as the self-indulgent theatrics of privileged women. By 1910 the WSPU was faltering, and in 1914, with the outbreak of the war, its pure politics of women's advancement looked ridiculous. The constitutionalists, on the other hand, thrived. Open to male support, they moved into the Labour Party fold and the mainstream of twentieth-century British politics. At the center of the British Empire, suffragists believed their successes—not yet secured but certainly auguring well for the future—affirmed their enlightened predominance and set the bar for women the world over.[46]

Outside Europe, in Asia, the Middle East, and Latin America, ideas sped along lines of missionary influence, colonial rule, and indigenous independence movements. In the British colonies, temperance beliefs and assumptions of Anglo-Saxon supremacy gave women's rights a moralizing colonialist cast. But colonized women also made the ideas their own, combined them with their own formulations, and pushed back. In India, for instance, women's rights gained ground among women educated in British schools and those committed to the independence movement.[47] Critiques of laws, customs, and institutions emerged—to be debated, denounced, and reworked outside the direct auspices of colonizers—in cities throughout the British Empire, but also in the Ottoman Empire

(Istanbul to Cairo), Iran, Ceylon, Vietnam, Korea, and the Philippines. In Cuba, Argentina, and Chile, women protested civil codes that denied them elementary civil rights, such as choosing one's own place of residence (separate from a husband or father). Where temperance was strong, the international authority of the WCTU could be called upon to amplify their protests. This was true in Japan in the 1890s, where Yajima Kajiko, the first president of Japan's WCTU, petitioned the government to end officially sanctioned prostitution and promote monogamy—an act of considerable courage that courted violent reprisals from the brothel industry.[48]

At the turn of the century and beyond, reformers and revolutionaries pushed for improvements in women's education, an end to male sexual license (as sanctioned by law and custom), and increased female employment opportunities. They tied these measures to the goal of modern nations freed from foreign rule, feudal despotism, and religious orthodoxy. Education promoted female writing: Circles of journalists broached the new ideas in newspapers and magazines (sometimes in their own separate publications), novels, and in some places—Egypt was one—the semi-public, semi-private institution of the salon, a theater for outspoken women since eighteenth-century France.[49]

Henrik Ibsen's *A Doll's House* (1879) flew around the world in translation for decades, a text that provoked discussions about the future of women wherever it touched down. At the end of the play, Nora walks out on her beloved children and the husband who both adores and infantilizes her—although she has no place to go. "I've been your doll-wife here," she informs the bewildered man, "just as at home I was Papa's doll-child." Nora is an unlikely New Woman: She has no talents, skills, or ambition. But she enacts the fundamental novelty of New Womanhood: the claim on oneself. Facing her husband's thundering admonition that she is a wife and mother before all else, she refuses: "I don't believe that any longer. I believe that before everything else I'm a human being—just as much as you are . . . or at any rate I shall try to become one."[50]

The question was, what was going to happen to her when she walked out the door? Did the New Woman really have a future? Detractors thought not. The Japanese feminists in Seitosha (Bluestockings), founded by Hiratsuka Raicho in 1912, were derided as Noras, self-deluded and silly. Left movements considered the play worriedly. When the play was translated into Chinese in 1918, radicals debated the meaning of Nora's actions. Nehru mentioned *A Doll's House* in a speech to Indian students in 1928.[51]

The divided response to Ibsen is one indication of the deeper ambivalence of anticolonial movements to New Women, figurative and real. Educated, modern women were necessary to independence struggles, but their challenges to male authority and traditional family structure were potentially disruptive, and a political liability with male supporters. One resolution was to summon up new varieties of national motherhood—a pattern of revolutionary imagination that, of course, went back to the American and French revolutions. Historian Afsaneh Najmabadi, writing about Iran, describes the arc elegantly. Despite women's contributions, the universal citizen in whose name the revolution was waged turned out to be male after all. After the revolution, women were demoted, and pushed back into domestic seclusion, a vulnerable population in need of manly protection from the battles and stresses of modernity. In Iran, Egypt, China, Japan, and Turkey, motherhood in the service of self-rule and nation building pushed away the aggravations of modern women's worrisome self-expression and autonomy. It was men, not women, who "were called upon at once to set the political injustices right and to reconstitute their manhood, to salvage national and sexual honor, to save the nation and manhood."[52] Yet women had an important role. They were to be symbols and upholders of the homeland and its traditions.

In the early stages of revolutionary upheaval, competing forces were in play and women's advocates had some room to maneuver. Because improved education could be so readily folded into model maternity, girls' schools were typically the first reforms to overcome the hostility of traditionalists.[53] By the same token, girls' education was a prime target when reactionary forces took power. In 1919, for instance, the modernizing king of Afghanistan, Amanullah, angered tribal rulers when he inserted a tax on polygamy and provisions for girls' education into the constitution he proposed; ten years later, after a trip to Europe and the Soviet Union, he banned the *burqah* and suggested, following Ataturk in Turkey, that women forgo the veil or wear a light covering. Queen Soraya, who traveled with him, adopted the Turkish veil. The king's edicts on women were a major cause of his overthrow by religious conservatives, who demanded after the coup that women and girls who were in school in Europe and Turkey be called home immediately and that all female education inside the country cease.[54]

Amanullah was unusual in his forthright enthusiasm. Male sympathizers were usually ambivalent, sometimes promoting women's demands, sometimes opposing them. In the French mandate in the Middle East after World War I, colonial administrators gave the vote to men and struck a kind of bargain: The French took the upper hand in certain domains in Syria and Lebanon, but they stepped back from family matters, ceding men their governing role in the name of Islamic tradition.[55] Everywhere that nationalists challenged European power, opponents undermined feminist claims by labeling them Western and promoting highly patriarchal family structures as tradition, belying the fact that on the eve of World War I, ideas slipped around the world too easily and transmogrified too often to be divvied up as native and foreign, East and West.

In the Middle East, for instance, there was no simple opposition between Westernizers and traditionalists in the controversy over veiling. Arguments turned on what kind of veil (how much of the body should be covered), religious authority (who was to judge the matter), personal choice and health, and interpretations of Islamic law.[56] In China, the case of footbinding shows how indigenous liberals and radicals took up ideas initially associated with the West and made them their own. Opposition to footbinding originated with Western missionaries in the mid-nineteenth century. Modernizing urban elites, Christian and non-Christian alike, responded and Chinese women added their own interpretations, so that by the early twentieth century, ideas of female equality coexisted with the belief that natural feet were a prerequisite for the efficient housewife whose domestic habits and goodness aided the nation. Anti-footbinding was a hard-and-fast principle of the 1911 revolution: The Nationalist government banned footbinding altogether and mostly ended the practice.[57]

These global changes occurred at a distance, emotional and geographic, from the American suffrage movement. Insofar as the rank and file knew about women outside Europe, it was from the temperance movement and returning missionaries who spoke of the cruelties of exotic patriarchies. Polygamy, child marriage, and backbreaking toil were what they assumed to be the lot of foreign women. When they considered their sisters in faraway lands supposedly so much less advanced, they plumped up an enhanced sense of their own efficacy in the face of a stultified political situation. Leaders returned from IWSA conventions abroad filled with pleasure at the spread of women's rights, but international awareness was filtered through the same worn-out leadership and tired ideas that held it hostage. Still, momentum elsewhere fostered a sense that women's rights had forged a partnership with modernity. The question was how to ride these energy currents to victory.

CHAPTER SIX

MODERN TIMES

Political Revival and
Winning the Vote

THE ADVENT OF the new century marked a sea change in feminism. We are in a new era, when assumptions changed drastically about differences between the sexes, human sexuality, the place of the market and paid labor in the life course, the obligations of marriage, and the legitimacy of male governance. Woman in the Twentieth Century, her rights and wrongs, possessed resources and rights that existed only on the far horizon for the generation born before the Civil War. By 1900, many of the demands broached at Seneca Falls had been tentatively won: college education, access to the professions, eased restrictions in property rights, child custody. And in 1920, American women won the vote, the prize finally gained after seventy years of work.

It happened because the suffrage movement changed. A younger generation churned the political waters, turning a polite, ladylike movement into a confrontational, contentious one. A new cultural style darted through the ranks, mixing the staid ethos of NAWSA with an urbane, resourceful sensibility. These newest of New Women spoke not so much about women's rights but about the human race, labor, democracy, and "feminism," the latter a French word gaining currency in the English lexicon. Indeed, this is the moment when "feminism" replaced the more cumbersome "women's rights" as the designation for emancipation. Feminists saw themselves as world changers, the insouciant young replacing the stolid Victorian matrons who had led women to a dead end.

These New Women turned suffragism into one of the largest and most diverse democratic forces in the country's history, strikingly different from the teetotaling civilizers and small-town uplifters who had until then dominated NAWSA. Socialists, trade unionists, African-Americans, immigrant radicals, and rebellious ladies of leisure joined in coalition with middle-class professionals, college graduates, and housewives. The enthusiasm was contagious, blending a romantic hope for transfigured class and sexual relations with an American faith that the new century would heap liberty and beauty on those loyal to modernity's promise. Liberals and progressives who ten years earlier would have been cool to the suffrage issue rose to the excitement of a different movement.

A string of male pundits proclaimed the value, importance, and necessity of votes for women. Walter Lippmann, a golden young man of liberal journalism and a card-carrying socialist since his Harvard days, wrote in *The New Republic* that a great and welcome change between the sexes was in the works. Lippmann advocated a no-more-nice-girls policy, a brief for the New Women. Change would not come as long as women did what they were supposed to do: "dancing well, dressing well, becoming adept in small talk, marrying an honest man, supervising a servant, and seeing that the baby is clean, healthy and polite"—so long as women were, in a word, nice. "They have to take part in the wider affairs of life."[1] This was what votes for women meant to one of the nation's most astute analysts in 1915: no longer a mildewed moral crusade, but a zestful demand made by emancipated women who were bound to transform not only their own lives but American culture and politics as well.

The newcomers to the suffrage fight were as likely to be gripped by issues of labor, poverty, and class as they were to be engrossed by the woman question. Many saw votes for women as an end to other causes. As the pace of urban reform quickened in the first decades of the century, left-leaning progressives searched for ways outside moral reform and charity to bridge the gap between the haves and the have-nots. Trade unions gained their support, and the Socialist Party attracted some, including idealistic college students and graduates. Urban settlement houses drew middle-class women interested in building a different kind of America, one that treated workers and immigrants as fellow citizens to be respected as well as helped.[2]

These overlapping milieus supported convictions about the rights of labor, the justice of the eight-hour day, the abolition of child labor, and regulation of women's working conditions, as well as the need for public parks and better housing codes. Between individuals and groups, the emphases and priorities differed, but what united them was the belief that the cause of women's emancipation could not be separated from other goals. Theirs was a feminism that was part of a broad democratic push. Until now, feminism in the United States, unlike its British counterpart, had few ties to working-class constituencies. Now they proliferated, to the great benefit of the suffrage movement.

In the public mind, suffragism's representative type was this generation's New Woman. Newspaper and magazine articles, cartoons, and silent films utilized the standard formula of New Womanhood—assertiveness, education, lofty goals, indifference to men, and plain clothing—but added twentieth-century enhancements: athleticism and physical daring, political acumen and diligence, and a penchant for adventure and travel. The New Woman imagery responded to and at the same time helped constitute a feminist avant-garde. Beneficiaries of much-enhanced opportunities for college education and slight openings in professional work and the arts, the self-described New Women of the early twentieth century tended to be college graduates who aspired to professional and vocational standing—lawyers, social workers, journalists, actresses, writers, and editors.

The association with labor was fundamental to this generation's understanding of women's need for productive work. "As human beings we must have work," advised Harriot Stanton Blatch, who came into her own in these years. "We rust out if we have not an opportunity to function on something." The public position was a principled disdain for domesticity. Charlotte Perkins Gilman's *The Home* (1903) turned an acerbic gaze on woman's sphere and found it to be an incubator of selfishness and antisocial sentiment—indeed, a barrier to the development of the human race. "It hinders, by keeping woman a social idiot," and the enterprise of supporting unproductive wives wore men down. Gilman called for cooperative kitchens and child care, to release both sexes from the torpor. Echoing Gilman, the South African–born Olive Schreiner's *Women and Labour* (1911), a sensation in Britain and influential in the United States, maintained that housewives risked turning into parasites. Modern homemakers had no social utility except as childbearers, since manufacturing and technology had taken over traditional domestic manufactures and the schools raised children. To regain usefulness in human progress, they must find work, and it would inevitably be work in men's sphere. Gilman and Schreiner still honored the maternal position. Race progress—an ostensibly universal term detached from racialist meaning—could be furthered by mothers, but only if their circumstances allowed them to act with dignity acquired through education and financial independence.[3]

The positive value given to paid work ran parallel to the labor movement's first serious efforts to organize women in the needle trades. These were years when women poured into the labor force, both in traditional manufacturing jobs and the burgeoning sector of low-level white-collar jobs. Although married women were present in compounding numbers, the prototypical female industrial worker was still young and single—which is to say, ripe for political activity. Middle-class feminists saw workingwomen as sturdy sympathizers, with aspirations for economic independence similar to their own—no longer forlorn and timid, the quintessential victims that Victorian feminists thought them to be. In 1903, the Women's Trade Union League (WTUL) formed, with branches in New York, Boston, and Chicago, dedicated to promoting contacts between middle-class "allies" and female industrial workers. The idea was that allies would support union organizing with social connections, writing skills, and legal aid. In the great garment workers' strike of 1909–10, the legendary "Uprising of the Twenty Thousand" carried on through a bitter New York winter, allies' help—which included walking the picket lines—was crucial. The "working women and the leisure women mix, on the whole, rather naturally," an American suffragist happily allowed to a British colleague.[4]

Workingwomen understood that the vote could put in office mayors, governors, and legislators sympathetic to the eight-hour day, health and safety measures in workplaces, and strike arbitration. In turn, the prospect of workingwomen's votes eased union antagonism. The American Federation of Labor (AFL) made formal gestures of support to suffrage in the early century. The Socialist Party, too, relented; although it did not endorse NAWSA, the party allowed members to create their own suffrage groups.[5]

Wage-earning women were often leery of suffragists, who were not immune to patronizing "girls" they considered simple and timid. "I feel as if I butted in wher[e] I was not wanted," complained Margaret Hinchey, a union representative, about a convention she attended. But there were productive ties, too. The New York feminists, in particular, incorporated working-class leaders such as Elizabeth Gurley Flynn and Dorothy Day. And overall the political convergence pushed suffrage into dialogue with new allies.[6]

Feminism was an approach to sexual equality that was at once political and psychological. *Féminisme* was a French coinage from the 1890s that described a version of women's rights that was avowedly feminine and thus different from the stodgy ideas (as the French saw the matter) of the clunky, mannish British movement. By 1910, "feminism" had taken on subversive connotations and migrated to Britain and the United States as a term analogous to other radicalisms of the day: anarchism, socialism, Zionism.[7]

Feminism was a metropolitan approach: It belonged to young women in London and New York (Paris invented it, then expelled it). The British and Americans competed to be the "storm center" of the movement, one group vying to outdo the other in militance. The British saw themselves as the avant-garde of the most civilized nation of the world, standing at the head of the empire as leaders of world democracy who exemplified the most advanced women's gains. For their part, Americans fancied themselves freed from Old World custom, empowered by their country's youth and revolutionary spirit.[8]

On both sides of the Atlantic, the outward trappings were similar: fashions that scorned Victorian fussiness (no gloves, corsets, or long skirts) and embraced smoking cigarettes, open love affairs before marriage, a college education and/or serious vocation as an artist or professional. Feminism lent a romantic, ingenuous cast to these self-styled daughters steeped in lyrical beliefs about the imminence of a thoroughgoing social revolution led by a vanguard "half-way through the door into tomorrow." The favored image was "a band of capable females, knowing what they want and taking it, asking no leave from anybody, doing things and enjoying life," as Floyd Dell, a bohemian admirer, described a New York City group in 1913.[9] The prized attitude was insouciance toward the world's limitations and rules, a willingness to experiment with what women could and could not do. It was an eloquent politics that could only have been embraced by those who styled themselves daughters, predicated as it was on freewheeling exemption from women's typical family obligations.

Feminism overlapped with suffrage, but it was not coterminous. Feminists assumed that suffrage was necessary, but votes did not really interest them as much as did subjective change. Psychological introspection and self-expression would clear the way for real equality. "We intend simply to be ourselves," avowed Marie Jenney Howe, a New Yorker who organized Heterodoxy, a club for feminists. "Not just our little female selves, but our whole big human selves." Feminists encouraged each other to throw off the constraints of mind and heart—what we would now call sex role socialization. Escaping femininity's decorum and limits of imagination, women would become their big human selves. Largeness was the operative trope, as if standard womanhood was impossibly small: "big spirited, intellectually alert, devoid of the old 'femininity,'" cheered Elizabeth Gurley Flynn, organizer for the Industrial Workers of the World.[10]

Feminism developed from the conviction that a life lived on equal terms with men was within reach. It was not so much a theory of male power as it was of the accidents of male power, and in its benign view of patriarchy, it departed from darker nineteenth-century views of male dominion. The assumption was that men's power over women was atavistic and would dissolve soon enough, given the right circumstances. Feminism would open the way to the reign of the "human sex," only incidentally divided into male and female. Feminists intended to live in a world where the sexes mingled (no more domestic sphere), consorting with male friends, lovers, and husbands as fellows in a world-building enterprise.[11]

The brothers would welcome them and do what they could to help emancipation along. It was a way to make a place beside men who were already established as artists, political leaders, writers, and cultural spokesmen.

Feminism thus eschewed the quiet realpolitik of the older women's movement, the Victorian assumption that a gulf divided most men from most women, that in education, work, interests, temperament, experience, and sexual desire, the sexes had little in common. The view was sanguine, not to mention wildly naïve, oblivious to the hard realities of motherhood, marriage, and male power. The twentieth century was expected to bring, if not utopia, then still something grand and shining between men and women. No dreary message about immovable laws and customs; here was a feminism that promised to propel women into a dazzling future with enthusiastic men at their side.

Crystal Eastman, a lawyer and something of a celebrity in bohemian New York, summed up the ethos. The modern woman "wants money of her own. She wants work of her own." But not just any work: fulfilling work. "Some means of self-expression, perhaps. Some way of satisfying her personal ambitions." Her aspirations did not stop there, though. She wanted a husband, home, and children, too. "How to reconcile those two desires in real life, that is the question." Feminism offered a double hope: meaningful work in the world and a rich intimacy with men. It was the marriage plot with a modern twist: Women's destiny was to live happily ever after, but in an equal partnership with a man. Eastman's question—"how to reconcile those two desires"—was intensely individualistic and self-referential and at the same time keenly aware of the needs of all women. Could freedom, full political and civil rights, the vote, education—all these goals of the nineteenth century—really lead to the realization of the two goals, and not one or the other? "How to reconcile those two desires in real life"?

The question, first broached in the 1910s, would be fundamental to twentieth-century feminism. It proved to be not quite answerable.[12]

The fascination with psychological development brings to mind Margaret Fuller's Romantic celebration of a transformed subjectivity and concord with men. Yet the historical antecedents were forgotten. The women knew about suffrage, but no feminist in 1912 would likely have known that others before her had connected democracy, socialism, the enlarged soul, and emancipation. Absent a history of women, these modernists could only believe that they worked with a clean slate.

Any twentieth-century political movement was liable to amnesia—modernity by definition instructs its protagonists that the past has little to offer—but feminists have been peculiarly liable to seeing their own generation's ventures as unique. The result is that thoughts and proposals have to be generated anew, mistakes are repeated, and few arguments are resolved. Although there is a complex, instructive feminist past, it has seldom been available to guide the present. This was going to be the case, too, with the valiant efforts of the 1910s to remake the human sex: soon abandoned, soon forgotten.

The feminist esprit worked its way into the suffrage movement. With the Southern strategy faltering in NAWSA and the old guard dying off, a space opened and women from progressive reform and the political left moved in. Young workers did an end run around the genteel tactics of the parlor to introduce a boisterous politics of the streets and flashy techniques of showmanship. The love of breaking rules, of making a spectacle of oneself, produced a repertoire of ways to stage feminism to the public.

Suffragists had always conducted their affairs inside, except for the New Departure challenges in 1872; the censure of the so-called public woman who exposed herself to strangers put street demonstrations and public gatherings off-limits. Now, for the first time, suffragists moved outside to express their views. Today, when women in many parts of the world march and take to the streets, it's difficult to grasp how daring was the act. When Harriot Stanton Blatch organized the first American suffrage parade in New York in 1910, her critics claimed it would set the cause back fifty years.[13]

In England, the WSPU pushed the entire question of suffragist propriety some degrees to the left. Thus the NUWSS could exploit its moderate reputation to hold an unprecedented march in London in 1907, although, as the suffragist Ray Strachey observed, "the vast majority of women still felt that there was something very dreadful in walking in procession through the streets" and believed they were risking public shame. But if they were exposing themselves, at least they weren't screaming at MPs as the Pankhursts were, and the march of some three thousand women set a precedent. In New York, Harriot Stanton Blatch orchestrated the 1912 parade as a pageant. Twenty thousand women marched before the eyes of an estimated half million watchers. Dressed in white and walking in step, they held their heads high, a tableau of noble mothers and valiant wage earners, spiced with a dash of stylishness and a strong dose of youthful good looks.[14]

Even so, marchers endured taunts from onlookers given to casual hatred of the kind a poison-pen writer expressed in a letter to Blatch's New York headquarters: "I don't wish you any bad luck, but I hope the sidewalk falls through and you all go to Hell." On the respectable end, contempt came from the likes of a prominent New York anti who judged the marchers morally bankrupt: "Your methods are utterly abhorrent to me at all times, but now, after the superb unselfishness and heroism of the men of the *Titanic,* your march is untimely and pathetically unwise." This was Annie Nathan Meyer, who was also the moving force behind the founding of Barnard College. Meyer believed in women's progress but thought that seeking the vote amounted to unseemly resentment of men. What the sinking of the *Titanic* had to do with voting rights, or why the men on the boat were more courageous than the women, did not need to be specified. Well-behaved women should always take the backseat.[15]

Regardless of the hostility, the parades were a hit. In New York, the resemblance of the marches to Broadway musicals brought to mind pretty chorus girls more than Amazonian viragoes. "A year ago 3,000 marchers and perhaps 70,000 onlookers. This year 20,000 marchers and 500,000 watching," reported a New York newspaper with something close to admiration. Marching in the company of thousands was a way to make a statement, not only about one's politics but one's stake in a different way of being female. It used to be the case, explained Gertude Foster Brown, middle-aged but nonetheless a woman of the Newest sort, that daughters learned "that self-distrust and shrinking from publicity were the most admirable of womanly qualities—'womanly modesty' was the phrase that covered it all, and this was thought to be the supremely desirable feminine characteristic." But that was over now; her generation was bringing about "a startling change."[16]

Between 1910 and 1915, suffrage spectacles swept the country, entertaining and enchanting. Suffragists organized automobile, trolley, and train "suffrage specials," put on street dances and outdoor concerts, launched hot-air balloons, staged shows in vaudeville theaters, stated their case on billboards, electric signs, and in store windows, and produced suffrage comedies and plays. The commercial media gave back in kind. Newspapers put up their doings in banner headlines, magazines gave them illustrated features, and the theater and silent film industry turned them into comic material. Top-billed actresses signed on to the cause: divas who were the equivalents of today's Hollywood stars, including the "divine" Sarah Bernhardt. In the cities, troupers climbed up on soapboxes—that platform for coarse politicians and dangerous radicals—to declaim to crowds. All were welcome, and it was a remarkably multigenerational moment, but youth, élan, and good looks were at a premium.[17]

On the West Coast, the innovative tactics contributed to the first big breaks. In Washington state in 1910, California in 1911, and Oregon in 1912, suffrage coalitions broke through the female apathy and opposition that had thwarted the issue for decades. The California campaign was the turning point. An assortment of clubwomen, former Populists, Socialist Party workers, and trade union women won the vote in the fastest-growing state in the nation, putting half a million women's votes into play and doubling the number of female voters nationwide. Suffrage expanded its class base. In Los Angeles, self-professed "women of leisure" gave tea parties for the "crème de la crème" of society. Simultaneously, working-class women, schooled in organizing tactics from union drives, held festive open-air meetings in parks, leading crowds in belting out suffrage songs. In San Francisco, Irish Catholics, Eastern European Jews, and the waitresses' union pitched in. Black women organized a suffrage league in the Bay Area. Socialists joined in Los Angeles. Californians utilized news-grabbing events, kicky stunts, and razzle-dazzle; they passed out doughnuts tagged with Votes for Women slips. There were parades and pageants on the English model, thick with drapery, costumes, banners, and speechifying. Workers traveled the state in automobiles to barnstorm for the referendum, a sensation when cars were rare and women driving them rarer still.[18]

Victories fanned out in the West: Arizona, Kansas, and Oregon in 1912; Alaska Territory in 1913; Montana and Nevada in 1914. Cross-class coalition politics made the difference. Where old-line suffragists casti-gated the horse-trading of elections and promised to purify the atmo-sphere at the polls, new suffragists saw power to be captured; where conservatives sniffed at the vulgar, ignorant male masses, suffragists saw allies; where the old guard drew back from divisive issues that might pull women from the high ground, these New Women spotted opportu-nities to attract followers of other causes. Harriot Stanton Blatch encap-sulated the change: "The old order of suffragist had kept youngsters 'in their place,' had left working women alone, had not 'bothered' with men bent on politics."[19] The new order was different. Those who forced the change were not always young in years (Blatch was forty-six when she returned to the United States and jumped into New York suffrage). But in their political psychology they occupied the position of the daughters.

American militance became a gesture of rebellion, not martyrdom as it had been with the Pankhursts. It was a demonstration of modern woman's determination to hold her ground in a man's world. A rash of silent films made comedy out of the presumption that such brazen women might as well be men. Charlie Chaplin turned his genius to play-ing a brawny suffragist in *A Busy Day* (1914); he brawled with police and walloped a pretty feminine rival who caught the eye of the suffragist's henpecked male companion. But to be the butt of a joke in a Chaplin film was far preferable to being invisible. Suffragists dipped into a popular culture brimming with visual media—silent films, newsreels, magazine and newspaper illustrations, and photographs—and turned spectacular behavior into a prerequisite for modern womanhood.[20]

It was as if they all had decided at once to disobey their mothers' steely injunction, "Don't make a spectacle of yourself." You could defy the rules of ladyhood all by yourself—Elsie Clews Parsons, future anthropologist, made a point of undressing in front of a window—or you could march in a suffrage parade. Or you could stage a spectacle by doing something in front of a crowd that would surely appall your mother. At San Francisco's 1915 Panama-Pacific International Exposition, Hazel Hunkins, a recent Vassar graduate, nervously clambered into an airplane to take a ride and shower the crowd with suffrage flyers—this at a time when few people had seen an airplane, let alone flown in one.

Such adventures in motion generated the publicity that came from risk and self-exposure. A cross-country automobile trip for suffrage that three women took from the San Francisco exposition to Washington, D.C., broke the rule against unchaperoned travel. The grueling journey along a chain of barely marked wagon roads was the high point of a practice that sent young women bombing around the countryside in automobiles to distribute flyers and make speeches. (In Britain, where distances were smaller and cars fewer, women were known to pedal around the countryside in cycling clubs to deliver the message and to travel in gypsy caravans for trips to out-of-the way villages.)[21]

While the image of the New Woman glowed and glittered in suffrage literature, and admiring onlookers praised the hijinks and valor, the realities were more complex. Despite their self-mythologizing, these New Women were no more exempt from the difficulties of ordinary life than any other women, New or Old. Committed, creative, and often reckless, they idealized modernity even as they lived amid the emotional clutter of history and the ordinary constraints of love and the female body. Careening along the fast track of politics beyond the usual limits, they could still not outrun the retributions of normal life. Inez Milholland, a beautiful and wealthy Vassar graduate and lawyer, ascended to celebrity status in the movement. Radiating devotion to the cause, she led parades clothed in flowing white robes and riding a splendid horse—mounted in a regular saddle, astride, no lady's sidesaddle. The image fused Joan of Arc with neoclassical nobility. But Milholland died tragically in 1916 at age thirty, from untreated pernicious anemia exacerbated by the exhaustion of the suffrage trail. Sara Bard Field exemplifies a more mundane mixture of vulnerability and political commitments. An Oregon divorcée and journalist, Field was obsessed with her long-running affair with a married man; stumping for suffrage in timber camps in the backwoods of Oregon was punishing work, but she won votes and she also found relief there from all-consuming obsession with a lover who promised much but delivered little.[22]

Maud Younger epitomizes the feminist temperament at its most ebullient and least conflicted. She was an unlikely New Woman when she joined the cause. A San Francisco heiress, forty years old and unmarried, she might have been a patron of the arts or a doyenne of better landscaping in public parks. Younger, though, mixed a rich girl's insouciance with serious politics of the first order. Prepared by her upbringing for a society lady's life, she instead took up residence in a New York settlement house in 1901, when she was thirty-one. Convinced that working people could best improve their lives by unionizing, she devoted herself to organizing a waitresses' union when she returned to San Francisco. As she fought city hall politicians who refused to enforce ten-hour-day laws already on the books, she discovered how much votes and elections mattered. Thus she moved easily from her labor commitments to the suffrage campaign. Reform women like her—and there were thousands—gave little credence to politics as a vessel for women's civilizing mission, the assumptions Younger mocked as carrying "the blessings of our civilization" to the downtrodden. Nor were they primarily interested in same-sex unity—either its emotional pleasures or its supposed political power. Younger's most spectacular suffrage feat—driving a six-in-hand team of white horses in a San Francisco parade—demonstrated the élan of a woman for whom men's tasks, even the most daunting technical feats of strength (like driving six horses in harness), were all in a day's work.[23]

Impressed by the renaissance in the West, Carrie Chapman Catt, a moving force in international suffrage for a dozen years, took up a leading role in NAWSA in 1913 and the presidency in 1915. Catt was brisk, single-minded, and practical. She was never a principled exponent of democracy, and with her essentially white middle-class outlook she brought elements of the older class-based movement into modern suffragism. She grasped, though, the lesson of the West Coast example: NAWSA must change its assumptions about who was in the movement and who was out. The white Southerners were definitely out; labor and white men were in (and soon, even black men's votes were in her sights), although African-American women were not. She set out to crack the Northeast, using Tammany Hall–style ward-by-ward organizing in New York and Boston. Eminently pragmatic, she once told a congressional committee that the rationale for voting didn't much matter. She didn't know whether suffrage was a right or a privilege, but "whatever it is, the women want it."[24]

With newly tolerant leadership at the top, cosmopolitan sympathies worked their way into the movement. In America, this meant openness to immigrants, exiles, and expatriates, many allied with the political left. In New York in 1912, a band of Chinese women students joined the New York suffrage parade. They were part of a milieu of Chinese students abroad that reached from Japan to New York. They were excited by the 1911 Revolution at home, where women's newspapers and suffrage sentiments were part of the insurgency. In Nanjing earlier that year, sixty women inspired by the Pankhursts' example had stormed the parliament of the new republic demanding the right to vote and stand for elective office. In New York, the spokeswoman for the marchers spoke glowingly of the connection between activity in the United States and China. A reporter from *The New York Times* noted wryly that it was odd that the United States hadn't given women the vote when China (implicitly so backward, so feudal) had. In New York City, international suffrage made for good publicity: A banner declared that America was "Catching Up with China."[25]

Catt learned to drum up suffrage sentiment among working-class immigrants using college women to canvass. To court men's votes and women's support, workers trudged up and down tenement stairwells and marched into factory yards. Soapbox speakers set up on street corners, sometimes with translators in Yiddish, Italian, and Arabic. On New York's Jewish immigrant Lower East Side during the 1915 state referendum on women's suffrage, the match paid off handsomely. Organizers brought in men's votes by winning over neighborhood women, courting labor sentiment, and appealing to immigrant ideals of democracy. Gertrude Brown, who worked there, found suffrage to be an exciting topic for everyone. A good time was had by all:.

> The East Side loved the night parades, with music, and great balls of yellow light bearing suffrage messages. Mothers . . . with babies on their hips, the green grocer, the delicatessen owner, all came out to watch. Children and dogs swarmed under foot, shrieking with joy at the lights and the bands, and it was all so lively and appealing that even tired housewives and young working girls fell in to help carry the banners.[26]

The work could be monotonous and discouraging—doors slammed in your face, harangues from antagonists. Florence Luscomb, a Bostonian who went out to Iowa, quipped that in one town she found everyone dead but unburied. But the travel was thrilling, the pleasures of the road intense, the comedy of odd encounters and unexpected sympathies exhilarating. There was a hint of elation when respectable women broke the rules of where they could go, what they could do, and how they should act. Suffrage work was fun. Maude Wood Park, a skilled NAWSA speaker, fell in with a traveling circus in rural Ohio and rolled into town behind the elephants, her car swathed in suffrage signs and streamers. Under the big top, she gave a speech, but the dog act in the next ring drowned her out with barking, so the helpful ringmaster had the clowns distribute her leaflets.[27] Spectacle and mobility created a buzz of zany energy, popularized arguments for the vote, and, in victorious state campaigns, built up the ranks of women voters.

Everywhere, men materialized as allies and co-conspirators. As the ideology of women's moral superiority abated, suffragists appealed more easily to working-class men. The need for support softened ingrained views of workers as drunks, wife beaters, and lugs who lacked the refinement and chivalry of middle-class men. Letters back to headquarters during four (unsuccessful) state campaigns in the East for suffrage referenda lingered over heartwarming encounters. "Men are the funny things!" marveled Florence Luscomb about her visit to a rubber boot factory. Luscomb was an architect with an MIT degree, and there was a touch of the upper-class charity lady in her description of "the dear creatures," but regardless, she delighted in the easy tone she established with the men once, in New Woman fashion, she assured them they could smoke in her presence.[28]

Enthusiasm for a common effort with men fostered faith that equality could be willed. By virtue of right feeling and feminist confidence, women could vault into easeful reciprocal relations with the sympathetic men who (in theory) awaited them, in labor and love. "Feminism Will Give—Men More Fun, Women Greater Scope, Children Better Parents, Life More Charm," rhapsodized Edna Kenton in a magazine article on attaining equity on men's terms. Feminism did stress women's unique character—their large souls, their nearly mystical capacity for sexual pleasure. Yet these differences were not seen as dividing women from men, but rather as explosive powers that would rocket them out of the domestic sphere into a cosmopolitan realm where they could do everything that men did. In the land of the human sex, the ancient battle of the sexes would finally end. A "true companionship and oneness" would blossom between the sexes, promised the Russian-born anarchist Emma Goldman, who became a sort of patron saint of revolutionary heterosexuality on the left-wing lecture circuit.[29]

The women-only habits of the older movement appeared stuffy and Victorian, useless for the lives that modern women planned as men's exuberant peers. Most assuredly men could be feminists, too. Some complied, stepping forward as New Men to meet the New Women in the as-yet-fantasized precincts of the human sex. In New York, a Men's League for Women's Suffrage enlisted prominent intellectuals and spawned men's clubs elsewhere. These turned out to be paper organizations, lists of members who turned out once in a while to march in suffrage parades. But feminists took their existence as a sign that women's suffrage was gaining a place in broad democratic debate. The suffrage worker Mary Beard was a partner in a New Woman/New Man marriage to fellow historian and progressive Charles Beard. She later became a pioneer historian of women, but in 1914 she was working for suffrage in New York state. To an inquiry from a political science journal about the tenor of the new politics, she observed that for her and her female colleagues, working with men was a hallmark of their efforts —even if they did do all the work, she joked. Nor were their collaborators only middle and upper class. "The men, in their beneficial societies, labor unions, Catholic and Jewish associations, etc., have all had their part, and it will be difficult to disentangle their activities from ours." All this was as it should be, insisted a female co-worker.[30]

This was nothing new for African-American women, who had always worked for suffrage with men's help. Now they too picked up the pace. In Western states where suffrage triumphed, black women went to the polls. The NACW had a suffrage department; black suffrage clubs sprang up in Tuskegee, Alabama, St. Louis, Memphis, Boston, Charleston, New Orleans, Los Angeles, and San Francisco. In 1913, Ida Wells-Barnett formed one in Chicago that suffered the standard racist rebuffs from NAWSA. Undeterred, the club went on to become a force in Chicago ward politics, helping to elect the first African-American alderman there in 1915 (Illinois women got the vote two years earlier). In 1914, the Baptist Women's Convention, led by Nannie Burroughs, convinced the main body of the Negro Baptist Convention, representing 2.5 million church members, to endorse votes for women.[31]

The National Association for the Advancement of Colored People (NAACP), founded by W.E.B. Du Bois in 1909, put women's suffrage on its agenda. "Votes for women, means votes for black women," Du Bois's journal *The Crisis* reminded readers in 1912. *The Crisis* gave extensive coverage to the issue, noting repeatedly the strength of support among black men. Mary Church Terrell used *The Crisis* to urge black men to join in: "For an intelligent colored man to oppose woman suffrage is the most preposterous and ridiculous thing in the world." Neither Du Bois nor Terrell harbored illusions about white women: "There is not the slightest reason for supposing that white American women under ordinary circumstances are going to be any more intelligent, liberal or humane toward the black, the poor and unfortunate than white men are," Du Bois wrote bluntly. But he reasoned that any expansion of democracy helped blacks, and that over the long run, white women, having known injustice firsthand, were likely to gain sympathy toward blacks where they were disenfranchised. He was unequivocal. "Every argument for negro suffrage is an argument for woman's suffrage; every argument for woman suffrage is an argument for Negro suffrage; both are great movements in democracy."[32]

With African-American men in the North and West casting votes for state measures that had a chance of passing, NAWSA leaders turned on a dime. In 1915, with thousands of black men's votes in play in the New York referendum and black women out in force, white leaders suddenly appealed to a biracial ideal of universal democracy. African-American women spotted hints of encouragement, not in any diminution of white women's prejudice, but in the prospect of the vote itself. Racism did not vanish, but collaboration with Jim Crow no longer set the tone and determined the direction of the movement.[33]

The companionship feminists imagined with men was in part erotic, with roots in the free-love tradition. The acceptance of premarital sex was part of a trend already in evidence in the American middle class (there had long been greater tolerance for nonmarital sexuality among working-class people, white and black). But feminists in the first decades of the century endowed love affairs with so many transformative meanings that they essentially revived free-love beliefs. The penchant for sexual freedom was expressed only elliptically, in florid romantic language, because frank discussion, particularly of female sexuality, remained impossible: Taboos were too strong. Even Emma Goldman and other Eastern European radicals, who inherited from the Russian nihilists a variant of nineteenth-century free love, kept to the high ground of generalities when they discussed sexual matters, assiduously avoiding any discussion of body parts or erotic acts. There were no feminist manifestos for free love in the 1910s, despite the tremendous emphasis feminists put on sex. Rather, the impulse toward sexual emancipation took the form of a call to legalize contraception.

Contraceptive devices, while widely available, could only be acquired on the black market. State laws and the federal Comstock law criminalized the sale and distribution of "obscene" matter—pornography and birth control devices (condoms and pessaries) and information. Poor and working-class women, who had little money for private doctors, had some difficulty getting the pessaries—diaphragm-like cups—that were the most reliable forms of contraception.[34] Beginning in 1912 and continuing up to America's entrance into World War I, feminists on the left agitated for legal contraception, fashioning themselves as champions of working-class men and women. "One of the most important and fundamental things we can do to-day to lighten the burden of women and strengthen the hands of laboring people is to distribute information which will teach them how to limit their families," Ida Rauh Eastman, a Greenwich Village lawyer, proclaimed to a rally in New York's Union Square. Socialists, anarchists, and feminists courted arrest by openly distributing information. Margaret Sanger, then a nurse and member of the Socialist Party, opened a birth control clinic in the poverty-stricken neighborhood of Brownsville, Brooklyn.[35]

Birth control—or family limitation, as Sanger called it—was distinct from the eugenics movement, which was allied with Social Darwinism and dedicated to ensuring that the fittest would multiply while the unfit would demographically dwindle away. It seems illogical, but eugenics advocates opposed contraception, on the grounds that educated white women should be reproducing instead of limiting their pregnancies.[36] In the twentieth century, birth control and eugenics activism would sometimes converge, but there was an inherent tension. Although feminist birth controllers believed that the poor should be able to limit their births, it was not because of population reduction, but because they believed that unwanted pregnancies afflicted women so terribly.

The birth control campaign spluttered out, to be revived by Sanger after World War I as a very different kind of crusade, an elite top-down effort tied to the medical profession. But regardless of the failure, a faint, quavering, and sublimated line of thought had emerged as a central demand for modern women. It was a step toward considering a form of women's self-sovereignty over the body that Stanton and utopian socialists had once called for. What later came to be called reproductive rights took shape in these years, and the legalization of birth control gave substance and a practical aim to the quest for self-realization that was becoming a paramount goal of feminism.

Even as the suffrage drive picked up momentum, tensions troubled relations between older and younger suffragists. The newcomers' enthusiasm for birth control and sexual emancipation, their support for workers and leanings toward socialism, their disinterest in separatism and enthusiasm for men were at best alien, at worst anathema to women formed by the nineteenth-century movement.

Yet in a culture that systematically stripped women of value and esteem as they aged, the mothers' need for respect and gratitude from their political daughters was large. Looking back to those who had prepared the way for them, and now forward, they counted on it being their time to be honored and consulted. They tried to instill in the young a regard for the founding mothers and an understanding of the obligations of generational succession. Middle-aged and elderly dignitaries lectured new arrivals on their "debt to the women who worked so hard for them," to make them understand "that one way to pay that debt is to fight the battle in the quarter of the field in which it is still to be won."[37] The lesson was to abide by the wisdom and direction of their seasoned predecessors.

The problem was that deference to the elders ran against the grain of modernist thought of all varieties, which construed the end of the nineteenth century as a sea change in history and the twentieth century as a time like no other. In feminism, the result was an outbreak of mother disdaining, mother contempt, and mother hating. Heartfelt testimonies to the need to live a life different from that of the mothers—the women this generation knew they never wanted to be—saturate the published and unpublished materials of the times. The "revolt of the daughters," first used in Britain in 1894 as the title of a magazine article, had flowed back and forth across the Atlantic as a literary trope for two decades and entered Anglo-American culture as a cultural truism. Now feminism made it a condition of political sophistication.

The escape from decorous womanhood took on a matrophobic edge. Young women wanted feminism to spring them loose from the encumbrances of the pure, morally superior, self-sacrificing nineteenth-century "angel in the house," as Virginia Woolf, who was young herself in these years, later encapsulated the idea, her tenderness mingled with something akin to scorn and something else not unlike fear. "She was so constituted that she never had a mind or a wish of her own, but preferred to sympathize always with the minds and wishes of others." Woolf wrote about her own beloved and long-suffering mother, but also about the pall an entire generation of self-denying and soul-stifling late Victorian women cast over their daughters. "It was she who bothered me and wasted my time and so tormented me that at last I killed her," announced Woolf of the metaphorical struggle of a younger self. Hostility toward fathers expressed itself in general criticisms of patriarchy, but feelings about mothers were personal and cutting. "Am I the Christian gentlewoman my mother slaved to make me?" bragged Genevieve Taggard, a poet and renegade from a missionary family. "No indeed."[38]

Feminism meant headlong flight from your mother's life. Older suffragists' appeal to tradition and obligation had little purchase among young women who saw themselves as inhabiting a century that could be lived only on its unique terms. Moreover, with such a pitiable record of success to show for the old guard's long struggle, it was unclear exactly what they had to teach. In the American movement, the older generation came up against unruly daughters who refused to be put in their place.

In the heady aftermath of the Western victories, two Americans who had been in England returned to the United States and joined NAWSA. Alice Paul was a Swarthmore graduate who had followed the well-trodden path from college idealism to settlement house work in London, where she fell in with the WSPU. Lucy Burns was working at Oxford University on a doctorate in history when she, too, joined. Both went the distance with the Pankhursts, to prison and on hunger strikes. Returning to the United States in 1911, they brought with them the WSPU creed of sensational action and (it turned out) going to jail. In Washington, D.C., they volunteered their services to NAWSA. Their special fiefdom was to be congressional work, an aspect of pushing for the federal amendment that lay quiescent. There was not even a NAWSA office in Washington, and the women's suffrage amendment had not made it out of congressional committee since 1896.

It was a propitious moment. In the 1912 presidential election, the Socialist Eugene Debs won a million votes and Theodore Roosevelt, running on the Progressive ticket, split the Republican vote, thereby handing victory to Woodrow Wilson and ending the Republicans' sixteen-year lock on the presidency. Southern Democrats greeted Wilson's win as a coup (Wilson was a Virginian) but the strength of the Socialists and Progressives showed there were left-liberal forces with which he would have to contend. With Republican hegemony gone, there were party rivalries to be exploited, but suffragists were so untutored in Washington politics that no one initially grasped that fact.

The gap in NAWSA leadership in the capital allowed Paul and Burns, two outsiders, to take over operations and in a short time wield inordinate influence. With a devotion so total it bordered on maniacal, they set about inserting women's suffrage into the excitement around the new administration, organizing a suffrage parade for the day preceding Wilson's inauguration. Five thousand marched, many in the requisite white dresses, including a contingent of African-Americans—a striking presence in a segregated Southern city. When the black women informed the organizers they were coming, they were told to march in the rear, but after protests poured in, NAWSA gave them a spot in the regular order. The parade was a huge success.[39]

Burns and Paul were shrewd enough to see the benefits of trolling the backwaters of Washington politics. They gathered around them a group of Washington insiders: political wives and daughters and female bureaucrats (women could not vote, but they could work in government). In less than two years they had enough strength to break out on their own, having offended Catt and NAWSA stalwarts with their brashness. "We have been having a pretty hard time with a lot of young women here who got their training under Mrs Pankhurst," Anna Howard Shaw confided to her Dutch friend Aletta Jacobs. Clashing generational styles, Old Guard versus Young Turks, militants versus moderates, mothers offended by heedless daughters: All these resentments converged. "They are all old members in this convention," wrote Margaret Hinchey to WTUL organizer Leonora O'Reilly of her appearance before NAWSA. "All the young people is gone over to the Congressial [Congressional] Union." From the NAWSA viewpoint, Shaw assessed the damage:

> I think by their unwisdom they have put us back ten years in Congress. It is pretty hard to work for years and years to bring the cause up to a point where it has some chance of going through and then have a lot of young things who never did any thing to build up the cause, attempt to run things their way being responsible to any one.[40]

In 1914, seven state referenda were in play and the Congressional Union for Woman Suffrage (CU)—the breakaway group Burns and Paul founded—pulled in volunteers, many with the means and willingness to travel. Women with a penchant for unconventional behavior attached themselves to the CU: Greenwich Village bohemians, for example, were a sizable contingent. Feminists with ties to labor tended to gravitate toward Paul's faction because the CU was interested in issues of equal pay for equal work, while NAWSA was indifferent. But beyond this core type, CU membership was as varied as the larger movement. Among those arrested in Washington in 1917 when the CU picketed the White House were matrons and grandmothers from old WASP families, rebellious heiresses, government workers, politicians' wives, immigrant factory workers, a golf champion, teachers, nurses, artists, college students, journalists, and university professors. At least one historic presence graced the picket line: Olympia Brown, frail, petite, and in her eighties, was a Universalist minister who had traveled with Stanton and Anthony in the Kansas campaign and worked with Stanton on *The Woman's Bible*.[41]

In those states in play, ordinary workers moved between the CU and NAWSA, oblivious to acrimony in the inner circles. After the burst of victories in 1910–12, wins did not come easily. Blocked by antis, liquor interests, and manufacturers fearful that women voters would strengthen labor laws, more than two thirds of the referenda went down to defeat.[42]

The dynamics of a federal political system, where state successes gave leverage at the national level, drove an upsurge. By 1916 there were some four million women's votes in play.[43] This meant that in Congress, supporting suffrage was no longer an automatic liability. The CU renamed itself the National Woman's Party (NWP) to signal an alliance of women voters. Congressmen and senators from the suffrage states recognized the importance of the new voters at a moment when margins of electoral victories were thin. Congressional support for the federal amendment rose incrementally with each state added to the column.

President Wilson was on record as disliking "unsexed, masculine females." But personal predilections were one matter, political calculations another. In 1915, he stated his personal support for the issue, but refused to put political muscle behind it. He was caught in his own party between two antisuffrage blocs: Southern Democrats and the urban political machines, whose opposition came from city Democrats' convictions that voting women equaled Republican women and temperance-favoring, antisaloon women. But once workingwomen got involved and the association between suffrage and middle-class prudishness dissipated, the urban machines did an about-face in the 1916 election and either endorsed suffrage or espoused neutrality. Wilson was freed up to maneuver around the diehard Southern Democrats.[44]

Success in a few states, however, would not have amounted to much had not suffragists been such quick studies in pressure politics. Both the

NWP and NAWSA set up full-time lobbying offices. They sacked the old methods of polite feminine persuasion and prowled the halls of Congress calling politicians to account. They kept meticulous notes on voting records, tracked the machinations of committee hearings, and lurked outside chambers and offices to buttonhole congressmen. "For three years every politician in Washington has been followed by a relentless feminine shadow," chuckled a writer in a women's magazine. Politicians' wives and daughters and Washington socialites wooed leading men. "Not only did we know each man's mind minutely from day to day, but we had their constituents on guard at home," boasted Maud Younger, who came to Washington to work for the NWP. They abided by feminine good manners. NAWSA instructed workers to avoid nagging or anger, and warned them not to stay too long. Nonetheless, they were relentless and politicians paid attention. "I'm with you; I'm for it; I'm going to vote for it," expostulated New York congressman Fiorello La Guardia when cornered. "Now don't bother me!"[45]

Wilson's 1916 reelection campaign was hard fought and close. The NWP made the gamble to oppose Democrats, every Democrat, even those who supported the cause—copying the WSPU tactic of holding the party in power responsible for the absence of suffrage. But intensifying debate over American intervention in World War I pushed women's suffrage to the margins of public attention. The strategy flopped. In fact, women voters were critical to Wilson's victory.

Something was needed to push the issue onto the front page. The NWP's mastery of the arts of spectacle led leaders to the insight—apparently no one else had ever had it—that they could use the sidewalk in front of the White House as a stage for protest. In January 1917, demonstrators gathered outside the iron fence on Pennsylvania Avenue. The well-dressed platoon stood as silent witnesses to the president's inaction. They came every day, a shifting collection of Washington stalwarts and pilgrims from out of town.

At first the demonstration was decorous. The women remained silent, hoisting signs with versions of their standard rhetorical question:

MR. PRESIDENT! HOW LONG MUST WOMEN WAIT FOR LIBERTY?

The president nodded cordially, a gentleman to the ladies, when he passed in his limousine; and one cold day he invited them to tea (they declined). The crowds were generally friendly and treated the pickets as a curiosity. But once the United States entered the war, the mood darkened. The NWP resolved to continue their campaign regardless. In June 1917, when envoys from the Kerensky government in Russia paid a call on Wilson, demonstrators unfurled a wordy banner denouncing the president and Secretary of State Elihu Root and urging the Russians to forgo an alliance with the United States.

PRESIDENT WILSON AND ENVOY ROOT ARE DECEIVING RUSSIA.

The episode had no effect on diplomatic negotiations, but it ended the president's willingness to tolerate them on his doorstep. Already engaged in stamping out antiwar dissent on the left, he apparently gave the go-ahead to shut down the demonstration. The D.C. police descended to throw picketers into paddy wagons and haul them off to jail. The next day, more women took the places of those arrested, and the police returned, and thus began a drama that lasted five months: picketers, police, arrests, paddy wagons, prisoners, leading to more picketers, police, arrests, etc.[46]

Thrown into the D.C. workhouse, the demonstrators—some two hundred were eventually arrested—endured abominable conditions (disgusting food, humiliating uniforms, manhandling by guards) that were the accustomed lot of the black women who were the usual residents. The prisoners ranged from factory workers to heiresses. Eva Weaver, a Connecticut munitions worker, was arrested along with her mother; Rose Gratz Fishstein, a Russian-born union organizer, went to jail with her sister-in-law; Caroline Spencer was a physician from Colorado Springs; the fabulously wealthy Louisine Havemeyer of New York City owned one of the finest art collections in the country; Kate Boeckh was an airplane pilot. Guards threw Dora Lewis, a fifty-five-year-old grandmother from Philadelphia's patrician Main Line, onto the floor of her cell so brutally that she was knocked unconscious and feared dead. Alice Paul went missing because authorities locked her up in the psychopathic ward of the D.C. jail.[47] The country was accustomed to police attacks on workingmen, but civil disobedience was as yet an unknown tactic and police abuse of middle-class white women was unheard of. Authorities further insulted them by breaking segregation policy to put them in cells with common criminals, that is, poor African-American women whose proximity was seen by authorities and white suffragists alike as degrading.

Throwing political prisoners in cells with ordinary felons—in a women's prison this usually meant prostitutes—was a tactic that dated back to the nineteenth century (and is still used around the world today). D.C. authorities added forced contact across the color line to their repertoire of punishments. "Not that we shrank from these women on account of their color," Doris Stevens, who was one of those arrested, wrote disingenuously. "But how terrible to know that an institution had gone out of its way to bring these prisoners from their own wing to the white wing in an attempt to humiliate us."[48] Two dozen women went on a hunger strike, emulating the Pankhursts. Even with war mobilization going on, the press was magnetized; coverage was divided between sympathetic treatments and the conviction that the prisoners were getting what they deserved.

The split between good girls and bad girls, responsible mothers and incorrigible daughters gave Wilson and Congress political cover. Carrie Catt presented herself as the reasonable older woman and became Wilson's de facto working partner, a new friend who deplored the insult the picketers threatened. The picketers aggravated her no end: She found their tactics extreme, counterproductive, and selfish. Catt was hardly a principled opponent of racism, but in Du Bois's *Crisis*, she denounced their outrage at being incarcerated with blacks. Privately, she complained bitterly to Aletta Jacobs that she was sick of the militants:

> Here am I working nights and days giving up my home and the beautiful country and living in one room in this hot city . . . taking no vacation and no rest and what I am doing hundreds of other women are doing for the government and yet all that counts for nothing as compared to a hysterical young girl or a fanatical woman waving a banner at the gate of the White House.[49]

But in the end, she benefited from the spectacle of the militants being carted off in paddy wagons. Their out-of-bounds behavior made it all the more apparent to the Wilson administration that Catt and NAWSA could be counted on to play ball. The despised radicals and their monopoly on the nation's attention actually put NAWSA in a position to exert pressure on Wilson and the Democratic Party. In Catt's memoir, she sails regally past the subject of picketers and hunger strikers without mentioning it, as though they had been no more to her than a bunch of unruly girls. In retrospect, though, it seems that she needed them and they needed her. The Nineteenth Amendment's passage finally came

about because of an unacknowledged common front, a mutual dependence between old and young, mothers and daughters, women's rights
practicality and feminist rebellion.

NAWSA members, who ostentatiously set aside their campaign to
devote themselves to the war effort, provided a useful symbol of national
will and self-sacrifice. Carrie Chapman Catt made a point of making
war readiness NAWSA's policy, repudiating the pacifist suffragists'
arguments—including those of Montana congresswoman Jeannette
Rankin, the first woman in Congress, who voted against the war resolution. In Britain, the Pankhursts threw themselves into the war effort and
thereby turned themselves from hysterical hunger strikers into mothers
and sisters who embodied female sacrifice for the nation and the men at
the front.[50] NAWSA benefited from a similar reversal of public opinion,
although given the United States' late entrance into the war and much
lighter burden of sacrifice, the change was less pronounced. Helen
Hamilton Gardener was a suffrage stalwart, a freethinker and popular
novelist whose involvement went back to *The Woman's Bible*. Now married to a well-to-do former army officer in Washington, Gardener was
President Wilson's friend and neighbor. She urged on him NAWSA's
argument for "real civilization based on a real democracy" that included
women. He was now a leader, perhaps *the* leader of the civilized world,
she reminded him. He needed to make the world and the country feel
"the keen edge of [his] disapproval of the present humiliating status of
American women."[51]

In 1918, Wilson went to Congress with an emphatic request in his
State of the Union speech to reward the women who, by throwing their
support and good offices behind the war, had shown themselves to be citizens worthy of recognition. "What shall we say of the women . . . their
aptitude at tasks to which they had never before set their hands; their
utter self-sacrifice. . . . The least tribute we can pay them is to make
them the equals of men in political rights as they have proved themselves their equals in every field of practical work they have entered."
He called in chips and twisted arms, continuing as the months wore on,
even from the Versailles peace table.[52]

Despite the president's support, the prospects were dim. A coalition
of strange bedfellows stood firm in opposition: Southern Democrats,
blue-blooded New England antis, and probusiness politicians.[53] When
the Nineteenth Amendment finally got to the floor of Congress, it

squeaked through the House by exactly the requisite two-thirds majority. In the Senate, it stalled for a year and a half, despite Wilson's appearance on the floor to ask for support. It finally passed the Senate late in 1919.

The insuperable obstacle was the South. So many campaigns for ratification were defeated there that it came down to a special session of the Tennessee legislature at the very last minute (before the ratification period expired). In a stifling chamber in August 1920, packed with suffragists and antis who flooded the town to line up votes, the Nineteenth Amendment passed by a two-vote majority.[54]

The Nineteenth Amendment was one of many suffrage measures around the world after the war, settlements that made women's votes a benchmark of enlightened liberalism and an ingredient of Wilsonian nationalism. In the twenty-four months after the Armistice, all belligerents except France, Italy, and Turkey gave votes to women: the United States, Britain (including Ireland, Wales, and Scotland), Germany, Austria, and the new Soviet government. The neutrals and occupied countries also made suffrage, or partial suffrage, part of the peace: Belgium, the Netherlands, Luxembourg, and Sweden. Czechoslovakia, Hungary, and Poland, former Hapsburg domains, incorporated female suffrage at their founding moments. The British colonies of Canada, East Africa, and Rhodesia followed the imperial example.[55] Enfranchised women entered their respective polities as sealants of national unity, gesturing to an identity that transcended ethnic and religious divisions.

As Europe staggered out of the catastrophe and regrouped for peace, much seemed open. "With continental regimes crumbling and politicians eying the new and untested 'women's vote' anxiously, even utopian schemes appeared possible," writes Susan Pedersen about Britain in the months after the war ended. The IWSA, decimated by the division between members on either side of the war, got a second wind and an infusion of members from previously unrepresented countries. At the 1920 conference in Geneva, delegates came from India, Turkey, Japan, Uruguay, Greece, the Baltics, Spain, and Ukraine. News arrived from hardy groups in Cuba, Brazil, Argentina, Mexico, Peru, and Iraq.[56]

International feminists hoped, too, that vigorous female citizens would join together as a force in international diplomacy, a women's lobby across borders that would stand as a guarantee against another war. The mothers of different nations eyed one another as upholders of the peace, partners in a great postwar reconstruction that would include pensions for mothers, publicly funded kindergartens, health clinics for women and children, and the means of family limitation. The newest of New Women looked across borders and spied partners in rebellion: fellow transgressors and convention defiers, workingwomen, birth control users, ultramodern sophisticates, and lovers of men on equal terms (and lovers of women—cosmopolitan lesbian circles glittered just under the surface of fashionable society in New York, Paris, London, and Berlin).

The triumph seemed unequivocal. For Americans, it was the single greatest act of mass enfranchisement in their history. For a fleeting moment, the habit of extravagant universalizing about the unity of women seemed based in historical fact.

Historical judgments, though, have been more skeptical. Later feminists like to point out the hollowness of a triumph that sent women into a male-dominated political system, only to stand on the sidelines for half a century. Was the vote worth the monumental struggle? Wouldn't it have come automatically, sooner or later? Critics note, correctly, that suffragists were blind to the reality that Jim Crow restrictions immediately separated white women from the African-Americans who campaigned with them for thirty years.[57]

But such criticisms fail to comprehend the immensity of the accomplishment, the limitations that suffragists overcame, and the possibilities the Nineteenth Amendment opened up. Indeed, the reason we can find fault now is because of what they did then; their achievement gives us the vantage point from which to criticize their undeniable shortcomings.

Suffrage dealt a huge blow to the disenfranchisers by removing the most comprehensive reason for exclusion since the republic's founding: sex. The fact was not lost on them. Defenders of the Southern way of life knew that women's suffrage represented a grave threat. "Pitchfork" Ben Tillman, Senate demagogue nonpareil from South Carolina, warned that toying with the woman question threw a wrench into white supremacy: "Experience has taught us that Negro women are much more aggressive in asserting the 'rights of the race' than the Negro men are." In Nashville, the fight galvanized aging champions of NAWSA's Southern strategy, who rallied once more—this time bitterly—to oppose suffrage and the democratic forces behind it. Kate Gordon rued the likelihood that votes for women would have the effect of dampening the violence necessary to withhold African-American political rights. White men wouldn't beat and maim black women as casually as they did men, she worried: "While white men would be willing to club negro men away from the polls, they would not use the club upon black women."[58]

One group jumped on the chance to close the gap between promise and reality. African-American women saw the gain the Nineteenth Amendment represented even as they knew the limits. Across the South, "colored women's vote leagues" formed. In November 1920, three months after ratification, knots of women went together to the polls. As they expected, white registrars turned them away. Some took the next step, lodging complaints with the NAACP, local officials, and Wilson himself, in letters protesting the violation of their rights under the Nineteenth Amendment.[59] Thus began another battle for the vote. Forty years later, these women and their daughters and granddaughters, still voteless, would form the rank and file of a civil rights movement that again took up the cause of universal democracy.

CHAPTER SEVEN

DEMOCRATIC HOMEMAKING AND ITS DISCONTENTS

Feminism in the Lost Years

WHAT WOULD A POST-SUFFRAGE feminism look like? Believers had long murmured about a woman's vote. In the early 1920s, ex-suffragists hoped that an alliance would come together. The question was, what could be accomplished by the eager, creative, energized citizens who helped push through the Nineteenth Amendment? Which ideas could be brought to fruition? "Men are saying, thank goodness that everlasting women's fight is over," Crystal Eastman noticed. "Women are saying, 'Now at last we can begin.'"[1]

But begin what? And where? Whatever agreement feminists had about goals dissipated after 1920. The irony was that the women's movement would never recoup the broad unity it had in the run-up to the Nineteenth Amendment. Enfranchised women now had to affiliate on the basis of shared ideology, not shared sex. Indeed, from 1920 to 1980, women's voting patterns faded into men's voting patterns. Not until the 1980s did women begin to coalesce into a distinct bloc, when they began to vote against the Republicans and for the Democrats in increasingly large numbers. The gap widened over time, materializing into a full-scale women's vote in 2008—nearly eighty years after the Nineteenth Amendment—when Hillary Rodham Clinton ran against Barack Obama in the Democratic primaries, and white and Hispanic women voted for her over Obama by wide margins.[2]

As a result, feminists found few visible outlets after 1920. In the years after World War I up to the early 1960s, women were active across the political spectrum—as liberal antifascists, socialists, Communists, trade unionists, civil rights activists, New Dealers, pacifists, Democrats, and Republicans. Voluntary organizations proliferated: the League of Women Voters (successor to NAWSA), parent-teacher associations, businesswomen's clubs and college graduates' clubs, civil rights groups, religious societies and mothers' organizations. These were decades of joiners and leaders. But they did not come together under feminist auspices. A young girl born in the 1920s who grew up wanting to change the world could find her principles and associates in many places, but she would not easily locate them in feminism. "Feminism," the word itself, once sleek and sophisticated, was a threadbare remnant of a bygone era, dowdy and vaguely suspect.[3]

Feminism did not die, but the organizational base drastically constricted. For one thing, the National Woman's Party (NWP), led by Alice Paul, appointed itself flag bearer but retracted into a hard core of single-minded devotees, narrowing its program to achieving another amendment to the Constitution that would abolish all legal distinctions of sex. This was the Equal Rights Amendment (ERA), which it introduced to Congress in 1923. Other ex-suffragists fanned out across the spectrum, some moving into international women's work, others into the League of Women Voters, still others into the two political parties. Those associated with progressive and labor causes gravitated to trade unions, local and state agencies for public welfare, and the Women's Bureau of the Department of Labor, established during World War I and directed by Mary Anderson, a former organizer for the Chicago WTUL. Retrospectively called social feminists, these women were active in public policy matters; they plowed their concerns into an agenda devoted to the needs of workingwomen. Social feminists came to play an important part in the 1930s in the New Deal and the trade unions; Frances Perkins, for instance, secretary of labor, came from this background.[4]

Explicit debate about feminist ideas dwindled. Uncoupled from political discourse, preoccupations with women's emancipation gravitated to popular culture. The most visible manifestations of female emancipation were the newest New Women: in the 1920s, the convention-spurning, cigarette-smoking, lipsticked and rouged, jazz-dancing, birth-control-using types known as "modern girls" or flappers. Modern girls also appeared in Britain (Virginia Woolf called the breed "crop-heads" for their bobbed hair), France, Germany, South Africa, India, and

Japan. A 1928 photographic portrait of the Syrian-born Queen Soraya of Afghanistan combines the signatures of the modern girl—bobbed hair, lipstick, and a flapperlike sleeveless chemise—with a regal tiara.[5]

Amnesia took hold, or at least massive forgetfulness. It was as if popular culture became the sanctuary for an abandoned purpose, with the high adventure of the political daughters played out in New Women narratives in film that turned on the premise that entrancing things could happen to daring women outside marriage. The fast-talking dames of the wonderful screwball comedies of the 1930s and '40s—Jean Arthur, Carole Lombard, Rosalind Russell, Myrna Loy, Katharine Hepburn—delighted audiences with the possibilities they proffered for a relationship with their handsome leading men that was both feisty and erotic.

During World War II, Rosie the Riveter was another kind of widely heralded figure of delightful competence, representing the sisters' valiant efforts on the home front to match the striving of their brothers in Europe and the Pacific. But after 1945, the feminist meanings of changed family roles and a briefly restructured labor market would be subdued and then virtually stamped out. Family ideology in the 1950s directed women back to the home, to take their place in the Cold War as homemakers for democracy. A placid, satisfied housewife would tend her darling children, basking in their dependence on an energetic, fully committed male breadwinner.

Away from the United States, though, the political history leading up to the 1950s looks quite different. First, the interwar years saw women's rights activity increase in the context of nationalist movements in India, Indonesia, Vietnam, China, and the Philippines. In the Middle East, the Egyptian Feminist Union, founded in 1923, held the first Pan-Arab Feminist Conference in 1944, which led to the establishment of the Arab Feminist Union. In Latin America, too, women's movements spread, with uneven success in reforming women's civil status and winning suffrage. International organizations were points of vital contact for feminist-minded women's around the world: the WCTU (still influential in Japan in the 1920s), the Young Women's Christian Association, the International Labor Organization, birth control and suffrage associations, and socialist and Communist international convocations. The Inter American Commission on Women gave Latin American women a platform in Washington and a position they used to press for women's inclusion in the founding documents of the United Nations.[6]

In the Soviet Union, women's rights were ensconced in economic

policies and legal codes. After World War II, the line was also implemented in Eastern bloc nations and in China after the Communist
victory there in 1949. Feminism—or more properly, women's rights,
divested of individualist connotations—was thus linked to various unifying projects: pan-Arab, pan-American, nationalist, Communist.

It is perhaps not so surprising, then, that in 1945 General Douglas
MacArthur, Supreme Commander of the Allied Powers (SCAP) in
Japan, should turn to women's rights for his own purposes, including a
section on women's rights as one of the five reforms he instructed the
prime minister to implement in the new constitution. MacArthur was no
feminist, but he saw the utility of women's rights; he envisioned wives
and mothers endowed with the franchise helping to advance a constitutional democracy—not that different from the United States. "Noble
womanhood and the home," he forecast, "which had done so much to
further American stability and progress," would uplift the barbaric
Japanese to a point where they could rejoin the family of nations.[7]

The paradox was that except for the Nineteenth Amendment, the
United States Constitution had nothing to offer. Beate Sirota, twenty-
six and one of two women with SCAP, turned to Germany's 1919
Weimar constitution for ideas. "Men and women are equal as human
beings" was the first sentence she wrote, a plain and powerful statement. Sirota tried to include provisions for social and economic rights,
but her superiors stripped the section down to suffrage and formal rights
in marriage: Women could choose their husbands, divorce, hold property, and inherit. Japanese leaders bridled, labeling the provisions an
imposition of American values, when in fact Japanese feminists—
although SCAP did not consult them—had been calling for these
reforms since the turn of the century. But the habitual association of
women's rights with Western domination, despite the thick history of
non-Western feminist organizing, gained added value in the back-and-
forth of postwar politics.[8]

The association of explicit women's rights with supposedly backward
decolonizing nations, or problematic ones like Japan, or ascetic,
deprived Communist countries was a leitmotif in the American press in
the late 1940s and '50s. When the topic surfaced, it was usually in connection with some foreign land or, alternatively, the United Nations.
Along with Japan, *New York Times* articles covered India, Turkey, Egypt,
Pakistan, Greece, Tunisia, Algeria, Argentina, Iran, and those "reluctant
Mexicans" who were ceding a few rights to women. The interest was

passing and condescending, working to assure Americans that in their own democracy, the need for such activity was moot.[9]

In the United States, the nexus of 1950s beliefs about female nature and family roles that Betty Friedan later called "the feminine mystique" resurrected the Victorian ideology of separate spheres. But 1950s domesticity thrived, too, on modernizing elements: consumerism, sexualized marriage, and civic activism. The idea was that men would work while women stayed home, to shop in stores where, unlike in devastated Europe, the aisles were overflowing. They would tend houses large enough for growing families—again, unlike Europe, where people were struggling to find housing, and they would heap on them the riches of consumer goods. In their spare time, they were to participate in benevolent causes, improving their communities and doing their part for democracy. They were to enliven their marriages with sexuality that drew in equal measure from girlish flirtatiousness and the seductiveness of the femme fatale.

The push back into the home came from above, with policies that forced women out of high-paying, high-skilled wartime jobs by giving preference to returning GIs. But neo-domesticity also came from below, from men's and women's desires for a bountiful private life freed from the demands of sacrifice for the nation. Private life held immense promise to a generation whose lives had been overwhelmed by world calamities, their childhoods shadowed by the Depression, their young adulthoods by war. Neo-domesticity was a cultural scenario peopled by whites, but its effects were more diffuse. Blacks and whites, working- and middle-class people were drawn to making families and remaking private lives. One can see the ideals, for example, floating through *Ebony*, the African-American women's magazine, where standard fare instructed readers on beauty and homemaking and celebrated domestic pluck.[10]

A postwar rise in the birthrate—only brief in Europe—turned into a sustained baby boom in the United States, reversing a 150-year downward trend. By 1957, the average family size of three to four children was 50 percent higher than in 1940; African-American families were at the high end, with an average of four children, and almost a fifth of black women had seven or more children.[11] Since women's duties at home multiplied with more children, full-time motherhood became for middle-class whites a logical way to incorporate the natalist push— although for most black female wage earners, this was not an option.[12]

If we see only a hegemonic neo-Victorian system, however, we miss the unpredictable elements of history. Chief among these was the contradiction between domestic ideology and the number of women, black and white, working outside the home. The image of a smoothly humming domestic apparatus of affection, with mother and children freed from worrying about money by a kindly male provider, disguised the reality that all groups of women continued to work in the paid labor force and did so in increasing numbers. Actually, women never stopped working after the war, they just took lower-paying jobs or, if they were middle class, quit for a while and then went back to work in the late 1950s. The number of female paid workers rose over the decade from 29 percent to a third of the labor force. More women stayed home than went to work, but the picture was changing. The big shift was with married women: Almost a third worked by 1960 and a fifth of all female workers were mothers with young children.[13] For African-Americans, this was nothing new, but for whites, the shift was historic. Among native-born whites and immigrants, daughters had always been the ones to work outside the house.

The beginnings of the transformation of the typical workingwoman into a mother meant that for millions, women's paid work no longer was a transitory stage in life. The trend had enormous implications. Even as neo-domesticity set in, women's double shift—working at a job and working at home—became a burden for white middle-class mothers, not just the unfortunate poor. Yet there were no provisions for them, nor acknowledgment of their needs. Nor was there, except for a few trade unions, recognition of the fact that their work was necessary to their families, not supplementary income or pin money for frivolities.

Overwhelmingly, they worked in jobs that were segmented by sex, although the variety of women's jobs had increased in the service and clerical sectors since the nineteenth century. Classified ads in newspapers specified male or female; employers bluntly informed women they would not earn as much as men doing similar work. Wages were low—60 percent of men's, on average—and women had little hope for advancement. Schoolteachers seldom became principals; waitresses did not become cooks or restaurant managers; secretaries did not move up to be office heads. Those were men's jobs. The reigning ideology tried to reconcile the contradiction between the female ghetto and the American faith in meritocracy by casting women's underpaid work as an emanation of special feminine choices. Teachers weren't in it for the money, but because they loved children; secretaries took pleasure in waiting on their bosses; waitresses enjoyed the sociability of meeting people and serving them; maids liked tidying up for others.[14]

Among workingwomen, though, the optimism and confidence they learned in wartime jobs did not disappear. Over the next fifteen years, as women moved into the service and clerical sectors, they found that white-collar work did not deliver its promised dividend of higher pay and less monotony. But a psychological legacy remained, a sense of self-worth and untested potential that the women who were booted out of high-paying skilled jobs in 1946 passed on to the younger ones who joined them in the labor force over the next fifteen years. One consequence was that for the first time, women joined trade unions in huge numbers. By the late 1950s, eighteen million union members in America included three million women, twice as many as in 1940. While the great majority of women were stuck in nonunion jobs, the surge nonetheless represented an important change. Substantial numbers of African-American female factory workers entered unions for the first time. In sum, women were crowded into a low-wage, feminized sector, but the increase in numbers and the presence of some in the unions opened up possibilities that had been lacking.[15]

In the professions, women were subject to the same downward pressures. Physicians and lawyers ended up pediatricians and estate attorneys; Ph.D.s in mathematics taught math to grade-schoolers. The numbers of women in learned professions—academics, medicine, and the law—declined slightly, the last two from proportions that were minuscule to begin with.[16] African-American women were more likely to become professionals than whites, but they were clustered in lower-paid, lower-status echelons: nursing, secondary school teaching, and social work. The romance of the New Woman professional, once flush with excitement, vanished; professional ambitions were treated as weird, condemning a woman to spinsterhood. The workingwomen on television who left flickering imprints on the collective subconscious were inevitably single and comically lonely: the sardonic Eve Arden, high school teacher on *Our Miss Brooks,* or Ann B. Davis as long-suffering Schultzy, adoring secretary to the debonair photographer and World War II vet in *Love That Bob.* Professional women were objects of intense scrutiny, monitored for possible infractions against femininity—acting like a man—and at the same time prey to derision for acting "just like a woman." On TV they were funny, or in real life they were sad: This was because they were alone. "The career woman is a statistical anomaly," definitively pronounced two sociologists in an essay on modern women's prospects.[17]

It was workingwomen who felt the strains most acutely, the contradictions of a system that placed tremendous value on women's labor in the family yet refused to support mothers with any social services; that encouraged lavish consumer spending yet remained sternly indifferent to families' needs for two earners to maintain culturally sanctioned levels of home ownership and domestic abundance; that consigned determined, talented professionals to menial work despite an ideology of meritocracy. But working women's grievances materialized only as grumbles and self-doubt.

The portrait of the 1950s is familiar: social conservatism, sexual repression, and conformist culture. Feminism's lost years. What few histories have noticed, though, is that underneath the surface, resistance stirred. With little space for women's advancement, a small, loosely associated network of sympathizers gained footholds in labor unions, women's organizations, and crevices in government bureaucracies. In the 1960s, when liberalism again gained force, their work came together and picked up speed. Then, for the first time since 1920, the rights and wrongs of women gained the attention of the public.

Neo-domestic ideology strained to incorporate mental habits bred by a war effort that had depended on women's full support. Unlike World War I, understood as a brother's war, World War II was seen as a mobilization of siblings, an arduous effort that pressed most heavily on men at the front but also called on the courage and labor of women at home. During the war, historian Judith Smith reminds us, "citizens were asked to serve their country, to put aside personal dreams, to risk their lives in the fight for democracy." Men and women encountered one another outside local and family contexts, new opportunities for friendships and sexual liaisons appeared, and "the scattering of families altered standards for male and female heroism."[18] The hardworking young woman—fiancée, recent bride—replaced the anxious mother-at-home as exemplar of domestic courage.

At its most benign, postwar life preserved these ideals in a different domestic script, one that replaced the rule of the fathers with a reciprocal arrangement of peers. Now that the troops were home, men too could embrace family as a life goal and enter marriages that were supposed to be companionships, unions of the long-separated brothers and sisters who had defeated fascism. Playful modern heterosexual chemistry replaced pious Victorian domesticity. A touch of the screwball plot remained in popular fancies, although the heroines seemed muted: Doris Day taking over for Carole Lombard, Lucille Ball, once a comic actress of high standing, playing a dame in *I Love Lucy* who was still fast talking but really dumb.[19]

True, the patriarchal dispositions of returning troops were evident, with veterans, pundits, and planners agreed on the need to reestablish normal male-headed families. Nonetheless, a discourse that valued women's independence and civic participation persisted into the 1950s: threads drawn out from the fabric of the common cause.

What Smith calls "visions of belonging," the "racially and sexually expansive cosmopolitanism" of the war years, dissipated, but the idea of a new bond between the sexes, sealed by a national purpose, remained. As the Cold War intensified, the imperatives of mobilizing against Communism gave the enterprise a different import. Men and women had joint work to do building their lives and households and, on a grand scale, defending democracy. The sexes were separate, but they were also joined in the public sphere, one people working to promote American values around the world.

Heterosexual amity presumptively allowed women to transcend the old grievances of women's rights. The Women's Bureau, for example, planning a conference in 1954, wanted to "avoid the old battle of the sexes idea and pitch a conference around the idea of men and women working together and maintaining the Nation's economy."[20] Women were equal, as African-Americans were equal: separate but equal. The comparison hardly occured to anyone, however, so separate did the situations of the two groups seem. White women could vote, and all women had in theory an array of life choices: the ability to go to college, hold property, practice a profession, and work for money. So the most fortunate and clear-sighted supposedly chose to contribute to civic life by staying home. In light of the dangers that faced the Cold War nation, feminism was a selfish and narrow preoccupation.[21]

This was a postfeminist ideology, an expression of a kind of antifeminism that was reconstructed on the basis of a superficial acceptance of sexual equality. Neo-domesticity did not set itself *against* feminism; it claimed to have *surpassed* feminism by building on what was substantial about women's rights and jettisoning what was silly: That would be the proposition that women could live like men. An awareness of the feminist past lurked in 1950s culture, with allusions to women's rights popping up in social commentary. The fight for suffrage was, after all, within living memory. But these were ghosts that bustling, voting, modern mothers would banish. The Nineteenth Amendment was continually bruited about as the ne plus ultra of modern womanhood, solvent of any residual stains of sexual inequality. "Wasn't the battle for women's rights won long ago?" sarcastically queried a reviewer annoyed by a book that hinted that there might still be problems. "Didn't women have the vote? Didn't they hold jobs in every imaginable human activity?"[22]

The idea that women's rights was passé came out of general agreement about "the end of ideology," a consensus that economic growth and prosperity made social conflict and the doctrines that explained it unnecessary. Feminism was associated with old ideologies, such as Marxism, which had "lost their 'truth' and their power to persuade."[23] The women's rights premise of conflict between the sexes no longer applied. Instead, women were "currently stressing a shoulder-to-shoulder stand with American men in a common enterprise and hope of the future," a summary of the state of American women judged. Like other interest group ideologies—including the class-based politics of the New Deal—feminism was antiquated and "the very fervor of the pioneers has become somewhat ludicrous."[24]

True, not all deliberations were so equable. Harsh, misogynistic views battened on to the worry that women had gotten out of hand during the war and couldn't adjust to normalcy. Women were said to choose homemaking, and undoubtedly many did; but those who tried to choose something else were condemned as selfish and maladjusted. *Ladies' Home Journal* was the flagship magazine of the American housewife, devoted to examining sympathetically her burdens and strengths, yet in 1958 the editorial staff saw fit to publish an article grappling with the question of whether women really deserved the vote after all.[25] Freudian psychologists, whose writings on child rearing, and marital problems were immensely influential, found evidence of a covert "sex war" waged by women who had not given up the worldly enticements of the war years. They were jealous of men's roles and refused to accept their own. Marynia Farnham, a psychiatrist who dabbled in cultural punditry, lambasted American women for their refusal to accept their domestic identity, which led to rivalry with men and low self-esteem.

Farnham made her name with a 1947 book, co-authored with journalist Ferdinand Lundberg, *Modern Woman: The Lost Sex*. The title makes the point. Addled by feminist propaganda, women lusted after men's jobs, competence, and orgasms (true women were supposed to ignore the clitoris) and lost sight of their existential mission, having babies. The jealous spinsters and ungrateful married women of the past bequeathed their penis envy to frigid juvenile-delinquent-producing housewives in the present. Farnham and Lundberg took a long detour through history to prove their case. They disinterred poor Mary Wollstonecraft and dragged her body through the mud. The founding of Vassar College, liberalized divorce laws, and the Nineteenth Amendment came in for baleful scrutiny.[26]

Such severe anxieties, rampant in the immediate postwar years, settled in the 1950s into a more placid discourse of "sex roles," which subdued the overt misogyny. While punitive portrayals of dissatisfied women persisted, popular writing stressed a more respectful acknowledgment of women's value to their families and the nation. Even the sternest evangelists of women's destiny as mothers agreed that domesticity wasn't a natural effusion of female nature but rather the result of labor. Women worked hard, as hard as their husbands, and they liked to see themselves as working with husbands, in "lives of shared responsibilities and fun," a journalist trilled about participants in a meeting staged by a women's magazine where "103 Women Sound Off." The role of wife and mother was ostentatiously roomy and companionable. "When my husband's lumber business was failing, I drove the trucks myself." "For a farmer's wife like me, there is nothing more wonderful than following your husband on another tractor." In turn, husbands pitched in around the house with dish washing, repairs, child care, and guests. Women's magazines gave ample space to housewives' complaints about their ceaseless round of cleaning, cooking, and tending children. Harried-housewives' writing was an insistently merry genre, but it registered the point: This was no life of Riley, sunk in a lotusland of space-age kitchen appliances and soap operas.[27]

To a nation obsessively calculating its assets and liabilities in the Cold War, the value given to women's labor entered calculations about mobilizing human potential against the Soviets. The worth attributed to housewives' work seeped across the line that separated them from workingwomen. Critical commentators scolded workingwomen for materialism—lust for consumer goods was said to drive them to abandon home and children for a paycheck's seductions. Kindlier observers, however, tried to reconcile women's jobs with the national interest. Working outside the home wasn't ideal, but it was still a way for women to fulfill their democratic obligations. In this vein, novelist John

Steinbeck pointed out proudly that while the Russians assumed that American prosperity bred indolent housewives—"overdressed, neurotic, kept women"—in truth, women ran farms, factories, and offices; in fact they helped run the country.[28]

The fight against communism was said to depend on the work of all citizens in their appointed places. The old grounds of opposition to woman's suffrage—that women would sully themselves with a dirty business—were gone. Now, when detractors of women in politics spoke out, they impugned their intelligence about the issues they were voting on. That was the gist of the *Ladies' Home Journal* forum about whether the Nineteenth Amendment was a good idea.[29]

Pundits' and experts' approbation reflected the fact that women of all classes and races took up small politics in the 1950s, continuing their customary roles in voluntary associations, involvements that sometimes led to more engaged action. They swelled the memberships of the League of Women Voters, the National Council of Negro Women (successor to the NACW), the National Federation of Business and Professional Women's Clubs, the American Association of University Women, the Young Women's Christian Association, civic groups, and federations of Protestant, Catholic, and Jewish women. At the lower levels of the Democratic and Republican parties, changes in rules after the Nineteenth Amendment gave women more positions on committees except for the key national nominating committees.[30] A new kind of woman party worker appeared: vivacious, well informed, and eager to shape her party's stand on the issues raised internationally by the Cold War and domestically by the civil rights movement. Phyllis Schlafly was such a person in the Republican Party, a self-described housewife who ran unsuccessfully for Congress in 1952 and went on to a stellar career on the far right; Ann Richards, who later became a beloved figure of the Democratic Party in Texas (and one-term governor), started her career as a teacher helping in liberal Democrats' state campaigns.[31]

One place where women had a toehold in leadership was the labor movement, where a few worked at the top of the auto, electrical, garment, and packinghouse workers' unions. The group included working-class daughters who had climbed up from the shop floor: Addie Wyatt, who started her working life in a Chicago meatpacking plant, took a national position in the union in 1954 as the first black woman (and later served as Martin Luther King, Jr.'s liaison to labor); Dorothy Haener of the United Auto Workers came from a poor Michigan farm and entered the workforce via a World War II bomber plant. Others were from elite backgrounds: Katherine Ellickson, who worked with the AFL-CIO, was a Vassar graduate from a well-to-do Manhattan family. Shared work, their frustrations with the men they worked with, and formal and informal attachments to the Women's Bureau kept them in touch with one another.[32]

The influx of working mothers into the unions in the 1950s pushed leaders to consider an agenda that combined women's needs in their homes with improving conditions on the job. They were instrumental in state and federal campaigns for equal pay and fair labor standards; and in the unions they broached the issue of paid maternity leave and discussed ways to ameliorate the dilemmas of combining family obligations and paid work. Several proposed, for example, a variety of the mother's pensions that had before been considered as help for impoverished women, but they recast the measure as a socially earned wage for domestic labor that benefited all. In the 1950s, they were the sole voices to call for government- and employer-funded child care. They staunchly defended women's dignity and needs as family breadwinners, fighting policies that made female jobs contingent on being young or unmarried. Meeting with some success in the unions, they paved the way for bigger accomplishments in the 1960s: the 1963 Equal Pay Act, the groundbreaking Title VII of the Civil Rights Act, and the 1966 extension of the Fair Labor Standards Act to women's jobs.[33]

Outside the labor movement, there were extensive assemblages of women, but they lacked the ability to put their concerns on any political agenda. Usually heralded as benevolent volunteers, these groups took on civic roles virtually unchallenged, so long as they abided by unspoken rules that roped off leadership for men. In the civil rights movement, for example, African-American women were involved at all levels, but their leadership was scarcely visible. "The movement of the fifties and sixties was carried largely by women," Ella Baker, legendary civil rights leader, flatly stated.[34] Montgomery, Alabama, is a well-known example. The local Women's Political Council, a group of black professionals founded by Jo Ann Gibson Robinson, an English professor at Alabama State College, organized and touched off the bus boycott in 1955 following the arrest of Rosa Parks. When the community rallied, however, the male clergy (including Martin Luther King, Jr.) moved to center stage.[35]

It was a society that valued women's civic involvements but barred them from power. To look squarely at the landscape was to confront frank expressions of male dominance, outcroppings of patriarchy supposedly abolished by post–Nineteenth Amendment modernity.

Thickets of limitations, rooted in the law, job discrimination, goverment policies, men's habits, education, children's dependency, and what people thought was common sense, kept women from the promised luxuriance of full social engagement. The Supreme Court had yet to affirm women's right to sit on juries. In any part of the country, you might never encounter a female veterinarian, police officer, surgeon, or judge. At most colleges you would never have a woman professor. There were housewives who didn't know how to write a check because their husbands believed only men should handle the money. Outside the large industrial unions, a woman usually lost her job when she was pregnant; at the height of the baby boom—when American women were giving birth, on average, to three children—there was no guaranteed right to pregnancy or maternity leave, even unpaid.[36] Neighbor women pounced on evidence that a workingwoman's children were having trouble: a playground fight or a daughter's looseness with boys was grist for the gossip mill.

Yet discussion of women's rightful place in American life never fell away. A *New York Times* writer in 1952 observed that questions about women's roles were perennial: Could women do men's work? Did men hold them back? Was it right that they gave free rein to their highest intellectual ambitions, or should they hunker down to be better wives and mothers?[37] In 1956, *Life* magazine, bellwether of the mainstream, announced that things were going so well for American women that someday the 1950s might be seen as the decade of a "feminist revolution," magically realized without the need for unpleasant conflict.[38]

This all goes toward explaining the surprising success of a new book about women, Simone de Beauvoir's *The Second Sex,* briefly an American bestseller in 1953. The book slipped through the neo-domestic consensus, riding undercurrents of restlessness and reaching readers who were skeptical about fixed ideas about women's place. It was at once the most definitive and exhaustive statement of women's wrongs since Mill's *On the Subjection of Women* and, paradoxically, a book severed from the feminist tradition. Beauvoir took pains to disassociate herself from anyone who had ever protested the very injustice she described. Feminism was a boring subject, she allowed, clearing her throat to begin. "Enough ink has been spilled in the quarrel over feminism." Now the whole controversy was practically over. "After all, is there a problem?" she asked disingenuously.[39]

Glittering with insights, *The Second Sex* laid out two premises that became the intellectual foundation of the feminism that was reborn ten years later. First, womanhood is a social role, not a biological given; and second, women's subordination is not simply a result of institutional forces—the law, education, politics, economics—but a consequence of the male-centeredness of all culture. *The Second Sex* was to play the role in the second half of the twentieth century that Mill's and Wollstonecraft's books played in the nineteenth. But like the *Vindication*, the ripple effects were more important than the initial splash. Published in America when the hunt for Communists was going full swing and domestic conservatism was riding high, the book struck Americans as an exotic thought experiment rather than a provocation for change.

A strange combination of ardor and detachment made Beauvoir just the right author for a time when some were willing to muse about injustice to women but not do anything about it. Trained in philosophy, she was a leading figure of Parisian intellectual society, the close colleague, friend, and onetime lover of Jean-Paul Sartre. She began writing *The Second Sex* in 1948. It was an odd book for a European intellectual to write. If there was ever a time and a place when the woman question was less pressing than other questions, this was it. Europe was a continent of graves. Thirty million dead; six million Jews murdered. Others took the catastrophe itself as their subject, training their powers of mind on understanding the character of fascism, the annihilation of the Jews, the nature of the Communist drive for domination: "rubble texts," a historian has called writings from these gray years, written from the ruins.[40]

Yet reading *The Second Sex*, you would never know it came from a ravaged city. Physically, Paris came through the war intact, its institutions functioning and its buildings not bombed, protected but also poisoned by the Nazi occupation. It took real effort for Beauvoir to pull down the blinds on what had happened and what was happening: French collaboration with the Germans, the destruction of the city's large Jewish community, the mutual recriminations of different factions of the Resistance, and acute food shortages. "The city lay under a black depression," remembered Saul Bellow, who lived there in 1948. "The gloom everywhere was heavy and vile."[41]

Nor would you know that France had finally just granted women the vote, almost the last European nation to do so (Switzerland, 1971, and Lichtenstein, 1984, brought up the rear). French suffrage represented a recognition of women's courageous activity in the Resistance, contributions that disproved the right's insistence that women were incapable of engaging meaningfully in politics and the left's judgment that women were reactionary Catholics who must be kept out. Beauvoir hardly mentioned French suffrage, displacing the subject of women's enfranchisement onto a brief discussion of American suffrage.

But the fact that the intellectuals' attention was elsewhere seems to have freed up something in this exceedingly proper woman. Despite all the trappings of the French avant-garde, Beauvoir was a "dutiful daughter"—a phrase she later used to title her memoir—who had long played to the hilt the role of exceptional woman in a circle of brilliant men. But as scores were being settled and politics reworked between 1946 and 1949, that tight male intellectual authority flagged and she took on an unorthodox subject that really only interested her, not them. It was as if she felt that no one was watching.

The questions she addressed were blunt. How is it that this world belongs to men and always has? And what is a woman, anyway? *The Second Sex* was a voluminous answer. Reading it now, the book seems to swoop through time and space. Beauvoir's commanding persona leaves the impression that she is taking up everything that ever mattered in women's relations to the world, men, and themselves. *The Second Sex* is social criticism in the grand manner, extending her philosophical gifts to survey biology, mythology and religion, literature, and history (medieval to modern), capped by a long section examining the stages of female development from girlhood to maturity.

But the book always circles around to light on one elegant, crystalline explanation of why women are second: the hierarchy men create between Self (male) and Other (female). The world belongs to men because they succeed in inundating the very terms of being, how the sexes view and experience life, with the opposition of male universal to female particular, male Normal to female Abnormal. "She [Woman] is defined and differentiated with reference to man and not he with reference to her; she is the incidental, the inessential as opposed to the essential. He is the Subject, he is the Absolute—she is the Other." She is the second term, the afterthought.[42]

Now, half a century later, feminists confidently propose that the social arrangements that divide human beings in two—men and women—are by no means natural but rather socially created, or constructed. Beauvoir originated this stunning idea but tucked it halfway through the book. "*One is not born, but rather one becomes, a woman*; no biological, psychological or economic fate determines the figure that the human female presents in society" (my emphasis).[43] Magisterially she explained how that "becoming" occurred, beginning in prehistory when men's awe of female fecundity engendered fear. Her range of subjects was extraordinary, from North American Indian potlatch rituals to ancient history, modern novels, and contemporary labor statistics. Leafing through the book now, even doubtful readers will encounter observations that still hold: her bleak description of how housework never ends, for example. "Few tasks are more like the torture of Sisyphus than housework, with its endless repetition: the clean becomes soiled, the soiled is made clean, over and over, day after day. The housewife wears herself out marking time: she makes nothing, simply perpetuates the present."[44]

This is not to say that *The Second Sex* transcends its time and place. The book is time-bound in many ways, not the least in the dour and dire view of its subject. More indictment of Woman than defense, it recapitulated the terms of 1950s misogynist thought even as Beauvoir criticized them. Woman-as-she-exists (the subject is always abstract Woman; Beauvoir seldom refers to actual people) is a sorry sort. Her body defines her, and it is a mess. Hormonal surges convulse her; menstruation disables her; fecundity swamps her; organs turn irritable and inflamed, swell and degenerate. "It escapes her control, it betrays her; it is her most intimate verity, but it is a shameful verity that she keeps hidden."[45] One can scarcely exaggerate how fraught are Beauvoir's descriptions with a language of distress and disgust, taken uncritically from the woman-despising medical profession of the time.

Beyond the bog of biology, the social and psychological facts only sink the sex deeper. Yes, Beauvoir sees women surviving in a world not of their own making, trapped in rigid structures of subordination. But they bear more than a little blame for their plight. Womanhood, that entropic state that drags one down into the debased "Other," is made from without but also from within. The accusations are relentless. Women make themselves vassals of male breadwinners. They are petty, unreasonable, timid, materialistic, "false, theatrical, self-seeking, and so on." They are bad with tools and they believe in astrology. They smile too much. "Man wants woman to be an object; she makes herself object."[46] The female reader can hardly exit the book without resolving with all her heart to be different, to get away from her pitiable sex. The text has no recourse to living women who might sustain a better future, except for the author herself. The only escape route seems to be modeling oneself on her.

Like Wollstonecraft, Beauvoir didn't much like women. True, present-day defenders show that, technically speaking, she did identify herself with the second sex—"If I wish to define myself, I must first of all say: 'I am a woman,'" she announced right off. But the declaration rings hollow, as if she were signing up by mail. The poet Stevie Smith, reviewing the British edition, joked that the book made one wonder how women could have survived their loathsome biology at all, let alone lived to be sometimes "brave, happy, active and occupied."[47]

In France, the book was caught in the crossfire between Communists who pilloried it as petty bourgeois and conservatives who found shocking all the talk about sex. The vitriol made it a succès de scandale, prompting the illustrious New York publishers Alfred and Blanche Knopf to purchase the English translation rights. When Knopf published it in 1953, American readers and critics responded warmly, enthralled by its learning and ambition. It was a "glorious and fantastic book," pronounced Elizabeth Hardwick from her perch as one of the very few women who mattered in the New York intelligentsia.[48] In a climate where feminism was moribund, the book's distance from any sense of political engagement in the here and now made it assimilable. A book that did not much like women, but that meant to defend them—that was a book that could make headway.[49]

The book's moment in the limelight spluttered out, and it dropped out of sight, as had *A Vindication of the Rights of Woman*. But the ideas did not vanish. Copies remained on shelves, repositories of a way of seeing the world that would become wildly relevant ten years later in the United States and a little later in France. *The Second Sex* was a diagnostic tool kit, ready for a time when women came to believe they could not only read but actually do something about always coming in second.

The National Woman's Party was the one organization in the 1950s to declare itself feminist and to press for an explicitly feminist measure—the ERA. Still led by the now-elderly Alice Paul, the NWP was an indefatigable lobbying group devoted to this one great cause. As drafted in 1923, the amendment read: "Equality of rights under the law shall not be denied or abridged by the United States or any state on account of sex." The framers thought it would abolish all sexism in the law at one swoop, and, by extension, all sexism, period. Its lobbyists were familiar habituées of the halls of Congress, with a presence in Washington that far outstripped the organization's actual importance.

Virtually all liberal organizations opposed the ERA. The crux of the conflict was over fair labor standards for women workers—protective legislation, as it was called. From the beginning of the twentieth century, social feminists fought for those very state laws. Arguing on the basis of the state's obligation to protect women's morals and health, they won legislation that required employers to give rest breaks to female employees, prohibited women from heavy lifting, and banned them from tending bar, working at night, and working long hours.[50] However counterproductive and paternalistic (or maternalistic) they may seem today, for nonunion workers, these laws were some of the only fair labor standards in play in the early part of the century. They were the signal achievement of American social feminists, who failed to secure other provisions—government-funded maternal and child health care, mothers' pensions, child care services—that their counterparts in Scandinavia, Britain, and France won in varying combinations (for many different reasons, few of them having to do with feminism). Some state laws were restrictive (bans on night work and maximum hour provisions, which effectively prevented women in union jobs from earning overtime pay). Others were predicated on protecting women's morals and their ability to bear children, laws that meshed with conservative gender norms but did little to improve workplace conditions. But others were beneficial, requiring employers to provide bathroom and lunch breaks, and stipulating safety and quality-of-workplace measures.[51]

The one thing both sides agreed on was that the ERA would abolish these statutes, since protective laws singled out women for special treatment. The NWP thought this was good, because protective laws interfered with women's freedom of contract and exercise of their full capabilities. Why should a workingwoman be barred from a job that required her to lift more than twenty pounds, the NWP demanded scornfully, if she wanted it? Who said she was so delicate? Labor feminists recognized the dilemma but insisted the laws meant protection for a vulnerable class, the only restraints to employers' demands on easily exploitable nonunion workers. "We settled for practical gains that made some difference to women who worked in factories and sweatshops, rather than striving for an ideal that was largely theoretical, given the social and political circumstances," explained Esther Peterson, a leader in the Amalgamated Clothing Workers and then the AFL-CIO.[52]

The standoff was also between different political venues. Officially the Woman's Party was nonpartisan, but by the 1950s, it incorporated a contingent of McCarthyites and segregationists along with garden-variety business Republicans. Its supporters in Congress included Richard Nixon, Barry Goldwater, and Strom Thurmond.[53] The organization refused to support the Fair Labor Standards Act or minimum-wage legislation. Its idea of woman leaned heavily toward the affluent and privileged, and its emphasis on liberty had to do primarily with liberty of contract: women's problems with inheritance and property rights, their difficulties in making their way in business and male-dominated fields.[54]

Insofar as women's issues entered politics in Washington, the standoff blocked any change. Each side had supporters in Congress, but the issue was low on male politicians' agendas (and politicians were almost exclusively male). Thoughtful women facing the problems of work and sex discrimination had to wonder: If the ERA was useless, what would be better? So things stood in Washington in 1960.

The balance shifted that year when John F. Kennedy was elected president. With a Democrat in office indebted to the labor vote, the unions had access to Washington they hadn't had since the New Deal. Kennedy appointed Esther Peterson as assistant secretary of labor, the administration's highest-ranking woman. Peterson, imbued with social feminist aims and union experience, had spent years in Scandinavia and was determined to import to America something of the spirit of experimentation with public resources for women—child care, maternal leave, household support—she saw there. She believed the time had come to put women's needs forward and persuaded the president to form a high-profile President's Commission on the Status of Women (PCSW). The PCSW would come up with a program of reforms that went beyond the "futile agitation about the ERA," she promised.[55]

With backing from the administration, women had a chance to create proposals linked to Kennedy's domestic policy. Peterson was not looking to reawaken a women's movement: She thought feminism was "an antiquated, more-than-slightly ridiculous notion."[56] Rather, she would utilize insider politics—connections to male patrons in the administration, Women's Bureau allies, and like-minded women in government positions. The immensely prestigious Eleanor Roosevelt was the commission's chair until she died late in 1962. Peterson, the vice chair and real administrator, chose the commissioners, some two dozen men and women from elites in government, business, academics, unions, and women's organizations. They included Dorothy Height, president of the

National Council of Negro Women; Mary Bunting, president of Radcliffe College (Harvard's then-sister school); the Princeton economist Richard A. Lester; union leaders; and leaders of Jewish, Catholic, and Protestant women's national organizations. Except for Marguerite Rawalt, a lawyer in a federal civil service position, Peterson kept out anyone associated with the Woman's Party.[57]

For the research committees that would do the real work of amassing information and writing the report, Peterson tapped a network of women in and around Washington. As individuals, they brought their own frustrations and grievances to bear on the problems at hand. A number had begun promising careers in the Roosevelt administration, only to be frozen in place (or frozen out) during the Truman and Eisenhower years.[58] Rawalt had been a lawyer in the Bureau of Internal Revenue since 1933, stalled at mid-level; Catherine East, similiarly blocked in the Civil Service Commission, came onto the commission as executive secretary. The House Un-American Activities Committee had hounded Mary Keyserling and her husband, Leon Keyserling, out of their positions as high-level government economic advisers; Mary was doing nonprofit consulting when Esther Peterson brought her in to join the research group on protective legislation. The next year, President Johnson appointed her to head the Women's Bureau when Mary Anderson retired.[59]

Pauli Murray, the moving force on the committee on the law, was another gifted professional wedged against a glass ceiling, the obstacles compounded in her case by race prejudice. Murray's memory of herself in the years leading up to the PCSW resonated with the stories of all these women: "I was standing on the corner, waiting for a movement to come along."[60] Born into a modest African-American family in North Carolina, Murray had been working since the 1930s in civil rights causes and labor causes, and had been around Washington since she attended law school at Howard University. She was a friend of Eleanor Roosevelt and was admitted to Howard with a recommendation from Thurgood Marshall, then chief counsel for the NAACP (and later an associate Justice of the Supreme Court). But despite her graduation as valedictorian of her class at Howard, an advanced degree from the University of California at Berkeley's Boalt Hall School of Law, and influential connections, Murray was unable to land a job in a law firm for many years. At the one corporate firm where she worked in New York, she was the only black attorney and one of three women. In 1960–61, she went to teach law in Ghana, where Nkrumah's socialist experiment was attracting African-American visitors and expatriates. Soon disillusioned, she returned to the United States; she was looking for a job when Peterson asked her to join the commission. For Pauli Murray, working on women and the law was a chance to turn a suppressed longing into tangible intellectual labor: a "kind of heaven," she remembered, "like throwing Brer Rabbit in the briar patch, because you see it was the first time in my life that I really sat down and researched the status of 'women.'"[61]

The results surprised her. "By the same token, this is where we began to discover all of this horrible sexism in the the law."[62] Starting in on the project at a moment when there was exactly one article she could locate on women and constitutional law, she saw herself as setting out into uncharted territory. And indeed, so meager was feminist history that Murray and her colleagues would have known little or nothing of the vociferous protests about the law's treatment of women that went back to 1848.

You can imagine, though, as if on a scrim, another image flickering behind the PCSW women at a conference table in some federal office building, burrowing into the law books to uncover the colossal matter of women's mistreatment at the hands of the law. That would be the tea table at Seneca Falls where Stanton, the lawyer's daughter, poured out to the others "all I had read of the legal status of women, and the oppression I saw everywhere."[63]

The committees piled up a mountain of data that showed that "horrible sexism" existed across American society. Copious statistics documented the prevalence of discrimination at work and in Social Security benefits, jury service, civil service positions, lack of representation in public office, and child-care burdens. Yet the commission took great care to avoid anything that smacked of feminist complaining. Two years in the making, the report, titled *American Women,* was released in October 1963, as well-mannered and supportive of American society as the female commissioners' appearance in hats and white gloves at the official ceremony of presentation to President Kennedy.[64] In calm, reasoned prose, the volume reiterated the consensual ideology that lay at the heart of postwar domestic hopes. Remedies for women's difficulties—the commission never went so far as to cast them as wrongs or injustices—would enhance the well-being of all.[65]

But the mild tone should not deceive us: Regardless of its prudence,

American Women marked a turning point. It was, after all, the first comprehensive enumeration of women's grievances to enter the discourse of national politics. The goals were twofold: to open opportunities to women in paid work and to bring social recognition and compensation to the work they did at home. A faith in the power of the federal government to identify and resolve problems, inherited from the New Deal, buttressed the willingness to propose big policy changes. The PCSW recommended publicly funded child care for all classes (not just the poor), which both workingwomen and homemakers could utilize; adult education so that women, as they grew older, could adapt to the requirements of a changing labor force; and income guarantees for the pregnant and unemployed.[66] On the legal committee, Murray worked out a lucid proposal to circumvent the entire ERA question by using the Fourteenth Amendment to argue for women's equal protection; the newly liberal, activist tilt of the federal courts and the NAACP's successes in civil rights litigation made this strategy look appealing. Finally, *American Women* suggested that President Kennedy issue an executive order encouraging (but not requiring) equal employment policies from employers taking federal funds.[67]

Despite its avoidance of the merest hint of protest, *American Women* wove demurral from neo-domesticity into the Great Society idiom by gesturing toward a more expansive, productive life for women. In the discussion of homemaking, for example, the report ramped up the consensus about the value of homemakers' labor into a definition of marriage as an economic partnership. Full-time homemakers should not be considered dependents on their husbands but equal contributors to the family's earnings. They deserved a fair share of family property in divorce and, if widowed, the full value of husbands' pensions.[68]

The commissioners' optimism that the spirit and perhaps even the letter of the major reforms they advocated could really come about—an optimism so odd and amazing to encounter now, when liberal hopes are much more constrained—came from confidence in the administration's policy of sustaining and improving upon the New Deal tradition: full employment, a stable working and middle class, and upward mobility through education. They wanted the federal government to provide services that would equip women to be effective citizens at every stage, whether as homemakers or full-time workers. Democracy in women's lives coincided with their freedom to choose—an articulation of the doctrine of personal choice that would later become a mantra of mainstream feminism. "Each woman must arrive at her contemporary expression of purpose," whether as homemaker, artist, thinker, scientist, or public servant.[69]

Respect for women's choices politely evaded the problems that choice entailed: How was a workingwoman to choose her work when she could get no child care; how was a homemaker to choose to stay home if her husband left her? But this early formulation was perhaps not so naïve as it sounds. In the background was an awareness, rooted in social feminism, that government must address women's dual responsibilities as collective, not individual, problems. The report was adamant about "the gross inadequacy of present child care facilities."[70] Yet it did not only focus on wage earners. It also acknowledged that domestic values played a role in life ambitions: Women desired both a secure home *and* a satisfying job.[71] The commission sought state services that would support a multiplicity of life patterns, all strengthened by education, job counseling and retraining, and optional child care. Hovering in the background was Sweden, where women could hire trained, well-paid "mother substitutes" and "homewatchers" from government agencies, augmenting their ability to combine work and family.[72]

Behind the moderate, calm recommendations lay considerable conflict. The minutes of commission meetings show that most present assumed that women preferred to stay at home, "to rear their children, to entertain the husband's boss, to have a nice home and to work in some volunteer committee activity," as Maurine Neuberger, senator from Oregon, put it primly (she seems to have squared all that with taking her husband's Senate seat when he died). Any hint that the recommendations, in easing working women's difficulties, might actually encourage mothers to work set off alarm. Some participants recoiled from any mention of European social welfare arrangements to aid mothers. Wilbur Cohen, an assistant secretary of health, education, and welfare, even repeated the 1950s canard that workingwomen raised juvenile delinquents—though Esther Peterson squashed the remark.[73]

Looking back, the PCSW's good manners seem timid when placed against the flashy confrontational feminism that shortly emerged with NOW's formation and the arrival of radical feminism. The commission held back from recommending direct government action in employment matters and instead urged voluntary compliance from private employers in egalitarian policies. They came nowhere near the sense of the urgent need for state intervention that gripped the civil rights movement. Even Peterson later described the commission apologetically as an exercise in "the art of the possible": "We did not propose to restructure society. Rather, we strove to fit new opportunities into women's lives as they were."[74] "Disappointing," one historian concludes—as if the report was supposed to address the needs of women in the twenty-first century, not in 1963.[75]

Regardless of its caution, though, the commission touched a nerve, simply by highlighting the gap between the much touted value of American women and the actualities of massive indifference to them. The challenge was not lost on the *New York Times* reviewer of *American Women*, Edward Eddy, president of Chatham, a women's college in Pittsburgh. He laid into the commission's "shocking" incapacity to honor women's essentially maternal nature. The PCSW had capitulated to nasty money issues like equal pay, pension equity, and job benefits that presumably subverted women's higher mission to love and nurture. The worst, he fumed, was the suggestion for paid maternity leave, a proposal beyond the pale that would put "the white adult American male in the disadvantaged group."[76] Thus in 1963 did the head of a women's college, historic sanctuary of American women's brains and ambition, fulminate in the nation's leading journal of opinion against the very thought of job equity.

The President's Commission sketched a female population poised for great things: determined, hopeful, and blessed with superior capabilities and plans. They only needed direction and government support to contribute mightily to the national good. Discrimination was a problem, but with proper attention, Americans could overcome old habits. The report emanated the hopefulness of that early autumn, 1963, following the great triumph of the March on Washington in August, a mood blasted within weeks by the assassination of the president.

High-level commissions always produce documents thick with compromises, not manifestos of logic and passionate purity. Peterson pulled together the existing forces for change inside the PCSW and consolidated disagreement into a set of recommendations that quietly challenged quietism. To see only the deficits is to neglect what was forward-looking and meaningful at the time: a high-profile discussion of women's potential, challenges to marital coverture, and a clear statement of the structural limitations to achieving women's equality. How different the country would look now, fifty years later, if those mild, sensible recommendations had come to fruition: publicly funded day care, universal paid maternity leave, equity in job benefits, and counseling for job retraining.

If the commission's *American Women* was the ego of women's politics in 1963, Betty Friedan's *The Feminine Mystique,* published the same year, was the id. The book's muckraking indictment of women's lives and family dysfunction in the suburbs was a sensation. Pitched as an exposé of hidden horrors, *The Feminine Mystique* purported to reveal "the problem that has no name," an epidemic of malaise among masses of housewives imprisoned in the "concentration camps"—Friedan actually used the image—of the suburbs. Friedan portrayed a female population awash in anomie: depressed, drug-addicted, obsessed with sex, besotted with consumer goods. The President's Commission pledged full integration of women into the common cause; Friedan blew open the whole scenario.

The feminine mystique was Friedan's term for neo-domestic ideology, a toxic blend of advertisers' blather, Freudian pronouncements on female nature, magazine pablum, social scientists' hokum theories on well-adjusted sex roles, and the baby boom mandate. Transposing the Cold War fascination with Communist brainwashing onto the psyche of the American housewife, Friedan depicted a mass of women who had fallen into catatonia or hysteria under the totalitarian pressures of neo-domesticity. The book trembled with premonitions of a national decline that originated with homemakers. Women were trapped in their well-stocked homes, isolated from real life, slaves to their appliances and children. Sons, subjected to domineering "mom-ism," turned into homosexuals. Husbands shrank from wives' insatiable sexual needs. It was a veritable holocaust of families: "If we continue to produce millions of young mothers who stop their growth and education short of identity, without a strong core of human values to pass on to their children, we are committing, quite simply, genocide, starting with the mass burial of American women and ending with the progressive dehumanization of their sons and daughters."[77]

Friedan knew her subject intimately. The mother of three and unhappily married (as she later confessed), she was living in the early 1960s in a suburb outside New York. She was not, though, a full-time homemaker. She carried on a busy although not especially lucrative career in New York as a freelance writer, churning out homilies on the gospel of femininity. But she was stranded, and her situation fell far short of her once-high ambitions and serious politics. An active antifascist student at Smith College, Betty Goldstein followed a left-liberal trajectory after graduating in 1942, traveling at the edges of Communist Party circles, working as a reporter for the *United Electrical Workers News* (published by a CIO union where women were gaining prominence), and marrying Carl Friedan, then a theater manager. In 1952, she left her union job to have a family. By the 1960s, she was one among many in the hustling (and sexist) world of New York journalism, looking to cash in with a big nonfiction book, her antennae out for a potentially bestselling subject.[78]

The Feminine Mystique capitalized on the polemical skills and heavy-handed rhetoric Friedan picked up in her earlier life from the Marxist-Leninist line. The central concept of a "mystique" came from the idea that capitalism duped, or mystified, workers with cheap rewards into colluding with their own oppression. The book's caustic account of domestic life drove home its points relentlessly, producing the most devastating portrait of women's sphere a feminist writer had ever offered. Not since Charlotte Perkins Gilman's *The Home* had anyone spoken so baldly of the claustrophobia of domestic life, the tedium of full-time child care, and the housewife's ennui. Even so, Gilman did not go as far as Friedan in her denunciations, partly because she wrote in the early century, when domestic servants did much of the work that Friedan's suburban housewives performed. Friedan slashed away at the sentimentality that encrusted the subject of the home, substituting melodramatic tales of mental illness and social pathology for the fantasies of the postwar agenda. Housewives teetered on the edge of drug addiction, alcoholism, and eating disorders, according to Friedan. Everywhere she spied "the lack of vitality, the deadly sameness of their lives, the furtive between-meal snacks, drinks, tranquilizers, sleeping pills."[79]

Today, *The Feminine Mystique* reads like a period piece, with its drug-addled zombies, sexual vampires, and wily shopaholics acting out the very misogynist assumptions Friedan was denouncing.[80] Friedan ignored the millions of women who were already at work—as if there were no one else living in America but suburban housewives and she, the truth teller. She offered no prospects for change, just a single-minded injunction to housewives to get a job. Women must refuse the seductions of the cushy suburban home and the sexy cocktail hour with their husbands. The solution? Nothing like the policy portfolio of the PCSW. There was one remedy and only one. Women had to go back to work—not just any work, but a "no-nonsense nine-to-five job, with a clear division between professional work and housework" (lest domesticity suck them back). The marching orders ignored patterns of discrimination and the lack of child care that made going to work hard or impossible for many. Hers was a thoroughly middle-class perspective: In one throwaway line, she suggested hiring a "cleaning woman" to do the housework, as if a cleaning woman did not count as an oppressed woman.[81]

What explains the book's instantaneous intellectual authority? For one, the earlier success of *The Second Sex* carved out a niche in postwar culture for champions of women who did not particularly like women, and Friedan was one (Margaret Mead was another). Yet unlike *The Second Sex, The Feminine Mystique* offered no architectonic theory. Nor did it probe the legal and political underpinnings of the gender order, as did Mill's *Subjection of Women*, or inject feminism into political theory, as did Wollstonecraft's *Vindication*. Rather, *The Feminine Mystique* succeeded by claiming to reveal the secrets of a hidden public. Packed with juicy testimonies from anonymous housewife-informants, the book articulated the gathering objections of college-educated women in the 1960s, as they looked to join working-class women in the labor force. By the end of the decade, Friedan's intensely self-referential white, middle-class perspective would limit her appeal. But for the moment the simplistic account got her message across. She offered readers the incitements of an American tradition of self-help through education, hard work, and willpower, a way to ride changes in the labor force already taking place.

The Feminine Mystique was a New York book, not a Washington book; it was geared to popular culture and media exposure, not policy and power. Later, Friedan dismissed the President's Commission as "talk, that's all it was, talk."[82] The habits of political analysis she took from her left-wing past underlay her disdain for government action as window dressing. But *The Feminine Mystique,* coming in the wake of *American Women,* marked out a new vantage point of criticism and dissent. It was a spirited intervention in a particular time and place, America 1963, a flag planted by an outrider on a battlefield where the armies were starting to assemble.

In the aftermath of President Kennedy's assassination in November 1963, national grief flowed into support for his civil rights agenda. Although passage of the Civil Rights Act (CRA) was by no means certain, President Lyndon Johnson made the bill his overriding priority, understanding that it spelled the loss of the white South to the Democratic Party. In the months leading up to the vote, LBJ used his peerless legislative skills to maneuver, putting together a coalition of Northern Democrats and moderate Republicans. Segregationist forces tried every means to stop it.

On the face of the matter, a civil rights bill could easily have included prohibitions against sex discrimination. Activated by the civil rights movement, the old parallel between race and sex discrimination had already popped up again in *American Women*. But Esther Peterson and others on the PCSW, the most likely people in the administration to push the matter, saw black civil rights as more urgent. Thus apparently no one mentioned to LBJ the possibility of including sex in the omnibus bill he sent to Congress in 1964.[83]

The relationship between race and sex soon surfaced, though, deployed and exploited by opponents. The Woman's Party, faced with a civil rights bill that had nothing to do with women, objected to legislation that supposedly gave exclusive advantages to black men. Southern Democrats in the House, failing in their efforts to block the bill, seized upon the sex discrimination issue the Women's Party handed them as a way to discredit the CRA. In debate on the floor of the House, the segregationist Virginia congressman Howard Smith tossed in a rider to the bill—Title VII—that outlawed sex discrimination in employment. His intention was to make the CRA look ridiculous. The point of the rider was that the very idea of discrimination was absurd: People got the jobs that they were suited for; there was nothing unfair about it. Presenting Title VII, Smith inquired of his colleagues with faux naïveté: If the government protected the rights of racial minorities (implicitly unqualified) to get jobs, well, why not protect the rights of spinsters (implicitly unlovable) to get husbands? The joke tickled representatives on both sides of the aisle. Chuckles and guffaws lightened the tense mood. Sexism was nothing if not a unifier of men.[84]

Smith was drawing water at the well of one of the deepest presumptions about women in American life. His joke followed the lines of the quip John Adams made two centuries before, when Abigail asked him to remember the ladies. If women were included in the provisions for full citizenship, why then, why not every servant, pauper, and apprentice boy? Anyone who subscribed to any kind of prejudice, anywhere, anytime, could always cite women's exclusion to buttress their position, because it appeared so natural. If you were going to protect the rights of racial minorities—this is what Smith's joke really came down to—well why not—heh heh—protect the rights of women, too?

But it was a fateful turn in the history of the joke. Martha Griffiths, an ERA supporter and well-respected Michigan Democrat, took the floor and like a veteran schoolteacher calling unruly boys to order put a stop to the hijinks. Griffiths supported Title VII for good reasons, not because she was trying to sabotage the CRA. But Griffiths too called up the turn-of-the-century paradigm of women being white. While she took care to note that black women also needed protection, she used racially differentiated language, playing to Southern members with the plea that the CRA was going to leave white women disadvantaged and unprotected. "When the colored woman shows up and she is qualified, she is going to have an open entrée into any particular field," and that was okay. But the problem was that black men would feast on antidiscrimination measures; black women would get a few bones; and white women would come up with nothing at all. "It would be incredible to me that white men would be willing to place white women at such a disadvantage except that white men have done this before," she scolded, calling up the nearly forgotten history of the rift over the Fourteenth and Fifteenth amendments.[85]

Liberal Democrats, the backbone of support for the CRA, objected to Title VII. They believed it would endanger the CRA's passage or, if it did pass, make the legislation too unwieldy to implement. In the end, though, Title VII survived in the House, voted through by a coalition of Southern Democrats and conservative Republicans. In the Senate, moderates of both parties, led by Margaret Chase Smith, Republican of Maine and one of only two female senators, shepherded the bill through without any further emendations.[86]

With such a compromised beginning, there would seem little to expect from Title VII. Yet the subsequent history shows how political outcomes can outrun their origins. The NWP began to come around. The organization would never be a principled exponent of civil rights, but as legal scholar Serena Mayeri points out, "Title VII helped to bring about a significant retreat from the explicitly racialist feminism the NWP had previously sponsored." "Today it is the negro women who will win for all of us equal rights," cheerfully observed member Meta Heller. "I only wish all women's organizations would get behind the civil rights movement, forgetting their prejudices for their own advancement."[87] More important, over the next three years workingwomen responded energetically. In the end Title VII belonged not to the Woman's Party or racist Southern congressmen but to the workingwomen—black and white—who responded in force and to the political movement they touched off, which no one could have forseen.

Immediately, women flooded the Equal Employment Opportunity Commission (EEOC), the agency set up to implement the CRA's provisions. There were more than two thousand complaints the first year, nearly one quarter of the total. Women wrote about the basics of hiring and pay, but also about promotions (more precisely, lack of promotions), differential health insurance and pensions, different job categorizations for the same work, and sex-segregated seniority lists. In an immediate sense, the complaints were futile, since the CRA's supporters had compromised with congressional opponents by stripping the agency of any enforcement power, thereby making it exclusively investigative. Moreover, EEOC commissioners themselves were divided about the legitimacy of the women's applications, with four out of the five responding with indifference or antipathy. Aileen Hernandez, from a trade union and civil rights background, was the only woman on the EEOC, and the one member who fought to implement the sex discrimination provision.[88]

There were two kinds of objections from liberals. One was that it was too confusing to deal with both sets of problems, and race discrimination was much more serious. The other was an unwillingness to interfere with supposedly natural differences. Obviously men and women belonged in different jobs, and if women got the short end of the stick, that was unfortunate but unavoidable. Unlike race differences, which they were willing to believe were products of prejudice, they saw women as biologically equipped for certain jobs that were somehow menial. Women's fingers were nimbler and men's clumsier (which was why they were clerical workers and men were their bosses); women were weaker and men stronger (which was why they were low-paid telephone operators and men were well-paid linemen). Fingers, muscles, and mysterious biological properties made men focused and analytical and women flighty and impressionistic. Jobs that required strength, decisiveness, and dependability—which happened to be men's jobs—paid better. That was the way things were.

If discrimination against women was a consequence of inalterable sex differences, the naysayers maintained, then Title VII held employers to a silly standard of sexlessness. Under the new law, how could a railroad turn down a woman who applied to be a locomotive engineer? What was an airline to do the day a licensed woman pilot applied for a job? And what about a Playboy Bunny: Could a man apply for that job? And could he complain to the EEOC when he was turned down? Title VII came to be known as "the Bunny problem," as if legions of men were clamoring to don rabbit ears and puffy tails and be pawed by customers in cocktail lounges. "You can't even safely advertise for a wife anymore," wisecracked *The New York Times* on the EEOC's quandaries with the Bunny problem.[89]

It was a sign of the protest gathering under the surface that the jokes bumped up against resistance, since this kind of humor normally floated free. "Let us have our fun out of the sex angle—if we must," Esther Peterson chided in a letter to *The New York Times* about the Bunny editorial. "But let us also treat the plight of the woman worker with the seriousness it deserves from a great newspaper."[90] The Johnson administration was divided, with some officials diffident or hostile to Title VII, and others—including LBJ himself and Secretary of Labor Willard Wirtz—avowing a commitment to putting the plight of the woman worker on the Great Society agenda. On the floor of the House, Martha Griffiths attacked jokes about Title VII as disrespectful of the law and actually drew applause.[91]

When the spotlight turned on the jokes, the unspoken assumptions behind them came under scrutiny. The old sexist clichés could be dressed up in contemporary motifs—men as Playboy Bunnies, how funny. But under pressure the humor was getting labored (what about a man who wanted to work in a corset shop?). Suddenly the setup of a woman wanting to be treated fairly in the workforce didn't seem so funny. Millions of women had jobs and paychecks that their families depended on. Why was it, again, that they could only work in certain jobs? And actually, yes, why *was* it that they couldn't fly airplanes or drive locomotives?

Women in labor unions had thought about these matters for years, but now the civil rights movement pushed issues of fairness and just deserts to the forefront of popular consciousness. The idea of segregation as something people were forced into rather than something they chose or just stumbled into made the vast congregations of women clustered in menial and badly paid jobs look suspicious, just as did the masses of black people congregated at the bottom of the labor market. Occupations deemed glamorous and feminine, preludes to marriage—secretaries, airline stewardesses, Playboy Bunnies—began to look like dead ends.

Employers fell back on the defense that some jobs truly required one sex or the other, a loophole the EEOC allowed as "*bona fide* occupational qualification exceptions," or BFOQs.[92] Sex discrimination was not illegal if sex was a BFOQ: A "house mother" in a college dormitory could only be a woman, went the reasoning, and possibly a Playboy Bunny required a bona fide female as well. But the obligation to spell out BFOQs opened up a Pandora's box, because the assumptions about why only the female sex could perform a job, once they were examined in the hard light of day, turned out to be insulting and contradictory to other views of American women that were woven through civic discourse.

That is, if you thought about the work a Playboy Bunny really did, one EEOC official pointed out, you'd conclude she served drinks.[93] Logically, a man could work as a Bunny drink server, unless someone spelled out that in truth the real Bunny job was to service men's sexual fantasies. Often BFOQs depended on stamping jobs with sexual components that were weird and disgusting once they were articulated. When the flight attendants' union complained to the EEOC that the airlines discriminated by refusing to hire men as attendants, newspapers joked that a passenger might have to ask a man instead of a woman for a pillow ("A Pillow, Please, Miss . . . Er, Mister," was the title of a bemused editorial on the subject). What was that about? What was the passenger supposed to be thinking when he asked for a pillow? The airlines' argument that they could only attract customers with pretty girls trained in the skills of "make up, hairdo, and even how to walk" began to look like high-level pimping—at a moment when the public was newly alert to the perfidy of racial stereotypes.[94]

Caught off guard, employers gave signs of backpedaling from sexual stereotypes even as they got tangled up in language that two years earlier was unobjectionable. "In our culture, a female is a target for a 'pass,'" a business executive noted about what we would call sexual harassment, putting the slang in quotes as if it were a word he himself would never use. "I probably should be more broad-minded—no pun intended," professed another, wanting to be sure readers wouldn't mistake him for a man who called women broads.[95]

The ideological justifications began to buckle under the analogy of race and sex. The EEOC dug in by searching for ways to justify sex discrimination rather than to address the outpouring of grievances. Commissioner Franklin Roosevelt, Jr., son of the late president, expressed a common opinion when he charged that the sex provision was there only because civil rights opponents had thrown it in to undermine the CRA's real intent.[96]

The renaissance of the women's movement in the 1960s is usually attributed to an explosion that was inevitable given the building pressure, or to the breaking of a "wave." In this version of the story, the President's Commission broached a few suggestions for improvement, *The Feminine*

Mystique took the lid off resentments, anger erupted, and women got organized. The account is useful in capturing the unexpected strength and suddenness of developments. Unquestionably, the feminism that emerged later in the decade marked a sea change in women's politics, generating a scrutiny of relations between the sexes that was more thoroughgoing than anything that came before. But the origins of the renaissance lay earlier; rather than amazing alchemy, the reappearance of women's rights can better be seen as a dialectic between Washington politics and popular politics, Democratic Party elites and workingwomen, and women with some access to power and those with none. That is, there was a longer, quieter route to the new feminism, one that is overlooked when historians are too quick to fasten on to the combustion of the late 1960s.

The impasse at the EEOC invited exasperation from women who worked in government agencies, especially PCSW veterans. Meetings and discussions continued after the commission closed up shop. Esther Peterson, Marguerite Rawalt, Catherine East, Martha Griffiths, Aileen Hernandez, and Mary Keyserling were in the thick of Washington politics, occupying (except for Griffiths, the one elected official) secure, if narrow niches and, through powerful male patrons, marginal positions in the Democratic Party. Rawalt, for example, was from Texas, and had long benefited—if "benefited" is the word for being stuck in a mid-level job—from her acquaintance with Lyndon Baines Johnson.[97] Beltway insiders, these women followed the imbroglio over Title VII closely.

The mood in Washington was fractious. As the Vietnam War escalated, LBJ made magnanimous and grandiose promises calculated to mollify various constituencies. In regard to top Democratic women, his vow to appoint fifty women within thirty days to top federal positions fizzled. He continued to hold back from forcing the EEOC to abide by Title VII.[98] Everywhere in the country—as well as among Democrats in Congress and in the administration—cynicism crept into views of the president, with opposition building on the left to the war, and hostility on the right to civil rights. At the edges—and women were one group at the edges—the liberal accord that had underwritten Johnson's Great Society unraveled. In the midterm elections in 1966, Congress turned sharply rightward, with the Democrats losing forty-eight House seats and four Senate seats.[99]

Thus when the Labor Department convened a meeting in 1966 to follow up on the PCSW, unrest was palpable. The commission had spawned state committees on women, and those veterans, too, came to Washington. Aggravation with the EEOC boiled over and malcontents huddled away from the main meeting to talk about the need for another organization, "an NAACP for women" that would push uncomfortable matters that Mary Keyserling, the new head of the Women's Bureau, was trying to keep in check, holding the line for the Johnson administration. The analogy between race and sex was irrepressible. The previous year, Pauli Murray and Mary Eastwood, another PCSW veteran, made a constitutional argument using the race-sex parallel in a groundbreaking law review article, "Jane Crow and the Law," using Murray's Fourteenth Amendment arguments as well as drawing on the United Nations Universal Declaration of Human Rights. Murray and Eastwood compared the Supreme Court's sanction of sex classifications in *Minor*, *Bradwell*, and *Muller v. Oregon* (1908) (which concerned a protective law) to the *Plessy* decision on separate but equal facilities for blacks.[100]

On the spot, the dissidents established the National Organization for Women (NOW) as a pressure group, a "select" association of influential women and men. Within months, they had three hundred charter members: lawyers, policy makers, federal officials, academics, and businesswomen. Members of state commissions were a large contingent. Kay Clarenbach, for instance, from the Wisconsin commission, was a college graduate and homemaker whose career path in short-term, part-time jobs typified one avenue into women's politics. While raising her children, she worked through the 1950s and early '60s in a series of jobs with no clear direction except a desire to be involved in women's issues. A veteran volunteer, she was a force in the League of Women Voters and a pioneer, at the University of Wisconsin, in adult education for women. A patient and kind woman with a gift for associational work, she was elected to a NOW office at the first meeting and stayed in the leadership, always a counterweight to the temperamental Betty Friedan, who became the first president. Other charter members were Gerda Lerner, then a graduate student in history at Columbia University and on the brink of a distinguished career as a pioneer of women's history; Marlene Sanders, the only high-ranking female television producer in New York; Muriel Fox, the one high-power female advertising executive in the city; and several nuns from Milwaukee and Chicago: Sisters Mary Claudine, M. Bernardin Deutsch, Mary Austin Doherty, and Mary Joel. Labor feminists were critical: Dorothy Haener of the United Auto Workers, to name just one, provided office support for the first year of NOW's existence. Thus to call NOW a middle-class white woman's organization, as many do, is to miss the nature of its early structural supports, the character of its founders, and the direction of their aims.[101]

Friedan's domineering and vain personality posed problems, many NOW colleagues privately agreed, in 1966 and long after. But she was the only one famous enough to draw national attention, and publicity was critical. Unlike some of the others, she had no solid experience as either a volunteer, a labor leader, or a professional in a workplace. She was a writer. "Betty had never organized anything in her life," Clarenbach put it bluntly. "And that made it difficult to work together."[102] Friedan's four-year tenure at NOW was tempestuous and often acrimonious, the feuds and splits worsened by her egotism. A fast, bold writer and speaker who didn't bother with details, she was never a diplomat or politician. She always left that to others, the worker bees to her queen.

But she was a diva who appeared at a critical juncture to identify those issues that could ignite mass protest. An extravagant personality, she turned into a talented speaker who could voice some of feminism's most uncomfortable truths in a way that listeners could easily grasp. In the 1980s, I introduced her at a speech at Princeton University. She plopped down on a chair in the middle of the stage—at this point she was too frail to stand—and, without notes, launched into a talk about the bad old days before NOW, when women wore girdles. "How many of you know what girdles are?" she asked the listeners, as if she were chatting over coffee. She maundered on, as confident as if she were delivering a spellbinding analysis of sexual oppression. But as rambling and banal as she was, she held an audience of several hundred young women rapt for over an hour.

The founding charter artfully wove criticisms of women's treatment into a clear and calm exposition of what needed to change. It carried over points from the PCSW: women's lengthened life spans, which meant they spent a small proportion of their lives raising children; girls' troublingly high dropout rates from high school and college. The language was tactful. "Nobody used the word oppression," Kay Clarenbach later marveled.[103] The tone was more direct and urgent than that of *American Women*. The time for study and deliberation was past. Enough commissions: Now was the moment for action to remedy the wage gap between the sexes that had increased since the war, the crowding of black women in the lowest-paid occupations, and the dismal average income of the female worker.

NOW parted ways with the PCSW's conciliatory nods to domesticity. In this the organization followed the lead of *The Feminine Mystique*. The charter insisted that full-time domesticity turned women into life-long dependents and stranded both sexes in an invidious half-equality.

Creating new arrangements was "a basic social dilemma which society must solve," not an individual woman's responsibility. National child care was practicable and possible. Social policies must allow women to meet their responsibilities in the world along with family obligations. "We do not accept the traditional assumption that a woman has to choose between marriage and motherhood, on the one hand, and serious participation in industry or the professions on the other."[104] A jolting idea then, and still contested today.

NOW's founders were marked by a no-nonsense willingness to work with men and a hard-boiled optimism about what one could achieve in their company. Five men were charter members, their presence testimony to the founders' background of working in mixed settings and the value they placed on male support.[105] Why men? NAWSA, after all, had never admitted men or solicited their commitment. But NOW made male membership a mark of its up-to-date orientation. Any woman who came to prominence in the 1950s had made her way through crowds of men, sometimes with their help, more often despite their disdain, indifference, and antagonism. Still, these women survived, often by bending over backward to give men credit for the slightest inclination toward fair play. As a generation, their experience disposed them to see female separatism as faintly Victorian: regressive and man-hating. In line with this sensibility, the NOW charter held up an egalitarian idea of marriage as a "true partnership between the sexes." The charter balanced action that was *for* women with activism that came *from* both sexes and would benefit all: a "we" composed of men and women.

The sensibility resonated with hopes for racial integration still burning bright. It also looked back to the early twentieth century, when feminists celebrated the human race and heterosexual partnership. But NOW was not an organization that tapped into the politics of daughters. Rather, it was responsible, productive marriages the founders championed, as if they were borrowing from African-American women's notions of industrious partnership in service to a common cause. Without ties to men, no action would proceed, nor would sex equality be complete.

The name was National Organization *for* Women, not National Organization *of* Women. It was always a difficult position to maintain, this loyalty to men, and it soon was evident that their incorporation was more symbolic than real. The emphasis would always limit NOW's ability to speak to and explain male opposition, such as that already flaring up in the conflict over Title VII. And the problem gathered strength as the politics spread outward. NOW soon veered toward separatism, but leaders retained their courteous attitudes about men, even when radicals mocked them as wishy-washy and deluded.

NOW founders used their influence with the administration to pressure President Johnson to expand an executive order requiring federal contractors to comply with equal employment policies including sex discrimination—thus going beyond JFK's analogous order that only banned sex discrimination in the federal civil service. Since federal contracts amounted to trillions of dollars of business, the order was actually much more effective than Title VII in intervening in prejudicial practices. LBJ's action effectively pushed the obdurate EEOC to attend to women's grievances.[106]

But the agency still would not budge on the issue of discriminatory want ads: "Female Help Wanted" and "Male Help Wanted." The practice was the exact analogue of "No colored need apply" designations, which were now highly illegal. The ads effectively nullified Title VII by throwing up a mental barbed-wire fence against female trespassers. The EEOC, though, refused to touch the ads, regardless of ruling that any other designations—race, religion, or national origin—were illegal.

No issue raised NOW's hackles more. Within a year, NOW spawned satellite chapters around the country, and in late 1967, the organization held demonstrations in six cities against EEOC policy. For a staid select organization of liberals, NOW grew impressively adept at moving outside official channels to embarrass the agency. The New York chapter, already savvy at attracting media attention, invaded the EEOC offices in the city with huge bundles of newspapers bound up in red tape. The newspaper companies started to cave in to pressure, the New York papers first, then papers in other cities. It took time and considerable effort, though. Not until 1973, when Pittsburgh NOW's challenge to sex-segregated ads in the local papers reached the Supreme Court, was the issue settled.[107]

In 1967, NOW was the sole feminist organization in the country. The fight over the EEOC gave form to what would otherwise have been inchoate grievances and drew liberal women into the fray. After 1967, as opposition to the administration intensified and the antiwar movement surged, NOW picked up the fervor of mass politics, outstripping its insider origins. Women joined from sectors where there was already agitation: union women, teachers, stewardesses, more nuns (radicalized by the war and the Catholic Church's rigidity about women in the priesthood), and housewives reassessing their lives.

Younger members arrived, too, brandishing 1960s weapons of street politics: ferocious controversy, stern moralizing, and finger-pointing at men and those women judged to be their collaborators. Feminism was tacking around, to head into far stormier waters than anyone in the select group foresaw in 1966. In 1968, the feminist movement broke open and a crowd of rowdy, riled-up daughters poured in, to help but also to criticize, judge, scold, and instruct the responsible mothers.

CHAPTER EIGHT

THE REVOLT OF THE DAUGHTERS

In 1968, the pace of feminist politics picked up—steadily, then astonishingly. Outside NOW, expatriates from the New Left and refugees from the counterculture jumped ship to join a radical movement dedicated to women. A feminist avant-garde appeared, given to flamboyant demonstrations and a lacerating critique of a society ruled by men. For the first time since the 1910s, the ranks teemed with young women, aggressive, swaggering, and brimming with bravado, aroused by new ideas about where sexual injustice was lodged—not only in wage work but in the inequities of housework and child rearing, the way men looked at women and talked to them, their selfishness in bed, their leers and wolf whistles on the street, the oppressiveness of trying to please them—in short, the multiple indignities borne by the second sex.

A feminist family quarrel flared up, to engulf a generation already given to pitched emotion in politics. Radical feminists ratcheted up a version of the revolt of the daughters into a fever of revolution. The aim was to topple patriarchy, not to make the EEOC comply with Title VII. But it was not the ultimate patriarchal authorities who drew the most fire. Rather, it was the brothers, whose complicities with oppression made them the enemies to be expelled. Mothers, too, came in for disdain, for their capitulation to a soul-crushing system, their timidity before male power, their compulsion to conscript their daughters into the same circumstances that crippled them. This was a politics with the habit of lashing out at intimates rather than august authority.

The mood of the late 1960s bequeathed a sense of momentous transformation. The writer Alice Munro captured the sensibility in a short story about a daughter's coming of age: "There is a change coming I think in the lives of girls and women," the vivid, sympathetic mother prophesies. "Yes. But it is up to us to make it come." The change did come, and no aspect of American life was untouched.

Women's liberation, as these politics were called, appeared in the midst of the 1960s turmoil that brought politics as usual to a halt. By 1968, fury at the escalation of the Vietnam War drove all before it, determining political alignments for and against. The Johnson administration's grandiosity and lack of credibility fed on each other, provoking massive distrust and anger, which spilled over from the antiwar movement into the broader public. Protest heated up all the more as a cultural revolution of sex, drugs, and rock and roll ripped through the student population. Searing denunciations of American society—attacks on racism, profiteering, warmongering, greed, imperialism—and apocalyptic visions of its collapse streamed through the New Left. Richard Nixon's election to the presidency that November stoked the sense of impending doom. Nothing like this had ever happened.

Radical feminism came out of this combustible mix. The recruits carried with them the New Left's precepts and applied them to women: that only revolutionary change could bring change; that the law and government were façades for class and racist rule; that the social fabric was rotten. Tuned to the millennial pitch of the left—the apocalyptic sense of perpetrators' wrongdoing and zeal to purge the world of sin—radical feminism was searing, melodramatic, and rambunctious. Its proposals to liberate women captured and transformed a national audience, a public alternately appalled and enthralled, scandalized and persuaded.

The newest feminists, largely middle-class white students and recent college graduates, scorned compromise. They took from the New Left a contempt for incremental change and electoral politics and cared nothing for working with men to change public policy. Rather, they identified the grounds of change as personal life; changes in hearts and minds would destroy patriarchal institutions. In discussions, revelations, and denunciations of the status quo, women's liberation generated countless pressure points of agitation, a myriad of ad hoc campaigns to change sexual mores, manners, men's expectations of women and women's expectations of themselves, and the very language of gender. "Many an office or kitchen has become a battlefield, strewn with male and female tears," wrote one witness from the fray.[1]

Initially, the ideas belonged to knots of expatriates from the New Left. But they spread quickly, electrifying thinking about women and among women. The politics of confrontation, catharsis, and personal transformation proved applicable to almost any situation.

The change seemed to come out of nowhere—of that everyone agreed. Yes, there had been *The Feminine Mystique*, the President's Commission, and NOW. But these all predicated their proposals on an orderly conception of pressure politics and appealed to women with families, who were accustomed to working in civic organizations. Women's liberation was proudly unorganized, sprawling, militant, and in-your-face, given to upheavals and accusation, not battles over the EEOC. Looking back, it seems inevitable—African-Americans mobilized, why not women? We know this story so well that it seems destined. But early in the 1960s, the possibility of a feminism as potent as the civil rights movement was so remote that no one ever anticipated a mass movement of women. What changed?

Women's unhappiness on the New Left surfaced early in the student wing of the Southern civil rights movement. There, the dangerous work of registering voters and running freedom schools conferred a rough reciprocity on dealings between the sexes. In the militant Student Nonviolent Coordinating Committee (SNCC), founded in 1960, women were prominent at every level, including veteran organizer Ella Baker, the organization's guiding genius, and the near-legendary young organizers Ruby Doris Smith Robinson and Diane Nash. "As SNCC developed a bold and brazen public image, bold and brazen women were attracted to it," writes Barbara Ransby, Baker's biographer. "And once they joined, no one sought to constrain them." The strength of female leadership in SNCC, however, did not extend into the Southern Christian Leadership Conference (SCLC), Martin Luther King, Jr.'s organization, despite the huge numbers of women in the campaigns and demonstrations. There, men did the leading.[2]

In SNNC, there were buried tensions. White women were in an especially vexed position. Because their very presence working and living with black men inflamed segregationists, they tended to work in the offices in cities rather than out in the countryside. African-American women were much more likely to run projects registering voters or running freedom schools. The divisions shouldn't be overstated. All SNCC workers considered themselves equals in a "beloved community": brothers and sisters, blacks and whites, friends, colleagues, and lovers, facing violence and possibly death together. Yet some women saw gradations that stood out against the guiding principle of strict participatory democracy. Men (white and black) usually called the shots in important political matters; and men subtly or not so subtly assumed that women performed the customary roles, cooking and cleaning in the communal houses where everyone lived, typing and mimeographing in the offices.

In 1964, in the aftermath of the bloody, tragic voter registration drive in Mississippi called Freedom Summer, two SNCC women submitted a short paper for discussion at a national meeting held to assess the future. The document, unsigned because the writers feared recriminations, challenged a bundle of assumptions about SNCC men's treatment of women. It began with a list of small insults—women were always asked to type and take minutes at meetings (as if they were secretaries); "girl" was sometimes appended to women's names on lists of organizers and attorneys, as if their lesser identity had to be noted. Then the memo went big by arguing that women's position vis-à-vis men was akin to that of blacks vis-à-vis whites. "Just as negroes were the crucial factor in the economy of the cotton South, women are the crucial factor that keeps the movement running on a day-to-day basis." Men's assumptions about their own superiority were as "widespread and deep-rooted and every bit as much crippling to woman as assumptions of white supremacy are to the Negro," the writers asserted, anticipating the ridicule that would ensue. But they ended with a jab at male self-satisfaction: The movement needed to learn "this is no more a man's world than it is a white world."[3]

This put male civil rights workers, black and white, in a position analogous to the white supremacists who ruled the Southern economy—an analogy that, on the face of it, was absurd. The comparison between women and blacks went back to the abolitionists, but it's doubtful that anyone in SNCC knew it, and even if someone did, the comparison was as disturbing in 1964 as it had been in the 1830s, since the writers aimed it at men who risked their lives working with black tenant farmers. One set of accounts (mostly white women's) recalls the memo drawing fire at the meeting, attacked as self-indulgent and melodramatic; another set of memories (black women's) recalls no reaction at all. Yet on balance, the evidence suggests that among white women (and perhaps surreptitiously among some black women), the memo struck a chord.[4]

Publicly, African-American women drew back with one accord from the brewing criticism. Black women experienced considerable day-to-day respect in SNCC and saw themselves as proud carriers of the same African-American tradition of high female competence and self-assertion that was at work among the poor Southern farm women SNCC worked with. The public face of the movement was male, but everywhere women were the backbone. "Women carried the movement, there is no doubt about it. I mean, there were some men who stood up, but it was a minority," testified James Miller, a participant in the Claiborne County, Mississippi, drive; his was a common observation.[5] In a milieu that depended so much on local women's initiative and courage, black SNCC women bridled at the memo's description of female deference, the assumption that all women took on the role of subservient field hands.

Decades later, a few African-American women who were in SNCC acknowledged that they too had complaints about how men dealt with women. At the time, though, they kept silent and routed their resentment into anger at white women. They felt themselves to be desexed, treated as men's neutered sisters, while white women were seen as objects of sexual attraction. "Our skills and abilities were recognized and respected, but that seemed to place us in some category other than female," Cynthia Washington remembered. She was a project director who had important responsibilities in the field, but she believed she paid a price for her prominence.[6] Both white and black men sought out white women as lovers; the interracial affairs aggravated and infuriated black women.

The sexual tension gave men, not women, power. "The negro girls feel neglected because the white girls get the attention," complained a black female staff member at the meeting where the memo was brought up. "The white girls feel misused."[7] White women felt mistreated because of their menial place in the work of the organization, and black women felt mistreated because of their menial place in heterosexual love. The men on top escaped with only a brush with criticism.

Two years later, SNCC became a separatist organization and white workers left. The new black-only incarnation soon ended, its members scattering into black power groups and community organizing. Meanwhile, the writers of the first memo, revealed to be respected veterans Mary King and Casey Hayden, rehashed the previous year's ideas in a document they sent to women in the antiwar movement around the country. The view that radical men were complicit in a system that oppressed women meshed with complaints building elsewhere.[8]

In the North and on the West Coast, too, radical black women also held back from the brewing conflict. From the perspective of black power politics, female solidarity across the color line was untenable. In a context where militant black separatism heightened faith in the potency of race solidarity, black women had no use for a revolt of the daughters in league with whites. Female radicals continued to voice pride in black women's independence and articulate a particular role in the struggle against racism, and a few black nationalist women's groups organized mothers and low-income women in order to improve day care and family services. But black women's politics were subsumed by a long-standing tradition of unity in defense of the race, and black women in the 1960s kept a studied distance between their own initiatives and anything labeled feminist.[9]

The drawing up of sides between black and white women had deleterious consequences for years to come, depriving mainstream feminism of the vibrancy of African-American women's contributions and cutting off black women from developments in which they had a profound interest.[10]

The New Left in general and its flagship organization Students for a Democratic Society (SDS) in particular professed noble principles of sexual equality. But from the founding of SDS in 1960, men were the public face of antiwar protest: the organizers who orchestrated demonstrations of tens of thousands; the speakers who harangued crowds; the self-styled revolutionaries who at late-night meetings brandished parliamentary procedure like weapons against those who disagreed with them. Half a world away, they were the soldiers who trucked through rice paddies, lives in the balance. Women, too, voiced hatred of the war, poverty, racism, and the hypocrisy of American life, and flocked to the cause. But they served by working in the offices, mimeographing pamphlets, sending out mailings, typing, and lining up speakers. Men wrote the pamphlets and gave the speeches.

Talented women faltered in the pressure cooker of male self-importance, revolutionary machismo (Che Guevara black leather jackets, spouting Marx and Lenin, Mao and Fanon chapter and verse), high-stakes bids for media attention, and sexual libertinism. The endemic disease of female self-doubt struck full force. Some—like the fabled Bernardine Dohrn, soon to go underground with the terrorist group Weatherman—responded by going macho themselves, sporting leather jackets and flaunting their sexual bravado and prowess. Others played the apprentice to male sagacity, humbling themselves before savants who expounded on the fine points of Marxist texts. "I often find myself frustrated and hamstrung by my own inadequacy," confessed Carol McEldowney, a talented organizer, to her friend Todd Gitlin in 1964. Gitlin was trying to get her to run for national office in SDS. "I often . . . lose my tongue when in a conversational situation with those of that superior ilk."[11] "That superior ilk" was, of course, men.

In 1967–68, arguments about the treatment of women broke out across the country; Casey Hayden and Mary King's memo had the effect of transforming individual women's complaints into a general problem. The fault line appeared at a moment when opposition to a hated war was of such depth and ferocity that it left few untouched whether for or against: outraged radicals whose protests mesmerized the nation, or prowar conservatives who, for the moment, fumed at the radicals but lay low and bided their time. In 1968, politics at the top buckled. The January Tet offensive in Vietnam led to LBJ's surprise announcement that he would not seek reelection. Martin Luther King, Jr., was murdered in April; students took over Columbia University's administration building and shut down the campus; student and worker demonstrations broke out across Europe in May and in Mexico City that fall, where police shot peaceful demonstrators, killing more than a hundred students. Robert Kennedy was assassinated in June, thus effectively ending any hopes for an antiwar candidate winning the presidency and putting an end to the war. Riots, looting, arson, and crowd violence broke out in more than a hundred American cities, with seventy-five thousand National Guard troops called out to restore order. The country roiled with fear, grief, anger, frustration, and contempt for the government.

It is impossible to understand the tone, tactics, and ideas of women's liberation without grasping this situation. Inside the left, outrage at one injustice fueled outrage at another, fury crackling through a moral circuitry and widening fault lines into fissures between moderates and militants, liberals and radicals, whites and blacks, and men and women. The unwillingness of New Left men to see their culpability in mistreating women seemed of a piece with the administration's unwillingness to admit its guilt in Vietnam. Denunciations of male behavior, enraged confrontations, and walkouts rocked the antiwar movement in New York City, Boston, Chicago, and the Bay Area. Fed up with the contradiction between professed egalitarianism and men's actual behavior, groups of SDS women broke away: "Our political awareness of our oppression has developed through the last couple years as we sought to apply the principles of justice, equality, mutual respect and dignity which we learned from the Movement to the lives we lived as part of the Movement; only to come up against the solid wall of male chauvinism."[12]

Radical feminism at first seemed merely another brand of over-the-top protest crashing onto the national scene. Amid war, assassinations, burning cities, and roaring crowds in the streets, women's liberation provided the public a kind of comic relief. The counterculture's love of attention-grabbing antics combined with a jaunty rejection of ladylike manners to produce a vaudevillian esprit. The first inkling came from TV news coverage of the 1968 Miss America pageant in Atlantic City, New Jersey, when a bevy of protesters from one of New York City's first radical feminist groups traveled down for the day to stage a demonstration on the boardwalk outside. Having alerted the New York newspapers and television networks, who sent crews to film them, they made the national news, dumbfounding viewers with indictments of women's enslavement to beauty standards and displaying a "Freedom Trash Can" into which demonstrators lobbed various "instruments of torture"—hair curlers, false eyelashes, girdles, and bras (the source of the enduring epithet "bra burner").[13]

Grouplets sprang up in cities and college towns along the two coasts and outposts in between.[14] They distanced themselves from NOW on the one hand and the antiwar left on the other, branding the former's reformist goals paltry and the latter's male radicalism self-serving and inadequate. In the spirit of the times, they called for revolution, led by a vanguard of women. The old order to be toppled was patriarchy, which subsumed capitalism, imperialism, and racism. Initially, the mood was utopian, expressive, exhilarating, and passionate, despite the surrounding political gloom. Looking back forty years later, Ann Snitow, an early *engagée* in New York women's liberation, spoke of the immediacy, desire on fire. "It was so exciting, you could die for this."[15] The elation came from the conviction, suddenly shared by many others, that women mattered in a way that they never had before. There was the excitement that came from finding that others shared one's difficulties. There was the assurance of sinking into a collectivity that was suddenly rendered important, even noble, by virtue of suffering at the hands of men, the satisfactions of joining one's fate and identity to others: the exalted state of belonging that politics can create among previously dispersed people.

An identification with any and all oppressed female persons inured radical feminists to charges of bourgeois feminism that former SDS comrades hurled. Feminists shot back that the same system that oppressed blacks, poor people, and workers of all colors subjugated women. "Our oppression is total, affecting every facet of our lives. We are exploited as sex objects, breeders, domestic servants, and cheap labor."[16] Bourgeois feminism was an epithet the left had used since the 1890s to warn its women away from the suffrage movement and any ideas that strayed from the dogma that class struggle was the fundamental task. Girding themselves against the accusation, radical feminists floated analogies that equated white middle-class women with their "sisters" in dire circumstances—North Vietnamese fighters, Chinese peasant women, and African-American mothers on welfare were favorite figures of comparison.

The extravagant likenesses worked to shore up the revolutionary bonds of womanhood in the face of men who saw themselves as the champions of the wretched of the earth. For what SDS heavy-hitting male was not on the side of Vietnamese and Chinese women? "We define the best interests of women as the best interests of the poorest, most insulted, most despised, most abused woman on earth," asserted New York Redstockings, one of the first radical groups. "She is what all women fear being called, fear being treated as and yet what we all really are in the eyes of men." A performance put on by the Chicago Women's Liberation Union was typical, an agitprop piece that evoked a procession of sufferers down a feminine via dolorosa: "the forty five year old file clerk, raped and strangled in her one-room walk up," the beaten girl whose mother was insane, the black prostitute, the Vietnamese guerrilla, the woman dying of an illegal abortion. These were the martyred figures on a frieze over the door to the future.[17]

There was no feminist history to speak of, so instead feminists concocted fables from Third World communism or the proletarian revolution that was supposed to begin soon.[18] The strained analogies were melodramatic and far-fetched, silly really, but they were also tools of self-defense against male scorn. The adolescent arrogance of New Left men was a cross between the puerile attitudes of fraternity boys and the hipster misogyny of the older Beats they emulated. Barely out of their teens, radicals quelled their own anxieties by pretending to be swaggering revolutionaries without a care for mere women. In 1969 one SDS chapter published a pamphlet in this mode of the devil-may-care Marxist libertine. It advised that "the system is like a woman; you've got to fuck it to make it change."[19] Of course in reality, these monsters of vanity and Marxist preening were the teenaged and twenty-something boyfriends, friends, and brothers of the women who bore the brunt of their idiotic posturing in New Left organizations. Ellen Willis, *The New Yorker*'s first rock music critic and founding member of New York Redstockings, wrote years later of women's difficulties around these truculent men. "It's hard to convey to people who didn't go through that experience how radical, how unpopular and difficult and scary it was just to get up and say, 'Men oppress women. Men have oppressed me. . . .' We were laughed at, patronized, called frigid, emotionally disturbed man-haters."[20]

But the break was with SDS and male comrades, not with the language and style. Women's liberation retained the male left's habits of sweeping indictment, the heavy-handed Marxist-Leninist theorizing, the scorn for compromise, the insistence that life was lived in blacks and whites and not in grays, the penchant for histrionic displays of outrage and suffering, the faith that sheer will could bring about a perfect—or near-perfect—society purged of wrongs, and the scorn for liberalism, electoral politics, and government. The impulse to make a clean sweep, to scour society of every vestige of sexism, came from faith in the powers of a revolution that would clean the Augean stables of exploitation. No place was free of sexist oppression, not the family, not work, not sex, motherhood, mind, psyche, or the inner sanctum of the spirit.

While the early groups, such as New York's Redstockings and Boston's Bread and Roses, vaunted ultrademocratic participation, they also retained the New Left's vanguard model: an enlightened cadre of the hypercommitted would forge ahead into a future whose perfect shape they, and they alone, could apprehend, leading the masses step by step toward a level of higher consciousness to match their own.[21] The persistence of New Left idioms explains some assumptions in women's liberation circles: for example, that all the isms were co-equals of sexism—imperialism, racism, capitalism. The fantasies about how women prospered under the regimes of various Communist dictatorships and military regimes: Cuba, the Soviet Union, China, and Vietnam. The contempt for electoral politics as bourgeois liberalism. The certainty that nothing short of feminist revolution would purge society of its inherent masculine violence, capitalist greed, racism, and imperialism. The dogma that nothing good, absolutely nothing, could come from the U.S. government, which was a shill for the (male) (white) ruling class.

The terminology was also more indebted to the Marxist lexicon than to the liberal feminist tradition (which was largely unknown), with heavy-handed phrases such as "male chauvinism" slung around to humble and impress. "This new exhortatory way of speaking," is how Alma Guillermoprieto describes the revolutionary vocabulary she encountered when she left New York to teach modern dance in Cuba in 1968. "These were sledgehammer words, of such enormous weight that I couldn't help paying attention to them, and they seemed to invite careful reflection. But I also experienced them as crushing words, without nuances or secrets." Women's liberation had its own sledgehammer words. Celestine Ware, living in New York in the late 1960s, complained about the turgid language that purported to capture women's experience: "The specialized vocabulary ... is psychologically confining, adapted as it is from black, New Left and hippie argot." As with Guillermoprieto's sledgehammer words, Ware thought that "rarely is there the inrush of feeling that occurs from a newly realized insight."[22] Women's liberation tried to illuminate the deepest recesses of the female psyche, but it had no room for the shimmering language of emotion, love, and sexual passion. That would only come later.

Feminism raced through radical circles, galvanizing defections and schisms. The ardor for a separate women's politics spawned discussion groups, underground newspapers, journals, and in 1969–70, "women's centers": low-rent storefronts and free space in college buildings made into gathering places for any and all who sought affiliation. Staffed by volunteers, furnished with ratty old couches, the walls plastered with posters of Vietnamese women toting guns and women worthies (Anaïs Nin, Emma Goldman, Simone de Beauvoir, Susan B. Anthony), the bulletin boards encrusted with notices of marches, abortion counseling, child-care needs, lectures, dances, and projects needing volunteers, the centers beckoned to the faithful as well as to neophytes who wandered in, curious about what all the excitement was about. An inquiring journalist found a "mixture of sorority house and campaign headquarters" in one in downtown New York.[23]

The impulse to associate was nearly irresistible to those women who came in contact with women's liberation, so various and idealistic were the projects, so captivating the faith that female citizens, on their own, could change so much. Myriad small groups focused on particular needs: publishing feminist newspapers, staging street theater, aiding women in prison, waging war on local Playboy Clubs. Many were called collectives, a term that came from the New Left lexicon denoting all-encompassing purpose, as in the Boston Women's Health Collective, which published in 1970 the first underground edition of what became the world-famous *Our Bodies, Ourselves,* a handbook for women's reproductive health and sexual well-being.[24] Other collectives published newspapers, ran free medical clinics for women, provided information about where to get an abortion or contraception, offered workshops on auto mechanics and carpentry (to free women from their dependence on men), and formed rock bands.

Commentators marveled at the speed with which radical feminism spread. "In less than two years, it [feminism] has grown in numbers and militancy, embracing a wide spectrum of women: housewives, professionals, students, women who are married, single, divorced, with children or childless," reported Sara Davidson, an enthralled California sympathizer, in 1969 in *Life,* the country's staple photo magazine.[25] By 1970, magazines and newspapers featured ideas that two years earlier were treated as the work of lunatics.

The slogan was "the personal is political." The insight was that women's oppression came from the family, marriage, and the bedroom, as well as the job market and courtroom. If you could transform the power dynamics of personal life, then everything else—the law, politics, education, work, marriage—would follow. The aim was ultimately structural: Radicals believed that institutions shaped and reproduced personal behavior, and only profound institutional change would really bring equality. But activity to effect institutional change was episodic and short-lived, while work on the personal insults of oppression proceeded steadily. The habitual orientation was psychological, changing gender inequities from the inside out, a perspective that cast NOW's preoccupation with public policy and the workplace as pitifully inadequate. The inward turn, away from the false promises of electoral politics and a liberal democratic system believed to be a sham, ran parallel to the civil rights movement, as black radicals turned away from institutional reforms to fix their attention on structural and cultural racism.[26]

An eye for the sexist perfidies that infested daily life became the radicals' stock-in-trade. The feminist press—pamphlets, journals, and underground newspapers—specialized in stripping down ordinary interactions to lay them bare. It was a roving third-degree interrogation, a vendetta to extirpate the deplorable practices that maintained the sexist status quo. Flirting, for example, was described in 1969 by the stern

Boston women's liberation paper *No More Fun and Games* as—indeed—fun that had to stop. Flirting might seem playful and innocuous, but really, the purpose was turning a woman into a sexual object. "The gestures pose as flattering, but they simultaneously say that she is defined once again not as an autonomous individual person."[27]

Once the interrogation began, there was no end to the treachery that had to be uncovered. Staple delicacies of an American white woman's upbringing were suddenly suspect. Under the glare of the third degree, not only frilly clothes and high heels, but Nancy Drew detective mysteries and romantic Hollywood movies were unmasked as brainwashing operations. Madeline Belkin, a self-proclaimed film addict, confessed that she liked to kiss her husband as if they were Hollywood lovers. "I hadn't thought about it until then, but I'd actually been up on my toes since my first kiss years ago, half waiting to be kissed the way Fred Astaire kissed Ginger Rogers, bent backwards over his knee." Smash mass-produced sexist fantasy! "We have been weaned on gross distortions of womanhood. . . .The positive images we must learn to accept and appreciate are the way we really look, who and what we really are."[28]

In Australia, Britain, France, Italy, and Germany, feminist movements were also emerging, but the historic ties of women's rights in those countries to the left and labor movements tempered the purity and self-righteousness with other commitments beyond the drama of Woman. The French movement would come slightly later, with its own ties to the left parties but also to the intellectual avant-garde.[29] But in the United States, there was a single-minded fervor that came from emotional sources in the American radical tradition, reaching back to the abolitionists and their politics of moral outrage and redemption. The feminist's task was to purge herself of false consciousness, distance herself from the unregenerate (men), and free others from oppression. Feminists saw themselves not so much as seeking power but as seeking rebirth: to live "clean," "unfettered by the inhibitions and the trade-offs necessary in mainstream politics," testified Dana Densmore of Boston's ascetic Maoist sect Cell 16. "It was like the anticipation of the end of the world for early Christians."[30] These convictions of moral purity and the desire to bring others to a new life fired up but also consumed political aims.

It was not the purist tenor of these early circles, however, but the ideas they generated, that gave feminism its strength and durability. The unworldly separatism petered out within a few years, relegated to a women's counterculture of communes and music festivals. But the penetrating critique of life-as-women-lived-it was a point of contact between strangers and far-flung sympathizers, even when other signs of affiliation were absent. This was what Jane O'Reilly meant in 1971 when she described the "click," feminist shorthand for the decisive moment when women's eyes met across a room, in unspoken recognition of some outrage disguised as normal life, men's petty dominion over women's time, attention, labor, and self-esteem, whether expressed in monopolizing a conversation or expecting a female employee to take notes at a meeting.[31] Life was saturated with political and moral meaning. The old rules were obsolete, but the new ones had yet to take root. By 1970, color-coded clothing for babies (pink for girls, blue for boys), the text of the marriage ceremony ("man and wife"), and the myth of the vaginal orgasm were all under indictment. In the turbulence of so many wrenching conflicts, resolution seemed to require nothing short of a clean sweep.[32]

In spring 1968, the murders of Martin Luther King, Jr., and Robert Kennedy, followed by the violence at the Democratic National Convention in Chicago and the Democrats' nomination for president of Hubert Humphrey—whom radicals scorned for his equivocation on the Vietnam War—marked the collapse of any hope of a left-liberal coalition. The terms of invective—womanhood as we know it must go!—recast NOW as the tired liberals, feminism's counterpart to Humphrey.

NOW was "hopelessly bourgeois," composed of appeasers who wanted a more equal share of the patriarchal-capitalist pie rather than a different pie altogether, a revolutionary pie.[33] Radicals took their in-your-face aversion into the heart of NOW. In one notorious episode, Cell 16 members forced their way into a big 1969 national meeting in New York that NOW called to unite all feminist organizations. Cell 16 presented a riveting demonstration of militance: One woman cut off another's luxurious long hair to illustrate what it meant to defy male-dominated beauty standards. From the audience, some women screamed with horrified dismay, others in wild approval. It was not what NOW had in mind.[34]

Typically, feminist liberals' identities and affiliations were already set in marriage and motherhood, professions and political commitments. They had histories in institutional settings—women's groups, government, universities, political parties, trade unions, and professional elites—and they were accustomed to dealing with men in these settings. NOW had officers, charters, and membership dues, and operated according to Robert's Rules of Order. Liberals pulled back from the rhetoric of revolution and the searing examinations of personal relations.

The radicals, clustered in big cities, college towns, and universities, were younger and more labile in their sense of family and work options: generally unmarried and without children, students and recent college graduates starting out in careers or making do with menial jobs and low-paid political work, living in the cheap, roomy apartments that were the unrecognized bounty of the era. Some came out of a half decade or more of work in the New Left or the civil rights movement. They were overwhelmingly white. The New Left veterans had experience with direct action and mass protest (street demonstrations and sit-ins), and they were skilled in the uses of polarization—the art of maximizing political disagreements in order to rally the faithful around a radical position. They brought to women's liberation a repertoire of protest tactics: large demonstrations, marches, dances, street theater, and daring "actions" accosting or attacking a purveyor of sexism. Women who had worked in the South brought skills in community organizing and civil disobedience. But as a political generation, they had virtually no experience—or interest—in pressure politics, legislative action, or elections.

As in the New Left, disdain for age and political experience reigned. Tensions between liberals and radicals simmered in the political semiconscious, breaking out in brawls such as the hair-cutting drama. Liberals assumed the role of prudent mothers, urging patience and diplomacy—including amicable relations with men. For their willingness to improve women's lives within capitalist society—instead of striving for revolution—they were treated as compliant housewives who fooled themselves that the system was receptive. Radicals were the daring daughters. "My friends and I thought of NOW as an organization for people our mothers' age. We were movement girls, not career women; NOW's demands and organizational style weren't radical enough," recalled Meredith Tax, in Boston at the time. "Besides, we were generational sectarians; we didn't trust anybody over thirty." Upstarts shoved aside veteran feminists who had worked for years in hard-pressed situations; they scorned the veterans' belief in democratic process and their willingness to work with men. "The gung-ho gals," Pauli Murray acerbically dubbed the radicals. Newcomers, she complained two years later, "tend to see older women as 'passé' and . . . do not have the same respect for and deference to older veterans as my generation does."[35] Depending on one's vantage point, radical feminism was new and revolutionary, and NOW was passé and stodgy. Or, from the other angle, women's liberation was self-destructive and foolish, and NOW was level-headed and practical.

Still, the embattled and precarious state of feminism, its novelty, and its astonishing growth put radicals and liberals into close contact, personally and ideologically, often with creative results. One essential element in feminism's astonishing takeoff was the fluidity of exchanges between the wings. Never entirely separate, these were more tendencies than clearly defined positions, sometimes merging in a force field across a center-left spectrum. A few leaders moved between the camps: The outré Flo Kennedy, a wisecracking African-American lawyer, was associated with NOW but shared the radical penchant for shocking conventional sensibilities. Lucinda Cisler headed NOW's task force to legalize abortion and maintained contact with women's liberation as well. The Italian-born actress Anselma Dell'Olio, cabaret performer and producer in New York, happily traveled between establishment uptown and bohemian downtown. She preferred the uptown women, with their marriages and dinner parties and professional accomplishments and connections, "if for no other reason [than that] the establishment women had a lot more to lose." But uptown or downtown, she later stressed, "there was an outpouring of ideas, brains, wit, and talent, the likes of which I have never experienced before."[36]

It was ideas and their application in personal circumstances that transmitted the identity of feminist. Ideology, with its connotations of dogma, is too strong a description; what spread was more a political sensibility, a disposition of the heart mixed with intellect. The inchoate mental structures were all the more important because women's liberation lacked organizational structure, designated leaders, and specific goals. "Structurelessness" was a point of pride, authorizing ad hoc groups without any formal underpinnings or leaders (in point of fact, there were plenty of leaders who did dominate, although the tenets of absolute democracy worked to obscure their very real power).

What accounts for the velocity with which the ideas moved out of urban circles and into the culture? One primary source of acceleration was the eager engagement of female journalists, whose age, metropolitan location, and college educations put them right in the center of the women's liberation demographic. In other words, the media itself was a feminist venue. At the time (and ever since), conventional wisdom judged the media to be implacably hostile, a villain in the dramaturgy of embattled women fighting the patriarchal minions. The evidence, though, speaks to a more complicated interaction. Previously sidelined female journalists brought a measure of respect and sympathy to the subject, increased the coverage, and urged the average woman to take the radicals seriously.

Media work was a daughter's profession, a field for New Women since the 1910s. Journalism had long had a reputation as a glamorous profession for tough, adventurous women. The delicious screwball comedies of the 1930s imprinted the image in film. *His Girl Friday* (1940), for example, features an imperious, handsome, and impeccably dressed Rosalind Russell as the paper's star reporter, striding through adoring crowds of men in the newsroom. The memory of the great female reporters and photojournalists of World War II—Martha Gellhorn, Janet Flanner, Margaret Bourke-White, Lee Miller—lingered, enticing the ambitious with the hope that with chutzpah and brains, a woman could really succeed in this man's world. In Vietnam, a few daring reporters, such as the swashbuckling *New York Times* Vietnam correspondent Gloria Emerson, embodied the legend.

But the promise was hollow. Women were overwhelmingly crowded at low levels in the print and broadcast media. An unwritten law divvied up jobs: The real writers, men, were on one side of the line, the researchers, women, on the other. Camaraderie—laced with the comforting fiction that men and women stood shoulder to shoulder in the task of getting out the news—tempered the inequalities, day by day. Friedan, a freelance writer and former reporter, knew the world firsthand and mentioned it in *The Feminine Mystique* as an example of frank discrimination that everyone, male and female, accepted. The woman journalist "doesn't get mad; she likes her job, she likes her boss. She is not a crusader for women's rights; it isn't a case for the Newspaper Guild. But it is discouraging nevertheless. If she is never going to get anywhere, why keep on?"[37]

Circa 1968–69, discrimination against women in the news media—flip that around, and you can call it preference for men—was the industry standard of the age: good-humored and unabashed. Editors turned down women who applied for reporters' jobs if they were married to men who worked for other papers, on the principle that professional rivalry would hurt their marriages. If women did become reporters and feature writers, it was likely to be for the women's or society section, covering fashion, recipes, and the goings-on of the rich and famous. Society was the one editor's slot a woman could get. A few who managed to escape the ghetto became reporters, never to advance to editors or bureau chiefs. The National Press Club in Washington—the venue routinely chosen by world leaders visiting the United States to deliver major speeches—banned female reporters from the floor and relegated them to a stifling balcony where there was only room to stand, not sit. Male reporters went out to lunch at men's clubs with male editors and the men they were interviewing.[38] Serious treatments of women's issues and women in the news was rare; they made it into the papers as party givers, consumers of recipes and fashion, and wives of famous men. Initially, the emerging women's movement was slated to be trivialized within these terms, treated with flippancy or not at all.

Journalism was thus a typically integrated field of the 1960s, laden with meritocratic promise but in actuality keeping hordes of women in dead-end jobs. Its very collegiality accentuated the contrast between smart, upwardly mobile men and smart, perpetually subordinate women. It was a hothouse of suppressed female resentments. Betsy Wade, who over two decades climbed the ladder to become a high-ranking editor—but never the managing editor—at *The New York Times,* described the atmosphere of jovial sexism when she took her first job as copy editor in 1956. The first woman ever to work in that position, she arrived the first day to find the men had put ruffles around the paste pot on her desk (copy editors cut up corrected galleys and pasted them on a proof sheet). They were gathered around waiting with a photographer to record the merry moment. Wade, looking back, mused on the photos from the day: "I look at those pictures now and I look at my face and I remember myself as I was so long ago, really unable—I couldn't do anything. I was in a cage. I couldn't pick up that paste pot and throw it in the wastebasket. I couldn't tell the people to go away, I couldn't tell them to stop taking my picture. I couldn't say, 'Just let me do what I have to do and let's see if I can be good enough for this job.'"[39]

Women in journalism were in a position to experience the contradictions of supposed meritocracy and equality firsthand. These were the contradictions that Title VII was supposed to fix, but the veneer of prejudice was so thick, the rationalizations for men's superiority so dense, that it was impossible to conceive a plan of attack. Complaints to the EEOC wouldn't do it. How to explain to male colleagues what was wrong with the little prank they played on Betsy Wade? Or, continuing with Wade, how could she object to the long-running show that a hostile male co-worker put on for her benefit for years? As a courtesy to the new woman, the management removed all the spittoons (a customary fixture of the hard-boiled male newsroom) when she started. But one man made his hostility known, by pointedly walking past her desk every day to dump the coffee can he used to spit in, now that the spittoons were gone. Wade's challenge was not to gag. "A man behind him, who ran the national copy desk, had said he would resign his job if they ever put a woman on his desk. So there was a lot of traditionalism, that was holding on there," Wade added, "despite the fact that I was not, I think, a conspicuous person."[40]

These structures meant that journalism was a field where the battle was joined early on. When feminism broke into the news in 1968, male editors (and editors were only male) assigned the subject to low-ranking women because it was "their" subject. What the men were not prepared for was that reporters liked and—worse— rallied to the new cause. In New York, the first overt challenge to sexism in the newspapers came from a young woman who stood right at the intersection of women's liberation and the profession. Lindsay Van Gelder, a reporter for the New York *Daily News*, was two years out of Vassar College and a cub reporter in 1969 when she touched off the first skirmish of what became a protracted war in the media by refusing a demeaning assignment. Nineteen sixty-nine was a big year for the New York Mets, and Van Gelder got the woman's job of interviewing pitcher Tom Seaver's wife—known as Mrs. Tom Seaver. When she balked, her editor assigned her Mrs. Gil Hodges the next week, to teach her a lesson. That time she refused flat out and the editor fired her on the spot, violating the union contract under Newspaper Guild rules. The entire newsroom, including the printers, walked out. The upshot was that Van Gelder got her job back and she never had to do the "wives interview" again.[41] A routine matter— sending a woman out to cover the wife of a famous man—suddenly turned objectionable. You could say it was a controversy that revolved around a young woman's sudden refusal to abide by the logic of the second sex.

Small clashes touched off big battles in a city where NOW and women's liberation were everywhere in evidence. Journalists were connected to both wings of the women's movement through friends, and by 1971, feminist complaints rippled through *The New York Times, Time, Newsweek*, television networks, publishing houses, and a score of smaller operations. Female employees filed grievances with the city's Human Rights Commission, as required by law, and then the EEOC.

Editors found themselves in a bind—accustomed to assigning anything about women to female reporters, they found that those same reporters were too sympathetic to what they were covering. The accusation of "advocacy—of being too close" dogged women journalists. "You practically had to go in and take an oath that you didn't believe in the women's movement in order to cover the women's movement," Wade recalled caustically.[42] It would have been unthinkable to deny an assignment to a reporter who was covering the civil rights movement, she pointed out, because he believed in desegregation. "But to have a woman cover the women's movement?" Editors concerned about objectivity picked women known for their doubts about feminism, thinking they were commissioning a critical article, but they came up short. "Women's Lib: The Idea You Can't Ignore" in the middlebrow magazine *Redbook* was such a conversion story. The writer Sophy Burnham testified that she went into the assignment put off by stereotypes of hairy-legged bra burners and came out on the other side an angry feminist. "Suddenly I see no reason why one whole group of humanity is given intellectual satisfaction and another is given the satisfaction of motherhood."[43]

Because New York set the terms for news coverage, local ties between feminists and journalists influenced the national picture. Women's liberation provided great material. Radicals revived the tactics of publicity-grabbing spectacle that feminists in the early century had used to such good effect. Certain groups could be counted on for wild theatrics, "freaky, neo-Dada actions," as the downtown art critic Jill Johnston described them. Take the 1970 Wall Street Ogle-In. A human interest story in the news that spring concerned boyish antics on Wall Street, where a crowd of men gathered around a particular subway stop to hoot and leer as a woman notorious for her large breasts came up the stairs on her way to work. Feminists bent on evening up the score descended on Wall Street one morning before the New York Stock Exchange opened, with a TV producer and crew along for the fun. The group ogled, whistled, hooted, and hurtled remarks about the physical endowments of bankers and traders as they hurried to work. In the terms of the times, this was direct action and guerrilla theater. But we could also see it as a tactic lodged deep in the memory of the sex, a latter-day enactment of the carnival pastime of turning the world upside down, the men turned into the mocked, women into the mockers.[44]

The actions were all the more exciting because it was women doing them. "Get the bra burning and the karate up front," editors were known to demand once they came around to the appeal. "Women's liberation is hot stuff this season, in media terms," reported the young feminist journalist Susan Brownmiller in 1970, not without satisfaction. Book editors dangled lucrative contracts before aspiring writers: Doubleday turned English professor Kate Millett's doctoral thesis in English literature, a polemic against the misogyny of male writers, into the bestselling *Sexual Politics* (1970). TV talk shows invited radical feminists to appear to explain themselves. The media attention was so aggressive that some groups took a disdainful attitude to the press, first banning male reporters and then banning all reporters.[45]

NOW also learned how to get media attention. Muriel Fox, a New York advertising executive and a charter member, made sure that protests and demonstrations made the news. On August 26, 1970, NOW staged a huge Women's Strike for Equality on the fiftieth anniversary of the Nineteenth Amendment's ratification, replete with slogans and sound bites that could survive hostile coverage.[46] The Women's Strike for Equality, which had sister demonstrations that day in cities across the country, combined the orderly march and list of demands with enticing hints of wildcat actions: Friedan announced that Boston women would distribute four thousand cans of contraceptive foam and that "we're going to bring babies for a baby-in to sit on the laps of city fathers to show the need for child care centers in New York." She hinted that women everywhere just might take the day off from ironing, cooking, and making love.[47]

Among both radicals and liberals, media-ready figures appeared, sometimes entrancing, sometimes fearsome but consistently newsworthy. Some were beautiful. Gloria Steinem, with long legs, a gorgeous mane of blond hair, and a model's sculpted features. Some were eloquent: Betty Friedan looked like a frowsy suburban housewife, but her imperious intonation was oddly mesmerizing. Some were slapstick comics: Rita Mae Brown, remembered as "a lesbian Huck Finn with curly short hair and intense dark eyes," a self-styled Southern rascal who on occasion upstaged Friedan herself; Flo Kennedy, a middle-aged lawyer who upended the stereotype of the respectable, socially conscious African-American lady with foul-mouthed wisecracks and harangues against "this fucking business" (i.e., sex) and "the chocolate covering on the shit of housewifery." Some were seasoned media personalities: Robin Morgan had been a child actress on television and radio in the 1950s. And some were scary, humorless zealots like the hard-core Cell 16 of Boston, who specialized in martial arts and required a vow of celibacy, so counterrevolutionary did they see any form of sex.[48]

What is remarkable is that the journalists managed to frame feminism as a serious matter, worthy of consideration. At the most basic level, the mainstream media provided information about what feminists were protesting, thereby disseminating the terms of grievance and widening the circle of the aggrieved. Articles in magazines from *Esquire* to *Ladies' Home Journal* to *Cosmopolitan* to *Time* presented a variety of voices and topics, from the silly and self-dramatizing to the serious and timely. *The Atlantic Monthly,* for instance, a genteel magazine of cultural and political commentary, published a special women's issue in 1970 covering a range of subjects, from the law to men's place in feminism to job discrimination. *The Atlantic* stressed more palatable issues and downplayed thornier ones. There were brisk, informative articles about combating discrimination in the labor market and the law, and cogent discussions of gender stereotypes, mixed in with a few mellifluous objections in order to lend balance. "The word feminism is outmoded," sniffed Catherine Drinker Bowen, a wealthy writer of an earlier generation who had made a successful career as a biographer of great men. Yet for all her haughty dismissal of the feminist hoi-polloi, she took the occasion to express her own resentment of the prejudices she had endured in her working life. Others in *The Atlantic* angled to position themselves in the emerging genre of middle-of-the-roaders, the smug "I'm an independent woman but I'm oh-so-happy in my marriage and family" testimonial.[49]

True, ridicule was the media's default pose. A *Time* article on the Women's Strike for Equality saw the march as a spectacle of sexiness: "They took over the entire avenue, providing not only protest but some of the best sidewalk ogling in years."[50] Exotic stereotypes made good copy. A portrait of a glowering Kate Millett in a karate outfit was *Time's* cover on the eve of the march. The lead article cast Millett as angry, hurt, and full of invective, spewing distrust and dislike of men. But even negative reportage spread the news to eager recipients who received it as anything but preposterous.

The coverage reached millions, far from the cities. Marlene Sanders, high-ranking producer and a NOW charter member, produced a documentary on women's liberation for ABC and inadvertently brought in converts. A teenager sent her a note scrawled in a juvenile hand: "can you give me some information on how I can joint The Womens Liberation and how do I write to. I am 15 years old. What do you think about it." Another viewer, a Kentucky woman who cared for other people's children for a living ("babysitting"), wrote to ask advice on how she could rectify her situation: "Miss Sander's I want to be literated also—will you please tell me what is an equitable wage for 10 hours— (a day). And how I should word my ad."[51]

It was a fruitful collaboration between activists, journalists, and an audience in formation. Veteran *New York Times* staffer Eileen Shanahan, the paper's star economic reporter, remembered covering the women's movement as "the happiest experience I ever had as a reporter." "It was as blissful for me as for any twenty-year-old, maybe more so, because I knew what discriminations were out there." The journalists gave militance a national platform, and women's liberation gave journalists a platform for their own fight. *Newsweek* women, for example, held a press conference to announce they were filing a grievance with the EEOC the same day in 1970 that the magazine's big feature "Women's Lib: The War on 'Sexism'" appeared.[52]

Journalists learned to make their own protests into media events. The collaboration underlay a famous 1970 sit-in at the *Ladies' Home Journal*. Media Women, having alerted the reporters and TV networks, descended on the magazine's offices with a crowd of a hundred women—journalists and sympathizers—to accuse editor John Mack Carter of injuring the entire sex by publishing the lies and delusions of standard women's magazine fare. The invaders occupied the office for ten hours, cameras rolling. The sit-in was notably free of rancor. In the newsreel footage, everyone seems to be having a good time, from the cheerful, occasionally bored-looking demonstrators to the handsome Carter, who lounges at his desk with his chair tilted back as he parries their charges, his body language connoting bemused condescension. The protesters' demands concerned both the asinine content of the magazine and its employment practices: a man as editor, women concentrated at the bottom of the hierarchy and pay scale, the absence of any African-American staff, and no child care.[53]

Here the attack was not only about discriminatory policies but also cultural stereotypes that the media purveyed. The demonstration unfurled like a "speak bitterness" session in China's Cultural Revolution, with prosecutorial leaders taking turns confronting Carter with articles and ads from the *Journal* while the crowd cheered and heckled. The list of evils included virtually every vicarious delicacy of women's magazine fare: pieces about celebrities, food, makeup, fashion, and "all articles oriented to the preservation of youth." The denunciation of beauty obsessions and the mandate to please men tied the charges together. The message, a demonstrator sneered, was "better stay young . . . beautiful . . . keep this marriage going."

Thus in two years' time the press became a local forum as well as a platform for the entire country. Feminists were heroines of a big story. The coverage emboldened women—both the subjects of the writing and the readers—drew in recruits, and charged up political action that much more. New protagonists pushed into the political community, women who had been on the margins of other 1960s radical movements or hadn't participated at all.

The process by which an individual put "the personal is political" into motion was called "consciousness-raising." Because women's liberation put so much stress on the psychological dimensions of sexism, consciousness-raising was more fundamental to being feminist than joining an organization or taking action. Raising consciousness *was* action, the pivotal action, because it was necessary to shear away so many assumptions. Before anyone could be effective as a feminist, she must see that her problems were not hers alone. The point was to realize that most women—perhaps all of them—had troubled, painful relationships with men: bosses, family members, teachers, and male authorities of any kind. Consciousness-raising could occur in many settings: when a woman was reading feminist literature, talking to friends, or writing in her journal.[54] Beginning with New York Radical Women in late 1968, feminists established small talking groups to make consciousness-raising systematic. The goal was to replace the false with the true.

The term was an offshoot of the Marxist concept of "false consciousness," the distorted view of the world that kept workers in thrall to capitalism instead of rising up in proletarian revolution. Culture was to blame, because misogyny pervaded all previous knowledge about women. Thus women themselves, speaking without inhibitions, were the sole repositories of truth. But in normal settings, patriarchal authorities blinded them to their oppression. In order to bring buried truths to light and apprehend the real state of things, they must listen to one another in a trustworthy setting. "We cannot rely on existing ideologies as they are all products of male supremacist culture," decreed Redstockings. "We question every generalization and accept none that are not confirmed by our experience."[55]

The point was changed consciousness, a comprehension of how structures of male power shaped the deepest, most intimate experiences. The aim was "to develop knowledge to overthrow male supremacy" in all its immensity. Yet personal experience was the slingshot that was to be aimed at this Goliath; thousands of slingshots together could bring down the behemoth. Redolent of the therapeutic encounter groups of the 1960s human potential movement, consciousness-raising (or "C-R") groups turned self-awareness into political pedagogy and, in theory, inspiration for action. Groups met in apartments and women's centers. A question kicked off the discussion, with members sharing their experiences in (supposedly) equal measure. "Discuss your relationships with men. Have you noticed any recurring patterns?" "When you think about having a child, do you want a boy or a girl?" Stories of families, marriages, love affairs, professional slights, men's emotional thuggery, mothers' wrongdoing, broken hearts, and thwarted ambitions entered a stream of political narrative, refashioned into home truths of sexist oppression, the dark side of American womanhood revealed. Grievance seeded grievance.[56]

The excitement of doing politics in an entirely novel way, so intimate, so different from the mass actions of the antiwar movement, crackled through the experiment. Women laughed over dating experiences, debated the pros and cons of being married or single, discussed their parents' marriages and their hopes for their own families. They talked about their bodies—feeling fat, feeling ugly—and being afraid to go out after dark. Some revealed that they had been raped or molested. Women mulled over their surnames, some deciding to shuck husbands' and fathers' names to announce their newfound independence. They talked about lack of confidence, their shame about sex, their resentments of brothers' seemingly better deal in the family, their gnawing timidity.

The groups, however, were seldom the loving communities of sisterly support that promoters described. The process could be embarrassing and intrusive. For all the claims that they were havens for authentic truth, they unquestionably laid down a party line. Some revelations counted, others were whisked aside. Testimonies to good-enough marriages, supportive fathers, and the pleasures of motherhood were not especially welcome. If an intrepid participant ventured something in this vein, the group tended to twist her story to bring it in line with prevailing wisdom.[57]

But despite the psychological clumsiness, consciousness-raising was inspired. The groups did much more than modernize the age-old women's practice of complaining to one another about men. They churned out a huge database on which feminists could draw, revelations about the hidden dramas of women's lives. The resulting critique of patriarchal society, elaborated many times over in writing, artistic work, and political dialogue, contained brilliant ideas about what, exactly, went into the making of modern womanhood and revealed a disturbing asymmetry between the fates of the brothers and the sisters in liberal, prosperous, meritocratic America.[58]

Discoveries were data for a burgeoning ethnography of the gendered self, a kind of top-to-bottom, inside-out, and outside-in account of femininity that developed at a breakneck pace. *The Second Sex* was a text of conversion. "Simone de Beauvoir's *The Second Sex* opened doors for me!" a self-described grandmother, an avowed convert, chirped to the women's liberation monthly *Off Our Backs* in 1972.[59] Almost certainly, more women knew about the book or owned the book than read the book. As *A Vindication of the Rights of Woman* had been in the nineteenth century, the volume was as much a flag that women planted to claim a position as it was a text absorbed chapter and verse. But its core insight, that women are made not born, was a reagent that worked its way through the tissue of women's lives, dissolving norms and assumptions that had only a short time before seemed facts of nature.

The making of women seemed bound up with the business of men: that is, the labor and thought women devoted to attracting, pleasing, and mollifying men, bearing and raising their children, tending their domestic, sexual, and psychological needs. While the business of men clearly involved fathers and male authorities, the stress was on peers—lovers, husbands, workmates, roommates, political comrades. It was above all the fictive brother-friends whom consciousness-raising exposed as woefully inadequate. Whereas liberals made the inclusion of men a point of pride, radicals sought to jettison the desire for male companionship as foolish and self-destructive.

> *The phantom of the man-who-would-understand,*
> *the lost brother, the twin—*
>
> *for him did we leave our mothers,*
> *deny our sisters, over and over?*

asked Adrienne Rich.

By the late 1960s, the patina of companionship and camaraderie that glossed different versions of twentieth-century heterosexuality for women was patchy, rubbed bare by the hypocrisy of the sexual revolution. On the left, the fantasies of the 1960s blended dreams of living happily ever after with utopian fancies of sexual freedom. Radicals spurned monogamy for its possessiveness and roots in bourgeois life and conflated marriage with the property relations of capitalism. The most advanced believed the future lay with multiple love affairs and communal households, as if they were channeling Fourier. But, as in the nineteenth century, free love was a mixed blessing for women, more of a license for men's traditional philandering than a new deal for sex. The double standard persisted; in the counterculture and SDS, nasty gossip swirled around female sexual adventurers while men gained in reputation for their erotic conquests and profligacy—usually at the expense of the women they slept with.

The sex could be had—as women testified in C-R groups—organized around men's needs, not women's. And in communal households, men slept around, did drugs, and pontificated on the coming revolution along with their female comrades; but when it came time to scrub the bathtub or put the children to bed, the responsibility was women's. No matter how disaffected or distanced from the American status quo, men were accustomed to seeing women in subordinate positions, and they defined themselves to some extent through their superiority, just like the fathers they maligned.

Marriage was thus an easy target for women's liberation. Blending the New Left's dislike of monogamy as bourgeois with a quickened understanding of male/female power relations, radical feminists produced a view of marriage as bleak and scabrous as any account since Mary Wollstonecraft wrote about the desperate women she saw dancing their fates out in the meat markets of English society balls. "Marriage is the model for all other forms of discrimination against women," asserted Sheila Cronan from New York, unknowingly evoking centuries of protest. Emotionally speaking, "wife" took shape as an inherently degraded identity. One divorced woman's dictum that "I have come to view marriage as a built-in self-destruct for women" was a commonplace sentiment.[60]

The 1960s critique bypassed older condemnations of marriage's legal and economic liabilities to stress the psychological infirmities that companionate marriage inflicted. Sardonic descriptions abounded of wives' service to male egos and the decimation that marriage wreaked on woman's sense of self. Habits of deference suffused middle-class marriages: "We stagger under the weight of cultural commandments. Thou

Shalt Not Compete With Him, Thou Shalt Not be Aggressive, Thou Shalt Seek Fulfillment Through Your Womb Not Your Head," wrote Ellen Maslow in a downtown New York journal. Given this state of things, anyone would want a wife, suggested Judy Syfers, herself married. And why not? She laid out the job requirements, putting herself in the place of a husband. "I want a wife who will work and send me to school. And while I am going to school I want a wife to take care of my children. I want a wife to keep track of the children's doctor and dentist appointments. And to keep track of mine, too."[61]

Underlying the contempt for marriage was distrust of heterosexuality itself—or, more precisely, of the men who made up one half of the enterprise. In many ways—some women said in all ways—men were oppressors and exploiters. At the very least they were a lot of work, even if you weren't married to one. "I realize now how completely you're expected to give to them in order to have them talk to you," reflected a woman in a consciousness-raising group. "You have to just *lavish* attention on them or else they just don't come around." The roundup of malefactors broke open the façade of family government and threw the spotlight on the men who headed the jurisdiction. Women learned to see their hopes for equality with boyfriends and husbands as inevitably self-deluding, luring them into amiable or, worse, tender and passionate relations with antagonists who disguised themselves as lovers. "It is hard to fight an enemy who has outposts in your head," confessed Sally Kempton in *Esquire* about the contradiction she experienced between being a feminist and being married. "At the risk of sounding naïve ... ," ventured a woman attending a 1968 consciousness-raising group, "I've been listening to this for an hour and no one has mentioned love." A transcript of the conversation records that her question set off a wave of "ferocious laughter."[62]

The bad habits of husbands and fathers, brothers and workmates, lovers and friends embodied personal failings magnified many times over in the failings of the entire sex. The left's indictment of the "military-industrial complex" and American racism and imperialism set the pattern: Radical feminism attacked "male chauvinism," which held women in line just as racism did blacks, imperialism did the Third World poor, and capitalism did workers. "All men receive economic, sexual, and psychological benefits from male supremacy." It was a scathing view of ordinary men's stake in an oppressive system. "We identify the agents of our oppression as men."[63] No surprise, then, that "the man-who-would-understand" was a phantom, that the brother/twin was lost.

Every man was a boss. This was a core insight of a feminism that owed much to the Marxist theory of labor exploitation. A labor system gave structural coherence to male dominance in the family; and the name of that system was housework, or, in Marxist terminology, reproduction. The assumption that housework and full-time child care sucked up women's time and turned them into drudges was an article of faith with feminists and had been since *The Feminine Mystique*. And historically, it was irrefutable that women always did the housework, men never did. Girls and women learned at home, as they had for centuries, that this was the way the world worked. From the 1920s on, modernity in the United States was always promising changes, not from men but from domestic technology, but the prospects for freedom vanished as standards of cleanliness rose with the new devices to keep things clean, and the bars for home decorating and cooking moved ever higher, actually increasing the time women spent in housework.

Since 1900, writers had lamented the encumbrances of domestic work, the magnitude and weight that kept women from taking a full part in the world—although it was seldom that they noticed that the working-class women who labored as their servants did most of it.[64] But Charlotte Perkins Gilman, Olive Schreiner, Beauvoir, and Friedan, while they detested housework, never considered the possibility that men could be asked—no, required—to help. The assumption was that those servants would step in so that middle-class women of the future could come home and kick off their shoes like men.[65] Now, for the first time, feminists questioned men's ancient exemption. Surely domestic drudgery wasn't a natural emanation of femininity. So why was it that only women did it?

The conclusion was obvious: The pretense that somehow housework was suitably female was a way men veiled the facts of exploitation. It was one of women's liberation's most potent ideas, with immediate consequences for gender relationships. There was a political economy to domestic labor, an organized system of power, not just a happenstance arrangement dictated by individuals' different skills ("I never learned to use the washing machine and you did"). The insights produced a revelatory account of just how much housework handicapped women. In a heterosexual pair, men's work always had more prestige and was more highly compensated, which meant that men's earnings counted as their domestic contribution, while women's lesser earnings—or lack of paid work altogether—landed them the job of caring for everyone and everything else.

Even the kindest of men in the 1960s seemed to feel in their very bones that women were born to do housework and they were not, that they, the men, had no reason to wipe off the stove; no know-how to wash dishes; no skill to diaper the baby properly or entertain fussy children. In the 1960s, a loving father who helped raise three children could proudly note to his daughter that he had never changed a diaper in his life: His freedom from what was literally shit work was, in his mind, a tribute to a smoothly functioning marriage. Young men justified the scummy bathtubs, sinks piled high with dirty dishes, and filthy kitchen floors with an antibourgeois ethic: They weren't "uptight" about cleanliness, and if some woman wanted to clean the place up, well then, no one would stop her. It was startling to see that men's feigned ignorance really masked their certainty that housework was beneath them, and that women, no matter how cherished, were made to muck around in the dirt and shit.

Perhaps it was a mental confrontation with the daily toll of living with men that only young women could have had, daughters who were new to this branch of the business, not yet socialized and thus incredulous about the double standard that their mothers tolerated. It was an area of crime in which the feminist third degree revealed a massive cover-up of men's privileges. "The Politics of Housework," a feminist parody widely circulated in the early 1970s, captures the cynical turn. A comic send-up of one ostensibly liberated man's responses to his girlfriend's pressure to share the housework, the piece proceeds as a point-counterpoint between his equivocations and her sardonic commentary. "'I don't mind sharing the housework' [he says], 'but I don't do it very well. We should each do the things we're best at.' MEANING [she says]: 'Unfortunately I'm no good at things like washing dishes or cooking.'" "'I don't mind sharing the work' [he says], 'but you'll have to show me how to do it.' MEANING [she says]: 'I ask a lot of questions and you'll have to show me everything every time I do it because I don't remember so good.'"[66]

Alongside the literature of confrontation in the household was a small body of work on how actually to improve domestic life with men. A few minority voices counseled acts of resistance rather than following Ibsen's Nora out the door. The assumption was that men—even men!— could learn a different way to be husbands and partners. But the process would bring discomfort and turmoil; it required a thick skin and a tough will. Don't let yourself get interrupted so easily, one writer admonished in this vein. Take yourself seriously. The same hopeful impulse, edged with realism about family dynamics, glinted in Alix Kates Shulman's notorious "Marriage Agreement." Shulman, a novelist and member of New York Redstockings, was a rare married woman in the feminist avant-garde, the mother of two small children, caring for them at home as she struggled to launch a writing career. In 1970, she published in a small feminist journal a contract she had drawn up with her husband, a successful businessman, to make their relationship and family life more equitable by dividing up housework.[67]

Shulman told a familiar tale, of a young couple who had some reciprocity at the beginning of their marriage that hardened, under the pressures of children and jobs, into a conventional and tiresome arrangement. Her husband's job kept him out late and often out of town, while she sank into a bog of housework and child care. "If I suffered from too much domesticity, he suffered from too little." When she came to see her situation from a feminist perspective, she realized that the only way the marriage could survive was "to throw out the old sex roles we had been living with and start again."

The "agreement" was a marvelously detailed, dry enumeration of the routine jobs of keeping a family going—jobs that mysteriously turned into women's jobs even in the best of marriages. The Job Breakdown was divided into two categories, Children and Housework. The jobs having to do with children included hallowed maternal tasks: "tucking them in and having night-talks; handling [them] if they wake and call in the night" and "answering questions, explaining things." The Schedule divided everything strictly and efficiently, and the "Principles" declared that the work that brought in more money (that is, the husband's) was not automatically more valuable and exempt from the claims of the family than the wife's, and that "each member of the family has an equal right to his/her own time, work, value, choices." Time was the currency of negotiation, as anyone knows who's ever taken serious care of small children and a household. The partners could make deals and swap, but the principle had to hold fifty-fifty.

Redbook reprinted the article in 1971; glitzy *New York* magazine followed with a how-to piece; the newly founded feminist *Ms.* picked it up. In 1972, Alix Shulman published her first novel, *Memoirs of an Ex-Prom Queen*, a runaway success, and the photo magazine *Life* ran a spread on the family with fetching photos of the lovely Alix (she really was an ex-prom queen), handsome husband, and beguiling children, captioned with apposite sections of the "Agreement" and enthusiastic testimonials from Martin Shulman and the children. "The Marriage Experiment," *Life* proclaimed on the cover, and for the moment, feminists had charge of the experiment and it seemed to be going well. Shulman, having sorted through two thousand letters that inundated *Redbook* in response to the article, found grounds for optimism: While 50 percent opposed the marriage contract, more than a third praised it and thought their own marriages would be better for such an agreement. "I received the unmistakable impression that changes are in the air," she concluded.[68] Change was in the air, and for the moment there was a chance that feminism would help direct it.

But successful experiments in domestic equity never really gained ground. Housework was a burden that virtually every woman experienced. The housework issue cut to the bone of their dealings with the men they lived with. Predictably, it had mass appeal among women and none among men. In a period of steeply increasing female employment, the unequal division of domestic work became a flashpoint in millions of relationships. And to this day, housework and child-care arrangements remain a source of simmering antagonism between the sexes, hashed out in quarrels all the nastier in their pettiness. Reading the contract now, the division of parental tasks at first looks outrageous—how could someone want to get out of tucking a child in bed at night, or answering her calls in the night? That is, until you imagine a married gay couple implementing it, rather than a woman and a man: Then the agreement seems practical, an efficient and considerate division of labor rather than an abrogation of maternal nature.

As members of the first generation to come of sexual age with reliable contraception, young feminists were imbued with views of how emancipatory sex should be. But they also had a backlog of experience of its disappointments, a corpus of grievances about men's erotic clumsiness and obtuseness. The mass confessions of consciousness-raising in 1968–70 stripped bare what seemed a common problem of male obliviousness to women's desires.

Since the nineteenth century, women had alluded elliptically to unhappiness in heterosexual sex. But the taboo against respectable women speaking frankly was too strong to bring specifics into the open. When New Women in the 1910s referred to erotic pleasure, they did so in vague mystical language, without naming the female orgasm or clitoris, or indeed, specifying in the least what two people did together in bed. In the 1960s, however, advice columnists, physicians, and psychiatrists began to bruit about details and options of the bedroom that had always before been veiled. In their corner of this conversation, feminists discovered in consciousness-raising that the sexual revolution that supposedly encouraged female desire and pleasure was, in fact, dishing out assignments to service men in bed. Complaints merged around a dawning awareness of the politics of female orgasm.

In 1966, the Kinsey Institute, a world-famous center for sex research, published its definitive finding that the clitoris was the sole organ of female climax. Kinsey researchers found that the vaginal orgasm, heralded by 1950s psychiatrists as the zenith of mature female sexuality, was in fact a fiction. All female orgasms originated in the clitoris, whether directly (through manual stimulation) or indirectly, from penile friction. The Kinsey research, however, had little success winning hearts and minds; everywhere in the midst of the sexual revolution, the belief persisted that the vaginal orgasm was normal and the clitoris was an embarrassing little extra that could be ignored. A typical marriage manual articulated the dogma: "Clitoral orgasm is immature, evades true feminine sexuality, and is considered a form of frigidity."[69]

In 1971, Anne Koedt, from New York Radical Feminists, revived the Kinsey research, disseminating her summary in a mimeographed pamphlet, "The Myth of the Vaginal Orgasm." It was an underground sensation, distributed through feminist newspapers and women's centers. Koedt did Kinsey one better: She went beyond the physiological findings to discern what was at stake in keeping the myth going. Koedt maintained that men's needs, not women's, defined what was taken as normal heterosexual coitus. Men were oblivious to female physiology and pressured their lovers, who ended up pretending to have vaginal orgasms as a tribute to phallic prowess, deferring to "whatever model of their sexuality is offered by men."[70]

The shift to this explicit discussion of erotic pleasure came as an embarrassment to liberals. Theirs was a cautious, reticent view of the trouble that erotic license could bring to women: a mother's view. Friedan, president of NOW, was deeply uncomfortable with sexual issues. Fighting her way out of the pervasive sexualization of the 1950s and the eroticization of the languorous housewife, Friedan saw women's desire as the residue of a humiliating feminine obsession best banished by useful work in the world. In *The Feminine Mystique*, sexual desire smacks of women's shameful needs, miasmic lusts, and needy bodies—factors that threaten to confirm the misogynistic images Friedan was trying to beat back. "The women's movement was not about sex, but about equal opportunity in jobs and all the rest of it," Friedan insisted to the end of her life. "Sexual politics was bad business."[71] The imbroglio over gay rights—a "minority" issue that became a majority one—was one factor that led to her leaving the NOW presidency in 1970.

But sexual politics overran liberal distaste in the long run, sending enhanced norms of female pleasure into a culture already booming with erotic images, confessions, needs, and profit motives. Whatever the unexpected outcomes, the step toward sexual knowledge was a little-noted but laudable contribution of women's liberation at its boldest. Radical feminism took a huge step in actually *naming* the source of female pleasure—a subject that had always been shrouded in euphemisms or hidden altogether. In a culture that was turning sexual satisfaction into a life goal, open discussion of women's erotic requirements and criticisms of men's sexual habits had influence well beyond the radicals who first proposed that orgasms, too, had politics.[72]

Beginning with the 1968 protest at the Miss America pageant, women's liberation held up the beauty industry as a major profiteer from women's distress about their bodies. The culturally induced fixation was another facet of the business of men. The female body itself, far from being a natural expression of irreducible difference, was revealed to be the product of exploited labor. The New Left and counterculture had prepared the ground, making a return to the natural body, including rejecting cosmetics and fashion, a prerequisite for repudiating bourgeois society. Revolutionaries wore work shirts, blue jeans, and India print skirts, not pleated skirts and blouses with Peter Pan collars. But feminism took the animus further, into an understanding of how beauty standards reinforced male domination. The labor of looking good came to seem a quintessential act of creating oneself as the other to the male subject, woman fashioning herself as object of man's desire.

A puritanical ethos of anti-beauty sat heavily on radical feminism in these years: Liberation was defined as abandoning makeup, stylish clothes, nylon stockings, high heels, and bras, all deemed trappings of heterosexual oppression. The act of renouncing, say, miniskirts or long hair—as in the political hair-cutting demonstration—became almost a requirement of seriousness. They were capitulations to patriarchy, emblems of false consciousness.[73]

It was an obsession particular to a movement of young women, for whom the rejection of beauty standards was as much a passion as fidelity to them would be for young women in the twenty-first century. "What's wrong with that one?" the bemused editor John Mack Carter asked with genuine puzzlement at the *Ladies' Home Journal* protest when a spokeswoman confronted him with an article on makeup techniques. "What's wrong with your natural face?" was the outraged rejoinder. Had he ever considered how useless and draining all that work was for ordinary women? She lectured him about the futility of it all: "You put on gook and make up and lipstick and eyeshadow" and all for naught. And "there isn't the glamour to accommodate it," she concluded tremulously.[74]

What to make of feminine beauty and fashion has always been a stumbling block for feminists. Since Mary Wollstonecraft, women's rights thinkers have had difficulty considering the desire to look good. Wollstonecraft was a lovely and sensual young woman, and surely a sight to behold when she was in the full flush of love. But she understood—as did many who came later—that beauty had its hidden, grim visage. Even for the blessed, it was only full-blown for a short time; and for the rest of womankind, the masses of ordinary-looking women, it was a mask that must be artfully prepared, because women's marriage prospects and thus their entire well-being depended on attracting men. Wollstonecraft, with her years spent at the edges of rich women's lives watching the marriage market grind on, learned to despise the artful getup of femininity as debased labor, and the "weak woman of fashion" as the lowest of the sex. "Taught from their infancy that beauty is woman's scepter, the mind shapes itself to the body, and roaming round its gilt cage, only seeks to adore its prison." Sarah Grimké, too, child of the South Carolina aristocracy, had only disparaging words for the "butterflies of the fashionable world" of the kind she would have known in planter society. "They are taught to regard marriage as the one thing needful, the only avenue to distinction; hence to attract the notice and win the attention of men, by their external charms, is the chief business of fashionable girls."[75]

Could women look good for any reason other than to please and attract men? In the 1960s, the answer was no. Did sexy clothes necessarily make you a slave to male fantasy? That women might want to attract other women was only barely considered, and then the assumption was that lesbians had no need to look sexy. Naomi Weisstein, showy, fearless, and funny keyboard player for the Chicago Women's Liberation Rock Band (and a Harvard Ph.D. to boot), looked back on the anti-beauty ethos of woman's liberation as marvelous. "It was no longer an imperative of nature that we paint our faces and squeeze our breasts into little cones."[76] No more hours in front of the mirror; no more worries about breasts that were too big or too small.

But the problem was that too many women fell out of feminist calculations because they wore lipstick and high heels. Certainly the dogma that no feminist should shave her legs had limited appeal. It was another divide between moderates and radicals, a tension between those who put on nylons, suits, and prim pumps as body armor and those who threw themselves into battle in jeans and peasant blouses, long hair flying, their contempt for looking good an advertisement for blazing noncompliance. Friedan, belligerently outspoken, sounded like a nagging mother when she put into words the disapproval that others of her generation felt, deploring the imperative "to *make yourself ugly*, to stop shaving under your arms, to stop wearing makeup or pretty dresses—any skirts at all." On the morning of the Women's Strike for Equality, an amused journalist reported that Friedan was late for her interview because she was held up at the hairdresser's. "I don't want people to think Women's Lib girls don't care about how they look," Friedan prissily informed *The New York Times*. "We should try to be as pretty as we can. It's good for our self-image and it's good politics."[77] Anti-beauty would always aggravate Friedan, who thought it a diversion from more important challenges the movement faced. She was not wrong. To shave your legs or not was the least of women's problems post-1968.

Yet the idea was powerful. In revealing how much labor went into looking naturally feminine, anti-beauty showed that the female body as women knew it was bound up with male power. The radicals were onto something, at *Ladies' Home Journal* and in general: The beauty industry makes fools of women, takes their money, and leaves them with last year's clothes and half-used jars of face cream, sooner or later "without the glamour to accommodate it."

The bald proposition that "men oppress women" contained the unspoken corollary that all men oppress all women. Never in feminism's long history had advocates given so little room to the prospects for working with *some* men for change. The early-twentieth-century idea of the human sex, the vibrant connection between New Women and New Men, was gone. Rather, women's liberation cast relationships with men as an unfortunate habit to be kicked. In contrast, liberals shied away from the purge mentality. They preferred to temper their criticisms of men with the language of roles, since role theory implied that both sexes were trapped in dysfunctional behavior and both sexes could change. NOW's position on including men as fellow fighters for equal rights remained strenuously "optimistic and consensual," writes Linda Kerber.[78]

For women's liberation, though, there was no debating the matter. The faith that it was just a matter of men relearning roles was pallid beside the dramaturgy of perfidious male chauvinism. Radical texts rebuked men for their loutish behavior in bed, their laziness when it came to housework, their cluelessness with children, their egotism, woeful characters, and selfish ways—in short, their characters and their persons. "Actually, being oppressive seems to be their natural state," agreed the middle-class college graduates featured in a *New Yorker* investigation of women's liberation. The worst men—wife beaters, rapists, misogynists—were in some sense Representative Men, "different in degree but not in kind from the behavior of most men."[79]

The exposé of "the masculine mystique," as Dorothy Sue Cobble calls it, was a breakthrough that promised more thoroughgoing change than when the burden was on women. The critique of masculinity gave emotional focus to an unstructured movement by creating a multitude of battlefields with easily identifiable antagonists. There was no "problem without a name," as Friedan had diagnosed the situation. The problem's name was sexism—the word first cropped up in 1968—and the men who profited from it.[80]

But in the short run, the ideology hardened into judgments that had little relation to women's actual lives, gay or straight. Men were the enemy, yet women continued to live with men in parallel time, constructing lives with fathers and brothers, male friends straight and gay, husbands, ex-husbands, co-parents, lovers, workmates, and co-conspirators. Virtually all women were connected to men in important ways. Yet feminism only acknowledged those valences that were negative and ignored women's investment in a better future. Lesbians remained marginally more open about relationships with men: The gay liberation movement was the one place on the left where feminists could acknowledge imagined brothers. Women's liberation exempted African-American men, too, from the general indictment. White feminists paid obeisance to the strength and importance of black men's and women's ties, but at the risk of constructing a spurious common cause with black men, whom they assumed to be exempt from male privilege, an idea that was highly irritating to black women.[81]

Modernity had long assigned a central role to the mixing of the sexes.

Radical feminism's contribution was to show that the collaboration was so asymmetrical that it was impossible to square with equality. But the inability to come to terms with heterosexual love and heterosocial friendship and kinship created a blind spot, which blocked a full and more complete vision of what feminist relations between the sexes might be in this world, not a distant utopia. Radicals were unable to create a language that looked to a life that women could honorably live with men—sexually, collegially, familially, parentally, and fraternally. Life and love with men, gay and straight alike, proceeded as underground activity, the yearning, amity, and—yes—tenderness across the sex line skirted in consciousness-raising circles, untheorized by the exciting ideas of the times.

Betty Friedan was aware of the tendency, having already been branded a sellout and homophobe for her friendly comments about heterosexuality. She tried to keep the lines open, assuring her public in 1973 that feminism "will make it possible in this world for men and women to make love, not war." Boston's ascetic Cell 16 reprinted Friedan's comment and contemptuously tagged it, as if with a graffiti smear, "NOW LESS THAN EVER!"[82]

In itself, the female separatism of women's liberation was unremarkable. What was distinct was the relegation of men to a useless, in fact an invidious, position. Earlier feminists were vague about the role individual men played in the institutions that oppressed them, preferring to protest the power of anonymous patriarchs rather than snoop around too much in any particular family jurisdiction. They generally treated husbands, brothers, and male friends as invited guests to a better world.

But could that world be composed of women alone? Of course not, which leads to the question: What were radical feminists thinking? Some of the extreme language was tongue-in-cheek. "Women of the World Unite—We Have Nothing to Lose but Our Men!" "A woman without a man is like a fish without a bicycle." Were men going to wither away, as the state was supposed to do after the proletarian revolution? Not really, although brash young women fed off one another's audacity to induce mass hallucination about what the future was going to look like.

Black power authorized the sardonic tone, because this was the attitude militants took at the moment toward whites, including liberal civil rights supporters. As the rage of black power shattered the beloved community, the rage of women's liberation separated the sheep from the goats, real feminists from the trimmers and weak sisters who put their priorities with women second. The stress on omnipresent racism and sexism forced attention on how deep both ran. But in terms of the alliances, compromises, and practical goals that propel liberal democratic politics, the attachment to denunciation and black-and-white moralizing was costly.

In this feminist family quarrel, sisterhood became the one metaphorical bond free of the taint of patriarchy. The title of *Sisterhod Is Powerful* (1970), Robin Morgan's bestselling anthology of women's liberation texts, gives a sense of the investment, ties between women accorded solidarity and strength nonpareil. For a short time in the headiest days, it seemed as though sisters born again in the grace of feminism could live in Herland, laying the foundations for a redeemed society to which others, once cleansed of false consciousness, could immigrate.

As sisterhood took on added meaning, lesbianism turned into a political statement—a tactic—for heterosexual refuseniks. "We must move out of our old living patterns and into new ones," announced The Furies, a lesbian-feminist vanguard group. "Monogamy can be cast aside; no one will 'belong' to one another."[83] Self-consciously political lesbianism overlapped with "woman-defined" ways of living and the promotion of the "woman-identified woman" as an ideal. Political lesbianism, however, was oddly detached from and at times even antagonistic to longtime lesbians.

In the first years of the women's movement, lesbian identity was muted, sometimes choked. With so much interest in male shortcomings, lesbians' grievances didn't count for much—after all, they were not living in the "belly of the beast." NOW gained a reputation as hostile to gay women, whose open presence threatened to compromise its respectability: Friedan would not even list the Daughters of Bilitis, a staid lesbian rights organization in existence since 1955, among the sponsors of a 1969 event in New York; she supposedly invoked a "lavender menace" that would ruin NOW. Gay radicals turned Friedan's lavender menace remark into a token of everything that was repressed and repressive about liberals.[84]

Once the 1969 Stonewall Rebellion launched gay liberation, though, lesbians took on a different role, as a heroic force for sexual liberation. Last of the radical movements to surface, gay liberation sent off fireworks of self-discovery, rapturous declarations, and bacchanalia. "It was a movement for the right to love," the critic Paul Berman admiringly observes. "The gay movement was the most romantic political campaign that ever existed." In the exhilarating atmosphere, lesbian lives seemed exalted: exclusively female and wonderfully sensuous and egalitarian, free of deadly phalluses and the sexists who sported them. Lesbian life blossomed outside the customary settings of gay bars and private parties in the more open air of a political subculture: Semi-political parties and dances, renowned for their sexy atmosphere, great dancing, and general good times, attracted gays, straights, and bisexuals. Knots of zealots—many of them new to lesbian life—promulgated the dictate that every woman could be a lesbian if she broke the chains of self-hatred forged in living with the oppressor. "It is the primacy of women relating to women, of women creating a new consciousness of and with each other which is at the heart of women's liberation," rhapsodized Radicalesbians.[85]

After 1969, lesbianism changed from a minority identity to be tolerated to an ideal and, among insiders, the one route for the truly committed. Anne Koedt advised in "The Politics of Orgasm" that if women understood that they didn't need penises to have pleasure, they might consider men expendable. "Lesbian sexuality, in rubbing one clitoris against another," Koedt expounded in her dry, clinical way, "could make an excellent case . . . for the extinction of the male organ." What Koedt phrased tentatively turned into the belief that lesbianism was the revolutionary choice, "the rage of all women condensed to the point of explosion," exhorted the manifesto "The Woman-Identified Woman." The spirit was evangelical, promising the grace of a woman-centered world. "Devote all your energies to women, in an extreme form, to lesbians alone. Radicalesbians hope to persuade 'straight' women to become lesbians and lesbians to a radical political position."[86]

And what of women who already were lesbians? Ironically, lesbian-feminism was less sympathetic to those who saw sexual desire for other women, rather than political conviction, as the core of their identity. By watering down lesbian sex to sensuous feelings rather than acknowledging a distinctive genital eros, the figure of the woman-identified woman masked a wariness of "dykes," as women with lesbian histories differentiated themselves from the politicals. Karla Jay, a Redstockings member who helped found the Gay Liberation Front, saw the apotheosis of the woman-identified woman as daring in some respects, but damaging in others. The idealization disguised, she believed, a discomfort with women having sex with women, eliding sexual pleasure with tender touching, and demoting genital pleasure as something male. Lesbians went along with the ideology because, Jay remembers, "our primary goal was to make a political point, and back then the vision of a lesbian in bed conjured up an image of perversion, not radicalism." Some politicals suggested that lesbianism itself might wither away in the coming revolution: When patriarchal constructs were gone, gay sex, too, would disappear and everyone could have sex with everyone else.[87]

In places where there was no critical mass of longtime lesbians, the self-styled woman-identified revolutionaries looked on older lesbians who frequented gay bars as perverted. In Dayton, Ohio, for example, feminists spurned the one lesbian bar as seamy, even as they heralded woman-centered sexuality. "Those lesbians weren't conscious lesbians," scoffed a woman who had discovered she was one. "They were old-world dykes—hard-drinking, hard people . . . [who] didn't give a hoot about feminism." Jay remembers her uneasiness with the disguised assumption that, in the absence of a penis, women lovers really "didn't do too much," and that any woman whose consciousness had been raised could become a lesbian, because feminism held that "our definition did not depend on sexual acts."[88]

Older lesbians had something to gain from women's liberation, although they could be uneasy with the brash style and habits of confrontation. But they bridled at the barely muted contempt for lesbian history and lives, especially for butch/femme women, judged to be trapped in patriarchal roles. "I had behind me a decade of lesbian living and loving that formed a complex sense of self—criminal, erotic, independent, exiled," wrote Joan Nestle, describing her discomfort with newly minted lesbian-feminists in New York in the late 1960s.[89] Nestle took exception to the 1970s idea—which persisted well into the next decade—that butch and femme identities were oppressive sex roles that older lesbians fell into because of false consciousness. The idea that lesbianism was a choice and a kinder, gentler form of eros was at first bothersome, then offensive, to those who had spent years protecting their intimate lives from humiliating and dangerous exposure and treasuring the desire that defined who they were. So was the idea that feminism was "the validating starting point of healthy lesbian culture" and that all that came before was vaguely twisted. It was an odd replication of mainstream homophobia in the name of a purified sisterhood.

The romance of the woman-identified woman stopped short of mothers. To a generation of daughters bent on resisting the housewife's degradation and the wife's ignoble compromises, it was difficult to see traditional motherhood as anything but a life sentence to patriarchy. The compulsion was to dissolve motherhood's centrality to feminine identity, to make it count less in time, emotional energy, and bodily wear and tear. Motherhood seemed to be about concessions to others, not revolution. It was most certainly the state that feminists wanted to escape, not that which they wanted to become. The tension runs deep in the tradition, but it was acute in the face-off between the generation of women who lived out the feminine mystique and their willful, wayward daughters. "The mother is the one ... through or against whom we figure out what we might have become," writes literary critic Nancy Miller.[90]

It was not that women's liberation was anti-mother, or that there were no actual mothers involved, but rather that motherhood seemed a state that was irrelevant, perhaps inimical, to sisterhood. "There was an under-the-surface condescension toward mothers," acknowledged Ellen Willis. "On some level was the ... feeling that women who were breaking with traditional roles were the ones who would be your *real* allies." Women's liberation perpetuated daughters in revolt, not mothers in thrall. "I saw having children as the great trap that completely took away your freedom," she added. The intensity differed across the country and the ocean—Lynne Segal, for example, writes of the importance of mothers in London women's liberation at the time. In the United States, some groups were more interested and sympathetic than others. But however protagonists assessed the feeling, it is undeniable that overall, discussion was indifferent or antipathetic. The Newest of New Women was unfettered, free of family obligations, endowed with the revolutionary fervor of picking and choosing and able to follow the dictates of raised consciousness wherever they might take her.[91]

The attitude was aggressively antisentimental, a caustic solvent to pieties about female destiny and child raising. The best-known summa of women's liberation, Shulamith Firestone's *The Dialectic of Sex* (1970), described pregnancy as "the temporary deformation of the body of the individual for the sake of the species." Firestone, a founding member of New York Redstockings, hoped for artificial wombs, "cybernation" that would free women from dangerous biology. Nor did she see things improving once the babies were born. Firestone made explicit what was a widely shared assumption in women's liberation, that the mother–child bond damaged both parties: She titled one chapter "Down with Children." Firestone's polemic pushed to the outer reaches of matrophobia, but regardless, the point is that no one publicly distanced women's liberation from these views. In other writings, too, childhood and femininity were crippled companions. "Wow! Listen, kids— liberation is just around the corner! No more moms oppressing you," advised the menacingly titled Boston journal *No More Fun and Games*, with a scary stab at playful prose. The family was the template of deforming demands, turning mothers into oppressors of their own children. "'Mother love' can usually be translated as a woman finding her identity through another person. That's a terrible burden on the child." "I feel that the more responsibility any one person bears for raising a child, the more anger that person will have for the child," one mother testified.[92]

Such doleful views were offshoots of the New Left's condemnation of the family as the incubator of individuals who would fit capitalist requirements. These conclusions were only explicit on the far left of women's liberation, but the angle of vision was common. In Germany, the New Left animus was ferocious, and led to even more draconian experiments in communal living and parenting. In the United States, feminism's dissent from motherhood was in some ways assimilable to the mainstream, providing a political rationale for an overall trend toward fewer children that had been going on since 1960. A radical vision of fewer children or no children meshed with the structural requirements of a society where more and more women were working full-time. Mainstream culture, too, inquired if motherhood was destiny. In 1970, *Look* magazine, a bellwether of the mass American psyche, published "Motherhood, Who Needs It," an astonishingly cavalier dismissal that today, in our zealously pro-natal times, could hardly be discussed politely, so incendiary does the question seem.[93]

"Most radical feminists were not anti-child, they simply ignored children," recounts Rosalyn Baxandall, in New York women's liberation at the time, who had a small son. And indeed, the tone seems to have differed from city to city: In Seattle and Cambridge, Massachusetts, for instance, there was organized pressure on universities to provide child care. But for women's liberation as a whole, the child-care issue, while important in theory, seemed remote. True, both radicals and liberals voiced a demand for twenty-four-hour free child care. But it was a demand in name only, since munificent child care on this model existed nowhere in the world except for the Israeli kibbutzim and was never a realistic goal in a country that lacked strong traditions of public support for workingwomen and families.[94]

More modest centers for children during the workday were possible at a time when the country was fascinated by ideas of early childhood development: The federally funded Project Head Start, created in 1965, remained a popular holdover from LBJ's Great Society. Child-care centers, however, would not bring the dazzling revolution that the toughest radicals wanted. Firestone scorned even twenty-four-hour child care, because "day-care centers buy women off. They ease the immediate pressure without asking why that pressure is on women." Mothers along with feminist fathers did organize parent-run facilities that in the radical spirit prided themselves on loose bohemian arrangements and lack of professional staff. They were determinedly separate from anything that might be construed as workplace-based child care. "As radicals we must understand that our goals for children are in conflict with those of the institutions—corporations and universities—from whom we will be demanding day care services." These centers instilled feminist principles: Boys and girls were to use both the Housekeeping Corner and the Carpentry Corner, and if the girls were playing with dolls but the boys weren't, a parent or two helpfully intervened. Yet their appeal was limited, since they demanded huge amounts of time from parents, more than people working eight-hour days could afford. They addressed the needs of students, artists, and the self-employed but not workingwomen who needed a standard routine. "The objection seemed to be that our nursery was non-institutional," acknowledged Baxandall, whose son was in a feminist/left-wing center. "Emphasis was placed on free play rather than structured learning. One Black mother did join the group but left because she didn't feel at ease with the other mothers who seemed like hippies to her."[95]

The most influential book on motherhood that came out of this construct of motherhood, Adrienne Rich's beautiful *Of Woman Born* (1976), both pulled at and confirmed the association between maternity and women's infirmities. Rich saw motherhood as the basis for all relations between human beings—mothers taught children what it was to be human. It was the mother's love, not the father's, that made the difference: The sensuous bond spun by suckling, holding, and soothing came from a maternal essence that was much superior to the paternal capacity to nurture. Rich lovingly evoked the exquisite details of a "continually changing dialogue between mother and child, crystallized in such moments, as when, hearing her child's cry, she feels milk rush into her breasts ... when the child's mouth, caressing the nipple, creates waves of sensuality in the womb where it once lay; or when, smelling the breast even in sleep, the child starts to root and grope for the nipple."

But Rich believed that patriarchal institutions deformed this natural capacity. The crushing isolation of mothers; the overwhelming burdens of children's dependencies; society's denigration of maternal work; the devaluation of women's longings independent of their identity as mothers: All these created anger and resentment that poisoned the generations.[96]

Of Woman Born evoked a tone established early in the 1970s, motherhood bleeding into injury and defeat. "Sometimes I seem to myself, in my feeling toward these tiny guiltless beings, a monster of selfishness and intolerance," Rich quoted from her 1960 journal of her days with three young sons, close in age. "Their voices wear away at my nerves, their constant needs, above all their need for simplicity and patience, fill me with despair at my own failures, despair too at my fate, which is to serve a function for which I was not fitted." She recorded desolation, monstrous antagonism, barely suppressed rage, which fueled debilitating depression. "And yet at other times I am melted with the sense of their helpless, charming and quite irresistible beauty." Rich's argument was not about motherhood itself, but the institution of motherhood as shaped by a society that put the entire burden of child rearing on women. Yet even so, this stunning poet of ordinary life could find little that was redemptive in the ordinary round of motherhood as women knew it in the here and now: meals given, confidences received, stories read, achievements praised. Motherhood in all its banality was the soil of tragedy.[97]

Since the turn of the century, the hallmark of New Womanhood, one secret sign of belonging, was the determination to live a life different from the mother. The 1960s revolt threw daughters into a headlong flight, propelled by a matrophobia that much more intense. The disinterest in maternity turned into dislike when feminists looked at their own mothers. When women's liberation investigated the scene of the patriarchal crime, it was mothers, not fathers, who were the chief suspects.

Disdain for the mother and sometimes outright mother-hating were set pieces of feminist novels of the 1970s, mass-market books that won popular audiences. "My love for her and my hate for her are so bafflingly intertwined that I can hardly see her," Erica Jong's wisecracking heroine of the bestseller *Fear of Flying* (1973) explains of her mother. "The umbilical cord which connects us has never been cut so it has sickened and rotted and turned black." Mothers were aggressive and emotionally stinting. "Any honor I received was tainted by a suspicion I saw in her eyes that the honor might not have been deserved," complains the heroine in Sara Davidson's lightly fictionalized memoir *Loose Change* (1977), about the intertwined lives of three footloose girls in Berkeley and New York in the 1960s.

Injured, thwarted mothers injured and thwarted their own daughters. In the most extreme formulations, old mothers and new mothers were locked in a death-dealing embrace. "It was as if I had got a sense of waste with my mother's milk," confessed a New York woman, "a sense of despair that women never seem to move as if they were in their own element." "I am angry at my mother for not mothering me," acknowledged Susan Griffin in 1974. Writing with halts and jerks, as if she could barely prise out of herself what she was admitting, she turned on her own daughter. "There, it is said. I am angry—this is harder to say—at my daughter for always interrupting me. Generation after generation it is the same story. My daughter says to me one night, 'You don't like me because I always bother you.' I carry this around with me, these words, a sorrow so deep to express it would be to fly apart."[98]

Matrophobia was a white woman's sentiment; among African-American and (later) Chicanas/Latinas, such views were unthinkable. Alice Walker's beautiful short essay "In Search of Our Mother's Gardens," first published in 1974 in *Ms.*, can be read at one level as a retort to white matrophobia, at another as laying a claim to an exemplary African-American feminism anchored by the mother–daughter bond. The essay tapped conventions of reverence for mothers and grandmothers that abound in black culture, but Walker's achievement was to bundle up those tributes and make them into the daughters' treasure.

Walker rehearsed the litany of black women's labors, honoring those who wore themselves out in poverty and overwork in the fields, the white kitchens and their own households, their creativity crushed by fatigue, worry, and the contempt piled on them—the "dear Mama" so embedded in black culture that one heard it later in hip-hop lyrics. But she pressed beyond, to reimagine the sainted figures as artists "who died with their real gifts stifled within them." At the end of the line of creative spirits stood Walker's own mother, a poor Southern farm woman who worked from dawn to dusk. "There was never a moment for her to sit down, undisturbed, to unravel her own private thoughts, never a time free from interruption." Yet she prevailed.

In a lyrical culmination, Walker described her mother's beautiful garden as art. "A garden so brilliant with colors, so original in its design, so magnificent with life and creativity, that to this day people drive by our house in Georgia—perfect strangers and imperfect strangers—and ask to stand or walk among my mother's art." As a mother, she gave unstintingly—sewing every stitch of clothing the children wore, quilting their blankets, battling landlords—but she gave as an artist, too: The legacies were fused. There was no bitter daughter's struggle for autonomy, no fight to claim from the world what the mother, being denied herself, would deny her. The daughter carries on where the mother left off—"in search of my mother's garden, I found my own."[99]

Later, Chicanas and Latinas picked up the valedictory strain in a "woman of color" feminism they distinguished from white women's liberation. In a 1981 collection that brought these efforts to a public beyond the founding circles of militants, Cherríe Moraga spoke of her connection to her mother as the bridge connecting her feminism to solidarity with all Mexican-Americans. "My mother. On some very basic level, the woman cannot be shaken from the ground on which she walks." Others chimed in.[100] Ironically, these essays became icons for white feminists, as if praise for the mother could exist only at a safe remove, contained and idealized within black and Hispanic culture.

Within African-American culture, this line of tributes to the mother was rarely challenged or significantly complicated until Toni Morrison's *Beloved* (1987), which turned on the anguished choice of a slave mother to murder her baby daughter, and later A. J. Verdelle's *The Good Negress* (1995), written in the voice of a wounded daughter who has escaped both an uncaring mother and a grandmother who cared too much.

Young black women would have none of the romance of sisterhood. Despite radical feminists' oft-stated antiracism, African-American militants remained suspicious of calls to sisterly solidarity.[101] Across the board, black women were put off by radical feminism's ideology of oppression, as they had not necessarily been by NOW's emphasis on job discrimination.

For one, it was difficult to honor white women's claims to extreme subordination. Black women were at the bottom of every hierarchy of prestige and status. In the 1970s labor market, they earned less than anyone else: significantly less than white women, and less than half what white men earned. Most telling, even black female college graduates earned less than a white man with an eighth-grade education. For another, middle-class white women were historically the employers of ill-paid black female domestic workers, the Miss Anns who got to be ladies while black women scrubbed their toilets. Black women developed "no abiding admiration of white women as a competent, complete people," Toni Morrison allowed in a stinging article on women's liberation in 1971.[102] Even though the postwar generation of educated black women was spared that fate, the low assessment of white women's character was branded in the collective psyche.

Nor was the vehement anti-male rhetoric appealing. Race politics gave no room for such denunciations, which easily ended up fodder for white condemnations of black men's failures. The old mantra of African-American female uplift politics, "Lifting as we climb," still held sub rosa. "Black women tended to want to raise their status and take the whole race with them," explained Frances Beal. "White women tended to go in a separatist direction and damn the men."[103] In no black power group was women's liberation welcome. Everywhere in the years following 1968, debate turned on the status of black manhood, with the model of the machismo revolutionary pushed to the fore. Even in the intellectual *The Black Scholar*, the talk was of guns, warriors, physical confrontation. "Will the real black man please stand up?" the journal's editors requested in a special issue on African-American men. Racism was described as an emasculating force, which could be countered by an army of proud black men who were backed by women's love and respect. "The black woman is, can be, the black man's helper, an undying collaborator, standing up with him, beside her man," advised this editorial confidently. But "we will not need a black women's liberation movement."[104] The real black man would restore race pride to the errant young whose crimes were tearing up urban communities and lead the fight to turn the ghettos back into decent neighborhoods.

From this perspective, feminism was "infiltration," a white plot to divide black women from men in the name of a spurious female unity. There were family quarrels within black radical circles, rifts and tensions between men and women, but over all the gravitational pull of race solidarity prevailed. Ida Lewis, editor of *Essence*, declared unequivocally in 1970 that "the role of Black women is to continue the struggle in concert with Black men for the liberation and determination of Blacks." Gerda Lerner ran into the common wisdom when she spoke in 1969 to a group of black women about sisterhood across the color line. Lerner, long committed to interracial politics, was dismayed by what she heard;

she tartly reported to her friend Pauli Murray that she refused to believe "that all black women are: 1) happily submissive to the male 2) emancipated and in a much better position than white women 3) uninterested in this issue."[105] Lerner would likely have heard a party line aimed at a white woman. But Fran Beal, too, a black SNCC veteran who was more sympathetic to feminism than most, insisted that "at this time Black women are not resentful of the rise of the power of Black men. We welcome it." Black women's job was supporting men whom white society tried to emasculate: They were partners in the struggle for race pride, as they had been since the 1890s, or, for that matter, the 1830s.[106]

Nonetheless, Beal cautioned—with a black nationalist audience in mind—that men should not ignore women's needs, blame them for emasculating them, or force them back into the kitchen. Eleanor Holmes Norton, appointed head of the New York City Human Rights Commission in 1970 and one of the most prominent black liberals in the country, similarly rejected automatic race solidarity. Norton called the task of black feminism "delicate"—an unusual word, because the left was deaf and blind to delicacy of any kind. Delicate because Norton wanted white feminists to acknowledge the simultaneous liberation of black women into economic independence and recognize their loneliness, their poverty, and their quarrels with men. Delicate because feminism must forget neither the damaging ways black men used their power over women nor the truths of men's own injuries.

Norton echoed the themes of black women in the 1890s—their unique relationship to modern womanhood, precisely because they stood so far outside conventional feminine roles; her convictions also resonated with Toni Morrison's beautiful tribute that year to black women's existential solitude and self-invention. Women's alienation endowed them with the ability, Norton argued, to do something remarkable, along with men and children: "We who are black have a chance for something better." The family romance of black politics blossomed in her imagination. Brothers and sisters, despite all the quarrels and held-in unhappiness, could lead the way. "We have a chance to pioneer in forging new relationships between men and women. We have a chance to make family life a liberating experience instead of the confining experience it more often has been. We have a chance to free woman and, with her, the rest of us."[107]

Pauli Murray had consistently maintained since 1963 that the two battles for civil rights should be linked. By 1969, she was one of the few prominent black women to argue for an interracial movement.

270 · *Christine Stansell*

Otherwise, she believed civil rights and feminism would die. Only black women could make the necessary, sustaining connection between the two. Thus she affirmed a key insight of many years of work. "The most essential instrument for combating the divisive effects of a black-only movement is the voice of black women insisting upon the unity of civil rights of women and Negroes as well as other minorities." Always an integrationist, Murray was convinced that separatism undermined effective democratic movements. Her 1970 article, "Liberation of Black Women," challenged men's monopoly on articulating African-American aspirations. She stressed the historic bond of the sexes in race politics but maintained that it was now the woman's era: "The Negro woman's fate in the United States, while inextricably bound with that of the Negro male in one sense, transcends the issue of Negro rights." She pushed it further. It was white women who were black women's "natural allies"—an unpopular position then, and unpopular ever since.[108]

Murray's devotion to feminism isolated her from younger black women, and her dedication to labor causes and civil rights separated her from young white women. Mixing up issues, weighing one set of concerns against another, and finding common ground made someone like Murray appear less feminist than the newly minted radicals, with their insistence on a sisterhood (on the one hand) or race solidarity (on the other) free of what were supposedly distracting and diluting concerns with other people's issues.

In NOW, Murray opposed decisions she saw as leading to a movement "confined almost solely to 'women's rights' without strong bonds with labor and civil rights." Long before academics invented theories of polyvalent identity and intersections between class, race, and gender, Murray insisted that people could not be fenced off in little plots. She was not only a woman, nor was she only black: "And since, as a human being, I cannot allow myself to be fragmented into Negro at one identity, woman at another, or worker at another, I must find a unifying principle in all of these movements to which I can adhere."[109] "The Liberation of Black Women," prescient in so many ways, made no ripples in the radical feminist press, which was preoccupied with racism in a different key—racial guilt and breast-beating, pointing fingers, soul-searching, and endorsing the far-fetched claims of male black militants.

In print, a few others mused on the benefits of allying with white women yet found it next to impossible. Celestine Ware, one of the few African-Americans in New York women's liberation, couched her reflections in hypotheticals: Both black and white women would have to change by altering their relationships to men. "If women of both races see their problems as originating in female dependency on men and in their self-contempt, then women will make a revolution."[110] The language of real gender identities, imported from black power's emphasis on authentic black manhood, surfaced the next year in Toni Morrison's biting distinction in *The New York Times* between white women, always fancying themselves ladies but really acting like children, and black women, the real women.

Yet at the same time, Morrison was alert: "The winds are changing, and when they blow, new things move." She was lyrical, and she was practical. She liked the recent formation of the National Women's Political Caucus and its goal of increasing female representation in Congress and the two parties. "A hard-headed power base," she believed, "something real: women talking about human rights rather than sexual rights." Something, she added, outside white men and women's family quarrel, "and the air is shivery with possibilities." Morrison thus expressed qualified interest—a reserve that was both critical and tinged with curiosity—about the feminist movement.[111]

Reading the reminiscences today, you can't fail to notice how wrong were the wrongs of women that radical feminists brought to light and how right they were to object. Men didn't do the housework, not one bit, and even loving fathers made a habit of squirreling out of anything except special Sundays with their children. Women faked orgasms and male lovers balked when partners asked them to change their ways. Little girls could not play baseball or much of anything at all, and teachers shoved them away from math and science. Those were stunning realizations, there in plain sight, but no one had really noticed before. The absence of the subject of women in the entire university curriculum, for instance: Women discovered that they could graduate from the best institutions of higher learning in the country and never read a book about women, or by a woman, in any discipline.

Under scrutiny, norms and practices buckled, and while victory was remote, benchmarks were set. With the New Left collapsing and the black power movement running aground, women's liberation was the 1960s survivor, entering the 1970s with powerful ideas and an ardent mass following. Yet the translation of stunning insights into bringing about changes in the here and now was hindered by the dogma that nothing short of absolute change would do. Radical feminists raised questions but came nowhere near wielding the power to demand that they be settled, and in important ways they refused to articulate any ways in which they could be resolved. The purist zeal, impatience with compromise, and cynicism about working with men meant that by default the liberals, who had room for all these impurities in their tactics, took over the job of doing politics on the inside. Women's liberation instead moved to a footing of permanent opposition. "The phenomenon of pushing a new issue forward and watching the vision play out pragmatically was a dilemma for them," mused Susan Brownmiller, who was, at the time, one of "them."[112]

In 1970, though, none of this mattered. Time and history seemed on the side of the daughters, conferring on them a heroic role in a drama of world-changing importance. A landmark article in New York's alternative paper *The Village Voice* by Vivian Gornick summed up the zeitgeist: "The Next Great Moment in History Is Theirs." When a feminist volume reprinted the essay, Gornick kicked off the traces and changed the pronoun: "The Next Great Moment in History Is Ours."[113]

CHAPTER NINE

POLITICS AS USUAL AND UNUSUAL POLITICS

CONFIDENCE CARRIED feminism into the next decade, a belief across the spectrum that, indeed, the moment belonged to women. The early successes were encouraging enough that at times rapprochement between generations took hold. Tensions remained, yet radicals and liberals sometimes worked in tandem in what came to be called the women's movement—a designation more neutral and anodyne than "feminist." Liberals depended on the militants to embolden the ranks and stir up publicity. Radicals gained credibility from the liberals' successes in law and legislation and used them as springboards to stake out new grounds for agitation. Encouraged by solid achievements, black feminists began to organize independently. A vast middle of onlookers massed on solid ground of sympathetic public opinion.

Success drew in more women, until by 1975 certain suppositions of the women's movement held across the culture. Even the New Right, which took on feminism with a vengeance in the 1970s, conceded the basic principle that women had a right to equal pay and equal treatment at the hands of the law. "Equal pay for equal work" turned into as unimpeachable a principle as the value of motherhood—never mind the vast ambiguities as to how to go about honoring the precept.

This sketch goes against most histories and memoirs, which tell a story of steep declension from the golden years of militance. And it is true that countercultural institutions and emblems disappeared or declined: women's centers, underground newspapers, bralessness, consciousness-raising groups. The 1970s women's movement sidelined the sensational assertions about beauty, marriage, men, and motherhood. Yet the collapse of the student left amid recriminations and infighting actually bequeathed a more flexible temperament, encouraging pragmatic skills that allowed some women to enter the high-stakes game of politics as usual in Congress and the state legislatures. The claims of 1970s feminism were less extravagant and shocking, the protagonists less colorful; mainstream adaptations blunted the most brilliant and incisive analyses and the bravura demonstrations. Many achievements were workaday compromises, dilutions of grander visions. But they were solid and enduring, with unanticipated consequences that gave feminism a strong voice in the country's life.

It was liberal feminism, with NOW as the standard-bearer, that modified and transmitted ideas that originated with women's liberation through a network that reached deep into the heartland.[1] No state except Hawaii lacked a NOW chapter. There were outposts in Lake Havasu City, Arizona; Anchorage, Alaska; Weld County, Colorado; Wilmington, Delaware; Moscow, Idaho; and Orlando, Florida. Predictably, groups cropped up in California and along the East Coast: California eventually counted forty-eight chapters, followed by New York state with thirty-eight and New Jersey with nineteen. The organization had a healthy presence in the South. Over the course of the 1970s, Florida actually outdid New Jersey, with twenty-six chapters; North Carolina had ten; Virginia, thirteen; Texas, twenty-one. Clusters of five to ten chapters even appeared in the Deep South, historic stronghold of antifeminism: in the big cities, of course (Memphis, New Orleans, Birmingham, Atlanta) but also in smaller places: Meridian, Mississippi; Huntsville, Alabama. West of the Mississippi, chapters were scarcer, and so all the more noteworthy: Kalispell, Montana, a ranching town of ten thousand near the Canadian border; Johnson and Wyandotte counties in Kansas (suburbs of Kansas City).[2]

The purpose and force of chapters varied. Some were as evanescent as women's liberation groups, twenty or so women coming together, publishing a newsletter, throwing a few rummage sales, signing on to NOW national campaigns and then folding. Others lasted years. One typical small chapter was in Knox County, Ohio, a classic middle-

American locale, where I happened to grow up. Knox County was forty miles north of Columbus, the state capital, but in the early 1970s it was distant from urban influences. The county seat, Mount Vernon, was a small manufacturing town, overwhelmingly white and highly conservative, ready to jail long-haired hippies simply for the crime of sitting on the town square—"disturbing the peace" by their very presence. The NOW chapter was based in nearby Gambier, a village built around the liberal outpost of Kenyon College.[3]

The members, mostly women employed by the college or attached through their husbands, typified the NOW demographic: workingwomen and liberal homemakers. The chapter formed in 1975, a year of uproar at Kenyon, when women faculty's bottled-up grievances tumbled out of backrooms into government agencies. A philosophy professor denied tenure filed a complaint with the EEOC; her action seems to have broken what amounted to a female vow of silence. In the next months, three women resigned, one sued the college, more complained to the EEOC, and the Ohio Civil Rights Commission launched an investigation of the college. By the end of the year, supporters discovered more complaints going back to 1971: eleven all told, in four years.[4]

Knox County NOW displayed a feisty spirit yet took few actions; when it did, it was about injecting the newly claimed identity of feminist into the social practices of the Midwest. The women offered workshops that sought to attract converts, the themes straddling the line between self-help and consciousness-raising: sex discrimination at work, employment rights, female sexuality, rape, and abortion. The emphasis on assertiveness training, not yet the cliché it later became, aimed to turn the psychology of the second sex into an insistence on decent treatment. The chapter newsletter alerted the troops to feminist victories nearby. Cleveland NOW was taking on the Cub Scouts because they wouldn't let a woman serve as Cub Master! The news appeared as a delightful vignette—so middle-American, the Cub Scouts—because it spoke of a gender order elsewhere being challenged, even as it would have seemed nearly immovable in Knox County.

Midwestern hatred of nonconformity put newly politicized women under tremendous social pressure in places like central Ohio. "Libber" was the epithet detractors hurled. Local chapters' connections to national NOW thus helped shore up positions that were treated at home as ridiculous or weird. Everywhere, but especially in middle America, NOW membership offered connections to a wider world: for one, travel to big cities, a precious perquisite of women's movements since the nineteenth century, when delegates went to regional, state, and national meetings. Stars from New York appeared at state conventions to stir up the faithful: Gloria Steinem and Flo Kennedy, great stump speakers, were favorites. National NOW distributed commercial knickknacks that conferred the dignity of insignia, protective regalia in a hostile environment: Susan B. Anthony note cards, bumper stickers and ashtrays with the Woman Power symbol, T-shirts, and calendars.

In cities and metropolitan areas, activity was more purposeful and concentrated. Greater numbers, a higher degree of political sophistication, and ties to major news outlets put these chapters at the forefront of the women's movement. Princeton, New Jersey, NOW, for example, composed mostly of academics and professionals, started a full-day child-care center that was a model of professional staffing and state-of-the-art facilities. The group helped produce a 105-page, richly detailed study of sex stereotypes and prejudice in high school civics textbooks, which became a pioneering work in the field of curriculum change. It was one spur to Congress to pass the Women's Educational Equity Act in 1974—a prime example of how local initiatives might end up helping secure major gains.[5]

Demonstrations with picket lines, chanting, and signs were relatively easy to stage in this era when left liberals retained the habit of taking to the streets. Some of the most enjoyable and successful were against men-only facilities, common in the early 1970s: the posh Oak Room in the Plaza Hotel in Manhattan; McSorley's Ale House, a bohemian haunt in downtown New York; the Polo Lounge in Beverly Hills; a businessmen's grill in a Minneapolis department store. Desegregation protests evoked the indisputable justice of 1960s civil rights battles against white-only restaurants. As Friedan told it, "Virtually every woman had experienced or known someone who'd been told, 'No, we don't serve women.'" Spirits were high in these affairs; the pleasure came from spurning good-girl manners and heckling male patrons, those middle- and upper-class businessmen and professionals who thought they were entitled to indulge in the simple pleasures of a stag bar where the only women were likely to be well-dressed prostitutes.[6]

Urban chapters had resources dense enough to support ongoing campaigns against sex discrimination, which smaller local chapters did not. Internal changes in NOW, spurred by Friedan's sense of feminism as a movement that stood on its own, had severed the links that bound the organization in its early years to organized labor; ties to the civil rights movement also atrophied. This meant that NOW members tended to be middle-class, nonunionized white women. Still, the connection to job issues remained strong. Cleveland, Ohio, NOW was typical in the several fronts on which members pursued fair employment. In 1973 the group pressured the chief of police to hire women after a local woman filed a lawsuit against the department's cadet program. The same year, they touted ads for jobs that were once male only but now open to women ("The National Guard Needs You!") and sought complainants who had been fired from the school system because they were pregnant.[7]

From the first stirrings of the women's movement during the Kennedy administration, liberals pondered how to translate ideas into political power. It was not easy. NOW learned in the 1960s how to bring pressure, but not how to initiate legislation and policy. As of 1970, feminists still had no standing in the political parties and no experience in creating bills and navigating them out of the hearing room and into the legislative mainstream. Yet, strangely, two years into the Nixon administration, the situation in Washington looked propitious for those willing to take the plunge. Although there were virtually no women in Congress, both parties harbored pockets of support for women's rights measures. Democrats controlled both houses and were generally sympathetic. On the one hand, the furious politics of the Vietnam War overwhelmed Washington, but on the other, the war distracted, allowing liberal social welfare and regulatory legislation to slip through: for example, the establishment of the Environmental Protection Agency, the expansion of Medicaid and Medicare, and the administration's support for affirmative action guidelines for minorities and women.[8]

As for Richard Nixon, the president had a distant and ambivalent attitude to feminism. He was "schizophrenic," a Republican feminist high up in the party in that era described him, not known for his interest but also not for his opposition.[9] Nixon was working all the while on crafting a new Republican majority, one that would use conservative positions on civil rights and social issues to pull away Northern ethnic and Catholic voters from their long allegiance to the Democratic Party. The plan was to merge these newly won voters with Southern whites who had broken with the Democrats over civil rights, as well as with traditional Republican constituents. But in the early 1970s, Republican strategists had not yet spotted opposition to the women's movement as an opportunity. Nixon equivocated on women's issues, sometimes signaling support, sometimes pulling back. The woman he appointed to head the Women's Bureau, Elizabeth Koontz, was an African-American associated with NOW, and in his second term he took care to appoint more women to federal office than any of his predecessors. He did not object to a decent women's plank in the Republican Party platform in the 1972 election, and he supported the ERA. Yet he attacked legal abortion when New York liberalized its law in 1969, a notable presidential meddling in a state matter.

It was very different from what began in the waning years of the Ford administration, when the far right ratcheted up opposition to the ERA and legal abortion as core elements of its takeover of the party. Under Nixon, that turn was yet to come. But the move that did presage the conflict was the president's veto of a popular bill for federally funded child care, the Comprehensive Child Development Act (CDA), which passed Congress in late 1971. Child care, an issue that cannot be separated from workplace equity for women, commanded support from a surprisingly wide and varied constituency: employers interested in cutting worker absenteeism, child development professionals enamored of the results of Head Start, advocates of the poor, workingwomen, and trade unions. The bill, hammered out by a consortium of civil rights, welfare rights, child advocacy, and liberal feminist groups, had solid bipartisan support in Congress when it was first introduced—"a political sure bet in the months preceding the 1972 election." Designed for the middle class as well as the poor, it provided for a network of federally funded community centers, with free care to the poorest families and everyone else paying on a sliding scale.[10]

The underpinnings of the CDA were promising. It was predicated on the idea that child care was an entitlement, like Social Security or Medicare. With the brief exception of World War II, when the need for women workers was so urgent that the federal government funded some child-care centers, programs in the United States were sparse, treated as a measure of last resort for the needy poor. In Europe, too, child care was stingy, although where it existed it was at least not always tied to poverty. Communist countries professed to offer a bounteous palette of services for workingwomen, although the reality behind the official line was inconsistent. Western European nations varied, with provisions waxing and waning, depending on what any given state thought the public interest (rather than women's interests) required. Notable exceptions were France, with a pro-natalist family policy that assumed public responsibility for young children's well-being, and Sweden, whose policies tilted toward encouraging women's labor force participation.[11] While never feminist, the European examples were at least alternatives to no government policy at all; the Swedish program in particular glimmered behind NOW's push for publicly funded child care. Nixon's own White House Conference on Children and Youth in 1970 recommended federal funding, pitched to needy families but not limited to them.[12] The CDA was by any measure a modest start, compared to the pie in the sky of free child care that NOW advocated. It was only a morsel, given the mammoth need. But from today's vantage point, what a morsel.

In the opening salvo, a coalition of Protestant evangelicals and the John Birch Society materialized—out of thin air, it seemed—in a full-out campaign against the bill. Conservative columnist James Kilpatrick rose to the attack, charging that the CDA was designed "to Sovietize our youth. . . . This bill contains the seeds for destruction of Middle America." It was a departure from the right's obsession with Communist subversion and the evils of integration. Nixon, looking to appease the far right wing of the Republican Party in the wake of his newly initiated policy of détente with China, vetoed the bill after initially giving it his full support. His stand against "government interference" in the family meshed nicely with his opposition to "government interference" in segregated schools. He announced he had stopped "the most radical piece of legislation to emerge from the 92nd Congress" and decried the attack on "the family centered approach." Yet so novel and untested at the time was hard-line opposition to women's issues that even the architect of the Republican New Majority strategy, Nixon aide Kevin Phillips, warned that the party risked losing a crucial slice of young workingwomen's votes.[13]

The New York Times voiced the widespread consternation Nixon's veto provoked among moderates: "The President's charge that day care weakens the family ignores the realities of much of modern family life," including the needs of parents at all levels of income. *The Washington Post* fastened on the cynical calculations behind his veto: "This message is a bone he has tossed to his critics on the far right, with next November in mind, and at the expense of mothers and children." The *Post* denounced the president for ignoring not only the will of Congress but popular support. But the outrage soon died down. Feminist attention was elsewhere, on the movement to legalize abortion. NOW did not rally protest and radicals were unmoved, since from a revolutionary perspective any legislation was, by definition, bound to be compromised and useless.[14]

The defeat of the CDA is a neglected episode in an era remembered for the furor over Vietnam, busing to achieve school desegregation, and, soon enough, Watergate. It was a skirmish of negligible interest to radicals on the left. But it was instructive to radicals on the right, who in 1971 were testing their political mettle, coming out of the years in the wilderness after the Goldwater debacle. Looking to take their politics away from the bastions of the segregated South and the anti-Communist fringe of the John Birch Society, they seized on the fight for the family— even though the interests of the family were precisely what the child care bill addressed.

At the time, no feminist anticipated that antifeminism would become a force in national politics. The immediate problem in Washington was the male makeup of Congress. In the Ninety-second Congress in 1971, there were fifteen women: two in the Senate, thirteen in the House— only two more than in the Eighty-third Congress of 1953–55.[15] Shirley Chisholm, Democrat from Brooklyn, took office in 1970 as the first African-American woman elected to Congress. The "coffin route"—a wife or political appointee appointed to a seat vacated by a man's death—was still the main way women got there. Margaret Chase Smith, one of two women in the Senate that year, was the only duly elected female senator ever. The four who preceded her had all arrived via the coffin route and as a rule refrained from doing serious congressional business. Arkansas's Senator Hattie Caraway, a famous example of the female senator as onlooker, took her husband's place in 1931 when he died unexpectedly and then shocked Southern Democrats by running the next year and winning. Despite her unexpected self-assertion in holding on to her seat, Caraway, jokingly called Silent Hattie, made it a point in her thirteen years in the Senate to avoid speaking on the floor. The approach suited her housewife persona—that was the joke; and "Silent Hattie" she's been ever since, a figure of fun. But as her posthumously published diary makes clear, that silence protected her from ridicule in a setting where she never knew whether she was saying too much or too little—not an unfamiliar experience for a token woman working in what was, in the 1930s, not yet called a male-dominated environment. Down Pennsylvania Avenue, the new secretary of labor, Frances Perkins, a much more accomplished and confident woman, struggled with the same worry during FDR's cabinet meetings.[16]

The National Women's Political Caucus (NWPC) was founded in 1971 to get more influence in Congress. The goal was to increase the representation of women in both parties at all levels, with the assumption that this would make the government more accountable to women's needs and demands. The tacit assumption was that having women office-holders would inevitably further the goals of feminism. (Once conservative opposition developed, this equation of Woman and Feminist would be a point of furious dispute.[17] The intention was to be nonpartisan, but in effect the NWPC was left-liberal, with a few moderate Republicans added in.[18]

Shirley Chisholm's presence on the NWPC executive board along with other black leaders signaled a willingness to sign on to a women's movement that was a big-tent consortium rather than an evangelical sect. For the first time, Latinas also allied themselves publicly with feminism. Chisholm saw the NWPC as a "big umbrella organization," a bloc to provide "the weight and muscle for those issues which the majority of women in this country see as concerns." Augmented by high-profile women from organizations that were not solely or explicitly feminist, the NWPC acted as a sort of Tammany Hall for women, mostly in the Democratic Party, brokering interests, opening channels of upward mobility, and distributing patronage. The influx of groups claiming to represent Woman is evident in a 1974 issue of the *Civil Rights Digest*, published by the US Commission on Civil Rights, which features articles on African-, Asian-, and Native American women, Chicanas and Puertorriqueñas, kicked off by a hopeful article on "Where Feminism Will Lead."[19]

In both political parties, the short-term results were dramatic. Disarray among Democrats over the war and school busing, along with power struggles between Republican moderates and conservatives, opened opportunities for women to move in. Their numbers at both 1972 presidential nominating conventions soared. Among Republicans, the percentage almost doubled from what it had been at the 1968 convention—to 30 percent. Among Democrats the percentage tripled from 13 percent to 40 percent. NWPC women engineered planks on women in both platforms.[20]

It was transformative, although not the peaceful revolution the NWPC sought. The 1972 conventions did embolden women to run for local and state offices, and over the decades, their numbers at those levels improved steadily. But in Congress, change was very slow, almost glacial. Among Democrats, the NWPC became an interest group of consequence and feminists flexed some muscle. But among Republicans, conservatives were devoted to marginalizing the moderate wing of the party, which encompassed most of the influential women. Overall, while the number of women elected to Congress remained low, they were more successful at local and state levels, where there were so many positions that a small corps of officeholders began to emerge. In the 1990s, they moved into national politics after long apprenticeships. For instance, Kay Bailey Hutchison was first elected to the Texas state legislature in 1972 and twenty years later won a Senate seat. Nancy Pelosi, daughter of a wealthy and influential Democratic father, became chair of the Northern California party branch in 1977 and chair of the California Democratic Party in 1981; she won her congressional seat in 1987 and twenty years later, in 2008, became the first female Speaker of the House.[21] It was not until 1992 that the pace in Congress accelerated, and then only among Democrats.

Again, the women's movement dreamed of a women's vote, and again the hope was vain. But far more than in the 1920s, the women's movement exerted force in Washington and state capitals after 1971—where before there was none. "The recent awareness, on the part of the general public, of women's raised consciousness has, it seems, lent credibility to the notion that angry women might damage a legislator's political career," observed a not entirely pleased writer about New York state abortion politics. NOW chapters were one source of organized pressure; members prided themselves on legislative savvy. The chapter in Charlotte, North Carolina, for example, alerted members to the wiles of a state legislator who courted female voters by supporting women's legislation that he knew would never get out of committee. Chapters tracked the fate of bills in state legislatures and the votes of representatives.[22]

In Washington, D.C., a small feminist policy network came together, amassing expert information and using it to press arguments on legislators. The combination of the NWPC plus professional lobbyists on Capitol Hill was enough to increase the importance of women's issues for politicians in 1972, a close election year. *Newsweek* reported uneasily that lawmakers faced "a feminist lobby that was far better organized than ever before—and the Realpolitik of an election year."[23]

The years 1972–74 saw this momentum result in a few legislative victories, one of them—Title IX—a landmark. The failure of the child-care bill was not repeated and, briefly, it seemed that feminist proposals were unobjectionable mom-and-apple-pie issues for politicians from both sides of the aisle. Feminists turned into familiar figures in the halls of Congress, knowledgeable about legislative minutiae. "It's all hard work and detail," commented a lobbyist. "And you get tired and it's a bloody bore. But if I don't do it and the rest of us don't do it, we won't have it. The people who win are the people who stay."[24]

It may seem like hard work and detail to read about them, too; and the wins may seem painfully prosaic, given how high the hopes ran outside the halls of Congress. None of these pieces of legislation turned the world upside down; none abolished sexism. But over the long run they proved much more important than their dry matter-of-fact descriptions reveal at first glance. They created preconditions for modest changes without which more dramatic changes could not have occurred; one measure, Title IX, actually touched off a revolution in women's athletics.

The Ninety-second and Ninety-third congresses passed four important bills and a constitutional amendment—the long-delayed Equal Rights Amendment. In addition, "they enacted a veritable cornucopia of legislation prohibiting sex discrimination" in a variety of publicly funded programs. Given the dearth of legislation in American history for women's rights, it was quite a record. Strong bipartisan majorities in both houses passed the bills, and two Republican presidents, Nixon and Ford, signed them into law.[25]

The Equal Employment Opportunity Act (1972) extended the protections of Title VII to public employees and strengthened federal enforcement powers. Passed almost unanimously in both houses of Congress, the Equal Credit Opportunity Act (1974) ensured women access to credit cards, bank loans, and mortgages, resources they had been effectively denied because of the tenacious prejudice of lending agencies. It was a vivid reminder of coverture, this reluctance to let women function as buyers and borrowers. Historian Flora Davis identifies the bind: "Single women were said to be poor risks because they might marry and stop working, and married women were poor risks because they might have a baby and stop working." The effects were pernicious, especially for women applying for business loans and mortgages. Or even for minor consumer credit, such as buying a couch on an installment plan.[26]

The Women's Educational Equity Act (1974) was so humdrum that Representative Patsy Mink concluded she could not get it out of committee, and tacked it on as a rider to an omnibus education bill. It provided federal money for projects creating sexual equality in schools and universities: training teachers (or retraining them out of habitual sexist practices), improving girls' success in math and science, and encouraging the newly minted field of women's studies. It was an under-the-radar bill that had considerable effects in the long run, setting up programs that encouraged girls to go into engineering and science, and injecting women's studies with doses of government money.[27]

Title IX (1972) turned out to be potent and controversial, although at the time it slipped through Congress as an innocuous rider to the Education Amendments of the Civil Rights Act. Title IX required educational institutions that received federal money—which is to say, virtually all schools, colleges, and universities—to provide equal treatment to girls and young women. The bill took its cues from a wave of lawsuits that women faculty filed, beginning in 1970, claiming their employers violated a 1965 executive order by President Johnson that prohibited federal contractors—in this case, universities receiving federal money—from discriminating on the basis of sex.[28]

The academics' actions inspired Democratic representative Edith Green of Oregon to hold hearings on sex discrimination in education. The seven days of testimony generated some thirteen hundred pages of evidence about pervasive, mean prejudice against women. The outcome, Title IX, closed loopholes that allowed professional schools, universities, and high schools to circumvent civil rights law. Quotas limiting women's admissions had to be abandoned and separate privileges for men came under scrutiny (for example, fellowships reserved for them), although there were exceptions made for religious institutions, military academies, and a few others.

The few others included Princeton, Harvard, Yale, and Dartmouth, anxious lest their continuing preference for men in admissions be curbed (although Princeton and Yale admitted women in 1969, both had quotas, as did Harvard, which had absorbed Radcliffe College for women; Dartmouth was still all male). Once the Ivy League schools got their exemption, concern about the bill disappeared.[29] The result was that the bill, unnoticed, retained clout in the area of athletics; it forced high schools and colleges to abandon their parsimony in funding women's athletics or risk losing federal funds. It was a dramatic break with discrimination so deeply rooted it seemed all but natural.

The segregation of athletics was universal and unabashed. While girls were present in most sports except football and wrestling, teams were pitifully underfunded and coaches subjected to the same woeful sex discrimination that affected other teachers. At the professional level, women's accomplishments occasioned interest—especially in tennis—but players, coaches, and the journalists who covered them were considered second string. Women's ambitions to compete at the level of men, or to compete with men, were treated with mockery and open hostility. When Wellesley College runner Kathrine Switzer quietly entered the Boston Marathon as "K. Switzer" in 1967 and started off with the men, an official, Jock Semple, spotted her and, incensed, lunged into the crowd of runners to tackle her, screaming, "Get the hell out of my race!"[30]

Title IX was an unwitting act of genius. Once the implications of the law dawned on the public, male coaches raised the alarm, as they saw athletic budgets stretched to cover girls' sports. Outraged, coaches and parents of boys claimed that equal treatment was desexing young people. "I think girls have a right to participate but to a lesser degree than boys," huffed a Wisconsin coach. "If they go too far with the competitive stuff, they lose their femininity." An official from a Midwest coaches' association raised the specter of brawny girls unmanning boys. "There is the possibility that a boy would be beaten by a girl and as a result be ashamed to face his family and his friends." "I wonder if anybody stopped to think what that could do to a young boy," he mused mournfully. Regardless of periodic assaults, girls' supporters succeeded in fending off forces that called for the bill's revocation.[31] It fostered a stunning change in a gender order in which the elements of athletics—throwing, running, jumping, catching, blocking, flexibility, and strength—had for centuries lain far outside girls' reach.

The ERA also passed Congress in 1972, by huge bipartisan majorities in both houses. At that juncture, it was popular and uncontroversial. By this time, even the trade unions, nucleus of historic opposition, had come around to support the amendment, agreeing that protective laws worked against women, not in their favor. The momentum seemed unstoppable. The Hawaii legislature, still in session because of the time difference when the Senate vote took place, ratified it the same day; five states ratified in the next two days. Within a year the ERA needed approval from only eight more states.[32] Amid the recriminations and anguish of these last years of the Vietnam War and, soon, the Watergate scandal, the proposal that "equality of rights under the law shall not be denied or abridged by the United States or by any state on account of sex"—the language is from the 1923 draft—was a rare opportunity for sunny consensus.

The fireworks of women's liberation spluttered out in the 1970s with the collapse of the New Left and the depletion of millennial expectations. But the way of seeing the world bequeathed by radical feminism, the great refusal to proceed with business as usual, endured in the psyche of a generation of daughters. Women's centers died, but feminism spread. Work was an arena for less spectacular militance. In a collaboration between liberals and radicals, mothers and daughters that went unremarked at the time, the newest of New Women were able to use new laws, policies, regulations, and court decisions to enter bastions monopolized by men and carve out a place for themselves there. This process stopped short of the hoped-for revolution; the decreasing strength of labor unions, the ascendancy of business conservatism in national politics, and the restructuring of the labor market impeded them. Nonetheless, the entry of feminist-minded women into the labor market and the professions drastically changed American workplaces.

In the professions, challenges from African-Americans had already ended some customary practices of an old boy network that ushered the "best" young men from the best preparatory schools into the best colleges and then the best professional schools and best firms and institutions. Now under pressure from the women's movement and (after 1972) Title IX, medical, law, and divinity schools and Ph.D. programs in the social sciences and humanities cracked open to women, reversing a pattern of discrimination established at the turn of the century, when professional schools had formally opened to women, only to keep their numbers down to a handful. The numbers are telling: 1,240 women graduated from law school in 1971; ten years later, 11,768. There were 809 women who received medical degrees in 1971; there were 3,833 in 1981. The number of women graduating from religious seminaries doubled.[33]

The integration of the professions had a tremendous impact on Americans' perceptions of women's abilities and prospects. It was as if Rosie the Riveter, figure of dazzling competence and valor, were reborn, this time as a physician, trial lawyer, or veterinarian. For the first time, Americans encountered women sitting on high, figuratively (and actually) perched in positions of authority long assumed to be wildly inappropriate for them: in the pulpits on Sunday morning, making hospital rounds trailed by interns and nurses. It was in the professions that the clothing of the workplace changed most dramatically: female ministers and judges in robes, female doctors in white coats; lawyers, business-women, and professors in the ubiquitous women's black pantsuits that served to signify a distinctive gender identity and at the same time tran-scend the frippery of professional women's fashion that was still de rigueur as late as the 1960s—little hats and white gloves, matching shoes and purses.[34]

Ambitious women did not sashay through these changes with impunity. Resentment and suspicion besieged them. The pace and pulse of opposition varied: Not all university disciplines were as intractable as history departments, not all sectors of medicine as hostile as surgery, not all legal specialties as antipathetic as corporate law. As a rule, the more prestigious or lucrative the domain, the more intense—or, alternatively, the more insidious—the antagonism.

The law provides a striking study, first, because its masculine exclusiv-ity was rooted in a rationale articulated by Justice Bradley's assertion in *Bradwell* that married women could not practice the law, and second, because some who surmounted the obstacles revolutionized the law itself in the 1970s. Over the course of the twentieth century, the ranks of female lawyers had increased so slowly that on the eve of the feminist insurgency in 1967, they were still only 3 percent of the total. Women mostly worked as mid-level government bureaucrats or partners in small offices, since partnerships in any of the big, posh firms were effectively out of reach, as were judgeships and professorships in major law schools.[35]

Discrimination was everywhere, but it was vicious at Harvard Law School, at the head of the profession. Harvard Law School only opened its doors to women (with much self-congratulation) in 1950, the last elite school to do so; but the number of female graduates was tiny. Ruth Bader Ginsburg, for instance, was one of only nine women who entered with some five hundred men in 1956. A decade later, little had changed: In 1967 there were thirty-two women in an entering class of 565.[36]

In the 1960s, the women students' status as anomalies was emphasized by the debonair sexist humor that was a trademark of Ivy League hau-teur. The faculty addressed the class as "gentlemen," and famed cur-mudgeon A. James Casner (model for the crusty professor in the 1973 film *The Paper Chase*) refused, on principle, to call on women in class. The jokes stemmed from the implicit agreement among men (what everyone already knew) that women didn't really belong at Harvard Law at all. Aristocratic disdain slid into sexual aggression (we would now call it harassment), sublimated in naughty digs about sex at the women's expense. The subject of rape law, for example, occasioned titters, played for laughs by professors while female students squirmed. Snickering male classmates turned to look up women's miniskirts as they entered the law school amphitheaters. Ridiculed because they were women, they were also mocked because they weren't real women: Male peers were wont to consider a woman, at best, just one of the boys.[37]

For decades, women law students had experienced these annoyances and indignities as inevitable burdens to bear. Through the prism of feminism, however, students began to see them as sexism: a set of unjust practices and attitudes that was remediable. The harsh treatment of well-placed and well-educated women was so extreme that once women's liberation entered public consciousness, a surge of daring, a touch of the radicals' fearlessness and bravado, overwhelmed the bred-in-the-bones discipline of even those raised to be hardworking nice girls. At Harvard, campus protests against the university's racism, class exploitation (its status as slumlord, for example), and complicity in the war (through ROTC programs and scientific research for the defense industry) exacerbated women's awareness of the injustices they endured. Soon they were complaining openly about the school's sexually segregated facilities.

While few considered themselves radical feminists, the orderly politics that liberals espoused seemed beside the point in these situations. The contempt for women's possibilities and talents was no longer Friedan's "problem that had no name." At Harvard and elsewhere, the problem did have a name: It was men, individualized as the professor who refused to call on women in class, or the one who enjoyed making fun of the female students on "Ladies' Days," or the irate caretaker of the squash courts who shooed away women, or the male classmate leering from his seat. For the brave and even the not so brave who found strength in numbers, confrontation and catharsis could be used with some effect to call individuals and officials to account.

In a student culture still geared to protest politics, these early classes of women, loosely bound together by their minority status, produced ad hoc groups precisely focused on particular local issues—a great source of strength—and strengthened by the lessons radical feminism gave as to why insults like Ladies' Days weren't trivial. There were tensions between those who aligned themselves with feminism and those who saw themselves as nonpolitical, only there to take advantage of opportunities finally opened up, as they saw it, on the basis of their own merit. But the tensions were productive, with feminists stirring up complaints that resonated with other women. Everywhere segregated facilities and male privileges came under attack, and some blatant ones collapsed. It was the fearless and brazen at Yale who took part in Operation Shit, the sit-in at the Divinity School that integrated the men's bathroom in the library stacks.[38] But even apolitical good girls could welcome the results, since women's rooms were as scarce as hens' teeth at Yale, Harvard, and Princeton—giving rise to the title of Marilyn French's 1977 bestseller about Harvard, *The Women's Room.*

The collaboration between liberals and radicals was unspoken but effective. Although students were oblivious to the implications of something as remote as a federal law, women's protests had real leverage because of Title IX. With the threat of legal action hovering in the background, administrators backed off from many provisions that, once women called attention to them, were indefensible. By 1974 they knew that any practice that smacked of overt discrimination was ripe for legal challenge. The gyms, swimming pools, and squash courts that were male only, or squeezed women into a few hours, disappeared; so did the fellowships and prizes reserved for men.

At Harvard Law, the graduating class in 1974 was more than 10 percent female and the proportion climbed every year thereafter. A souring economy was still sufficiently robust to absorb newcomers in entry-level jobs. The number of practicing lawyers in the country increased by a third between 1960 and 1969. Admissions to law schools and the bar followed the curve of demand, almost doubling. Across the country, what had been in 1963 a population of 1,800 women in law school soared by 1975 to almost 27,000.[39]

A new kind of student appeared, her hopes for a life beyond the marriage plot shaping her sense of professional opportunity. The blighted stereotype of the 1950s career woman—sad and anomalous—dissolved. Enough students, male and female, were caught up in the imaginative moment that it was common to speak of vocational goals that accompanied marriage and children or superseded them. In the elite undergraduate programs from which Harvard law students came, the goal of going to college in order to be an educated wife and mother, a once near-universal ambition for young women, was suddenly unusual. A Stanford poll that year found that fewer than 1 of every 25 women graduating saw homemaking as their choice and only 7 percent said they would stop working to raise children. This reversed the poll's findings from seven years earlier, when 70 percent of Stanford's female graduates said they would stay home while their children were young.[40]

Female law students across the country called for classes on women and the law. The subject simply did not exist in the curriculum or scholarship. When Pauli Murray began working in 1964 on "Jane Crow and the Law," she found only one article on constitutional issues of sex discrimination; "not a burdensome venture" was how Ruth Bader Ginsburg drily described the task of mastering everything there was to know on the subject in 1969. But with the influx of women, student demand led to new courses, often cooked up on the fly by a marginal woman assigned the task by male faculty. In a felicitous instance, Ginsburg, then a law professor at Rutgers, taught one of the first courses on women and the law anywhere in 1970.[41]

The fate of these classes marked a break with the past. Larger numbers meant students could see themselves as a "body of women" (as one administrator put it) rather than as the oddities that Ginsburg and her classmates were, when the dean of the law school invited them to dinner and courteously inquired what they were doing "taking a place that could be held by a man." Ten sex discrimination lawsuits in the 1970s against elite corporate firms resulted in settlements in which the firms agreed to alter their hiring practices. The result was a wave of interest in women. At Harvard in 1974, a higher proportion of women took jobs in corporate firms than did men. It was the first time that, upon graduation, demotions were not issued on the basis of sex.[42]

Across the professions—in medicine, business, academics, and the clergy—a partnership between generations and political temperaments took hold. Mothers who came up through the ranks as a stigmatized minority welcomed legions of daughters as co-conspirators. Typically, older women, schooled in the stoicism of an earlier era but energized by the newcomers' indignation, would organize a separate women's caucus in their professional association and generate a fact-finding committee on the status of women. The formal imprimatur of these fact-finding groups—enhanced by eminent men recruited to serve on them—helped impress on the organization's members the necessity of changing the most egregious practices. A tiny female presence grew to a modest one, always much larger in entry-level positions at the bottom than at the top.[43]

Business schools, the research sciences, and engineering were hold-outs: Not until the late 1980s, and in some cases the '90s, would the numbers of women in those fields and their treatment once they got there seriously improve. But elsewhere in the professions, thousands of young women taking up positions in the 1970s as lawyers, doctors, ministers, and professors had a lasting effect on American beliefs that a revolution had occurred between the sexes.[44]

Against considerable resistance (often from close male associates), and aided by the new pressures that female clients, patients, parishioners, and students brought to bear, these women also modified the content and practices of their respective professions. They broached profound questions. Art historian Linda Nochlin's "Why Have There Been No Great Women Artists?," a groundbreaking 1971 essay, analyzed the institutional barriers that kept women from exercising a full range of creativity, no matter what their talent. "What if God is a woman?" was a query that went the rounds of theological seminaries and religious studies departments. Freudian theory was organized around a model of male development; women psychologists and psychotherapists observed. The measure of the success of these ideas can be gauged by how unexceptional they seem in the twenty-first century: Accepted wisdom of the culture now, they were provocative and outrageous in the 1970s.[45]

In medicine, for example, female physicians joined with intense feminist popular health discussions to challenge the condescending treatment of female patients, especially in obstetrics and gynecology; the construction of childbirth as a pathological event always requiring sedation; the absence of gender controls in trials of drugs; the dangers of IUDs (intrauterine devices) and high-estrogen birth control pills. By the late 1970s, a woman who studied up on the effects of birth control pills in *Our Bodies, Ourselves* might well locate a female gynecologist sympathetic to her concerns.[46]

These patterns were powerfully evident in the nation's churches and synagogues. Women aspiring to spiritual leadership criticized patriarchal readings of sacred texts and questioned liturgies littered with symbols, practices, and language that encoded contempt for women. "YOU ARE NOT MY GOD, JEHOVAH!" thundered the Reverend Peggy Way in a sermon at the University of Chicago chapel in 1970. "I will not worship a god who only trusts his priesthood and his power and his prophecy to men. . . . I will not serve . . . a god for whom a woman's mission is to listen and a man's mission to speak." As if she were summoning up Sarah Grimké, she ended by affirming a Christ "in whom there is neither Jew nor Greek, slave nor free, male nor female." In Judaism, Reform seminaries were the first to ordain women as rabbis in 1972, followed by Conservatives and Reconstructionists. Although most mainstream Protestant denominations had allowed female ordination since the nineteenth century, female ministers were always oddities. Now women flocked to seminaries, transforming them in a manner akin to the law schools.[47]

The impact was uneven across denominations. Traces of Saint Paul's admonitions—"let your women keep silent in the churches"—lingered. The process of integrating the clergy was protracted, the opposition haughty but subtle, rooted in centuries of doctrine. Depending on the particular church, women could be kept out for years. When the Reverend Sue Anne Morrow arrived at Princeton as the assistant chaplain in 1981, twelve years after the university admitted women as undergraduates, no one of her sex had ever preceded her up the stairs of the very lofty pulpit in the very grand chapel.[48]

In the Episcopal Church, the battle was ferocious. Women could serve as deacons but not priests. But seminary-trained candidates pressed for admission to the priesthood, backed by liberal parishioners and clergy. In 1974, three retired bishops irregularly ordained the "Philadelphia Eleven," women who had trained for the priesthood and met all qualifications except for gender. The event touched off an uproar. The church hierarchy invalidated the ordinations and entertained charges against the dissident bishops. The rebellion overcame formal opposition, and in 1976, the General Convention voted to ordain women. Some dioceses, however, resisted church government and have continued to hold out into the twenty-first century. In fact, the battle over women's ordination forecast the civil war over the ordination of gays, a struggle that as of 2010 threatens to break apart the Anglican Church worldwide.[49]

In the Catholic Church, an upswelling of hope after Vatican II came to nothing. So striking was the gap between the changing needs of the Church and its bars to women's authority that the head of the normally conservative Council of Catholic Women issued a protest: "As the participation of laymen in liturgical and ecclesiastical affairs continues to increase, it becomes painfully obvious that women are being left behind in a class by themselves."[50] The American cardinals suppressed and finally extirpated uprisings among liberal priests and nuns calling for women to be admitted to the priesthood, or, at the minimum, to be allowed an expanded liturgical role.

These accounts of open conflicts, however, give little sense of the minefields the newcomers traversed when they crossed the gender line on the job. A woman in the most innocuous position could loom in the fantasies of co-workers and clients as a menace to the way things should be done, an impostor, a dangerous, sexless creature on a mission to destroy real femininity. Women ministers could not be trusted to preach the word of God without distorting it for nefarious purposes; female police officers endangered public safety by pretending they could do the job under fire. Better that they should be Sunday school teachers and traffic cops: Now *those* were jobs for women. A lowly assistant professor in a small college, hired to teach the new scholarship on women's history, ran into the accusation that she was trying to indoctrinate students. The course "was more like a consciousness-raising session," a pair of offended students reported to college authorities; the professor was waging a vendetta against femininity, informing students in class, so they claimed, that "women who wear make-up and high heels deserve to be raped." At work, a generation of hotheaded daughters had to learn how to walk through minefields and proceed with caution.[51]

Integration, it's clear, made little headway in altering working relationships in male dominated fields. Employers were unrepentant, ignorant, and indifferent when it came to the many obstacles that stood in women's way; male co-workers were discouraging and, often enough, combative. Women were fired for being pregnant, sexually harassed, and discouraged from trying for promotions. The same law firms that seemed magically welcoming to young women in the mid-1970s proved, within a few years, to be arid and inhospitable: A chronicle of Harvard Law graduates shows that women started dropping out in short order— to have families or work in less high-pressure kinds of law.[52]

Across the class spectrum, a few intrepid women sued employers for sex discrimination, in the process expanding the purview of legislation beyond its original intent. Often, it was female lawyers who represented these clients and in the process enlarged the powers of Title VII and the Equal Pay Act. They changed the atmosphere of courtrooms. The late Catherine Roraback, a New Haven, Connecticut, attorney, described the scene in court in the 1960s: "The judges were men, the bailiffs, the marshals, the sheriffs were men; they were all male. The court reporters were men; [the] clerks were men." But with many more female attorneys appearing in court and serving as clerks for judges, it was more difficult to assume, as the liberal Warren Court did as late as 1961 in *Hoyt v. Florida* (which concerned sex discrimination in mandatory jury duty), that they were essentially creatures of the home: "The center of home and family life," reasoned the Court then. Moreover, a boom in articles in legal journals about feminist issues, occasioned by litigation as well as the interest of law students, contributed to the readiness of appellate judges to see matters in a different light.[53]

The changes were spotty, but overt forms of disdain and exclusion in legal culture began to buckle. The male counsel arguing for the state of Texas in *Roe v. Wade* got caught out, for example, when he began his argument in 1972 before the Supreme Court with a sexist pleasantry about the two female attorneys representing the plaintiff. "When a man argues against two beautiful ladies like this, they are going to have the last word." No one laughed, and Chief Justice Warren Burger glared at him.[54]

To grasp the dynamics of feminist litigation, however, we need to understand not only the lawyers and judges but also the plaintiffs who came forward in the 1970s. They represented a range of profiles, motives, and temperaments, from avowed feminists to people who simply wanted a square deal: parents whose daughters couldn't play Little League baseball, women forced to take mandatory (unpaid) pregnancy leaves or were fired for being pregnant, a widower denied a Social Security benefit that routinely went to widows, and a mother whose daughter was barred from competing in the Soap Box Derby.[55] Thousands of women, about whom next to nothing is known, took the first step by filing complaints with the EEOC. Even that minor action required breaking with potent habits of deference to employers.

Taking the next step to go to court meant trouble, expense, public disapproval, and possibly loss of a job. Eileen Shanahan was one of seven named plaintiffs in a class-action suit filed against *The New York Times* in 1974 for sex discrimination. She summed up the warning her husband gave her when she told him what she was considering:

> Basically, he said, "Well, of course, it's your decision to make. But you've got to think about what you're getting into and the consequences because going public with complaints against your employer is something that they will be furious at, any employer will be. You will be exposing yourself to resentment that is reserved for people who criticize the boss or the company in public."[56]

As he calculated it, there were few gains and high costs. His most dire prediction, that she would never again work in newspapers, proved correct: Shanahan left journalism during the lawsuit and went to work for the federal government.

Nonetheless, Shanahan pushed ahead on the sheer force of principle. She recalled her decision as not so much a choice made for herself but for her daughters. "I didn't think I could ever look my daughters in the eye again if I ran away from this just because I was afraid of the consequences for myself." A language of generational interconnectedness runs through her account of the lawsuit. "Well, I wasn't young," she stressed. She was forty-seven when the women filed suit, yet she remembered the moment as one of youthful exultation. "But to see the possibility of change at that time," she reflected. "I guarantee you it was as blissful for me as for any twenty-five-year-old, maybe more so, because I knew what discriminations were out there."[57]

Workingwomen with much less money and much sparser resources stepped up in some very tough cases. Lorena Weeks, plaintiff in the first famous case against AT&T, was a telephone operator for the Southern Bell division in Wadley, Georgia. She was looking to move up to a much better paid switchman's job—working on the phone lines—when she applied for a posted opening. In 1966, AT&T provided job security and good benefits, but promotions for women were nil, since managers always came from the ranks of linemen. Southern Bell turned her down, openly admitting she was rejected because she was a woman, even though she had more seniority and experience than the man who got the job. Stunned by the reactions of not only management but friends and family (why was she stirring up trouble and trying to take a good job away from a man?), she went to the EEOC, which assigned her a local lawyer. When she lost in court, he told her she would lose her job.[58]

Weeks v. Southern Bell is a good example of the gains that could result from collaborations of feminist lawyers and otherwise luckless female clients. Marguerite Rawalt was by this time heading NOW's legal task force. Rawalt believed that a favorable ruling in the case would close the huge BFOQ ("bona fide occupational qualification") loophole in Title VII (Southern Bell argued only a man had the strength for a switchman's position). Rawalt contacted Sylvia Roberts, a feminist attorney in Baton Rouge, Louisiana, NOW, who took on the appeal. In federal court, the tiny Roberts hoisted a forty-pound bench and walked around the room as she spoke: The point was that forty pounds was not much for any woman used to hauling around small children and groceries.[59] In a landmark 1969 decision, the Fifth Circuit Court denied the validity of the BFOQ in Weeks's case and set a higher bar for "bona fide" reasons to discriminate.[60]

Regardless of their fate in court, individual lawsuits could do nothing to change mammoth structures of job discrimination. Sympathetic EEOC attorneys confronted the fact that the complaint-by-complaint approach was like draining a swamp with a teaspoon. The worst problems had to do with discrimination so sweeping that it stretched as far as the eye could see and thus looked normal. In feminized sectors of the labor force—offices, retail, and low-level service work—differences in compensation were harder to spot; where the sexes didn't work together, there was no readily apparent comparison. Habitual structures of preference—unconscious, semiconscious, and explicit—favored men for promotion, divided jobs by sex, and valued men's work more highly than women's. These hierarchies overlapped with racial hierarchies. A prime offender was AT&T, which accounted for 7 percent of all the EEOC's complaints by 1970. The Weeks case was not enough to make a dent. Seizing on a technicality, the EEOC brought a legal challenge to AT&T's discriminatory practices, winning a 1973 settlement that required the company to pay millions of dollars in back wages to some 13,000 women and 2,000 minority men. Over the next year, the number of women in management increased by 25 percent, and the number in skilled jobs—the kind that had been denied Lorena Weeks—rose by 78 percent. It proved over time an empty victory, however, when deregulation effectively broke up AT&T and rearranged the corporate structure.[61]

Gains were unsatisfactory and compromised, laced with employers' and co-workers' ill will even when plaintiffs prevailed. Many a woman who sued an employer left for another job, whatever the outcome. Plaintiffs retained the stigma for years; usually they ended up saddled with legal fees, however generous the attorneys; seldom were they hailed as heroines; often they were forgotten. "It takes enormous courage," observed Harriet Rabb, who specialized in some of the earliest and nastiest cases in New York. "It is a long, slow, painful, difficult, and ego-destroying process." In large part, she found, the plaintiffs "do it for the women who come after them." Sally Frank, an undergraduate at Princeton University, began her ten-year battle in 1979, when she was a sophomore, to desegregate the all-male undergraduate eating clubs. Although she opened the way for hundreds to dine and network in the posh clubs, in the collective Princeton female historical memory either she figured as an unpleasant troublemaker who had done something embarrassing but necessary, or she figured not at all.[62]

The story of the class-action suit against *The New York Times*—Eileen Shanahan's suit—is about a case that involved Herculean patience and courage. The gains benefited those who followed, but did little to help the plaintiffs themselves. It was a lawsuit so gargantuan in time, expense, and personalities that it came to be known as the "Title VII World Series."[63]

The New York Times saw itself as an enlightened institution. Publisher Arthur Ochs Sulzberger and the editors —almost all men—prided themselves on their relations with female employees and saw the *Times* offices as above the fray of feminist agitation that was overtaking other New York media outlets. Yet there were gross dissimilarities in pay and rank. "It was clearly masculine, all masculine," said Betsy Wade.[64] Practices such as lunching at all-men's clubs melted into just-the-way-things-were, jolly sexist bonhomie: late hours, drinking, palling around. A few star female reporters and writers—Eileen Shanahan, architecture critic Ada Louise Huxtable, Vietnam reporter Gloria Emerson, and Charlotte Curtis, editor of the society/women's page—stood at a pinnacle where it seemed any woman could climb by dint of hard work and talent. Thus was created a myth of meritocracy, imagined rewards beckoning to the best and the brightest who could muscle their way past the others on the trek to the top.

In 1972, a group organized a women's caucus and presented a list of grievances to the dumbfounded management. Women elsewhere in the New York media—at *Time, Newsweek, Reader's Digest,* and NBC—had taken legal action earlier, but *The New York Times,* with its heavy traditions of loyalty to the paper, remained pleasantly unruffled. The caucus changed that. "We all began to poke around . . . three or four of us in unison, to lift up the corners and see what was under the rug, " recounted Betsy Wade. "And we found incredible situations." A female sports reporter, for example, a champion golfer herself, earned a secretary's salary covering women's golf—because both she and the subject were deemed less valuable than the man who covered men's golf.[65]

The caucus learned that under Newspaper Guild rules, they could have access to payroll data so long as names were erased. The inequities turned out to be appalling, gaps of thousands of dollars. The data stunned even veterans: Shanahan had long been aware of discrimination as a blur in the background, but never had to face the exact figures.

Women's promotions to top jobs were virtually nonexistent: There were upward trajectories, but they were gradual and long, while men climbed straight up the ladder. Nan Robertson, a former *Times* reporter who wrote about the lawsuit, noted how the dynamic affected a brilliant woman like Betsy Wade. "It was obvious from the beginning how talented she was. She rose through the ranks, making good copy better and bad copy passable; she was known to be cool in a crisis and a superb judge of what news was important and what was not." Many people at the paper believed she would make a superb managing editor. "But somewhere that upward trajectory flattened out." Everyone had versions of this story: lower salaries than their peers or men who were far less experienced, few rewards and promotions. Eventually, economic statisticians discovered that men at the *Times* were paid an average of $5,000 more a year than women: in 1970s dollars, the equivalent of a year of a child's college tuition at a private school, or more than $40,000 as of this writing. Jane Brody, who wrote a column on health and had a degree in biochemistry, found she was making one hundred dollars a week less than the lowest-paid man in the science department. Eighty-eight women signed a letter of complaint.[66]

Tense negotiating sessions followed, sweetened by the management's attempts at good-natured joshing and promises to address the problems with pay and promotions. "Confucius say, 'When they've got you by the balls, don't struggle,' " Sulzberger joked. At work, he genially announced that "we must have equal pay for equal work, full use of the talents and training of women employed at the *Times*, initiatives in hiring greater proportions of women." A few women got raises and there were studies of the problem. Shanahan referred to this period as the " 'hey, these are decent folks, we can work this out' phase." She remembered assuring the others that now that the facts were known, management was sure to fix things. The comity of the workplace, in which they all had an investment, made it impossible to contemplate a bitter falling-out. But nothing really happened.[67]

A year later, the women hired Harriet Rabb, head of a new employment discrimination project at Columbia. Rabb, a steely and determined litigator, had already taken on several class-action suits from women in the New York media and brought suit on behalf of women law students against ten Wall Street firms. In 1974 the *Times* women sued the newspaper under Title VII in federal court. Five hundred and sixty female workers joined the class, headed by the seven named plaintiffs representing a range of jobs.[68] Eileen Shanahan and Betsy Wade were the most visible, both high up in the *Times* hierarchy. Wade reflected on their careers, satisfying yet short-circuited, and the mental journey that landed them in court:

> I think that if the *Times* could not take someone with the capac-
> ities and the record and the performance of Eileen Shanahan
> and give her everything that was required to run the Washington
> bureau if she wanted to do that, or be national news editor if she
> wanted to be that, then they weren't able to do anything. In a lot
> of ways, I consider Eileen to be my cognate in her area of the
> paper. We both arrived with honed skills, we both demonstrated
> ourselves thereafter, we progressed and unfolded, we improved
> upon our performance, we kept going. And if they couldn't give
> us the jobs that we wanted, then there had to be an explanation,
> and there was really only one explanation.[69]

Andrea Skinner, an African-American, worked on the fashion page. Skinner was categorized as a wardrobe mistress, despite a college degree, years of experience, and her smashing redesign of the children's fashion section. Louise Carini was in accounting; superb at her job, she had trained four men who worked under her to become her boss. Carini was the most surprising plaintiff, from a conservative, Catholic Italian-American family: antiunion, gripped by a deep fear of litigation, uncomfortable with the other women, and by no stretch of the imagination a feminist. Yet she signed on at the urging of her brother, who told her, as she remembered, "If your manager doesn't think enough of you to appreciate what you're doing, then he's not a good manager and he doesn't respect you. Go for it!"[70]

Management struck back by assailing the women's competence, character, and standing with their peers. Shanahan, who was held in high esteem by everyone at the paper including the publisher, found her work ethic and reputation smeared. Management's deposition described her as argumentative, difficult to work with, and narrow. "They couldn't just say I was lousy in my job," she recalled. "They just couldn't, given all my internal awards. So what they said was, well, yes, I did what I did very well but I was a narrow expert. I couldn't do just everything the way a *New York Times* reporter should be able to do everything."[71] Rabb, who had heard scurrilous accusations against her clients when she went up against New York's white-shoe law firms, was shocked by the charges that executive editor Abe Rosenthal hurled: "This one was a drunk, that one slept around, the other one couldn't write, the other one couldn't report." The women stuck it out, and eventually the suit was settled out of court for a nominal sum, attached to a serious plan the plaintiffs secured to hire women.[72]

A pattern developed that appeared in other litigation as well. The instigators received few rewards. The actions were emotionally exhausting and financially costly, "like wading through a huge vat of oatmeal mush," as one woman described the process. At the *Times,* the lawsuit did lead to hiring more women. Yet newcomers came in featured as the freshly turned-out good girls in contrast to the sour old bad ones. Wade described the shift with mordant irony: "I do think that sometime thereafter, they began to look around and say, 'Well, gosh, now we're going to have to find some women who aren't these women.'" Women who came into workplaces in the wake of discrimination battles were often indifferent or unaware of the history that had opened the way. "There is no sex discrimination at the *Times,*" a young reporter declared firmly in 1980. "I got here on my merits and I'm going to get ahead on my own merits."[73]

Women's suspicions that the media was fundamentally sexist, not just accidentally prejudiced, reinforced the effects of employees' battles. NOW chapters in the early 1970s monitored local television and newspapers on the quantity and quality of reporting about women, the fairness of presentation of women's issues, and the numbers of female journalists.[74] Scrutiny highlighted the use of demeaning language, sometimes converging with women employees' own objections. In fact, the first time female employees protested anything at *The New York Times* was when they objected to a 1970 editorial titled "The Henpecked House," about the passage of the Equal Rights Amendment by the House of Representatives. "Would you call something the 'Nigger-loving House'?" they demanded. The point was indisputable, but regardless, plenty disputed it. What came to be called sexist language was supposedly only innocuous and well-meaning. In 1974, the *Times,* riled on this point, mocked another publisher's efforts to avoid language that treated women as the exception rather than the norm by raising what the *Times* writer saw as the reductio ad absurdum: Would someday "Betty Co-ed" simply be called a *student?* Would people say that boys grew to *adulthood* rather than *manhood?* Others were less belligerent and backed away. Preempting conflict at his own newspaper, the editor of *The Washington Post* instructed his reporters to desist from using words such as "brunette," "divorcée," "cute," or "grandmother" to describe women unless they used parallel descriptions of men.[75]

The double pressure—from female staff inside, from audiences and readers outside—had visible effects on the media. In the 1972 presidential primaries, women reporters worked on the floor of the conventions for the first time.[76] New sections directed to female readers appeared in newspapers, abrogating the silliness of the society and women's pages for retooled, ostensibly gender-free features on fashion and food, packaged as lifestyle reading. In New York, discontent with the women's magazines led to *Ms.* magazine, launched in 1972, devoted to bringing feminism to a mainstream audience. *Ms.*, glossy, cheerful, and ebulliently pluralistic, mixed human interest and glossy advertising with devotion to liberal causes—the ERA, legal abortion. Pushing a political version of the self-improvement ethic, *Ms.* became the woman's magazine of choice for the enlightened female masses.

Litigants in lawsuits were the shock troops in a legal revolution spearheaded by feminist lawyers in Washington and New York. They kept tabs on a busy, buzzing field, looking for cases like Lorena Weeks's that could be used to change law and policy. The process worked from the bottom up, with plaintiffs searching to bring new sorts of matters to court, and from the top down, with legal thinkers searching for cases to use in crafting appeals. Reva Siegel and Robert Post capture the creativity of the times in constitutional law: "Working with a variety of resources inside and outside the formal legal system—with principles, precedent, collective memory, social movement organizing, the party system, congressional legislation, constitutional lawmaking, and litigation—feminism in the 1970s helped change the meaning of the Constitution."[77]

In 1970, the American Civil Liberties Union (ACLU), the premier organization for legal reform in the country, decided to pursue litigation on women's issues. Dorothy Kenyon, a moving force on the ACLU executive board since 1930 and a lifelong feminist, had long urged the organization to take a role in fighting for women's rights. When Pauli Murray joined the board, she acquired an ally. Their pressure led to the ACLU's Women's Rights Project, which Ruth Bader Ginsburg, newly appointed to the Columbia Law faculty, helped launch in 1972. Ginsburg and Brenda Feigen Fasteau, a recent graduate of Harvard Law School, were co-directors. The Women's Rights Project opened a channel between the women's movement and the considerable financial and legal resources of the ACLU. There was enough money to push cases as far as they could go and brilliant talent to call upon, including Ginsburg's women students at Columbia.[78]

The problems went beyond job discrimination. Differentiation between the sexes pervaded the law. A labyrinth of sex discriminations was embedded in statutes and government regulations. For example, they littered Social Security provisions and the tax codes. Judicial treatment of cases involving sex discrimination ranged from poor to abysmal, judged two scholars in 1971 who reviewed the record. While judges had largely freed themselves from thinking that could be called racist, " 'sexism' . . . is as easily discernible in contemporary judicial opinions as racism ever was." Prejudice reigned. Judges "have failed to bring to sex discrimination cases those judicial virtues of detachment, reflection and critical analysis which have served them so well with respect to other sensitive social issues."[79]

Judges partook of a romantic paternalism, as ACLU director Mel Wulf dubbed the mindset, jovial and ostensibly well disposed toward women. Ginsburg is worth quoting at length on the tenor of the law at the end of the 1960s and into the 1970s:

> [L]egislators and judges, in those years, were overwhelmingly white, well-heeled, and male. Men holding elected and appointed offices generally considered themselves good husbands and fathers. Women, they thought, had the best of all possible worlds. Women could work if they wanted, or they could stay home. They could avoid jury duty if they were so inclined, or they could serve if they elected to do so. They could escape military duty or they could enlist. [80]

Federal courts invalidated statutes based on race discrimination on Fourteenth Amendment grounds, but they consistently refused to extend that logic to sex discrimination. Ginsburg recalled beginning the Women's Rights Project determined but pessimistic: "The possibility of getting a favorable decision seemed nil. The Supreme Court had held the line so long."

A recent example was *Hoyt* in 1961, when the justices upheld a Florida law that allowed women, but not men, to exempt themselves from jury service. The justices reasoned that sex discrimination in jury service was benign, designed to protect women from the stresses of public life so that they could function in their ordained sphere of the family, echoing the *Bradwell* decision of a century earlier and articulating what Ginsburg characterized as "these gross lines between men and women."[81] She sought a Supreme Court decision that would hold sex discrimination to the same standard of strict scrutiny from the Court as was used in examining race discrimination.

Linda Kerber, who has written the classic history of these years, gives a dramatic account of the 1970s as a legal revolution that "first established the principle that discrimination on the basis of sex was a burden, not a privilege, [and] challenged law and custom in virtually every sector of American life." There was a great deal of work at the appellate level and in trial courts. "Everything was coming together," Ginsburg told Kerber. "The Equal Rights Amendment, the Women's Rights Project, teaching, the casebook, litigation." "It was really exhilarating," she summed up. "But we were always tired." Meanwhile, the ERA was pending, but Ginsburg followed Pauli Murray's theory in "Jane Crow and the Law" that the Supreme Court could use Fourteenth Amendment guarantees of equal protection to strike down discrimination without the huge effort of securing the ERA's passage. As Murray had earlier enunciated the point of pressure to a colleague:

> [W]hat I am after, of course, is to get a clear cut decision from the Supreme Court . . . that the Fourteenth Amendment is applicable to discrimination because of sex, and to get a clarification of the term "reasonable classification" as applied to women against the backdrop of mid-twentieth century notions of democracy.[82]

The number of cases percolating through the courts meant there were rich resources for planning a line of attack. Basing her approach on Pauli Murray's work, Ginsburg's plan was to bring a series of carefully chosen cases up through the appeals process, "each maximally suited to a favorable court response, each serving as a foundation for its immediate successor and each taking the reasoning one step closer to constitutionally guaranteed sexual equality."[83] Ginsburg was seeking a decision that women were a "suspect classification" in the law, and that statutes discriminating on the basis of sex would be, like those using race to discriminate, subject to "strict scrutiny" to determine that there was a rational basis for the distinction.

The precise requirements for an opening move came together in *Reed v. Reed* (1971), which tested a seemingly innocuous but altogether discriminatory Idaho law that concerned a separated couple's dispute about who could administer their dead son's estate: Automatic preference went to the father. Ginsburg and the ACLU, representing the mother, Sally Reed, persuaded the Court to rule that although Idaho's different treatment of men and women—supposedly a neutral provision designed for administrative convenience—was not without some legitimacy, it could be a denial of women's Fourteenth Amendment right to equal protection. She didn't convince the justices to apply strict scrutiny to the classification of Sally Reed as a woman to determine her qualifications (like race), but the Court, in reversing the lower court's decision, seemed to indicate that it was "somewhat suspect."[84]

Two years later, Ginsburg submitted an amicus brief for the ACLU, arguing before the Court on behalf of Sharron Frontiero, a married air force officer who had run afoul of a law that provided additional employment benefits to dependent wives of male officers, but not to husbands of female officers. Ginsburg's brief for *Frontiero v. Richardson* (1973) was "stunning," co-counsel Brenda Feigen writes in her memoir. Historical amnesia obliterated most of the feminist tradition, but Ginsburg wove together what shreds she could find to survey centuries of legal opinion about and social attitudes toward women. In *Reed v. Reed* she acknowledged her own historical debt by listing Dorothy Kenyon and Pauli Murray on the amicus ACLU brief, even though they had not contributed directly. And in the brief, she unveiled the backstory to a Court that had never had to consider the history of women's subordination. She reminded them of coverture; traced the close association in America between slaves and women, abolition and women's rights; trotted out old chestnuts of misogyny to show how outrageous they were; and quoted extensively from Sojourner Truth's "Arn't I a Woman" speech. She stressed the forward-looking hopes of the President's Commission on the Status of Women and the relevance of the civil rights struggle to the contemporary women's movement. She quoted the now-ludicrous reasons the 1873 Court gave to deny Myra Bradwell the right to practice law and the equally absurd rationale it used to evade the question of women's enfranchisement in *Minor v. Happersett*. In oral argument, she ended with Sarah Grimké's ringing declaration. "I ask no favor for my sex. All I ask of our brethren is that they take their feet off our necks."[85]

The Court ruled for Sharron Frontiero, for the first time articulating a heightened standard of judicial scrutiny when classifications of sex were involved. Justice William Brennan, writing for a plurality of the Court, pointed to the burst of lawmaking from the Ninety-second Congress the previous year to buttress its conclusion that "classifications based upon sex are inherently invidious." Moreover, Brennan's opinion recognized—for the first time—America's "long and unfortunate history of sex discrimination." *Frontiero* was a major step toward making sex a category of discrimination analogous to race and bringing the full implications of the equal protection clause of the Fourteenth Amendment to bear on the rights of women. Although it fell short of the strict scrutiny classification the Women's Rights Project sought, it was a landmark decision, an indication of the Court's new openness to feminist claims.[86]

The gains were remarkable, and they were also shaky. A revolution that had barely been on the horizon in 1963 swept through the culture. Young women went out into the world with a soaring faith in their own possibilities and a determination to live as they imagined men did. As the heady days of women's liberation faded, a détente with men took hold—although it never entered the realm of theory or ideas. For the lucky, the circumstances of work itself—the shared burdens and aspirations, the rhythms of labor and leisure, the pride in tasks well done—seemed to offer a footing for reciprocal relationships between the sexes, practically a guarantee of sexual equality. Soon, a genre of high-class soap operas emerged on TV depicting the shifting liaisons, romances, marriages, and friendships of male and female workmates in police stations, hospitals, and law firms.

But after 1975, further gains in Washington eluded feminism. The structural changes in work that would have created lasting support did not materialize. The wage gap between men's and women's incomes, with black women at the bottom of every index, hardly budged. While educated women moved into professional and managerial positions, a much larger stream poured into low-wage, nonunionized women's jobs: the ever-voluminous pink-collar ghetto. Sex discrimination law lumbered along, but it was unwieldy, cumbersome, and expensive to pursue; the weakening of labor unions meant that in general, employers found ways to circumvent restrictions. The effect was to move prejudice against women into a subtler register. Through the 1970s and thereafter, workingwomen moved into the labor force with no publicly funded support for child care or other family matters.[87] The PCSW's recommendations for public policies that would accommodate women's work and family lives, so conservative compared to the proposals of radical feminism, were by 1980 artifacts of a bygone era, expectations of state largesse now inconceivable.[88]

As a result, five and ten years into the great transformation, the old order had weakened but not toppled. New structures of discrimination emerged, more difficult to challenge because they were more covert. Ironically, given the matrophobia of the late 1960s, motherhood proved to be a great undoer of the daughters' romance of work. Faced with structures geared to men who usually had families but had few household obligations, they ended up in less prestigious and lower-paying jobs. Forced to circumvent the most demanding levels of careers and professions, some dropped out and others were pushed out by employers who claimed that their family involvements disqualified them. Men proved disappointing feminist partners. Friendly male co-workers were cold to the importance of changing routines in order to accommodate mothers' responsibilities. The sexual division of labor at home failed to budge; studies showed that women with full-time jobs did as much or more housework than did full-time homemakers, while male partners' contributions dwindled to negligible. An ideology of choice emerged as the explanation for why highly trained, ambitious women in high-power jobs failed to achieve the goals that, given the momentum of change up to 1975, had seemed within reach.

By 1975, there was much that feminism had changed in the three decades after the end of World War II—more than anyone in 1945 could have dreamed. Indisputably the old order was beyond resurrection. But what would take its place? There was also much that, by 1975, had not changed—and still hasn't. All of us, men and women, live with the aftereffects: the bright enduring hopes, the second thoughts, the revisions and reactions, the compromises and defeats.

Everywhere, among those who thought of themselves as feminists and those who didn't, the insights and claims of the women's movement shaped expectations of themselves and others. No longer were girls told so readily that their arms weren't made to throw balls and that their fingers destined them to be typists. Antipathy toward women could no longer swagger about in the public square without repercussions. It often had to walk more softly and rephrase its boasts and slurs in an idiom of reason and good feeling. The task of conservatives over the next quarter century would be to refashion family government, with all its embedded scorn for women, into a modern, efficient setup. For a time they succeeded, and gained an influence in politics that was unprecedented. In the years leading up to Ronald Reagan's election in 1980, the successes of feminism and antifeminism were entwined and the victories of the women's movement became food for the antifeminist feast.

CHAPTER TEN

POLITICS AND THE FEMALE BODY

A FEW WEEKS AFTER the Supreme Court heard arguments in the *Frontiero* case, it handed down its decision in *Roe v. Wade*. A seven-justice majority held that a Texas statute banning abortion violated women's constitutional right to privacy. An all-male Court thereby brought the power of the Constitution to affirm what by then was a passionately sought goal of the women's movement.

When *Roe* was announced in January 1973, the women's movement had already changed the Republican and Democratic nominating conventions, popular feminism was building, and the ERA was trooping along blithely picking up one ratification vote after another. Far-flung approval greeted *Roe*'s announcement. None of this amounted to a feminist revolution. Radicals were lukewarm to *Roe*, which seemed a modest decision that came nowhere near the call for free abortion on demand. But if the whole loaf was not in evidence, a steady output of half loaves seemed guaranteed.

The campaign to legalize abortion did not begin as a feminist cause, as is often assumed. The movement to legalize abortion actually dates back to the 1950s. It included a range of viewpoints, from left-liberal to conservative—although it was liberals, eventually joined by feminists, who were the mainstays. Until 1967, men dominated the movement, and they continued to play a major part through the *Roe* victory and beyond.

Lucinda Cisler, who led NOW's work for legal abortion, acknowledged that feminists entered belatedly a movement that others started: "The abortion issue is one of the very few issues vital to the women's movement that well-meaning people outside the movement were dealing with on an organized basis even before the new feminism began to explode."[1]

Initially, physicians, psychiatrists, and family planning professionals sustained the campaign. For fifty years, physicians had seen illegal abortions as a threat to public health. This was one reason why the American Medical Association (AMA), a prime mover of illegalizing abortion in the nineteenth century, did an about-face and came to endorse legalization in 1970.[2] Family planning professionals also reversed their view. In the 1910s and '20s birth control advocates kept the abortion issue at arm's length, counterposing the goal of safe, available contraception to the plague of secret murders of unborn children. But in the late 1950s, a few figures from the Planned Parenthood Federation (PPF), heir to Margaret Sanger's campaign, broke with the standard line to join with physicians concerned about the devastating effects of illegal abortion. The PPF called for laws allowing "therapeutic" abortions, to be authorized by committees of physicians upon application of a pregnant woman whose life was in danger.

Abortion was common in the United States and everywhere else, as it is today. It is a universal of women's experience and always has been: Evidence of abortion dates back to the beginnings of recorded history. But the numbers of abortions have waxed and waned in response to the availability of contraceptives and social circumstances that encouraged or discouraged childbearing. During the Great Depression, when childbearing was unthinkable for many, abortions skyrocketed. One large study found that white middle-class married women aborted one in every four pregnancies in the 1930s. The numbers dropped during World War II, when birth control devices (condoms, diaphragms, vaginal foam) circulated widely, but in the late 1950s, the rate started to climb.

For doctors and medical workers, the woman bleeding from a botched abortion was a familiar figure in hospital emergency rooms in the 1950s and '60s. Entire wards were given over to patients suffering from septic abortions. Women tried to abort themselves with abortifacients or irritants administered as douches: Lysol, soap, kerosene, vinegar, powdered mustard, bleach, among others. They used, or others used on them, garden hoses, syringes, telephone wire, coat hangers, nut picks, pencils, catheters, and chopsticks. They were brought into hospital wards by the hundreds, bleeding from perforated uteruses. In 1962, for instance, Cook County Hospital in Chicago treated nearly five thousand women for abortion-related complications. Police crackdowns forced women to self-abort or resort to untrained specialists, with the result that deaths increased, doubling in New York City between 1951 and 1962. In the 1960s, they accounted for nearly half of maternal mortality.[3]

The idea of therapeutic abortion gained force in the early 1960s, winning support from physicians, nurses, liberal Protestants and Jews, lawyers, psychiatrists, social workers, and advocates of zero population growth. Bands of reformers formed across the country, pushing liberalizing measures in state legislatures. Two panics about birth defects intensified awareness of the need for legal abortions and broadened the idea of therapeutic from the mother's life to her health, including her mental health (which would be threatened by the birth of a damaged child). One was the revelation that thalidomide, a drug prescribed to pregnant women from 1957 to 1961, caused severe malformations in fetuses. The other was a measles epidemic in 1965, rubella also having devastating effects on the fetus. The health exception drew additional legitimacy from Britain's passage of a therapeutic law in 1967. In the late 1960s, reformers succeeded in securing laws for therapeutic abortion in a number of states, which set up complicated processes heavily supervised by medical committees that allowed women to end pregnancies in "hardship cases" involving rape, incest, the probability of a deformed child, or the threat of death.[4]

In 1965, a sea change came about in government regulation of sexuality and reproduction when the Supreme Court in *Griswold v. Connecticut* struck down a draconian 1879 Connecticut statute that criminalized both the use and prescription of contraception. The decision was the fruit of four decades' worth of militant challenges mounted by Connecticut women from the Birth Control League—a Sanger-led organization—and its successor, the PPF (Katharine Houghton Hepburn, a suffragist and mother of the film star Katharine Hepburn, started the fight in the 1920s). They periodically opened clinics for poor women to distribute contraception and birth control literature, only to be shut down by the police, arrested, tried, and found guilty. The latest conviction went on appeal to the Supreme Court and the Court struck down the Connecticut law, ruling that married couples had a right to privacy that included the right to make decisions about childbearing and contraception free of government intrusion.[5]

Griswold's right to privacy, even though it initially pertained only to the "sacred precincts of marital bedrooms," changed the field of activity and thought around the politics of the body. Although *Griswold* did not make all contraception legal (that happened only in 1972, with the Court's decision in *Eisenstadt v. Baird* that the state could not prohibit the distribution of contraceptives to unmarried people), the decision had the effect of loosening up access for everyone. Law students and liberal attorneys were fascinated by the broader implications of the privacy right. Among reformers, the interest began to swing from winning laws for therapeutic abortion to repealing all laws that prohibited abortion— that is, to legalizing abortion, period.

Even before feminism took off, an argument emerged that women had a right to determine if and when they bore children. In 1963, the biologist Garrett Hardin, leading spokesman for zero population growth, proposed that abortion was a matter in which a woman, and a woman alone, should make the decision: "Any woman, at any time, should be able to procure a legal abortion for herself *without even giving a reason.* The fact that she *wants* it should be reason enough."[6] After 1967, an awareness of the connection to feminism pushed public discussion beyond the exclusive emphasis on abortion as a public health measure to abortion as a necessity for women's freedom.

Given the fury of anti-abortion politics in the decades after *Roe v. Wade,* it is hard now to grasp how mainstream the legalization movement was in the 1960s. Initially based in professional circles, it soon persuaded a moderate public, inspired by awareness of the changing needs of American families and, at the borders, protofeminist rationales such as Hardin's. In 1966–67, the middlebrow *Saturday Evening Post* ran "We Should Legalize Abortion" and *The New York Times* editorialized for legalization. The physician who wrote for the *Post* stressed that a large number of married women sought abortions. But he pulled no punches about single women, arguing that no teenage girl, either—even if she had sex by choice and thus fell outside the hardship provisions—should be forced to carry a child she did not want. This writer proposed the modified choice position, that any woman should be able to have a pregnancy terminated should she want to, provided that her husband and doctor agreed.[7]

The modified choice position, which spread among liberals, scaled down the autonomy of a woman's decision: Abortion was not quite a woman's right to decide but rather a marital, family, and medical matter. The proposed reform was an improvement on the absolute prohibition of abortion, but it left women still within the jurisdiction of male authority, either husbands' or physicians'. Once feminists joined the cause, they denounced these consent provisions.

Rationales for abortion reform ranged widely. Advocates cited population control, economic prudence in limiting family size, the suffering caused women and families by unwanted births, and the freedom of physicians to care for their patients as they saw fit. For all these reasons, the call for total or partial repeal of the abortion ban attracted wide support in numerous state campaigns: New Mexico, California, New York, New Hampshire, New Jersey, Connecticut, Arizona, Georgia, Indiana, Nebraska, and others.

The backdrop to the swelling chorus was the sexual revolution. Birth control pills initially came on the market in 1960, at first readily available only to middle-class married women through private physicians. Their use strengthened the idea that pregnancies could be planned— which was a more palatable way of saying that sex could be freed from the fear of pregnancy. The linked demographic dynamics of smaller family size and growing numbers of working mothers encouraged couples to view the decision to terminate an unwanted pregnancy as their own. In this context, the state's interference appeared atavistic, a vestige of a moralistic Victorian past.

But the sexual revolution was not the only force propelling support for legalization. People who lived outside the sexual revolution, culturally, morally, and socially, could also agree that abortion should be legal, not because they advocated women's rights but because they saw abortion as a birth control measure of last resort. Physicians, whatever their politics, were generally moved to support legalization because they saw the devastating consequences of illegal abortions. Ministers and rabbis witnessed the strains unwanted pregnancies put on members of their congregations and many came to see the choice of abortion as a matter of individual conscience.

One thread of conservative support came from eugenics advocates, who held that poverty could be alleviated if the poor limited their births, thus lowering numbers on the welfare rolls. Eugenics had always had a complex relationship to birth control. Early in the century, proponents objected that legal contraception would allow "fit" women, who should be replenishing the population, to limit their births instead. But with eugenics' reputation to salvage after the horrors of Nazi race policy, promoters moved closer to supporting birth control in their desire to curb what they saw as a population explosion in poor countries—the "population bomb"—which, they maintained, would result in catastrophic resource scarcity. This meant that when oral contraceptives were first tested in the 1950s, it was in Puerto Rico, America's corner of the Third World. In Puerto Rico, abortions were available, too; it was so easy to get one there that American women with the money for plane tickets traveled there routinely.

The racism and class prejudice of eugenics was close to the surface. From this perspective, abortion was a way to keep "unfit" mothers—supposedly hypersexual black women, slutty poor whites, and feckless teenagers—from having babies and lolling about on the welfare rolls to raise them. Among abortion reformers, tensions between the eugenics view on the right and the pro-woman position of feminists on the left were at first muted: Feminists, too, championed abortion as a way for impoverished women to lessen their burdens. Indeed, this empathy across lines of class and race was one reason that feminists, once they took command of the battle, invented the slogan "free abortions on demand"—the idea being that no woman should have to bear an unwanted child because she didn't have money for an abortion.[8]

The black power movement reacted by conflating all abortion reform with eugenics and branding legal abortion as a genocidal plot against African-American families. The Black Panther Party newspaper in 1970 laid into legal abortion as "a victory for the oppressive ruling class who will use this law to kill off Black and other oppressed people before they are born." One reason was distrust of population control programs as the only form of low-cost health care the government was willing to make available to African-Americans. But this was a male-dominated movement, and the imperative to put women in their place was unmistakable. "Black women love large families," insisted the writer for the Panther newspaper, "and the only reason they would want to eliminate them is to rid them of the pain and the agony of trying to survive." Opposition to legal abortion merged with opposition to birth control, period. In Pittsburgh, black power militants closed a family planning clinic with bomb threats; in Cleveland they burned one. Whitney Young, leader of the moderate Urban League, reversed his organization's long-standing support for family planning, and the head of the Florida NAACP asserted that "our women need to produce more babies, not less."[9]

The vehemence of an African-American leadership composed chiefly of men represented a historic reversal. Except for the Garveyites, twentieth-century black organizations—the NAACP, the Urban League, women's clubs—had long supported family planning as a means of racial uplift. The militant posture—writer Michele Wallace dubbed it "black *macho*" in 1979—prompted some women's irritation and sarcasm. In fact the response in the pre-*Roe* period was one of the first articulations of a distinct African-American feminist voice in this chapter of the women's movement. Representative Shirley Chisholm dispatched the genocide argument with tart efficiency. "To label family planning and legal abortion programs 'genocide' is male rhetoric; for male ears. It falls flat to female listeners and to thoughtful male ones." Chisholm linked the *lack* of safe legal abortion to class and racist structures. At a 1969 news conference she was unequivocal. From her own experiences in family planning centers in Brooklyn, her own New York City district, she maintained that black women too believed they had a right to abortion. Chisholm was typical of the African-American mainstream: Black politicians and newspapers supported abortion reform steadily. In New York and Wisconsin, it was African-American representatives who introduced repeal bills in legislatures.[10]

The National Welfare Rights Organization (NWRO), composed predominantly of black women, resisted the black power line. Johnnie Tillmon, executive director in 1971, asserted that "nobody realizes more than poor women that all women should have the right to control their own reproduction." A Pittsburgh NWRO group ran out an interloper—it turned out he was on the payroll of the Catholic Church—who was trying to recruit them to demonstrate against local family planning clinics. "Why should I let one loudmouth tell me about having children?" one woman demanded. Frances Beal touched on an older African-American assumption about women's reproductive control as a matter of racial uplift when she insisted, "Black women have the right and responsibility to determine when it is in *the interest of the struggle to have children or not to have them and this right must not be relinquished.*"[11] In the idiom of African-American politics, Beal phrased her eloquent call as a race matter, a family matter, a point of common interest where men must cede the grounds of the decision to women—but in the "interest of the struggle." It was an instance, perhaps the first, when some black women publicly contested the militant line and vied with male leaders to shape public opinion.

Organized opposition came principally from the Roman Catholic Church. Since the 1920s, the Church had been *the* major opponent of contraception, holding that it interfered with the primary function of sexual intercourse and thus with natural law. The "child is the primary purpose of marriage," Catholic teaching held, not the bond between husband and wife.[12] But after *Griswold*, Catholic doctrine conflicted with the law of the land and stood at a far remove from the demographic trends of modern family life. For millions of American Catholics, pious practice in this matter coexisted uneasily with a recognition that contraception was widely used and legal. Priests taking confession struggled with parishioners' overwhelming predilection to disobey. Social surveys found that Catholics used birth control almost as routinely as did non-Catholics.

For a time, hopes rose that the Catholic hierarchy would take a more flexible position on sexual matters. The winds of change blew through the Church in 1962 with the Second Ecumenical Council of the Vatican convened by Pope John XXIII, known as Vatican II. Vatican II was the pope's invitation to make the Church a force of modernity and transformation. "The gathering of bishops and theologians from around the world set an unpredictable dynamic in motion," religious historian John McGreevy writes. "Enveloping the whole was a new sense of the church moving through history . . . directly addressing the problems of the current age." In the United States, laypeople called on Vatican II's spirit of tolerance to argue for recognizing the religious freedom of their fellow citizens to adapt a different ethics of reproduction. Boston's Cardinal Cushing took this approach in 1965 when he refrained from opposing legislation that revised Massachusetts's ban on birth control, distinguishing between Church law and civil law and stating that the former did not require enforcing the observance of Catholic doctrine on others.[13]

Vatican II's spirit of coexistence could have been the basis for the Church taking a hands-off position with non-Catholics in regard to abortion as well as birth control. But the post–Vatican II stand on all sexual matters hardened. The commission on contraception appointed by Pope John XXIII overwhelmingly recommended a change in teaching on contraception. But after his death, Pope Paul VI reaffirmed the hard line, dashing hopes for a shift toward moderation in sexual and reproductive matters.

The American Church was thus backed into a corner on contraception. Retreating from a battle over contraception they clearly could not win, American prelates shifted their efforts to upholding the ban on abortion. They were extremely successful, at first pulling in Catholic conservatives but also liberals who ignored the prohibition on contraception yet accepted the teaching that abortion was the destruction of innocent life. In the wake of Vatican II's emphasis on Catholics' duty to the poor, liberals brought to the anti-abortion campaign an ethical imperative for the Church to work for social conditions that would welcome every child into the world and alleviate the burdens of childbearing and child rearing on poor women. This liberal view, tying opposition to abortion to genuine concern for women and children, would not survive long.

In every state where there was a significant Catholic presence, the hierarchy instituted a parish-by-parish effort to block reform bills. By 1970, a bellicose Catholic-driven opposition was up and organized into right-to-life groups. The Church went to great lengths, aggressively lobbying legislators by threatening to work against their reelection if they voted the wrong way. But despite the huge resources the Catholic Church had at its disposal, there was an insoluble problem: Its influence stopped short of federal appeals courts, and the courts were issuing sympathetic decisions on abortion cases with increasing frequency.[14]

The result was a standoff. In many states, reformers won some kind of physician-supervised therapeutic abortion. But therapeutic laws did nothing to lower the numbers of illegal abortions: Pregnant women found it too hard to face intrusive and judgmental questions from hospital committees and went their own way, to find practitioners operating outside the law. In truth, the reformed laws were geared to protecting physicians from legal repercussions, not to helping women. Hospital abortion committees strained to keep the numbers of procedures they approved as low as possible. There were horror stories. A woman not allowed to terminate her tenth pregnancy, although she had nine living children she could not afford to support. A pregnant woman confined to her bed with polio, denied an abortion. A middle-class African-American woman from Long Island, pregnant with a rubella-scarred fetus, was approved for a therapeutic abortion, but once in the hospital had the bad luck to fall into the hands of a Catholic attending physician. He tricked her into believing the fetus was normal and sent her home, and she bore a child with multiple birth defects. Finally, there was only a minuscule number of women who actually qualified for a therapeutic abortion on the grounds of hardship: because they would otherwise die, or because they had been raped, or were victims of incest, or were bearing a malformed fetus—compared to the numbers seeking abortion for what reformers drily called "socio-economic reasons."[15]

By the late 1960s, reformers could see that the strategy of state-by-state change was fruitless. Catholic groups tirelessly drove back reform bills. This happened in Arizona, North Dakota, and Michigan.

Consolidating forces in 1969, reformers organized the National Association for the Repeal of Abortion Laws (NARAL) and targeted several states where prospects looked good to repeal the abortion ban altogether. New York state was at the top of the list, because of the moderate Republican governor Nelson Rockefeller and liberal strength in the legislature. The battle in New York turned out to be savage. A supporter in the state assembly, the Republican Constance E. Cook, mentioned later that she had not expected an explosion when the bill came to the floor: "I didn't really have a sense at that time that we had done something momentous, since it was long overdue." Catholic opposition knew no bounds, presaging right-to-life tactics routinely used in the next decade. On the day the bill passed, the Republican majority leader wept as he read aloud the "Diary of an Unborn Child," a literary legacy of a fetus, which concluded: "Today, my parents killed me." Regardless of the attacks, however, NARAL's careful, patient lobbying strategy paid off: The New York bill was the first actually to legalize abortion, and the most liberal in the country. Between 1970 and 1973, women seeking abortions traveled to New York City by the thousands. Alaska and Hawaii followed New York.[16]

Immediately, the Catholic hierarchy launched a drive to revoke the New York law. To reformers, it was evident that if lasting victory could not be secured even in New York, the legislative strategy was pointless. Physicians and repeal groups stepped up to the task of pushing on the legal front, bringing test cases crafted to maximize the chances of favorable decisions in the courts—the one realm where Catholics could make no headway. In one day alone in May, federal courts issued four declaratory judgments. In an era rife with every kind of protest, referring women for abortions and performing them became acts of civil disobedience, the arrests intensifying the legal action. A. Frans Koome, for example, a Seattle physician who worked with a local abortion rights group, notified the governor of Washington that he was performing abortions and would continue to do so. (Police refrained from arresting him to avoid a cause célèbre.) Whenever reporters contacted him over the next year, he provided a tally: 22 done the week he sent the letter to the governor, 29 the next week, 3,000 over the course of the year.

Civil disobedience was no lark: It involved substantial risks, especially for physicians. That spring, Jane Hodgson, an obstetrician and chair of

Minnesota's American Medical Association committee on abortion, asked the federal district court to enjoin Minnesota from applying state law so that she could perform a therapeutic abortion on a young mother of three who was pregnant with a rubella-scarred fetus but whose application a hospital committee had denied. When the court refused on procedural grounds, Hodgson went ahead anyway, announcing the news to the press and notifying the police. Her May 1970 arraignment was the first time a licensed physician was indicted for performing an abortion in a hospital. Subsequently tried and convicted, Hodgson was at risk of losing her medical license until the *Roe* decision mooted the trial's outcome.[17]

With a number of favorable rulings in appeals courts, hopes rose for a judicial remedy, a ruling from the Supreme Court that would legalize abortion in one swoop.

Women's liberation entered the abortion battle relatively late. At first radicals left the issue to NOW: Even the repeal demand was reform, not revolution, and it involved the painstaking, slow business of changing the law, an accession to the power structure. On the fringe, Shulamith Firestone's vision of test tube babies for the modern woman supplanted interest in working for reproductive rights for the same old female bodies that had been getting pregnant and giving birth for centuries.[18]

But in 1968–69, radical feminists jumped into the fight, accelerating the action and changing the terms of debate. While strong proponents like Garrett Hardin insisted unequivocally that the abortion decision was a woman's to make, and a woman's alone, they saw doctors' and husbands' consent provisions as a politically necessary compromise. The male professionals who led the repeal movement had always framed it as altruistic, coming to the aid of needy women and their families. Radical feminists changed the tenor of popular action from a battle to rescue somebody else (the pregnant woman) to one led by women fighting for themselves. They pushed out and strengthened the principle of a woman's right to autonomous decision-making and infused it with a militant rejection of all measures short of total repeal of the abortion ban. The principle was that a woman had the right to choose abortion at any time, including late pregnancy, whatever the reason. She belonged to herself; the state—or her husband or doctor—had no right to tell her what to do with her body.[19]

Sharp differences broke out over tone and tactics. But the arguments engendered dynamic combinations rather than rifts. A united front came together, in fact the most cohesive front this second wave of feminists ever formed. Feminist referral groups linked up, for instance, with the already vigilant Clergy Consultation Service, founded in 1967 by Howard Moody, pastor of the liberal Judson Memorial Church in New York City's Greenwich Village, an organization that came to involve more than a thousand clerics nationwide. Rabbis and Protestant ministers operated openly in defiance of the law, sending women to willing physicians or providers, with local abortion reformers and sympathetic lawyers ready to step in if and when there was trouble. Ties developed among counselors, repeal groups, and the older, secretive world of physicians providing abortions outside the law. In Chicago, a women's liberation group founded Jane, an underground service that referred scores of women to physicians. When they discovered that some of the practitioners were not accredited, they decided to train themselves to provide abortions. Jane claimed to have performed thousands of procedures.[20]

Full-fledged militance arrived when New York Redstockings disrupted a 1969 public forum in Manhattan about the bill then pending in the state legislature. Redstockings denounced the panel of experts slated to speak, a lineup consisting of only one woman—who was a nun—and fourteen men. "The only real experts on abortion are women," avowed a leaflet the protesters distributed. "Women who have known the pain, fear, and socially imposed guilt of an illegal abortion. Women who have seen their friends dead or in agony from a post-abortion infection. Women who have had children by the wrong man, at the wrong time, because no doctor would help them." The New York hearing was the first event where women insisted on putting themselves at the center of the proceedings. A month later, Redstockings held its own evening of testimonials from women who themselves had had abortions. Intimate material, already familiar from consciousness-raising groups, went public. Predictably, the stories were electrifying: humiliations at the hands of doctors, the shame of bearing an illegitimate child, lovers' betrayals. It was a turning point. After this, feminists' determination to make the female self the final point of reference of the debate—rejecting the perennial position of the Other whom male leaders referred to—was the driving dynamic of legalization politics.[21]

Once women's liberation was involved, the political daughters rephrased abortion from a family issue involving a married couple to an issue that concerned single women and sexual freedom. Of course, single women had always sought abortions, but because sexually active women outside marriage were viewed as morally tarnished figures, repeal discourse shunted them to the side. Wives and mothers, shadowed by concerned husbands and physicians, were the featured figures of sympathy.[22] But radical feminists brought home the tight connections between abortion and young women's lives in the sexual revolution. In pro-repeal rhetoric after 1969, sympathy for the hard-pressed mother, disastrously pregnant again, merged with a defense of the rights of adventurous, lovelorn, and traduced young women—girlfriends, lovers, and casual pickups—dismayed to find themselves pregnant. The scenarios in Lucinda Cisler's 1969 description of how women unintentionally got pregnant came from dramas of courtship and pleasure, not marital negotiations: Women didn't want to appear cheap with a new lover, Cisler explained, so they pretended they were swept away by passion and didn't use birth control. A young woman might use pregnancy as a factor to negotiate with a man about commitment, bringing an ambiguous relationship to a crisis point of decision.[23]

The shift from she-who-was-described to she-who-speaks injected fresh evidence of the centrality of bodily integrity to women's freedom. In Garrett Hardin's lacerating objections in 1968 to compulsory pregnancy, the pregnant woman still existed at a remove from the writer, described as an abstract figure who found herself in an abstract dilemma.[24] With the turn to personal testimony, the abortion-seeking woman took on a life, dragging life's messy details into the debate. Women got pregnant for a myriad of reasons, and there were a myriad of reasons why unwanted children would be intolerable burdens.

The stories unleashed a storm of female honesty—never something a culture welcomes. Feminists showed how entirely the predicament bore down on the woman herself, disrupting her entire existence. They wrenched the decision about what to do away from the dyad of doctor/patient, or husband/wife, or man/woman and made it hers alone. An intrepid man at the Redstockings hearing tried to stem the tide of stories by bringing in a man's rights—what were his rights over a fetus he fathered? he demanded. He was told unequivocally: "Women have the ultimate control over their own bodies." Physicians testifying in *Abele v. Markle,* a feminist-initiated challenge to a Connecticut statute, talked about their experiences treating actual women with unwanted pregnancies, describing the impact on persons worthy of respect. The law "operated to treat women as chattel, as breeding animals without regard for their rights as human beings and with complete disregard of decent everyday respect," contended the chief of obstetrics and gynecology at Mount Sinai Hospital in New York.[25]

The maxim of a woman's right to choose lit a fire under a great pile of misogynist and patriarchal assumptions and laws. As it spread, it became one of the most attractive ideas that second-wave feminism bequeathed—not only to the country but to the world. For one, it brought to light an age-old assumption buried in women's cultures: that it was up to the pregnant woman to decide whether to continue her pregnancy. For another, it moved body politics formally into the regime of rights and pressed the question of self-ownership, raised in the nineteenth century by Stanton and Mill as one of legal and economic standing, into the realm of corporeal dignity. Body politics turned into a political principle with wings, poised to fly across borders and oceans in widening feminist discussions in the 1970s and '80s.[26]

Insistence on physical integrity as a prerequisite for women's liberty went back to Mary Wollstonecraft's desire to see little girls running around like boys. The Owenites, Fourierists, and Stanton in her advocacy of voluntary motherhood; Margaret Sanger, Emma Goldman, and the birth control movement they led in the 1910s: These were the historical antecedents. But the abortion campaign was more assertive than any previous movement, because it was grounded in radical feminism's frank assertion that female sexuality was desirable in itself and could be separated from childbearing. The insight was that enforced pregnancy closed the door on any assurance women might have that they could exist outside the family jurisdiction. The threat that an unintended pregnancy had to be carried to term effectively consigned them to the possibility that involuntary motherhood could descend at any moment, putting childbearing before the requirements of the female self.

On these grounds, liberals and radicals converged, and the legalization movement became a collaboration of political mothers and daughters. It was one flashpoint where NOW, early on, was willing to join the radicals in a daughterly, defiant stance. Already at the second NOW national convention in 1967, the adoption of a strong plank for repeal precipitated a walkout by moderates who thought it was too much for middle America and wanted to work in a more "patient, determined and diplomatic" mode.[27] But the majority of members tolerated the schism and held to the pro-repeal position.

Feminists across the spectrum made the central question that of women's choice. They drove home the point: It was a woman's body;

why should a husband or a doctor have to vet her decision? By 1970, the checks and balances that took the decision away from women included combinations of physician's agreements, mandatory hospitalization, husbands' and parents' consent, and state residence requirements—cumbersome regulations that made abortion more difficult to get and more expensive. The anxiety that underlay all qualifications was that legal abortion would prompt women to have sex willy-nilly, knowing that if something went wrong they could end their pregnancies any old time. The requirement to make getting an abortion hard, supervised by supposedly responsible people like husbands and doctors, was a particular issue in the state legislatures, which because of the dearth of female office-holders—this was 1970–71—were overwhelmingly male. One Colorado lawmaker traced the fault line. The public was comfortable, he thought, if the question was put in terms of balancing two rights, between the woman's health and welfare and the potential life of the fetus. "But if one asks whether a woman ought to have the unfettered right to control her reproduction," he maintained, the response was a resounding no.[28]

Yet the evidence points the other way. Feminists in the early 1970s won a strong public following on the abortion question, even as the right-to-life movement ramped up its crusade. Americans moved toward, not away from a woman's right to choose. Mainstream Protestant denominations began to come around. In 1969–70, for example, the United Methodist Church came out for decriminalization and abortion "on request"; the Presbyterians went on record supporting abortion in hardship cases, and the liberal wing of the Lutheran Church affirmed that a woman could responsibly choose an abortion. Even the Baptist General Convention, later a bastion of right-to-life politics, called for change.[29]

Physicians, overwhelmingly male, took the rap from feminists for wanting to maintain control and refusing to recognize women's autonomy. And it is true that although a solid majority of doctors supported legal abortion and were instrumental in the reform movement, they tended to believe that they should be the wise, benevolent gatekeepers and supported physicians' consent provisions. One point in the 1970 AMA debate on which doctors could agree was that they should not provide abortions "in mere acquiescence to the patient's demands"— that is, the wishes of the irresponsible, impulsive female patient who couldn't be trusted with such a grave decision. Yet a poll of thirty-three thousand physicians taken immediately after the *Roe* decision was announced showed that while the majority had "deep reservations," the picture changed radically when one looked at the generations: Seventy-five percent of doctors thirty-five years or under were in favor.[30]

With watered-down repeal bills passed in several states in 1970, the future seemed to lie with heavily hedged legalization. Regardless, feminists ratcheted up their language, stressing the negative implications of moderate reform. They attacked opponents as not only antimodern, antisexual, antifamily, and antiliberal, but also as antiwoman. Hospitalization and residency requirements drew fire. Residency was not a requirement for any other medical procedure, feminists pointed out; you did not have to live in a state to get a tonsillectomy there. As for being in a hospital, most abortions were straightforward, simple procedures, easily performed in outpatient clinics.

NOW made free abortion on demand one of three planks of the 1970 Women's Strike for Equality march.[31] Abortion on demand was an over-the-top proposal, with no chance of becoming a reality. Like the call for twenty-four-hour child care (another demand) in a country that had scarcely given a penny for any kind of child care, *free* abortion was a delusory goal when you could hardly get a Pap smear for free. It was surely one of the worst slogans that ever circulated in the women's movement; it practically begged for opposition to materialize. The last part, "on demand," raised the psychological stakes, imbuing feminist abortion politics with the absolutist tone of late 1960s antiwar politics and early 1970s race politics.

On the other hand, as pure propaganda the slogan resonated, a hammer hitting steel, with the newly discovered bedrock certainty that women had a right to determine their reproductive lives. And "free"—as in "no cost"—had its own logic, not entirely off the mark when funding for Medicare and Medicaid made publicly supported health care seem within reach. Free abortion also gestured toward poor and working-class women's needs for low-cost, nonintrusive procedures. Indeed "free" and "on demand" rallied the troops at just the points where the right to abortion, once it was secured constitutionally, turned out to be the most vulnerable. Once antichoice zealots had to contend with *Roe v. Wade*, they would turn to chipping away the unimpeded access that "on demand" and "on request" affirmed by inserting parental and spousal consent provisions into state laws everywhere they could find a crack. The abortions that Medicaid provided for poor women and girls were the closest abortion came to being free; and they would be the first to go when conservatives regrouped and trained their sights on depleting *Roe*'s meaning.

In 1970, the Supreme Court agreed to hear two abortion cases. *Doe v. Bolton* from Georgia and *Roe v. Wade* from Texas began with the troubles of two poor women, Sandra Bensing in Atlanta and Norma McCorvey in Dallas. Each woman's plight came to the attention of repealers, who convinced them to take legal action, connected them to a wider world of advocacy, and put money and legal resources into the litigation. In other words, the cases were joint creations of reformers and hard-pressed women, neither entirely crafted by legal activists nor simply outgrowths of protest politics, but rather products of what can be seen as constitutionalist collaborations.

In 1970, the same day the physician Jane Hodgson filed her appeal of her conviction in Minnesota, a complaint filed on behalf of "Mary Doe" hit the news in Georgia. Signing the complaint with Mary Doe were the organizers and initiators of the action, some two dozen doctors, nurses, and hospital social workers, Atlanta Planned Parenthood, and the Georgia group for abortion repeal. Mary Doe was the legal pseudonym of Sandra Bensing, whose compelling case presented a worst-case scenario that was, in fact, the best-case scenario to test the law.

Bensing's situation, while extreme, was by no means atypical of women without the money to travel to Mexico, Puerto Rico, or Sweden to get an abortion. A twenty-two-year-old high school dropout down on her luck, she was into her fourth pregnancy and married to a violent and abusive drifter who was a convicted child molester. The couple had given up one child for adoption and the other two were in foster homes. Bensing applied for a therapeutic abortion at an Atlanta hospital, went through five sessions of interviews and examinations, and was denied.[32]

In Texas, Norma McCorvey also agreed to sign on to a suit constructed and carried forward by activists. The movement in Texas dated back to 1968, when a group of Austin feminists started a birth control counseling service near the University of Texas campus and found themselves fielding women's requests to help them find abortions. Once they set up a connection with a safe and reputable clinic in Mexico, they asked Sarah Weddington, a recent law school graduate and native Texan, to investigate their legal standing. Weddington, underemployed at the time, had been a star student at the University of Texas School of Law. But graduating in 1965 as one of four women in a class of 120, she had no job offers. Thus in 1968, when the others approached her, she had time on her hands to pursue an interesting question, one that might relate to the *Griswold* decision that had so intrigued her generation of law students.[33]

Weddington contacted a law school friend, Linda Coffee, who was involved in Dallas NOW. Drawn together by an interest in women's causes, they mused about bringing a challenge to the 1859 Texas statute, the most extreme in the country, which prohibited abortion for any reason (including rape and incest) except when a woman's life was in danger. They found their plaintiff through a lawyer friend when Norma McCorvey contacted him to ask for help getting an abortion. McCorvey was single and a high school dropout; she had one child and did not want another. She was working as a waitress and knew she would lose her job if she were pregnant. Although desperate, a woman like McCorvey, because she was healthy, had absolutely no chance of getting a therapeutic exception. The lawyer told her he could not help with the abortion but put her in touch with the two lawyers who were interested in abortion. McCorvey, moved by their explanation of how many women found themselves in her plight and touched by their respectful manner, agreed to be a plaintiff.[34]

NOW members and Protestant and Jewish women's groups pitched in to raise money and get sympathetic local publicity. Dallas women produced two more plaintiffs. Marsha King had recently had a traumatic experience getting an abortion in Mexico; she volunteered along with her husband, David, to join McCorvey, or "Jane Roe," adding the dimension of the marital right to privacy affirmed in *Griswold*. McCorvey, an unstable figure and hard to locate in her vagabond life, remained in the shadows, while the Kings, respectable, articulate, and middle-class, represented the lawsuit to the Texas public; they remained anonymous but spoke eloquently to the press. Although they stood for the moderate position, conjuring up responsible spouses making a careful decision to terminate an unwanted pregnancy, that did not mean they pulled back from the tougher feminist claims. David King movingly enunciated the implications of their participation: "We don't really stand for two people who, because of our particular situation, found abortion necessary. We stand for everybody—for women's right to freedom of choice."[35]

Roe was blessed with legal luck from the start. Weddington's petition for a declaratory judgment reached federal district court at just the moment the membership of the AMA voted to support repeal of the abortion ban. The three-judge panel, which included Judge Sarah Hughes, one of the few female federal judges in the country, took five minutes to decide the case. In a succinct nine-page opinion, the judges ruled the statute unconstitutional.[36]

The arguments and strategies in the Texas and Georgia cases drew from a crowded field of legal activity where women were directing the action. On the East Coast, feminists were organizing lawsuits in which hundreds, rather than one carefully chosen perfect plaintiff like Mary Doe or Jane Roe, challenged the law. The approach was inspired by Redstockings' use of women's experiences. With New York women in the lead in a powerfully argued case, *Abramowicz v. Lefkowitz*, feminist lawyers challenged statutes in New Jersey, Connecticut, Pennsylvania, Massachusetts, Rhode Island, and Tennessee. Hundreds of women signed on. These large actions changed the dynamics of litigation. *Abramowicz* went to court with 350 female plaintiffs represented by five women lawyers, whose "presence in the courtroom startled male judges and lawyers alike," recalled one of the attorneys, Nancy Stearns.[37]

The process of recruiting plaintiffs was in itself a politicizing activity, because so many women from different backgrounds joined and because their stories dramatized all the more the urgent need for change. The group that brought the Connecticut suit, *Abele v. Markle* (called Women versus Connecticut in the women's movement), sent out speakers with plaintiff forms to women's groups. The dictate of the-personal-is-political kicked the process into gear. "We thought that you went from the personal to the political, so everywhere we went, we told things that were hard to tell strangers," recounted Ann Hill, an organizer. "And they in turn told things that were hard to tell." It was consciousness-raising on a grand scale. "Everybody had either had an abortion or had a friend who had had an abortion or went to school with somebody who suddenly wasn't in school anymore, and they'd hear they were in some home for pregnant teens and banished from society." The momentum conferred a sense of agency and efficacy: Women might be able to shape the law to their needs. "We broke down our feelings of isolation and said, 'It's time that we did something about this.'"[38]

Before *Abramowicz* went to trial in 1972, courts considered the rights of physicians, since they were the ones subject to sanctions, not the rights of women. The new wave of challenges forced courts to refocus their attention. Judges could bridle at the shift, which involved an all-female cast of characters. In *Abramowicz*, the three-judge panel balked at the lineup of women ready to testify in court and ruled that they must instead present written depositions. In Rhode Island, two judges walked out before witnesses were even called. In the Connecticut case, however, a panel of judges heard testimony and the influence on the decision was clear. Ruling for the plaintiffs, the district court agreed that "the decision to carry and bear a child has extraordinary ramifications for a woman" and went on to speak of economic burdens, the interruption of education, the stigma of illegitimacy, and the physical strains of pregnancy.[39]

When the Supreme Court agreed to hear the Texas and Atlanta cases, a dispersed legal network snapped into action. At the center was Roy Lucas, the man responsible for crafting the strategy that moved the fight to the courts. Like Sarah Weddington, Lucas was a recent law school graduate who had been deeply affected by the civil rights movement and fascinated by *Griswold*'s implications. He was first struck by the creative uses of *Griswold* in a civil rights case, *Loving v. Virginia*, in which the Supreme Court struck down a Virginia anti-miscegenation law.[40]

At New York University Law School, Lucas wrote a bold paper using *Griswold* to mount a frontal attack on abortion statutes. Lucas argued that abortion was "a fundamental right of marital privacy, human dignity, and personal autonomy reserved to the pregnant woman acting on the advice of a licensed physician." Published in 1968 in a law review, the article drew the attention of Harriet Pilpel, who had been representing defendants in test cases of anti-birth-control statutes for four decades (since she worked in the 1930s as a junior associate in the firm of Morris Ernst, who was Margaret Sanger's counsel). Pilpel was looking to move the action out of state legislatures and welcomed the innovative approach. In 1968, Lucas began to coordinate challenges from across the country under the auspices of a Manhattan public interest law organization.[41]

To prepare for *Roe*, Weddington moved to New York to work with Lucas. Her attorney husband, Ron Weddington, quit his job to join her. Lucas's small staff orchestrated the amicus curiae briefs—forty-two in all, from organizations that included the AMA, American Psychiatric Association, and Zero Population Growth. Lawyer friends in Austin pitched in from a distance. The many lawyers working on amicus briefs, the mix of men and women, the fraught partnership of Southerners (Texans and Georgians) with New Yorkers, the distance, and the heat all frequently brought tensions to a boil.

One testy issue was the prominence of women, a question linked to who would argue the case before the Court—a feather in any attorney's cap, and for Lucas, the chance to make good on work that had consumed him for years. But by 1971, feminists had reframed abortion as a woman's issue and recast the culture of the male courtroom as itself needing change. The mood was not generous toward men in general, and particularly men slow to comprehend the demands of drastically revised gender etiquette. Lucas, while in large measure responsible for giving intellectual and practical coherence to national litigation, was known for his arrogance and high-handedness. He managed to offend several parties to *Roe,* including plaintiff Marsha King, who pulled a new word out of the hat and complained that he was a sexist. For a change, this was the woman's hour, and Lucas was forced to step aside to let two women serve as lead attorneys: Sarah Weddington and *Doe*'s Margie Hames of Atlanta. At twenty-six, Weddington, the law school graduate who couldn't find a law-firm job, was possibly the youngest person ever to argue before the Supreme Court.[42] It was almost certainly the first time two women argued before the Court.

The argument for the plaintiffs invoked numerous sources of constitutional authority for the right to abortion. The attorneys cited the Fourth, Fifth, Eighth, Ninth, Fourteenth, and Nineteenth amendments and proposed an extension of *Griswold*'s right to privacy in contraceptive choice. "Liberty talk and equality talk were entangled, as emanations of different constitutional clauses," Reva Siegel observes.[43] Pilpel, representing the ACLU, and Nancy Stearns, on behalf of New Women Lawyers (associated with *Abramowicz*), submitted amicus briefs that reinforced those aspects of the argument that spoke to the social meanings of compulsory pregnancy for women: the inordinate responsibilities that fell on them, the adverse effects on their prospects for education and financial well-being, the burdens of maternity that forced mothers into dependence on men and the state.

Stearns's brief was sweeping, tough, and to the point. It is the custom that amicus briefs go for broke, making the claim in the strongest terms possible, and Stearns did not disappoint. A tincture of women's liberation outrage suffused the elegant reasoning from the first sentence: "During the past two years the question of the constitutionality of abortion laws—of the right of a woman to control her own body and life—has become one of the most burning issues for women throughout the country." Stearns quoted women's personal testimony and detailed meticulously the crippling effects of forced pregnancy. She cited a host of laws upheld by the courts that affected pregnant women and new mothers adversely: statutes that denied them their jobs and unemployment insurance, expelled them from school, and gave them no help in getting child support from fathers. She put the Nineteenth Amendment into play, pointing out the historical dilemma of a class of people subject to laws made prior to the time they could vote. The broadly gauged approach stressed women's historical entanglement in a nexus of laws, customs, and assumptions that condemned them to a subject position—a time-honored argument of feminist thinkers, now turned to maximum effect. Stearns and Pilpel both stressed the importance of the choice and timing of childbearing as a necessity for women to function fully in the wider world, an argument from the fullest interpretation of the Fourteenth Amendment's guarantee to equal protection.[44]

In January 1973, the Court issued its decision, written by Justice Harry Blackmun, a Nixon appointee. A modest man, Blackmun insisted later that "*Roe* against *Wade* was not such a revolutionary opinion at the time." The demurral has truth to it, if one considers the high bar of free abortion on demand. But at the time the ruling was "stunning," as Ruth Bader Ginsburg wrote in 1985. A "thunderbolt," a leading reformer heralded *Roe,* going "beyond what anyone would have predicted." Pilpel, who had appeared in court arguing for reproductive rights longer than anyone else involved, marveled that the decision "scaled the whole mountain. We expected to get there, but not on the first trip."[45]

In a 7–2 decision, the Court extended *Griswold* to pertain to "the personal privacy of the abortion decision." The justices ruled that a woman, guided by her physician's medical judgment, had a constitutionally protected right to terminate a pregnancy, anchored to a concept of personal autonomy. *Roe* reached across the field of pro-abortion arguments, sorted through them, and collected the moderate ones into an affirmation that the right to privacy pertained to a woman's judgment about her pregnancy.

Blackmun, however, rejected the claim that "the woman's right is absolute and that she is entitled to terminate her pregnancy at whatever time, in whatever way, and for whatever reason she alone chooses." He sought rather to balance the woman's desire to end the pregnancy with the state's interest in her health—a woman's health being the traditional justification for nineteenth-century statutes banning abortion. He thus introduced a medical dimension, famously blurring the distinction in *Roe* between which right is being upheld: the doctor's right to protect a patient's health or the patient's right to terminate a pregnancy for her own reasons. Because the state did have a "compelling interest" in preserving and protecting a woman's health, her right to an abortion was not absolute. The state was justified in intervening with increasing degrees of restraint as the pregnancy proceeded and the issues of her health became more complex. It is here that the now famous system of trimesters came into play, whereby Blackmun turned the guidelines used by obstetrical studies into legal distinctions, with the second and third trimesters involving increasing degrees of state regulation. In the third trimester, the viability of the fetus entered in, although in obstetrics, the viability of a fetus is not fixed, but a medical judgment. Blackmun made viability a hard-and-fast legal designation, like age eighteen for voting. Choosing to "regulate, and even proscribe, abortion, except where necessary." Even so, no question of fetal life was involved, but rather, the increasing risk of later-term abortions to the woman's health.[46]

Blackmun's trimesters, however, were probably the only practical solution that over the long run could hold firm against the anti-abortion movement's claim that from the moment of conception the fetus had an absolute right to be carried to term. The first trimester designation had the additional merit of lining up with "quickening," when the fetus moves in utero, a sign recognized for centuries by women, midwives, and physicians as the moment when the fetus becomes a human being.[47] And, to repeat: Even the trimester system was there to protect the woman from the increasing risks of later abortions, not to differentiate degrees of human life. In fact, to the lay reader today, the mild-mannered concern about protecting the woman's health—and thereby justifying state intervention—stands in surprising contrast to the lurid dramaturgy of fetal personhood that became the antiabortion movement's stock-in-trade. While the Court recognized a state's interest in protecting "the potentiality of human life," it rejected the Texas claim that the fetus was a person and thus protected under the Fourteenth Amendment (Sarah Weddington pointed out that no U.S. census had ever counted fetuses).

Blackmun was not deaf to women's voices in the arguments: "Maternity, or additional offspring, may force upon the woman a distressful life and future." There could be psychological harm, he noted; child-care burdens that taxed mental and physical health; the stress of bringing a child into a family without the means to care for it. Nancy Stearns recognized language from her brief in Blackmun's opinion: "The experiences of women got through. Our decision to influence the law by presenting the experiences of women was successful."[48] Others disagree and say that Blackmun ignored feminist claims. Certainly he veered away from the challenge of imagining women's lives to the safer exercise of conjuring up the doctor's office: "All these are factors the woman and her responsible physician will consider in consultation."[49]

Roe at one stroke turned repeal into the law of the land. It fell short of the boldest demand for women's unrestricted right to abortion. Blackmun's apparatus of trimesters seemed cumbersome and threatening, as if it were going to be the foundation of a counterattack (as in fact, it proved to be). Poor women's needs were the first to go, once Catholics succeeded in revoking Medicaid funding in New York state, a tactic that led three years later to the Hyde Amendment, which denied Medicaid funds for abortion services.[50]

The mainstream papers declaimed wildly on the decision's importance, but radical feminists were lukewarm: Anything that came from the American government, let alone a Supreme Court composed of nine men, was bound to be unsatisfactory. Suspicion and caution set the tone. It was understandable, given the constant setbacks the movement for abortion had suffered in legislatures, yet the response seriously underestimated the importance of *Roe*. *Off Our Backs*, the newspaper of Washington, D.C., women's liberation, groused about the meagerness of the half loaf: Abortion was not free and it was still not available on demand. In New Haven Women's Liberation that January, the announcement at a big meeting occasioned scarcely a murmur, so cynical were the radicals around Yale about change that emanated from the courts. The victory seemed inevitably compromised by the fact it was won by a coalition: "a quiet back-burner issue promoted by a handful of stray radicals and moderate reformers," in the patronizing view of Susan Brownmiller.[51] And the most knowledgeable supporters could scarcely celebrate before they started to worry about what came next, and with good reason, given what happened in New York state. Lucinda Cisler warned with prescience that the battle was not over: "The concept that fetuses have priority over women was not completely rejected by the court, while the concept of fully human autonomy for women was clearly not affirmed," she observed cogently.[52]

But regardless of its weaknesses, *Roe* was a historic achievement. Along with Title VII and Title IX, these were the piers sunk to support a bridge to the future for both mothers and daughters, a far-reaching feminism that touched men and women, middle-aged and young, the well-off and the poor (for a time, until Medicaid funding was denied), and black, brown, and white.

If not everyone agreed on the reasons, they agreed enough. That is the definition of a successful coalition. Out of the polarized 1960s, a consortium of groups held together, despite tensions, and exerted pressure that changed the law in ways that would be experienced by every American woman, couple, and family. Mothers and daughters sank their energies into the crusade, and plenty of political brothers helped, too: the men in the repeal movement, the lawyers who helped construct the arguments, the physicians who provided abortions at great risk to themselves and who went to court as defendants, witnesses, and plaintiffs. While the judges were deliberating their decision, polls showed that the number of Americans who supported legalization rose to 65 percent, a solid majority that had been building for a decade and has remained a given of electoral politics ever since. After *Roe*, "the popular base for radically altering the abortion status quo seems to be lacking," observed two political scientists in 1983 with studied neutrality, even though high-level candidates, including presidential contenders, would be forced after 1973 to take equivocal or antagonistic positions on *Roe*.[53]

The United States, whose policies for women fell short in most areas of family support compared to Western Europe and Scandinavia, now compared more than favorably, with one of the more liberal abortion laws in the world. A 1987 survey showed that only twenty-three countries, comprising about 40 percent of the world's population, permitted abortion on request: These included most Communist states (China, the Soviet Union, Cuba, parts of Eastern Europe), half of Western Europe, and most of Scandinavia. Only two African countries and no Latin American nation permitted abortion on request. Half of the 30–50 million abortions that took place each year around the world were illegal.[54] In other words, the U.S. women's movement had scored a major victory in the most powerful country in the world: won, moreover, in the face of a fully mobilized Catholic Church.

Opponents were determined to obliterate the gain. Antichoice radicals, at this point led and financed by the Catholic hierarchy, geared up for a national campaign. In 1973, they were a highly effective and vociferous group of extremists, their dogmatic, shrill, and intolerant views overwhelming any liberal Catholic arguments for social justice that persisted from the 1960s. Their intolerance never abated, and over the next twenty years, they diversified their ranks to include evangelical Protestants, shifted ideological ground, and pushed their dogma to the center of U.S. domestic politics.

There was no undoing *Roe*—at least for the moment. The Church faced a rare defeat. In a pastoral message a month later, the bishops called for civil disobedience, an action unprecedented in recent memory, and reaffirmed their position that any woman who had an abortion would be excommunicated. Several groups of Catholics proposed that Justice William Brennan, a Catholic who had voted with the majority on *Roe*, be excommunicated.[55] Reversing *Roe*, however, was a possibility that existed only faintly on the far horizon. In fact, as of this writing, it has still not happened, although right-to-life forces have seriously weakened abortion rights and women's and girls' access.

Unlike *Roe*, though, the ERA could still be stopped. Recall that at the end of 1973 the amendment was well on the way to being ratified (with thirty states having passed it out of a necessary thirty-eight). Notwithstanding their previous indifference to the amendment, conservatives now ginned up an analogy between the forced equality the ERA engineered and the forced equality of school busing. They were astoundingly successful in ramping up what had been an apple-pie issue into a referendum on defeating feminism. By 1977, the ERA was foundering. It died in 1982 when a second deadline for ratification expired.

The innovator who discovered the political gold in antifeminism was Phyllis Schlafly, who had never before concerned herself with women's issues. Schlafly found in opposition to the ERA an issue that stirred up conservative women, becalmed in the backwaters of the Republican Party for years. By seizing the identity of Woman in the name of traditional housewives in Stop ERA, the organization she founded, Schlafly challenged feminism's claims to speak for universal needs and rights. She indicted feminism as a monstrous aberration, an attack on women rather than a defense. "Women's libbers are radicals who are waging a total assault on the family, on marriage, and on children as the basic unit of society," she announced—a generality that she and her followers reworked a thousand times over.[56] Feminists were dreadful people, unloved, shrill, and whiny, harridans who begrudged married women their happiness and wanted to ruin it by sowing discontent. The defense of the family, which Nixon fiddled with and Schlafly put up in lights, gave a new dimension to the Cold War crusade, projecting an America to be saved from godless feminism along with godless Communism.

Schlafly was from the far right wing of the Republican Party. She was a zealous Cold Warrior and, in the 1960s, a rabid critic of nuclear deterrence. Her foreign policy views were so apocalyptic that the logic would have led directly to nuclear war with the Soviet Union. In the 1960s, she maintained that Franklin Delano Roosevelt was despicable, America should have stayed out of World War II, wealthy Eastern moderate Republicans like the Rockefellers were secretly working with the Soviets, and segregation was a sane and workable system. As president of the Illinois Federation of Republican Women, she made a splash with a self-published book, *A Choice Not an Echo,* which became an underground bestseller on the right-wing lunatic fringe. The book purported to expose a secret cabal of "persons high in finance, government and the press" on the East Coast who were aiding the Soviets. Her conspiracy-mongering and hyperbole were so extreme that in 1964, even the Goldwater campaign tactfully rebuffed her offers to help.[57]

Initially indifferent to feminism, Schlafly found her way into women's politics through the backdoor. Narrowly defeated in 1966 by a moderate for the presidency of the National Federation of Republican Women, Schlafly nearly fomented a schism within the ranks but pulled back and formed her own organization of virulent anticommunists by exploiting gender resentments of the ruling male cabal. Schlafly presented a spirited brief for the role and power of women that weirdly echoed NOW's. The time was past, she declared, "when the women of the Republican party are merely doorbell pushers." So they were ready to become "important in their own right, and not merely as the mirrored reflection of their masculine counterparts."[58]

Ironically, it was the incipient spirit of the women's movement that gave Schlafly her entrée to a career with much greater influence. Followers saw her as a powerful figure proclaiming a new era of female clout in the party, a "demonstration of fearlessness and candor of women." Taking great care to present herself as a reluctant leader, a housewife whom the pressing demands of the times had thrust on the public stage, she appealed to those who sank their lives and sense of self in the home. "Your ability and enthusiasm really did inspire us in our local efforts," wrote a disciple who heard her speak in a Chicago suburb. "The example of your busy schedule leaves little alibi for us young mothers to shirk the responsibility of safeguarding our freedom." "Don't ever let anyone persuade you to 'tone down,'" urged another. In the early 1970s, as Republican feminists in and around the women's movement stepped up pressure for more power in the party, she kept her distance, but she nonetheless reaped the benefits of their labors to increase female leadership.[59]

In 1972, Schlafly departed from her harangues on foreign policy to lambast the ERA, attacking the amendment as a Soviet-style assault on women's traditional role in the family. She did so in terms identical to those the right had used the previous year to torpedo the Child Development Act. Initially, condemning the ERA was difficult, as she herself acknowledged, since the idea of equal rights was widely accepted as a guarantee of fairness. "Most people mistakenly believe that 'equal rights' means simply 'equal pay for equal work,'" and she was all for that, she assured readers of her *Phyllis Schlafly Report,* signaling her support for more job opportunities, equal pay for equal work, more women in medical school, even more appointed to "high positions."[60]

But the goal of equality had already been reached, she asserted. Then came the pernicious ERA, which caught Congress off guard. A few noisy, maladjusted women were trying to wreck a chivalric system that had evolved over centuries to rescue America's women from drudgery and place them under the kindly protection of men. She declared war on those who threatened this system, which was the most benevolent, sumptuous, life-enhancing regime available to women in the entire world. The ERA was a plot to brainwash American women into believing that they were second-class citizens rather than pampered consorts.

About the need for justice, she noted: The idea that the ERA would bring justice to women could not be further from the truth! Politicians simply hadn't heard "from the millions of happily married women who believe in the laws which protect the family and require the husband to support his wife and children." Men were ready to shower women with love and support to ease their lives.

> A man's first significant purchase is a diamond for his bride, and the largest financial investment of his life is a home for her to live in. American husbands work hours of overtime to buy a fur piece or other finery to keep their wives in fashion, and to pay premiums on their life insurance policies to provide for her comfort when she is a widow.[61]

Elevated to their position as treasured homemakers and mothers, dripping with furs and diamonds, their lot eased by ample goods and labor-saving devices provided by the American free enterprise system, the right to a husband's financial support guaranteed by law: No sane woman would want to throw away the housewife's bounty for the dystopian nightmare of sexual conflict the ERA would bring on.

Like any dogmatist, Schlafly presented ideology as fact. The reality was that housewives were losing face. Male-headed households were buckling in the 1970s; among African-Americans, the numbers of female-headed families had been climbing since 1940, and the trend was now evident among whites, too. The role of the wife/mother/homemaker touted in the 1950s was frayed from the wear and tear of divorce and rising rates of female employment; and feminists were not the only women who treated housework as drudgery. Matrophobia was in the air: The stay-at-home wife was a debased Other whom bright young American women were running hard to escape. Schlafly rallied true believers by insisting the housewife's future was golden, that their fortunes would turn, provided the enemy was crushed. If under the law, "the man is *always* required to support his wife and each child he caused to be brought into the world," then "why should women abandon these good laws?" Why, indeed? She articulated phobic fantasies about the catastrophic effects of female independence and channeled them into a crusade to shore up family government, presented as benign dictatorship.[62]

Schlafly, a Catholic, went beyond the traditional purview of Republican women's organizations by recruiting highly traditional working-class and lower-middle-class women from Protestant evangelical churches as the storm troopers of Stop ERA, which she created in 1972. The overwrought style diverged from the genteel ladies' decorum of mainstream Republican women. In states where the amendment was up for ratification, they inundated legislatures with feverish warnings about the pernicious effects of the ERA. "Long before the birth of the Moral Majority," Tanya Melich notes, "Schlafly's women of the Religious Right were fixtures in the capitals of southern states, walking the halls with their Bibles and strongarming legislators to understand that 'women weren't meant by the Lord to be equal.' "[63]

The Stop ERA campaign capitalized on the highly American analogy between uppity women and uppity blacks. "Forced busing, forced mixing, forced hiring. Now forced women. No thank you," declaimed a North Carolina woman. The ERA was said to legislate unisex toilets, prohibit all-female organizations such as sororities, mandate that women be drafted into the military along with men, and outlaw any female advantages in divorce—alimony, child custody. For reasons that are unclear, Schlafly at first did not harp on the *Roe* decision, although she brought in legal abortion from time to time as Exhibit C for feminism's attack on childbearing. "Women's libbers are trying to make wives and mothers unhappy with their career. . . . Women's libbers are promoting free sex instead of the 'slavery' of marriage. They are promoting Federal 'day-care centers' for babies instead of homes. They are promoting abortions instead of families."[64]

Stop ERA and its male allies rerouted the Republican Party away from its historic support for the ERA (since 1940). President Gerald Ford withstood them, his resolve stiffened by his staunchly feminist wife, Betty, who took a heavy beating from the right for her principles. But Ford was the last Republican president to do so. Ronald Reagan ran for president in 1980 on explicit opposition to the ERA and *Roe*.[65]

Despite feminist successes in Congress, the women's movement was unable to mount a successful counterattack. One problem was that the ERA itself had so few concrete meanings that tangible truths were scarce to use in countering Stop ERA's fantastical charges. The dual feminist legal strategy in the 1970s—pushing Fourteenth Amendment appeals as the ERA campaign continued—obviated the original intent of the amendment, since courts were already striking down sexually discriminatory laws. The effect of the legal revolution was that most laws that ERA supporters in 1972 cited as unjust were found unconstitutional within ten years anyway.[66]

The dearth of substantial issues emptied out public debate, which came to rest on two decontextualized issues. First, there was the question of whether or not men protected women. Stop ERA charged that the amendment would throw the traditional harmony of male independence/female dependence out of whack and encourage men to abandon their obligations. In line with denunciations of coverture stretching back centuries, ERA supporters maintained that male protection was a myth and women needed legal equity to take care of themselves.

Second, there was the potential that the ERA would make women liable for the draft, a vastly exaggerated scenario at a time when the United States had pulled out of Vietnam and was demobilizing its armed forces. Yet feminists got caught up in a hypothetical tangle. Unwilling to abandon principle, they insisted that an equal opportunity draft was better than a discriminatory one. But because the women's movement was so strongly antimilitarist, ERA supporters lacked any real commitment to grapple with the nature of military obligation and men's domination of the armed services. Thus their reasoning lacked the appeal of practical outcomes. There were already women in the military, for example: Would the ERA do anything to improve their situation? American citizenship brought obligations as well as rights. What were women's obligations to the nation, besides paying taxes and obeying laws? Was military service one of them? Feminists were loath to engage these questions.

The ERA's demise in 1982 completed a shutdown on feminist hopes in Washington that was already in progress once Reagan took office. Radical feminists, uninterested in electoral politics to begin with, retreated from the dismaying trends of the Reagan years. Liberals who in the earlier 1970s had seen the road through institutions open to them lost heart as conservatives blocked them at every turn. As the New Right seized national and state office, small-scale local actions—dubbed "grassroots"—proved more appealing. Feminists in politics either retired from the rout, settled in for the long haul, or took up positions in liberal enclaves where they could wield influence: foundations, the media, universities, professional organizations, and Democratic Party venues. Among the highly committed looking for accessible and immediate issues to bring about change, a set of new concerns with body politics—issues that lay beyond birth control and abortion—proved fertile ground.

As coalition politics, the campaign to legalize abortion paid the women's movement enormous dividends. "A woman's right to choose," with its attendant belief in the integrity of the female body, moved into the mainstream of the culture after 1973, even as it fueled what was already a powerfully organized opposition. The justice of *Roe* was an adamantine belief for feminists of all dispositions: "The one thing I care about in politics," a generally nonactivist woman told me sometime in the 1980s. "Just about the only thing I care about," she added. Millions put off by the New Right's ascendancy but cynical and disillusioned about taking action could have echoed her sentiment.

The core principle of women's right to bodily dignity, free of coercion, undergirded reproductive rights discourse. It also generated other issues: activism against rape, domestic violence, and sexual harassment. These newly accentuated wrongs of woman—newly accentuated, not newly discovered, because protests against male domestic and sexual violence went back to the eighteenth century—dramatized men's power, formally and informally maintained by law, economics, and government, to use, abuse, exploit, and wreak havoc on women's bodies. These particular expressions of body politics had the advantage of circumventing the polarities of the abortion debate. Images of abused and traumatized women tapped into a traditional moral scheme of female virtue and male vice. The very familiarity of the moral outrage these campaigns against male violence inspired gained them support from constituencies outside feminism and even opposed to feminism.

Like abortion rights, body politics brought together women across generations—mothers and daughters—and across the color line. Susan Brownmiller's *Against Our Will* (1975), a feminist bestseller, touched off a furor by demonstrating how enmeshed rape was with normal male behavior. At every level, Brownmiller showed, rape victims were subject to hostility, shaming, and distrust from police, judges, neighbors, and even sometimes family and friends. *Against Our Will* presented a comprehensive view of male power in its most violent manifestations. The grievances had been circulating in the women's movement for years, but Brownmiller's book broke open the subject for a mainstream audience and galvanized the formation of groups dedicated to changing the abuse of rape victims by police and courts and ensuring that rapists were prosecuted. These rape crisis centers, while small and scattered, spurred research and revelations on the scandalously low number of convictions and the horrible assumptions that led judges and juries to assume victims were "asking for it." In league with scholars, antirape activists challenged the stereotype of rape as a crime of black men against white women, a scenario that went back to the nineteenth-century South. They publicized the facts: Most rape was intraracial and the rapist was more likely to be an acquaintance than a stranger.

Feminist lawyers worked for reform in standards of evidence and treatment of victims' testimony—for one, arguing strenuously that the victim's sexual history was irrelevant and should be inadmissible in court. Marital rape, which women's rights advocates had long decried, came under pressure; and state laws for marital exemptions crumbled. The first trials of men for raping their wives occurred in 1978 and marked the beginning of the end of one of the last formal vestiges of coverture.[67] While the idea was fodder for jokes ("If you can't rape your wife, who can you rape?" ran one old chestnut), the radical insight that a woman could deny sex to any man, including a husband or boyfriend, led to the new category of date rape, which became a mandatory topic for discussion in college freshman orientations across the country in the 1980s. Awareness of domestic violence spread at the same time and along the same pathways, spurred by similar convictions about how courts, police, and families looked away from violence against women.

Body politics could be conducted locally, within cities, towns, and institutions. And like the abortion battle, body politics generated generational and sometimes cross-racial coalitions. Funding for shelters, counseling services, and crisis hotlines came from local, state, and federal government. During the administration of President Jimmy Carter, the Justice Department funded some 1,500 antirape projects; 400 of them were feminist rape crisis centers. Battered women's shelters won backing from states and a few localities; President Carter introduced a bill to Congress that would have funded a national network of shelters, sponsored research, and established a federal agency. But conservatives blocked it, and after 1980 it was a dead issue.[68] The results were striking, if always unsatisfying in the end. Over time, feminists succeeded in revamping police procedures and in rescuing some endangered girls and women.

It was easier to invoke feminism when it meant protecting women than when it meant ensuring they could protect themselves from the adverse consequences of sex. In a time when antifeminism was on the rise, these forms of body politics, which stressed women's vulnerability to male coercion and violence, were more palatable to local governments, donors, and supporters than was the defense of women's sexual freedom and their right to make their own choices about pregnancy and childbearing. A view of sexual traits as inherently male or female, with male "sexuality" innately violent and predatory, crept into corners of body politics and from there into popular understanding. The views drew legitimacy from assumptions that went back to the temperance movement. Male sexuality was at the very least aggressive—as in sexual harassment—and at the worst murderous, as in rape and domestic violence.

Nowhere were the historical sources clearer than in the antipornography movement, that form of body politics whose object—male titillation—was the most ephemeral and dubious. For a time, antipornography activism even garnered sympathy from conservatives, reviving old themes of social and sexual purity and the crusade against male vice. Centered in Los Angeles and New York City, Women Against Pornography, formed in 1979, drew initially favorable press coverage and the support of mainstream feminist venues such as *Ms.* magazine. The rallying point was the conviction that male consumption of pornography was a potent source of misogyny—indeed, the main source—a rationale for mundane sexual exploitation as well as an incentive to pathological violence. Zealots conflated pornography with violent pornography, and violent pornography (as in depictions of sexual sadomasochism) with actual rape, torture, and murder. The uses male hipster culture made of images of misogynistic violence to sell not only pornography but rock and roll provoked one of the first demonstrations, led by Women Against Violence Against Women in Los Angeles, to call for the removal of a billboard advertising the Rolling Stones' new album *Black and Blue*. Floating high above Sunset Boulevard was a supersize woman, scantily clad, bound with ropes and bruised and captioned "I'm 'Black and Blue' from the Rolling Stones—and I love it!"

"Pornography is the theory, rape is the practice," the legal scholar Catharine MacKinnon declared; MacKinnon lent antipornography politics the credibility of her first-rate intellect and sensationalist depictions of the viciousness of male power. Antipornography ideology drew its sensational appeal from a black-and-white moral allegory which equated the most savage masculine cruelty with normal male propensities. The view of men's systematic erotic tyranny at times came close to suggesting that heterosexual intercourse, too, was something that men forced on women, who only pretended to like it. The moralistic politics attracted conservatives: In Indianapolis, antipornography campaigners allied with Republicans on the city council to ban the sale of pornography within city limits (a federal court struck down the ordinance on First Amendment grounds); a similar measure passed in Bellingham, Washington, but failed in Minneapolis and Cambridge, Massachusetts.

As the women's movement splintered into the components of American identity politics—Latina, Asian-American, lesbian, and African-American "feminisms," all counterposing themselves to the white heterosexual mainstream—these groups more or less existed amicably. But the division between antipornography crusaders and their opponents, the "pro-sex" radicals, was bitter and irreconcilable. Each side accused the other of advocating ideas that would destroy feminism. Pro-sex feminists decried the self-righteous morality of the antipornography forces and its animus to free speech; the latter accused their critics of being brainwashed by patriarchal sexuality and ignoring the deadly injuries pornography inflicted on millions of voiceless women. Antipornography zealots denounced First Amendment defenses. "A defense of pornography is a defense of the brute use of money to encourage violence against a class of persons who do not have—and have never had—the civil rights vouchsafed to men as a class," preached Andrea Dworkin, the obsessed melodramatic polemicist of the movement.[69] Women were pure and menaced; men were dirty and dangerous.

Ellen Willis, a sex radical whose clarity about feminist means and ends was unsurpassed, identified the neo-Victorian elements at work in the Women Against Pornography (WAP) chapter in New York. WAP was conducting tours of commercial sex spots in Times Square, then a red-light district, for all the world as if they were evangelical crusaders against brothels in the 1830s. "Self-righteousness has always been a feminine weapon, a permissible way to make men feel bad," Willis wrote. "Ironically, it is socially acceptable for women to display fierce aggression in their crusades against male vice, which serve as an outlet for female anger without threatening male power." Substitute pornography for demon alcohol, she observed, and you have the antipornography movement in a nutshell: a reenactment of nineteenth-century temperance ideology.[70]

On the one hand, body politics could not have flourished without the popular front that supported abortion. On the other, initiatives against rape and domestic violence prospered because they circumvented the abortion movement's most challenging assertions. Women as victims of violent men could be conceived as adamantine moral innocents; pregnant teenagers could not. Bad men, injured women and girls: The story was imprinted in cultural memory, a scenario that was the historic centerpiece of conservative feminism. Rights-bearing female citizens were never as assimilable to traditional scenarios. Thus the defense of rape and incest victims and battered women could draw support from across the political spectrum: It appealed to middle-of-the-road, nonfeminist opinion in part because it was free of any tincture of interest in women's autonomy. These were immensely worthy, important initiatives, but they were born of constrained political circumstances.

In 1976, the abortion issue cropped up for the first time in presidential politics, in the race between Jimmy Carter and incumbent president Gerald Ford. Henry Hyde's amendment to an appropriations bill to ban Medicaid funding for abortion, once Carter was in office, introduced the issue in Congress.[71] As the controversy roiled on, the utility of right-to-life sentiment became unmistakable to the New Right, just getting its legs in national politics. In 1979, Paul Weyrich (who was Catholic) and Howard Phillips (who was Jewish) met with evangelical minister Jerry Falwell and others to form the Moral Majority, a united front to defend "family values." Falwell had never spoken publicly about abortion until the previous year, but now the defense of the unborn and the restoration of traditional family roles became a rallying cry for the crusade against what New Right ideologues denounced as creeping "secular humanism." Gearing up for the 1980 election, New Right operatives enlisted Phyllis Schlafly, who now jumped on the issue with a pamphlet, *The Abortion Connection.*[72]

In 1980, Ronald Reagan defeated Carter in a landslide. While the Democrats did not lose control of Congress until 1994, and liberals continued to hold a majority on the Supreme Court, Reagan's skillful use of social conservatives brought far right domestic concerns into the mainstream. Despite touting conservative obeisance to pro-family policies, the right vehemently opposed federal funding for real family policies, like child care or health care. There was no major legislation that originated with the women's movement until the Clinton administration, when Congress passed the Family and Medical Leave Act (1993) and the Violence Against Women Act (1994).[73]

Yet paradoxically, feminism as sensibility, daily practice, and micropolitics reached into ever-larger areas of American culture. Cultural institutions became the province of left liberals barred from influence in politics. The revolution in the arts and popular culture that began in the 1960s continued unabated, despite conservative attacks on universities and federal funding for the arts and humanities as fronts for the pointy-headed liberal third column. Feminism was a chief target for the anti–"political correctness" vigilantes. Yet in the production of ideas and art, images, symbols, scholarship, and stories, the generation of the 1960s and their heirs excelled. The result was something of a standoff. The liberals got Lincoln Center, the joke went; the conservatives got the Defense Department; the liberals got rock and roll; the right got to bust unions. And feminists got women's studies in colleges and universities, while antifeminists got to destroy sex education in public schools.

Reflections upon feminism ran through spectacular work in these years in dance, theater, fiction, poetry, the visual arts, and intellectual work. Women artists and thinkers, whether or not self-consciously political, explored the imaginative world that feminism opened up: fascination with ties between women, a spirit of skeptical inquiry about motherhood and marriage, the rich secrets of female bodies and erotic desires, men's subtle and overt manipulations of power, and the phenomenal discovery of a Lost Continent of women's interior lives.

True, stressing the momentum fails to take into account the undercurrents, the ways American culture distorted and attacked feminist ideas and the New Women who championed them even as it absorbed them. Hollywood, in particular, rounded on feminism as if by common consent among writers, directors, and producers to put independent women in their place. In films of the 1980s, heroines of unusual ideas and unconventional behavior were bound to end up alone, insane, murdered, or left in the dust by younger, perkier, more pliant rivals who snag the man while the heroines falter and flop (sassy Melanie Griffith in *Working Girl* [1988] stealing the man and the job out from under icy executive Sigourney Weaver). Worse, they could turn psychotic. The most notorious New Woman transformation was that of Glenn Close in *Fatal Attraction* (1987), in which she played a successful, beautiful, rich executive-turned-stalker who invades her married lover's home and boils the pet bunny after he dumps her.[74] Such were the wages of sin for a successful, seductive beauty, with the money to live alone in a gorgeous apartment—weath and autonomy being mortal sins for women.

On balance, though, there is no question that feminism set in motion hopes, preoccupations, obsessions, dreams, and fantasies that streamed through art and intellect in the last two decades of the century. But to lay out these lists of artists, thinkers, and achievements against the comparable roster of accomplishments in politics, policy-making, economics, and diplomacy is to see a problem. A few women worked in the highest echelons of American politics, but except for Madeleine Albright, secretary of state under President Clinton, and First Lady Hillary Rodham Clinton, they operated at a remove from feminism. Worldwide, the same could be said of the handful of female leaders—most notably Margaret Thatcher, Reagan's Conservative partner in Britain. Even New Right women did not make it to the top. Phyllis Schlafly never got a diplomatic or cabinet post, and Republican women failed to keep up with their Democratic peers' slow but steady gain of seats in Congress.

The result was an American women's movement whose cultural wing was populous, assured, and flashy and whose political wing was drab and sparse. American women could imagine themselves as the fount of modern feminism, with their rich body of investigations—aesthetic and scholarly—of women's lives, their utopian proposals, their ever-bubbling artistic creations, and their brilliant analyses of sexism in every corner of the culture. They fanned out through the labor force and populated the professions. Many kinds of liberties survived and flourished. Yet power at the top eluded them.

The weak feminist presence in Washington gave credence to the venerable conviction that politics were the province of men and that nothing short of revolution would change this. "There are many of us who know on a 'gut level' that elections are not 'where it's at,'" proclaimed Mary Morgan, a leader in Dayton, Ohio, voicing a sentiment that had long been commonplace.[75] With women making no major inroads into upper-level government positions until the 1990s, women's politics operated of necessity at the grassroots, and great significance was given to small-scale attempts, whether or not they were consequential.

The social transformations feminism nourished were revolutionary. The sexual revolution rumbled on, with sex outside of wedlock no longer an open secret. Free love went mainstream, helped by the rising numbers of men and women who openly declared themselves gay. Legal contraception and abortion (albeit highly constrained) provided a material basis for the possibility that girls and women could approach the erotic freedom that boys and men had long had. Other long-term trends continued: Growing numbers of married women with small children entered the workforce and increasing numbers raised children alone, without male partners. Even as the AIDS epidemic devastated the gay community, the vicissitudes faced by anguished lovers who lacked legal standing as spouses or family members fueled a drive that would lead to the first successes in securing marriage rights for same-sex couples in the early years of the twenty-first century. A baby boom among lesbian couples created a sense of urgency to legitimate household ties. The impress of gay households on family life, while still the imprint of a minority, moved households even further away from the gendered positions that family government and coverture had long dictated.

Everywhere, among those who thought of themselves as feminists and those who didn't, the insights and clamor of the women's movement shaped expectations of themselves and others. The great change in the lives of girls and women that Alice Munro predicted had come to pass. No longer would girls be told their arms weren't made to throw balls; women thought of themselves as capable of doing just about any man's job, whether or not they applied for it and whether or not they got it. True, the reigning public discourse simply drove many kinds of prejudices underground. But the fact that prejudice and misogyny had to disguise themselves, creep about furtively rather than proudly and arrogantly, was itself a huge change, representing some space for women. Successive waves of young women who dubbed themselves "postfeminist" dashed past the older generation pell-mell, seeing themselves as leaving behind the mothers stumping along with their loads of ancient grievances.

The success of feminism and the success of antifeminism were antipathetic, bitter companions. Posing as reluctant political actors thrust out of the haven of the family by the urgent demands of the times, conservative women cast themselves as the saviors of motherhood and family, taking back the initiative from feckless, ungrateful, irresponsible daughters, whose heads had been turned by sex and wild ideas. While antifeminists did not succeed in some of their grander aims, they succeeded in many of their more modest ones, including radically limiting access to abortion and turning "feminist" into an epithet that few young women, whatever their aspirations, wanted to embrace. What was to be done?

CHAPTER ELEVEN

GLOBAL FEMINISM

The Age of Reagan and Beyond

Ronald reagan's presidency gave the conservative movement an unprecedented power to redirect the nation. With the rightward turn affecting states and municipalities as well, feminist legislative and policy initiatives collapsed. Who truly spoke for the masses of women? Antifeminists now insisted they did, and many believed them.

One response was to retreat to those sanctuaries of art and culture that harbored feminist aims. Another was to reorient political ambitions to women's movements abroad. Stymied at home, American feminists projected themselves onto a global stage. A flourishing international women's movement seemed a venue that could use American energies and ideas. This expansion—both the spread of women's rights ideology and American women's faith that they could lend a hand throughout the world—was one result of institutional structures laid down by four great United Nations World Conferences on Women: meetings in Mexico City in 1975, Copenhagen in 1980, Nairobi in 1985, and Beijing in 1995. The meetings brought together thousands and created international networks of reformers. By 1990, global feminism, heavily sponsored and underwritten by U.S. feminists and foundations, was from the American point of view a triumph in an otherwise vexed and clouded period. Americans, endowed with goodwill and strong convictions about the nature of women's rights and wrongs, played a leading role in bringing this international lobby into being.

The idea of a cosmopolitan body of women whose loyalties to the sex transcended their national identities dated back to the International Woman Suffrage Association in the early twentieth century. That organization, though, was almost exclusively European and American before World War I. When it regrouped in the 1920s, scattered women from outside the West joined and energy rippled through the organization. Although little about the quality of international dealings can be gleaned from the cheerleading reports, it is clear that despite the infusions of heterogeneity, the Europeans and Americans remained firmly in command.[1]

The next time around in the 1980s, Americans were more aware of the pitfalls of Western domination. The changed demographics of the American movement helped, since feminists in international work could be African-American, Hispanic-American, or heir to any number of American immigrant identities—Korean, Mexican, Chinese, South Asian, or Caribbean. Americans strained to distance themselves from the older model of themselves as mothers and older sisters to the world's women. A zealous adherence to cultural relativism took hold, with a concomitant reluctance to judge, assess, or criticize non-Western beliefs, including political ideologies. "Difference" was the watchword— described as cultural, racial, class, and/or ethnic (at this point, seldom did religious differences figure in feminist contemplations of the world situation).[2]

Difference was one way to grapple with the erosion of a universal project in the United States. As the women's movement splintered along lines of race, sexuality, ethnicity, generation, and political priorities, Americans disavowed the unifying paradigms that came from faith in sisterhood. Metaphors of assortment reigned: Feminism was a patch-work quilt, a gumbo, a mosaic. Yet a yearning for universal Woman was secreted inside the ethic of difference. If the proper stance could be struck, if enough differences could be acknowledged, if merit could be found in enough points of view, then surely some sort of sisterhood, however tenuous, would emerge. The international conferences, gathered under the banner of the extravagant likeness of all women, furthered the hope.

Global feminism was a creature of globalization, a shorthand for the acceleration of capital and labor flows and neoliberal economic policies around the world, beginning in the 1980s. Investments, markets, and labor recruitment penetrated remote rural areas in Latin America,

South Asia, and Africa, pulling poor people the world over into volatile markets. The end of the Cold War and the collapse of the Soviet Union in 1989 opened up Eastern Bloc countries and Central Asia to aggressive investment, creating jagged vectors of winners and losers and sending migrants across the world searching for work. Neoliberal economic policies issued by international banking and lending organizations restructured the economies of the Third World—promising rising levels of income for the masses, entrepreneurial opportunity, capital accumulation for local elites, and a steady decline in poverty in return for conditions favorable to foreign investors and stringency in government expenditures, including social services. Travel, immigration, Hollywood movies, brand names, and (once the Internet and cellphones arrived) a communications revolution increased the pace and frequency of interactions among people around the world.[3]

The term "global feminism" was coined in the age of Reagan, appearing in the title of a 1983 workshop in Rotterdam, The Netherlands, on international "sexual slavery."[4] At the moment, sisterhood could not be found at home in the United States with women of the New Right. Nor, more troubling, could it always be found among the postfeminist young who in the 1980s began to publish articles criticizing their feminist predecessors as frumpy, sour has-beens. The perennial daughters of 1960s women's liberation found themselves ignominiously pushed into the role of pleasure-denying mothers as they reached middle age, accused by the self-appointed spokeswomen for a new generation of being censorious about men, overcautious about sexual danger, negative and self-defeating about their prospects in the workplace, and lamentably closed to the joys of domestic life. "They tend to see women as a homogeneous sisterhood with the same political opinions and values, men as misogynistic predators, sexuality as a weakness, and real freedom as problematic," wrote one of the carping daughters, Karen Lehrman, in *The Lipstick Proviso* (1997). One after another, a postfeminist pundit of the moment magnetized media attention with her neofeminine manifesto, extolling the ease with which she and her friends planned to have it all: meteoric success in the work world combined with domestic bliss, men's devotedness, and great sex.[5]

But while relations on the home front were vexed, it was possible to project cherished ideas and goodwill on women farther afield, those whose travails seemingly made them receptive to a message of revolution inherited from the 1960s. Global feminism implicitly required participation from women of the Third World—or "the global South," a new term. A meeting with Americans, Germans, and Dutch didn't quite count as global unless delegates from, say, the Philippines or South Africa or Nicaragua were there. Global feminist optimism bounded around the world, in part sponsored by American universities, foundations, and church groups, who provided major funding for conferences, collaborations, university fellowships, student internships and exchanges, and visiting lecturers. Thus public health workers in Thailand read about their Ugandan and Brazilian colleagues' successes fighting HIV transmission; reports on the horrors of sex trafficking traveled through circles of women from the United States to the Netherlands to Southeast Asia and back again; African lawyers took a year in England or America on a university fellowship reserved for a feminist from abroad; American filmmakers made documentaries about Filipino women's groups. These contacts and the relationships that grew from them occurred within a feminist frame of connecting differences, which at heart was a hope that differences could be overridden.

For three decades, the U.N. conferences provided institutional coherence and durability. Six thousand participants met in Mexico City; the Nairobi conference drew fifteen thousand; and the gargantuan meeting in Beijing capped off the series with some thirty thousand attending. Regional and topical meetings to assess progress punctuated the years between conferences: the 1994 International Conference on Population and Development, in Cairo, for instance. The consequences were sweeping and pervasive. "Feminism is no longer viewed as relevant only to the industrialized nations of the North," asserted Jo Freeman, an astute observer, after the meeting in Beijing. "In all but the most conservative of countries, the feminist message that women are people, not just wives and mothers, is taken seriously." Feminism was not a unitary phenomenon, she hastened to add, but one riddled with differences: "not the same movement in every country" but rather coherent and sophisticated in some places, ragged and rudimentary in others.[6]

The Mexico City conference was staid, with official delegations dominating the proceedings, packed with wives of government officials. In contrast, the gatherings in Nairobi and Beijing were sprawling extravaganzas of nationalities, personalities, and nonofficial along with official groups. Outside the mammoth official sessions, there were discussions, soapbox oratory, socializing, and wandering through a bazaar of thousands of presentations. Delegates spoke of the exhilaration of working with so many women from so many places, the incredible learning, and the newfound understanding of commonalties. "A virtual city of female people," exulted Robin Morgan about Beijing in *Ms.* magazine. She described a happy multicultural hodgepodge. "Turbans, caftans, sarongs, kente cloth, blue jeans. Workshops—on microcredit, caste, women's studies, 'comfort' women, solar stoves, refugees, you name it. Round-the-clock networking. . . . First-timers, euphoric at the sheer numbers, finally feeling part of a vast global movement."[7]

Two streams of women flowed into the meetings. One was an emerging class of experts, government officials, and bureaucrats devoted to pursuing and documenting women's issues. After Mexico City, the U.N. began to require member states to file periodic reports on the status of women. Governments had to show a commitment to women's affairs in health, employment, and education. These efforts varied widely in their success—sometimes they existed only on paper—but the government sector provided jobs and careers for a new group of female professionals. The demographics of international policy making changed, too, beginning with the United Nations, as contingents of women transformed parts of an institution notorious for its sexism, including sexual harassment and frankly discriminatory pay scales. The Decade of Women conferences bound U.N. agencies to furthering their goals, and programs that turned on women's rights filtered through any number of bureaucracies in the vast, sprawling institution: the U.N. Economic and Social Council (ECOSOC), the Development Fund for Women (UNIFEM), and the World Health Organization (WHO), for example. In 1977, two years after the Mexico City conference, the World Bank created an administrative section for development aid for women.[8]

There were many consequences, but one simple one was that for the first time, the world's women were carefully counted. Comparative international statistics had always subsumed them under husbands' or fathers' households. But after 1975, international agencies began to count many things about women's lives, including maternal mortality, life expectancy, fertility, years of education, agricultural productivity, literacy, employment, and marital status. It was these statistics, in fact, that allowed the economist Amartya Sen to uncover the astonishing fact that more than one hundred million women had gone missing. "These numbers tell us, quietly, a terrible story of inequality and neglect leading to the excess mortality of women," Sen concluded in 1990.[9] Girls and women disappeared because of malnutrition, HIV/AIDS, childbed mortality, female infanticide, and, where sonograms were available, sex-selective abortion. It was a story that was not previously known.

The other stream that flowed into the international conferences came from proliferating women's nongovernmental organizations (NGOs): groups that worked for specific causes (seed cooperatives for women farmers, job training for ex-sex workers) or responded to dire situations (resettlement of refugees, medical treatment for rape victims of war). Over the last quarter of the twentieth century, NGOs gained in importance. In some places, they spurred civic activity where dictatorships and single-party rule had closed down dissent and social activism. In the many countries ruled by weak states or harsh regimes indifferent to the populace, they supplemented or substituted for government social functions by providing medical care, housing, schools, and road building.

International agencies, looking to avoid the pitfalls of imposing their own agendas on clients or dealing with corrupt states, found NGOs useful in mediating between local needs and funding. In 1993, the World Bank channeled half its funds through NGOs and in 1995, the year of the Beijing conference, more than a third of the bank's funds went to gender concerns. Better known NGOs were magnets for international interest and contributions from individuals, states, development agencies, and foundations. The effects were visible in the makeup of the international conferences. At the Mexico City conference, delegates generally came from the official women's wings of ruling parties. But at Beijing, NGO women held their own separate conference and played a major role in the general sessions.[10]

Feminist impact on poor countries came mainly through NGOs. Women the world over had little power or status in governments and party systems—this was as true in the United States as it was true, say, in Tanzania, Peru, and Thailand—but they proved to be adept organizers of NGOs. "In an unequal world, civil society participation often offers the best, sometimes the only, means by which women can make their voice heard," judged a British enthusiast.[11] When they worked well, NGOs gave women a bit of social power by pooling their scarce resources into cooperatives, encouraging group solidarities in the face of obstructions (for example, male relatives' reprisals for individuals' assertions of independence), and helping them make demands on obdurate state institutions. A good deal of the success came from the single-sex structure; participants spoke of working together, not having to defer to men, and gaining respect and power as a group that would have been otherwise inconceivable. "Just seeing that the national government officials came to see not the men of the village, but the women—made women seem like powerful people who can do things," remarked Martha Nussbaum of a visit she made to a women's cooperative in India.[12]

Governments that in 1970 paid little attention to women by the 1990s had incorporated mazes of women's departments, funds, bureaus, and offices, with official and quasi official functions overlapping with NGOs. There was an explosion of organizing outside women's traditional sectors of charities, religious associations, and auxiliaries of ruling parties. The women's movement in South Asia was among the world's most robust, with roots going back to the nineteenth century, but the economist Bina Agarwal's description of its interlaced groupings captures the dense heterogeneity that existed more sparsely elsewhere:

> autonomous women's groups that were formed in the 1980s in larger cities, some (especially in India and Bangladesh) also with rural links; women's fronts of political parties, women's committees in mass-based mixed-sex organizations (including working-class and poor peasant organizations); groups implementing various types of projects for women (income-generating, educational, health, etc.) . . . women's journalistic and publishing ventures, academic women's associations; and the thousands of individual women struggling for gender equality in diverse ways in diverse areas.[13]

Agarwal found much to applaud in the intricate weave of NGOs and feminist-inspired development projects in her study of women's land rights in South Asia. NGOs were able to give women farmers credit when traditional lenders bypassed them, pool resources to purchase seeds and fertilizers, and encourage group solidarities in the face of difficulties and obstructions. NGOs were also more flexible than programmatic, top-down development projects in encouraging women to press for goals beyond the economic—for health and education, for example, and freedom from violent attacks from landlords and male relatives. Agarwal attributed a good deal of the success to the fact that NGOs were participatory and that paid staff and managers were female. Another analyst of women's movements in India lends support to the judgment: While international forces usually provided the funding and urban middle-class women sometimes dominated women's organizations, "it has often been the case that some of the most radical and important issues have been brought forward by the movements of poor women."[14]

India, however, is a stable democracy with a women's movement that is deeply rooted in political culture. Its NGOs were typically strong and self-directed, with considerable abilities to use international funding and still chart their own course. Ifi Amadiume's description of the Nigerian women's movement gives a different picture of contending groups within a multilayered women's movement in a notoriously corrupt and violent state, striated with divisions between rich women and impoverished ones; women allied with elites and elite women allied with labor and socialist movements; women who didn't want to rock the boat and women who believed that making waves was the only way to move forward. In Nigeria, the lion's share of government largesse in the 1990s went to the wives of two successive dictators, who established women's programs that funneled funds and patronage into the ruling circle and its clients. Maryam Abacha, wife of the infamous Sani Abacha, de facto president from 1993 to 1998, effectively controlled the Nigerian delegation to the Beijing conference and used her position as head of a foreign donor-funded immunization program to extend her influence and extortion capabilities further into government ministries.[15]

Thus the field of activity was made up of starkly varied political contexts. It ranged from countries with decent institutions of civil society where NGOs actually wielded power, to those where NGOs masked the near absence of women's rights in any meaningful sense, to failed states where NGOs by default supplied basic human services and substituted for civil society. Western feminists' enthusiasm for NGOs, however, overrode these distinctions. In reality, to assess the integrity or importance of any particular venture required sophistication and knowledge about the politics, divisions, and needs of particular countries. The view from global feminism, however, picked out continents and regions, not nations; "Africa" blurred together, as did "Southeast Asia." Certain places stood out: Nicaragua (because of the war) and South Africa, for example—but mostly it was a blur.

The NGO-ization of international politics unloosed a thrilling feminist populism, with the worldwide web of NGOs imagined as a sort of Herland, the female utopia Charlotte Perkins Gilman described in her 1915 novel, a society where men were seldom seen. Enthusiasts hailed participants as something like the Amazons of a new world order. Yet the idea that NGOs could compensate for or win power, especially from despotic and corrupt regimes, had severe limitations. Emma Rothschild has pointed out that the dependence on NGOs, which are nonaccountable institutions and not democratic ones, can have the effect of excusing, in the eyes of powerful Western nations, the lack of strong state institutions that are citizens' only lasting chance for political and economic security.[16] The same, of course, is true for women.

Still, in the last two decades of the century, as barriers to democracy, social well-being, and women's rights were thrown up everywhere, NGOs were in many places the only footholds for feminist activity. Even Amadiume, as acerbic as she is about the Nigerian movement, notes that women's organizations supported by international church groups made admirable strides in conducting business on democratic principles.[17] Despite their considerable limitations and the superficial international sentiment that backed them, NGOs' alliances, supports, and funding pushed approval for feminism's projects deeper into conceptions of the common good. Operating with some reference to international norms, goals, and laws, NGOs were experiments in universalism, drawing on a cosmopolitan repertoire of feminist ideas to give direction and coherence to their work: "on the eve of the 21st century, the eruption of the voice of women."[18] The voice was faint or strong depending on whether the speakers could command a local audience, local personnel, and local alliances, as did the South Asian cooperatives. On the one hand, global feminist involvements were seldom efficacious if Western participants did not understand local contexts: Vociferous good intentions and certainties could swamp women's needs in Western fantasies of helpfulness. On the other, global feminism provided resources for women to act for themselves when the odds were stacked against them.

Intellectually, global feminism unleashed in the enclaves of international development work and the United Nations a spirit of exploration. Here, too, a vast unknown continent of women attracted the curious and intellectually intrepid. Recalling the excitement of the first feminist breakthroughs in universities in the 1970s, discoveries spread through policy circles as researchers focused for the first time on women as economic and social actors rather than as victims or ciphers. Thick studies and surveys came out of ECOSOC, UNIFEM, and the World Bank. It was women's studies in the policy world, loosely allied with feminist academic work in economics, political science, law, medicine, sociology, public health, and anthropology. Just as historians discovered that half the population did not appear in the reigning scholarship, and literary scholars realized that virtually no women novelists or poets were taught in literature courses, researchers in policy and development studies exposed huge blank areas in international programs that treated half the world's population as if they hardly existed.

They dug up mines of data that created a quite different profile of the object of study. In development economics, the breakthrough book was *Woman's Role in Economic Development* (1970), by the distinguished Danish economist Ester Boserup. Boserup showed that far from being household dependents, women did more than 70 percent of the world's agricultural labor and that in many parts of the world, including the whole of sub-Saharan Africa, they were the primary farmers. The book uncovered a hidden world of women—intricate trade-offs, negotiations, and obligations of labor and love threaded through kin and household groups. Boserup identified huge patterns of work and family that held across continents, and at the same time delved sympathetically into the intimate details of domestic economies: how hardworking Yoruba women in Nigeria, for instance, encouraged husbands to take second wives so they could get help with tiresome jobs.[19] Portraying women as diligent, calculating, and intelligent, balancing their many obligations with forethought, Boserup discredited the common view of development experts that they were inert traditionalists mired in unproductive household work, impediments to modernization.

The new object of aid came into view at a moment when modernization strategies had fizzled and the field opened to "pro-poor" approaches. Women, now highlighted as crucial household members, were treated as good risks for social investment. After the Mexico City conference, many agencies installed Women in Development programs that concentrated on female labor power. The programs ran into resistance from male colleagues. The derisive charge was that women-centered initiatives were trying to take Western feminism to African huts. At international conferences, though, the changed view triumphed: The 1980s image of a multitasking producer with multiple responsibilities replaced Mexico City's passive, homebound, uneducated housewife with too many children, needy of the world's largesse. The new wisdom was that busy, tireless, responsible women the world over were worthy citizens who held the future of the world in their hands. Foreign-aid programs began to treat them as central—as farmers in Africa and Asia, as breadwinners and mainstays of their households everywhere, and as incipient entrepreneurs in their roles as market women and petty producers.[20]

In a nutshell, studies on women as workers found that they represented half of the world's adult population and one third of the official labor force; they performed nearly two thirds of all working hours; yet they received only one tenth of the world's income and owned less than 1 percent of property. In no country were they treated as well as men: Men went to school more, were far more likely to be literate, were paid more, better nourished, subjected to less violence, and lived longer. Women's sexuality was exponentially more likely than men's to have injurious consequences: in pregnancies (with high childbirth mortality in poor countries) and children to care for, in social ostracism for non-marital sex, and (in worst-case scenarios) in retributive violence and death (as in honor killings of sexually active or raped daughters). In sum, they did so much, yet they benefited so little. "All too often women are not treated as ends in their own right, persons with a dignity that deserves respect from law and institutions," Martha Nussbaum reflected gravely in 1998. "Women in much of the world lose out by being women." Judgments like this, based in the grim facts of the world situation, deepened the sense of the liabilities of being the second sex.[21]

Over time, evidence accumulated for another revelation: Income that went directly to women, which they continued to control, raised the standard of living of the entire household, including children's education. The insight had a history. During World War I, the British government paid soldiers' allowances for their dependents directly to the wives of men at the front. In working-class neighborhoods, British social workers (many of them female) observed that this income notably improved the care of children and raised the entire family's standard of living. But over the years, the record the world over showed that the same was not true for men. A women's microfinance bank in India observed that "if a woman earns 100 rupees, 90 rupees goes into mouths and medicine and schoolbooks for children; with a man only 40 rupees comes back." Policy makers everywhere rediscovered this simple social fact. In Brazil, for instance, children who lived with employed mothers had a twenty times greater chance of surviving childhood than those who lived with an employed father and an economically dependent mother.[22]

In their newly acquired role in development thought as providers, poor women were critical to theories of neoliberal "shock therapy" administered to debt-ridden poor nations. The World Bank and International Monetary Fund (IMF) imposed structural adjustment programs on poor nations, tying loans to requirements that aimed to jolt nations into economic growth by imposing strict debt repayment provisions, lowering trade barriers, and opening them to foreign investment. Experts agreed there would be short-term hardship, since giving priority to debt repayment necessitated slashing social welfare programs. In what planners called "crossing the desert," women's work caring for others in the face of plummeting incomes and loss of social services was supposed to cushion the blows. Their Herculean capacities for work and their patience for unpaid, low-status work—that is, child care, tending the old and the sick, and domestic labor—figured in these schemes as a way to reconcile populations to poverty while at the same time urging them forward into education, entrepreneurship, and labor migration. When the fund for school uniforms was slashed, theorists assumed, women would scrounge and save and cut back on expenditures to find secondhand uniforms or make them. When the program to bring a water line into the village crumbled, well, women and girls could be counted on to make the trek to the spring. When food was scarce, mothers would compensate by spreading their share around (a phenomenon that, taken to the extreme, is recognized by nutritionists as maternal "autostarvation").[23]

In the 1990s, attention shifted to women's abilities to generate cash income. One wing of policy makers believed that the key to poverty reduction lay in maximizing the cash value of women's labor. They warned against march-across-the-desert programs that stressed women's unpaid labor at the expense of earning income. From this emphasis on women's access to markets came the vogue for microfinance, which began in the 1990s, funding banks that would give minute loans to impoverished borrowers to support cash-producing ventures—small businesses, workshops, farms—on the strength of guarantees given by NGOs and women's cooperatives. "Women don't need charity, they need access," firmly stated Nancy Barry, a graduate of Harvard Business School and former World Bank executive who joined the newly founded Women's World Bank in 1990. It was an attractive proposition to Americans, raised to believe that hard work counted and individuals could pull themselves up by their bootstraps. Global feminism amplified the significance: Microfinance was not only going to enhance the well-being of households, but provide a floor for democracy and development. "There can be no democracy or development without women," maintained an executive from a microfinance fund in 1993. "We're showing how strengthening the condition of women is a strategic investment."[24]

At its best, microfinance brought development policies down to tangible needs, putting money in the hands of local women who had concrete goals and giving them flexibility in using it, small as the amounts were. By the mid-1990s, the disastrous results of top-down structural adjustment policies were becoming clear. A paper from the Ministry of Foreign Affairs in the Netherlands, a leader in development, bluntly declared in 1991, "Economic and political development processes have in general had no beneficial effect on the position of women." Widespread acknowledgment of neoliberalism's failures to reduce poverty resulted in strategies designed from the vantage point of poor women, rather than the agencies that sought to exploit or harness their labor. Feminist advocates insisted that poor women step forward in these poverty reduction schemes. When asked what they needed, women in Africa or Asia were likely to put forward realistic, sensible schemes— a village water tap, sewing machines, schools for girls, sturdy market stalls.[25]

But women's emergence as stars of development concealed very real hazards. In many ways, it was their strengths as community members and household mainstays that were their undoing. Their sociability, their habits of altruism, their self-abnegation in the face of children's needs: All these skills were hard-won and immensely admirable. But experts and reformers saw them as resources not because women themselves were worthy objects of aid but because they could be used in so many different ways. Women in developing countries became a target group who planners thought could make up for huge deficiencies in states' abilities to deliver basic resources. Female farmers, for instance, hailed as the "missing link" in development policies, were to serve many ends: "The cure for Africa's food crisis, child welfare, environmental degradation and failures of structural adjustment policies are all sought in women," two economists drily remarked.[26] Unsupported by legal changes in land rights, inheritance, and ownership, and lacking educational opportunities (scarce in any case, and typically reserved for sons), women remained stranded within drastically asymmetrical divisions of labor and societies that severely undervalued their humanity. No microfinance loan, no matter how successful, was going to address that problem. Americans, though, eager for the quick fix, leapt on incremental changes as auguring something much greater. The idea that investing in women was strategic was by 1993 unassailable.

In truth, feminist principles of women's well-being were not identical with notions of investment. Could women be an investment simply in themselves? For one, that would mean an international commitment to female education, and education was a longer-term institutional project that necessarily depended on governments and political will more than on NGOs and donors. Regardless of the fact that the correlation between women's education and lowering birthrates had been known and repeatedly demonstrated since 1926, planners and population experts veered away from the insight that population planning required respect for women's individual integrity and needs.[27] Educating women seemed somehow less practical than deploying their enormous capacities for hard work and self-sacrifice. Thus the celebration of women's savvy and hard work stopped short of supporting efforts to honor their dignity as individuals and nourish their minds.

Celebrants of global feminism hoped that women were becoming the honest brokers of international politics and diplomacy, advisers and advocates who stood apart from national rivalries and interests. "I go to Nairobi committed to the necessity of global feminism and excited by the promise of learning more from other women because I believe that the greatest hope for life in the next century lies in the number of women's voices that are being raised where once there was silence," avowed Charlotte Bunch, a leader in international work in the United States. "Global feminism is not a luxury activity for the elite but a necessity for effective action." The world conferences represented for many "the coming of age of the international women's movement, with women playing key roles in the inter-governmental negotiations as delegates, advisors, and advocates."[28]

At their most callow, pronouncements about the potency of global feminism unknowingly echoed the views of another era that maternal character could solve the world's problems. After World War I, the International Woman's Suffrage Alliance put forth women as the vanguard of a new order of international governance. Similarly, in the 1980s and '90s, enthusiasts believed that global feminism created among women "lateral identifications with each other across national boundaries for the sake of human survival." "It has to do with the grounding in the family," a veteran of Beijing explained, a grounding that distinguished women from men. "It has nothing to do with whether we are better or worse. It has everything to do with the fact that we are different."[29]

The proposition that "sisterhood is global," title of a popular 1984 compendium by veteran feminist Robin Morgan (published fourteen years after her landmark *Sisterhood Is Powerful*), appealed to converts to the international project. "SISTERHOOD IS POWERFUL! INTER-NATIONAL SISTERHOOD IS MORE POWERFUL!" exhorted Diane Russell the next year, calling the troops to battle.[30] In the United States, global sisterhood became a rallying point for what was, by the time of the Beijing conference, a venture of moderate churchwomen, Marxists committed to anti-imperialist politics, and hard-line radical feminists. To socially concerned Protestants, global feminism was a matter of helping the less fortunate around the world; it called forth modern versions of the nineteenth-century impulse of Christian womanly protection. To feminists on the left, it promised the bygone satisfactions of socialist and anti-imperialist solidarity, all the more precious after 1989 when Communism crumbled and Third World revolutions ran aground. To radical feminists, the desperate straits of so many women worldwide seemed to vindicate their dire judgments of female oppression and men's wrongdoing.

Global feminism in the American lexicon was a general approach, focusing on no one place but on any and all places outside the West. Gone were the pragmatic solidarity groups with women in beleaguered socialist countries that dotted American left-wing feminism in the 1970s: Action for Women in Chile, for example, a New York–based feminist group that gave financial support to refugees fleeing Pinochet's Chile and publicized the plight of prisoners and the disappeared.[31] Solidarity work, rooted in Marxist internationalism, depended on thick knowledge of local conditions: prisoners' situations, distinctions among political parties, the details of government repression. The new global feminism, unmoored from any particular place, slid around on a glaze of thin knowledge. In the United States, it called up habits of analogizing that American women had used since the antebellum years, when women first imagined themselves sisters to enslaved women. She—so different from me in most respects—is really like me in fundamental ways, because we are both women and we both contend with the power of men. "Am I not a woman and a sister?" The abolitionist slogan could be modernized to apply to the secretary in an office in Denver, propositioned by her boss, or to a village girl in a garment factory in Manila, propositioned by her boss.

Global feminism, heavily dependent on Western countries for funding and publicity and especially tied in with America, also met with considerable resistance and outright antagonism in the many places where women's rights thinking was reviled as colonial ideology. Feminists in Asia, Latin America, and Africa had difficulty countering the charge that patriarchalism was rooted in indigenous custom and tradition. The corollary of this wave of antifeminism was that male dominance was a proud feature of culture and religious piety. Feminist assertions were said to introduce Western individualism, anticommunalism, and selfishness that undermined the will and soul of the postcolonial nation.

Human rights politics aided local feminists in changing the terms of argument by strengthening feminism's universalist claims beyond the West. It seems counterintuitive that women had never fully been enveloped in human rights declarations: Were they not human? But then, they had never been included in development discussions, either. The foundation of the human rights movement, the Universal Declaration of Human Rights (UNDHR, 1948), did not specifically address the human rights of women but rather folded them into generic Man—although Latin American women were at least successful in getting women as a group recognized in the United Nations' founding documents. The United Nations fully acknowledged the specific entitlements of women as a vulnerable population only in 1979, when, in the wake of the Mexico City world conference, the General Assembly adopted the Convention on the Elimination of All Forms of Discrimination Against Women (CEDAW).[32] CEDAW was a giant ERA, a world bill of rights for women. The treaty provisions summed up most of the classic goals of the women's movement since Mary Wollstonecraft—the rights to education, equal pay, ownership of property, divorce, child custody, the end of legal disabilities in marriage—as well as new ones that were the product of modernity, such as access to family planning and equal participation in government. CEDAW declared, for instance, that a woman should not have to give up her nationality if she migrated with her husband or married a man from another nation, a common practice that could render a woman a stateless refugee should the husband die or desert her.[33]

CEDAW's enforcement mechanisms were nonexistent and the ratification process was drawn out, spotty, and halting. By 2010, 185 countries have signed (over 90 percent of U.N. members), although nearly one third noted reservations, meaning they retained the right to ignore requirements that didn't suit them. Reading through the reservations is a world tour of patriarchy, with the lion's share devoted to those sections of the treaty pertaining to men's governance of women and children. A Turkish feminist nailed the problem: "The patriarchal system is at its most intractable in its resistance to reforming the institutions of marriage and the family."[34] Many of the reservations were about those measures pertaining to marriage and family law. For instance, provisions that attracted reservations were those that accorded women the same rights as men to determine the nationality of their children and to choose their own domicile. Islamic states, especially but not exclusively, objected to provisions that interfered with sharia, or religious law. The United Arab Emirates (UAE) lodged so many reservations that Sweden registered a reservation about those reservations, complaining that they were so numerous that they effectively nullified the UAE's status as signatory.

President Carter signed CEDAW in 1980 but the Senate never ratified it; once Reagan took over, conservatives blocked CEDAW every time it was introduced. Taking their cues from the charges that the Stop ERA campaign invented, American opponents called CEDAW an insult to women with traditional values, who wanted to be protected and cared for by their husbands in their homes, not have their rights meddled with by international treaties. As of this writing, the United States still has not ratified the agreement, a position that puts America in the company of Iran, Sudan, Somalia, and several small Islamic states and Pacific islands.[35]

The long section of reservations signaled CEDAW's limitations. Those states whose laws CEDAW contravened put the world on notice they had no intention to abide by it. Nonetheless, the convention announced the presence of women as a class in international law, and it had positive, although uneven, effects. In places where governments and left-wing and nationalist parties derided women's rights as bourgeois and Western, CEDAW's international stature gave feminist dissidents some legitimacy in phrasing their demands as basic requirements of modern nations. Women's advocates could seize on local abuses otherwise untouchable in order to publicize them as abrogations of an international agreement. In Ghana, Nigeria, and Sierra Leone, for instance, CEDAW gave women a platform from which to demand the reform of inadequate laws against domestic violence. In Kenya, tribal governance coexisted with the modern state and posed a major constraint on women: Tribal laws limiting women's inheritance, for example, overrode civil law. CEDAW's provisions gave women and their supporters some power to pressure states to bring their legal codes into line. In Argentina, after the junta collapsed in 1983, a women's movement emerged and used CEDAW to revamp longstanding laws: New measures decriminalized birth control and permitted remarriage after divorce. And CEDAW's existence, although hardly common knowledge, was enough to alert a few that patriarchal systems that seemed otherwise unbreachable were under pressure, even if the source of pressure was remote.[36]

The treaty was a palimpsest of earlier moments, of basic demands that had been achieved in some places, but achieved for too few; or achieved and undone; or never achieved at all. Provisions were nonenforceable, and implementation depended on countries' self-reporting. CEDAW was a doubled image: of feminism's failures in the modern era and its abiding promise that justice to women was necessary for a better world. On the one hand, there was an international agreement whereby parties assented to bring their laws into conformity with a list of basic rights. On the other, the United States—a major repository of modern feminism—refused to ratify: That could be taken as an indication that nothing was ever won, that the same ground had to be staked out and fought for again and again. Little about the position of women was entirely settled, in part because, as Catharine MacKinnon pointed out, CEDAW does not challenge the premises of the system it aims to change. Nowhere does the agreement state that male supremacy is unjustifiable. "Sexism remains clothed, sexual politics ungrounded," she concluded. The further feminism reached—the more it promised—the more it became clear that the very fundamentals were still not secure.[37]

After 1980, human rights organizations multiplied, adding to their staffs, expanding the scope of their investigations, and branching out in their understanding of who it was they were defending. Despots, war, authoritarian regimes, whipped-up ethnic hatred, genocide, and mass murder fueled the cause: Cambodia, Afghanistan, Chechnya, El Salvador, Guatemala, Congo, Iran, Rwanda, Saudi Arabia, the Soviet Union, Yugoslavia, South Africa, Uganda, Iran, Iraq, North Korea, China, Cuba, Nigeria, and many more countries were the scenes of massive cruelty and political repression. In the 1980s, American foundations poured millions of dollars into the movement. Global feminism was a major beneficiary.[38]

The victims who came to light included both sexes, but initially men were much more prominent in the concerns of human rights groups such as Amnesty International, because these organizations championed victims of state-sponsored repression in the public sphere: Journalists, opposition leaders, and prominent dissenters were mostly male. It was not a question of ignoring women, but rather a selectivity dictated by the nature of the enterprise. As stories and testimonials piled up from around the world, though, it became evident that civil and political definitions of human rights did not begin to cover much of the systematic brutality being reported.

In 1993, feminists at the World Conference on Human Rights in Vienna, held to amend and extend the cornerstone UNDHR, succeeded in expanding the Vienna Declaration and Programme of Action to affirm "the human rights of women and of the girl-child." The Vienna Declaration's commitments to women went beyond CEDAW: It held not only states but private individuals accountable for human rights violations. Catherine MacKinnon, who shifted the focus of her theoretical work and activism from a dissolving antipornography movement into human rights work, elucidated the problem: Violence against women was conscious and systematic, yet it had no salience in international law when the perpetrators were men in civil society and not state actors—officials, soldiers, or police.[39] The new human rights provisions challenged the shibboleths of family integrity and tradition, holding that domination and supra-exploitation of women in the family and ordinary economic and social life were violations of their human rights: physically abusing women and girls, trafficking them for the purposes of prostitution or coerced labor, sexually harassing them, using them for purposes of pornography and forcibly impregnating them as a weapon of war (a practice that Serbian forces were using at the time in the Bosnian War).[40]

The Vienna Declaration was not an international convention like CEDAW; it had no binding power. Regardless, after 1993, public and professional interest in women's human rights quickened. Human Rights Watch compiled a massive 1995 *Global Report on Women's Human Rights*, which laid out a dreadful array of violations: girls forced to undergo virginity exams (Turkey), rape used as a weapon of war (Bosnia, Somalia, Kashmir, Peru), sexual trafficking (Nepal, Bangladesh, Burma), states with no laws against domestic abuse or informally condoning it (Russia, South Africa), and wife murder (Brazil).

In the next ten years, human rights publicity turned the sentence by a sharia court in Nigeria of a woman to be executed by stoning into an international cause célèbre and brought world attention to the plight of Korean women enslaved as sex workers by the Japanese military during World War II—the so-called comfort women. Both of these became matters for serious diplomatic negotiations.[41] American papers published articles on dowry deaths in India, clitoridectomy in Somalia, forced sterilization in China, and military rapes in Peru and Burma as violations of human rights, worthy of attention and redress.

Victims who caught the attention of local advocacy groups might find legal help and kick up public support; the fortunate attracted the interest of sympathetic journalists who brought the case to the notice of newspaper readers—fortunate being an ironic status, because it was the severity of the woman's fate that made her newsworthy. Spirited resistance to horrors that were unfamiliar and exotic in the West made the news, such as the fight put up by Miriam Willingal, who defied tribal law in the highlands of Papua New Guinea in 1997. Willingal was part of a complex compensation package offered to the clan of a murdered leader by the clan of the murderer: Willingal was offered in marriage, along with money and livestock. Willingal, who had ambitions—she wanted to finish high school and work as a typist—refused to play her part. She found a sympathetic woman lawyer in a nearby town who pushed her case up through the regular judicial system, making it a test of highland people's rights to force women into bride payments. Amnesty International and then *The New York Times* picked up the story, and the Papua New Guinea high court eventually upheld her constitutional right to choose her own husband and ordered tribes to abandon the practice.[42]

Attacking human rights abuses perpetrated by families was often the most radical and dangerous work feminists did, undertaken in the face of hostile officials, indifferent police, judges, and menacing guardians of supposed tradition—often male elites and politicians with a stake in preserving power over wives and daughters. Most victims did not have access to Western sympathizers. It was local feminists—individuals and organizations—who brought the scandals and cases to light, gave sanctuary to victims, provided support and legal help, and put in the work to fight laws and police practices. The feminist movement in India, for example, was notable for tackling cruelty and murder and unmasking officials who rationalized criminal behavior. The political dynamics came from a productive dialectic between urban, middle-class and rural women. Over several decades, feminists made public the suppressed scandal of dowry deaths, of systemic, quasi-sanctioned rape—including habitual rape by police and landlords—and of sex-selective abortions, which by 2000 were badly skewing the sex ratios of India and China (with a huge portion of the world's population between them), as well as of Singapore, Taiwan, and South Korea.[43]

High-profile cases were tried in international courts. A turning point came after the Bosnian war, with the first international prosecutions of sexual slavery and rape as crimes against humanity. The 1949 Geneva Convention designated rape a crime of war, but the indictments at Nuremberg did not include any for rape and the Tokyo trials gave rape only cursory attention.[44] What happened in Bosnia was related to customary practices but intensified. The Serbian command encouraged soldiers to commit mass rape—as many as twenty thousand women may have been assaulted—as one way to terrorize civilians, force them into flight, and impregnate Bosnian Muslim women. Serbian soldiers took women captive, imprisoned them in camps used to torture and execute men, and raped them over periods ranging from days to months.[45] Determined lawyers and victims brought charges in the International Tribunal for Crimes in the Former Yugoslavia (ITCFY) in The Hague.[46]

A collaboration between NGOs in Bosnia and feminists based in New York and London helped victims make the atrocities known, drawing outraged attention to practices that had long been judged regrettable, horrible, but unavoidable. The ICTFY in The Hague issued some forty-six indictments. Although in the end only four men were convicted and sentenced to prison, the vital contact among Bosnian women, American and European feminists, and jurists trained in international law was a turning point in human rights litigation and the international understanding of rape.[47]

Revelations about Bosnia meant that the mass rapes of the Rwandan genocide would be seen in a very different light, as instrumental, not incidental. In 1995, the new government, staggering out of the mass murder, incredibly and heroically pulled together a report to the Beijing conference that counted the number of rape victims at fifteen thousand in the first ten days of the killing (an estimate we now know was far too low) and went into some detail about the Hutu militias' use of rape as a weapon. The influence of women's human rights ideas can be seen in Rwanda's 2000 decision to put rape and sexual slavery in the category of the most serious crimes—along with multiple murders and organizing the genocide—to be tried in the country's massive effort to bring justice. The International Criminal Tribunal for Rwanda (ICTR) in Arusha, Tanzania, also issued multiple indictments for rape as a crime against humanity, including one of a woman, Pauline Nyiramasuhuko. Nyiramasuhuko was minister for women's affairs under the Habyarimana government. Eager to make a name for herself, she helped organize the genocide in and around the university town of Butare, allegedly calling the militias to rape Tutsi women before they killed them and, in one episode, urging soldiers to rape as a prelude to burning the victims alive.[48]

These trials were points when the women's lobby mobilized the power of international law and diplomacy, trials that made something visible that had long been invisible or occluded. But rape as a weapon of war was a dramatic instance of brutality, a rallying point around which any sane person would gather. More difficult to challenge were practices embedded in laws and family relations, especially men's control over women's sexuality. The defense of these forms of patriarchal power summoned up custom and culture. Practices such as child marriage, the argument went, were regrettable, but inseparable from honorable traditions, religious beliefs, and national or ethnic folkways. To oppose them was to introduce alien Western values. Human rights language pushed past this impasse by gesturing instead toward international norms.

Sometimes issues that would have otherwise gone unmentioned, staying below the radar of international relations, became points of negotiation. Feminists in Turkey, for instance, were able to use the 1995 Human Rights Watch report about virginity exams (forced on girls and unmarried women, including schoolgirls, security guards, and government employees) to create an outcry inside and outside the country as Turkey was gearing up to renew its application for admission to the European Union. The bad publicity led the government to ban the practice in 2002. Brazilian feminists used human rights language to strip away the veneer of custom and machismo that accrued around their society's extensive pattern of male domestic abuse; at one point in the 1980s in São Paulo, they had enough power on the city council to establish a police precinct staffed by female officers specially trained to deal with sexual violence.[49]

Generally, though, the overriding problem was that feminists' reach was so limited in states where the worst violations occurred. In the Democratic Republic of Congo (formerly Zaire), for instance, where 5.5 million people died in the war and its aftermath between 1998 and 2008, the violence continues, and today rape and sexual torture are legion. In the conservative Muslim world, aggression against women and women's movements mounted after the 1979 Iranian revolution; there, human rights pressure, CEDAW, and Western public opinion were of little use to beleaguered women imprisoned, tortured, and forced underground or into exile. Even in Afghanistan during the U.S.-led occupation in 2004, with Kabul awash in donor money and peppered with NGOs, Ann Jones, an American who worked there for several years, noted impatiently that the monthly meeting about violence against women set up by UNIFEM moved down a predictable path, everyone beginning by agreeing that atrocities were widespread and proceeding to a consensus that the issue should not be raised publicly lest it cut into conservative support for the government.[50]

The ubiquity of violence against women was American feminists' signal contribution to international discussions. A popular—indeed a prevalent—subject of concern in the United States in the 1980s, violence against women became over the last two decades of the century a copious designation, which included rape, domestic violence, murder, forced marriage, sexual trafficking, sexual harassment, homophobia, and clitoridectomy. It was here that American feminists spied the most atrocious abrogations of women's human rights and the most urgent international issues. And who could not agree that violence against women must end? The subject did not materialize in deliberations at the Mexico City conference in 1976, but it emerged the next year in an International Tribunal on Crimes Against Women held in Brussels, funded by American donors. At the Nairobi conference in 1985, the topic generated scores of workshops and thousands of pamphlets. At the Beijing conference, sexual violence "transcended race, class and cultures, and united women worldwide in a common cause," reported a pleased participant: "There were so many different workshops on violence . . . that one could not have attended them all in nine days."[51]

It was an approach to women's wrongs indebted to radical feminism's insistence on the profound estrangement of women from men. In the United States, the modus operandi of the personal as political had allowed feminism to kick open the door of the family jurisdiction to investigate private activity that was sometimes criminal activity, as in domestic abuse, incest, and marital rape. Nowhere else in the world was that investigation so thorough as in American circles in the late 1960s and early '70s; nowhere else did it cut so deep into the tissue of human relations usually seen as formed from love. Yet by the same token, the American project of ending violence against women was, by 1980, effectively cut off from struggles for economic and social improvements in women's lives; indeed the most vociferous wing had veered into the fight to abolish pornography. The attraction to hyperbolic renditions of male abuse, decontextualized, meant that American-driven analyses marched across continents, indifferent to differences between political regimes, social classes, and economic systems, precisely those distinctions that provide clues about the exact nature of the violence women face and, even more important, where they can find remedies.

The designation of violence spread outward, an oil slick of male evil. "Crimes against women," which at the 1976 Brussels conference comprised Third World poverty, domestic violence, pornography, and discrimination against lesbians, had metamorphosed by 1983, the year of an international conference on sexual slavery in Rotterdam, into "violence against women"—which essentially meant sexual violence. "Forced prostitution" turned into the centerpiece of activism: now termed "female sexual slavery," which at the conference extended to marriage and normative heterosexuality along with commercial sex.[52] At the Vienna conference in 1993, sexual violence again expanded to include the all-encompassing category of "sexual exploitation."

For women outside the West, the issue was electrifying because it illuminated just how entrenched female subjugation was. Liberal emphases on job equity and property rights could not do the same work. In Africa, women across the continent responded with excitement. Bread-and-butter issues such as sexual discrimination at work and lack of opportunities in higher education were irrelevant to the vast majority of rural African women. But beatings, rapes, and child marriage were familiar elements of their lives, daily enactments of men's power untrammeled by any contravening force of law or social norms, and backed by tribal or religious law in states with mixed judicial systems. The new attention pulled these debilitating, deadly exercises of power out of the obscure realm of what men did to women and gave those protesting them some credibility, as well as international norms to draw upon for legitimacy.

It is possible that violence against women was actually rising around the world, deployed against those very feminist initiatives that global feminism nurtured. Thus an analysis that took the full measure of misogyny as a political dynamic was necessary to understand the outbreaks. But a framework that isolated women as the victims of choice was also inadequate. Sex-specific violence was inextricable from the plague of wars and insurgencies that laid waste to entire populations. Rape, torture, mutilation, and female captivity and enslavement were standard procedures of marauding insurgents in Africa, from Liberia and Sierra Leone to Congo, northern Uganda, Rwanda, Sudan, and Somalia. Prostitution across borders—sexual trafficking in women and girls—also stepped up in intensity, following patterns of labor recruitment and forced migration. Everywhere, violence was inseparable from politics: Islamic extremists in Afghanistan, Nigeria, Saudi Arabia, and Iran, for example, wielded power by implementing draconian interpretations of sharia to harass, brutalize, and murder alleged female offenders against codes of sexual propriety.

The appalling death of Hauwa Abubakar in Nigeria is a good example of an individual tragedy that came to public attention because the attention to violence against women made intolerable what once would have been seen as a terrible but inevitable by-product of religious and cultural tradition. Hauwa's case became a cause célèbre among feminists and antigovernment protesters in 1987, the outcry lasting for months at the collusion of officials, police, and medical personnel in her death and the subsequent cover-up. At issue was not simply violence against women but child marriage, an ongoing battle for Nigerian feminists.

Betrothed at nine to a cattle farmer in the Islamic state of Bauchi, Hauwa Abubakar was married at twelve and sent to live with her husband. She repeatedly ran away; the husband, to punish her, cut off her fingers. The next time she tried, he cut off her legs with a cutlass rubbed with poison, so that the stumps were infected. Moved back and forth between the hospital and local healers, the child died after several months. The husband was charged with homicide and indicted in a Nigerian criminal court, but Hauwa's father, who had paid off a debt to him by giving his daughter in marriage, professed sympathy with the man's travails and asked that the case go to a sharia court as a family matter. The hospital also minimized the husband's culpability, declaring that the child died of shock not from the amputation but from refusing to eat.

Where violence was systemic, as it was in Nigeria, the efficacy of opposition depended on first of all raising potent questions of why. Why here, why now, and to what ends? Defenders of the government cautioned protesters to stay away from such a sensitive subject as a husband's rights in a Muslim state. While male dissidents and feminists raged at the "male cartel" of the Nigerian legislature, the official women's organization and the Federation of Muslim Women's Associations in Nigeria rushed to cover up the outcome of a system that operated to bestow virgin girls on older men. Hauwa's case was a lurid and tragic illustration of the miseries of child marriage. From there, feminists proceeded to denounce the plague of reproductive injuries that ensued even without violence, as when girls were married and impregnated at menarche.[53]

Women's movements such as Nigeria's tied violence to the context that produced it rather than isolating sexual violence as a unitary phenomenon that could be separated from other vectors. "The cultural clash between extremist Muslims and the West is not about democracy but about women's equality," advised *Ms.* magazine in 2004, naïvely assuming the two could be separated; but for women and men fighting Islamic fundamentalists in Nigeria, as elsewhere, feminism was about democracy.[54] This was enveloping feminism in a thick understanding, which took account of particular places, times, casts of characters, histories, and power relations—as opposed to a thin one that depended on a floating paradigm of gender relations issuing from the West. Thus: sexual violence and child marriage. Violence and land rights. Violence and sharia. Violence and state concessions to religious parties. Rape and genocide. Rape and the political uses of ethnic antagonism. Violence against women condoned by regimes and ruling parties in exchange for clerical and conservative male support. Linking violence against women to other issues also led to remedies that otherwise might seem extraneous. Women's rights to land, for instance, denied and violated in many places, turned out to be a major protection against domestic abuse. And finally, tradition and culture, and the interest of antidemocratic male elites in using both against supposedly Westernized feminists.[55]

In America, however, the fascination with sexual violence typically thrived on thin understandings. Violence against women seemed instantly recognizable, something that could be understood without recourse to knowledge about the region, locality, or nation. Stories about domestic horror, escapes, captures, violations, torture, and dishonor, featuring many varieties of male villains, inspired sympathy yet demanded little effort to understand. Feminist advocates saw this tendency to homogenize all violence against women as unproblematic. To the contrary, the identifications were a positive force: "Despite vast differences in the way violence is manifested, be it as domestic battery or rape during wartime, the omnipresence of violence in women's lives provides them with a unifying agenda." Violence was a way to link women across the divides of fortune: the class they were born into, the places and the group identities that claimed them.[56]

Why was sexual violence so compelling an issue? Why sexual trafficking in women (the old issue of the white slave trade put in the new bottle of globalization) and not labor battles—including the major form of trafficking, the international trade in female workers? Why clitoridectomy and not vaginal fistula, a devastating condition attendant on injuries in childbirth (which inordinately affects postpuberty brides) that is endemic in Africa? Why domestic beatings, and not women's lack of land rights? There were so many terrors, hardships, sorrows, and injustices that afflicted women the world over: Why this particular set? For one, sexual violence was, literally, sexy, calling up prurient fascination. For another, the preoccupation stirred up the passions of the political semiconscious, calling forth the fantasy of the powerful rescuer, transposing a late Victorian allegory of innocence and evil into twentieth-century globalism. Women in the late nineteenth century lumped together polygamy and the harem with child marriage, sati, and footbinding. The fascination ran deep. Incredibly, in 1939, at the last meeting before World War II, as Hitler was marching into Poland, the International Women's Alliance (formerly the IWSA) made a resolution linking the threat of war to an increase in prostitution its main piece of business. Likewise, in the 1990s, feminist college students dreamed of traveling to Cambodia and India to extricate girls from brothels.

In the United States, the fixation on international expressions of sexual violence bundled together many issues, some related, some unrelated. Clitoridectomy, for example, riveted popular feminist attention in the 1980s. Reduced by polemicists to a savage enactment of men's fear of female sexuality, clitoridectomy is, in reality, a complex practice that varies by locale in technique, severity, and meaning. Bound up with rites of kinship and adulthood, and enacted by women, it may or may not be violent for the individuals involved.[57] As for prostitution, another subject conflated with violence, not all prostitution is violent, and not all commercial sex is coerced—except in the sense that poverty drives women into prostitution, as it drives them into other demeaning and exploitative employments. Not all trafficking is sexual trafficking. Not all states are the same in their treatment of rape, or of domestic abuse. The treatment of victims in the United States and judicial procedures was (and remains) flawed and biased. The law, however, allowed some latitude of prosecution and formally recognized rape as a crime. In rape and other matters of violence, the situation of women in liberal democracies has to be distinguished from that of women beset by religious extremists backed by local authorities. In a dramatic instance of resistance in 1987, Indian feminists exposed a sati, or widow-burning, in the state of Rajasthan as an event engineered by the Hindu extremist political party, using a frightened teenage widow—and drugging her to boot—to demonstrate the supposed reverence of the villagers for tradition. Feminists showed that the ceremony was cooked up not by pious peasants but by very modern politicians vying for power.

In those places where extremist parties held sway, atrocities went unopposed. In Pakistan, authorities turned a blind eye on honor killings, when brothers, uncles, and cousins murdered women whose supposed sexual transgressions shamed the family. In the Iraq War, there was no Iraqi government opposition, even rhetorical, to an epidemic of honor killings of teenagers who were abducted by rival Shia or Sunni militias, raped, and returned to "shame" their families.[58]

As a result, the American furor over violence remained oddly apolitical and divorced from present realities, in contrast to feminist protest in Nigeria or India, for example. Knowing little or nothing about the stakes and the contenders, it was impossible to take political positions, since male violence in the international arena was seen as an autonomous force, not a practice of a particular militia or army, supported by a mix of political forces. The problem became striking after the terrorist attacks of September 11, 2001, when long-standing controversies over the treatment of women by Islamic extremist parties and movements moved to the center of international politics. One result of Western deference to multiculturalism was a reluctance to level any but limited and temperate criticism, lest it be construed as neo-imperialist. Indeed, not until Afghan women succeeded in drawing liberal American feminists into their cause in 1997 after the hard-line Taliban seized power was there a sustained outcry against a fundamentalist regime. More typically, protest flared up over an isolated incident, such as the 2002 sentence of death by stoning meted out to Amina Lawal Kurami, convicted of adultery for conceiving a child out of wedlock in Katsina, another Muslim state in northern Nigeria. There a conjunction of international politics, human rights pressure, protest in Nigeria against Islamicization, and feminist activism—including the dedicated lawyer Hauwa Ibrahim—converged; the sharia court overturned the sentence.[59]

In American politics, the issues were tailored for a conservative age. In the 1990s, church groups joined with veterans of the antipornography crusade to target sex trafficking as a major cause of the global oppression of women.[60] When George W. Bush took office, he made it the centerpiece of his foreign policy on women's issues, even as he implemented draconian restrictions on American funds for family planning, with restrictions that decimated programs throughout the Third World. In Cambodia, American attempts to stop trafficking were the issue of the day, some said the *only* issue the American ambassador cared about—in a country of one-party rule by a political strongman where all indices of health and welfare (child mortality, crop yields, education, income levels) were plunging. Yet the cause was irrefutable: Who would not want to stop forced prostitution in Cambodia? Moderates, liberals, and feminists alike could agree that ending violence against women was a good thing, and that Americans should do their best to stop it. In a time when feminist power in the United States was an oxymoron, it was an appealing fantasy indeed.

Reproductive rights was the American issue that was perhaps the most transformed in its migration through global feminist networks. In a fruitful exchange, American women's devotion to abortion rights entered global feminism in the 1980s to transform the agendas of women in other countries and, in turn, to be itself transformed into something much broader. By 1993, reproductive rights had become "reproductive health," an approach to well-being that feminists succeeded in implementing in world health organizations, development agencies, and the U.N.

The success was enormous in international policy-making circles. It was not easily won. The freedom of choice to bear or not to bear children was, after all, denied women by conservative religious authorities across the world—above all the Catholic Church—as well as antagonists who saw this power as an imposition of Western values on women who were said to value unlimited childbearing above all. Americans were at a disadvantage, because their presence in the debate brought to mind the long history of U.S.- backed population programs that used Third World women as guinea pigs and sought population reduction at any cost, with little or no concern for their health. The programs left a trail of abuse and catastrophes: experimental trials of oral contraceptives with dangerous side effects, painful and dangerous IUDs, and sterilizations.

In the 1980s, the truculent spirit of Americans fighting to hold on to abortion rights entered the international campaign for reproductive rights. There was reason to make abortion central. Abortion was never simply a Western women's preoccupation, a charge that both the religious right and the far feminist left made. Worldwide, there were some fifty million abortions every year, over half illegal, making the need for legal abortion an urgent international issue.[62] Abortion continued (and continues) to be a basic form of birth control used the world over, yet it was (and is) criminalized in most places.

In international women's circles, exchanges across borders in the 1980s were rich, with those from Africa, Latin America, and the Caribbean taking the lead in amplifying ideas of what women needed. A woman's right to choose had to include the ability to bear children as well as not bear them; and thus reproductive health programs must attend to the conditions that bred pelvic infections and made sterility so extensive in poor countries. In Africa, one couldn't talk about a woman's right to choose without first discussing the need for more protein in their diets, or the prevalence of vaginal fistulas, which made them unable to bear more children. In India, researchers found that measures to improve women's gynecological and reproductive health needed to take into account the dearth of sanitary napkins and toilets—modesty leading them to reuse dirty napkins and retain urine, with chronic gynecological infections as a result.[63] Indeed, the insight about the importance of cheap sanitary napkins traveled around the world. In Africa today, evidence suggests that menstruation, with its attendant fears of embarrassing leaks and stains, creates frequent absences from school for girls without the money for pads; the absences increase drop-out rates.

Openness to new information from particular contexts, rather than an intent on proving that women in India were like women in Guatemala, made political understanding more supple. The principle of a woman's right to choose could only be meaningful if women were free from the threat of disease, hunger, high child mortality, and dangerous childbirth. Nor could choice be considered apart from the pressures behind choices. In places where sons were more prized than daughters— notably China and India—women had the right to choose, but sex-selective abortion was a threat to female life.[64]

Human rights language broadened feminism's abilities to think beyond the Western situation, filling up universal claims with concrete details, such as what a reliable supply of sanitary napkins could mean. Feminists in international health campaigns moved from contraception and abortion to a concern with the health and sexuality of both sexes, as HIV/AIDS, initially seen as an epidemic among gay men, widened into a pandemic. In the 1990s, the number of affected women skyrocketed: By 2000 they constituted more than 50 percent of cases in sub-Saharan Africa. The feminization of the epidemic demanded a reorientation of treatment and prevention programs to women, children, and adolescents. Health professionals and advocacy groups pressed knowledge about the gender-specific patterns of AIDS on experts and a public who were slow to grasp the changing realities. They changed prevention and treatment programs by calling attention to the practices of sexual subordination that made women so vulnerable: for instance, men's assumptions that having sex without condoms was a marital right. In Brazil, a great success story of the 1990s, women's groups and gay rights organizations influenced the government to provide free drugs and universal treatment, cutting the infection rate in half.[65]

In short, this was a feminism that learned to speak about men as subjects and beneficiaries and about women in relation to men. Like women in development work, feminists in the reproductive rights movement found that a model that assumed a unity of interests between men and women was useless, but so was one that assumed their total separation or violent antagonism.[66] Policy makers could not improve the general welfare without improving the lives of women, the argument went, but women's needs could not be addressed as separate, either, from those of men and children. The uses of body politics were elastic, connecting women to AIDS sufferers, husbands, sons, and lovers—rather than cordoning them off as an interest group of victims, women-without-men. A special issue of a journal about reproductive health worldwide tackled the subject of men, but not with the usual litany of accusations and dark revelations about violence. There were a few articles on domestic abuse, but others showed an inquisitive spirit: essays from Sweden on fatherhood, Nigeria on men's and women's perceptions of reproductive disease, China on improving condom use, Kenya on improving vasectomy services, and "Making Space for Young Men in Family Planning Clinics."[67]

The broad understanding of women's reproductive health made headway in powerful circles. A turning point was the 1994 International Conference on Population and Development, held in Cairo, where feminist delegates from around the world managed to convince demographers, population control experts, and environmentalists to change their goals from lowering birthrates by any means to providing a full range of health services—including maternity care as well as contraception—for women, men, and adolescents. At Cairo, principles of women's bodily integrity conjoined with pro-poor development strategies to sideline the

Malthusian goal of population reduction as the cure-all for the developing world's ills. Women's advocates at Cairo pushed not the sturdy American mantra of a woman's right to choose, but rather a view of body politics as a basis for all human engagements. "Health, wellness and sexual pleasure" were present "not as individualistic concerns, but as inseparable from women's full and equal participation in all aspects of social life." The sexual pleasure angle was remarkable, given the fact that the main body of delegates were men from development agencies such as the World Bank and environmentalists concerned about overpopulation. "Reproductive and sexual rights are inseparable from a broader framework of enabling conditions," explained Rhonda Copelon and Rosalind Petchesky, long active in the American reproductive rights movement, describing the results of the Cairo meeting.[68]

The program worked out at Cairo was far from ideal—while pleased, feminist participants noted the tendency of population planners simply to make feminist principles an instrument to achieve population reduction more effectively. As for the latter, they muttered about "extremist feminist groups" hijacking the proceedings.[69] The idea of aiming for human well-being was strange and, for some, off-putting. The headway that feminists made in the preliminary sessions alarmed the Vatican. Before the meeting, Pope John Paul II personally wrote heads of state, including a reproachful message to President Clinton suggesting that the United States was trying to impose abortion and individualistic, antifamily, materialistic ethics onto the world's poor. Clinton stood his ground. The threat of a worldwide movement for legal abortion moved the Holy See to look to Islamic regimes, reaching out to Libya and Iran. Sudan and Saudi Arabia withdrew from the proceedings, with Sudan claiming the conference was a front for the West to limit population growth in the Muslim world. Among those who remained, the Holy See led a successful effort to block a clear statement about women's right to abortion.[70]

In the end, the Vatican could not muster a solid bloc of Catholic states to stand behind it at Cairo—Mexico, Brazil, and even conservative Poland held back.[71] The coalition with the Islamic right, while shaky at first, resurfaced in Beijing, where the Vatican marched into the conference determined to roll back the merger of women's reproductive health with the needs of the poor. It was a purely opportunist alliance of strange bedfellows, since in general suppressing birth control was not on the agenda of Islamic states. While fundamentalist parties and regimes were intent on their own campaigns to suppress women, most did not oppose contraception and abortion; indeed, Iran, with a large population to support and an economy weakened by the Iran-Iraq War, had instituted a family planning program. At the Beijing conference, supporters of reproductive health partially outmaneuvered the Vatican's alliance with Iran, Sudan, Libya, Egypt, and Kuwait, by winning support from some Catholic countries and adding strong voices from Africa. The conference platform affirmed the importance of bodily integrity to all the world's women. It was the best of body politics, writ large.[72]

In the 1990s, veterans of global feminist meetings believed that feminists had arrived as players on the world stage. Substantively in the case of the reproductive health lobby, dubiously in that of the violence-against-women movement, writers and activists saw women's involvement in world affairs as growing and efficacious. Reports from that decade are packed with celebrations of resolutions passed and new agencies created. The acronyms swarm, as bureaucracies and NGOs for women reproduced. Yet we can ask, did it matter? And how much?

There was an unfortunate conjuncture of feminist claims to influence in world affairs with the shattering of the postwar international order. In the global arena, feminists gained power and prestige in some parts of the United Nations as overall the power and prestige of many of its agencies—and certainly the General Assembly—slumped and, after 2000, the administration of George W. Bush did its best to marginalize it.[73] Women made it into human rights declarations at a time when atrocities, genocide, torture, and mass anguish dominated world events. The Bush administration wreaked havoc on reproductive health worldwide when the president, in one of his first acts in office, restored the global gag rule, which had been rescinded by President Clinton in 1993. It made U.S. family planning funds for programs abroad contingent on refraining from providing or discussing abortions.[74]

Although feminist institutions were ubiquitous, their rise coincided with the spread of failed and authoritarian states: through corruption, the devastations of war, and economic disaster. Throughout Africa, the Middle East, and Asia, states were increasingly less willing and able to guarantee security and social resources to their citizens. "Private time and money are constantly filling in for government refusals to protect its citizens from ill health or poverty or old age," observed Ann Snitow, an American whose commitments took her to women's groups in Eastern Europe.[75] Small, weak NGOs tried to compensate for and ameliorate the confusion and anguish generated by crashing state structures.

Feminist NGOs abroad could sometimes respond to local women's needs in the absence of government services, but they could also be driven by the preoccupations of donor nations—for example, sexual violence. High-profile issues such as trafficking in women drew money and support, but issues that were chronic, mundane, and low-intervention (for instance, the dearth of sanitary napkins and toilets, or the need for running water) had a much harder time getting donors' attention. The vogue for microfinance obscured the fact that women's access to lenders and aid could not substitute for state-sponsored health care, electrification, sewage programs, and irrigation. Women might get microfinance loans to sell food at local markets, but if roads were washed out or bandits patrolled them, they could not get there. Snitow's colleagues in Poland and Hungary asked why it was so easy to get money for antiprostitution and antitrafficking work but so difficult to drum up outrage in the West about the unregulated flows of capital and labor, in which "women make choices under terrible new economic pressures."[76]

The limitations of global feminism were evident in the months after 9/11, when the United States invaded Afghanistan. The country harbored training camps for Al Qaeda, and terrorist leader Osama bin Laden was rumored to be there, but the broader U.S. goal was to oust the Taliban regime that harbored him. Afghanistan was a place of tragedy, a battleground for a Soviet-American proxy war for twenty-five years, riven by warlord factions ever since and inundated with arms. Hundreds of thousands of Afghans were in exile, including most of the professional middle class. Before 1979, the year the Soviets invaded and the war began, Afghanistan was a multiethnic society divided between city dwellers and highly local peasants. The elite was tiny and the number of employed women minuscule—in 1979 only about 150,000 women in a country of 20 million had jobs. Nonetheless, in Kabul, a city that was a historic crossroads of trade and migration, women wore miniskirts in the streets and the country had one of the highest proportions of women physicians in the Middle East.[77]

After the Afghans drove out the Soviet invaders in 1989, warlords plunged into a fierce struggle for power. The Taliban was one faction, backed by the United States because it was anti-Iranian as well as anti-Soviet. The Taliban were religious extremists tied to a fanatical interpretation of Islam that made the suppression of women's liberties the central pillar of the program. Heavily composed of young men from the rural south who had grown up in exile in Pakistan attending all-male religious schools, the Taliban despised the cities for moral laxity and rampant infidelism, summed up in the liberties taken by the women who lived in them. In 1996 they welcomed back bin Laden, who had a long association with militant extremists in the rugged border region between Afghanistan and Pakistan.

When the Taliban marched into Kabul in 1996 and took power, they cracked down brutally on women's employment, dress, and freedoms. Edicts forbade women from wearing Western clothes or veiling lightly with headscarves. The *burqah*, the dress of conservative rural women, was mandatory.[78] A kind of shroud with a slit covered by latticework for the eyes, the *burqah* caused headaches and dizziness and made women vulnerable to traffic accidents because they lost peripheral vision. Children could not recognize their mothers if they got separated from them on the streets. The Taliban proscribed female work outside the home, closed girls' schools, and shut down public baths for women. Morals squads roamed the streets with whips, ready to set upon women for wearing sandals or violating the prohibition against appearing in public without a male family member—a terrible burden for the legion of war widows who could not set foot outside their households to search for food or work because they had no male relative nearby.

Afghanistan, and especially Kabul, was ground zero for women, a place where fanaticism that was subject to restraint elsewhere took off unbridled. Nonetheless, until 1998 Washington supported the Taliban through its allies Saudi Arabia and Pakistan, because the Taliban was anti-Iranian, and (supposedly) anti-poppy and anti-opium. The journalist Ahmed Rashid covered the Taliban takeover and ruefully noted, "There was not a word of US criticism after the Taliban captured Herat in 1995 and threw out thousands of girls from school."[79]

News leaked out slowly, largely through the efforts of courageous women inside the country smuggling information to exiles who then disseminated it. In 1999, Afghan women found a vociferous and energetic partner in the United States in the Feminist Majority Foundation. Led by Mavis Leno, a Hollywood liberal and wife of a television celebrity, studded with Hollywood stars, and augmented by a letter-writing campaign of some forty-five thousand women—the advice columnist Abigail Van Buren, "Dear Abby," even got involved—the organization made the plight of Afghan women its cause. Leno and her associates took advantage of the Clinton administration's cooling sentiments in the aftermath of Al Qaeda's 1998 bombing of the U.S.

embassies in Tanzania and Kenya to work for a change in American pol-icy toward the government that was hosting bin Laden's group.[80] First Lady Hillary Rodham Clinton contributed speeches. Democratic sena-tor Barbara Boxer of California introduced a resolution calling for the United States to refuse recognition of the regime. *Ms.* magazine publi-cized the issue.[81] The pressure helped bring about a change already in the works in the Clinton administration. It was a consequential inter-vention in international affairs, possibly the most consequential in fem-inism's long history. "The U.S. rejection of the Taliban was largely because of the pressure exerted by the feminist movement at home," wrote Rashid.[82]

But it was only in part a useful intervention. Western opprobrium rained down on the Taliban, who relaxed their iron rule only slightly. Terrible things took place. A man convicted of sodomy was executed by bulldozing a wall to bury him alive. The regime made executions in Kabul a spectator sport, with thousands watching a woman convicted of adultery stumble onto a field with a toddler in her arms. Guards removed the child and shot the woman in the head. A feminist with a video cam-era under her *burqah* filmed the episode and smuggled it out, to be dis-tributed on the Internet by a group of women in exile.

For Americans, the impact of the campaign was to transform a rav-aged country, one among many, into a site of focused concern. In the aftermath of 9/11, public awareness of the depredations the Taliban had inflicted on women in the 1990s allowed the Bush administration to define the U.S. invasion of Afghanistan as having a moral aim entwined with the military mission to eliminate Al Qaeda. In Congress, liberal Democrats joined Republicans in condemning the Taliban's gruesome violations of women's human rights. Two weeks after the invasion of Afghanistan, Senator Kay Bailey Hutchison, Texas Republican, intro-duced a bill with bipartisan backing from all the female senators to authorize educational and health care assistance to Afghan women and children. The bill tied humanitarian intervention to Bush's vision of the new world order and even evoked a little global sisterhood in the Senate. "See, Mr. President, this is what the terrorists don't understand," proudly declared Senator Barbara Mikulski, Democrat of Maryland. "They can't stop us. We are the red, white, and blue party. If you look at Hutchison, Mikulski, and the other 11 women of the Senate, the Taliban can't stop us from helping the women of the world."[83]

The declarations framed the intervention in traditional terms, as a war to protect women, not to restore their rights.[84] Yet regardless of the ruts in which the discussion ran, an expectation of restoring women's freedom and securing a place for them in civil society hovered over the American public's vision of Afghanistan's future. The war was not only supposed to protect women and save mothers—traditional rationales for military force—but restore a society where women had previously gone to school, worked, and walked the streets freely. When the coalition forces took over Kabul, American papers featured photographs of female students walking together on the university campus, faces uncovered, *burqahs* thrown over their heads as makeshift *hijabs,* and women washing laundry in the river for the first time in four years. Hillary Clinton, now senator from New York, called for giving women a central role in political and social reconstruction.[85]

President George W. Bush was no feminist, and the main story of the invasion lay elsewhere, with the war on terror, the U.S. need to assert secure control over oil transport, and the need for a stable and U.S.-friendly neighbor to Iran. But the Bush administration's hypocrisy should not distract us from an essential insight: Feminism arrived on the world stage in 2001, as a factor to be used and brokered in geopolitical considerations. The ideological mission of spreading democracy had never so assertively promoted the rights of women. The concerns of a tiny group of democratic radicals at the edges of the French Revolution had migrated to the center of calculations of the world's most powerful nation.

As to support for the intervention, though, American feminists were quiet. Could there be a war with feminist aims? The question was almost unthinkable, impossible to voice. This was despite the fact that historically, women's rights was not a pacifist tradition. Feminism was embroiled with the French Revolution; women's rights advocates were staunch Unionists in the Civil War; British and American feminists heralded World War I (however embarrassing the fact is now); and women in anti-imperialist and independence wars in the twentieth century fought for their rights as part of nationalist struggles. But American feminists, appalled as they were by the Taliban, were so habituated to criticizing U.S. foreign policy and opposing armed force that they could barely bring themselves to ask if the invasion could bring about results they favored. The Bush administration's mendacious, heedless rush to war in Iraq made the question all the more difficult to consider. Yet the situation in Afghanistan was catastrophic: Only 2 percent of children were in school, the childbed mortality rate was among the highest in the world, and Human Rights Watch, assessing the situation, found that "more than 70 percent of Afghan women suffered from major depression, nearly two-thirds were suicidal, and 16 percent had attempted suicide."[86]

Trumped by the war in Iraq, the war in Afghanistan became the forgotten conflict for five years. But its impact on sexual equality and its possibilities for a peace hospitable to women's aspirations were largely lost in the tsunami of anti-American, anti-Bush sentiment. The prospects for pushing for better funding, more troops, and solid backing for the new government went largely unconsidered in the women's movement.[87]

As for Afghan women, they had brought about an alliance across borders that prepared the way for Western intervention, but they had also witnessed the calamity that America had fostered for twenty years with its covert and then overt funding for the anti-Soviet insurgency; they saw thugs turned into national liberation heroes with CIA money, including, most recently, the Taliban. Their country was devastated. So while there was relief that the Taliban were ousted, and immediate efforts to organize as civic life awoke and exiles and expatriates returned, their reactions were ambivalent. Sonali Kolhatkar, an exile and soon-to-be radio journalist in California, spoke for the exile group Revolutionary Association of the Women of Afghanistan when she welcomed the war but insisted "this combat against terrorism cannot be won by bombing this or that country."[88] They, too, focused on the urgent needs of putting women in positions to hold power in the reconstruction.

The problem was that the war, with too few troops and underfunded, underequipped, and badly pursued, dragged on, and reconstruction faltered. Women in Kabul could function again with some normalcy; NGOs flooded the city. Afghan women won some representation inside the government: The new constitution formally recognized their rights. But the country's ordeal continued. The Taliban regrouped in strongholds in the south and along the border with Pakistan; rural women were never free from the threat. NGOs built girls' schools in the countryside, and girls came from miles around to attend, but when coalition troops left the area, the Taliban came and burned the buildings down or threw acid on the little girls who dared defy them.[89] Global feminist concern strengthened Afghan women's position, but the attention was inconstant. The intolerable discomfort over American intervention coupled with raging protest against the war in Iraq made it difficult for those outside the country to focus on what they might do to help women inside the country.

In the distant past, international feminists had always made solidarity between women seem as easy as dropping by the neighbor's to lend a hand with the baby. Did not all women suffer from lack of power and recognition vis-à-vis men, ruling groups, and states? Did not all women suffer from war? Was it not indisputable that the world would be a better place if their ideas were implemented and their needs honored? And this, of course, was the message of global feminism in the twenty-first century.

Yet even as feminist questions moved to the center of international deliberations, the assumptions of unity that underlay this stance seemed threadbare. The bank secretary whose supervisor pressed her to go out with him was not in the same situation as the Cambodian rice farmer whose access to water depended on giving sexual favors to the village headman who controlled irrigation. Pakistani physicians and lawyers were not in the same relation to upholders of Muslim tradition as were Afghan women of all classes under the Taliban. Some of the most murderous ethnic and religious conflicts of the last decade of the century involved zealous women perpetrators: the Hutu genocide of the Tutsi minority in Rwanda, and Hindu violence against Muslims in India in 1992–93.

What was the best course for Western democracies to take? Feminists deflected the difficult task of answering that question onto the easier task of denouncing the United States and the Bush administration. What might a feminist-minded foreign policy look like—not in utopia, when the world will be peopled by angels, but in the here and now? What would an efficacious feminist opposition to the use of terror be, not in the great hereafter but in the real world? The habitual position of criticism was from outside governments, in permanent opposition to male power. But this meant that feminists stood aside from any advocacy of state responses. The problem became acute as Muslim women under duress battled against religious extremism. Denunciations of the West, the global North, neo-imperialism, American hegemony, and right-wing Christians were louder among American feminists after 2001 than condemnations of Islamic extremists and their attempts to extirpate long-standing women's rights movements throughout the Middle East.

These were large impasses before grave questions, and women's difficulties in negotiating them reflected feminism's coming of age. Could the rights of women be a basis for power in the affairs of this world?

Could women's rights generate the pragmatic alliances to wield power, rather than to criticize power or oppose the use of power? Could feminists aspire to state power, as socialists and democrats had before them?

No longer simply a family romance, the commitment to women in this century when so much is at stake depends undeniably on the fact that women must take their place with a new generation of brothers in a struggle for the world's fortunes. Herland, whether of virtuous matrons or daring sisters, is not an option. Many of the stumbling blocks to women's full participation are the same; but the stakes of success are that much higher. In the twenty-first century, the well-being and liberty of women cannot be separated from democracy's survival.

CONCLUSION

FEW FEMINISTS sign on for life. Like others, I was a curious and intrigued but reticent recruit when, in 1969, I first began to call myself a feminist. Friends say that their plunge into the women's movement was like falling in love, but for me it was more like an abduction. I could not have dreamed that I would be writing a book on the subject so many years later. I anticipated a quick exit, because the cause seemed so indisputably just and the remedies so obvious. Surely it couldn't take too long. Knowing nothing about the history of feminism—really nothing!— except that Victorian ladies once campaigned for the vote, I assumed that a chastened American public would rise to meet the challenge, pushed and pulled along by the millions like me who were suddenly blazing to abandon womanhood as we knew it for something much bigger. We were after the business of being fully human. And in the late 1960s, achieving full humanity seemed like the most natural thing in the world.

Forty years later, the expectation of imminent, thoroughgoing change is gone. And there has been no quick exit, for me or anyone else. Feminists, to be sure, won some stunning victories. The issues of women's rights have moved into the heart of the great struggles of liberal democracy: for economic parity, religious tolerance, human rights, sexual expression, bodily ease and health, education, and the dignity of human attachments. The morning papers bring news about the devastation of illegal abortion in Africa, the Taliban's bombing of girls' schools in

Pakistan, Iranian women's massive turnout in the tumultuous 2009 presidential election, and the feminist features of American foreign policy under a new secretary of state who has made the human rights of women a centerpiece. A year ago in 2008, that same secretary of state, Hillary Clinton, fought for the Democratic Party's presidential nomination, the first time an American woman made a serious run for the executive (although readers will recall that Belva Lockwood and Victoria Woodhull gave it a go). Clinton's candidacy, which started out carefully distanced from gender issues, over time and under fire brought ideas about fair treatment for women into the center of the campaign. The desire for a new deal for women migrated out of a female constituency and won over a huge portion of the Democratic electorate, men as well as women.

But the centrality of women's issues to national and international concerns and debates, impossible to foresee in 1969, does not mean that the classic wrongs of women have been righted. Women are still handicapped and excluded in innumerable ways. True, their sorrows and social difficulties are not removed from the human condition—men, too, suffer from poverty, the psychological debilities of a multitude of prejudices, and many forms of political tyranny. Manhood can be more of a burden than a privilege in a world where traditional sources of male confidence and esteem in breadwinning and communal authority are eroding. But while many of women's difficulties are not entirely their own, the basic injustices done to them over the last two centuries persist.

You, the reader, may be familiar with some of them. The psychology of gender: Men talk a lot—a lot! Women complain about it to one another, and they respond more often than not to the problem by cutting themselves off, compressing what they're saying, minimizing its importance in order to squeeze into their allotted time. Sexuality: Women's magazines offer endless articles on how to please men; men's magazines dish up more fare on how women can please men. Virginia Woolf's observation about this asymmetry still bears thought: "Women have served all these centuries as looking-glasses possessing the magic and delicious power of reflecting the figure of man at twice its natural size." The deference and erotic subservience that Wollstonecraft deplored is still with us, modernized into self-actualizing sexuality that still hinges on male approval.

Labor discrimination: Outside the home, women are no longer boxed into a tiny number of occupations—the classic source of nineteenth-century discrimination. Now they are dispersed through more sectors of the labor force, but they are still underpaid. Men earn more money—much more, despite all the laws and policies and talk about fair pay; they still dominate public office and high-status employment. Household labor and child rearing: Women do more housework and take care of children more than their male partners do, even when they are also working outside the home. Go into supermarkets: They are full of women of all races and ethnicities. They are sitting in pediatricians' and clinic offices; there they are out front of schools to pick up children, buzzing about the merits of teachers and trading playdates while the stray man shifts about uneasily on the sidelines.

Marriage has been more amenable to change. Feminism has certainly helped make marriage something better than the prison for women that it was in the 1800s, in part by making nonpunitive divorce readily available. The women's movement also helped foster the idea that marriage can provide psychological and sexual intimacy and a place to nourish the life aspirations of both spouses, a change in the psychology of the institution that has contributed to the appeal of gay marriage.

At the same time, marriage still matters less to men than it does to women. Divorce is easily an economic and social calamity for women and children, while for men it is a financial boon (despite the stories about men depleted by alimony). In many ways, we live in a post-patriarchal society, where decreasing numbers of men worldwide live with women and children, because of divorce, desertion, and labor migration. Many men meet their obligations as fathers and partners from afar or not at all, while preserving traditional patriarchal privileges. For working-class women across the board, single motherhood is so common and divorce so frequent that marriage and stable longterm heterosexual companionship are rapidly becomes scarce goods.

None of these divisions between the sexes are hard and fast. Other relations of subordination come into play. The male immigrant restaurant worker defers to the female manager; he most likely earns more, though, than the maid at a nearby hotel. And the less power a man has, the more his plight resembles a woman's. Ill-paid janitors and busboys clean up after people, as women have been doing for centuries; downsized professional men find themselves taking part-time, uninsured, sporadic work to get by, joining educated women who have been doing this work for years. Yet women, taken together, still earn only about three-quarters of what men do. When you factor in part-time work, the proportion has hardly budged since the women's movement publicized the figure of sixty-nine cents for every dollar in 1970.

———————

One has only to consider the prospects for American girls to see how much things have changed, and how much remains to be changed, and how ideals come up against ideologies that bear little relationship to social facts. For forty years, since Title IX began to enforce equal treatment in secondary schools, America has been turning out gifted girls—star athletes, student leaders, artists, writers, science whizzes. They are mostly the coddled daughters of the middle class, but immigrant and minority girls, too, slip through the barriers into the privileged world of the gifted and talented. Cheered on by parents, teachers, coaches, and demanding mothers, they go to college and do brilliantly. Routinely, they head off to graduate and professional schools and then to demanding positions in business, medicine, the law, and teaching.

They do everything asked of them and more, but unaccountably, as they draw closer to the future for which they've long been preparing, a cloud gathers. By turn hectoring and anxious, a gloomy chorus of relatives, friends, and journalists, reinforced by the norms of popular culture, announces that success will deplete them of love and cheat them out of the families they want to have. As girls turn into women, they falter; they pull back; they take themselves out of the picture. Too often, no one steps in to stop them, because too many people believe this is true. New Womanhood collapses; a late-twentieth-century version of traditional womanhood steps in—baffled, beleaguered, and quietly conflicted.

None of this is supposed to matter, because American women—once yearning, ambitious girls—now can supposedly choose, as adults, with their own free will to work for money or remain at home as full-time wives and mothers. Their choices are assumed to translate into blessed lives free of the threats of lost love, desertion, and divorce. Antifeminism at the turn of this century, like its earlier expressions, has enfolded gains that are here to stay (women's education and contraception) into a neodomestic ideal that fundamentally opposes women's desires to be fully in the world. The result is a mishmash of objections to equality that takes the guise of being pro-woman.

Looking around the world, the American obsession with a single question—can women who work outside the home sustain a satisfying family life?—looks disturbingly static. Flurries of controversy recur in five-year cycles, kicked off when some new apostle of affluent neo-domesticity appears in the press (or on the Internet), briefly makes merry with lighthearted anecdotes about the romps and pratfalls of her charmingly wacky postmodern family, and slides into irrelevance. Feminists in so many places work in an entirely different theater of gender politics, where the fate of women rests on the fate of the auto-cratic, corrupt, and dysfunctional regimes that control them. The questions they face are among the most important ones in the world; the answers are by no means obvious. How to stop the plague of sexual violence and terror that afflicts central and east Africa? And how to halt the feminized epidemic of HIV/AIDS on the continent? In the Islamic world, feminists argue with one another and the public about religious piety and secularism, nationalism and cosmopolitanism, modernity and tradition. Basic questions are up for grabs about interpretations of the Koran and Muhammad's teachings on women's rights and duties. These are not academic matters.

Yet the situation is fluid. Who really ever cared before about girls' schools except feminists and the students and their parents, but now in Afghanistan for instance, these schools start to appear as institutions worth fighting for; for their own sake, yes, but also for what their existence means to an entire people. Thus, fleetingly, questions about human liberty and prosperity are fused with the destiny of women in new and unprecedented ways.

The copious feminist past, replete with achievements and fluent adaptations—as well as mistakes and second thoughts—has often dropped out of sight. Historical amnesia always has consequences, and feminism has suffered through compulsive repetitions of old mistakes, old arguments, old quandaries. Seldom has a new generation, however elated and inspired, set forth with a sense that the past was backing them up, that this time (to paraphrase Seamus Heaney) history and hope might rhyme.

But this need not be. Certainly many of the paths modern feminism has traveled have trailed off. Yet other roads open, if we have the curiosity and conviction to follow them. I've written this book for the twenty-first century, that it may transport the riches and assurances of the past, along with its sobering lessons, to the women and men who now take up the task of making good on feminism's democratic promise.

Acknowledgments

I owe a great deal to the advice, encyclopedic knowledge, and intellectual company of colleagues: Martha Nussbaum, Rosalind Petchesky, and Ann Snitow; Carla Hesse, Susan Pedersen, David Nirenberg, and Philip Nord; Dorothy Sue Cobble, Ellen Carol DuBois, and Dirk Hartog; and especially Nancy Cott and Susan Faludi. Stephanie McCurry has read and mulled over virtually every argument and interpretation of the book.

Leon Wieseltier, my friend and editor of many years, gave me the idea for the book. To his devoted care and intellectual passion, I owe the chance to explore these issues first in the pages of *The New Republic*.

The Radcliffe Institute gave me a year to write the book in the best of circumstances. A year's stay in Cambridge also provided the peerless delight of working with the fine staff of the Schlesinger Library.

Janette Gayle and Alix Lerner brought precision, creativity, and curiosity to difficult tasks along with mundane ones. Cary Franklin lent me her scrupulous and extensive understanding of legal history.

I thank Sean Wilentz for his support, counsel, and abiding engagement with my ideas. James Wilentz embodies the feminist promise of a new generation every day. To my daughter, Hannah Wilentz, and the dear friends with whom I have shared so much happiness and so many satisfactions in life and work, I dedicate the book.

NOTES

Short biographies of many individuals discussed in the book can be found in *Notable American Women: A Biographical Dictionary,* ed. Edward T. James and Janet Wilson James (Cambridge, Mass., 1971) and the subsequent volume 4, *The Modern Period,* ed. Barbara Sicherman and Carol Hurd Green (1980), and volume 5, *Completing the Twentieth Century,* ed. Susan Ware (2004); and in *Black Women in America: An Historical Encyclopedia,* ed. Darlene Clark Hine, Elsa Barkley Brown, and Rosalyn Terborg-Penn (Bloomington, Ind., 1993).

Chapter One: Wild Wishes

1. "The Waggoner's Lad" (trad.), as performed on Debra Cowan, Acie Cargill, Susan Brown, with Kristina Olsen and Ellen and John Wright, *The Songs and Ballads of Hattie Mae Tyler Cargill* (Folk-Legacy Records, 2001); Anna Bijns, "Unyoked Is Best! Happy the Woman Without a Man," in *Women Writers of the Renaissance and Reformation,* ed. Katharina M. Wilson (Athens, Ga., 1987), p. 382.

2. Natalie Zemon Davis, "Women on Top," *Society and Culture in Early Modern France* (Stanford, Calif., 1975), p. 145.

3. Ibid., pp. 124–51.

4. Blackstone's commentaries on marriage can be found at http://avalon .law.yale.edu/18th_century/blackstone_bk1ch15.asp.

5. On Poullain de la Barre, see Karen Offen, *European Feminisms, 1700–1950: A Political History* (Stanford, Calif., 2000), p. 34; Astell, *Reflections upon Marriage* (1706), reprinted in *The First English Feminist: Reflections upon Marriage and Other Writings by Mary Astell*, ed. Bridget Hill (New York, 1986), p. 76; Offen, "How and Why the Analogy of Marriage with Slavery Provided the Springboard for Women's Rights Demands in France, 1640–1848," in *Women's Rights and Transatlantic Antislavery in the Era of Emancipation*, ed. Kathryn Kish Sklar and James Stewart (New Haven, Conn. 2007), pp. 57–81.

6. This is the argument of Lynn Hunt, *The Family Romance of the French Revolution* (Berkeley, Calif., 1992), chapter 1.

7. Paine, *Rights of Man, Common Sense and Other Political Writings*, ed. Mark Philip (New York, 1995), pp. 29, 194. The argument about parricide was made by Winthrop D. Jordan, "Familial Politics: Thomas Paine and the Killing of the King, 1776," *Journal of American History* 60 (September 1973), pp. 294–308; see also Edwin G. Burrows and Michael Wallace, "The American Revolution: The Ideology and Psychology of National Liberation," *Perspectives in American History* 6 (1972), pp. 167–308; Hunt, *The Family Romance*, p. xiv.

8. Linda Kerber, " 'I Have Don . . . Much to Carrey on the Warr': Women and the Shaping of Republican Ideology After the Revolution," in *Women and Politics in the Age of Democratic Revolution*, ed. Harriet B. Applewhite and Darline G. Levy (Ann Arbor, Mich., 1993), pp. 250–51.

9. Barbara Taylor, *Mary Wollstonecraft and the Feminist Imagination* (Cambridge, U.K., 2003), passim; Linda K. Kerber, *Women of the Republic: Intellect and Ideology in Revolutionary America* (1980; New York, 1986), p. 28 and chapter 1 in general.

10. Alfred F. Young, *Masquerade: The Life and Times of Deborah Sampson, Continental Soldier* (New York, 2004); Mary Beth Norton, *Liberty's Daughters: The Revolutionary Experience of American Women, 1750–1800* (Boston, 1980).

11. Rachel Wells's petition is reprinted in full in Kerber and Jane Sherron De Hart, *Women's America: Refocusing the Past*, 4th ed. (New York, 1995), p. 89. Kerber discusses the petition in *Women of the Republic*, p. 87.

12. On women's speech and writing in France, see Carla Hesse, *The Other Enlightenment: How French Women Became Modern* (Princeton, N.J., 2001), chapter 1. For contrast, see Kerber, *Women of the Republic*, p. 74; also Young, "The Women of Boston: 'Persons of Consequence' in the Making of the American Revolution," in *Women and Politics in the Age of Democratic Revolution*, ed. Applewhite and Levy, pp. 181–226.

13. In a speech opposing the Stamp Act, Otis momentarily wandered into the far reaches of radical republican logic as he worked out who, exactly, had to consent in order for a government to be legitimate. Otis queried—one gets a sense that he got carried away by his hypotheticals—why it was that apple

women and orange girls, i.e., poor street sellers, had not "a natural and equitable right to be consulted in the choice of a new King or in the formation of a new original compact or government." Otis, "The Rights of the British Colonies Asserted and Proved" (1764), reprinted in *Pamphlets of the American Revolution, 1750–66*, ed. Bernard Bailyn (Cambridge, Mass., 1963), pp. 420–21.

14. Paine, *Rights of Man, Common Sense*, p. 11.

15. Adams to James Sullivan, May 26, 1776, *Papers of John Adams*, vol. 4., ed. Robert J. Taylor (Cambridge, Mass., 1979), p. 210.

16. Abigail Adams to Isaac Smith Jr., April 20, 1771, *The Adams Papers, Series II: Adams Family Correspondence*, vol. 1, ed. L. H. Butterfield (Cambridge, Mass., 1963), p. 76.

17. Abigail to John Adams, March 31, 1776, ibid., p. 370.

18. Reva Siegel, "'The Rule of Love': Wife Beating as Prerogative and Privacy," *Yale Law Journal* 105 (June 1996), pp. 2121–24.

19. For a brisk summary on the relations of the common law to familial authority, see Siegel, "She the People: The Nineteenth Amendment, Sex Equality, Federalism, and the Family," *Harvard Law Review* 115 (February 2002), pp. 980–81.

20. John to Abigail Adams, April 14, 1776, *Adams Papers*, ser. 2, vol. 1, p. 382.

21. Adams to Sullivan, May 26, 1776, *Papers of John Adams*, pp. 208–9.

22. Ibid., p. 211.

23. Abigail Adams to Mercy Otis Warren, April 27, 1776, *Adams Papers*, ser. 2, vol. 1, pp. 397–98. Warren's father was James Otis, he who asked ten years earlier why poor women street sellers could not vote; by this time he was confined to a lunatic asylum.

24. Kerber, *No Constitutional Right to Be Ladies: Women and the Obligations of Citizenship* (New York, 1998), p. 8.

25. Norma Basch, *Framing American Divorce: From the Revolutionary Generation to the Victorians* (Berkeley, Calif., 1999), p. 23; Nancy F. Cott, *Public Vows: A History of Marriage and the Nation* (Cambridge, Mass., 2000), pp. 48–49.

26. Ibid., pp. 16–17.

27. The exception was New Jersey, where women with the same qualifications as enfranchised men voted (that is, single women and widows with property,

since married women could by definition own none). But this ended in 1807. See Joan Hoff, *Law, Gender, and Injustice: A Legal History of U.S. Women* (New York, 1991), pp. 98–103; Kerber, *No Constitutional Right,* p. 33.

28. Adams to Sullivan, *Adams Papers,* p. 210.

29. Kerber, *Women of the Republic,* chapter 7.

30. "Introduction," *Women, the Family, and Freedom: The Debate in Documents,* vol. 1, 1750–1880, ed. Susan Groag Bell and Karen M. Offen (Stanford, Calif., 1983), pp. 13–19.

31. Joan Landes, *Women and the Public Sphere in the Age of the French Revolution* (Ithaca, N.Y., 1988), pp. 16–38, 58 (on the salons and *Journal des Dames*); Kerber, *Women of the Republic,* pp. 18–39 (on Enlightenment writers and the differences between the French and the British). On women and the French Revolution, see also Bonnie G. Smith's interpretation in *Changing Lives: Women in European History Since 1700* (Lexington, Mass., 1989); Karen Offen's in *European Feminisms;* Joan Wallach Scott, *Only Paradoxes to Offer: French Feminists and the Rights of Man* (Cambridge, Mass., 1996). *Women in Revolutionary Paris, 1789–1795,* ed. Darline Gay Levy, Harriet Branson Applewhite, and Mary Durham Johnson (Urbana, Ill., 1980) is a collection of documents.

32. Dominique Godineau, "Daughters of Liberty and Revolutionary Citizens," in *A History of Women in the West,* volume 4, *Emerging Feminism from Revolution to World War,* ed. Genevieve Fraisse and Michelle Perrot (Cambridge, Mass., 1993), p. 24; Gary Kates, "'The Powers of Husband and Wife Must Be Equal and Separate': The Cercle Social and the Rights of Women," in *Women and Politics in the Age of Democratic Revolution,* ed. Applewhite and Levy, p. 167.

33. Condorcet, "Sur l'Admission des femmes au droit de cité," reprinted in translation in *Women, the Family, and Freedom,* ed. Bell and Offen, p. 97.

34. Gouges, "The Rights of Woman," reprinted in *Women in Revolutionary Paris,* ed. Levy, Applewhite, and Johnson, pp. 89–96.

35. Scott, *Only Paradoxes,* p. 42.

36. Louis-Marie Prudhomme, in Offen, *European Feminisms,* p. 63; Landes, *Women and the Public Sphere,* pp. 116–17.

37. Among passive citizens were women, men under twenty-five years, domestic servants, convicted felons, bankrupts, and those men who did not pay direct taxes equivalent to three days' local wages. Effectively this meant that about one third of adult males were excluded from active citizenship. Literacy was not a qualification. Eventually Jewish men were admitted to full

citizenship, provided they met the other qualifications. Free blacks of color in the colonies were also relegated to passive citizenship, although there was back-and-forth on the issue until the abolition of slavery in 1794.

38. Smith, *Changing Lives,* p. 110.

39. Arianne Jessica Chernock, "Champions of the Fair Sex: Men and the Creation of Modern British Feminism, 1788–1800" (Ph.D. diss., University of California at Berkeley, 2004), pp. 31, 34 35.

40. Wollstonecraft, in Janet Todd, *Mary Wollstonecraft: A Revolutionary Life* (New York, 2000), pp. 35, 124.

41. Lyndall Gordon, *Vindication: A Life of Mary Wollstonecraft* (New York, 2005), pp. 130–32, 144.

42. Taylor, *Mary Wollstonecraft,* chapter 2, p. 86.

43. Wollstonecraft, *A Vindication of the Rights of Woman,* ed. Carol H. Poston (1792; New York, 1988), pp. 19, 34.

44. Ibid., p. 34.

45. Ibid., p. 175.

46. Ibid., p. 41.

47. See Taylor, *Mary Wollstonecraft,* pp. 15–21, for more analysis of Wollstonecraft's misogyny; Wollstonecraft, *Vindication,* pp. 19, 192.

48. Wollstonecraft, *Vindication,* pp. 150, 35; Taylor, *Mary Wollstonecraft,* p. 17.

49. Wollstonecraft, *Vindication,* p. 77.

50. Ibid., p. 57.

51. Imagining a young woman writer starting out, Woolf envisions "the bishops and the deans, the doctors and the professors, the patriarchs and the pedagogues going at her shouting their warnings and advice. 'You can't do this and you shan't do that!' . . . So they kept at her like the crowd at a fence on the race-course, and it was her trial to take her fence without looking to right or left. If you stop to curse you are lost, I said to her; equally, if you stop to laugh. Hesitate or fumble and you are done for. Think only of the jump, I implored her. . . ." Woolf, *A Room of One's Own* (1929; New York, 1957), p. 97.

52. Wollstonecraft, in Todd, *Mary Wollstonecraft,* p. 332.

53. Godwin and Wollstonecraft, in ibid., pp. 438–39.

54. Burke, Walpole, in Barbara Taylor, *Eve and the New Jerusalem: Socialism and Feminism in the Nineteenth Century* (New York, 1983), pp. 11, 14.

55. Taylor, *Eve and the New Jerusalem*, pp. 59–60; Margaret McFadden, "Anna Doyle Wheeler (1785–1848): Philosopher, Socialist, Feminist," *Hypatia* 4 (Spring 1989), pp. 91–101.

56. Clarence Cook, *A Girl's Life Eighty Years Ago: Letters of Eliza Southgate Bowne* (New York, 1882), pp. 61–62. Southgate's letter is reprinted in *Root of Bitterness: Documents of the Social History of American Women*, ed. Nancy F. Cott et al. (1972; Boston, 1996), pp. 101–2.

57. Excerpts from the *Vindication* were widely reprinted in the United States, along with two American editions; the ideas circulated widely. Clare A. Lyons makes the case for Philadelphia and summarizes the scholarship in *Sex Among the Rabble: An Intimate History of Gender and Power in the Age of Revolution, Philadelphia, 1730–1830* (Chapel Hill, N.C., 2006), pp. 242–43.

58. Fuller, *Woman in the Nineteenth Century and Other Writings*, ed. Donna Dickenson (New York, 1994), p. 46; Woolf, *The Common Reader*, 2nd ser., "Mary Wollstonecraft" (1925; New York, 1932), p. 163. See also Elaine Showalter, *Inventing Herself: Claiming a Feminist Intellectual Heritage* (New York, 2001). Showalter traces the thread of Wollstonecraft as exemplar and inspiration.

59. In Cook, *A Girl's Life*, pp. 61–62.

60. Barbara Taylor, "Mother-Haters and Other Rebels," *London Review of Books*, January 3, 2002, p. 3.

CHAPTER TWO: BROTHERS AND SISTERS

1. Grimké, "Letters to Catharine Beecher," *The Liberator* (Boston), October 13, 1837.

2. Sean Wilentz, *The Rise of American Democracy: Jefferson to Lincoln* (New York, 2005), p. 495.

3. Signatories to Constitution of the PFASS, December 14, 1833, Minute Books, Historical Society of Pennsylvania, Philadelphia. For information on the female societies see Blanche Glassman Hersh, *Slavery of Sex: Feminist Abolitionists in America* (Urbana, Ill., 1978); Shirley Yee, *Black Women Abolitionists: A Study in Activism, 1828–1860* (Knoxville, Tenn., 1992); Paul Goodman, *Of One Blood: Abolitionism and the Origins of Racial Equality* (Berkeley, Calif., 1998), chapters 13–14; Deborah Gold Hansen, *Strained Sisterhood: Gender and Class in the Boston Female Anti-Slavery Society* (Amherst, Mass., 1993); Nancy A. Hewitt, *Women's Activism and Social Change: Rochester, New York, 1822–1872* (Ithaca, N.Y.,

1984); Carolyn Williams, "The Female Anti-Slavery Movement: Fighting Against Color Prejudice and Promoting Women's Rights in Antebellum America," in *The Abolitionist Sisterhood*, ed. Jean Fagan Yellin and John C. Van Horne (Ithaca, N.Y., 1994); Kathryn Kish Sklar, *Women's Rights Emerges Within the Anti-Slavery Movement, 1830–1870: A Brief History with Documents* (Boston, 2000). On the Massachusetts industrial towns, see Bruce Laurie, *Beyond Garrison: Antislavery and Social Reform* (New York, 2005), chapter 1.

4. American Anti Slavery Society, "Petition Form for Women" (1834), *Letters of Theodore Dwight Weld, Angelina Grimké Weld, and Sarah Grimké 1822–1844*, vol. 1, ed. Gilbert H. Barnes and Dwight L. Dumond (New York, 1970), pp. 175–76.

5. See Elizabeth Heyrick on abolitionist women's sympathies, in Claire Midgeley, *Women Against Slavery: The British Campaigns 1780–1870* (London, 1992), p. 94 and passim for the trajectory of the British women in relation to the male-dominated movement.

6. Pugh, in ibid., p. 161.

7. Chandos Michael Brown, "Mary Wollstonecraft, or, the Female Illuminati: The Campaign Against Women and 'Modern Philosophy' in the Early Republic," *Journal of the Early Republic* 15 (Fall 1995), pp. 389–424.

8. What is known about Stewart comes primarily from the prefatory letters and her own introduction to her last publication, *Meditations from the Pen of Mrs. Maria W. Stewart (Widow of the Late James W. Stewart)* (Washington, D.C., 1879). The reference to the girl is in Alexander Crummell, prefatory letter, *Meditations*, p. 11. For a biographical sketch see *Maria W. Stewart: America's First Black Woman Political Writer: Essays and Speeches*, ed. Marilyn Richardson (Bloomington, Ind., 1987), pp. xiii–xvii, 3–27.

9. On Garrison and Stewart, see Garrison, prefatory letter, *Meditations*, p. 6, and Henry Mayer, *All On Fire: William Lloyd Garrison and the Abolition of Slavery* (New York, 1998), pp. 119–20. "Loveliest of women" is from Louise C. Hatton, prefatory letter, *Meditations*, p. 8. The pamphlet is Stewart [Maria W. Steward], *Religion and the Pure Principles of Morality: The Sure Foundation on Which We Must Build* (Boston, 1831), published by Garrison & Knapp.

10. *Maria W. Stewart*, ed. Richardson, p. 38, refers to the African Meeting House. The First African Baptist Church is named in Stewart's pamphlets published by Garrison & Knapp. "Pots and kettles" is in *Religion and the Pure Principles of Morality*, p. 16.

11. Catherine Brekus, *Strangers and Pilgrims: Female Preaching in America, 1740–1845* (Chapel Hill, N.C., 1998), pp. 183–211; Louis Billington, "'Female Laborers in the Church': Women Preachers in the Northeastern United States, 1790–1840," *Journal of American Studies* 19 (December 1985), pp. 369–94.

12. Celia Morris Eckhardt, *Fanny Wright: Rebel in America* (Cambridge, Mass., 1984), pp. 171, 186–87; "Mrs. Stewart's Farewell Address to Her Friends in the City of Boston Delivered September 21, 1833," *Productions of Mrs. Maria W. Stewart Presented to the First African Baptist Church & Society of the City of Boston* (Boston, 1835), p. 82.

13. Stewart, "Farewell Address," *Productions,* p. 75; Nell Irvin Painter, *Sojourner Truth: A Life, a Symbol* (New York, 1996), chapters 14, 18. Painter shows that it was Frances Dana Gage, an abolitionist, who invented from memory and attributed the phrase to Truth in 1863.

14. Stewart, "Farewell Address," *Productions,* p. 76.

15. John Adams, *Woman, Sketches of the History, Genius, Disposition, Accomplishments, Employments, Customs and Importance of the Fair Sex in All Parts of the World Interspersed with Many Singular and Entertaining Anecdotes by a Friend of the Sex* (1790; Boston, 1807); Stewart, "Farewell Address," *Productions,* pp. 75–78. On Stewart's use of the book, see Jennifer Rycenga, "A Greater Awakening: Women's Intellect as a Factor in Early Abolitionist Movements, 1824–1834," *Journal of Feminist Studies in Religion* 21 (Fall 2005), pp. 47–50.

16. Charles Capper, *Margaret Fuller: An American Romantic Life,* vol. 1, *The Private Years* (New York, 1992), p. 106. Stewart did not publish again until after the Civil War. She left Boston for New York and joined the African-American female literary society there. She worked as a teacher in New York and Baltimore, and in 1863 moved to Washington, D.C., where she also taught school. She was an active Episcopalian in Washington, often tangling with a conservative pro-Southern white ministry. She led prayer meetings, by her account attracting many followers. In 1879 she was matron of the Freedman's Hospital in Washington, D.C. This was when she reissued the Boston book with an autobiographical preface. See Crummell's prefatory letter on the New York years and Stewart's account of her post-Boston life, *Meditations,* pp. 13–23.

17. Paul Starr, *The Creation of the Media: Political Origins of Modern Communication* (New York, 2004), pp. 47–82.

18. Kumari Jayawardena, *Feminism and Nationalism in the Third World* (London, 1986), pp. 64–66, 176–77, 263. See Joan Judge's moving account of Chinese women reformers' use of national motherhood in "Talent, Virtue, and the Nation: Chinese Nationalisms and Female Subjectivities in the Early Twentieth Century," *American Historical Review* (June 2001), pp. 765–803. The history of female education in France is an especially clear illustration of the fit with republicanism and the complications it engendered. See Karen Offen, "The Second Sex and the Baccalaureat in Republican France, 1880–1924," *French Historical Studies* 13 (Fall 1983), pp. 252–86.

19. Fuller, *Woman in the Nineteenth Century* (1844; Oxford, U.K., 1994), p. 61; Capper, *Margaret Fuller: An American Romantic Life*, vol. 2, *The Public Years* (New York, 2007), pp. 34, 116.

20. Martha Vicinus, *Independent Women: Work and Community for Single Women, 1850–1920* (Chicago, 1985), chapter 4; David Rubinstein, *Before the Suffragettes: Women's Emancipation in the 1890s* (Brighton, Sussex, U.K., 1986), chapter 11; Rachel G. Fuchs and Victoria E. Thompson, *Women in Nineteenth Century Europe* (New York, 2005), p. 97.

21. The remarks of President Lawrence Summers ignited a firestorm of controversy that eventually led to his resignation. See Robin Wilson, Paul Fain, and Piper Fogg, "The Power of Professors," in *Chronicle of Higher Education*, March 3, 2006, pp. A10–A13; "Harvard Chief Defends His Talk on Women," *New York Times*, January 18, 2005.

22. Susan Zaeske, *Signatures of Citizenship: Petitioning, Antislavery, and Women's Political Identity* (Chapel Hill, N.C., 2003), chapter 5; pp. 69, 119.

23. Angelina Grimké, *Slavery and the Boston Riot [A Letter to Wm. I. Garrison]* (Philadelphia, 1835). On the Grimkés, see Gerda Lerner, *The Grimké Sisters from South Carolina* (1967; New York, 1998); Mark Perry, *Lift Up Thy Voice: The Grimké Family's Journey from Slaveholders to Civil Rights Leaders* (New York, 2001).

24. Ryan P. Jordan, "Slavery and the Meetinghouse: Quakers, Abolitionists, and the Dilemma Between Liberty and Union, 1820–65" (Ph.D. diss., Princeton University, 2004), chapter 1.

25. *The Public Years of Sarah and Angelina Grimké: Selected Writings 1835–1839*, ed. Larry Ceplair (New York, 1989), p. 31.

26. Grimkés to Sarah Douglass, February 22, 1837; to Weld, May 18, *Letters*, vol. 1, ed. Barnes and Dumond, pp. 363, 387. The proceedings of the meeting are reprinted in *Turning the World Upside Down: The Anti-Slavery Convention of American Women . . . in New York City, May 9–12, 1837*, ed. Dorothy Sterling (New York, 1987), p. 19.

27. AG to Weld, *Letters*, vol. 1, ed. Barnes and Dumond, August 12, 1837, p. 414.

28. AG, "Letters to Catharine Beecher," *Liberator*, October 13, 1837; Beecher, *An Essay on Slavery and Abolitionism, with Reference to the Duties of American Females* (Boston, 1837), pp. 101–2.

29. AG to Jane Smith, July 25, 1837, *The Public Years*, ed. Ceplair, p. 117. The movement of abolitionist women into women's rights sentiment has been well studied. See Hersh, *Slavery of Sex*; Anne M. Boylan, *The Origins of Women's*

Activism (Chapel Hill, N.C., 2002); *Women's Rights and Transatlantic Slavery in the Era of Emancipation* (New Haven, Conn., 2007), ed. Kathryn Kish Sklar and James Brewer Stewart; Yee, *Black Women Abolitionists;* Hansen, *Strained Sisterhood;* Jean Fagan Yellin, *Women and Sisters: The Antislavery Feminists in American Culture* (New Haven, Conn., 1989); *The Abolitionist Sisterhood: Women's Political Culture in Antebellum America,* ed. Jean Fagin Yellin and John Van Horne (Ithaca, N.Y., 1994); Julie Roy Jeffrey, *The Great Silent Army of Abolitionism: Ordinary Women in the Antislavery Movement* (Chapel Hill, N.C., 1998).

There is a rich biographical and memoir literature, as well as republished materials, e.g., Linda L. Geary, *Balanced in the Wind: A Biography of Betsey Mix Cowles* (Lewisburg, Penn., 1989); Ira V. Brown, *Mary Grew: Abolitionist and Feminist* (Selinsgrove, Penn., 1991); *Two Quaker Sisters . . . From the Original Diaries,* ed. Elizabeth Buffum and Lucy Buffum Lovell (New York, 1937); *Elizabeth Buffum Chace,* ed. Lillie B. Wyman and Arthur Wyman (New York, 1914); Otelia Cromwell, *Lucretia Mott* (New York, 1958); *Selected Letters of Lucretia Mott,* ed. Beverly Wilson Palmer (Urbana, Ill., 2002); Sarah H. Southwick, *Reminiscences of Old Slavery Days* (privately printed, 1893). Laurie, *Beyond Garrison,* opens up new ways to look at women's activities on the race question.

Information on African-American female abolitionists is harder to come by. See Anne Bustill Smith, "The Bustill Family," *Journal of Negro History* 10 (1925), pp. 638–44; Janice Sumler-Lewis, "The Forten-Purvis Women," *Journal of Negro History* 66 (1981–82), pp. 282–88; Julie Winch, *Philadelphia's Black Elite* (Philadelphia, 1988) and *A Gentleman of Color: The Life of James Forten* (New York, 2002); *Speak Out in Thunder Tones: Letters and Other Writings by Black Northerners, 1787–1865,* ed. Dorothy Sterling (New York, 1973).

30. Stephanie McCurry, *Masters of Small Worlds: Yeoman Households, Gender Relations, and the Political Culture of the Antebellum South Carolina Low Country* (New York, 1995), pp. 220–25. See also *Ideology of Slavery: Proslavery Thought in the Antebellum South, 1830–1860,* ed. and intro. by Drew Gilpin Faust (Baton Rouge, La., 1981), p. 119; Faust, *Mothers of Invention: Women of the Slaveholding South in the American Civil War* (Chapel Hill, N.C., 1996), pp. 5–6.

31. "Pastoral Letter of the General Association of Massachusetts (Orthodox) to the Churches Under Their Care," reprinted in *The Liberator,* August 11, 1837, and more accessibly in *Up from the Pedestal: Selected Writings in the History of American Feminism,* ed. Aileen S. Kraditor (Chicago, 1968), pp. 50–52.

32. His friends and intimates were all men, beginning with the cherished patron and friend Charles Stuart, who in 1832 paid for him to train for the ministry, and extending through the cadre of abolitionist brothers he worked with at Lane Seminary and then in the AASS. Barnes and Dumond summarize Weld's biography and his relationship to Charles Stuart and the Lane rebels in their Introduction to *Letters,* pp. xix–xxiv.

33. Weld to SG and AG, Aug. 26, 1837, *Letters,* vol. 1, ed. Barnes and Dumond, p. 433; SG and AG to Weld and John Greenleaf Whittier, ibid., August 20, 1837, pp. 429–30.

34. AG to Weld, in Sklar, *Women's Rights Emerges Within the Antislavery Movement*, pp. 125–26.

35. Ibid.

36. AG to Jane Smith, August 10, 1837, in *The Public Years*, ed. Ceplair, pp. 133–34.

37. An 1833 edition was published by A. J. Matsell in New York. Matsell was possibly a freethinker associated with Frances Wright's earlier visit and the Workingmen's Party. On Wright in New York City, see Sean Wilentz, *Chants Democratic: New York City and the Rise of the American Working Class, 1788–1850* (1984; New York, 2004), pp. 176–83. On Mott's copy see Cromwell, *Lucretia Mott*, pp. 28–29; the strike is recounted in Christine Stansell, *City of Women: Sex and Class in New York, 1789–1860* (New York, 1982), p. 134.

38. Grimké, *Letters on the Equality of the Sexes*, ed. Elizabeth Ann Bartlett (1837; New Haven, Conn., 1988), p. 100.

39. Ibid., p. 98.

40. Ibid., p. 35.

41. Biblical commentary is scattered throughout the text. For extended passages see ibid., Letters I and II (on the Fall), and Letters XIII–XV, which consider the problem of Paul, in *The Feminist Thought of Sarah Grimké*, ed. Gerda Lerner (New York, 1998).

42. *Right and Wrong in Boston: Report of the Boston Female Anti Slavery Society; with a Concise Statement of Events, Previous and Subsequent to the Annual Meeting of 1835* (Boston, 1836), p. 6.

43. Sklar, *Women's Rights Emerges*, p. 40.

44. In *Colored American* (New York) see "Ladies Beware," May 18, 1839; "Thoughts on Miss S. M. Grimke's 'Duties of Woman,'" September 22, 1838; "Colored Females," November 17, 1838; "Whisper to a Wife," March 18, 1837; "Counsel for Ladies," September 8, 1838; "Daughters," September 25, 1841.

The shift away from women's rights in the female leadership—and in the next generation—is a question that has not been studied.

45. Aileen S. Kraditor, *Means and Ends in American Abolitionism: Garrison and His Critics on Strategy and Tactics, 1834–1850* (New York, 1969), chapter 3; Laurie, *Beyond Garrison*, pp. 35–40.

46. The London meeting is famously described by Stanton in her autobiography, *Eighty Years and More: Reminiscences 1815–1897* (1898; Boston, 1993),

pp. 78–84; see also *History of Woman Suffrage* (hereafter *HWS*), vol. 1, ed. Elizabeth Cady Stanton, Susan B. Anthony, and Matilda Joslyn Gage (New York, 1881), pp. 53–62. My revision of Stanton's account, which is the accepted account, comes from Lori D. Ginzberg, *Elizabeth Cady Stanton: An American Life* (New York, 2009), pp. 34–41.

Dramatic on-the-ground evidence of women's difficulties in the movement after the onset of violence in Philadelphia and growing animus in the AASS is in the Abby Kelley Foster Papers, American Antiquarian Society, Worcester, Mass. Dorothy Sterling captures the tenor of the late 1830s and early 1840s in *Ahead of Her Time: Abby Kelley and the Politics of Antislavery* (New York, 1991).

Chapter Three: New Moral Worlds

1. Brown to Stone, September 22, 1847, *Friends and Sisters: Letters Between Lucy Stone and Antoinette Brown Blackwell, 1846–93*, ed. Carol Lasser and Marlene Deahl Merrill (Urbana, Ill., 1987), p. 31. Another classmate was Sally Holley, who would never marry: See *A Life for Liberty: Anti-Slavery and Other Letters of Sallie Holley*, ed. John White (Chadwick, N.Y., 1899). Holley's life is a particularly interesting example of one track of female abolitionism before and after the Civil War. More Stone-Blackwell correspondence is in *Soul Mates: The Oberlin Correspondence of Lucy Stone and Antoinette Brown 1846–1850*, ed. Lasser and Merrill (Oberlin, Ohio, 1983). Both went on to marry; Stone left a stirring protest against coverture in the marriage agreement she drew up with her husband, Henry Blackwell. She did not take his name, a defiance of coverture that was almost unheard of. The agreement is reprinted in *Feminism: The Essential Historical Writings*, ed. Miriam Schneir (New York, 1972), pp. 103–5.

2. Fourier, quoted in Taylor, *Eve and the New Jerusalem*, p. 29. For a recent treatment of Fourier, see D. Graham Burnett, "Contra Naturam," *Lapham's Quarterly* (Summer 2008), available at www.laphamsquarterly.org/magazine/book-of-nature.php. The standard intellectual biography is Jonathan Beecher, *Charles Fourier: The Visionary and His World* (Berkeley, Calif., 1986).

3. Claire Goldberg Moses, *French Feminism in the 19th Century* (Albany, N.Y., 1984), pp. 41–59, 61–87, 47–48. Bonnie Anderson sees Saint-Simonianism as influencing radicals outside France through the vogue for Fourier. *Joyous Greetings: The First International Women's Movement, 1830–1860* (New York, 2000), pp. 73–74.

4. Owen, *The Life of Robert Owen, Written by Himself* (London, 1857), p. 349; in Taylor, *Eve and the New Jerusalem*, pp. 39–40.

5. J.F.C. Harrison, *Quest for the New Moral World: Robert Owen and the Owenites in Britain and America* (New York, 1969), "Anatomy of a Movement," pp. 195–232.

6. On Anna Wheeler, see Taylor, *Eve and the New Jerusalem,* pp. 59–65 and passim; McFadden, "Anna Doyle Wheeler," pp. 91–101; Anderson, *Joyous Greetings,* p. 74.

7. Taylor, *Eve and the New Jerusalem,* chapter 4; Linda Gordon, *The Moral Property of Women: A History of Birth Control Politics in America* (1974; Urbana, Ill., 2007), pp. 45–46.

8. Dolores Dooley examines their relationship in *Equality in Community: Sexual Equality in the Writings of William Thompson and Anna Doyle Wheeler* (Cork, Ireland, 1996). Thompson is an extraordinary figure, understudied as a major feminist thinker because he is a man. The best biographical information is Richard K. P. Pankhurst, *William Thompson (1775–1833): Pioneer Socialist, Feminist, and Co-Operator* (London, 1954).

9. Mill's essay on government is reprinted in *James Mill: Political Writings,* ed. Terence Ball (New York, 1992), p. 27. Thompson, *Appeal of One Half the Human Race* (1983; London, 1825), p. 86.

10. Carlyle, in Kathryn Gleadle, *The Early Feminists: Radical Unitarianism and the Emergence of the Women's Rights Movement* (New York, 1995), p. 35. The radical Unitarians also had international connections. The exiled Italian leader Giuseppe Mazzini stayed with them when he lived in London in exile in the 1830s, and may have absorbed something of their hospitality to women's emancipation. Later in 1849–50 Mazzini and Margaret Fuller were drawn to each other and worked together during the Roman revolution: Fuller stayed with the Unitarians on her European trip. Ram Mohun Roy, a pioneering Bengali thinker and reformer, encountered the Unitarians on a trip to London; he would have found resonances among them with his own condemnations of the treatment of women in Hindu society. Writing in the 1820s, Roy denounced child marriage and polygamy and waged a campaign against sati, the sacrifice of a widow on her husband's funeral pyre. On Roy, see Martha C. Nussbaum, *Women and Human Development: The Capabilities Approach* (Cambridge, U.K., 2000), pp. 48, 197, 222; Susobhan Sarker, *Bengal Renaissance and Other Essays* (New Delhi, India, 1970), p. 9; Lata Mani, *Contentious Traditions: The Debate on Sati in Colonial India* (Los Angeles, 1998), pp. 56, 74–75; Kumari Jayawardena, *The White Woman's Other Burden: Western Women and South Asia During British Colonial Rule* (New York, 1995), p. 71. On Mazzini, see Gleadle, *The Early Feminists,* p. 41; Capper, *Margaret Fuller,* vol. 2, pp. 302–3.

11. Gleadle, *The Early Feminists,* chapter 4.

12. Karl Marx and Friedrich Engels, *The Communist Manifesto* (1848; New York, 1967), "Critical-Utopian Socialism and Communism," pp. 46–47.

13. Ibid. Trembling, chains, and the world to win come in the conclusion, p. 52. For an analysis of how Marx's and Engels's views developed vis-à-vis the followers of Fourier and Owen on the margins of working-class politics,

see Harold Benenson, "Victorian Sexual Ideology and Marx's Theory of the Working Class," *International Labor and Working Class History* 25 (Spring 1984), pp. 1–23.

14. For Fourierist communities, see Emily Bingham, *The Mordecais: An Early American Family* (New York, 2003), pp. 210–12; *Free Love in America: A Documentary History,* ed. Taylor Stoehr (New York, 1979), pp. 485–548. Charles Capper notes that social (not sexual) Fourierism was so much the vogue among the Boston intelligentsia in the 1840s that Fuller and Emerson used the phalanx as a metaphor for the intermeshed relationships of life: *Margaret Fuller,* vol. 2, p. 602. Bronson Alcott tried to stamp out the implications of Fourier for the reformed family and preserve the authority of the male head in a Boston debate in 1848; see F. B. Sanborn and William T. Harris, *A. Bronson Alcott,* vol. 2 (Boston, 1893), pp. 412–13. Lydia Maria Child's ruminations on Fourier and phalanxes are another perspective from Boston: Child was taken with the idea of passionate attraction and worked to domesticate it for native uses: "I think Fourier means that society ought to be so constructed that every passion will be excited to healthy action on suitable objects." *Lydia Maria Child: Selected Letters, 1817–1880,* ed. Milton Meltzer and Patricia G. Holland (Amherst, Mass., 1982), pp. 165–66. On the American free-love tradition more generally see John C. Spurlock, *Free Love: Marriage and Middle-Class Radicalism in America, 1825–1860* (New York, 1988); Joanne E. Passet, *Sex Radicals and the Quest for Women's Equality* (Urbana, Ill., 2003); Jean L. Silver-Isenstadt, *Shameless: The Visionary Life of Mary Gove Nichols* (Baltimore, 2002).

15. Thomas Hertell first introduced a resolution to appoint a committee to produce a bill in 1836. Hertell was a follower of Frances Wright, and his effort conjoined with those of Ernestine Rose. The bill was voted down in 1840 and reintroduced later. See Judith Wellman, *The Road to Seneca Falls: Elizabeth Cady Stanton and the First Woman's Rights Convention* (Urbana, Ill., 2004), pp. 145–53.

16. Ellen Carol DuBois, "The Pivot of the Marriage Relation: Stanton's Analysis of Women's Subordination in Marriage," in *Elizabeth Cady Stanton: Feminist as Thinker,* ed. Ellen Carol DuBois and Richard Cándida Smith (New York, 2007), pp. 83–84; Stanton tells her story of the law office in *Eighty Years and More,* pp. 31–32.

17. "Margaret Fuller," *HWS,* vol. 1, p. 801. Stanton wrote the bulk of the material for the first volume, and the stirring stentorian voice sounds like hers. Stanton does not mention having heard Fuller lecture, although her residence in Boston overlapped with Fuller's last years there. See Capper, *Margaret Fuller,* vol. 2, pp. 37–39, on Fuller's criticisms of the Garrisonians and theirs of her.

18. Fuller, *Woman in the Nineteenth Century,* pp. 81, 49. On the Barmbys see Taylor, *Eve and the New Jerusalem,* pp. 172–82.

19. Fuller, *Woman in the Nineteenth Century,* p. 79.

20. Ibid., pp. 75, 3.

21. She imagined a ponderous male critic accusing her of taking his wife away from the kitchen to vote at the polls and preach from the pulpit. Ibid., pp. 11, 14.

22. Ibid., pp. 20, 22, 24–25, 78.

23. It is unclear how much women's rights were openly discussed, however. When Flora Tristan, once a Saint Simonian, visited London in 1840, women recoiled at any mention of Wollstonecraft. *The London Journal of Flora Tristan,* trans. Jean Hawkes (1840; London, 1982), p. 253.

24. Capper, *Margaret Fuller,* vol. 2, chapter 8.

25. On Germany and Anneke, see Henriette M. Heinzen, in collaboration with Hertha Anneke Sanne, "Biographical Notes in Commemoration of Fritz Anneke and Mathilde Franziska Giesler Anneke," Typescript, 1940, Wisconsin State Historical Society; Sanne and Heinzen, "Mathilda Franziska Anneke," Written for the National League of Women Voters Honor Roll, Typescript, ibid. For the Vésuvienne declaration, see Laura S. Strumingher, "The Vésuviennes: Images of Women Warriors in 1848 and Their Significance for French History," *History of European Ideas* 8, no. 4/5 (Winter 1987), pp. 454–55.

26. Strumingher, "Vésuviennes," p. 457; Honoré Daumier, *Liberated Women: Bluestockings and Socialists,* cat. and ed. Jacqueline Armingeat (London, 1990).

27. Fuller, in Capper, *Margaret Fuller,* vol. 2, p. 419. On Deroin and Roland, including Proudhon's gibe, see Anderson, *Joyous Greetings,* pp. 7, 9; chapter 1, passim; pp. 157–63.

28. Documents from the hospital controversy are reprinted in *Margaret Fuller: Transatlantic Crossings in a Revolutionary Era,* ed. Charles Capper and Cristina Giorcelli (Madison, Wis., 2007), Appendix, pp. 241–50. On being an ambassador, see Capper, *Margaret Fuller,* vol. 2, p. 419. Fuller's dispatches from Rome are reprinted in *The Woman and the Myth: Margaret Fuller's Life and Writings,* ed. Bell Gale Chevigny (Old Westbury, N.Y., 1976).

29. Wilentz, *Rise of American Democracy,* pp. 610–11, 620–21.

30. Stanton to Elizabeth W. McClintock, July 14, 1848, *The Selected Papers of Elizabeth Cady Stanton and Susan B. Anthony,* vol. 1, *In the School of Anti-Slavery 1840 to 1866,* ed. Anne D. Gordon (New Brunswick, N.J., 1997), p. 69 (hereafter *Selected Papers*).

31. Stanton was invested by this time in describing Seneca Falls as if it emerged full-blown from the mind of Zeus (or Athena). See *HWS*, vol. 1, pp. 67–75.

32. The number of attendees is unknown, but the organizèrs were surprised by the crowd. See Wellman, *Road to Seneca Falls*, pp. 194–97, 201. The "Declaration of Sentiments" at the end was signed by one hundred people, a third of them men. "Appendix," *HWS*, vol. l, pp. 809–10.

33. An accessible reprinting is in *The Feminist Papers: From Adams to De Beauvoir*, ed. Alice S. Rossi (Boston, 1973), pp. 413–21. The original is in *HWS*, vol. l, pp. 70–73.

34. Moses, *French Feminism in the Nineteenth Century*, p. 142.

35. Lori Ginzberg, *Untidy Origins: A Story of Women's Rights in Antebellum New York* (Chapel Hill, N.C., 2005). Earlier that year, in the jockeying that preceded the formation of the Free Soil Party, Stanton's cousin Gerrit Smith had called for women's suffrage at the convention of a splinter group of the Liberty Party. See Wellman, *Road to Seneca Falls*, pp. 150–53, 175–76. For a general discussion of the intellectual vectors of the moment, see Nancy Isenberg, *Sex and Citizenship in Antebellum America* (Chapel Hill, N.C., 1998).

36. *HWS*, vol. l, p. 73; "Letter to Henry Clay," *North Star* (Rochester, N.Y.), December 3, 1847. Douglass published a glowing report about Seneca Falls, followed by a long, enthusiastic account of the Rochester women's rights convention held the next month. Ibid., July 28, August 11, 1848. Ginzberg discusses the impact of the state constitutional convention in *Untidy Origins*. See Ginzberg also on the suffrage resolution at Seneca Falls in *Elizabeth Cady Stanton*, pp. 61–62.

37. Douglass, March 31, 1888, *The Frederick Douglass Papers: Series One: Speeches, Debates and Interviews*, ed. John W. Blassingame (New Haven, Conn., 1992), vol. 5, p. 53. I draw the quote and the interpretation of Douglass from Ann D. Gordon, "Difficult Friendships: Frederick Douglass and the Woman Suffrage Movement," unpublished paper in my possession.

38. A surge came in 1850, when leading Garrisonian men joined by Ralph Waldo Emerson and Bronson Alcott added their names to the call for a convention in Worcester, Massachusetts. With the provisions of the Compromise of 1850 fresh in the public mind and looming conflict over the Fugitive Slave Act, more than a thousand people, three times the number at Seneca Falls, showed up in Worcester. The Call and Proceedings are reprinted at www.assumption.edu/whw/old/On-line%20Archive.html.

Elizabeth Stanton, among others, called attention to the horrors of the Fugitive Slave Act, whose implications were dramatized shortly thereafter in Boston, on October 25, when two slave catchers, sent by an owner emboldened by the federal act, showed up to repossess antislavery celebrities

William and Ellen Craft, who had escaped slavery in Georgia two years earlier. See Wilentz, *Rise of American Democracy,* pp. 645–46.

39. See the strong case for the similarities, from the point of view of the slaves, between masters and mistresses in Thavolia Glymph, *Out of the House of Bondage: The Transformation of the Plantation Household* (New York, 2008).

40. *The Salem, Ohio 1850 Women's Rights Proceedings,* ed. Robert W. Audretsch. Typescript on deposit at Public Library, Salem, Ohio.

41. Ginzberg, *Untidy Origins,* p. 66; Call to Worcester Convention, online at www.assumption.edu/whw/old/On-line%20Archive.html.

42. The Sheffield Female Reform Society authored the petition. Anne Knight, an abolitionist who was more feminist than many in the British movement, was involved. Knight corresponded regularly with American women. See Anderson, *Joyous Greetings,* p. 8; Jutta Schwarzkopf, *Women in the Chartist Movement* (New York, 1991), pp. 248–55.

43. Anderson, *Joyous Greetings,* pp. 8–9, 69, 180. The letter is reprinted in *HWS,* vol. 1, pp. 234–37, although without the excited punctuation, Anderson points out.

44. Andrea Moore Kerr, *Lucy Stone: Speaking Out for Equality* (New Brunswick, NJ, 1992).

45. Ruth Bogin, "Sarah Parker Remond," *Essex Institute Historical Collections* 110 (April 1974), pp. 120–50; Dorothy Porter, "Sarah Parker Remond, Abolitionist and Physician," *Journal of Negro History* (1935), pp. 287–93; Carla L. Peterson, *"Doers of the Word": African-American Women Speakers and Writers in the North 1830–1880* (New York, 1995); Bettye Collier-Thomas, "Frances Watkins Harper: Abolitionist and Feminist Reformer 1825–1911," in *African-American Women and the Vote 1837–1965,* ed. Ann Gordon et al. (Amherst, Mass., 1997).

46. Barbara Caine, *English Feminism 1780–1980* (New York, 1997), pp. 94–98; "Women and Work" (1857), in *Barbara Leigh Smith Bodichon and the Langham Place Group,* ed. Candida Ann Lacey (New York, 1986), pp. 36–72; Sheila R. Herstein, *A Mid-Victorian Feminist: Barbara Leigh Smith Bodichon* (New Haven, Conn., 1985); Jane Rendall, "Langham Place Group," *Oxford Dictionary of National Biography,* online ed., Oxford University Press, May 2007, www.oxforddnb.com/view/theme/93708.

47. Bodichon, *An American Diary 1857–58,* ed. Joseph W. Reed (London, 1972), p. 61.

Chapter Four: Loyalty's Limits

1. Whitman, *Specimen Days*, in *Walt Whitman: Complete Poetry and Collected Prose* (New York, 1982), p. 779.

2. Anthony to Stanton, December 23, 1860, pp. 451–52, to Martha Coffin Wright, January 7, 1861, p. 453; Henry B. Stanton to Stanton, January 12, 1861, pp. 454–55; Martha Coffin Wright to Anthony, March 31, 1862, p. 474, in *Selected Papers*, vol. 1.

3. "To the Women of the Republic," ibid., p. 483; Editorial Note, ibid., p. 480.

4. Dall's objections can be inferred from Stanton's replies, April 22, May 7, 1864, ibid., pp. 514–15, 518–22.

5. Meeting of the Loyal Women of the Republic, May 14, 1863, ibid., p. 490; Women's National Loyal League statement, May 14, 1863, ibid., p. 499.

6. Wendy Hammond Venet, *Neither Ballots nor Bullets: Women Abolitionists and the Civil War* (Charlottesville, Va., 1991), chapters 5–6; Zaeske, *Signatures of Citizenship*, pp. 168–72; Nina Silber, *Daughters of the Union: Northern Women Fight the Civil War* (Cambridge, Mass., 2005), pp. 150–61.

7. Correspondence with Sumner is in *Selected Papers*, vol. 1, passim; Stanton to Dall, ibid., April 22, 1864, p. 514.

8. Ibid., May 7, 1864, p. 519. Just as in the South, "soldier's wife" was a new self-designation that for yeoman women emblematized their political salience. See Stephanie McCurry, *Confederate Reckoning: Power and Politics in the Civil War South* (Cambridge, Mass., 2010).

9. Resolution, Eleventh National Woman's Rights Convention, *Selected Papers*, vol. 1, p. 585; James Mott, ibid., p. 587; Stanton, " 'This is the Negro's Hour,' " *National Anti-Slavery Standard*, December 26, 1865, *Selected Papers*, vol. 1, p. 564. DuBois details the tensions surrounding the new organization. See Ellen Carol DuBois, *Feminism and Suffrage: The Emergence of an Independent Women's Movement in America, 1848–1869* (Ithaca, N.Y., 1978), pp. 63–64.

10. Eric Foner, *The Story of American Freedom* (New York, 1998), p. 111.

11. Stanton, in DuBois, *Feminism and Suffrage*, p. 61.

12. Stanton to Truth, March 24, 1867, *Selected Papers*, vol. 2, p. 47; Truth, in proceedings, American Equal Rights Association (AERA), May 9, 1867, *HWS*, vol. 2, p. 193; Martha Wright, Eleventh National Woman's Rights Convention, May 10, 1866, *Selected Papers*, vol. 1, p. 588.

13. New York State Equal Rights Convention, November 20, 1866, *Selected Papers*, vol. 1, p. 601.

14. *Selected Papers*, vol. 2, p. 9 n2, p. 113 n15. It was apparently an AERA petition.

15. For example, in the Senate, an amendment to remove "male" from the franchise bill for the District of Columbia in December 1866 was introduced by a Democrat and supporter of Andrew Johnson. The nine affirmative votes came from five Democrats and four Republicans. Ibid., notes on pp. 7–9.

16. Truth, AERA meeting, May 9, 1867, *HWS*, vol. 2, pp. 193–94.

17. The classic account of the Kansas campaign is DuBois, *Feminism and Suffrage*, chapter 3. For documents see *HWS*, vol. 2, chapter 19.

18. On the fracas after Sumner's speech, see William Lloyd Garrison to Helen Garrison, October 9, 1862, *The Letters of William Lloyd Garrison*, vol. 5, *Let the Oppressed Go Free: 1861–1867*, ed. Walter M. Merrill (Boston, 1979), p. 120; *Boston Daily Journal*, October 6, 7, 10, 15, 1862. On Train's politics, see Ann Gordon's cogent editorial note in *Selected Papers*, vol. 2, pp. 94–95 n11, which characterizes him as occupying "a space somewhere between brilliance and insanity."

19. Twain, "Letters from Washington, Number VII," *Territorial Enterprise* (Virginia City, Nev.), February 27, 1868. He also lampoons Train in "Information Wanted," *New York Tribune*, January 22, 1868, and the *Chicago Republican*, March 1, 1868.

20. Entry on Train in *Dictionary of American Biography*, vol. 9 (New York, 1964), pp. 626–27. The *DAB* gets some points wrong; more accurate and illuminating is Patricia G. Holland, "George Francis Train and the Woman Suffrage Movement, 1867–70," *Books at Iowa* 46 (April 1987), pp. 8–29.

21. Train published a kind of scrapbook of the campaign speeches, put together from his own memories, notes, stenographic transcriptions, and newspaper accounts. One ditty is: "In the age of Shoddy / A busy little body, / Kept dancing a legislative gig; / But while riding his hobby, / He kicked and threw poor Snoddy, / And elected Sebastopol, the nig." *The Great Epigram Campaign of Kansas . . . Thirty Speeches in Two Weeks in All Parts of Kansas* (Leavenworth, Kan., 1867).

22. DuBois, *Feminism and Suffrage*, p. 97; *Selected Papers*, vol. 2, p. 104 n5; Appendix B (tabulation of votes cast by county), pp. 643-44.

23. Stanton to Ellen Eaton, December 17, 1867, *Selected Papers*, vol. 2, p. 117; quoted in Holland, "George Francis Train," p. 5.

24. Stanton to Eaton, December 17, 1867, *Selected Papers*, vol. 2, p. 118; Anthony to Olympia Brown, ibid., January 1, 1868, p. 122.

25. Garrison to Anthony, January 4, 1868, ibid., p. 124; Douglass, meeting of the AERA, May 14, 1868, ibid., p. 138; *New York World* account of meeting, ibid., p. 137.

26. Douglass, AERA meeting, May 1869, *HWS,* vol. 2, p. 382.

27. Douglass and respondents, ibid.; Benjamin Quarles, "Frederick Douglass and the Woman's Rights Movement," *Journal of Negro History* 25 (January 1940), pp. 39–41. For a private expression of the same sentiments, see Douglass's letter to Josephine Griffing, September 27, 1868, in Joseph Borome, "Two Letters of Frederick Douglass," *Journal of Negro History* 33 (October 1948), pp. 469–70.

28. Amy Dru Stanley, *From Bondage to Contract: Wage Labor, Marriage, and the Market in the Age of Slave Emancipation* (Cambridge, U.K., 1998), pp. 52–54. Frances Dana Gage and Sojourner Truth were the exceptions. Gage worked in freedpeople's camps on the Sea Islands during the war, and Truth worked in a refugee camp in Washington, D.C. Both complained that freedmen tried to dominate and "master" the women. AERA meeting, May 9, 1867, *HWS,* vol. 2, pp. 193, 197.

29. Harper, AERA meeting, May, 1869, *HWS,* vol. 2, p. 391.

30. Stanton's gibe was at Caroline Dall. See ibid., p. 187 n5.

31. "The Sixteenth Amendment," April 29, 1869, ibid., pp. 236–38.

32. For an old instance that came out of the conventional wisdom of the 1960s left, see Warren Hinckle and Marianne Hinckle, "A History of the Unusual Movement for Women Power in the United States 1961–1968," *Ramparts,* February 1968, pp. 22–43.

33. Rosalyn Terborg-Penn, "Nineteenth-Century Black Women and Woman Suffrage," *Potomac Review* 7 (Spring–Summer 1977), pp. 16–17; Rosalyn Terborg-Penn, *African American Women in the Struggle for the Vote, 1850–1920* (Bloomington, Ind., 1998), pp. 34–35; Painter, *Sojourner Truth,* pp. 232–33. Charlotte Ray, to name a less-known black woman, attended the NWSA convention in 1876, possibly because the organization's activities in Washington, D.C., where she practiced, attracted black women. Entry in *Black Women in America: An Historical Encylopedia,* ed. Darlene Clark Hine, Elsa Barkley Brown, and Rosalyn Terborg-Penn (Bloomington, Ind., 1993), p. 965 (hereafter *BWA*). See *Selected Papers,* vol. 2, Appendix C for listings of biracial activity for suffrage in Washington, D.C.

34. Blackwell's pamphlet was "What the South Can Do. How the Southern States Can Make Themselves Masters of the Situation." See *Selected Papers,* vol. 2, p. 51 n10. On Blackwell's statistical argument, see Marjorie Spruill

Wheeler, *New Women of the New South: The Leaders of the Woman Suffrage Movement in the Southern States* (New York, 1993), pp. 113–14.

35. Anthony to the Editor, *New York Times,* June 4, 1869, *Selected Papers,* vol. 2, p. 247; Emil Hoeber's criticism at an NWSA meeting was reported in *The New York Times,* ibid., p. 248 n3. A typical Stanton speech using caricatures is "Manhood Suffrage," December 24, 1868, ibid., pp. 194–99.

36. See my "Missed Connections: Abolitionist Feminism in the Nineteenth Century," in *Elizabeth Cady Stanton,* ed. DuBois and Smith, pp. 41–47, on this point.

37. Stanton to Martha Coffin Wright, March 21, 1871, *Selected Papers,* vol. 2, p. 426. Davis was also Wright's relative, because he was married to her niece.

38. Quarles, "Frederick Douglass and the Woman's Rights Movement," p. 42; Gordon, "Stanton and the Right to Vote: On Account of Race or Sex," in *Elizabeth Cady Stanton,* ed. DuBois and Smith, pp. 122, 127. In 1888, at the founding convention of the International Council of Women, organized by Stanton and Anthony, Douglass gave an opening address and again elegiacally recalled his involvement at Seneca Falls: "There are few facts in my humble life to which I look back with more satisfaction than to the one, recorded in the History of Woman Suffrage, that I was sufficiently enlightened at that early day, and when only a few years from slavery, to support Mrs. Stanton's resolution for woman suffrage." *Report of the International Council of Women . . . 1888* (Washington, D.C., 1888), p. 329. "All good causes are mutually helpful," he concluded. Ibid., p. 330.

39. Arguments that universal suffrage might have come to fruition are DuBois, *Feminism and Suffrage,* chapter 3, and Ann D. Gordon, "Difficult Friendships."

40. Remarks, "Western Woman Suffrage Association," September 10, 1869, *Selected Papers,* vol. 2, p. 266.

41. DuBois, *Feminism and Suffrage,* pp. 103–4 and passim; Twain, "Letters from Washington," *Territorial Enterprise.*

42. Proceedings of Tenth National Woman's Rights Convention, May 10–11, 1860, *HWS,* vol. 1, pp. 723–29. On the newspapers see editorial notes in *Selected Papers,* vol. 1, p. 431. Ernestine Rose defended her friend. DuBois attributes Stanton's newfound assertiveness on the subject to her friendship with Rose, a former Owenite. " 'The Pivot of the Marriage Relation': Stanton's Analysis of Women's Subordination in Marriage," in *Elizabeth Cady Stanton,* ed. DuBois and Smith, pp. 83–84.

43. Hendrik Hartog rescues the case from the terms in which it's usually discussed—which are inherited from Stanton's account in *The Revolution*—to

restore the fascinating detail, including the fact that Abby had established a modest career as an actress and "public reader." *Man and Wife in America: A History* (Cambridge, Mass., 2000), pp. 221–23 and passim. See also Stanton's speech reprinted in *Elizabeth Cady Stanton/Susan B. Anthony: Correspondence, Writings, Speeches,* ed. Ellen Carol DuBois (Boston, 1981), pp. 125–30.

44. Stanton, Speech on the Richardson-McFarland case, May 17, 1870, *Selected Papers,* vol. 2, pp.336–56; "true union" is on p. 349.

45. Hartog, *Man and Wife,* p. 169.

46. Stanton, speech on Richardson-McFarland case, *Selected Papers,* vol. 2, p. 342; Stanton to Josephine White Griffing, December 1, 1870, ibid., p. 382.

47. Rebecca Edwards, *Angels in the Machinery: Gender in American Party Politics from the Civil War to the Progressive Era* (New York, 1997), chapter 2; Melanie Susan Gustafson, *Women and the Republican Party, 1854–1924* (Urbana, Ill., 2001).

48. Jill Norgren, *Belva Lockwood: The Woman Who Would Be President* (New York, 2007).

49. Anthony's initiatives were clumsy and ill timed. See DuBois, *Feminism and Suffrage,* chapter 5.

50. Alice Kessler-Harris, *Out to Work: A History of Wage-Earning Women in the United States* (New York, 1982), chapters 5–6; for Europe, see Smith, *Changing Lives,* chapter 7.

51. Arnell, in Norgren, *Belva Lockwood,* pp. 38–39.

52. Norgren, *Belva Lockwood,* p. 63.

53. On their need for "new men," see Olympia Brown to Anthony, January 3, 1868, *Selected Papers,* vol. 2, p. 123. Capsule biographies of women's rights marriages and professional partnerships can be found throughout the editorial notes of ibid., vols. 2 and 3. For John Hooker see Stanton to Isabella Beecher Hooker, July 5, 1876, *Selected Papers,* vol. 3, pp. 242–43; on the Olneys, Anthony to the Editor, *Ballot Box,* ibid., September 21, 1877, p. 322.

54. Robert C. Post and Reva B. Siegel, "Legislative Constitutionalism and Section Five Power: Policentric Interpretation of the Family and Medical Leave Act," *Yale Law Journal* 112 (June 2003), pp. 1982–83.

55. DuBois, "Outgrowing the Compact of the Fathers: Equal Rights, Woman Suffrage, and the United States Constitution, 1820–1878," *Journal of American History* 74 (December 1987), p. 844; Belle Squire, *The Woman Movement in America: A Short Account of the Struggle for Equal Rights* (Chicago, 1911), pp. 123–25.

56. On the Minors, see Monia Cook Morris, "The History of Woman Suffrage in Missouri, 1867–1901," *Missouri Historical Review* 25 (October 1930–July 1931), pp. 67–82; Kerber, *No Constitutional Right*, pp. 103–4; *HWS*, vol. 2, pp. 407–11. The origins of the name are unclear. It anticipated the Democratic Party's "New Departure" policy of 1872, which announced acceptance of the Thirteenth, Fourteenth, and Fifteenth amendments, conceding that postwar constitutional change and black suffrage were irreversible. See David Montgomery, *Beyond Equality: Labor and the Radical Republicans, 1862–1872* (New York, 1967), p. 354. For Stanton's shift to the Fourteenth Amendment strategy, see *Selected Papers*, vol. 2, p. 413 n3.

57. Kerber, *No Constitutional Right*, pp. 88–90. Protests in six Connecticut towns occurred in 1871. The information is in *Selected Papers*, vol. 2, Appendix C, pp. 645–54. The best analysis is Ellen Carol DuBois, "Taking the Law into Our Own Hands: *Bradwell*, *Minor*, and Suffrage Militance in the 1870s," in *Visible Women: New Essays on American Activism*, ed. Nancy A. Hewitt and Suzanne Lebsock (Urbana, Ill., 1993), pp. 19–40; see also Terborg-Penn, *African-American Women in the Struggle for the Vote*, pp. 44–47.

58. Siegel, "She the People," pp. 972–73; Barbara Goldsmith, *Other Powers: The Age of Suffrage, Spiritualism, and the Scandalous Victoria Woodhull* (New York, 1998), pp. 211–12, 248–51.

59. The Republican campaign even offered Stanton and Anthony money to travel on Grant's behalf. Edwards, *Angels in the Machinery*, p. 51; DuBois, "Taking the Law into Our Own Hands," pp. 19–40. The plank in the Republican platform is the fourteenth, on the party's obligations to the "loyal women of America." www.presidency.ucsb.edu/ws/index/php?pid=29623.

60. *Selected Papers*, vol. 3, p. 21 n4; Gordon, "Difficult Friendships"; Norgren, *Belva Lockwood*, pp. 57–63. Most famously, Susan B. Anthony presented herself at her polling place in her hometown of Rochester, New York, and was arrested. She wanted to be tried and found guilty so she could appeal the case to the Supreme Court. She was short-circuited by a technicality that prevented her from appealing beyond federal district court. *Selected Papers*, vol. 2, p. 590 n1.

61. James Bradwell served one term in the Illinois House of Representatives. He sponsored successful bills making women eligible to be elected to school boards and appointed notary publics. See "James Bradwell," *American National Biography Online*, www.anb.org/articles; *Selected Papers*, vol. 2, pp. 220 n3, 309 n2; Hoff, *Law, Gender, and Injustice*, pp. 163–64.

62. He noted that single women could make contracts, but that the Court could not make law on the basis of exceptions. *Bradwell v. Illinois*, 83 U.S. 130 (1873).

63. Amicus curiae brief of American Civil Liberties Union, *Frontiero v. Richardson*, 411 U.S. 67 (1973).

64. *Minor v. Happersett,* 88 U.S. 162 (1875); *Selected Papers,* vol. 3, p. xix; Norma Basch, "Reconstructing Female Citizenship: *Minor v. Happersett,*" in *The Constitution, Law, and American Life: Critical Aspects of the Nineteenth-Century Experience,* ed. Donald Nieman (Athens, Ga., 1992), pp. 52–66; DuBois, "Taking the Law into Their Own Hands," p. 33.

65. Adams, in Alexander Keyssar, *The Right to Vote: The Contested History of Democracy in the United States* (New York, 2000), p. 122.

66. Gordon, "Stanton and the Right to Vote," in *Elizabeth Cady Stanton,* ed. DuBois and Smith, p. 112; Stanton, "National Protection for National Citizens," January 11, 1878, *Selected Papers,* vol. 3, pp. 346–67.

67. Stanton, Speech to the Women Taxpayers' Association of Rochester, New York, October 31, 1873, *Selected Papers,* vol. 3, pp. 7–8 ; Gordon, "Stanton and the Right to Vote," in *Elizabeth Cady Stanton,* ed. DuBois and Smith, p. 113.

68. Elsa Barkley Brown, "'To Catch the Vision of Freedom': Reconstructing Southern Black Women's Political History, 1865–1880," in *African-American Women and the Vote 1837–1965,* ed. Ann Gordon et al. (Amherst, Mass., 1997), pp. 66–99; see also Steven Hahn, *A Nation Under Our Feet: Black Political Struggles in the Rural South from Slavery to the Great Migration* (Cambridge, Mass., 2003), p. 185; Terborg-Penn, *African-American Women and the Struggle for the Vote,* pp. 44–45. In South Carolina, Charlotte Rollin advocated suffrage on the floor of the state legislature in 1869; Rollin was from a wealthy free black family in Charleston and her two sisters, Frances and Louisa, were active in Reconstruction politics in the 1870s. Frances Rollin married William J. Whipper, who advocated for women's suffrage as a delegate to the state constitutional convention. In 1870 Lottie Rollin was secretary of the South Carolina Women's Rights Association, and she represented her state to the AWSA in 1872.

69. Brown, "'To Catch the Vision of Freedom,'" pp. 84–85.

70. Hahn, *Nation Under Our Feet,* p. 166. Nancy Bercaw points out that it is more accurate to speak of reconstructed households rather than families, since domestic living groups were flexible, including blood relationships (mothers/children), heterosexual pairs (marriages, "taking up," "sweethearts"), fictive kin (uncles, aunts, grandparents), and orphans, single people, and the elderly. See *Gendered Freedoms: Race, Rights, and the Politics of Household in the Delta, 1861–1875* (Gainesville, Fla., 2003), chapter 4.

71. Laura Edwards, *Gendered Strife and Confusion: The Political Culture of Reconstruction* (Urbana, Ill., 1997), chapter 1; Stanley, *From Bondage to Contract,* chapter 5.

72. Hannah Rosen, "The Rhetoric of Miscegenation and the Reconstruction of Race: Debating Marriage, Sex, and Citizenship in Postemancipation

Arkansas," in *Gender and Slave Emancipation in the Atlantic World*, ed. Pamela Scully and Diana Paton (Durham, N.C., 2005), pp. 289–309.

73. National Woman Suffrage Association, "Memorials," January 15, 1874, *Selected Papers*, vol. 3, p. 34.

74. Eleanor Flexner, *Century of Struggle: The Woman's Rights Movement in the United States* (1959; New York, 1974), p. 31; Glenda Elizabeth Gilmore, *Gender and Jim Crow: Women and the Politics of White Supremacy in North Carolina, 1896–1920* (Chapel Hill, N.C., 1996), pp. 37, 33; Paula Giddings, *When and Where I Enter: The Impact of Black Women on Race and Sex in America* (New York, 1984), pp. 76–77; entry on Bethune in *BWA*, pp. 113–26.

75. Virginia Drachman, *Sisters in Law: Women Lawyers in Modern American History* (Cambridge, Mass., 1998), p. 30, and *Women Lawyers and the Origins of Professional Identity in America: The Letters of the Equity Club, 1887–1890* (Ann Arbor, Mich., 1993); Kerber, *No Constitutional Right*, p. 172. On African-American physicians, see *BWA*, vol. 2, pp. 488–91; on attorneys, *BWA*, vol. 2, p. 245.

76. Quoted in Drachman, *Sisters in Law*, p. 48.

77. Joyce Antler, "The Educated Woman and Professionalization: The Struggle for a New Feminine Identity, 1890–1920" (Ph.D. diss., State University of New York at Stony Brook, 1977), p. 208; Mary Roth Walsh, *"Doctors Wanted: No Women Need Apply"* (New Haven, Conn., 1979), p. 186.

78. Stanton to Martha Coffin Wright, March 8, 1873, *Selected Papers*, vol. 2, pp. 597–98; quoted in Kathi Kern, *Mrs. Stanton's Bible* (Ithaca, N.Y., 2001), p. 133. For a revealing analysis of the transatlantic impact of the European visits, see Sandra Stanley Holton, "'To Educate Women into Rebellion': Elizabeth Cady Stanton and the Creation of a Transatlantic Network of Radical Suffragists," *American Historical Review* 99 (October 1994), pp. 1112–37.

79. Ian Tyrrell, *Woman's World, Woman's Empire: The Woman's Christian Temperance Union in International Perspective, 1880–1930* (Chapel Hill, N.C., 1991), p. 22; Ruth Bordin, *Woman and Temperance: The Quest for Power and Liberty, 1873–1900* (Philadelphia, 1981), p. 141; Elizabeth Battelle Clark, "The Politics of God and the Woman's Vote: Religion in the American Suffrage Movement, 1848–1895" (Ph.D. diss., Princeton University, 1989), chapters 4–5. Clark's dissertation is the most probing analysis of the conflict between liberal and maternalist feminism, never published as a book because of her untimely death.

80. "By the revelation of her place in His kingdom, He lifted to an equal level with her husband the gentle companion." Anna A. Gordon, *The Beautiful Life of Frances E. Willard* (Chicago, 1898), p. 132.

81. Bordin, *Women and Temperance*, pp. 98, 89, 94.

82. Ibid., pp. 56–63; Suzanne M. Marilley, *Woman Suffrage and the Origins of Liberal Feminism in the United States, 1820–1920* (Cambridge, Mass., 1996), chapter 4; Faust, *Mothers of Invention*, pp. 248–54. Willard visited the South and encouraged African-American temperance. Willard's own abolitionist roots—her father attended Oberlin—made her a sympathetic figure in the eyes of black women, a rare contact across the color line. Gilmore, *Gender & Jim Crow*, pp. 47, 45–59; Gordon, *Beautiful Life*, p. 32.

83. Vivian Gornick, *The Solitude of Self: Thinking About Elizabeth Cady Stanton* (New York, 2005), p. 120.

84. Brian Donovan, *White Slave Crusades: Race, Gender, and Anti-Vice Activism, 1887–1917* (Urbana, Ill., 2006).

85. Marilley, *Woman Suffrage*, p. 113; Clara Parrish, in Tyrrell, *Woman's World*, p. 125; Rumi Yasutake, "Men, Women, and Temperance in Meiji Japan: Engendering WCTU Activism from a Transnational Perspective," *Japanese Journal of American Studies* 17 (2006), passim; Bordin, *Woman and Temperance*, p. 114.

86. Tyrrell, *Woman's World*, pp. 133–35.

87. Crystal Feimster, *Southern Horrors: Women and the Politics of Rape and Lynching, 1835–1930* (Cambridge, Mass., 2009); LeeAnn Whites, "Rebecca Latimer Felton and the Problem of 'Protection,' in the New South," in *Visible Women*, pp. 41–61; Wheeler, *New Women of the New South*, pp. 89–103.

88. Willard admonished French suffragists, presumably because socialist women were in their ranks, that "the emancipation of women if not based on religious principles and feelings is doomed to hell." Tyrrell, *Woman's World*, p. 68.

89. Stanton, "Woman Suffrage," May 30, 1874, *Selected Papers*, vol. 3, pp. 82–83. When her son Theodore married in 1881, she wrote him a touching letter of advice, tempered by her own experiences of how the institution of marriage could distort the best intentions. "Men and women can do a great deal to elevate and intensify each others lives and quite as much to enfeeble and degrade each other." Stanton to Theodore W. Stanton, April 21, 1881, *Selected Papers*, vol. 4, p. 64.

90. Restless with the constraints of the Americans, she and Anthony formed an International Council of Women (ICW), which met for the first time in Washington, D.C., in 1888, drawing together women they had met when they traveled in Europe and during Stanton's long sojourns in England. They saw the ICW as having many unifying functions, but certainly Stanton hoped to use it to recruit women who were willing to join a "Woman's Bible" committee that would employ liberal Bible commentary to make a female critique of

scripture. See Kern, *Mrs. Stanton's Bible*, p. 104; *Report of the International Council of Women . . . 1888* (Washington, D.C., 1888).

CHAPTER FIVE: THE POLITICS OF THE MOTHERS

1. The stress on motherhood was not entirely a retreat from the fight for sexual equality. Demands for higher education and access to the professions continued, justified as the means to outfit women for their civilizing jobs. Nor did suffragists stop insisting that women could live full and important lives outside the family. They honored single women as leaders and cultural icons: Frances Willard and above all, Susan B. Anthony, known in NAWSA as "Aunt Susan," who by 1900 was ascending to the status of a symbolic mother to the movement. NAWSA's litany of female achievement included teachers and lawyers, writers, physicians, and ministers, along with honored wives and mothers: all worthy professions for cultivated women who, whether or not they were biological mothers, would diffuse the highest traits of the race and spread the virtues of the home. "A woman, all by herself, and without any man to help her, can, if she likes, transform a house into a home," instructed Mary Livermore, a suffragist writer, in a staple speech she gave on the lyceum circuit. See Aileen Kraditor, *Ideas of the Woman Suffrage Movement, 1890–1920* (New York, 1965), p. 129; Livermore, "Homes Built by Women," AM1 3484 in Livermore Papers, Rare Books and Manuscripts, Princeton University.

2. Kern, *Mrs. Stanton's Bible*, pp. 83–85.

3. Stanton, "The Solitude of Self," reprinted in *Elizabeth Cady Stanton/Susan B. Anthony*, ed. DuBois, pp. 246–54. Given before the House Judiciary Committee, January 18, 1892. See also DuBois's discussion of the speech, ibid., and Gornick's analysis in *Solitude of Self*, pp. 3–7.

4. Gordon, "Difficult Friendships"; see Kern, *Mrs. Stanton's Bible*, pp. 217–22, on Stanton's last years.

5. Mary Putnam Jacobi, *"Common Sense" Applied to Woman Suffrage* (New York, 1894), pp. 201–2; Reverend Ida C. Hultin, 1897 NAWSA convention, *HWS*, vol. 4, p. 285; Isabella Beecher Hooker, 1892 NAWSA convention, ibid., p. 194. Jacobi's book is an illustration of how suffragists routinely mixed the expediency and justice arguments that Aileen Kraditor argued were separate and opposed. Indeed, this had been the case since the demand for suffrage was first raised at Seneca Falls. See Kraditor, *Ideas of the Woman Suffrage Movement*, passim.

6. Louise Newman, *White Women's Rights: The Racial Origins of Feminism in the United States* (New York, 1999), chapter 1.

7. Cooper, *A Voice from the South* (1892; Oxford, U.K., 1998), p. 44.

8. Williams, "The Intellectual Progress of the Colored Women of the United States Since the Emancipation Proclamation," in *The World's Congress of Representative Women,* ed. May Wright Sewall (Chicago, 1894); see also the responses from Cooper, Fannie Jackson Coppin, Sarah J. Early, Hallie Q. Brown, and Frederick Douglass; Williams, "The Woman's Part in a Man's Business," *The Voice of the Negro* 1 (November 1904), pp. 543–47; Giddings, *When and Where I Enter,* p. 96; Morrison, "What the Black Woman Thinks About Women's Lib," *New York Times,* August 22, 1971.

9. Paula Giddings, *Ida: A Sword Among Lions: Ida B. Wells and the Campaign Against Lynching* (New York, 2008), chapter 9.

10. Willard, in ibid., p. 266; see also Patricia A. Schecter, *Ida B. Wells-Barnett and American Reform 1880–1930* (Chapel Hill, N.C., 2001).

11. Anna Julia Cooper had also been pushing from within the WCTU for the organization to take a stand on lynching, but with no success. Wells used the leverage of moral arbiters who had influence with Willard, including British luminaries and Frederick Douglass. Willard reopened the "colored work" department she had shut down over Cooper's objections. Willard, in Giddings, *Ida,* pp. 266–69, 301; Bettye Collier-Thomas, "Frances Ellen Watkins Harper: Abolitionist and Feminist Reformer 1825–1911," in *African-American Women and the Vote,* ed. Gordon et al., pp. 57–59. The account of the uproar comes from Giddings, *Ida,* pp. 256–68, 291–92. Ruffin, quoted in "Josephine St. Pierre Ruffin," *BWA,* p. 995.

12. Edwards, *Angels in the Machinery,* pp. 35–38; Giddings, *When and Where I Enter,* pp. 93, 135–36; Collier-Thomas, "Frances Ellen Watkins Harper," in *African-American Women and the Vote,* ed. Gordon et al., p. 59; Gilmore, *Gender & Jim Crow,* chapter 6.

13. Williams, quoted in Terborg-Penn, "Discrimination Against Afro-American Women in the Woman's Movement, 1830–1920," in *The Afro-American Woman: Struggles and Images,* ed. Sharon Harley and Terborg-Penn (Baltimore, 1997), p. 24. On Logan, see Giddings, *When and Where I Enter,* p. 121, and Adele Logan Alexander, "Adella Hunt Logan, the Tuskegee Woman's Club, and African Americans in the Suffrage Movement," in *Votes for Women! The Woman Suffrage Movement in Tennessee, the South, and the Nation,* ed. Marjorie Spruill Wheeler (Knoxville, Tenn., 1995), p. 99; on Ruffin, see Flexner, *Century of Struggle,* pp. 191–92; Fannie Barrier Williams, "A Northern Negro's Autobiography," *The Independent* (July 14, 1904), pp. 91–96. See also entries on Ruffin, Logan, and Williams in *BWA.*

14. On the General Federation of Women's Clubs endorsement, see Sara Hunter Graham, *Woman Suffrage and the New Democracy* (New Haven, Conn., 1996), p. 67; on the NACW see Terborg-Penn, *African-American Women in the Struggle for the Vote,* ed. Gordon et al., p. 88.

15. Burroughs, "Not Color but Character," *The Voice of the Negro* (July 1904); Williams, "The Colored Girl," ibid. (June 1905); Terborg-Penn, *African-American Women and the Struggle for the Vote,* pp. 66–68.

16. Ellen Carol DuBois, "Woman Suffrage: The View from the Pacific," *Pacific Historical Review* 69 (November 2000), pp. 539–51; Raewyn Dalziel, "Presenting the Enfranchisement of New Zealand Women Abroad," in *Suffrage and Beyond: International Feminist Perspectives,* ed. Caroline Daley and Melanie Nolan (New York, 1994), pp. 42–64

17. Marilley, *Women's Suffrage,* chapter 5.

18. See for example James S. Clarkson, Benjamin Harrison's campaign manager, in Edwards, *Angels in the Machinery,* p. 83.

19. Ibid., pp. 133–49.

20. Gordon, in Wheeler, *New Women of the New South,* p. 118, on Blackwell's statistical argument see ibid., pp. 115–16, and Marilley, *Woman Suffrage,* pp. 162–64.

21. Mildred Rutherford, J. B. Evans, in Wheeler, *New Women of the New South,* pp. 25–26. Hostility to women's rights was strongest in the Black Belt, where white supremacist rule was strongest. See Elna Green, *Southern Strategies: Southern Women and the Woman Suffrage Question* (Chapel Hill, N.C., 1997), p. 45.

22. Wheeler, *New Women of the New South,* chapter 3.

23. *Woman's Journal,* March 28, April 4, April 11, 1903; Anthony to Douglass, June 25, 1893, Stanton-Anthony Papers, Rutgers University.

24. *Woman's Journal,* March 28, April 4, April 11, 1903. Williams's letter is discussed in Terborg-Penn, *African-American Women in the Struggle for the Vote,* pp. 91–92.

25. Keyssar, *The Right to Vote,* passim; DuBois, "1869 Redux: Gender and Race Politics in the Democratic Race," *Dissent,* online archive (Winter 2008).

26. Terborg-Penn, *African American Women in the Struggle for the Vote,* pp. 66–68. Terborg-Penn notes that women made distinctions in who was to blame. Terrell, for example, pointed out that it was white men who drove the corrupt political system. For a range of views, see Cooper, *Voice from the South,* pp. 139–40; Burroughs, "Black Women and Reform," *The Crisis* 10 (August 1915),

p. 1871; Giddings, *When and Where I Enter,* pp. 122–23; Barbara Savage, *Your Spirit Walks Beside Us* (Cambridge, Mass., 2008), p. 169; Terrell, *The Progress of Colored Women* (Washington, D.C., 1898), p. 15.

27. Shaw, in Kraditor, *Ideas of the Woman Suffrage Movement,* p. 126; Catt, in Wheeler, *New Women of the New South,* p. 115; for a general view of women's suffrage's relationship to disenfranchisement, see Keyssar, *The Right to Vote,* chapter 6.

28. Wheeler, *New Women of the New South,* p. 27.

29. Susan E. Marshall, *Splintered Sisterhood: Gender and Class in the Campaign Against Woman Suffrage* (Madison, Wis., 1997), pp. 64, 88–89; Rep. James Thomas Heflin (D-Alabama), *Congressional Record,* 63rd Congress, 3rd Session 1914/1915, Jan. 12, 1915, p. 1465; Rep. Frank Clark (D-Florida), p. 1412.

30. Graham, *Woman Suffrage and the New Democracy,* pp. 18–21; Eileen L. McDonagh and H. Douglas Price, "Woman Suffrage in the Progressive Era: Patterns of Opposition and Support in Referenda Voting, 1910–1918," *American Political Science Review* 79 (June 1985), pp. 415–35.

31. Rep. Stanley Bowdle (D-Ohio), *Congressional Record,* 63rd Congress, 3rd Session 1914/1915, Jan. 12, 1915, p. 1456. Antisuffragists dined out on former president Grover Cleveland's contention in a leading women's magazine that any kind of public activity, even women's clubs, was "a weapon of retaliation upon man." See Cleveland, "Woman's Mission and Woman's Clubs," *Ladies' Home Journal,* May 1905; "Menace to the Home," *Washington Post,* April 24, 1905; "Replies to Cleveland: Susan B. Anthony Defends the Equal Suffrage Clause," *Washington Post,* April 26, 1905; "Cleveland and the Women: Alice Stone Blackwell in Reply," *Washington Post,* May 8, 1905; "Sees No Good in Suffrage: The Former Mrs. Cleveland Opposes the Ballot for Women," *New York Times,* June 2, 1915.

32. Meyer, in Newman, *White Women's Rights,* p. 72.

33. Flexner, *Century of Struggle,* chapter 16.

34. Harriot Stanton Blatch and Alma Lutz, *Challenging Years: The Memoirs of Harriot Stanton Blatch* (New York, 1940), p. 92; Shaw to Aletta Jacobs, February 24, 1905, in *Politics and Friendship: Letters from the International Woman Suffrage Alliance, 1902–1942,* ed. Mineke Bosch with Annemarie Kloosterman (Columbus, Ohio, 1985), p. 59.

35. Antoinette Burton, *Burdens of History: British Feminists, Indian Women and Imperial Culture, 1865–1915* (Chapel Hill, N.C., 1994); Pamela Scully, "White Maternity and Black Infancy: The Rhetoric of Race in the South African Women's Movement, 1895–1930," in *Women's Suffrage in the British Empire: Citizenship, Nation, and Race,* ed. Ian Christopher Fletcher, Laura E. Nym Mayhall, and Philippa Levine (New York, 2000).

36. See the introduction to *Politics and Friendship*, ed. Bosch and Kloosterman, on the ambitions of the International Woman Suffrage Alliance.

37. Daniel Rodgers, *Atlantic Crossings: Social Politics in a Progressive Age* (Cambridge, Mass., 1998), pp. 35–36.

38. Marilyn J. Boxer, "Rethinking the Socialist Construction and International Career of the Concept 'Bourgeois Feminism,'" *American Historical Review* 112 (February 2007), pp. 131 58; Charles Sowerwine, *Sisters or Citizens? Women and Socialism in France Since 1876* (New York, 1982). Ellen Carol DuBois has made a different argument, more sympathetic to socialism, in "Woman Suffrage and the Left: An International Socialist-Feminist Perspective," *New Left Review* 186 (March–April 1991), pp. 20–45.

39. Richard Stites, *The Women's Liberation Movement in Russia: Feminism, Nihilism, and Bolshevism 1860–1930* (Princeton, N.J., 1978), chapters 7–8; *International Encyclopedia of Women's Suffrage*, ed. June Hannam et al. (Santa Barbara, Calif., 2000), p. 257.

40. DuBois, "Woman Suffrage and the Left," pp. 20–45; Richard Evans, *The Feminists: Women's Emancipation Movements in Europe, America and Australasia 1840 1920* (London, 1977); Martin Pugh, "The Rise of European Feminism," in *A Companion to Modern European History*, ed. Pugh (London, 1997), pp. 154–73.

41. In Rubinstein, *Before the Suffragettes*, p. 147; Sandra Holton, *Feminism and Democracy: Women's Suffrage and Reform Politics in Britain, 1900–1918* (New York, 1986); Caine, *English Feminism*, p. 161. See also Martin Pugh, *The March of the Women: A Revisionist Analysis of the Campaign for Women's Suffrage 1866–1914* (Oxford, U.K., 2000). In 1906 the Liberals came back into power, but Asquith, soon to be prime minister, was implacably opposed to women's suffrage.

42. On working-class women's involvement, see Jill Liddington and Jill Norris, *One Hand Tied Behind Us: The Rise of the Women's Suffrage Movement* (London, 1978).

43. Women taxpayers could already run for local elections. See Holton, " 'To Educate Women into Rebellion' " pp. 1121–22.

44. Laura E. Nym Mayhall, *The Militant Suffrage Movement: Citizenship and Resistance in Britain, 1860–1930* (New York, 2003); Martin Pugh, *The Pankhursts* (London, 2001).

45. Vicinus, *Independent Women*, chapter 7.

46. Ibid.; Caine, *English Feminism*, pp. 158–66.

47. Burton, *Burdens of History;* Nupur Chaudhuri, "Clash of Cultures: Gender and Colonialism in South and Southeast Asia," in *A Companion to Gender*

History, ed. Teresa A. Meade and Merry E. Wiesner-Hanks (Oxford, U.K., 2004), pp. 431–35; Jayawardena, *White Woman's Other Burden,* pp. 90–94.

48. Chaudhuri, "Clash of Cultures," p. 434; Vera Mackie, *Feminism in Modern Japan: Citizenship, Embodiment, and Sexuality* (Cambridge, U.K., 2003), p. 30; Yukiko Matsukawa and Kaoru Tachi, "Women's Suffrage and Gender Politics in Japan," in *Suffrage and Beyond,* ed. Daley and Nolan, p. 174; Sheldon Garon, *Molding Japanese Minds: The State in Everyday Life* (Princeton, N.J., 1997), pp. 98–104; Sima Bahar, "A Historical Background to the Women's Movement in Iran," in *Women of Iran: The Conflict with Fundamentalist Islam,* ed. Farah Azari (London, 1983), pp. 175–76.

49. Louise Edwards, "Women's Suffrage in China: Challenging Scholarly Conventions," *Pacific Historical Review* 69 (November 2000), p. 620; Sharon H. Nolte and Sally Ann Hastings, "The Meiji State's Policy Toward Women, 1890–1910," in *Recreating Japanese Women, 1600–1945,* ed. Gail Lee Bernstein (Berkeley, Calif., 1991), pp. 151–74; Joanna Liddle and Sachiko Nakajima, *Rising Daughters: Gender, Class, and Power in Japan* (London, 2000); Elizabeth B. Frierson, "Women in Late Ottoman Intellectual History," in *Late Ottoman Society: The Intellectual Heritage,* ed. Elisabeth Özdalga (New York, 2005), pp. 154–56; Jayawardena, *White Woman's Other Burden,* passim, and *Feminism and Nationalism in the Third World,* pp. 17–19, for a succinct overview of journals; Margot Badran, "Competing Agendas: Feminists, Islam, and the State in Nineteenth- and Twentieth-Century Egypt," in *Global Feminisms Since 1945,* ed. Bonnie G. Smith (New York, 2000), p. 15.

50. "A Doll's House," in Henrik Ibsen, *A Doll's House and Other Plays* (1879; New York, 1965), p. 228.

51. Laurel Rasplica Rodd, "Yosano Akiko: The Taisho Debate over the 'New Woman,'" in *Recreating Japanese Women,* ed. Bernstein, p. 177; Jayawardena, *Feminism and Nationalism in the Third World,* pp. 14, 18, 184–85, 223, 284–85; Barbara Molony, "Frameworks of Gender in Twentieth-Century Asia," in *A Companion to Gender History,* ed. Meade and Wiesner-Hanks, p. 535; Jung-Soon Shim, "Recasting the National Motherhood: Transactions of Western Feminisms in Korean Theatre," *Theatre Research International* 29 (Spring 2004), p. 145; Barbara Sato, *The New Japanese Woman: Modernity, Media, and Women in Interwar Japan* (Durham, N.C., 2003), p. 15. Jayawardena notes the importance of Ibsen but also mentions other writers male and female whose work became lightning rods for controversy about feminism and New Women in particular regions and countries. *Feminism and Nationalism,* p. 18.

52. Najmabadi, *The Story of Daughters of Quchan: Gender and National Memory in Iranian History* (Syracuse, N.Y., 1998), p. 183. See also Joan Judge, "Talent, Virtue, and the Nation," pp. 765–803; Judith Tucker, "Rescued from Obscurity: Contributions and Challenges in Writing the History of Gender in the Middle East and North Africa," in *Companion to Gender History,* ed. Meade and Wiesner-Hanks, pp. 399–404. The 1907 autobiographical play of

Kalliroi Siganou-Parren, a Greek feminist writer, exemplifies the pull of national motherhood on the New Woman. See her "The New Woman," in *Modern Woman Playwrights of Europe,* ed. Alan P. Barr (New York, 2001), pp. 50–84. On New Women more generally, see my *American Moderns: New York Bohemia and the Creation of a New Century* (New York, 2000) and Mary Louise Roberts, *Disruptive Acts: The New Woman in Fin-de-Siècle France* (Chicago, 1992).

53. Jayawardena cites multiple examples of this connection in *Feminism and Nationalism.*

54. Ludwig W. Adamec, *Afghanistan's Foreign Affairs to the Mid Twentieth Century: Relations with the USSR, Germany, and Britain* (Tucson, Ariz., 1974), pp. 90, 132–34, 137, 140, 183; Hammed Shahidian, *Women in Iran: Gender Politics in the Islamic Republic* (Westport, Conn., 2002), pp. 36–37; Leon B. Poullada, *Reform and Rebellion in Afghanistan, 1919–1929: King Amanullah's Failure to Modernize a Tribal Society* (Ithaca, N.Y., 1973), pp. 82–86. Soraya's photograph is on p. 83. For a first-person account after Amanullah's abdication see Kohrab K. H. Katrak, *Through Amanullah's Afghanistan: A Book of Travel with Illustrations* (Karachi, Pakistan, 1929; 1963), pp. vi, 27. See too the Afghan exile Sima Wali's account of her country's history in an interview with Gayle Kirshenbaum, "A Fundamentalist Regime Cracks Down on Women," *Ms.,* May–June 1997, p. 34.

55. Elizabeth Thompson, *Colonial Citizens: Republican Rights, Paternal Privilege, and Gender in French Syria and Lebanon* (New York, 2000).

56. Ibid., chapters 6–7.

57. Dorothy Ko, *Every Step a Lotus: Shoes for Bound Feet* (Berkeley, Calif., 2001); Alison Drucker, "The Influence of Western Women on the Anti-Footbinding Movement," in *Women in China: Current Directions in Historical Scholarship,* ed. Richard W. Guisso and Stanley Johannesen (Youngstown, N.Y., 1981), pp. 179–99; Margot Badran, "Competing Agendas," in *Global Feminisms Since 1945,* ed. Smith, pp. 17–18.

CHAPTER SIX: MODERN TIMES

1. Lippmann, Editorial, *New Republic,* October 9, 1915, p. 5.

2. Stansell, *American Moderns,* pp. 60–61; Maureen A. Flanagan, "Gender and Urban Political Reform: The City Club and the Woman's City Club of Chicago in the Progressive Era," *American Historical Review* 95 (October 1990), pp. 1032–50; Kathryn Kish Sklar, *Florence Kelley and the Nation's Work* (New Haven, Conn., 1995), pp. 171–205.

3. Blatch, in Stansell, *American Moderns,* p. 241; Gilman, *The Home* (New York, 1903), pp. 315, 321; Schreiner, *Woman and Labour* (New York, 1911), p. 126;

Ellen DuBois, "Woman Suffrage: The View from the Pacific," p. 545; DuBois, *Harriot Stanton Blatch*, p. 67.

4. Stansell, *American Moderns*, pp. 244–45; Nancy Schrom Dye, *As Equals and as Sisters: Feminism, the Labor Movement, and the Women's Trade Union League of New York* (Columbia, Mo., 1980), p. 5; Frances Bjorkman, in Lucy Delap, *The Feminist Avant-Garde: Transatlantic Encounters of the Early Twentieth Century* (Cambridge, U.K., 2007), p. 84.

5. On the AFL, see Flexner, *Century of Struggle*, p. 246; Philip Foner, *Women and the American Labor Movement from Colonial Times to the Eve of World War I* (New York, 1979), pp. 300–301.

6. Hinchey, in Kraditor, *Ideas of the Woman Suffrage Movement*, p. 160; Mari Jo Buhle, *Women and American Socialism, 1870–1920* (Urbana, Ill., 1981), pp. 214–45; Blatch and Lutz, *Challenging Years*, p. 95; Kraditor, *Ideas of the Woman Suffrage Movement*, p. 160.

7. Nancy F. Cott, *The Grounding of Modern Feminism* (New Haven, Conn., 1987), chapter 1; Stansell, *American Moderns*, chapter 7.

8. Delap, *Feminist Avant-Garde*, chapter 2; for British hauteur toward Americans in the previous decade, see Holton, "To Educate Women in Rebellion," p. 1120.

9. *New York Sun*, 1917, and Dell, in Stansell, *American Moderns*, pp. 231, 234.

10. Howe, in Cott, *Grounding of Modern Feminism*, p. 39; Flynn, in ibid., p. 38.

11. Ibid., p. 38; Stansell, *American Moderns*, pp. 271, 274; Delap, *Feminist Avant-Garde*, pp. 27–29.

12. Eastman, in June Sochen, *Movers and Shakers: American Women Thinkers and Activists, 1900–1970* (New York, 1973), p. 51.

13. See Ellen Carol DuBois, *Harriot Stanton Blatch and the Winning of Woman Suffrage* (New Haven, Conn., 1997), pp. 110–11, for other horrified reactions.

14. Strachey, in Lisa Tickner, *The Spectacle of Women: Imagery of the Suffrage Campaign 1907–14* (Chicago, 1988), p. 78; Susan A. Glenn, *Female Spectacle: The Theatrical Roots of Modern Feminism* (Cambridge, Mass., 2000), p. 133.

15. Anonymous and Meyer, in *Women's Suffrage in America: An Eyewitness History*, ed. Elizabeth Frost and Kathryn Cullen-DuPont (New York, 1992), p. 304; Blatch and Lutz, *Challenging Years*, p. 181.

16. The point about the evocation of Broadway musical theater is from Glenn, *Female Spectacle*, p. 149 and chapter 5; *New York Tribune*, in *Women's Suffrage in*

America, ed. Frost and Cullen-DuPont, p. 305; Gertrude Foster Brown, in Glenn, *Female Spectacle*, p. 132; Biographical Introduction to Gertrude Foster Brown Papers, Schlesinger Library.

17. Glenn summarizes the rich literature on suffrage techniques in *Female Spectacle*, chapter 4; DuBois, *Harriot Stanton Blatch*, pp. 148–56.

18. Gayle Gullett, "Constructing the Woman Citizen and Struggling for the Vote in California, 1896–1911," *Pacific Historical Review* 69 (November 2000); Susan Englander, *Class Conflict and Coalition in the California Woman Suffrage Movement, 1907–1912* (Lewiston, N.Y., 1992).

19. Blatch and Lutz, *Challenging Years*, p. 109.

20. The Chaplin film has been reissued. For the general subject see Kay Sloan, "Sexual Warfare in the Silent Cinema: Comedies and Melodramas of Woman Suffragism," in *History of Women in the United States: Historical Articles on Women's Lives and Activities*, ed. Nancy F. Cott, vol. 19, "Woman Suffrage," part 2 (Munich, 1994), pp. 514–38.

21. On Parsons, see Delap, *Feminist Avant-Garde*, p. 42; on Hunkins, see Christine A. Lunardini, *From Equal Suffrage to Equal Rights: Alice Paul and the National Woman's Party, 1910–1928* (New York, 1986), pp. 78–79; on the British caravans and bicycles, see Liddington and Norris, *One Hand Tied Behind Us*, pp. 133–35; Susan Pedersen, *Eleanor Rathbone and the Politics of Conscience* (New Haven, Conn., 2004), pp. 118–19.

22. Milholland appears throughout the suffrage literature. On the 1913 New York parade see DuBois, *Harriot Stanton Blatch*, p. 153; on the Washington, D.C., parade see Linda G. Ford, *Iron-Jawed Angels: The Suffrage Militancy of the National Woman's Party 1912–1920* (Lanham, Md., 1991), p. 49. On Field, see Stansell, *American Moderns*, pp. 278–79; Sara Bard Field Oral History, Online Archive of California, http://ark.cdib.org/ark; Sara Bard Field Collection, Huntington Library, Pasadena, California.

23. Younger, "Revelations of a Woman Lobbyist," *McCall's Magazine*, September 1919, p. 7; Katherine Marino, "Maud Younger and the San Francisco Wage Earners' Suffrage League: Standing Firmly for Working-Class Women," *California Historian* (Fall 1997), pp. 17–23.

24. Catt, in Kraditor, *Ideas of the Woman Suffrage Movement*, p. 45.

25. On the women students who went abroad to study in Japan, see Judge, "Talent, Virtue, and the Nation," pp. 765–83. On New York see "Chinese Women to Parade for Woman Suffrage," *New York Times*, April 14, 1912. Columbia University had strong ties to China, so the women may have been at Barnard College. On the feminists at the Nanjing parliament, see Louise Edwards, *Gender, Politics and Democracy: Women's Suffrage in China* (Stanford,

Calif., 2008), pp. 74–83. See also "China," in *International Encyclopedia of Women's Suffrage,* ed. Hannam et al., pp. 63, 295; DuBois, *Harriot Stanton Blatch,* pp. 142–43. Carrie Chapman Catt and Aletta Jacobs, international suffrage leader from the Netherlands, made a world tour in 1911–12 exploring women's rights movements and were thrilled by the feminist activity in China. See *Politics and Friendship,* ed. Bosch, p. 95.

26. Graham, *Woman Suffrage and the New Democracy,* p. 64; Brown, in Elinor Lerner, "Jewish Involvement in the New York City Woman Suffrage Movement," *American Jewish History* 70 (June 1981), p. 452.

27. Graham, *Woman Suffrage and the New Democracy,* pp. 75–76.

28. Luscomb in ibid., pp. 67–68; see also Field Oral History.

29. Kenton, "Feminism Will Give—Men More Fun, Women Greater Scope," *Delineator* 85 (July 1914), p. 17; Goldman, *Anarchism and Other Essays* (1917; New York, 1969), p. 239.

30. Beard, "The Legislative Influence of Unenfranchised Women," *Annals of the American Academy of Political and Social Science* 56 (November 1914), pp. 54–61; Michael S. Kimmel, "Men's Responses to Feminism at the Turn of the Century," *Gender and Society* 1 (September 1987), p. 274; Men's League for Woman Suffrage of the State of New York, Letter Collection, Woodsen Research Center, Fondren Library, Rice University, Houston, Texas.

31. Terborg-Penn, "Nineteenth Century Black Women," p. 21; Giddings, *When and Where I Enter,* p. 120; "The Suffrage," *The Crisis,* November 1914, p. 15; Savage, *Your Spirits Walk Beside Us,* p. 169.

32. Du Bois, "Votes for Women," *The Crisis,* September 12, p. 234; August 1914, pp. 179–80, April 1915, p. 285; Terrell, "The Justice of Woman Suffrage," *The Crisis,* September 1912, p. 243.

33. Contributions from Anna Howard Shaw, Carrie Chapman Catt, and Mary Garrett Hay, "Symposium," *The Crisis,* November 1917, pp. 19–20; Suzanne Lebsock, "Woman Suffrage and White Supremacy: A Virginia Case Study," in *Visible Women,* ed. Hewitt and Lebsock, pp. 62–100.

34. However, Andrea Tone shows persuasively that the birth control movement, for political purposes, greatly overstated the lack of access. See Tone, *Devices and Desires: A History of Contraception in America* (New York, 2001), pp. 80–81.

35. "Birth Control Demonstration on Union Square," *Mother Earth* 11 (June 1916), p. 526; Stansell, *American Moderns,* pp. 234–41.

36. A view that President Theodore Roosevelt, for example, articulated in his 1903 speech warning that native-born women were guilty of "race suicide" in

pulling back from marriage and childbearing, thus putting the country in danger of being overrun by nonnative stock. See Gordon, *Moral Property of Women*, p. 86. Matthew Connelly, *Fatal Misconception: The Struggle to Control World Population* (Cambridge, Mass., 2008), chapters 2–3, delineates the tensions between the birth control and eugenics movements.

37. Maude Wood Park, in Graham, *Woman Suffrage and the New Democracy*, p. 46.

38. Woolf, "Professions for Women: A Paper Read to the Women's Service League," in *The Death of the Moth and Other Essays* (London, 1981), p. 150; Pedersen, *Eleanor Rathbone*, p. 57. See Barbara Taylor, "Mother-Haters and Other Rebels"; Genevieve Taggard, in *These Modern Women*, ed. Showalter, p. 66.

39. Previous histories state that black women were excluded, but this appears to have been a claim replicated from one source to another without verification. *The Crisis*, April 1913, pp. 267, 297, reports on the protest and the upshot. On the parade more generally, see Lunardini, *From Equal Suffrage to Equal Rights*, chapter 2.

40. Hinchey to O'Reilly, in Kraditor, *Ideas of the Woman Suffrage Movement*, p. 160; Shaw to Jacobs, March 19, 1914, in *Politics and Friendship*, ed. Bosch, pp. 132–33.

41. List of suffrage prisoners, in Doris Stevens, *Jailed for Freedom: American Women Win the Vote* (New York, 1920), pp. 205–11; Kern, *Mrs. Stanton's Bible*, p. 145.

42. Graham, *Woman Suffrage and the New Democracy*, p. 73.

43. Flexner, *Century of Struggle*, p. 276.

44. Christine A. Lunardini and Thomas J. Knock, "Woodrow Wilson and Woman Suffrage: A New Look," *Political Science Quarterly* 95 (Winter 1980–81), p. 656; McDonagh and Price, "Woman Suffrage in the Progressive Era," pp. 415–35; John D. Buneker, "The Urban Political Machine and Woman Suffrage: A Study in Political Adaptability," *The Historian* 33 (February 1971), pp. 264–79.

45. Editor's preface to Younger, "Revelations of a Woman Lobbyist," pp. 32–33; Graham, *Woman Suffrage and the New Democracy*, p. 97.

46. Lunardini, *From Equal Suffrage to Equal Rights*, pp. 113–21.

47. Stevens, *Jailed for Freedom*, pp. 111–19, 121–28. Appendix 4 is a partial list of those arrested with descriptions. Sara Bard Field, who went to jail, pointed out that the youth of those arrested was exaggerated; among those she mentioned as middle-aged was Mary Beard. Field Oral History; Havemeyer,

"The Suffrage Torch," *Scribner's* 72 (May 1922), pp. 528–29; "The Prison Special," *Scribner's* (June 1922), pp. 661–76.

48. Stevens, *Jailed for Freedom,* p. 109. An oral history done in 1975 with one NWP member, Hazel Hunkins Hallinan, elicited more extensive comments on the uses of racism in the D.C. jail than can be found in the printed accounts. Hallinan recalled that Alice Paul never wanted the prisoners to discuss their fears of the black male prisoners whom, as she remembered, wardens allowed to roam the hallways of the women's lockup. Interview, January 22, 1975, in Washington, D.C., pp. 221–22, at http://content.cdlib .org/xtf/view?docId=kt2r29n5pb&doc.view=frames&chunk.id=d0e16106&t oc.depth=1&toc.id=&brand=oac.

49. A balanced account of Catt's political reasoning is Robert Booth Fowler, *Carrie Catt, Feminist Politician* (Boston, 1986), pp. 145–53; Catt, entry in "Votes for All: A Symposium," *The Crisis,* November 1917, p. 20; Catt to Jacobs, 1917, in *Politics and Friendship,* ed. Bosch, p. 165.

50. Fowler, *Carrie Catt,* p. 139; Nicoletta F. Gullace, *"The Blood of Our Sons": Men, Women, and the Renegotiation of British Citizenship During the Great War* (New York, 2002), p. 161.

51. Gardener to Wilson, November 27, 1918, *The Papers of Woodrow Wilson,* vol. 53, ed. Arthur S. Link (Princeton, N.J., 1986), p. 217; Lunardini and Knock, "Woodrow Wilson and Woman Suffrage," pp. 655–71. On Gardener see Kern, *Mrs. Stanton's Bible,* p. 141.

52. Wilson's evolution can be traced in *Papers of Woodrow Wilson,* vol. 53, in letters of November 9, November 29, December 2, 1918, and January 11, March 2, March 22, April 5, April 30, May 6, 1919. The letters are mostly between Wilson and his private secretary, Joseph Tumulty, on whom he relied as presidents do now on their chiefs of staff. See also diary entries of Dr. Cary Grayson, Wilson's physician and friend, May 8, 1919, and of Ray Stannard Baker, May 9, 1919. The State of the Union endorsement is ibid., p. 277. See also Lunardini and Knock, "Woodrow Wilson and Woman Suffrage," pp. 655–56.

53. Flexner, *Century of Struggle,* chapter 22.

54. The surprise vote came from Harry Burn, a Republican from the eastern part of the state whom the antis counted in their column. His mother wrote him ordering him to vote for suffrage. Flexner, ibid., pp. 303, 317–24. Mrs. Burn's missive is quoted on p. 323. Burn, a Republican, represented McMinn County, which was Unionist during the Civil War but riven by savage partisan warfare, with women on the home front inevitably pulled into the reprisals and counterreprisals. Nothing is known about Mrs. Burn; she may have inherited her suffrage sentiments from a Republican family, or she may have come to the issue via the WCTU. On McMinn County see Noel C.

Fisher, *War at Every Door: Partisan Politics and Guerrilla Violence in East Tennessee, 1860–1869* (Chapel Hill, N.C., 1997), pp. 80–84.

55. Evans, *The Feminists*; Pugh, "Rise of European Feminism," pp. 155–73. Suffrage was in several cases granted only to portions of the female population.

56. Pedersen, *Eleanor Rathbone*, p. 152. A list of "Countries in Which Women Vote" in 1920 is in Stevens, *Jailed for Freedom*, p. 204. On postwar plans see Cott, *Grounding of Modern Feminism*, pp. 66–73; on the British, see Pedersen, *Eleanor Rathbone*, p. 185 and in general chapter 10. For the Geneva conference see the IWSA's newspaper *Jus Suffragii* (London), July 1920; Adele Schreiber and Margaret Matheson, *Journey Towards Freedom: Written for the Golden Jubilee of the International Alliance of Women* (Copenhagen, 1955).

57. Graham, *Woman Suffrage and the New Democracy*, p. 145

58. Letter from Tillman reprinted in *The Crisis*, January 1915, p. 141; Gordon, in Graham, *Woman Suffrage and the New Democracy*, p. 118.

59. Gilmore, *Gender & Jim Crow*, p. 224.

CHAPTER SEVEN: DEMOCRATIC HOMEMAKING AND ITS DISCONTENTS

1. Eastman, in Kerber, "On the Importance of Taking Notes (And Keeping Them)," *Voices of Women Historians: The Personal, the Political, the Professional*, ed. Eileen Boris and Nupur Chaudhuri (Bloomington, Ind., 1999), p. 58.

2. Cott, "Across the Great Divide: Women in Politics Before and After 1920," in *Women, Politics, and Change*, ed. Louise Tilly and Patricia Gurin (New York, 1990), pp. 153–76; Marjorie Connelly, "How Americans Voted: A Political Portrait," *New York Times*, November 7, 2004, section 4, p. 4; for the women's vote since 1990 see Stansell, "Feminism and Misogyny in the Primaries," *Dissent* (Fall 2008), p. 37.

3. Cott, *Grounding of Modern Feminism*, chapter 3. On the distance of pure feminism, even the most appealing kind, from antifascism and anticolonialism, see Susan Pedersen, "Women's Stake in Democracy: Eleanor Rathbone's Answer to Virginia Woolf," The Harry Ransom Humanities Center Papers in British Studies, University of Texas at Austin, 2000; and "Satire and the Civilizing Mission: Winifred Holtby Looks at Africa," paper delivered at the Conference on Women, Art and Politics in the Twentieth Century, Princeton University, April 2005.

4. Seth Koven and Sonya Michel, *Mothers of a New World: Maternalist Politics and the Origins of Welfare States* (New York, 1993).

5. Modern Girl Conference, Schlesinger Library, Radcliffe Institute, Harvard University, March 2007; Poullada, *Reform and Rebellion in Afghanistan,* p. 83.

6. Badran, "Competing Agenda," *Global Feminisms,* ed. Smith; Ellen Fleischman, "Nation, Tradition, and Rights: The Indigenous Feminism of the Palestinian Women's Movement, 1929–1948," in *Women's Suffrage in the British Empire,* ed. Fletcher, Mayhall, and Levine; Anna Macias, *Against All Odds: The Feminist Movement in Mexico to 1940* (Westport, Conn., 1982). International conferences were also structured by other national rivalries and power imbalances. As fascism and total mobilization for war absorbed Japanese suffragists in the 1930s, for example, the uplifting of women in primitive Asian states became one rationale for Japanese imperialism. One woman explained her idealistic motives for what she saw as a Japanese rescue of the women of Asia: "When I went to China, I saw girls who were blinded with needles at birth, who were sold to Hong Kong, or who played music by the side of the road. In India the situation of women was awful. . . . So, I hoped for the awakening of all women in Asia, including Japan." Kora [Wada] Tomi, quoted in Mackie, *Feminism in Japan,* pp. 108–9. On the Latin Americans, see Ellen DuBois and Lauren Derby, "The Strange Case of Minerva Bernardino: Pan American and United Nations Women's Rights Activist," *Women's Studies International Forum,* www.elsevier.com/locate/wsif; Megan Threlkeld, "The Pan American Conference of Women, 1922: Successful Suffragists Turn to International Relations," *Diplomatic History* 31 (November 2007), pp. 801–974.

7. Sirota's parents were European Jews; her father, a renowned pianist, went to Japan in the 1930s to teach and stayed on in order to escape the Nazis. Beate was sent to the United States for the duration, where she went to Mills College. See Beate Sirota Gordon, *The Only Woman in the Room: A Memoir* (Tokyo, 1997), pp. 103–39. In 2004, a panel of the governing party denounced the women's rights article in the constitution as promoting "egoism in postwar Japan, leading to the collapse of family and community." See "A Women's Cause in Japan: Rights Drafter Returns to Rescue Her Legacy," *International Herald Tribune,* May 30, 2005.

Having grown up in Japan, Sirota was intensely sympathetic to the situation of Japanese women. The draft she wrote guaranteed women economic and social entitlements as well as juridical rights, public assistance for pregnant and nursing mothers, and the prohibition of the widespread practice whereby husbands forced their wives to adopt children of concubines. The sections on social rights were omitted from the final draft. See Mackie, *Feminism in Modern Japan,* pp. 120–22; Molony, "Frameworks of Gender in Twentieth-Century Asia," pp. 535–38; Garon, *Molding Japanese Minds,* pp. 180–82.

The article won support from the Japanese suffrage movement, which had collapsed in the 1930s. Ichikawa Fusae, the leader and chief spokesperson, had grown to political adulthood in the 1910s in the shadow of the daring feminism of her New Woman predecessors in Seitosha (Bluestockings). Fusae, while blacklisted by SCAP, supported the constitution. See Takeda Kiyoko, "Ichikawa Fusae: Pioneer for Women's Rights in Japan," *Japan Quarterly* 31 (Oct.–Dec. 1984), p. 413.

8. Mackie, *Feminism in Modern Japan,* pp. 120–23, 130–36; Mire Koikari, "Exporting Democracy? American Women, 'Feminist Reforms,' and Politics of Imperialism in the U.S. Occupation of Japan, 1945–1952," *Frontiers: A Journal of Women's Studies* 23 (Winter 2002), p. 29; William Manchester, *American Caesar: Douglas MacArthur, 1880–1964* (Boston, 1978), p. 440; Douglas MacArthur, *Courage Was the Rule: General Douglas MacArthur's Own Story* (New York, 1964), pp. 204–5; James D. Clayton, *The Years of MacArthur,* vol. 3, *Triumph and Disaster, 1945–1964* (Boston, 1985), pp. 134–35.

9. The news reflected movement in many countries. The 1950s marked intense activity among Egyptian feminists, for example, who broadened their class base and presence on the left, and entered the workforce at all levels, incurring the denunciations of religious conservatives for their adoption of supposedly Western values. See Badran, "Competing Agenda," in *Global Feminisms Since 1945,* ed. Smith, pp. 23–26. The patterns of reporting on women's rights are evident in scanning major newspapers between 1946 and 1955: the *New York Times, Washington Post, Boston Globe,* and *Los Angeles Times.*

10. Joanne Meyerowitz, "Beyond the Feminine Mystique: A Reassessment of Postwar Mass Culture, 1946–1958," *American Historical Review* 79 (March 1993), passim.

11. Elaine Tyler May, *Homeward Bound: American Families in the Cold War Era* (New York, 1988), pp. 120–21, 137; Susan Householder Van Horn, *Women, Work, and Fertility, 1900–1986* (New York, 1988), chapter 7; Giddings, *When and Where I Enter,* p. 240.

12. Suggestive comparisons about the meaning of family and private life can be found in Donna Harsch's arguments about women in postwar Communist bloc countries. See *Revenge of the Domestic: Women, the Family, and Communism in the German Democratic Republic* (Princeton, N.J., 2007).

13. *America's Working Women: A Documentary History—1600 to the Present,* ed. Rosalyn Baxandall, Linda Gordon, and Susan Reverby (New York, 1976), p. 405; Kessler-Harris, *Out to Work,* p. 301.

14. On employment patterns, see Robert Self, *American Babylon: Race and the Struggle for Postwar Oakland* (Princeton, N.J., 2003), p. 44; Ruth Milkman, *Gender at Work: The Dynamics of Job Segregation by Sex During World War II* (Urbana, Ill., 1987), pp. 100–101.

15. Dorothy Sue Cobble, *The Other Women's Movement: Workplace Justice and Social Rights in Modern America* (Princeton, N.J., 2004), chapter 1.

16. From 1950 to 1960, female college and university faculty declined from 25.0 to 22.0 percent of the total, lawyers from 3.5 to 3.3 percent, and physicians from 6.1 to 6.0 percent. Figures in Cott, *Grounding of Modern Feminism,* p. 219.

17. Arnold W. Green and Eleanor Melnick, "What Has Happened to the Feminist Movement?," in *Studies in Leadership: Leadership and Democratic Action,* ed. Alvin W. Gouldner (New York, 1950), p. 291.

18. Judith Smith, *Visions of Belonging: Family Stories, Popular Culture, and Postwar Democracy, 1940–1960* (New York, 2004), pp. 2–3.

19. See Maria DiBattista, *Fast-Talking Dames* (New Haven, Conn., 2003), which remains the best book on women in popular culture in the 1930s and '40s.

20. Women's Bureau, in Leila Rupp and Verta Taylor, *Survival in the Doldrums: The American Women's Rights Movement, 1945 to the 1960s* (New York, 1987), p. 49.

21. See the calls for a "new feminism" in the immediate aftermath of the war quoted in Susan M. Hartmann, *The Home Front and Beyond: American Women in the 1940s* (Boston, 1982), p. 157.

22. Orville Prescott, review of *Women Today: Their Conflicts, Their Frustrations and Their Fulfillments,* ed. Elizabeth Bragdorn, "Books of the Times," *New York Times,* May 11, 1953, p. 25.

23. The classic essay is Daniel Bell, "The End of Ideology in the West" (1960), reprinted in *The American Intellectual Tradition: A Sourcebook,* vol. 2., ed. David A. Hollinger and Charles Capper (New York, 2001), pp. 339–44.

24. Green and Melnick, "What Has Happened to the Feminist Movement?," p. 278.

25. *Ladies' Home Journal,* February 1958, p. 6.

26. Ferdinand Lundberg and Marynia F. Farnham, *Modern Woman: The Lost Sex* (New York, 1947), pp. 240–41. Historians cite the book as a locus classicus of a hegemonic 1950s misogyny, enthusiastically greeted, but in fact the critical reception was mixed. Margaret Mead wrote a highly critical review for the *New York Times* (January 26, 1947). Green and Melnick, in the Gouldner volume cited above, gently mocked Farnham for her comically strenuous advocacy of full-time domesticity (p. 283); her influence seemed already to be waning in 1951, when they wrote. By that year, Farnham had shifted to writing about adolescents—the clinical population she was trained to treat—and toned down her invective against women. See "Talk with Dr. Farnham," *New York Times,* September 30, 1951. See also Meyerowitz, "Beyond the Feminine Mystique," p. 1476.

27. Selma Robinson, "103 Women Sound Off," *McCall's* (1959), reprinted in *Women's Magazines 1940–1960: Gender Roles and the Popular Press,* ed. Nancy A. Walker (Boston, 1998), pp. 186–87. Farnham herself, in reprising "The Lost Sex" in a 1952 collection of essays about women, turned to more anodyne prescriptions that women should learn home economics and become active in

their children's schools, maybe even go back to college and take a part-time job. "The Lost Sex," in *Women, Society, and Sex*, ed. Johnson E. Fairchild (New York, 1952), pp. 33–52.

28. Steinbeck quoted in Meyerowitz, "Beyond the Feminine Mystique," p. 1469.

29. See, for instance, the intriguing comment on "Should Women Vote?" in the "Letters" column, *Ladies' Home Journal*, February 1958, p. 6. On the LWV, see Susan Ware, "American Women in the 1950s: Nonpartisan Politics and Women's Politicization," in *Women, Politics and Change*, ed. Tilly and Gurin, pp. 281–99.

30. For the roots of small politics in the 1940s, see Hartmann, *The Home Front and Beyond*, pp. 149–57. A political scientist looking at the parties in a 1947 survey found that women party workers had "virtually preempted the bottom of the political ladder" as election clerks, assistant precinct captains, and poll workers, although most complained that they had no influence on party matters and no patronage to dole out. Melnick and Green's comments on the 1947 study, in "What Has Happened to the Feminist Movement?," p. 281. The study is Marguerite J. Fisher, "Women in the Political Parties," *Annals of the American Academy of Political and Social Science* 251 (May 1947), pp. 87–93, and an article by Florence Allen in the same volume, "Participation of Women in Government," pp. 94–103. See also Jo Freeman, *A Room at a Time: How Women Entered Party Politics* (Lanham, Md., 2002), chapters 1 and 9 and passim; Catherine E. Rymph, *Republican Women: Feminism and Conservatism from Suffrage Through the Rise of the New Right* (Chapel Hill, N.C., 2006), chapters 4–6.

31. Donald T. Critchlow, *Phyllis Schlafly and Grassroots Conservatism: A Woman's Crusade* (Princeton, N.J., 2005), pp. 48–61.

32. Cobble gives capsule biographies of the principals in *The Other Women's Movement*, chapter 1.

33. Ibid., chapter 6.

34. Baker, quoted in Giddings, *When and Where I Enter*, p. 259.

35. Jo Ann Gibson Robinson, *The Montgomery Bus Boycott and the Women Who Started It* (Knoxville, Tenn., 1987).

36. On maternity provisions see Cobble, *The Other Women's Movement*, pp. 127–30.

37. Lucy Freeman, "The Distaff Side," review of *Women, Society, and Sex*, ed. Fairchild, *New York Times*, July 27, 1952.

38. "Introduction by Mrs. Peter Marshall," *Life*, December 24, 1956, pp. 2–3.

39. De Beauvoir, *The Second Sex* (1952; New York, 1989), p. xix.

40. Anson Rabinbach, *In the Shadow of Catastrophe: German Intellectuals Between the Wars* (Berkeley, Calif., 1997), p. 206.

41. Philip Roth, "'I Got a Scheme!' The Words of Saul Bellow," *New Yorker*, April 25, 2005, p. 72. See also Paula Fox, *The Coldest Winter: A Stringer in Wartime Europe* (New York, 2006).

42. Beauvoir, *The Second Sex*, p. xxii.

43. Ibid., p. 267.

44. Ibid., p. 451.

45. Ibid., p. 619.

46. Ibid., p. 615.

47. Smith, "The Devil's Doorway," *The Spectator* (London), November 20, 1953, pp. 602–3.

48. Elizabeth Hardwick, "The Subjection of Women," *Partisan Review* 20 (1953), pp. 321–31; see also *Atlantic Monthly* 191 (April 1953); Clyde Kluckhohn, "The Female of Our Species," *New York Times Book Review*, February 22, 1953, p. 3; see the advertisement in the *New York Times Book Review*, March 1, 1953, p. 14; bestseller lists in issues of March 15, April 5, 1953. Beauvoir's name was used in the crossword puzzle in the *New York Times Sunday Magazine*, September 5, 1954; and in a jingle, *New York Times*, December 23, 1954. See also William Phillips, "A French Lady on the Dark Continent," *Commentary* 16 (July 1953), pp. 25–29. The continuing controversy over Howard Parshley's English translation is described in Sarah Glazer, "Lost in Translation," *New York Times Book Review*, August 22, 2004, pp. 13–14.

49. Judith G. Coffin, "Historicizing the Second Sex," *French Politics, Culture & Society* 25 (Winter 2007), pp. 123–48.

50. Trade unionists, social feminists, and civil rights activists—the entire spectrum of American reformers—saw the NWP as something close to a collection of monomaniacs, "little old ladies in tennis shoes," in Pauli Murray's words. Pauli Murray transcript, Leila Rupp–Verta Taylor interviews, p. 9, Schlesinger Library.

51. Cobble, *The Other Women's Movement*, p. 184.

52. Peterson, "The Kennedy Commission," in *Women in Washington: Advocates for Public Policy*, ed. Irene Tinker (Beverly Hills, Calif., 1983), p. 29. She added that the 1950s courts were hostile to any labor legislation, so labor leaders

and women's advocates believed it was important to keep in place what standards already existed.

53. Rupp and Taylor, *Survival in the Doldrums*, p. 62. On McCarthyism, red-baiting, anti-Semitism, and calculated racism, see chapter 7; Kerber, *No Constitutional Right*, p. 139.

54. Peterson sums up the case against the NWP in "The Kennedy Commission," in *Women in Washington,* ed. Tinker, pp. 21–34.

55. Peterson, in Jo Freeman, "How 'Sex' Got into Title VII: Persistent Opportunism as a Maker of Public Policy," adapted from *Law and Inequality: A Journal of Theory and Practice* 9 (March 1991), p. 4, available at www.jofreeman .com/lawandpolicy/titlevii.htm.

56. Peterson, "The Kennedy Commission," in *Women in Washington,* ed. Tinker, p. 21.

57. See Alice Kessler-Harris's careful account of the commission in *In Pursuit of Equity: Women, Men, and the Quest for Economic Citizenship in 20th-Century America* (New York, 2001), pp. 213–26.

58. Hartmann, *American Women in the 1940s,* pp. 154–55.

59. Cobble, *The Other Women's Movement,* pp. 54–55, 171.

60. Murray Transcript, Rupp-Taylor Interviews, p. 20. Murray was one of three African-American women to serve on the PCSW. The others were Dorothy Height, an appointed member of the commission, and Addie Wyatt, in one of the working groups.

61. Ibid., p. 18. Murray's extensive early history as a political activist is detailed in Glenda Elizabeth Gilmore, *Defying Dixie: The Radical Roots of Civil Rights* (New York, 2007), pp. 250–55 and passim.

62. Murray transcript, Rupp-Taylor interviews, p. 20.

63. Stanton, *Eighty Years and More,* p. 148.

64. The photo is reproduced in Cobble, *The Other Women's Movement,* p. 169.

65. *American Women: Report of the President's Commission on the Status of Women 1963* (Washington, D.C., 1963).

66. Winifred D. Wandersee, *On the Move: American Women in the 1970s* (New York, 1988), p. 17; Cobble, *The Other Women's Movement,* p. 169. The interest in continuing education is evidence of the presence of Mary Bunting, who,

when she was president of Douglass College at Rutgers, instituted continuing education there.

67. Serena Mayeri, "Constitutional Choices: Legal Feminism and the Historical Dynamics of Change," *California Law Review* 92 (May 2004), p. 768; *American Women*, p. 30. Cobble, *The Other Women's Movement*, pp. 170–71, summarizes the recommendations. For a critical analysis of the commission, see Kessler-Harris, *In Pursuit of Equity*, pp. 213–34.

68. *American Women*, pp. 42, 47.

69. Ibid., p. 2.

70. Ibid., p. 19.

71. See the union leader Kitty [Katherine] Ellickson on this point, quoted in Cobble, *The Other Women's Movement*, p. 160.

72. Ibid.; *American Women*, p. 22.

73. Kessler-Harris provides an account of the behind-the-scenes discussions, based on detailed archival research. *In Pursuit of Equity*, p. 213–38; Neuberger and Cohen, in ibid., p. 218.

74. Peterson, "The Kennedy Commission," *Women in Washington*, ed. Tinker, p. 29.

75. Ruth Rosen, *The World Split Open: How the Women's Movement Changed America* (New York, 2000), p. 67.

76. Eddy, "On Being Female," *New York Times*, August 1, 1965.

77. Friedan, *The Feminine Mystique* (New York, 1963), p. 364.

78. Daniel Horowitz, *Betty Friedan and the Making of "The Feminine Mystique": The American Left, the Cold War, and Modern Feminism* (Amherst, Mass., 1998).

79. Friedan, *Feminine Mystique*, pp. 252, 256.

80. Kenon Breazeale sees Friedan drawing on the popular magazine *Esquire*'s mockery of the pill-popping housewife. "In Spite of Women: 'Esquire' Magazine and the Construction of the Male Consumer," *Signs* 20 (Autumn 1994), pp. 1–22.

81. Friedan, *Feminine Mystique*, pp. 349–50.

82. Ibid., p. 382. This is the "Epilogue," added in a later edition.

83. Donald Allen Robinson, "Two Movements in Pursuit of Equal Employment Opportunity," *Signs* 4 (Spring 1979), pp. 414–16; Flora Davis, *Moving the Mountain: The Women's Movement in America Since 1960* (New York, 1991), p. 44.

84. *House Congressional Record* 110, February 8, 1964, p. 2577.

85. Ibid., pp. 2578–80; Carl M. Brauer, "Women Activists, Southern Conservatives, and the Prohibition of Sex Discrimination in Title VII of the 1964 Civil Rights Act," *Journal of Southern History* 49 (February 1983), pp. 37–56; Freeman, "How 'Sex' Got into Title VII," pp. 163–84; Rupp and Taylor, *Survival in the Doldrums,* p. 160.

86. Robinson, "Two Movements in Pursuit of Equal Employment Opportunity."

87. Mayeri, "Constitutional Choices," p. 775; Heller, in ibid., p. 773.

88. Nancy MacLean, *Freedom Is Not Enough: The Opening of the American Workplace* (Cambridge, Mass., 2006), pp. 123, 125, 127; Davis, *Moving the Mountain,* pp. 22–23. Confronted with complaints from the airline stewardesses (given the same job as stewards, but with a different title and at lower pay, and fired when they married or turned thirty-two), one commissioner stated that he was certain Congress never intended the EEOC to abolish distinctions between the sexes.
   On Hernandez see Marjie Driscoll, "Another Minority Group—Women," *Los Angeles Times,* April 18, 1969; "In a Fair First: Old Stereotypes Are Her Target," *Washington Post,* May 25, 1965, p. D1; Maggie Savoy, "NOW Lib Group Leader Too Busy to Be Angry," *Los Angeles Times,* June 3, 1970, p. E1.

89. "De-Sexing the Job Market," *New York Times,* August 21, 1965, p. 20.

90. "Letters to the Editor," ibid., September 3, 1965.

91. "Mockery of Law Seen," *Christian Science Monitor,* June 25, 1966, p. 5.

92. Davis, *Moving the Mountain,* pp. 45–47.

93. Richard K. Berg, deputy counsel to EEOC, quoted in John Herbers, "For Instance, Can She Pitch for the Mets?," *New York Times,* August 20, 1965, p. 1.

94. "A Pillow, Please, Miss . . . Er, Mister: Unions Say Men Should Be Cabin Attendants on Planes," *New York Times,* May 29, 1966, p. S20.

95. "Pandora's Box," *Chicago Tribune,* July 8, 1965.

96. "Protest Proposed on Women's Jobs," *New York Times,* October 13, 1965.

97. Judith Paterson, *Be Somebody: A Biography of Marguerite Rawalt* (Austin, Texas, 1986), p. 123.

98. Davis, *Moving the Mountain*, p. 57.

99. http://clerk.house.gov/art_history/house_history/partyDiv.html; www .senate.gov/pagelayout/history/one_item_and_teasers/partydiv.htm.

100. Cobble, *The Other Women's Movement*, pp. 184–85; Murray and Eastwood, "Jane Crow and the Law: Sex Discrimination and Title VII," *George Washington Law Review* 34 (December 1965), pp. 232–56.

101. Kay Clarenbach Oral History, Midwestern Origins of the Women's Movement Project, Typescript, Schlesinger Library; NOW list of charter members, September 1966, NOW Papers, ibid., Box 1, Folder 29. Pauli Murray describes Dorothy Haener's provision of UAW support in a letter to Clarenbach, November 21, 1967, Murray Papers.

102. Clarenbach Oral History, Midwestern Origins of the Women's Movement, p. 274.

103. Ibid., p. 278.

104. Charter of the National Organization for Women, http://feminist.org/ research/chronicles/early1.html.

105. List of charter members, NOW Papers.

106. Davis, *Moving the Mountain*, p. 57.

107. Ibid., p. 63; *Pittsburgh Press Company v. Pittsburgh Commission on Human Relations*, 413 U.S. 376 (1973).

CHAPTER EIGHT: THE REVOLT OF THE DAUGHTERS

1. Ellen Maslow, "I Dreamed I Took Myself Seriously," *Up from Under* 1 (May–June 1970), p. 22.

2. Barbara Ransby, *Ella Baker and the Black Freedom Movement: A Radical Democratic Vision* (Chapel Hill, N.C., 2003), p. 297; see also p. 367 for Baker's protofeminism. See also Anne Standley, "The Role of Black Women in the Civil Rights Movement," in *Women in the Civil Rights Movement: Trailblazers & Torchbearers 1941–1965,* ed. Vicki L. Crawford, Jacqueline Anne Rouse, and Barbara Wood (Bloomington, Ind., 1993), pp. 183–202. The prevalence of local women also contributed to a sense of women's importance. Fannie Lou Hamer is the best-known grassroots organizer, but there were others from the rural South who came to the fore. Chana Kai Lee notes that Hamer "did not

regard herself as a feminist, not by anybody's definition." Yet "she was a 'non-feminist' whose life and powerful presence had undeniably feminist conse-quences. In this sense, she was like many other black women of her generation and of other historical periods and places." *For Freedom's Sake: The Life of Fannie Lou Hamer* (Urbana, Ill., 1999), p. 172.

3. The writers were Mary King and Casey Hayden, respected white members of SNCC. There is speculation that African-American women were also involved, but that King and Hayden were the only writers willing (eventu-ally) to come forth. See "SNCC Position Paper," reprinted in Mary King, *Freedom Song: A Personal Story of the 1960s Civil Rights Movement* (New York, 1987), pp. 567–69. King's account of the episode is ibid., chapter 12.

4. Winifred Breines, *The Trouble Between Us: An Uneasy History of White and Black Women in the Feminist Movement* (Boston, 2006), pp. 23–40; King, *Freedom Song;* Sara Evans, *Personal Politics: The Roots of Women's Liberation in the Civil Rights Movement and the New Left* (New York, 1979), pp. 85–87; Lynne Olson, *Freedom's Daughters: The Unsung Heroines of the Civil Rights Movement from 1830 to 1970* (New York, 2001), pp. 332–36.

5. Exhibit on 1965–66 voter registration drive, Claiborne County, Mississippi, courthouse, August 2007.

6. Wini Breines relates the furious retrospective debates among former SNCC workers when Sara Evans's account of SNCC appeared in *Personal Politics. The Trouble Between Us,* chapter 1; Washington, in Alice Echols, *Daring to Be Bad: Radical Feminism in America 1967–1975* (Minneapolis, 1989), p. 32; Olson, *Freedom's Daughters,* p. 309. See *Freedom's Daughters,* p. 309, and Echols, *Daring to Be Bad,* pp. 29–34, for nuanced accounts of the tensions. Many par-ticipants, including King and Hayden themselves, insisted that Evans over-stated the women's criticisms.

7. Unidentified staffer, in Olson, *Freedom's Daughters,* p. 309.

8. "A Kind of Memo from Casey Hayden and Mary King to a Number of Women in Other Freedom Movements," reprinted in King, *Freedom Song,* pp. 571–74. It reached women in Students for a Democratic Society (SDS) right before the big SDS "rethinking" conference at the University of Illinois in December 1965: Todd Gitlin, personal communication. *Liberation,* a leading New Left magazine at the time, reprinted the memo in April 1966.

9. Rosalyn Baxandall traces one thread of African-American activity in "Re-Visioning the Women's Liberation Movement's Narrative: Early Second Wave African American Feminists," *Feminist Studies* 27 (Spring 2001), pp. 225–45.

10. Years later, a few black women voiced second thoughts. See Cynthia Washington and Faye Bellamy, in Olson, *Freedom's Daughters,* pp. 335–36.

11. McEldowney, in Rosen, *World Split Open,* p. 119; more of the passage is in Gitlin, *The Sixties: Years of Hope, Days of Rage* (New York, 1987; 1993), p. 368.

12. SDS Women, "To the Women of the Left" (1967), in *Dear Sisters: Dispatches from the Women's Liberation Movement,* ed. Rosalyn Baxandall and Linda Gordon (New York, 2000), p. 28.

13. There are so many stories that the event is legendary. For a good first-person account, see Carol Hanisch, "Two Letters from the Women's Liberation Movement," in *The Feminist Memoir Project: Voices from Women's Liberation,* ed. Rachel Blau DuPlessis and Ann Snitow (New York, 1998), pp. 197–202.

14. Including Boston and Washington, D.C.; Chicago and Minneapolis; San Francisco and Seattle.

15. Snitow, in Rosen, *World Split Open,* pp. 200–201.

16. Karla Jay's memory of a statement that began a meeting with Redstockings. Jay, *Tales of the Lavender Menace: A Memoir of Liberation* (New York, 1999), p. 53. The phrasing replicates a point in the Redstockings Manifesto, reprinted in *Sisterhood Is Powerful: An Anthology of Writings from the Women's Liberation Movement,* ed. Robin Morgan (New York, 1970), p. 533.

17. Boxer, "Rethinking the Socialist Construction and International Career of the Concept 'Bourgeois Feminism,'" pp. 131–58; Meredith Tax, "Woman and Her Mind: The Story of Everyday Life," pamphlet in Nancy Grey Osterud Collection, Schlesinger Library; New York Radical Women, "Principles," in *Sisterhood Is Powerful,* ed. Morgan, p. 520; Amy Kesselman, with Heather Booth, Vivian Rothstein, and Naomi Weisstein, "Our Gang of Four: Friendship and Women's Liberation," in *The Feminist Memoir Project,* ed. DuPlessis and Snitow, p. 44.

18. The one available book on the history of feminism was Eleanor Flexner's *Century of Struggle* (1959). Everywhere that one finds accounts of the history of women's rights in these years, there are traces of the Flexner volume. Ruth Bader Ginsburg, for example, called upon it in her summary of the history of women's rights in her brief for *Frontiero v. Richardson* (1973), the groundbreaking Supreme Court case on sex discrimination.

19. Quoted in Echols, *Daring to Be Bad,* p. 120.

20. Willis, in ibid.

21. Gitlin, *The Sixties,* p. 3.

22. Guillermoprieto, *Dancing with Cuba: A Memoir of the Revolution* (New York, 2005), p. 38; Ware, *Woman Power: The Movement for Women's Liberation* (New York, 1970), p. 140.

23. Marilyn Bender, "Women's Lib Headquarters," *New York Times,* July 1, 1970.

24. Kathy Davis, *The Making of "Our Bodies, Ourselves": How Feminism Travels Across Borders* (Durham, N.C., 2007), pp. 20–23.

25. Davidson, "An 'Oppressed Majority' Demands Its Rights," *Life,* December 12, 1970, pp. 66–78.

26. For example, "The analogy is racism, where the white racist compensates his feeling of unworthiness by creating an image of the black man . . . which is inferior to him." See Anne Koedt, "Myth of the Vaginal Orgasm," pamphlet, Schlesinger Library. There are several versions of the Koedt essay.

27. *No More Fun and Games,* no. 3 (November 1969), p. 60.

28. Belkin, "Scarlett O'Hara and Me," *Up from Under* 1 (January–February 1971), p. 18; Doris Conklin, "Investigating Nancy Drew," ibid., pp. 22–23.

29. Arthur Marwick, *The Sixties: Cultural Revolution in Britain, France, Italy, and the United States, c. 1958–c.1974* (New York, 1998), chapter 13. In Germany, where radical feminism emerged a few years later, the pitch of anger was closer to the Americans', driven by fervent need to repudiate the sins of the fathers in fascism. See Dagmar Herzog, *Sex After Fascism: Memory and Morality in Twentieth-Century Germany* (Princeton, N.J., 2005), chapter 4.

30. Densmore, "A Year of Living Dangerously: 1968," in *Feminist Memoir Project,* ed. DuPlessis and Snitow, p. 72.

31. O'Reilly, "The Housewife's Moment of Truth," *New York,* December 20, 1971; the article was reprinted in the spring 1972 issue of *Ms.* See Amy Erdman Farrell, *Yours in Sisterhood: Ms. Magazine and the Promise of Popular Feminism* (Chapel Hill, N.C., 1998), pp. 161–62, 222.

32. Judith Hole and Ellen Levine, writing at the time, allude to the obvious fact of women radicals' indifference to formal politics. See Hole and Levine, *Rebirth of Feminism* (New York, 1971), pp. 91–92.

33. Susan Brownmiller, " 'Sisterhood Is Powerful': A Member of the Women's Liberation Movement Explains What It's All About," *New York Times Magazine,* March 15, 1970, p. 129.

34. This is another oft-recounted event. Densmore gives her account from the Cell 16 end in "Year of Living Dangerously," in *Feminist Memoir Project,* ed. DuPlessis and Snitow, p. 85.

35. Jane Kramer, "Founding Cadre," *New Yorker,* November 28, 1970, p. 54; Tax, in Rosen, *World Split Open,* p. 84; Murray to Aileen Hernandez,

September 18, 1969, Folder 1895, Box 105, Murray Papers; to Al Reitman, November 24, 1971, Box 2, Folder 30, Murray Papers.

36. Dell'Olio, "Home Before Sundown," in *Feminist Memoir Project,* ed. DuPlessis and Snitow, p. 157.

37. At *Newsweek* in 1970, when female employees filed a grievance with the EEOC, 34 of the 35 researchers were female and 1 of 52 reporters was a woman. See Davis, *Moving the Mountain,* pp. 110–11; Friedan, *Feminine Mystique,* p. 185.

38. See Nan Robertson, *The Girls in the Balcony: Women, Men, and The New York Times* (New York, 1992), for an overview of the situation of women. There was a high-profile exception to the rule in broadcasting—Barbara Walters, whom NBC promoted in 1965 to a leading spot on the *Today* show. Walters's ascendancy prompted Gloria Steinem, then a journalist, to take notice, and concoct a list of how-tos about how to replicate "the patterns of the few who have made it." See Steinem, "Nylons in the Newsroom," *New York Times,* November 7, 1965.

39. Wade interview, Washington Press Club Foundation, Women in Journalism Oral History Project, Schlesinger Library, p. 133.

40. Ibid., p. 68.

41. Phone interview with Lindsay Van Gelder, April 8, 2005.

42. Wade interview, Women in Journalism Oral History Project, p. 142. For a description of how these charges could fly at even a distinguished veteran, see Eileen Shanahan interview 9, ibid., p. 177.

43. Sophy Burnham, "Women's Lib: The Idea You Can't Ignore," *Redbook,* September 1970, p. 191. A famous reversal occurred in 1970 at *Newsweek,* where a feature writer—one of the few women on staff—wrote an article on feminism the editors rejected as biased. They then brought in from the outside a writer with no experience covering politics—but married to an editor—to rewrite it. She, too, confounded the editors by producing an approving piece, capped with an announcement that she was now a feminist. See Helen Dudar, "Women's Lib: The War on 'Sexism,' " *Newsweek,* March 23, 1970. Flora Davis recounts the episode in *Moving the Mountain,* pp. 110–11.

44. Jill Johnston, in Susan Brownmiller, *In Our Time: Memoir of a Revolution* (New York, 1999), p. 179; Anselma Dell'Olio, "Home Before Sundown," in *Feminist Memoir Project,* ed. DuPlessis and Snitow, p. 158; Jay, *Tales of the Lavender Menace,* pp. 133–35; Brownmiller, *In Our Time,* p. 45.

45. Brownmiller, " 'Sisterhood Is Powerful,' " p. 27 and passim; Alix Kates Shulman, "A Marriage Disagreement, or Marriage by Other Means," pp. 285–86,

and Dell'Olio, "Home Before Sundown," p. 160, in *Feminist Memoir Project*, ed. DuPlessis and Snitow, on the media attention in New York. I myself, an ingenue from Ohio, was interviewed by the *CBS Evening News* when I came to Princeton University in fall 1969 as one of the first "coeds" on that historically all-male campus. The next year, with nothing remarkable in hand except admission to Princeton, I was invited to chat about feminism on a New York talk show, along with the brilliant New York feminist Catharine Stimpson, then a Barnard professor, and Celestine Ware, the author that year of a pathbreaking book on black women and feminism.

46. Post and Siegel, "Legislative Constitutionalism and Section Five Power," p. 1998.

47. *Time,* September 7, 1970, pp. 16–23; *New Yorker,* September 5, 1970; *Life,* September 4, 1970; Judy Klemesrud, "Coming Wednesday: A Herstory-Making Event," *New York Times Magazine,* August 23, 1970. Klemesrud tried in a half-humorous way to quell the rumors: "Although some of the feminists have vowed to withhold sex from their men on Wednesday, most regard abstention as an unimportant part of the day's activities." Klemesrud died in 1985 at the age of forty-six. At her funeral, Friedan said, "We were hers and she was ours." Friedan, *Life So Far: A Memoir* (New York, 2000), p. 241.

48. On Brown, see Brownmiller, *In Our Time,* p. 71. Karla Jay describes Brown as the Jay Gatsby of the movement, a personality ever transforming her biography and origins. Jay, *Tales of the Lavender Menace,* pp. 47–48. Brownmiller has her born in rural Pennsylvania, but in 2006 Rita Mae Brown alluded to patrician origins on her website, mentioning the foxhunting country of Virginia. On Kennedy, see Flo Kennedy, *Color Me Flo: My Hard Life and Good Times* (New York, 1976).

Diane Gerrity provides a view of Cell 16's martial arts training in "Miss Superfist," *Atlantic Monthly* 225 (March 1970), pp. 91–93. For sheer sensation, however, no one topped Valerie Solanas, author of the SCUM Manifesto, a former prostitute and borderline personality turned performance artist who was a hanger-on in the avant-garde circle around Andy Warhol and followed up on the SCUM Manifesto's agenda ("SCUM will kill all men who are not in the Men's Auxiliary of SCUM") by shooting Warhol and a male associate in a showdown intended to eliminate several of the avant-garde men who had badly used her. It was a crime committed by a disturbed woman against misogynist men, and in its melodrama it was a deeply New York episode, but for a time Solanas was a feminist heroine, and important figures like Flo Kennedy rose to her defense.

49. "Woman's Place," *Atlantic Monthly* 225 (March 1970), pp. 18–126; Bowen, ". . . We've Never Asked a Woman Before," ibid.; for the middle-of-the-road positions see Elizabeth Janeway, "Happiness and the Right to Choose," pp. 118–19; Anne Bernays, "What Are You Supposed to Do if You Like Children?," pp. 107–9.

50. "Women on the March," *Time,* September 7, 1970.

51. Marlene Sanders Collection, Folder 5194, Schlesinger Library.

52. Shanahan Interview 6, Women in Journalism Oral History Project, p. 108. Top editors of both sexes at *Harper's,* a monthly journal of opinion, walked out in protest over the exclusion of women from an important meeting. See *New York Times,* June 4, 1970, p. 47; *Newsweek* action described in Davis, *Moving the Mountain,* pp. 110–11. For a summary of the important media protests in 1970 see Hole and Levine, *Rebirth of Feminism,* pp. 252–70.

53. *Ladies' Home Journal* Writers' Collective, "Inside *Ladies' Home Journal,*" newsreel at Schlesinger Library. See Jay's recollections of the event in *Lavender Menace,* pp. 113–20; Brownmiller, *In Our Time,* pp. 84–92. What stands out for Jay and Brownmiller is the moment Shulamith Firestone jumped on Carter's desk. Whether this was before or after the newsreel was shot is unclear. See also Echols, *Daring to Be Bad,* pp. 195–96.

54. Rosen, *World Split Open,* p. 212; Echols, *Daring to Be Bad,* p. 83.

55. "Redstockings Manifesto," reprinted in *Sisterhood Is Powerful,* ed. Morgan, p. 535.

56. Brownmiller, " 'Sisterhood Is Powerful,' " p. 230; Brownmiller, *In Our Time,* p. 5; Jay, *Tales of the Lavender Menace,* p. 51. Jay's account avoids the idealizations of most remembrances and combines sympathy with an acute awareness of the groups' callowness and clumsiness with many of the difficult confessions that participants made and the mental health issues they raised.

57. Jay, *Tales of the Lavender Menace,* p. 53. Jay had the good fortune to join a group overseen by the novelist Alix Kates Shulman, then a prominent member of New York Redstockings, whose curiosity and kindness helped the women open up to one another. See also Nora Ephron's funny essay on her New York group in *Crazy Salad* (New York, 1975), pp. 69–75.

58. Lauren Berlant chronicles and analyzes the expression of this age-old practice in depoliticized form in the early twenty-first century in *The Female Complaint: The Unfinished Business of Sentimentality in American Culture* (Durham, N.C., 2008).

59. Letters to the Editor, *Off Our Backs,* October 25, 1970.

60. Cronan, "Marriage," *Notes from the Third Year* (New York, 1971), p. 65; interviewee, in Brownmiller, " 'Sisterhood Is Powerful,' " p. 136.

61. Maslow, "I Dreamed I Took Myself Seriously," p. 22; Judy Syfers, "Why I Want a Wife," *Notes from the Third Year,* p. 13, reprinted in *Ms.* (December 1971); "Putting Hubby Through," *Off Our Backs,* November 1972; *No More Fun and Games* 4, p. 34. For a fascinating reconsideration of the essay from a lesbian

whose spouse is a stay-at-home partner, see Sara Sarasohn, "Once Political, Now Just Practical," *New York Times,* August 30, 2009, Style section, p. 8.

62. Friday Night Study Group Excerpts, April 3, 1970, *No More Fun and Games* 4, April 1970, p. 109; Kempton, "Cutting Loose," *Esquire,* July 1970, p. 57; Shulamith Firestone, "Women Rap About Sex," *Notes from the First Year,* ed. New York Radical Women (New York, 1968), pp. 8–10.

63. Redstockings Manifesto, *Sisterhood Is Powerful,* ed. Morgan, p. 534.

64. The exception was Virginia Woolf, who wrote movingly about charwomen sinking their souls into their own kitchens in *A Room of One's Own* (1929). Alison Light points out that the domestic servant was the New Woman's invisible twin in the 1910s and examines Woolf's ambivalence. See *Mrs. Woolf and the Servants: An Intimate History of Domestic Life in Bloomsbury* (New York, 2008).

65. Friedan, *Feminine Mystique,* pp. 342, 348.

66. Redstockings [Patricia Mainardi], "The Politics of Housework," in *Liberation Now! Writings from the Women's Liberation Movement,* ed. Deborah Babcox and Madeline Belkin (New York, 1971), pp. 110–13.

67. Maslow, "I Dreamed I Took Myself Seriously," p. 22; Shulman, "A Marriage Agreement," *Up from Under* 1 (August/September 1970), pp. 5–8.

68. "The Marriage Experiment," *Life,* April 28, 1972; Susan Edmiston, "How to Write Your Own Marriage Contract," *New York,* December 20, 1971; *Ms.,* Spring 1972. See Shulman, "A Marriage Disagreement, or Marriage by Other Means," in *Feminist Memoir Project,* ed. DuPlessis and Snitow, pp. 284–303; she sums up the publication history on p. 294; "A Challenge to Every Marriage," *Redbook,* September 1972, pp. 89 ff. Shulman identified the extremes as "Hallelujah!" on the one one hand; "revolting" and "against God and Nature" on the other. Most letters came from thoughtful readers who "seemed to be testing it against the circumstances of their own lives to see whether it [the Agreement] might make any sense for them." Whether or not they thought it was a good idea, most—far more than Shulman expected—thought equality was necessary between spouses. The public response reiterated the companionate ideal; the question was how to achieve it.

69. Marie Robinson, *The Power of Sexual Surrender* (1959), in *Off Our Backs,* March 1972, p. 9.

70. Koedt, "The Myth of the Vaginal Orgasm," reprinted in *Radical Feminism,* ed. Koedt, Ellen Levine, and Anita Rapone (New York, 1973), pp. 198–207. See also Susan Lydon, "The Politics of Orgasm," reprinted from *Ramparts* as a mimeographed pamplet c. 1971, Schlesinger Library, and in *Sisterhood Is Powerful,* ed. Morgan, pp. 197–205. Judy Davis's bleak first-person account

from 1972, reprinted in *Dear Reader*, ed. Baxandall and Gordon, pp. 155–57, describes the act of faking an orgasm.

71. Friedan, *Life So Far*, pp. 223, 249.

72. Susan Brownmiller mentioned that "Have you ever lied about an orgasm?" became a popular question in consciousness-raising groups. " 'Sisterhood Is Powerful,' " p. 134.

73. The haircutting incident is reported in many places. See Brownmiller, *In Our Time*, p. 63; see also Friedan, *Life So Far*, p. 220.

74. *Ladies' Home Journal* Collective, Newsreel. The pernicious influence of women's magazines was a common topic in the feminist press, stemming from their omnipresence in middle-class homes as well as Friedan's emphasis on their role in upholding the Feminine Mystique. For a typical women's liberation critique, see "Women's Magazines and Womanhood, 1969," *No More Fun and Games* 3 (November 1969), pp. 30–31; no. 4 (April 1970), pp. 34–42.

75. Wollstonecraft, *Vindication*, p. 44; Sarah Grimké, *Letters on the Equality of the Sexes*, p. 56.

76. Weisstein, in Kesselman, "Our Gang of Four," in *Feminist Memoir Project*, ed. DuPlessis and Snitow, p. 40.

77. Friedan, *It Changed My Life*, pp. 138, 249–50; "Leading Feminist Puts Hairdo Before Strike," *New York Times*, August 27, 1970, p. 30.

78. See, for instance, Lucy Komisar, *The New Feminism* (New York, 1972), p. 21, a major summary of liberal feminism that stresses how oppressive sex roles can be for men and discusses the "sensitivity" of teenage boys. "Optimistic and consensual" is Linda Kerber's description of Pauli Murray's writing in the early and mid-1960s. *No Constitutional Right*, p. 193.

79. In Kramer, "Founding Cadre," p. 85; a description of rapists in a special "Rape!" section, *Off Our Backs* (March 1972), pp. 8–9.

80. Cobble, *The Other Women's Movement*, pp. 172–73. The *Oxford English Dictionary* attributes the first use of "sexism" to Caroline Bird, in a speech she gave before the Episcopal Church Executive Council in Greenwich, Connecticut, on September 25, 1968. The first Library of Congress entry using the word in its title, a U.S. Senate study on women's employment in Congress called *Sexism on Capitol Hill*, appeared two years later. A LOC search reveals that between 1973 and 1983 there were roughly three to four books published each year whose titles contained the word; the first book to be placed under the subject heading "sexism" in the LOC catalog was Vivian Gornick's *Women in Sexist Society* (1971).

81. On marriage and heterosexual relations, Ellen Willis commented to Alice Echols that "there was this rebellion and resentment against the lives that in many ways we were, in fact, living." In Echols, *Daring to Be Bad*, p. 146. In the 1970s, the dogma that men were enemies reached its reductio ad absurdum on the fringe, when organizers of a feminist countercultural music festival debated whether to ban boy children (including babies and toddlers) and ended up confining them and their mothers at night to a campsite fourteen miles away from the festival grounds. See Sara Evans, *Tidal Wave: How Women Changed America at Century's End* (New York, 2003), p. 153.

82. *No More Fun and Games* 6 (May 1973), p. 140. See Alice Wolfson's comments on this tendency in "Clenched Fist, Open Heart," in *Feminist Memoir Project*, ed. DuPlessis and Snitow, pp. 277, 281.

83. Rita Mae Brown, "Living with Other Women," *Radical Therapist* (1971), quoted in Evans, *Tidal Wave*, p. 103.

84. See Brown's bemused reminiscences of NOW's homophobia in *Rita Will*, p. 228. The fullest account is in Davis, *Moving the Mountain*, pp. 264–67. Susan Brownmiller thought NOW's fear of lesbians was overblown, although she showed her own disparaging attitudes in disputing it: "A lavender herring, perhaps, but surely no clear and present danger." See Brownmiller, "'Sisterhood Is Powerful.'"

85. Paul Berman, *A Tale of Two Utopias: The Political Journey of the Generation of 1968* (New York, 1996), p. 165; Echols analyzes the implications of the shift in *Daring to Be Bad*, pp. 214–18; Radicalesbians, "The Woman-Identified Woman," in *Liberation Now!*, ed. Babcox and Belkin, pp. 287–93.

86. Koedt, "Myth of the Vaginal Orgasm," mimeographed pamphlet in my possession. Interestingly, this wording was toned down in the published versions, with "extinction of the male organ" removed. See "The Woman-Identified Woman," in *Liberation Now!*, ed. Babcox and Belkin, pp. 287–92; "The Soul Selects: A Separate Way," *Off Our Backs* (January 1972), p. 7.

87. Jay, *Tales of the Lavender Menace*, p. 141. "Political lesbians," one angry group of "real lesbians" charged, were uninterested in actually having sex. "Anonymous Realesbians, Politicalesbians and the Women's Liberation Movement," in *Dear Sisters*, pp. 109–10.

88. Judith Ezekiel, *Feminism in the Heartland* (Columbus, Ohio, 2002), p. 53; Jay, *Tales of the Lavender Menace*, pp. 141–42.

89. Nestle, "A Fem's Feminist History," in *Feminist Memoir Project*, ed. DuPlessis and Snitow, p. 340; "Butch-Femme Relationships: Sexual Courage in the 1950s," *A Restricted Country* (1987; New York, 2003), pp. 95–99.

90. Miller, "Public Statements, Private Lives: Academic Memoirs of the Nineties," *Signs* 22 (Winter 1997), p. 999.

91. Willis, in M. Rivka Polatnick, "Diversity in Women's Liberation Ideology: How a Black and a White Group of the 1960s Viewed Motherhood," *Signs* 21 (Spring 1996), p. 691; Segal, *Making Trouble: Life and Politics* (London, 2007).

92. Firestone, *The Dialectic of Sex: The Case for Feminist Revolution* (New York, 1970), chapter 4, pp. 226–29; "Day Care Centers," *No More Fun and Games* 3, p. 105; Polatnick, "Women's Liberation Ideology," p. 692; Vicki Cohn Pollard, "The Five of Us (With a Little Help from Our Friends)," in *Dear Sisters*, ed. Baxandall and Gordon, pp. 222–24. See also Dana Densmore's candid comments on the antimother views of Cell 16, which published *No More Fun and Games*. "A Year of Living Dangerously," in *Feminist Memoir Project*, ed. DuPlessis and Snitow, p. 87.

93. Betty Rollin, "Motherhood: Who Needs It?," *Look*, September 22, 1970. The article took off from feminist sociologist Jessie Bernard's research that fathers could be just as good as mothers at mothering; a child could prosper with multiple caretakers; and maternal instinct was a myth.

94. Baxandall, "Catching the Fire," in *Feminist Memoir Project*, ed. DuPlessis and Snitow p. 219; Lauri Umansky, *Motherhood Reconceived: Feminism and the Legacies of the Sixties* (New York, 1996), pp. 34–38; Lucy Komisar, *The New Feminism*, p. 59. For two different views of the importance of child care and respect for mothers, see Barbara Winslow's recollections of Seattle and Alice Wolfson's of Washington, D.C., in *Feminist Memoir Project*, ed. DuPlessis and Snitow, pp. 271, 278.

95. Firestone, *Dialectic of Sex*, p. 233; Louise Gross and Phyllis Taube Greenleaf, "Why Day Care?," in *Dear Sisters*, ed. Baxandall and Gordon, pp. 234–36. Baxandall argues that child care and motherhood were much more important than has been allowed, and stresses the efforts of early black women's rights groups around children and child care. "Re-Visioning the Women's Liberation Movement's Narrative," p. 234; also Baxandall, in Hole and Levine, *Rebirth of Feminism*, p. 312. Evans describes centers that focused on sex role socialization in *Tidal Wave*, p. 56.

96. Rich, *Of Woman Born: Motherhood as Experience and Institution* (1976; New York, 1995), p. 36. Marianne Hirsch's *The Mother/Daughter Plot: Narrative, Psychoanalysis, Feminism* (Bloomington, Ind., 1989) movingly explores these intellectual patterns and the psychic undertow. See especially chapters 4 and 5 on the "feminist family romance."

97. Rich, *Of Woman Born*, p. 21. On the tragic view of motherhood more generally in feminist literature of the period see Nancy Chodorow and Susan Contratto, "The Fantasy of the Perfect Mother," in *Rethinking the Family: Some Feminist Questions*, ed. Barrie Thorne and Marilyn Yalom (New York, 1982).

98. Kramer, "Founding Cadre," p. 72; Griffin, "Feminism and Motherhood," in *Mother Reader: Essential Writings on Motherhood*, ed. Moira Davey (New York, 2001), p. 33. The evolution of feminist writing on mothers can be seen in this collection, which ends in 2000. See also Rosen, *World Split Open*, pp. 36–40.

99. Walker, *In Search of Our Mothers' Gardens: Womanist Prose by Alice Walker* (New York, 1983), pp. 231–43. See also *Double Stitch: Black Women Write About Mothers & Daughters*, ed. Patricia Bell-Scott et al. (Boston, 1991). For scholarly expressions of the viewpoint, see Gloria J. Joseph, "Black Mothers and Daughters: Their Roles and Functions in American Society," and Jill Lewis, "Mothers, Daughters, and Feminism," both in *Common Differences: Conflicts in Black & White Feminist Perspectives* (Boston, 1981), pp. 75–150.

100. Moraga, "Preface," *This Bridge Called My Back: Writings by Radical Women of Color* (Watertown, Mass., 1981), p. xviii.

101. One opposing intellectual current was the discourse of militant black manhood. See Robert O. Self, *American Babylon: Race and the Struggle for Postwar Oakland* (Princeton, N.J., 2003), p. 173. See also the rejoinder of Floyd McKissick, from CORE, to Pauli Murray, in Kerber, *No Constitutional Right*, p. 195.

102. Morrison, "What the Black Woman Thinks About Woman's Lib," p. 43. The median wage for white men was about $9,000, for minority males, $6,600, for white women, $5,500, and for minority women, $4,600. A summary of the labor force statistics is Aileen Hernandez, "Small Change for Black Women," *Ms.*, August 1974, pp. 16–18.

103. Beal, "Speaking Up When Others Can't," *Crossroads*, March 1993, p. 5; Charlayne Hunter, "Many Blacks Wary of 'Women's Liberation' Movement in U.S.," *New York Times*, November 17, 1970, p. 47.

104. "Will the Real Black Man Please Stand Up?," *Black Scholar* 2 (June 1971), pp. 32–35. On the effects of black power on militant women, see Echols, *Daring to Be Bad*, p. 106.

105. Lerner to Murray, Murray Papers, Folder 1895, Box 105.

106. Beal, "Double Jeopardy: To Be Black and Female," in *Sisterhood Is Powerful*, ed. Morgan, p. 342. A short biography of Beal is in *Significant Contemporary American Feminists: A Biographical Sourcebook*, ed. Jennifer Scanlon (Westport, Conn., 1999), pp. 22–27.

107. Morrison, "What the Black Woman Thinks About Women's Lib"; Norton, "For Sadie and Maude," *Sisterhood Is Powerful*, ed. Morgan, pp. 356, 359.

108. Pauli Murray, "The Liberation of Black Women," in *Voices of the New Feminism*, ed. Mary Lou Thompson (Boston, 1970), pp. 98, 101, 102.

109. Murray to Clarenbach, November 21, 1967, Murray Papers, Box 51, Folder 99.

110. Ware, *Woman Power,* pp. 98–99.

111. Morrison, "What the Black Woman Thinks About Women's Lib," p. 66.

112. Brownmiller, *In Our Time,* p. 113.

113. Gornick, "The Next Great Moment in History Is Theirs," *Village Voice,* November 27, 1969; "The Next Great Moment in History Is Ours," in *Liberation Now!,* ed. Babcox and Belkin, pp. 25–38.

CHAPTER NINE: POLITICS AS USUAL AND UNUSUAL POLITICS

1. For an excellent analysis of NOW in the 1970s, see Wandersee, *On the Move,* chapter 3.

2. Chapter Reports, NOW Papers, Schlesinger Library. The membership increased from 1,122 and 14 chapters in 1967 to 125,000 and 700 chapters in 1978. See Joyce Gelb and Marian Lief, *Women and Public Policies: Reassessing Gender Politics* (Charlottesville, Va., 1996), p. 27.

3. NOW Papers, Ohio/Knox County folder.

4. *Kenyon Collegian,* October 23, 30, 1975; February 26, April 1, 8, 1976; and passim.

5. University/NOW Child Care Center survives today, geared to the needs of parents with full-time jobs and eight-hour workdays. The study of stereotypes is Jennifer S. Macleod and Sandra T. Silverman, *"You Won't Do": What Textbooks on U.S. Government Teach High School Girls* (Pittsburgh, 1973); Arvonne S. Fraser, "Insiders and Outsiders: Women in the Political Arena," *Women in Washington,* ed. Tinker, p. 130.

6. *Feminist Chronicles 1953–1993,* ed. Toni Carabillo, Judith Meuli, and June Bundy Csida (Los Angeles, 1993), p. 53; Evans, *Tidal Wave,* p. 57; "Debbie Millenson," New Orleans Chapter Newsletter, November 1972, NOW Papers, p. 4; Friedan, *Life So Far,* pp. 199–200.

7. *Women Unite Now* (Cleveland), Jan.–May 1973, NOW Papers.

8. The early 1970s constituted a "window of opportunity for federal involvement in social policy." See Kimberly Morgan, "A Child of the Sixties: The Great Society, the New Right, and the Politics of Federal Child Care," *Journal of Policy History* 13 (2001), p. 221.

9. Tanya Melich, *The Republican War Against Women: An Insider's Report from Behind the Lines* (New York, 1996), p. 27.

10. On support for child care, see for example Komisar, *The New Feminism,* p. 59. On Nixon and Congress, see Melich, *Republican War Against Women,* pp. 13–35; Morgan, "A Child of the Sixties," p. 223.

11. Morgan, "Child of the Sixties," p. 215; Sonya Michel, *Children's Interests, Mother's Rights: The Shaping of America's Child Care Policy* (New Haven, Conn., 1999); Morgan, *Working Mothers and the Welfare State: Religion and the Politics of Work-Family Policies in Europe and the United States* (Stanford, Calif., 2006); *Child Care Policy at the Crossroads: Gender and Welfare State Restructuring,* ed. Michel and Rianne Mahon (New York, 2002); Celia Winkler, *Single Mothers and the State: The Politics of Care in Sweden and the United States* (Lanham, Md., 2002).

12. Urie Bronfenbrenner and Jerome Bruner, "The President and the Children," *New York Times,* January 31, 1972, p. 41. Bronfenbrenner and Bruner were child development specialists.

13. Kilpatrick quoted in Morgan, "Child of the Sixties," p. 234; Edward F. Zigler and Jody Goodman, "The Battle for Day Care in America: A View from the Trenches," in *Day Care: Scientific and Social Policy Issues,* ed. Edward F. Zigler and Edmund Gordon (Boston, 1982), pp. 338–50; Melich, *The Republican War Against Women,* pp. 27–28.

14. *New York Times,* December 11, 1971; *Washington Post,* December 12, 1971. Friedan mentions the lackluster interest of NOW in child care in *Life So Far,* p. 200.

15. "Women in the U.S. Congress 1917–2008," Fact Sheet, Center for American Women and Politics, National Information Bank on Women in Public Office, Eagleton Institute of Politics, Rutgers University.

16. http://womenshistory.about.com/library/lists/bl_list_senate.htm; www.cawp.rutgers.edu/Facts/Officeholders/senate.pdf. Two women were appointed but did not serve because Congress was not in session. Rebecca Latimer Felton, the first woman to be appointed to the Senate (in 1922), served for only one day. Rose McConnell Long was the other senator appointed to a husband's seat and subsequently reelected. A humorous woman, Hattie Caraway harbored a low opinion of the masculine sex that came from an utterly conventional acceptance of separate spheres. Her diary from 1932 is a sardonic chronicle of the experience of sitting for hours listening to men who loved to hear themselves talk. "Pure bunk" was a typical summary of a colleague's speech. See *Silent Hattie Speaks: The Personal Journal of Senator Hattie Caraway,* ed. Diane D. Kincaid (Westport, Conn., 1979); Kristin Downey, *The Woman Behind the New Deal: The Life of Frances Perkins, FDR's Secretary of Labor and His Moral Conscience* (New York, 2009), p. 136.

17. Davis, *Moving the Mountain,* pp. 187–90.

18. National Women's Political Caucus Newsletter 1, December 10, 1971, Schlesinger Library. They were Democratic congresswomen, NOW officers, powerful women in the media, Democratic and a few Republican notables, and high-ranking staff from the Johnson and Nixon administrations. The congresswomen included Bella Abzug and Shirley Chisholm (D-N.Y.) and Patsy Mink (D-Hawaii). The NOW leaders were Friedan and the new president, Wilma Scott Heide, along with Gloria Steinem, editor of *Ms.* The presidential staff members were Liz Carpenter (former press secretary to Lady Bird Johnson) and Jill Ruckelshaus (aide to Nixon). See Rona F. Feit, "Organizing for Political Power: The National Women's Political Caucus," in *Women Organizing: An Anthology,* ed. Bernice Cummings and Victoria Schuck (Metuchen, N.J., 1979), pp. 184–208; Susan Carroll, "Women's Rights and Political Parties: Issue Development, the 1972 Conventions, and the National Women's Political Caucus," M.A. thesis, Political Science, Indiana University (on deposit in Schlesinger Library). For Republican feminists' use of the NWPC, see Rymph, *Republican Women,* pp. 207–8.

19. Davis, *Moving the Mountain,* p. 186; Chisholm quoted in Evans, *Tidal Wave,* p. 73; *Civil Rights Digest* 6 (Spring 1974). The NWPC board included Myrlie Evers, Fannie Lou Hamer, Dorothy Height, and Beulah Sanders of the National Welfare Rights Organization; those allied with Hispanic-American politics included Evelina Antonetty, Cecelia Suarez, and Lupe Anguiano. See Feit, "Organizing for Political Power," in *Women Organizing,* ed. Cummings and Schuck, pp. 185, 207.

20. Davis, *Moving the Mountain,* p. 186; Evans, *Tidal Wave,* p. 72.

21. Wandersee, *On the Move,* p. 35.

22. Emily C. Moore, "Abortion and Public Policy: What Are the Issues?," *New York Law Forum* 17 (1971), p. 418; *Act Now Newsletter* (Charlotte, N.C.), June 1973; NOW Newsletters, Box 20, NOW Papers.

23. The array of groups was funded by a combination of the Ford Foundation (known for supporting women's causes), left-liberal political groups, and older organizations like the League of Women Voters. See Gelb and Palley, *Women and Public Policies,* p. 44; Evans, *Tidal Wave,* chapter 3; Anne N. Costain, "Lobbying for Equal Credit," in *Women Organizing,* ed. Cummings and Schuck, p. 83; "Woman Power," *Newsweek,* April 3, 1972, p. 28; Fraser, "Insiders and Outsiders," in *Women in Washington,* ed. Tinker, passim.

24. In Mary Ann Millsap, "Sex Equity in Education," in *Women in Washington,* ed. Tinker, p. 117.

25. A comprehensive list is in Post and Siegel, "Legislative Constitutionalism and Section Five Power," p. 1996 n 159. See Richard Nixon, Statement About

Signing the Equal Opportunity Act of 1972, reprinted by John Woolley and Gerhard Peters in the American Presidency Project, University of California at Santa Barbara, www.presidency.ucsb.edu/ws/?pid=3358.

26. Davis, *Moving the Mountain*, p. 148 and passim. Eileen Shanahan recalled that her daughter graduated from Harvard Law School in 1975 and could not get credit to buy a couch; Shanahan Interview, Women in Journalism Oral History Project, p. 149. A political scientist who studied the legislative process in depth concludes that without the organized efforts of women's lobbies to shepherd the credit bill through the convoluted path to passage, it would have failed, even given the overwhelming support it ultimately received when it came up for a vote. Costain, "Lobbying for Equal Credit," in *Women Organizing*, ed. Cummings and Schuck, pp. 82–110.

27. Davis, *Moving the Mountain*, pp. 213–14.

28. Ibid., pp. 212–13; Sheila Tobias, *Faces of Feminism: An Activist's Reflections on the Women's Movement* (Boulder, Colo., 1997), pp. 105–6. LBJ's order was forgotten until 1970, when Bernice Sandler, a college teacher and recent recipient of an advanced degree at the University of Maryland, realized that women could put the executive order to use against universities' overt and covert sexist practices in hiring. In short order, some 250 female academics filed suits along with Sandler.

29. Davis, *Moving the Mountain*, pp. 212–13.

30. Kathrine Switzer, *Marathon Woman: Running the Race to Revolutionize Women's Sports* (New York, 2007), p. 91, and chapter 7. Semple grabbed her but failed to rip her number off. Switzer, stunned, managed to keep running, and her teammates blocked him, throwing him to the sideline.

31. Coaches, in Davis, *Moving the Mountain*, p. 215; Millsap, "Sex Equity in Education," in *Women in Washington*, ed. Tinker, p. 94.

32. The vote in the House was 354–23; in the Senate, 84–8. See "Woman Power," *Newsweek*, April 3, 1972, p. 28; Melich, *Republican War Against Women*, p. 30; Critchlow, *Phyllis Schlafly*, p. 203.
   The NOW legal task force was of two minds. The Fourteenth Amendment strategy Pauli Murray had in the PCSW mapped out continued to appeal as a more practical route to legal equality, with the advantage that it tied women's causes to African-Americans'. NOW's lawyers, however, were unwilling to give up on a measure that promised so much, since in one stroke the ERA would remove all discriminatory laws. The lawyers pushed ahead with a dual strategy, pursuing cases under the Fourteenth Amendment at the same time that NOW mobilized to press ratification of the ERA. See Mayeri, "Constitutional Choices," p. 792; Davis, *Moving the Mountain*, pp. 123, 387.

33. National Center for Education Statistics, "Digest of Education Statistics," http://nces.ed.gov/programs/digest/d07/tables/dt07_269.asp; Mark Silk, "Is God a Feminist?," *New York Times*, April 11, 1982.

34. Cynthia Fuchs Epstein, *Women in Law* (Urbana, Ill., 1981), pp. 312–14.

35. In 1970, fewer than two hundred of the country's ten thousand judges were women and only one of them was a federal appellate judge. Ibid., pp. 1–13; D. Sassower, "The Legal Profession and Women's Rights," *Rutgers Law Review* 25 (1970), pp. 60 ff.

36. Kerber, *No Constitutional Right*, p. 203.

37. See Brenda Feigen's vivid account of her years at Harvard Law School in the 1960s, *Not One of the Boys* (New York, 2000), pp. 5–21; Jill Abramson and Barbara Franklin, *Where They Are Now: The Story of the Women of Harvard Law 1974* (New York, 1986); Kerber, *No Constitutional Right*, chapters 4–5.

38. Entry for Carol Christ (an early female graduate student in religious studies), in *Feminists Who Changed America 1963–1975*, ed. Barbara J. Love (Urbana, Ill., 2006), p. 83.

39. On the impact of Title IX on the law schools, see Epstein, *Women in the Law*, p. 95; NYU Law Women's Conference, videotape of the proceedings, March 30, 2005, Schlesinger Library. The NYU women's challenge to a male-only scholarship is also mentioned in Diane Schulder, "Women and the Law," *Atlantic Monthly*, March 1970, p. 103. The Vietnam War also had an impact once the draft was instituted and male law students were eligible, but less so than has been thought, given that most of the draftees and volunteers were working class, not the demographic group bound for law school. See Epstein, *Women in Law*, pp. 16, 53; Donna Fossum, "A Lawyer-Sociologist's View on Women's Progress in the Profession," in *Women Lawyers: Perspectives on Success*, ed. Emily Couric (New York, 1984), pp. 245–59.

40. Stanford survey cited in *Feminist Chronicles*, ed. Carabillo et al., p. 62.

41. Kerber, *No Constitutional Right*, p. 191; Fred Strebeigh, *Equal: Women Reshape American Law* (New York, 2009), pp. 14–15.

42. Dean Albert Sacks of Harvard, in Abramson and Franklin, *Where They Are Now*, p. 2; on hirings, see ibid., pp. 22–23. Ginsburg anecdote about the dean is in Kerber, *No Constitutional Right*, p. 202; and elaborated in Strebeigh, *Equal*, p. 36.

43. At a meeting of the American Historical Association, for example, young feminists attacked the profession for erasing women from written history and treating them with condescending stereotypes. Men responded with

incredulity, accusing the panelists of political bias. Evans, *Tidal Wave*, p. 83, describes the 1970 panel, which included Linda Gordon, then a member of Boston Bread and Roses and eventually a major feminist force in American history. The committee that issued the first report on the status of women named overt sex discrimination as the root cause of the dearth of women in history departments. The 1970 committee frankly maintained that the appalling statistics—almost as bad as the law, with only two women history professors among the ten largest departments—were "no accident, that they were the result of intention, and that intentions were shaped by prejudice, misjudgment, and perverse ideology." Kerber, "On the Importance of Taking Notes," in *Voices of Women Historians*, ed. Boris and Chaudhuri, pp. 52–53; Renate Bridenthal, "Making and Writing History Together," in *Voices of Women Historians*, ed. Boris and Chaudhuri, pp. 76–85.

44. On academic degrees in the social sciences and history, see Digest of Education Statistics, http://nces.ed.gov/programs/digest/d07/tables/dt07 _305.asp, Table 305; for medicine, dentistry, and law, ibid., Table 269. The number of M.D. degrees conferred on women increased from 809 in 1970–71 to 3,833 in 1980–81; L.L.B.s or J.D.s from 1,240 to 11,768; history/social science Ph.D.s from 507 to 848.

At the Massachusetts Institute of Technology, a shocking 1999 report on the situation of female professors revealed a dismaying picture of women scientists' treatment at the institution. The report's findings prompted an unprecedented agreement in 2001 between the presidents of nine top research universities to conduct equity reviews of women in the sciences in their own institutions. See *Chronicle of Higher Education*, April 2, June 11, December 3, 1999.

45. The intellectual ferment is legendary. One of the first anthologies of essays on academic disciplines and intellectual questions offers a glimpse: *Women in Sexist Society*, ed. Vivian Gornick and Barbara K. Moran (New York, 1971), which includes Nochlin's essay.

46. Davis, *The Making of "Our Bodies, Ourselves,"* passim.

47. Way, "You Are Not My God, Jehovah!," in *Dear Sisters*, ed. Baxandall and Gordon, pp. 103–5; Evans, *Tidal Wave*, p. 84.

48. Sue Anne Steffey Morrow, personal communication, October 2, 2002, Princeton, N.J.

49. Conflict over ordaining gays commenced immediately after the General Convention vote. The 1977 ordination of Ellen Barrett, a gay activist, provoked a storm of opposition. See Paul Moore, Jr., *Take a Bishop Like Me* (New York, 1979).

50. Quoted in Mary Daly, "Toward Partnership in the Church," in *Voices of the New Feminism*, ed. Thompson, pp. 147–48.

51. Personal papers, evaluation for reappointment in Social Studies, Bard College, 1979.

52. Abramson and Franklin, *Where They Are Now,* chapter 2.

53. Roraback, in Amy Kesselman, "Women Versus Connecticut: Conducting a Statewide Hearing on Abortion," in *Abortion Wars: A Half Century of Struggle, 1950–2000* (Berkeley, Calif., 1998), p. 54. Roraback represented Estelle Griswold in *Griswold v. Connecticut.* She did not argue before the Court because she and other lawyers for the plaintiff agreed that a woman would lessen the chances of a favorable ruling. Dean Harold Koh, talk at memorial for Roraback, Conference on *Roe v. Wade,* Yale Law School, October 2008; *Hoyt v. Florida,* 368 U.S. 57 (1961).

54. Ruth B. Cowan, "Women's Rights Through Litigation: An Examination of the American Civil Liberties Union Women's Rights Project, 1971–76," *Columbia Human Rights Review* (1976), p. 381; the moment in *Roe* is recounted in David J. Garrow, *Liberty and Sexuality: The Right to Privacy and the Making of Roe v. Wade* (Berkeley, Calif., 1994).

55. *Feminist Chronicles,* ed. Carabillo et al., pp. 58, 67, and passim.

56. Shanahan interview 9, Women in Journalism Oral History Project, p. 166.

57. Ibid., interview 6, p. 108.

58. Judith Paterson interviewed Lorena Weeks for her biography of Marguerite Rawalt, *Be Somebody,* pp. 184–85.

59. Roberts's activities are mentioned throughout the chapter newsletter of Baton Rouge NOW. See the announcement of "Major Victory in Lorena Weeks Case" in vol. 1, no. 2 (April 1971), NOW Papers. The relationship between Weeks's evolving case and NOW is described in Lois Herr, *Women, Power and AT&T: Winning Rights in the Workplace* (Boston, 2003), pp. 43–46. See also Evans, *Tidal Wave,* pp. 64–65.

60. "No longer would a demonstration that many, or even most, women could not perform a specific job requirement justify such a restriction. Instead, employers (and states) would have to show that all or 'substantially all' women could not do so." Thus a woman who was exceptionally strong could not be barred from a job that required lifting weights that most women could not lift. Evans, *Tidal Wave,* pp. 64–65. Annabelle Walker, an Atlanta NOW leader, discusses the impact of the Weeks decision in an oral history. "'Walker Talks About *Weeks v. Southern Bell,*" Georgia Women's Movement Oral History Project, Georgia State University Library, www.library.gsu.edu/spcoll/pages/pages.asp?ldID=105&guideID=534&ID=3512.

61. The EEOC was able to intervene because AT&T was effectively doing business with the government and had asked for a rate increase from the Federal Communications Commission in 1970. See Herr, *Women, Power and AT&T,* pp. 146–48, 156.

62. On the upshot of Lorena Weeks's victory, see *Feminist Chronicles,* ed. Carabillo et al., pp. 58–59; Rabb, in Robertson, *Girls in the Balcony.* Frank's case ended when the Supreme Court refused to hear Ivy Club's appeal. *Frank v. Ivy Club,* A. 2d 1142 (N.J. Superior Ct. App. Div. 1988); 576 A. 2d 241 (N.J. 1990).

63. Robertson, *Girls in the Balcony,* pp. 141–48, 199. See also Judith Coburn, "Women Take the *New York Times* to Court," *New Times,* October 2, 1978, pp. 20–27.

64. Wade interview, Women in Journalism Oral History Project, p. 68.

65. Ibid., p. 191.

66. Robertson, *Girls in the Balcony,* pp. 86, 181, 190. Professor Orley Ashenfelter of the economics department at Princeton did the statistical analysis.

67. Shanahan interview 9, Women in Journalism Oral Project, pp. 164–65; Wade interview, ibid., p. 201; Robertson, *Girls in the Balcony,* p. 156.

68. Robertson, *Girls in the Balcony,* pp. 185–86; Finding Aid, *New York Times* Women's Caucus Papers, 1969–1986, Schlesinger Library. On Rabb, see Strebeigh, *Equal,* pp. 164 ff.

69. Wade interview, Women in Journalism Oral History Project, p. 235.

70. The named plaintiffs were Betsy Wade (copy editor), Eileen Shanahan (Washington correspondent), Louise Carini (accounting), Grace Glueck (art critic), Joan Cook (reporter, women's section), Nancy Davis (classified advertisements), and Andrea Skinner (clerk in fashion section). On Carini, see Robertson, *Girls in the Balcony,* pp. 169–72.

71. Shanahan interview 9, Women in Journalism Oral History Project, p. 179.

72. Coburn, "The *Times* Avoids Trial," *New Times,* October 30, 1978, p. 7. The large monetary settlements women won in discrimination suits against *Newsweek* and *Reader's Digest* were the exceptions. See "*Newsweek* Charged with Sex Bias by 50," *New York Times,* May 17, 1972, p. 34; "Time Inc. and State Agree on Job Policy for Women," *New York Times,* February 7, 1971; Shanahan interview 9, Women in Journalism Oral History Project, p. 179.

73. Quoted in Wandersee, *On the Move,* p. 110; unidentified newcomer in Robertson, *Girls in the Balcony,* p. 212; Coburn, "Women Take the *New York*

Times to Court." Outside the legal route, Media Women, which sponsored the invasion of *Ladies' Home Journal*, adapted the women's liberation tactic of exposure, public embarrassment, and denunciation to publish reports on the treatment of female employees inside news organizations and publishing houses. See Media Women's Association, *Rooms with No View: A Woman's Guide to the Man's World of the Media*, ed. Ethel Strainchamps (New York, 1974).

74. Channels in Detroit and Pittsburgh were among those targeted by NOW, which agreed to change programming and employment practices.

75. "The Hen-Pecked House," *New York Times*, August 12, 1970; Hole and Levine, *Rebirth of Feminism*, pp. 263–64.

76. *Feminist Chronicles, 1953–1993*, ed. Carabillo et al., p. 62.

77. Post and Siegel, "Legislative Constitutionalism and Section Five Power," p. 1985.

78. Kerber, *No Constitutional Right*, pp. 169–70, 194; Biographical Note, Dorothy Kenyon Papers, Sophia Smith Library, http://asteria.five colleges.edu/findaids/sophiasmith/mnsss35_main.html; Hartmann, *The Other Feminists*, pp. 53–56. NOW's legal committee, chaired by Marguerite Rawalt, was also set up to appeal cases, but NOW's financial resources were much slimmer than the ACLU's.

79. John D. Johnston, Jr., and Charles L. Knapp, "Sex Discrimination by Law: A Study in Judicial Perspective," *New York University Law Review* 46 (1971), pp. 675–76.

80. Ginsburg, "Remarks for the Celebration of 75 Years of Women's Enrollment at Columbia Law School, October 19, 2002," *Columbia Law Review* 102, pp. 1441–48.

81. Ginsburg, in Kerber, *No Constitutional Right*, p. 202. An account of the *Hoyt* case is in chapter 4.

82. Ginsburg, in ibid., p. 204. Murray quoted in ibid., p. 190.

83. Cowan, "Women's Rights Through Litigation," p. 389.

84. See Nan D. Hunter's analysis of the judges' correspondence in Justice Blackmun's recently opened papers in "Twenty-First Century Equal Protection: Making Law in an Interregnum," *Georgetown Journal of Gender and Law* 12 (2006), pp. 141–69. See also Jane Mansbridge, *Why We Lost the ERA* (Chicago, 1986), p. 49; Strebeigh, *Equal*, chapters 2–3.

85. Feigen, *Not One of the Boys*, pp. 79–89; Brief of American Civil Liberties Union, Amicus Curiae; Oral Argument of Ruth Bader Ginsburg on behalf of

Amicus Curiae, *Frontiero v. Richardson,* p. 855. Ginsburg's oral argument can be heard on www.oyez.org/cases/19701979/1972/1972_71_1694/argument/. Although there was almost no women's history to draw on, Ginsburg used the *History of Woman Suffrage* and took her Sojourner Truth quotes from Flexner's *Century of Struggle.*

86. *Frontiero v. Richardson,* 411 U.S. 677. At this writing the intermediate standard of scrutiny still falls short of the strict scrutiny given to the drawing of racial differences in statutes, although in practice the Court has generally invalidated statutes that discriminate on the basis of sex.

87. The Pregnancy Discrimination Act provided that discrimination on the basis of pregnancy, childbirth, or related medical conditions constituted unlawful sex discrimination under Title VII but it did not guarantee maternity leave. The Family and Medical Leave Act of 1993 protected a worker's job security should she take maternity leave or time to care for a sick family member but it did not provide for compensation. Institute for Women's Policy Research, "Maternity Leave in the United States" (2007), www.iwpr.org/pdf/parentalleaveA131.pdf.

88. For another assessment of feminism's problems in the 1970s, see Alice Echols, *Shaky Ground: The '60s and Its Aftershocks* (New York, 2002).

CHAPTER TEN: POLITICS AND THE FEMALE BODY

1. Cisler, "Abortion Law Repeal (Sort of); A Warning to Women," *Notes from the Second Year* (1969), reprinted in *Dear Sisters,* ed. Baxandall and Gordon, p. 141. "The recent movement in the United States for liberalization of state abortion laws encompasses a great variety of issues and has made for strange bedfellows." Moore, "Abortion and Public Policy," p. 420.

2. The Trustees of the AMA recommended in 1970 that abortion be treated as a private matter between doctor and patient. The position of the organization, however, was a compromise between liberals and conservatives (primarily Catholics), retaining the provisions of therapeutic abortion—that the procedure be performed in a hospital, and with consultation of two other physicians—but widening the reasons an abortion could be performed for other than medical reasons that accorded with a patient's welfare and giving the physician considerable wiggle room. Garrow judges it essentially a pro-repeal position. *Liberty and Sexuality,* pp. 455–56. See also Hole and Levine, *Rebirth of Feminism,* p. 290.

3. For a list of items used to abort, see Cynthia Gorney, *Articles of Faith: A Frontline History of the Abortion Wars* (New York, 1998). On rates, see Gordon, *Moral Property of Women,* pp. 15–16; Leslie Reagan, *When Abortion Was a Crime: Women, Medicine, and Law in the United States, 1867–1973* (Berkeley, Calif., 1997), chapter 1, pp. 132–37, 209–14, and passim. Reagan points out that middle-class

women had higher abortion *rates* than did working-class women, but the latter group "had a greater *number* of abortions because they were pregnant more often." Ibid., p. 136 (emphasis in orginal).

4. "Hardship cases" is the phrase of Garrett Hardin, used ironically. See "Abortion—or Compulsory Pregnancy?," *Journal of Marriage and the Family* 30 (May 1968), p. 246.

5. Garrow, *Liberty and Sexuality,* chapter 1.

6. Hardin, quoted in ibid., p. 293. Hardin elaborated his views in "The History and Future of Birth Control," *Perspectives in Biology and Medicine* (Autumn 1966), pp. 1–18; see also "Abortion—or Compulsory Pregnancy?"

7. For an overview, see Alice S. Rossi and Bhavani Sitaraman, "Abortion in Context: Historical Trends and Future Changes," *Family Planning Perspectives* 20 (November–December 1988), pp. 273–81, 301; William B. Ober, M.D., "We Should Legalize Abortion," *Saturday Evening Post,* October 8, 1966. *Abortion in a Changing World: Proceedings of an International Conference Convened in Hot Springs, Virginia . . . 1968 by the Association for the Study of Abortion* (New York, 1970), is a two-volume compilation of essays.

8. Support came from unexpected quarters. For example, a survey of Mississippi physicians, a heavily white group not known for their liberalism by virtue of their race and residence, after the *Roe* decision showed very strong support for legalization. Typically, support was strongest for abortion when a woman's life was at risk or in cases of rape, incest, or deformity, and tapered off thereafter, to just over a third when it was an issue of "financial strain on parents." See Paul T. Murray and Herman Jew, "Mississippi Physicians' Attitudes Toward the Supreme Court Abortion Decision," *Journal of the Mississippi State Medical Association* 15 (July 1974), pp. 291–94.

On eugenics, see Connelly, *Fatal Misconception,* chapter 4; on the pill in Puerto Rico, see Gordon, *Moral Property of Women,* p. 287.

9. Brenda Hyson, "New York City Passed New Abortion Law," *Black Panther,* July 4, 1970; Gordon, *Moral Property of Women,* p. 290; Loretta J. Ross, "African-American Women and Abortion," in *Abortion Wars: A Half Century of Struggle 1950–2000* (Berkeley, Calif., 1998), ed. Rickie Solinger, p. 180.

10. Wallace, *Black Macho and the Myth of the Superwoman* (New York, 1979). Flo Kennedy, *Color Me Flo,* pp. 143–48, sums up the black feminist case against the genocide charge. For an example of a local group that defied the black power position, see Polatnick, "Diversity in Women's Liberation Ideology," p. 704; see also Myra McPherson, "MDs File Abortion Lawsuit," *Washington Post,* September 30, 1969, p. B1. On Chisholm, see Ross, "African-American Women and Abortion," in *Abortion Wars,* ed. Solinger, p. 183.

Judge Ruth Bader Ginsburg wrote of giving a speech on sex equality and constitutional law in 1971 that did not mention the abortion cases then pending but nonetheless provoked a storm of questions from black men in the audience about abortion and genocide. "Some Thoughts on Autonomy and Equality in Relation to *Roe v. Wade*," *North Carolina Law Review* 65 (1984–85), pp. 376–77.

I am indebted to Nicola Beisel for my understanding of mainstream black political support.

11. Tillmon, in Premilla Nadasen, *Welfare Warriors: The Welfare Rights Movement in the United States* (New York, 2005), p. 215; Ross, "African-American Women and Abortion," in *Abortion Wars*, ed. Solinger, pp. 181–84; Beal, "Double Jeopardy," In *Sisterhood Is Powerful*, ed. Morgan, p. 349; Kennedy, *Color Me Flo*, pp. 143–48.

12. National Catholic Welfare Conference, quoted in John T. McGreevy, *Catholicism and American Freedom: A History* (New York, 2003), p. 235.

13. Ibid., pp. 236–38.

14. Ibid., p. 274; Marion Faux, *Roe v. Wade: The Untold Story of the Landmark Supreme Court Decision That Made Abortion Legal* (New York, 1988), p. 190.

15. Roy Lucas, "Federal Constitutional Limitations on the Enforcement and Administration of State Abortion Statutes," *North Carolina Law Review* 46 (1967–68), pp. 734, 741. Garrett Hardin pointed to this problem—a huge one—in "Abortion—or Compulsory Pregnancy?," pp. 246–47. On the woman denied an abortion that was already approved, see Marion K. Sanders, "The Right Not to Be Born," *Harper's*, April 1970, pp. 92–99. On protecting physicians, see Eva R. Rubin, *Abortion, Politics, and the Courts: Roe v. Wade and Its Aftermath* (Greenwood, Conn., 1982), p. 26.

16. Cook, quoted in 2000 in her obituary. Dennis Hevesi, "Constance E. Cook, 89; Wrote Abortion Law," *New York Times*, January 24, 2009; McGreevey, *Catholicism and American Freedom*, pp. 274–76; Bill Kovach, "Final Approval of Abortion Bill Voted in Albany," *New York Times*, April 11, 1970, pp. 1, 17.

17. Faux, *Roe v. Wade*, pp. 188, 255–62; Melich, *Republican War Against Women*, p. 28; Brownmiller, *In Our Time*, pp. 132–33; Garrow, "Abortion Before and After *Roe v. Wade*: An Historical Perspective," *Albany Law Review* 62 (1999), pp. 833, 840; Garrow, *Liberty and Sexuality*, pp. 384, 428–32; "Dr. Adriaan Frans Koome (1929–1978)," ww.historylink.org/index.cfm?DisplayPage=output.cfm&file_i d=2642H; "Marilyn Ward Recalls the Campaign to Reform Washington's Abortion Law," www.historylink.org/index.cfm?DisplayPage=pf_output.cfm &file_id=2675; Hodgson, "The Twentieth-Century Gender Battle: Difficulties in Perception," in *Abortion Wars*, ed. Solinger, pp. 300–301. Linda J. Greenhouse describes the challenges in New York that preceded legalization in "Constitutional Question: Is There a Right to Abortion?," *New York Times*, January 25, 1970.

18. See, for example, "The New Feminism/3," *Guardian*, April 19, 1969, p. 11; Hole and Levine, *Rebirth of Feminism*, p. 92.

19. Faux, *Roe v. Wade*, pp. 192–93.

20. Davis, *Moving the Mountain*, p. 165; Hole and Levine, *Rebirth of Feminism*, p. 284. On Jane, see Garrow, *Liberty and Equality*, p. 361; Laura Kaplan, "Beyond Safe and Legal: The Lessons of Jane," in *Abortion Wars*, ed. Solinger, pp. 33–41. On the technology, see Brownmiller, *In Our Time*, p. 106; Reagan, *When Abortion Was a Crime*, pp. 224–27. Providers abandoned the old D&C method, performed with a surgical instrument, for vacuum aspiration, a simple procedure for first-trimester pregnancy that a paramedic could perform.

21. Susan Brownmiller, "Everywoman's Abortions: 'The Oppressor Is Man,'" *Village Voice*, March 27, 1969; "Talk of the Town," *New Yorker*, February 22, 1969, pp. 28–29. The unsigned piece was written by Ellen Willis, the magazine's rock critic, a Redstockings member who was at both evenings. The famous Redstockings protest was preceded by a now-forgotten action at a state hearing on reform on February 13. See Alfred Miele, "Gals Squeal for Repeal, Abort State Hearing," New York *Daily News*, February 14, 1969.

22. Roy Lucas's foundational legal strategy described the client group in this way. Lucas, "Federal Constitutional Limitations," pp. 730–78.

23. "The New Feminism/3."

24. Hardin, "Abortion—or Compulsory Pregnancy?"; ibid., "The History and Future of Birth Control."

25. Brownmiller, "Everywoman's Abortions"; Dr. Michael Baggish, in Kesselman, "Women Versus Connecticut," in *Abortion Wars*, ed. Solinger, p. 57.

26. The phrase "a woman's right to choose" first appeared in the major East Coast papers in 1969. See Myra McPherson, "MDs File Abortion Lawsuit," *Washington Post*, September 30, 1969, p. B1. In 1972, Women's Abortion Action Coalition used the slogan to call for a march protesting the attempted rollback of the New York state bill: "Abortion Must Be a Woman's Right to Choose," *New York Times*, May 14, 1972, p. E5.

27. Elizabeth Boyer, in Davis, *Moving the Mountain*, p. 67. The dissidents founded the Women's Equity Action League.

28. In Moore, "Abortion and Public Policy," p. 419.

29. Faux, *Roe v. Wade*, pp. 196–97.

30. "AMA Abortion Position Legalized," *American Medical News*, July 6 1970; "33,000 Doctors Speak Out on Abortion," *Modern Medicine*, May 4, 1973, p. 31.

The *Journal of Obstetrics and Gynecology* voiced no objections; its concern was with *Roe*'s ambiguity about the cutoff point for late abortions, and with the possibility that freestanding clinics might not be safe enough and hospitals might better be the prescribed venue. See Robert E. Hall, M.D., "The Supreme Court Decision on Abortion," *American Journal of Obstetrics and Gynecology* 116, no. 1 (May 1, 1973), pp. 1–8.

31. Linda Charlton, "Women March Down Fifth in Equality Drive," *New York Times,* August 27, 1970, p. 1.

32. Garrow, *Liberty and Sexuality,* pp. 426–27, 444–47. Bensing later remarried and as Sandra Bensing Cano became active in antiabortion politics, repudiating her part in *Doe v. Bolton* and claiming that her lawyer and family coerced her into an abortion. See Cano et al. amici brief in *Gonzales v. Carhart,* 530 U.S. 914.

33. Sarah Weddington, *A Question of Choice* (New York, 1992), pp. 51–53.

34. Faux, *Roe v. Wade,* pp. 11–16, gives an excellent account of the first contacts between the lawyers and McCorvey. McCorvey, like Sandra Bensing, became active in the antiabortion movement. See www.leaderu.com/norma/; Weddington's restrained account of McCorvey's circumstances is in *A Question of Choice,* pp. 51–53; she notes that lawyer/client privilege prohibits her sharing confidential information. McCorvey's account differs substantially.

35. Garrow, *Liberty and Sexuality,* pp. 400–407; Faux, *Roe v. Wade,* p. 167. The initial challenge also included a physician plaintiff charged with providing an illegal abortion in Texas.

36. Garrow, *Liberty and Sexuality,* p. 453.

37. Nancy Stearns, "*Roe v. Wade:* Our Struggle Continues," *Berkeley Women's Law Journal* 1 (1988–90), pp. 4–5; Rubin, *Abortion, Politics, and the Courts,* pp. 46–53.

38. Hill, in Kesselman, "Women Versus Connecticut," in *Abortion Wars,* ed. Solinger, p. 50.

39. Stearns, "*Roe v. Wade:* Our Struggle Continues"; Rubin, *Abortion, Politics, and the Courts,* pp. 45–46; Kesselman, "Women Versus Connecticut," in *Abortion Wars,* ed. Solinger, pp. 53–54, 60–61.

40. A South Carolinian by birth, Lucas took the train to Washington in 1964 to hear Solicitor General Archibald Cox argue the constitutionality of the Civil Rights Act in two cases from Atlanta and Birmingham before the Supreme Court. Garrow, *Liberty and Sexuality,* pp. 335–37.

41. Lucas, "Federal Constitutional Limitations," p. 756. Pilpel defended women from the Connecticut Birth Control League arrested in 1939 under

an 1879 statute for distributing contraceptives at a clinic the organization established. Garrow, *Liberty and Sexuality,* pp. 67–69, 71, 334–39. On Lucas, see obituary, "Roy Lucas, 61, Legal Theorist Who Helped Shape Roe Suit," *New York Times,* November 7, 2003.

42. Garrow, *Liberty and Sexuality,* p. 515. The tension between Lucas and the other lawyers is discussed in Faux, *Roe v. Wade,* pp. 220–32.

43. Siegel, "Sex Equality Arguments for Reproductive Rights: Their Critical Basis and Evolving Constitutional Expression," *Emory Law Journal* 56 (2007), p. 823, available at http://ssrn.com/abstract=993308.

44. Ibid., pp. 823–26. Pilpel wrote the amicus curiae brief for Planned Parenthood, Inc., in *Roe v. Wade;* Stearns wrote the one for New Women Lawyers.

45. Blackmun, in Garrow, *Liberty and Sexuality,* p. 599; Pilpel, in Faux, *Roe v. Wade,* p. 304; Ginsburg, "Some Thoughts on Autonomy and Equality," p. 381.

46. *Roe v. Wade,* 410 U.S. 113 (1973).

47. Gordon, *Moral Property of Women,* p. 26.

48. Stearns, in Brownmiller, *In Our Time,* p. 134.

49. A ringing affirmation of personal liberty did come from Justice William O. Douglas, who, in his concurrence, lyrically invoked *Griswold*'s right to privacy. "Freedom to care for one's health and person, freedom from bodily restraint or compulsion, freedom to walk, stroll, or loaf" led logically to freedom of choice: "Elaborate argument is hardly necessary to demonstrate that child birth may deprive a woman of her preferred life style and force upon her a radically different and undesired future." Yet Justice Douglas, too, ignored the particularities of pregnancy, presenting the pregnant woman as Everyman in his discussion of the right to privacy.

50. Garrow, *Liberty and Sexuality,* pp. 636–37.

51. *Off Our Backs* 3 (February–March 1973); *Female Liberation Newsletter,* February 26, 1973, p. 4; "The New Feminism/3." The account of New Haven is my recollection of the meeting, which I attended; Brownmiller, *In Our Time,* p. 102.

52. Cisler, "Abortion: A Major Battle Is Over: But the War Is Not," *Feminist Studies* 1 (Autumn 1972), p. 127.

53. Donald Granberg and James Burlison, "The Abortion Issue in the 1980 Elections," *Family Planning Perspectives* 15 (September–October 1983), pp. 231–38.

54. Marie Costa, *Abortion: A Reference Handbook* (Santa Barbara, Calif., 1991), pp. 76–77.

55. Rubin, *Abortion, Politics, and the Courts,* p. 88.

56. *The Phyllis Schlafly Report* (February 1972), n.p.

57. Schlafly, *A Choice Not an Echo* (Alton, Ill., 1964), pp. 107, 113, and passim; Critchlow, *Phyllis Schlafly,* chapter 5.

58. Critchlow, *Phyllis Schlafly,* pp. 139–40. A new book, *Safe—Not Sorry,* chronicled the chicanery that pushed her out. An illustration showed a woman standing before the door to Republican Party headquarters with a sign reading "Conservatives and Women Please Use Servants' Entrance." See Rymph, *Republican Women,* pp. 176–84; the illustration is discussed on p. 184.

59. Critchlow, *Phyllis Schlafly,* pp. 140–41. Tanya Melich, one of the feminists who tried to open the Republican Party to women in the Nixon era, notes wryly that Schlafly, the antifeminist, actually embodied a feminist model, "a self-assured woman with a cause." "Gender was no impediment to Schlafly.... It didn't matter that her actions and beliefs stood in harsh contradiction." *Republican War Against Women,* pp. 45–46.

60. *Phyllis Schlafly Report* 5 (February 1972), p. 4.

61. Ibid., pp. 1–2.

62. Carole Shammas, *A History of Household Government in America* (Charlottesville, Va., 2002), p. 174, Table 8. *Schlafly Report* (February 1972), pp. 1–2. On differences over the status of the homemaker, see Mansbridge, *Why We Lost the ERA,* pp. 98–112.

63. Melich, *The Republican War Against Women,* p. 46.

64. In ibid., p. 48; "What Is Wrong with 'Equal Rights' for Women," *Schlafly Report* (February 1972).

65. Davis, *Moving the Mountain,* p. 393.

66. Champions cited the amendment's theoretical ability to uproot tenacious structures of sexual inequality such as the wage gap between men and women. But Title VII was already in place. At best, the ERA might have encouraged judges to interpret the statutes and Fourteenth Amendment cases bearing upon workplace practices and treatment in ways more consistently favorable to women. See Mansbridge, *Why We Lost the ERA,* p. 57.

67. In the first case, the spouses were living apart; in the second, the spouses were living together. See David Finkelhor and Kersti Yllo, *License to Rape: Sexual Abuse of Wives* (New York, 1985), p. 172.

68. Davis, *Moving the Mountain,* pp. 314–17, 321–22.

69. Dworkin, "For Men, Freedom of Speech; for Women, Silence Please," in *Take Back the Night: Women on Pornography,* ed. Laura Lederer (New York, 1980); "We Protest," flyer to protest the 1982 Barnard Conference, The Scholar and the Feminist, in my possession; "The *Powers of Desire,* edited by Ann Snitow et al., includes articles and editorials that misrepresent and distort the analysis and activism of feminists," undated flyer protesting the publication of *Powers of Desire: The Politics of Sexuality* (New York, 1983), ed. Snitow, Stansell, and Sharon Thompson. *Powers of Desire* and *Pleasure and Danger: Exploring Female Sexuality* (New York, 1984), ed. Carole Vance, were the major publications on the pro-sex side of what came to be known as the feminist sex wars.

70. Willis, "Feminism, Moralism, and Pornography," *Beginning to See the Light: Pieces of a Decade* (New York, 1981), p. 225.

71. Rubin, *Abortion, Politics, and the Courts,* p. 106. Both were personally opposed in a mild sort of way: Ford wanted the states to handle abortion; Carter opposed Medicaid funding but wanted poor women to have alternatives.

72. The consolidation is described in Robert Post and Reva Beth Siegel, "*Roe* Rage: Democratic Constitutionalism and Backlash," *Harvard Civil Rights–Civil Liberties Law Review* 42 (Summer 2007), pp. 373–434.

73. Granberg and Burlison, "The Abortion Issue in the 1980 Election," pp. 231–38.

74. Susan Faludi chronicles the making of *Fatal Attraction* and the changes made to the script in *Backlash* (New York, 1991), chapter 5.

75. Ezekiel, *Feminism in the Heartland,* p. 61. For a sense of the issues that rocked feminism in the United States in this period, and the political perplexities that surrounded them, see Katha Pollitt's incisive essays in *Reasonable Creatures: Essays on Women and Feminism* (New York, 1994).

CHAPTER ELEVEN: GLOBAL FEMINISM

1. *Jus Suffragii* (London). See the issues for the 1920s.

2. *Is Multiculturalism Bad for Women? Susan Moller Okin with Respondents,* ed. Joshua Cohen, Matthew Howard, and Martha C. Nussbaum (Princeton, N.J., 1999), is an elegant exploration of feminist multiculturalism, with attention paid to religion.

3. *Global Women: Nannies, Maids, and Sex Workers in the New Economy,* ed. Barbara Ehrenreich and Arlie Hochschild (New York, 2003).

4. Global Feminist Workshop to Organize Against Traffic in Women, Rotterdam, April 1983; *International Feminism: Networking Against Female Sexual Slavery . . . Report of the Global Feminist Workshop,* ed. Kathleen Barry, Charlotte Bunch, and Shirley Castley (New York, 1984).

5. Susan Bolotin, while distancing herself from antifeminism, announced the trend in "Voices from the Post-Feminist Generation," *New York Times Magazine,* October 17, 1982. For responses see Susan Bolotin Collection, Schlesinger Library; Lehrman, *The Lipstick Proviso* (New York, 1997). Lehrman's was a lesser-known entry in a genre whose best known exponents were Camille Paglia, Katie Roiphe, and Christina Hoff Sommers.

6. Arvonne Fraser, "Becoming Human: The Origins and Development of Women's Human Rights," *Human Rights Quarterly* 21 (1999), pp. 895–909; Jo Freeman, "Beijing Report: The Fourth World Conference on Women," www.jofreeman.com/womenyear/beijingreport.htm; initially published as "The Real Story of Beijing," *Off Our Backs,* no. 26 (March 1996).

7. *Meeting in Mexico: The Story of the World Conference of the International Women's Year* (New York, 1975); Susan Tiff, "The Triumphant Spirit of Nairobi," *Time,* April 12, 1985; Morgan, "Dispatch from Beijing," *Ms.* 6 (January/ February, 1996), p. 16. A collection of materials from Beijing is in the Wendy Thomas Collection, Papers from the Fourth World Conference on Women, Schlesinger Library.

8. Judith P. Zinsser, "From Mexico to Copenhagen to Nairobi: The United Nations Decade for Women, 1975–85," *Journal of World History* 13 (Spring 2002), p. 140; *Women, Politics, and the United Nations,* ed. Anne Winslow (Westport, Conn., 1995).

9. Sen, "More Than One Hundred Million Women Are Missing," *New York Review of Books,* December 20, 1990; Zinsser, "United Nations Decade," pp. 22–23. Extrapolating from Sen's figures, roughly 44 million women went missing in China, 36.7 million in India, and 4.4 million in Latin America. An astonishing 13 percent of Pakistani women were unaccounted for and 8.5 percent of Iranian women. See Martha Nussbaum, *Women and Human Development: The Capabilities Approach* (Cambridge, U.K., 2000), p. 4. In India in 1991, where sex-selective abortion has received much attention, the sex ratio was 927 females per 1,000 males.

10. Shahrashout Razavi and Carol Miller, *From WID to GAD: Conceptual Shifts in the Women and Development Discourse,* United Nations Research Institute for Social Development, 1995, p. 32; Barbara Crossette, "The Second Sex in the Third World," *New York Times,* September 10, 1995, p. E1; Joan Dunlop et al., "Women Redrawing the Map: The World After the Beijing and Cairo

Conferences," *SAIS Review* 16 (Winter–Spring 1998), available at www.iwhc .org/resources, p. 6; Virginia Allan, Margaret E. Galey, and Mildred Persinger, "World Conference of International Women's Year," in *Women, Politics, and the United Nations,* ed. Winslow, p. 33.

11. Patricia Daniel, "Is Another World Possible Without a Woman's Perspective?," www.opendemocracy.net/democracy-africa/wsf_4257.jsp

12. Nussbaum, *Women and Human Development,* p. 287.

13. Bina Agarwal, *A Field of One's Own: Gender and Land Rights in South Asia* (Cambridge, U.K., 1994), p. 493; see also Mary Fainsod Katzenstein, "Organizing Against Violence: Strategies of the Indian Women's Movement," *Pacific Affairs* 62 (Spring 1989), pp. 54–60.

14. Agarwal, *A Field of One's Own,* pp. 482–93. See also Nussbaum's eloquent account of the Self-Employed Women's Association in India, in *Women and Human Development,* pp. 15–17 and passim; Gail Omvedt, *Women in Popular Movements: India and Thailand During the Decade of Women* (Geneva, 1986), p. 2.

15. Ifi Amadiume, *Daughters of the Goddess, Daughters of Imperialism* (London, 2000), pp. 248–53.

16. Rothschild, "The Quest for World Order," *Daedalus* 124 (Summer 1995), pp. 77–83.

17. Amadiume, *Daughters of the Goddess,* chapter 12.

18. Rosiska Darcy de Oliveira, "On UN World Conferences," in *A Commitment to the World's Women: Perspectives on Development and Beyond,* ed. Noeleen Heyzer (New York, 1995), p. 258.

19. Boserup, *Women's Role in Economic Development* (London, 1970).

20. Claudia Von Braunmuhl, "Mainstreaming Gender—A Critical Revision," *Common Ground or Mutual Exclusion? Women's Movements and International Relations,* ed. Marianne Braig and Sonja Wolte (London, 2002), pp. 55–79; Zinsser, "From Mexico to Copenhagen to Nairobi," pp. 149–51. Third World women organized Development Alternatives for Women in a New Era (DAWN) to push for policies that worked in the interests of women, rather than those that used women to work toward some larger national or international goal. See Deborah Stienstra, *Women's Movements and International Organizations* (New York, 1994), p. 122. For an analysis of the shifting uses of feminist perspectives in development models, see Razavi and Miller, *From WID to GAD.*

21. From the mid-decade Copenhagen Programme (1980), in Zinsser, "From Mexico to Copenhagen to Nairobi," p. 154; Nussbaum, *Women and Human Development,* pp. 2–3, 298.

22. On family allowances in Britain, see Pedersen, *Eleanor Rathbone*, p. 143; Agarwal, "Gender and Land Rights Revisited: Exploring New Prospects via the State, Family and Market," *Journal of Agrarian Change* 3 (January–April 2003), p. 194; Debra Sherman, "Banking on a Woman's World," *Ms.,* September/October 1991, p. 15. The pattern has now become a given of studies of household economics, in both developed and Third World societies. See Shelley J. Lundberg, Robert A. Pollak, and Terrence J. Wales, "Do Husbands and Wives Pool Their Resources? Evidence from the United Kingdom Child Benefit," *Journal of Human Resources* 32 (Summer 1997), pp. 463–80; Shelley A. Phipps and Peter S. Burton, "What's Mine Is Yours? The Influence of Male and Female Incomes on Patterns of Household Expenditure," *Economica,* New Series 65 (November 1998), pp. 599–613; Rae Lesser Blumberg, "Income Under Female Versus Male Control: Hypotheses from a Theory of Gender Stratification and Data from the Third World," *Journal of Family Issues* 9 (Winter 1988), pp. 51–85.

23. Ellen Ross, *Love and Toil: Motherhood in Outcast London, 1870–1918* (New York, 1993), pp. 54–55; Razavi and Miller, *From WID to GAD,* p. 18.

24. Razavi and Miller, *From WID to GAD,* pp. 22–25; Barry, in Crossette, "Second Sex in the Third World"; Helen Zia, "The Global Fund for Women—Money With a Mission," *Ms.,* July 1993, p. 21.

25. Ministry of Foreign Affairs, in Margaret Snyder, "The Politics of Women and Development," in *Women, Politics, and the United Nations,* ed. Winslow, p. 111; Stienstra, *Women's Movements and International Organizations,* p. 122; Crossette, "Second Sex in the Third World."

26. Razavi and Miller, *From WID to GAD,* p. 8.

27. Tarak Nath Das, an Indian nationalist and scholar of political science, suggested the correlation at a 1926 international birth control conference organized by Margaret Sanger. Demographers subsequently demonstrated the correlation statistically. See Connelly, *Fatal Misconception,* pp. 65, 95, and passim. See also Amartya Sen, "Fertility and Coercion," *University of Chicago Law Review* 63 (1996), pp. 1052–53.

28. Bunch, "U.N. World Conference in Nairobi: A View from the West," *Ms.,* June 1985, p. 80; Dunlop, "Redrawing the Map," p. 1.

29. Quoted in Janice Auth, "Pittsburgh Success Stories," *To Beijing and Beyond: Pittsburgh and the United Nations Fourth World Conference on Women,* ed. Auth (Pittsburgh, 1998), p. 189; Margaret McIntosh, "Comment on Irene Tinker's 'A Feminist View of Copenhagen,'" *Signs* 6 (Winter 1981), p. 772.

30. "Preface," Russell and Nicole Van de Ven, *The Proceedings of the International Tribunal on Crimes Against Women* (Millbrae, Calif., 1976), p. xv.

31. "By raising the demands of Chilean women in their struggle against imperialism we are raising the demands of all oppressed women. By freeing our sisters in Chile, we are freeing ourselves." Action for Women in Chile, *Women's Packet on Chile* (c. 1976), Schlesinger Library.

32. Two international covenants in 1966 translated the principles of the UNDHR (1949) into legally binding form. They clearly state that the rights put forward are applicable without distinction of sex, thereby positing sex as a ground of impermissible distinction; each covenant also binds ratifying states to undertake to ensure that women and men have equal right to the enjoyment of the rights they establish. However, the United Nations recognized that "the fact of women's humanity proved insufficient to guarantee them the enjoyment of their internationally agreed rights" and established the Commission on the Status of Women to define and elaborate guarantees of non-discrimination. The CSW produced several conventions and recommendations between 1952 and 1965, but CEDAW was the first comprehensive document.

33. See Cott, *Public Vows,* chapter 6, on the history of these laws in the United States.

34. Pinar Ilkkaracan, *Women's Movement(s) in Turkey: A Brief Overview,* Women for Women's Human Rights Reports, no. 2, p. 16. The English-language text of CEDAW along with the reservations is available at www.un.org/womenwatch/daw/cedaw/text/econvention.htmarticle#9.

35. www.un.org/womenwatch/daw/cedaw/states.htm. See Ann Elizabeth Mayer, "Cultural Particularism as a Bar to Women's Rights: Reflections on the Middle Eastern Experience," in *Women's Rights, Human Rights: International Feminist Perspectives,* ed. Julie Peters and Andrea Wolper (New York, 1995), pp. 178–79, on the gutting of CEDAW.

36. Akua Kuenyehia, "Economic and Social Rights of Women: A West African Perspective," *Common Ground,* ed. Braig and Wolte, p. 164; Marysa Navarro, "Argentina: The Long Road to Women's Rights," in *Women's Rights: A Global View,* ed. Lynn Walter (Westport, Conn., 2000), pp. 1–14; also Gratzia Villarroel Smeall, "Bolivia: Women's Rights, the International Women's Convention, and State Compliance," in *Women's Rights,* ed. Walter, pp. 17–20; Wolte, "Claiming Rights and Contesting Spaces: Women's Movements and the International Women's Human Rights Discourse in Africa," in *Common Ground,* ed. Braig and Wolte, pp. 174–77, 80, and passim.

37. MacKinnon, *Are Women Human? And Other International Dialogues* (Cambridge, Mass., 2006), p. 11; see "The Promise of CEDAW's Optional Protocol," pp. 64–67, on the amendment that allows women to make direct complaint against ratifying countries to a treaty body ("the Committee") that enforces the convention.

38. Kenneth Cmiel, "The Emergence of Human Rights Politics in the United States," *Journal of American History* 86 (December 1999), pp. 1231–50.

39. MacKinnon, *Are Women Human?*, pp. 22–23; Charlotte Bunch and Niamh Reilly, *Demanding Accountability: The Global Campaign and Vienna Tribunal for Women's Rights* (New Brunswick, N.J., 1994).

40. www.unhchr.ch/huridocda/huridoca.nsf/(Symbol)/A.CONF.157.23.n.

41. Ilkkaracan, "Do Women and Girls Have Human Rights?," www.opendemocracy.net/globalization_institutions_government/girls_rights_43 86.jsp; *The Human Rights Watch Global Report on Women's Human Rights* (New York, 1995); Sarah Aejin Seo, "The Contested Historical Memory of the Korean Comfort Women" (senior thesis in history, Princeton University, 2002). U.N. Special Rapporteurs came to Korea twice, in 1996 and 1998, and submitted two separate reports on the "comfort women" scandal.

On a more mundane level, human rights ideology put up in lights what seemed Promethean struggles against banal kinds of male cruelty. A book on human rights doctrine cites an example of a police officer in Moldova who protested his assignment to the domestic violence unit. "But when his superiors told him that Moldova had to comply with international human rights standards and that the United Nations had stated unequivocally that violence against women, including domestic violence, violated the fundamental human rights of women, he began to experience what can only be described as a personal transformation," seeing his work imbued with dignity and added importance. See James Dawes, *That the World May Know: Bearing Witness to Atrocity* (Cambridge, Mass., 2007), pp. 128–29.

42. *New York Times,* May 6, 1997; http://web.amnesty.org/library/index/engasa340042006.

43. Indira Jaising, "Violence Against Women: The Indian Perspective," in *Women's Rights, Human Rights,* ed. Peters and Wolper, pp. 53–54; Omvedt, *Women in Popular Movements,* pp. 21–27; Connelly, *Fatal Misconception,* pp. 356–57; Jean Drèze and Amartya Sen, *India: Development and Participation,* 2nd ed. (New York, 2002), pp. 257–62; Jeff Jacoby, "Choosing to Eliminate Unwanted Daughters," *Boston Globe,* April 6, 2008.

44. Testimony and documentation of rape was presented at the Nuremberg trials, but never prosecuted. In Tokyo, rape was included in the general list of crimes in the indictment, but only minimal attention was paid to the charge. Tokyo was a precedent, however, in international prosecution. See Julie A. Mertus, *War's Offensive on Women: The Humanitarian Challenge in Bosnia, Kosovo, and Afghanistan* (Bloomfield, Conn., 2000), p. 77.

45. The story of Omarska, a main camp where women were held, is recounted in the remarkable documentary *Saving the Ghosts*, which also chronicles the trip of several women to testify in the ICTFY in The Hague.

46. Kate Nahapetian, "Selective Justice: Prosecuting Rape in the International Criminal Tribunals for the Former Yugoslavia and Rwanda," *Berkeley Women's Law Journal* 126 (1999), p. 130. The "Foca indictment" of 1996 was the first ICTFY indictment to deal specifically with rape and sexual assault. It charged eight Bosnian Serb police and military officers with the rape and sexual assault of at least fourteen Bosnian Muslim women in the town of Foca.

47. A count of the information up to 2007 from the Netherland Institute of Human Rights (University of Utrecht) yielded these numbers: www.unhchr.ch/huridocda/huridoca.nsf/(Symbol)/A.CONF.157.23.En. For a comprehensive statement of the revised view of rape's importance, see Dorothy Q. Thomas and Regan E. Ralph, "Rape in War: Challenging the Tradition of Impunity," *SAIS Review* 14 (Spring 1994), pp. 81–99; Catharine MacKinnon, "Rape, Genocide, and Women's Human Rights," *Harvard Women's Law Journal* 17 (1994), pp. 5–16.

48. *Rapport du Rwanda aux Nations Unies pour la Quatrième Conférence Mondiale sur les Femmes . . . Beijing* (Kigali, Rwanda, 1995). Since 2000, Rwanda has designated rape and sexual slavery in Category One of genocide crimes, the most serious class.

49. *Washington Post,* January 27, 1998, p. A18; *New York Times,* January 8, 1998, p. A3, January 12, 1998, p. A20, June 19, 2002, p. A22; Chante Lasco, "Virginity Testing in Turkey: A Violation of Women's Human Rights," *Human Rights Brief* 9, no. 3, brief 10 (2002); Mary Geske and Susan C. Bourque, "Grassroots Organizations and Women's Human Rights: Meeting the Challenge of the Local-Global Link," in *Women, Gender, and Human Rights: A Global Perspective,* ed. Marjorie Agosín (New Brunswick, N.J., 2002), p. 257.

50. Ann Jones, *Kabul in Winter: Life Without Peace in Afghanistan* (New York, 2006), p. 155. Jones's grim meditation on the prevalence of violence against women in Afghan society during the war is on p. 173.

51. Freeman, "Beijing Report," p. 12; Fraser, "Becoming Human," pp. 901–2.

52. Sexual slavery was "present in *all* situations where women or girls cannot change the immediate conditions of their existence; where, regardless of how they got into those conditions they cannot get out, and where they are subject to sexual violence and exploitation." *International Feminism: Networking Against Female Sexual Slavery,* ed. Barry et al., pp. 8–9.

53. Amadiume, *Daughters of the Goddess,* pp. 125–31; Paulina Makinwa-Adebusoye, "Hidden: A Profile of Married Adolescents in Northern Nigeria,"

pp. 16–17, available at www.actionhealthinc.org/publications/downloads/ hidden.pdf. Blaine Harden, "Child Bride's Killing Shocks Nigerians," *Washington Post,* May 3, 1987. Amadiume gives the most searing account of the politics around the case; the *Post* reports outrage from Muslims and Christians alike.

54. *Ms.* (Spring 2004), pp. 3, 47.

55. Agarwal, "Gender and Land Rights Revisited," p. 214. On the bad faith swirling around the defense of tradition, see the penetrating work by Uma Narayan, especially *Dislocating Cultures: Identities, Traditions, and Third-World Feminism* (New York, 1997), notes to pp. 614–16.

56. Elizabeth Friedman, "Human Rights: The Emergence of a Movement," in *Women's Rights, Human Rights,* ed. Peters and Wolper, p. 21.

57. Western feminist debate on clitoridectomy, especially in the United States, proceeded in a bubble in the 1980s, with little interest in the views of African women. The problem of self-involved Westerners winds in and out of arguments in Egypt and East Africa. For a concise summary, see Melanie McAlister, "American Feminists, Global Visions, and the Problem of Female Genital Surgeries," in *Americanism: New Perspectives on the History of an Ideal,* ed. Michael Kazin and Joe McCartin (Chapel Hill, N.C., 2006). An especially illuminating study of a particular case is Ellen Gruenbaum, "The Islamic Movement, Development, and Health Education: Recent Changes in the Health of Rural Women in Central Sudan," *Social Science Medicine* 33, no. 6 (1991), pp. 637–45. Isabelle R. Gunning, "Arrogant Perception, World-Travelling and Multicultural Feminism: The Case of Female Genital Surgeries," *Columbia Human Rights Law Review* 23 (1991–92), pp. 189–248, expresses the dilemmas of an American feminist at a point of transition in the discourse. A sober assessment of the problem is Carla Makhlouf Obermeyer and Robert F. Reynolds, "Female Genital Surgeries, Reproductive Health and Sexuality: A Review of the Evidence," *Reproductive Health Matters* 7 (May 1999), pp. 112–20. See also the essays in *Genital Cutting and Transnational Sisterhood: Disputing U.S. Polemics,* ed. Stanlie M. James and Claire C. Robertson (Urbana, Ill., 2002).

58. Sheila Dauer, "Indivisible or Invisible: Women's Human Rights in the Public and Private Sphere," in *Women, Gender, and Human Rights,* ed. Agosîn, pp. 75–79; Deborah Ellis, *Women of the Afghan War* (Westport, Conn., 2000), pp. 67–68, 85, 104; Anne Garrels, "Concern Grows over Iraqi 'Honor Killings,'" report from Iraq on National Public Radio, www.npr.org/templates/ story/story.php?storyId=5043032; Fadia Faqir, "Intrafamily Femicide in Defence of Honour: The Case of Jordan," *Third World Quarterly* 22 (February 2001), pp. 65–82; Suzanne Ruggi, "Commodifying Honor in Female Sexuality: Honor Killings in Palestine," *Middle East Report* 206 (Spring 1998), pp. 12–15. On the sati case in India, see Madhu Kishwar and Ruth Vanita, "The Burning

of Roop Kanwar," *Manushi*, no. 43 (1987), pp. 18, 20; "Deorala Episode: Women's Protest in Rajasthan," *Economic and Political Weekly* 45 (November 7, 1987); Radha Kumar, "From Chipko to Sati: The Contemporary Indian Women's Movement," *The Challenge of Local Feminisms: Women's Movements in Global Perspective*, ed. Amrita Basu (Boulder, Colo., 1995), pp. 79–82.

59. "Respite for Woman Who Faces Stoning," *New York Times*, June 4, 2002, p. A10; "As Stoning Case Proceeds, Nigeria Stands Trial," *New York Times*, January 26, 2003. Information on Amina Lawal Kurami from Amnesty.org.

60. Flanders, "C. MacKinnon in the City of Freud," *Nation*, August 9/16, 1993, pp. 174–77.

61. Connelly, *Fatal Misconception*, passim.

62. Legal abortion was far from what literary critic Gayatri Spivak, speaking as a feminist of the Third World, derided as a "master symbol" of Western feminists who made it their "alibi . . . to keep the world order as it is." Spivak's talk at the International Conference on Population and Development, Cairo 1993, is reported in Loes Keysers, "Reflections on Reproductive and Sexual Rights During the ICPD," *Newsletter—Women's Global Network for Reproductive Rights* 47 (July–September 1994), p. 5. The International Conference on Safe Abortion gave updated statistics in 2007; the number had dropped to 42 million, with 68,000 women dying every year. Jane Gabriel "The Choir," *Open Democracy*, October 25, 2007, www.opendemocracy.net.

63. R. A. Bang et al., "High Prevalence of Gynecological Diseases in Rural Indian Women," *Lancet* (January 14, 1989), pp. 85–87; Nicholas D. Kristof and Sheryl WuDunn, "Why Women's Rights Are the Cause of our Time," *New York Times Magazine*, August 23, 2009, pp. 36, 38. The strength of women's movements in Africa is discussed throughout the essays in *African Women's Movements: Transforming Political Landscapes*, ed. Aili Marie Tripp, Isabel Casamiro, Joy Kwesiga, and Alice Mungwa (New York, 2009).

64. Rhonda Copelon and Rosalind Petchesky, "Toward an Interdependent Approach to Reproductive and Sexual Rights as Human Rights: Reflections on the ICPD and Beyond," in *From Basic Needs to Basic Rights: Women's Claim to Human Rights*, ed. Margaret Schuler (Washington, D.C., n.d.), p. 346.

65. Petchesky, *Global Prescriptions: Gendering Health and Human Rights* (London, 2003), chapter 3.

66. Razawi and Miller, *From WID to GAD*, p. 17

67. *Reproductive Health Matters* 4 (May 1996), Special Issue on Men.

68. Dunlop et al., "Women Redrawing the Map"; Copelon and Petchesky, "Toward an Interdependent Approach," pp. 346–47.

69. The phrase of Princeton demographer Charles Westhoff, in Connelly, *Fatal Misconception,* p. 364.

70. The letter to the president was followed by a highly unusual attack on Vice President Al Gore, accusing him of lying about the American position on abortion. "Letter released on April 5, 1994, by the U.S. Embassy to the Vatican," available at www.ewtn.com/library/PAPALDOC/ JP2CLINT.HTM; *New York Times,* September 1, 1994; Betsy Hartmann, "The Cairo 'Consensus': Women's Empowerment or Business as Usual?," *GeoJournal* 35, no. 2 (1995); Keysers, "Cairo plus Five—Business as Usual?," *Newsletter—Women's Global Network* 65 (1999); "The Sudan Withdraws from U.N. Cairo Conference on Population," *New York Times,* August 31, 1994.

71. Rosemary Radford Ruether, "Vatican Alliance with Muslims Did Not Materialize in Cairo," *National Catholic Reporter,* October 14, 1994.

72. On the alliance of the Holy See with conservative Muslim states, see Marge Berer, "Images, Reproductive Health, and the Collateral Damage to Women of Fundamentalism and War," *Reproductive Health Matters* 9 (November 2001), p. 6; "Introduction," *Globalization, Gender, and Religion: The Politics of Women's Rights in Catholic and Muslim Contexts,* ed. Jane H. Bayes and Nayereh Tohidi (New York, 2001), pp. 1–6.

73. Susan A. Cohen, "Global Gag Rule: Exporting Antiabortion Ideology at the Expense of American Values," *Guttmacher Report on Public Policy* 4 (June 2001).

74. Berer, "Images, Reproductive Health, and the Collateral Damage to Women of Fundamentalism and War," p. 6.

75. Snitow, unpublished manuscript in my possession (2002).

76. Ibid.

77. Carla Power, "City of Secrets," *Newsweek,* July 13, 1998; Veronica Doubleday, *Three Women of Herat* (London, 1988). Doubleday's book is about 1976, when she spent a year in Herat living in a family household. For the long war, see Deborah Ellis, *Women of the Afghan War* (Westport, Conn., 2000).

78. Nancy Hatch Dupree, "Afghan Women Under the Taliban," in *Fundamentalism Reborn: Afghanistan and the Taliban,* ed. William Maley (London, 1998); Rosemarie Skaine, *The Women of Afghanistan Under the Taliban* (London, 2002); Jan Goodwin, *Price of Honor: Muslim Women Lift the Veil of Silence on the Islamic World* (New York, 1994), chapter 4.

79. Ahmed Rashid, *Taliban: Militant Islam, Oil & Fundamentalism in Central Asia* (New Haven, Conn., 2001), p. 177; chapter 8, "A Vanished Gender," pp. 105–16.

80. Rashid, *Taliban*, pp. 180–82; Abby Van Buren and Mavis Leno, "Dear Abby," *Ottawa Citizen*, July 23, 1999, p. B6 (and many other newspapers where Dear Abby was syndicated). Skaine chronicles the campaign in *Women of Afghanistan*, pp. 128–34.

81. Senator Sam Brownback (R-Kans.) co-sponsored the resolution, S. 68. *Congressional Record* (Senate), March 17, 1999, pp. 2871–72; see the important interview with Sima Wali in "Regime Cracks Down on Women"; also Beena Sarwar, "Women Pay as Fundamentalism Grips Pakistan," *Ms.*, June–July 1999, pp. 15–17 (on Taliban influence in Pakistan); Haleh Anvari, "Asylum Denied," *Ms.*, March 2001, pp. 26–27 (on the plight of women refugees). After 9/11 and the onset of the war, *Ms.* also published updates.

82. Rashid, *Taliban*, p. 182.

83. *Congressional Record* (Senate), October 25, 2001, Introduction of S. 1573, pp. S11105–S11109.

84. First Lady Laura Bush, too, spoke of fighting brutality against the women and children of Afghanistan.

85. Janelle Brown, "Any Day Now," Salon.com, www.salon.com/mwt/feature/2001/12/03/afghan_women.

86. Institute for War and Peace Reporting, Jan. 17, 2003, citing Physicians for Human Rights, "Women's Health and Human Rights in Afghanistan: A Population-Based Assessment," December 31, 2001, http://physiciansforhumanrights.org/library/report-2001afghanistan.html.

87. Sharon Lerner, "What Women Want: Feminists Agonize over War in Afghanistan," *Village Voice*, October 30, 2001; Brown, "Any Day Now"; *The W Effect: Bush's War on Women*, ed. Laura Flanders (New York, 2004); *Nothing Sacred: Women Respond to Religious Fundamentalism and Terror*, ed. Betsy Reed (New York, 2002). *September 11, 2001: Feminist Perspectives*, ed. Susan Hawthorne and Bronwyn Winters (Melbourne, Australia, 2002), includes American authors.

88. Sonali Kolhatkar, "Chain of International Violence in Afghanistan: An Interview with RAWA," *Said It* 3 (February 2002), p. 2, http://saidit.org/archives/feb02/article3.html.

89. Dexter Filkins, "Afghan Girls, Scarred by Acid, Defy Terror, Embracing School," *New York Times*, January 14, 2009. An excellent chronicle of women's lives inside the country, the struggles of female politicians, and the work of NGOs can be found in the reports of the organization Women for Afghan Women, www.womenforafghanwomen.org.

INDEX

CHRISTINE STANSELL is Stein-Freiler Distinguished Professor of History at the University of Chicago. Her previous books include *American Moderns: Bohemian New York and the Creation of a New Century* and *City of Women: Sex and Class in New York 1789–1860*. She writes widely about matters of feminism and American history in journals and newspapers, including *The New Republic,* Salon, and The Daily Beast. Among other awards, Stansell has received a John Simon Guggenheim Foundation Fellowship. She has been a Fellow at the Institute for Advanced Study in Princeton, New Jersey, and the Mary Bunting Fellow at the Radcliffe Institute for Advanced Study.